FESTIVAL AND SPECIAL EVENT MANAGEMENT

THIRD EDITION

This book is dedicated to the memory of Ms Molly McDonnell BA, BSW

WILEY AUSTRALIA TOURISM SERIES

FESTIVAL AND SPECIAL EVENT MANAGEMENT

THIRD EDITION

JOHNNY ALLEN

WILLIAM O'TOOLE

ROBERT HARRIS

IAN McDONNELL

With special acknowledgements to Robyn Stokes,
Queensland University of Technology
who prepared chapter 7 and chapter 8

WILEY

John Wiley & Sons Australia, Ltd

Third edition published 2005 by
John Wiley & Sons Australia, Ltd
42 McDougall Street, Milton, Qld 4064

Offices also in Sydney and Melbourne

First edition 1999
Second edition 2002

Typeset in 10.5/12 pt New Baskerville

National Library of Australia
Cataloguing-in-Publication data

Festival and special event management.

   3rd ed.
   Includes index.
   ISBN-13   978 0 470 80470 4.
   ISBN-10   0 470 80470 X.

   1. Festivals — Management. 2. Special events —
   Management. I. Allen, Johnny.

394.26068

Cover images: © Image Disk Photography (crowd at
sporting event), PhotoDisc Inc. (crowdsurfer), PhotoDisc Inc.
(fireworks), Corbis Corporation (Sydney Harbour)
Internal images: © PhotoDisc Inc., Corbis Corporation

Printed in Singapore by
Kyodo Printing Co (S'pore) Pte Ltd

10 9 8 7 6 5

ABOUT THE AUTHORS

Johnny Allen

Johnny Allen was director of the Australian Centre for Event Management (ACEM) at the University of Technology, Sydney. He was event manager for the Darling Harbour Authority from 1989 until 1996, and has an extensive career in event planning. Prior to his position at the ACEM, he was the special event manager for Tourism New South Wales. Johnny has now retired but remains involved with event management and event education.

William O'Toole

William O'Toole has been creating and managing events for over 30 years. He has developed courses in event project management for a number of universities, including his alma mater, the University of Sydney. He trains event managers in countries around the world, such as Malaysia, Bahrain, the USA, China and the European Union countries. His company, EPMS, has worked with organisations as diverse as the Australia Taxation Office and the Al Ain Economic Development Department (UAE) to develop their event management systems. Currently, he is the senior adviser to the International Event Management Body of Knowledge project based in the USA, the United Kingdom and South Africa.

Rob Harris

Rob Harris is a senior lecturer and director of continuing professional education at the School of Leisure, Sport and Tourism at the University of Technology, Sydney. He has been involved in event management, training and research for the past nine years, and has developed undergraduate, postgraduate and TAFE programs in the area. He is also a founding director of the New South Wales Festivals and Events Association and a member of the editorial board of the academic journal, *Event Management*.

Ian McDonnell

Ian McDonnell is a senior lecturer in the Faculty of Business's School of Leisure, Sport and Tourism at the University of Technology, Sydney, where he teaches management and marketing of leisure and tourism services.

CONTENTS ···

PREFACE

In the past decade, event management has shifted from being a field of dedicated and resourceful amateurs to being one of trained and skilled professionals. There are several reasons for this shift.

First, event management has emerged as the umbrella profession for a diverse range of activities that were previously viewed as discrete areas. These activities include festivals, sporting events, conferences, tourism and corporate events. This change has led to the need for a methodology broad enough to service this wide range of event types, but also flexible enough to encompass their individual needs and differences.

Second, the environments in which events operate and the range of stakeholder expectations have become much more complex and demanding. This change has led to the need for a robust methodology that is responsive to change and able to manage and encompass risk.

Third, corporate and government involvement in events has increased dramatically, in terms of both companies mounting events for their own purposes, and companies and governments investing in events through sponsorship and grants. This change has led to the need for management systems that are accountable and able to measure and deliver return on investment.

In response to these challenges, the event industry has relatively quickly developed a body of knowledge of industry best practice, supported by training and accreditation. To do so, it has borrowed much from other disciplines and adapted this knowledge to the event context.

This textbook attempts to capture and refine this emerging body of knowledge, and to document it in a useful form for both researchers and practitioners in the field. As authors, we each bring to the textbook the benefits of our own discipline and perspective, reflecting the many facets of event management. In developing this body of knowledge, we have also relied on colleagues in academia and industry — in fields as diverse as marketing, tourism, project management, business studies, law and accounting — who have assisted us in applying these disciplines in the event context.

Teaching event management throughout Australia, and in locations as diverse as Kuala Lumpur, Beijing, Edinburgh, Auckland and Cape Town, has helped us to develop a global perspective on events, which is reflected in the range and diversity of case studies and examples in this textbook.

Event management is still evolving as an industry and as a profession; hopefully, the third edition of *Festival and Special Event Management* will contribute to this evolution and to a better understanding of how events enrich our lives.

Johnny Allen
Bill O'Toole
Ian McDonnell
Rob Harris

October 2004

ACKNOWLEDGEMENTS ···················

The authors and publisher thank Robyn Stokes for her revisions of chapters 7 and 8 in the third edition. The authors and publisher would also like to thank the following copyright holders, organisations and individuals, for permission to reproduce copyright material in this book.

Images
- p. 67: © Events Tasmania 2004 • p. 123: Associate Professor Leo Jago • p. 145: Cognizant Communication Corp. • p. 154: R. Clark 1992, *Australian Human Resource Management 2nd edn*, McGraw-Hill Book Company, Sydney, p. 236 • p. 163: R. Stone 1998, *Human Resource Management 3rd edn*, John Wiley & Sons, Brisbane • p. 168: T. Connors, *The Volunteer Management Handbook*, John Wiley & Sons New York • p. 169 (top): J. Wood et al 2004, *Organisational Behaviour: a global perspective 3rd edn*, John Wiley & Sons Australia, Ltd • p. 169 (bottom): Adapted and reprinted by permission of Harvard Business Review, from F. Herzberg, *One More Time: How Do You Motivate Employees?* 01/03, p. 90 • p. 193: Adapted with permission of The Free Press, Division of Simon & Schuster Adult Publishing Group, M. Porter, *Competitive Strategy: Techniques for Analyzing Industries & Competitors.* © 1980, 1998, by The Free Press. All rights reserved • p. 203: Morgan, *Marketing for Leisure and Tourism*, Pearson Education Limited • p. 209: F. Brassington & S. Pettitt 1957, 'Ansoff Matrix', *Strategies for Diversification.* © by the Harvard Business School Publishing Corporation; all rights reserved • p. 212: Lovelock, Patterson, Walker, *Services Marketing 3rd edn* © Pearson Education Australia, 2004, p. 222 • p. 236: Fit Sponsorship/Sponsormap.com • p. 241: T. Meenaghan, *Psychology & Marketing*, vol. 18, John Wiley Inc. • p. 291: Event Project Management System Pty Ltd • p. 300: EPMS/Source www.epms.net • p. 327: Department of Premier & Cabinet/Arts Victoria Do-It-Yourself Economic Impact Kit for Festivals & Events © State of Victoria • p. 329: *Project Management: Planning and Control, 2nd edn*, John Wiley & Sons Chichester. © John Wiley & Sons Limited. Reproduced with permission • p. 362: *Corporate Event Project Management*, O'Toole, 2002, John Wiley & Sons Inc.

Text
- p. 26: Lismore City Council • p. 37: Sustainability Programs Division of Department of Environment & Conservation NSW • p. 43: Lexmark Indy 300 • p. 63: Lars Blicher-Hansen, Danish Tourist Board, Copenhagen, Denmark • p. 73: http://www.iccaworld.com • p. 74: Nymagee Outback Music Festival/ Dunne 2003 • p. 77: Crown copyright material is reproduced with the permission of the Controller of HMSO and the Queen's Printer for Scotland • p. 103: Edinburgh International Book Festival — www.edbookfest.co.uk • p. 118: Michelle Morgan • p. 136: Camilla Rountree, Producer • p. 146: David Brettel, former Program Manager, Venue, Staffing and Volunteers, Sydney Olympic & Paralympic Games 2000, presently Chief Executive, Australian

Cancer Research Foundation • p. 151: California Traditional Music Society • p. 152: Courtesy of Botanic Gardens Trust Sydney • p. 156: National Folk Festival • p. 159: School of Volunteer Management, 2004 • pp. 161, 171: T. Connors, *The Volunteer Management Handbook*, John Wiley & Sons New York. This material is used by permission of John Wiley & Sons. Inc. • p. 162: Rob Harris • p. 167: California Traditional Music Society • p. 205: Morgan, *Marketing for Leisure and Tourism*, Pearson Education Limited • p. 217: Reproduced from Lovelock, Patterson and Walker 2001, *Services Marketing 2nd edn*, © Pearson Education Australia, table 9.2, p. 255 • p. 225: Bill Proud • p. 253: Country Energy Sponsorship Guidelines • p. 256: Cognizant Communication • p. 265: Terri Ferguson, Manager Sponsorship • p. 280: Robin Robertson/*Australian Financial Review* • p. 309: Neil Timmins • p. 359: Folk Federation of South Australia • p. 367: Commonwealth Copyright Administration, 1995, 'Work, health and safety', report no. 47, Canberra • p. 369: Tait Leishman Taylor • p. 372: Jo Hatton, Manager Special Projects, Australia Day Council of NSW • pp. 387–8, 390, 396: Woodford Folk Festival • p. 392: Peter Monley, Northern Rivers Folk Festival • p. 397: State Government of Victoria • p. 399: Dennis Wheeler, Senior Transport Planner Roads and Traffic Authority NSW • p. 403: Oxfam Community Aid Abroad • p. 464: Steve Kaless • p. 467: Margaret Deery, Associate Professor and Director, Victoria University • p. 494: John Chrispijn, Hobart City Council.

Every effort has been made to trace the ownership of copyright material. Information that will help to rectify any error or omission in subsequent editions will be welcome. In such cases, please contact the Permissions Section of John Wiley & Sons Australia, Ltd, who will be happy to pay the usual permission fee.

PART 1

EVENT
CONTEXT

The first part of this book looks at the history and development of events, and the emergence of the event industry in Australia. It examines the impacts of events, including their social/cultural, physical/environmental, political and tourism/economic impacts. This part also deals with the nature and importance of event tourism.

1

What are
special events?

LEARNING OBJECTIVES

After studying this chapter, you should be able to:

- define special events

- demonstrate an awareness of why special events have evolved in human society

- describe the role of special events in Australia and the Australian tradition of special events

- describe the rise of the community arts movement and its effect on the development of festivals and public events

- discuss the growth of state events corporations and the emergence of an event industry

- distinguish between different types of special event

- list and describe the components of the event industry

- discuss the attributes and knowledge requirements of a special event manager

- list the types of organisation involved in the delivery of event management training.

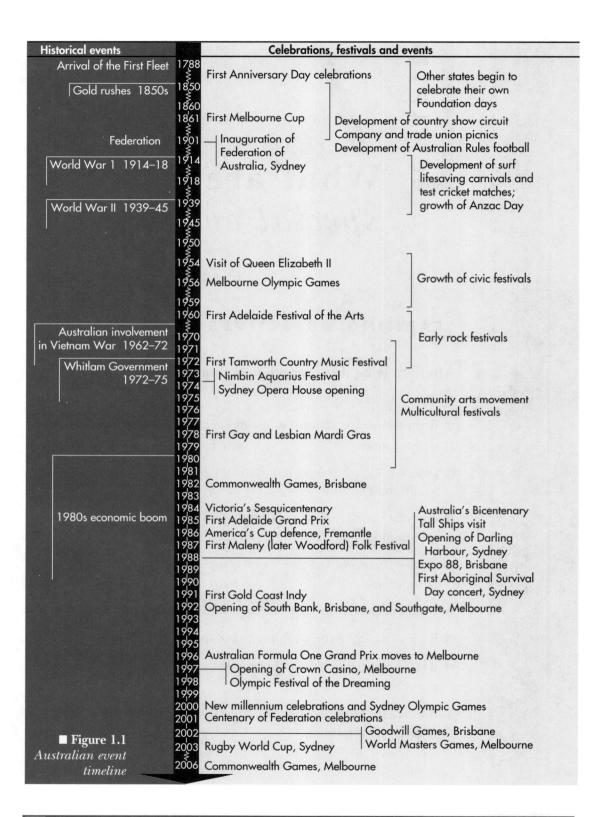

Historical events		Celebrations, festivals and events
Arrival of the First Fleet	1788	First Anniversary Day celebrations
Gold rushes 1850s	1850	Other states begin to celebrate their own Foundation days
	1860	
	1861	First Melbourne Cup — Development of country show circuit
Federation	1901	Inauguration of Federation of Australia, Sydney — Company and trade union picnics — Development of Australian Rules football
World War 1 1914–18	1914	Development of surf lifesaving carnivals and test cricket matches; growth of Anzac Day
	1918	
World War II 1939–45	1939	
	1945	
	1950	
	1954	Visit of Queen Elizabeth II
	1956	Melbourne Olympic Games — Growth of civic festivals
	1959	
	1960	First Adelaide Festival of the Arts
Australian involvement in Vietnam War 1962–72	1970	Early rock festivals
	1971	
Whitlam Government 1972–75	1972	First Tamworth Country Music Festival
	1973	Nimbin Aquarius Festival
	1974	Sydney Opera House opening
	1975	Community arts movement Multicultural festivals
	1976	
	1977	
	1978	First Gay and Lesbian Mardi Gras
	1979	
	1980	
	1981	
	1982	Commonwealth Games, Brisbane
	1983	
1980s economic boom	1984	Victoria's Sesquicentenary — Australia's Bicentenary
	1985	First Adelaide Grand Prix — Tall Ships visit
	1986	America's Cup defence, Fremantle — Opening of Darling
	1987	First Maleny (later Woodford) Folk Festival — Harbour, Sydney
	1988	Expo 88, Brisbane
	1989	First Aboriginal Survival
	1990	Day concert, Sydney
	1991	First Gold Coast Indy
	1992	Opening of South Bank, Brisbane, and Southgate, Melbourne
	1993	
	1994	
	1995	
	1996	Australian Formula One Grand Prix moves to Melbourne
	1997	Opening of Crown Casino, Melbourne
	1998	Olympic Festival of the Dreaming
	1999	
	2000	New millennium celebrations and Sydney Olympic Games
	2001	Centenary of Federation celebrations
	2002	Goodwill Games, Brisbane
	2003	Rugby World Cup, Sydney — World Masters Games, Melbourne
	2006	Commonwealth Games, Melbourne

■ **Figure 1.1**
Australian event timeline

INTRODUCTION

Today, events are central to our culture as perhaps never before. Increases in leisure time and discretionary spending have led to a proliferation of public events, celebrations and entertainment. Governments now support and promote events as part of their strategies for economic development, nation building and destination marketing. Corporations and businesses embrace events as key elements in their marketing strategies and image promotion. The enthusiasm of community groups and individuals for their own interests and passions gives rise to a marvellous array of events on almost every subject and theme imaginable. Events spill out of our newspapers and television screens, occupy much of our time, and enrich our lives. As we study the phenomenon of events, it is worth examining where the event tradition in Australia has come from, and what forces are likely to shape its future growth and development. As events emerge as an industry in their own right, it is also worth considering what elements characterise such an industry, and how the Australian event industry might chart its future directions in an increasingly complex and demanding environment.

SPECIAL EVENTS AS BENCHMARKS FOR OUR LIVES

Since the dawn of time, human beings have found ways to mark important events in their lives: the changing of the seasons, the phases of the moon, and the renewal of life each spring. From the Aboriginal corroboree and Chinese New Year to the Dionysian rites of ancient Greece and the European carnival tradition of the Middle Ages, myths and rituals have been created to interpret cosmic happenings. To the present day, behind well-known figures such as Old Father Time and Santa Claus lie old myths, archetypes and ancient celebrations. The first Australians used storytelling, dance and song to transmit their culture from generation to generation. Their ceremonies were, and continue to be, important occasions in the life of the community, where cultural meaning is shared and affirmed. Similarly, in most agrarian societies, rituals were developed that marked the coming of the seasons and the sowing and harvesting of crops.

Both in private and in public, people feel the need to mark the important occasions in their lives, and to celebrate milestones. Coming of age, for example, is often marked by a rite of passage, as illustrated by the tribal initiation ceremony, the Jewish bar and bat mitzvahs and the suburban twenty-first birthday.

At the public level, momentous events become the milestones by which people measure their private lives. We may talk about things happening 'before the new millennium', in the same way that an earlier generation talked of marrying 'before the Depression' or being born 'after the War'. Occasional events — Australia's Bicentenary, the Sydney Olympics and the new millennium — help to mark eras and define milestones.

Even in the high-tech era of global media, when many people have lost touch with the common religious beliefs and social norms of the past, we still need larger social events to mark the local and domestic details of our lives.

THE MODERN AUSTRALIAN TRADITION OF CELEBRATIONS

In the cultural collision between Aboriginal people and the first Europeans, new traditions were formed alongside the old. Probably the first 'event' in Australia after the arrival of the First Fleet was a bush party to celebrate the coming ashore of the women convicts in 1788:

> ■ Meanwhile, most of the sailors on *Lady Penrhyn* applied to her master, Captain William Sever, for an extra ration of rum 'to make merry with upon the women quitting the ship'. Out came the pannikins, down went the rum, and before long the drunken tars went off to join the convicts in pursuit of the women, so that, Bowes remarked, 'it is beyond my abilities to give a just description of the scene of debauchery and riot that ensued during the night'. It was the first bush party in Australia, with 'some swearing, others quarrelling, others singing' (Hughes 1987, pp. 88–9). ■

From these inauspicious beginnings, the early colonists slowly started to evolve celebrations that were tailored to their new environment, so far from Georgian Britain. Hull (1984) traces the history of these early celebrations, noting the beginnings of a national day some 30 years later:

> ■ Governor Macquarie declared the 26th of January 1818 a public holiday — convicts were given the day off, a ration of one pound of fresh meat was made for each of them, there was a military review, a salute of 30 guns, a dinner for the officers and a ball for the colony society. ■

This may have been the first festival celebrated by the new inhabitants of Australia. Although 'Anniversary Day', as it was known, was not to become a public holiday for another 20 years, the official celebration of the founding of the colony had begun with the direct involvement and patronage of the government that exists to this day. In contrast to government-organised celebrations, settlers during the nineteenth century entertained themselves with balls, shows and travelling entertainments as a diversion from the serious business of work and survival. The rich tradition of agricultural shows and race meetings such as the Melbourne Cup survives today. The Sydney Royal Easter Show, after surviving from the mid-nineteenth century, has reinvented itself as 'The Great Australian Muster'.

At the turn of the century, the celebration of Australia's Federation captured the prevailing mood of optimistic patriotism:

■ At the turn of the year 1900–1 the city of Sydney went mad with joy. For a few days hope ran so high that poets and prophets declared Australia to be on the threshold of a new golden age ... from early morning on 1 January 1901 trams, trains and ferry boats carried thousands of people into the city for the greatest day in their history: the inauguration of the Commonwealth of Australia. It was to be a people's festival (Clark 1981, p. 177). ■

At the beginning of the twentieth century, the new inhabitants had come to terms with the landscape of Australia, and the democratic ritual of the picnic had gained mass popularity. This extended to guilds, unions and company workers, as demonstrated by the following description of the annual picnic of the employees of Sydney boot and shoe manufacturers McMurtie and Company, at Clontarf in 1906:

■ 'The sweet strains of piano, violin and cornet... added zest and enjoyment to the festive occasion', said the Advisor. 'Laughter producers were also in evidence, several of the company wearing comical-looking hats and false noses so that even at the commencement of the day's proceedings hilarity and enjoyment was assured.' The enjoyment continued as the party disembarked to the strain of bagpipes, and the sporting programme began ... The 'little ones' were provided with 'toys, spades, balls and lollies'. The shooting gallery was well patronised, and when darkness fell dancing went on in the beautiful dancing hall. Baby Houston danced a Scotch reel to the music of bagpipes. Miss Robinson sang *Underneath the Watermelon Vine*, and little Ruth Bailey danced a jig.

At 8 pm, the whistle blew and the homeward journey commenced with 'music up till the last' and a final rendering of *Auld Lang Syne* as the *Erina* arrived at the Quay (Pearl 1974). ■

However, Australians had to wait until after World War II before a home-grown form of celebration took hold across the nation. In the 1940s and 1950s, city and town festivals were established, which created a common and enduring format. Even today, it is a safe assumption that any festival with an Aboriginal or floral name, and that includes a 'Festival Queen' competition, street parade, outdoor art exhibition and sporting event, dates back to this period. Sydney's Waratah Festival (later replaced by the Sydney Festival), Melbourne's Moomba, Ballarat's Begonia Festival, Young's Cherry Festival, Bowral's Tulip Time, Newcastle's Mattara Festival and Toowoomba's Carnival of Flowers all date back to the prolific era of local pride and involvement after World War II. Moomba and Mattara both adopted Aboriginal names, the latter word meaning 'hand of friendship'.

Holding such a festival became a badge of civic pride, in the way that building a School of Arts hall had done in an earlier era, or constructing an Olympic swimming pool would do in the 1950s and 1960s. These festivals gave the cities and towns a sense of identity and distinction, and became a focus for community groups and charity fundraising. It is a tribute to their importance to communities that many of these festivals continue after half a century.

Alongside this movement of community festivals was another very powerful model. In 1947 the Edinburgh Festival was founded as part of the post-war spirit of reconstruction and renewal. In Australia, the Festival of Perth (founded in 1953) and the Adelaide Festival of the Arts (founded in 1960) were based on this inspiring model. The influence of the Edinburgh Festival proved to be enduring, as shown by the resurgence of arts festivals in Sydney, Melbourne and Brisbane in the 1980s and 1990s.

By the 1970s, however, with the coming to power of the Whitlam Government and the formation of the Australia Council, new cultural directions were unleashed that were to change the face of festivals in Australia.

The Community Arts Board of the Australia Council, under the leadership of Ros Bower, developed a strategy aimed at giving a voice to the voiceless and taking arts and festivals into the suburbs and towns of Australia. Often for the first time, migrants, workers and Aboriginal people were encouraged to participate in a new cultural pluralism that broke down the elitism that had governed the arts in much of rural and suburban Australia. Sensing the unique cultural challenge faced by Australia, Bower (1981) wrote:

> ■ In terms of our national cultural objectives, the re-integration of the artist into the community is of crucial importance. Australia lacks a coherent cultural background. The artist needs to become the spokesman, the interpreter, the image-maker and the prophet. He cannot do it in isolation or from an ivory tower. He must do it by working with the people. He must help them to piece together their local history, their local traditions, their folk-lore, the drama and the visual imagery of their lives. And in doing this he will enrich and give identity to his work as an artist. The arts will cease to be imitative, or preoccupied with making big splashes in little 'cultured' pools. They will be integrated more closely with our lives, our history, our unique environment. They will be experimental and exploring forces within the broader cultural framework. ■

The 1970s involved not only the emergence of multiculturalism and the 'new age' movement, but also the forging of the community arts movement and a new and diverse range of festivals across Australia. Examples of the rich diversity spawned by this period are the Aquarius Festival staged by the Australian Union of Students at Nimbin in northern New South Wales, the Lygon Street Festa in Melbourne's Carlton, the Come Out young people's festival held in alternate years to the Adelaide Festival, the Carnivale celebration of multiculturalism across Sydney and New South Wales, and Sydney's Gay and Lesbian Mardi Gras. Festivals became part of the cultural landscape and connected again to people's needs and lives. Every community, it seemed, had something to celebrate and the tools with which to create its own festival.

THE BIRTH OF AN EVENT INDUSTRY

Through the 1980s and 1990s, certain seminal events set the pattern for the contemporary event industry as we know it today. The Commonwealth Games in Brisbane in 1982 ushered in a new era of maturity and prominence for that city and a new breed of sporting events. It also initiated a career in ceremonies and celebrations for former ABC rock show producer, Ric Birch, which led to his taking a key role in the opening and closing ceremonies at the Los Angeles, Barcelona and Sydney Olympics. The Olympic Games in Los Angeles in 1984 demonstrated that major events could be economically viable. The organisers managed to combine a Hollywood-style spectacular with a sporting event in a manner that had not been done before, and that would set a standard for all similar events in future. The production and marketing skills of the television industry brought the Olympics to an audience wider than ever before. Television also demonstrated the power of a major sporting event to bring increased profile and economic benefits to a city and to an entire country.

The entrepreneurs of the 1980s economic boom in Australia soon picked up on this potential, and the America's Cup defence in Perth and Fremantle in 1986–87 was treated as an opportunity to put Perth on the map and to attract major economic and tourism benefits to Western Australia. By 1988, there was a boom in special events, with Australia's Bicentenary perceived by many as a major commemorative program and vehicle for tourism. This boom was matched by governments setting up state events corporations, thereby giving public sector support to special events as never before. In Brisbane, the success of Expo 88 rivalled the Bicentennial activities in Sydney, and Adelaide managed a coup by staging the first Australian Formula One Grand Prix.

The Bicentenary caused Australians to pause and reflect on the Australian identity. It also changed forever the nature of our public celebrations:

> ■ I would argue that the remarkable legacy of 1988 is the public event. It is now a regular feature of Australian life. We gather for fireworks, for welcome-home marches for athletes and other Australians who have achieved success. We go to large urban spaces like the Domain for opera, rock and symphonic music in our hundreds of thousands. The Sydney Festival attracts record numbers. The Gay Mardi Gras is an international phenomenon ... Whatever the nature of debate about values, identity and imagery, one certainty is that Australians are in love with high-quality public events that are fun and offer to extend the range and experience of being Australian (McCarthy 1998). ■

The Bicentenary also left a legacy of public spaces dedicated to celebrations and special events and of governments supporting events for their perceived social and economic benefits. Sydney's Darling Harbour opened to welcome the Tall Ships on 16 January 1988 and provided the city with a major leisure centre. Darling Harbour incorporates dedicated celebrations areas, tourist attractions, a festival marketplace and convention and exhibition centres, all adjacent to the Sydney Entertainment Centre and the Powerhouse and National Maritime museums. Likewise, Brisbane's riverside Expo 88 site was converted into the South Bank Parklands, and Melbourne followed suit with the Southbank development on the Yarra River.

Whatever its economic causes, the recession of the late 1980s and early 1990s put a dampener on the party mood and the seemingly endless growth of events — that is, until 4.27 am on 24 September 1993 when International Olympic President Juan Antonio Samaranch spoke those memorable words: 'And the winner is ... Sydney!'

Many said the recession ended the day Sydney was awarded the Olympic Games of the new millennium. Certainly, it meant the event industry could once more look forward with optimism, as though the recession had been a mere pause for breath. Event corporations formed in the late 1980s and early 1990s started to demonstrate that special events could generate economic benefits. This led to competition between the states for major events, which became weapons in an event war fuelled by the media. Australia approached the end of the century with a competitive events climate dominated by the Sydney Olympics, the new millennium and the Centenary of Federation celebrations in 2001. This enthusiasm for events has continued well into the first decade of the new century, with the staging of the Goodwill Games in Brisbane in 2001, the World Masters Games in Melbourne, the International Gay Games in Sydney in 2002, the World Rugby Cup in venues around Australia in 2003 and the Commonwealth Games due to be staged in Melbourne in 2006.

The corporate world was quick to discover the marketing and image-making power of events, and events became established through the 1990s and early this decade as an important element of the corporate marketing mix. Companies and corporations began to partner major events, such as AMP's links with the Olympic Torch Relay in 2000 and the Centenary of Federation Journey of a Nation in 2001. Other corporations created events as vehicles for their own marketing — for example, One Summer of Sport presented by Uncle Tobys, St George Bank and the 10 Network, which toured nationally in 1999–2000. By early this decade, corporate involvement in events had become the norm, so sponsorship was perceived as an integral part of staging major events. Companies became increasingly aware of the role that events could play in promoting their image and increasing their market share, but they also became more focused on event outcomes and return on investment. It became common for large companies to have an in-house event team, focused not only on the company's involvement in public events, but also on the internal role of events in staff training and morale building. Events became not only a significant part of the corporate vocabulary, but also a viable career option with employment opportunities and career paths.

This brief outline of the history of modern events relates primarily to the Australian situation, but a similar story has been replicated in most post-industrial societies. The balance between more traditional festivals and contemporary corporate events changes according to the nature of the society in a given geographic area. Nevertheless, events are a growing phenomenon worldwide, suggesting they fulfil a basic need in human society. Australia is widely recognised as a leader in the event field, with state governments' events corporations and the staging of the Sydney Olympics being regarded as international benchmarks for best practice in the field.

WHAT ARE SPECIAL EVENTS? ·····················

The term 'special events' has been coined to describe specific rituals, presentations, performances or celebrations that are consciously planned and created to mark special occasions or achieve particular social, cultural or corporate goals and objectives. Special events can include national days and celebrations, important civic occasions, unique cultural performances, major sporting fixtures, corporate functions, trade promotions and product launches. It seems at times that special events are everywhere; they have become a growth industry. The field of special events is now so vast that it is impossible to provide a definition that includes all varieties and shades of events. In his groundbreaking work on the typology of events, Getz (1997, p. 4) suggests special events are best defined by their context. He offers two definitions, one from the point of view of the event organiser and the other from that of the customer or guest:

■ 1. A special event is a one-time or infrequently occurring event outside normal programs or activities of the sponsoring or organizing body.
2. To the customer or guest, a special event is an opportunity for a leisure, social or cultural experience outside the normal range of choices or beyond everyday experience. ■

Among the attributes that he believes create the special atmosphere are festive spirit, uniqueness, quality, authenticity, tradition, hospitality, theme and symbolism.

TYPES OF EVENT ·····················

There are many different ways of categorising or grouping events, including by size, form and content, as discussed in the following sections. This text examines the full range of events that the event industry produces, using the term 'event' to cover all of the following categories.

■ Size

Special events are often characterised according to their size or scale (figure 1.2). Common categories are mega-events, hallmark events, major events and local/community events, although definitions are not exact and distinctions can be blurred.

■ **Figure 1.2**
Categorisation of events

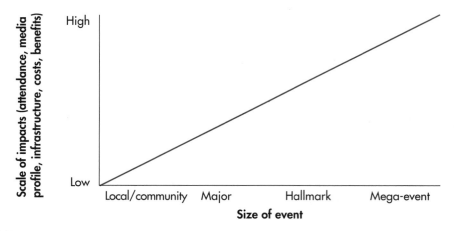

Mega-events

Mega-events are those events that are so large they affect whole economies and reverberate in the global media. They include Olympic Games and World Fairs, but it is difficult for many other events to fit into this category. Getz (1997, p. 6) defines mega-events in the following way:

> ■ Their volume should exceed 1 million visits, their capital costs should be at least $500 million, and their reputation should be of a 'must see' event . . . Mega-events, by way of their size or significance, are those that yield extraordinarily high levels of tourism, media coverage, prestige, or economic impact for the host community or destination. ■

Hall (1992, p. 5), another researcher in the field of events and tourism, offers this definition:

> ■ Mega-events such as World Fairs and Expositions, the World Soccer Cup final, or the Olympic Games, are events which are expressly targeted at the international tourism market and may be suitably described as 'mega' by virtue of their size in terms of attendance, target market, level of public financial involvement, political effects, extent of television coverage, construction of facilities, and impact on economic and social fabric of the host community. ■

By these definitions, the Sydney Olympic Games in 2000 was perhaps Australia's first true mega-event. The Melbourne Olympics in 1956 belonged to an earlier era of far less extensive media coverage and smaller television audiences, although in relative terms it may qualify as a mega-event of its era. Even Brisbane's Expo 88 was officially a 'B' class Expo, and events such as the

Commonwealth Games in Brisbane in 1982 and the America's Cup defence in Perth and Fremantle in 1986–87 would struggle to meet Getz's criteria. More recently, the Rugby World Cup in 2003 may qualify in terms of media coverage and profile.

Hallmark events

The term 'hallmark events' refers to those events that become so identified with the spirit or ethos of a town, city or region that they become synonymous with the name of the place, and gain widespread recognition and awareness. Tourism researcher Ritchie (1984, p. 2) defines them as:

> ■ Major one-time or recurring events of limited duration, developed primarily to enhance awareness, appeal and profitability of a tourism destination in the short term and/or long term. Such events rely for their success on uniqueness, status, or timely significance to create interest and attract attention. ■

Classic examples of hallmark events are the Carnival in Rio de Janeiro, known throughout the world as an expression of the vitality and exuberance of that city, the Kentucky Derby in the USA, the Chelsea Flower Show in Britain, the Oktoberfest in Munich, Germany, and the Edinburgh Festival in Scotland. Such events, which are identified with the very character of these places and their citizens, bring huge tourist dollars, a strong sense of local pride and international recognition. Getz (1997, pp. 5–6) describes them in terms of their ability to provide a competitive advantage for their host communities:

> ■ The term 'hallmark event' is used to describe a recurring event that possesses such significance, in terms of tradition, attractiveness, image, or publicity, that the event provides the host venue, community, or destination with a competitive advantage. Over time, the event and destination become inseparable. For example Mardi Gras gives New Orleans a competitive advantage by virtue of its high profile. Stratford, Ontario, has taken its tourism theme from the successful Shakespearean Festival. Increasingly, every community and destination needs one or more hallmark events to provide the high levels of media exposure and positive imagery that help to create competitive advantages. ■

Examples in Australia might include the Sydney Gay and Lesbian Mardi Gras, the Australasian Country Music Festival at Tamworth, the Melbourne Cup and the Adelaide Festival, all of which have a degree of international recognition and help to identify the ethos of their host cities.

Major events

Major events are events that are capable, by their scale and media interest, of attracting significant visitor numbers, media coverage and economic benefits. Melbourne has developed the Australian Open tennis tournament and the Australian Formula One Grand Prix into significant annual major events, and will host the Commonwealth Games in 2006. Perth has developed a portfolio of major events, including the Hyundai Hopman Cup in tennis and the Telstra Rally Australia. Brisbane hosted the Goodwill Games in 2001, and the Gold Coast has the annual Indy Grand Prix. Cultural events can also be contenders, such as the Adelaide, Sydney and Melbourne arts festivals, and regional festivals such as 10 Days on the Island in Tasmania, the Queensland Music Festival and the Margaret River concerts in Western Australia.

Local or community events

Most communities produce a host of festivals and events that are targeted mainly at local audiences and staged primarily for their social, fun and entertainment value. These events often produce a range of benefits, including engendering pride in the community, strengthening a feeling of belonging and creating a sense of place. They can also help to expose people to new ideas and experiences, encourage participation in sports and arts activities, and encourage tolerance and diversity. For these reasons, local governments often support such events as part of their community and cultural development strategies.

Janiskee (1996, p. 404) defines them as:

> ■ ... family-fun events that are considered 'owned' by a community because they use volunteer services from the host community, employ public venues such as streets, parks and schools and are produced at the direction of local government agencies or nongovernment organizations (NGOs) such as service clubs, public safety organisations or business associations. ■

Janiskee also comments that community festivals can become hallmark events and attract a large number of visitors to a community. Janiskee estimates that community celebrations in the USA have been increasing at an annual rate of 5 per cent since the 1930s, and it is reasonable to assume that they have increased at a similar rate in Australia.

■ Form *or content*

Another common means of classifying events is by their form or content. Festivals are a universal form of events that pre-date the contemporary event industry and exist in most times and most societies. Sports events have grown out of similar roots to become a sizable and growing sector of the event industry. MICE (Meetings, Incentives, Conventions and Exhibitions) events, sometimes called business events, are an established arm of the event industry, and generate considerable income for their host cities and, increasingly, for regional centres.

Festivals

Festivals are an important expression of human activity that contribute much to our social and cultural life. They are also increasingly linked with tourism to generate business activity and income for their host communities.

The most common type of festival is the arts festival, which can encompass mixed art forms and multiple venues — such as the capital city arts festivals — or single art forms such as the Queensland Bicentennial Music Festival, the Sydney Biennale or the Melbourne Writers Festival. The most popular form of arts festival is the music festival, which can range from classical music festivals such as the National Chamber Music Festival in Canberra, to jazz festivals such as the Melbourne International Jazz Festival, to folk and blues festivals such as the East Coast Blues and Roots Music Festival at Byron Bay and the Woodford Folk Festival in Queensland, to rock festivals such as the Big Day Out, Livid and Homebake.

Another type of festival that has become universally popular is the food and wine festival. These range from large festivals in the capital cities to local festivals showcasing regional cuisine. Other festivals such as the Tropfest short film festival and the Big Day Out have become multi-state festivals, while festivals such as Floriade in Canberra and the Sydney Gay and Lesbian Mardi Gras approach hallmark status in their respective cities. Regional festivals, too, are a growing phenomenon, with many large and small towns expressing their unique character and distinctiveness through well-honed festivals and community celebrations. Festivals have become a pervasive feature of our cultural landscape and constitute a vital and growing component of the event industry.

Sports events

The testing of sporting prowess through competition is one of the oldest and most enduring of human activities, with a rich tradition going back to the ancient Greek Olympics and beyond. Sports events are an important and growing part of the event industry, encompassing the full spectrum of individual sports and multi-sport events such as the Olympic, Commonwealth and Masters games. Their ability to attract tourist visitors and to generate media coverage and economic impacts has placed them at the fore of most government event strategies and destination marketing programs. Sports events not only bring benefits to their host governments and sports organisations, but also benefit participants such as players, coaches and officials, and bring entertainment and enjoyment to spectators. Examples of sports events can be readily identified in each of the size categories listed earlier.

The MICE industry, or business events

Another long-established component of the event industry is the MICE industry, now often called business events. This sector is largely characterised by its business and trade focus, although there is a strong public and tourism aspect to many of its activities. Meetings can be very diverse, as revealed by the definition of the Department of Industry Tourism and Resources (1995, p. 3):

■ … all off-site gatherings, including conventions, congresses, conferences, seminars, workshops and symposiums, which bring together people for a common purpose — the sharing of information. ■

The MICE industry market is worth an estimated $7 billion per year (Johnson, Foo & O'Halloran 1999). The scale and value of large MICE events is illustrated by the following two examples. The International Genetics Congress staged in Melbourne in 2003 attracted 2700 delegates, including elite scientists and leading researchers, and generated $23 million for the city (Melbourne Convention and Exhibition Centre 2003). The Lions Club International Convention to be hosted in Sydney in 2010 is expected to attract 25 000 people from more than 100 countries, and to generate more than $91 million for the city (Nori 2003).

Another lucrative aspect of the MICE industry is incentive travel, defined by the Society of Incentive Travel Executives (1997) (cited in Rogers 1998, p. 47) as 'a global management tool that uses an exceptional travel experience to motivate and/or recognise participants for increased levels of performance in support of organisational goals'. Australia's colourful and unique locations and international popularity as a tourism destination make it a leading player in the incentive travel market.

Last, but not least, exhibitions are a considerable and growing part of the MICE industry. Exhibitions bring suppliers of goods and services together with buyers, usually in a particular industry sector. They can be restricted to industry members — in which case they are referred to as trade shows — or open to the general public. The International Motor Show, the Home Show and the Boat Show are three of the largest exhibitions in Sydney, each generating tens of thousands of visitors. Major convention centres in most Australian cities and many regional centres now vie for their share of the thriving MICE industry market.

THE STRUCTURE OF THE EVENT INDUSTRY

The rapid growth of events in the past decade led to the formation of an identifiable event industry, with its own practitioners, suppliers and professional associations. The emergence of the industry has involved the identification and refinement of a discrete body of knowledge of industry best practice, accompanied by the development of training programs and career paths. The industry's formation has also been accompanied by a period of rapid globalisation of markets and communication, which has affected the nature of, and trends within, the industry. Further, it has been accompanied by an era of increasing government regulation, which has resulted in a complex and demanding operational environment. The following sections describe the key components of the event industry.

■ Event *organisations*

Events are often staged or hosted by event organisations, which may be event-specific bodies such as the Festival of Sydney or the Adelaide

Festival. Other events are run by special teams within larger organisations, such as the City to Surf fun run organised by *The Sun-Herald* newspaper in Sydney, or the Sydney to Hobart Yacht Race organised by the Cruising Yacht Club of Australia. Corporate events are often organised by in-house event teams or by project teams within the companies that are putting on the event.

■ Event *management companies*

Event management companies are professional groups or individuals that organise events on a contract basis on behalf of their clients. The Australia Day Council, for example, may contract an event management company to stage an Australia Day ceremony, or the Microsoft Corporation may contract an event manager to stage the launch of a new product. The specialist companies often organise a number of events concurrently, and develop long-term relationships with their clients and suppliers.

■ Event *industry suppliers*

The growth of a large and complex industry has led to the formation of a wide range of specialist suppliers. These suppliers may work in direct event-related areas, such as staging, sound production, lighting, audiovisual production, entertainment and catering, or they may work in associated areas, such as transport, communications, security, legal services and accounting services. This network of suppliers is an integral part of the industry, and their increasing specialisation and expertise assist the production of professional and high-calibre events.

■ Industry *associations*

The emergence of the industry has also led to the formation of professional associations providing networking, communications and liaison within the industry, training and accreditation programs, codes of ethical practice, and lobbying on behalf of their members. Because the industry is so diverse, multiple associations have arisen to cater for specific sectors of the industry. Some are international associations with affiliated groups in countries such as Australia; others are specific to their region or country. Some key industry associations relevant to the interests of event managers are described below:

- *International Festivals and Events Society (ISES)* (www.ises.com 2003). Headquartered in the USA, the ISES has established chapters in Europe, Canada, South Africa and Australia (Sydney and Melbourne). It stages an annual Conference for Professional Development, and offers accreditation as a Certified Special Events Professional (CSEP).
- *International Festivals and Events Association (IFEA)* (www.ifea.org.au). Also headquartered in the USA, the IFEA has affiliated organisations in Europe, Asia and Australia. It runs a Certified Festival and Event Executive (CFEE) program. It also organises an annual convention and

seminars. Festivals and events associations exist in some Australian states. The one in Sydney, for example, stages regular educational seminars and networking events, and has staged biennial conferences since 1999.

- *Meetings Industry Association of Australia (MIAA)* (www.miaa.net.com). The MIAA provides training for the meetings sector of the industry and offers an accreditation program that operates at two levels — Accredited Member of the Meetings Industry Association of Australia (AMIAA), covering all segments of the meetings industry, and Accredited Meetings Manager (AMM), applying only to meetings managers.
- *Exhibitions and Events Association of Australia (EEAA)* (www.eeaa.org.au). The EEAA promotes the value of exhibitions as well as the professionalism of its members. It conducts industry research, conducts an annual conference and runs an occupational health and safety assurance program for its members.

■ External *regulatory bodies*

As noted, contemporary events take place in an increasingly regulated and complex environment. A series of government and statutory bodies are responsible for overseeing the conduct and safe staging of events, and these bodies have an integral relationship with the industry. Many local councils now require a development application for the staging of outdoor events. This application may cover regulations governing the erection of temporary structures, traffic plans, noise restrictions and so on. Councils also often oversee the application of state laws governing the preparation and sale of food, street closures, waste management and removal. In addition, events organisers have a legal responsibility to provide a safe workplace and to obey all laws and statutes relating to employment, contracts, taxation and so on. The professional event manager needs to be familiar with the regulations governing events and to maintain contact with the public authorities that have a vested interest in the industry.

EVENT MANAGEMENT, EDUCATION AND TRAINING

As the size and needs of the event industry have grown, event management training has started to emerge as a discrete discipline. In the early years of the industry, leading up to the mid-1990s, the field was characterised by a large number of volunteers. Those few event managers who obtained paid positions came from a variety of related disciplines, drawing on their knowledge gained from that discipline and skills learnt on the job. Many came from allied areas such as theatre and entertainment, audiovisual production and film, and adapted their skills to events. Others came from working for event suppliers such as staging, lighting and sound production companies, having discovered that they could expand and build on their existing skills to undertake the overall management of events. However, as the use of events by government and industry has grown, event budgets have increased, and the logistics of events have become more complex, the need has emerged for skilled event professionals who can meet the industry's specific requirements. Education and training at a number of levels have arisen to meet this need.

■ Identifying *the knowledge and skills required by event managers*

In addition to generic management skills, Getz and Wicks (1994, pp. 108–9) specify the following event-specific areas of knowledge as appropriate for inclusion in event management training:

■ • History and meanings of festivals, celebrations, rituals and other events
  • Historical evolution; types of events
  • Trends in demand and supply
  • Motivations and benefits sought from events
  • Roles and impacts of events in society, the economy, environment and culture
  • Who is producing events, and why?
  • Program concepts and styles
  • Event settings
  • Operations unique to events
  • Management unique to events
  • Marketing unique to events ■

Perry, Foley and Rumpf (1996) describe the attributes and knowledge required by event managers based on a survey of the views of 105 managers who attended the Australian Events Conference in Canberra in February 1996. Seven attributes were frequently mentioned, of which vision was listed as the most important, closely followed by leadership, adaptability, and skills in organisation, communication, marketing and people management. Knowledge areas considered most important were project management, budgeting, time management, relating to the media, business planning, human resource management and marketing. The graph in figure 1.3 (page 20) shows some of the results of the survey. Respondents were asked to indicate how strongly they agreed or disagreed with a statement such as, 'An events manager requires skills in project management'.

Further studies by Harris and Griffin (1997), Royal and Jago (1998), Harris and Jago (1999) and Arcodia and Barker (2002) confirmed the importance of these knowledge/skill domains. Despite occasional differing emphases and nuances, therefore, the field generally agrees on the specific body of knowledge of best practice appropriate to the training of professional event managers.

■ Figure 1.3
*Knowledge
required
by event
managers —
respondents
to survey*

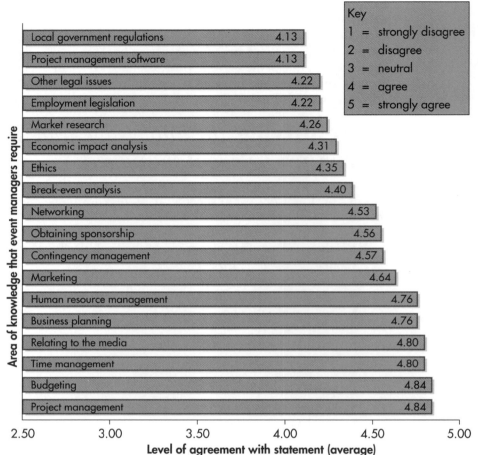

Key
1 = strongly disagree
2 = disagree
3 = neutral
4 = agree
5 = strongly agree

Area of knowledge that event managers require	Level of agreement
Local government regulations	4.13
Project management software	4.13
Other legal issues	4.22
Employment legislation	4.22
Market research	4.26
Economic impact analysis	4.31
Ethics	4.35
Break-even analysis	4.40
Networking	4.53
Obtaining sponsorship	4.56
Contingency management	4.57
Marketing	4.64
Human resource management	4.76
Business planning	4.76
Relating to the media	4.80
Time management	4.80
Budgeting	4.84
Project management	4.84

Level of agreement with statement (average)

■ Training *delivery*

As training has become needed, it has been delivered in a range of formats by a variety of institutions.

Industry associations

The major event industry associations have all been involved in the delivery of training and certification programs. These programs typically involve a points system whereby accreditation can be gained from a mix of participation in the association, contribution to the industry, attendance at conferences and seminars, and often a written paper or examination. Pre-requisites often include membership of the association, industry experience and allegiance to a written code of conduct or ethics. Accreditation programs are usually supported by educational provisions such as seminar training programs, online training courses and self-directed learning resources.

Universities and other tertiary education institutions

Universities have also recently become involved in event education, with most offering event management or marketing subjects as part of tourism, hospitality, recreation and/or sport management programs. The George Washington University in Washington DC was an early pioneer in offering a concentration in event management within a graduate program; in 1994 it commenced a complete certification program in event management (Getz and Wicks 1994).

Harris and Jago (1999) conducted a census of event-related subjects offered in Australian universities by assessing the courses listed on each university's website. Of the 29 universities examined, 17 offered at least one subject that was identified as belonging to the events/meetings sector. The majority of subjects were offered as electives within tourism, hospitality, sport management and human development programs, with others offered in marketing, communication and fine art programs. The study identified only four universities that offered specialisations in the events/meetings sector. The study also found that the offering of the tertiary and further education (TAFE) and private college sector was similarly limited to the inclusion of elective units in existing programs or, in some cases, to specific streams comprising up to four units. However, an integrated training package, under development by TAFE NSW at the time of the study, has now been implemented, and event courses have continued to proliferate and expand in Australian and overseas universities.

CAREER OPPORTUNITIES IN EVENTS

As demonstrated above, events are an expanding industry, providing new and challenging job opportunities for people entering the field. A national study of over 100 web-based job advertisements (Arcodia and Barker 2002) found a concentration of jobs along the Australian east coast, with the majority (54 per cent) located in Sydney, followed by Melbourne (17 per cent) and Brisbane (4 per cent). The most common types of employer were event companies (26 per cent), followed by the hotel and resort industry (13 per cent), non-profit organisations (8 per cent), financial management companies (6 per cent) and government agencies, including local government (5 per cent). The study confirmed the skill requirements listed earlier but also identified personal attributes specified by employers, including motivation (29 per cent), positive attitude (16 per cent), dynamism and energy (13 per cent), commitment (12 per cent), creativity (12 per cent) and initiative (12 per cent).

A successful career in events depends on applicants identifying their own skills and interests, and then matching these carefully with the needs of prospective employers. Areas of expanding activity — such as corporate events, conferences, local government and tourism — may be fruitful areas to examine. Employers often look for a mix of qualifications and experience, so intending job seekers may be advised to consider taking entry-level positions to take that important first step towards a satisfying and rewarding career.

EVENT PROFILE

Australian Centre for Event Management

The Australian Centre for Event Management (ACEM) was established at the University of Technology, Sydney, in 1999. It aims to provide research and training services to the event industry and to position Sydney and Australia as centres of excellence in the development of skills and knowledge associated with the creation, conduct and evaluation of events.

The following are some of the education and training programs provided by ACEM:

- Executive Certificate in Event Management — a seven-day intensive course tailored to the needs of people working in or wanting to enter the event industry
- event and venue management seminars — a series of one-day seminars on current topics and issues in event and venue management, delivered by industry practitioners
- Master of Management in Event Management — a masters program in event management, delivered by the university's Faculty of Business. The program covers all aspects of event management and may be taken at the graduate certificate and graduate diploma levels, as well as the full masters level.
- event management short courses — short courses in event management, delivered by the centre in association with university partners around Australia and overseas. Such courses have been delivered in Melbourne, Brisbane, Perth, Hobart, Edinburgh, Auckland and Kuala Lumpur.
- in-house training — training programs in event management tailored to the needs of specific government and industry clients. Clients have included Tourism New South Wales, the NSW Department of State and Regional Development, the NSW Attorney-General's Department, artsACT, Canberra Arts Marketing and Casula Powerhouse.
- research — ACEM conducts research on core issues in event management, and provides a research service to clients in government and industry. Clients have included Sydney Olympic Park Authority, Playbill Venues at Fox Studios in Sydney and artsACT.
- event research conference — a biennial international research conference in event management. The first conference, 'Events beyond 2000: setting the agenda', was conducted in 2000, with keynote speakers including noted event educators and authors Dr Joe Jeff Goldblatt and Professor

Donald Getz. The second conference, 'Events and place making', was conducted in 2002 with keynote speakers including Sandy Hollway, the former chief executive officer of SOCOG; Peter Kenyon, director of the Bank of IDEAS; and event director John Aitken. ACEM also conducted a one-day conference, 'The art of celebration', in Sydney in 2002, Canberra in 2003 and Gosford in 2004.

- publications — a range of event management resources published on the centre's website, including full conference proceedings of the above conferences and a complete Australian and international bibliography of event management publications. The website (www.acem.uts.edu.au) also provides details of current ACEM research and training programs and activities.

SUMMARY

Special events perform a powerful role in society, and they have existed throughout human history in all times and all cultures. The Australian Aboriginal culture had a rich tradition of rituals and ceremonies before the arrival of the Europeans. The event tradition in modern Australia began in a primitive way with the arrival of the First Fleet, and developed through the late eighteenth and nineteenth centuries as the colony prospered and the new inhabitants came to terms with their environment. The ruling elite often decided the form and content of public celebrations, but an alternative tradition of popular celebrations arose from the interests and pursuits of ordinary people. During the twentieth century, changes in society were mirrored by changes in the style of public events. The post-war wave of civic festivals and arts festivals was strongly influenced by the community arts movement in the 1970s, along with multiculturalism and the 'new age' movement. Notions of high culture were challenged by a more pluralistic popular culture, which reinvigorated festivals and community events.

With the coming of the 1980s, governments and the corporate sector began to recognise the economic and promotional value of special events, and state events corporations spearheaded a new level of funding, profile and professionalism. Events can be classified by size — including mega-events, hallmark events, major events and local or community events — and by form or content — including festivals, sporting events and MICE (or business) events. With increasing expansion and corporate involvement, events have emerged as a new growth industry, capable of generating economic benefits and employment.

Significant components of this industry include event organisations, event management companies, event industry suppliers, industry associations and external regulatory bodies. In response to the requirement for professional event management training, industry associations, universities and other tertiary institutions have developed programs. Intending entrants to the industry are advised to study the industry carefully to match their own interests and skills with those required by prospective employers.

Questions

1   Why are special events created? What purpose do they serve in society?

2   Do special events mirror changes in society, or do they have a role in creating and changing values? Give examples to illustrate your answer.

3   Why have special events emerged so strongly in recent years in Australia?

4   What are the key political, cultural and social trends that determine the current climate of events in Australia? How would you expect these trends to influence the nature of events in the coming years?

5   Identify an event in your city or region that has the capacity to be a hallmark event. Give your reasons for placing it in this category.

6   Examine the structure of the event industry in your area and identify local examples of the components outlined in this chapter.

7   Do you agree with the attributes and knowledge areas required by event managers identified by the studies in this chapter? Create a list of your own attributes and skills based on these listings.

Lismore Festival
and Events Strategy

Background

Lismore is a regional city in the Northern Rivers region of New South Wales. It has a robust tradition of diverse festivals and special community events, as well as hosting a dynamic touring program. The Lismore City Council serves the urban and rural constituency of more than 50 000 residents.

In the 1990s, the tourism manager and the Tourism Advisory Panel of Lismore City Council decided the city should develop and adopt an event strategy that could nurture and represent the community. The council recognised that the community festivals in the city's annual events calendar celebrate a sense of place through diverse, inclusive activities in specific, safe environments. These festivals and events are an outward manifestation of the city's identity. They offer opportunities for artistic development, cultural vitality, social wellbeing and economic growth. They make the city a stimulating and enjoyable place in which to live and work. They also provide a vehicle for the community to host visitors and share activities that reflect communal values, interests and aspirations. The council recognised that its portfolio of festivals and events comprised events that were:

1. home grown, low key, and essentially geared for the local community, or
2. professionally developed, addressing special interests of residents and visitors, or
3. large scale, attracting substantial numbers of locals and visitors, and sometimes featuring imported entertainment and held in significant locations.

Developing the strategy

With all this in mind, the council engaged a team of consultants to develop a formal strategy for use by the council, event managers and others involved in or affected by festivals and events in the region. The consultants canvassed the complex issues and environmental factors affecting festivals in the Lismore region by holding a series of focus groups and surveys, and undertaking desktop and media analysis. Among the consultants' tasks were dealing with fragmented and often contradictory social structures, identifying distinctive geographic locations, canvassing specific community resources (including special entrepreneurs), and establishing the willingness of residents to share with visitors.

The strategy document was intended to encourage best practice, creativity, excitement, fun, integrity and an appropriate unique selling proposition (USP) for each event, fitting in with a brand used by the city more broadly. The council wanted documentation that would provide event promoters and the general public with appropriate information and guidance through the complex range of approvals, processes, public safety implications and consent procedures involved when hosting an event.

(*continued*)

A holistic approach drove the planning, management and marketing strategies outlined in the strategic document. The following were among the guiding principles:

- Any festival and events strategy must articulate into broader cultural, economic and environmental policy to foster a positive civic identity.
- The policy must be grounded in an exploration and expansion of Lismore's character and context in the interests of the city's long-term development.
- The policy should develop cultural tourism.
- The policy should generate and sustain a cultural heritage that fosters understanding and appreciation of identity, history and aspirations for generations to come.

Lismore City Council could realise its policy aims partly through a festival and event strategy. The event strategy is an important part of the Council's overall cultural policy and needed to reflect the values held by its constituency: integrity, customer focus, continuous improvement, accessibility and equity, responsiveness, involvement and partnership, accountability.

The strategy

The council adopted the strategy developed by the consultants in 1998. The aim and objectives are reproduced below.

LISMORE CITY COUNCIL'S FESTIVAL AND SPECIAL EVENT STRATEGY

Aim
To assert Lismore's position as the region's premier location for quality festivals and special events

Objectives
To satisfy the interests and needs of residents to celebrate their culture, heritage, lifestyle and meet their recreational needs
To encourage partnerships with the community, commercial sectors and regional agencies to enhance the attractiveness of Lismore as a destination known for festivals and special events
To increase awareness of the economic benefits accrued from festivals and special events and increase the value to the regional economy of hosting these
To establish a Festival and Events Secretariat

(**Source:** *Lismore City Council 1998.*)

Broadly, the strategy reflected that local government:

- is important in the development and promotion of tourism
- is instrumental in economic development, the creation and maintenance of infrastructure, and encouraging cooperation among community stakeholders
- can assist underresourced community groups, particularly, with the provision of professional administration
- can support community interests, the private sector and individuals to contribute to the quality of festivals
- can increase awareness of the economic benefits accrued from festivals, conferences and special events, and increase the value to the regional economy of hosting these.

Lismore City Council established a Festival and Events Secretariat as part of its strategy. The employment of community event coordinators within local government allows policy and practice to be tackled in a transparent and equitable manner. The secretariat's role encompasses (among other tasks):

- liaising with event organisers, developing regional alliances (working on a regional events strategy) and liaising with existing professional networks and government agencies
- facilitating training for the non-profit community sector, which convenes most events in the city
- assisting the business community to capitalise on events in the city
- identifying marketing opportunities and promoting collaborative marketing and advertising
- working with Lismore Tourism on annual promotions
- sourcing funds and sponsorship from agencies such as Tourism NSW, Festivals Australia, the NSW Ministry for the Arts, Sport and Recreation, the Area Consultative Committee and the Heritage Office
- preparing and facilitating bids to attract special events to the city.

Outcomes

Lismore Council's Tourism and Economic Development Advisory Panels have monitored the outcomes of the strategy. Significant rigour in the planning, management and marketing of Lismore events is evident as a result of the centralising of many functions. The council has developed a cultural policy and plan that supports the strategy. A one-stop shopfront location for information sharing, administration and logistical support has ensured a cohesive presentation of Lismore's events to the public. Regional media have worked closely with other stakeholders to promote, sponsor and encourage professional marketing of events. The appointment of regional arts development officers has provided a wider regional framework for Lismore's community cultural activities. A three-year strategy review indicates that the keystone secretariat does not need to 'magic' up new events — the time taken to do this would distract from the greater strategic issues. The secretariat is actively involved with the management of two flagship events: the Rainbow Region Masters Games and the Northern Rivers Herb Festival. It now comprises a full time events coordinator, a part time assistant event coordinator and a shared receptionist, and is located within the council's Economic Development Unit in Lismore's central business district. Staff offer varying levels of support to a diverse annual calendar of events that can include the following:

December/January	Gay and Lesbian Social Clubs' New Year's Eve parties — Tropical Fruits Lismore Showgrounds
January	State under 12 Cricket Carnival
April	'Northern Stars . . . under the big top' — public education performing arts spectacular Northern Rivers Performing Arts (NORPA) series of public performances

(*continued*)

May	APEX National Conference
	Northern Rivers Career and Job Expo
	Under 17 State Hockey Championships
	SOLO's motorhome network rally, in conjunction with Casino campervan event
June	Rural Lands Protection Board State Conference
	Lismore's Lantern Parade from the city centre to Riverside Park for fireworks and performances
July	4WD Caravan and Camping Show, Lismore Showgrounds
	Musica Viva concert series
August	Northern Rivers Herb Festival, Riverside Park
September	Annual Racing Carnival, including the Lismore Cup
	Lismore Rainbow Region Masters Games — numerous venues
	Southern Cross University graduations
October	North Coast National Show
December	Carols by Candlelight at Southern Cross University, Lismore campus

(**Source:** *Ros Derrett, Southern Cross University, based on Lismore City Council 1998.*)

These events are representative of regular features of the annual calendar, and the Council's events secretariat considers each in terms of its commitment of advice, facilitation or direct action.

Ros Derrett, Southern Cross University

Questions

1 Discuss the value that Lismore's local government perceives in connecting with the event sector.

2 What might the job description of the event coordinator comprise under Lismore's strategy?

3 How do you think the relationship between individual event organisers and organisations and Lismore's event secretariat can work effectively?

REFERENCES

Arcodia, C & Barker, T 2002, 'A review of web-based job advertisements for Australian event management positions', in *Events and place making: proceedings of International Research Conference held in Sydney 2002*, eds L Jago, M Deery, R Harris, A Hede & J Allen, Australian Centre for Event Management, Sydney.

Bower, R 1981, 'Community arts — what is it?', *Caper*, vol. 10, Community Arts Board, Australia Council, Sydney.

Clark, M 1981, *A History of Australia*, vol. 5, Melbourne University Press, Melbourne.

Commonwealth Department of Tourism 1995, *A national strategy for the meetings, incentives, conventions and exhibitions industry*, Australian Government Publishing Service, Canberra.

Getz, D 1997, *Event management and event tourism*, Cognizant Communication Corporation, New York.

Getz, D & Wicks, B 1994, 'Professionalism and certification for festival and event practitioners: trends and issues', *Festival Management and Event Tourism*, vol. 2, no. 2, pp. 108–9.

Hall, CM 1992, *Hallmark tourist events: impacts, management and planning*, Belhaven Press, London.

Harris, R & Griffin, T 1997, *Tourism events training audit*, Prepared for Tourism New South Wales Events Unit, Sydney.

Harris, R & Jago, L 1999, 'Event education and training in Australia: the current state of play', *Australian Journal of Hospitality Management*, vol. 6, no. 1, pp. 45–51.

Hughes, R 1987, *The fatal shore*, Collins Harvill, London.

Hull, A 1984, 'Feasting on festas and festivals', Paper delivered to the Association of Festivals Conference at the Caulfield Arts Centre, Victoria.

Janiskee, R 1996, 'Historic houses and special events', *Annals of Leisure Research*, vol. 23, no. 2, pp. 398–414.

Johnson, L, Foo, LM & O'Halloran, M 1999, *Meetings make their mark: characteristics and economic contribution of Australia's meetings and exhibitions sector*, BTR occasional paper no. 26, Bureau of Tourism Research, Canberra.

Lismore City Council 1998, *Lismore festival and events strategy*, Lismore, New South Wales.

McCarthy, W 1998, 'Day we came of age', *The Sun-Herald*, 25 January, p. 46.

Melbourne Exhibition and Convention Centre 2003, 'International Genetics Congress worth $23 million in Victoria', Media release, Melbourne, 25 July.

Nori, S 2003, 'The lion's roar — Sydney to host $91 million conference', Media release of Sydney Convention & Visitors Bureau, Sydney, 15 April.

Pearl, C 1974, *Australia's yesterdays*, Readers Digest, Sydney.

Perry, M, Foley, P & Rumpf, P 1996, 'Event management: an emerging challenge in Australian education', *Festival Management and Event Tourism*, vol. 4, pp. 85–93.

Ritchie, JRB 1984, 'Assessing the impact of hallmark events: conceptual and research issues', *Journal of Travel Research*, vol. 23, no. 1, pp. 2–11.

Rogers, T 1998, *Conferences: a twenty-first century industry*, Addison-Wesley Longman, Harlow.

Royal, CG & Jago, LK 1998, 'Special events accreditation: the practitioner's perspective', *Festival Management and Event Tourism*, no. 5, pp. 221–30.

CHAPTER 2

The impacts
of special events

LEARNING OBJECTIVES

After studying this chapter, you should be able to:

- explain the role of the event manager in balancing the impacts of events

- identify the major impacts that events have on their stakeholders and host communities

- describe the social and cultural impacts of events and plan for positive outcomes

- describe the physical and environmental impacts of events

- discuss the political context of events

- discuss the tourism and economic impacts of events

- discuss why governments become involved in events

- describe the use of economic impact studies in measuring event outcomes.

INTRODUCTION

Events do not take place in a vacuum — they touch almost every aspect of our lives, whether the social, cultural, economic, environmental or political aspects. The benefits arising from such positive connections are a large part of the reason for the popularity and support of events. They are increasingly well documented and researched, and strategies are being developed to enhance event outcomes and optimise their benefits. The recent explosion of events, along with the parallel increase in the involvement of governments and corporations, has led to an increasing emphasis on an economic analysis of event benefits.

Understandably, governments considering the investment of substantial taxpayers' funds in events want to know what they are getting for their investment and how it compares with other investment options. This climate has given rise to economists' detailed studies of events and to the development and application of increasingly sophisticated techniques of economic analysis and evaluation. However, events can also have unintended consequences that can lead them to have public prominence and media attention for the wrong reasons. The cost of event failure can be disastrous, turning positive benefits into negative publicity, political embarrassment and costly lawsuits. An important core task in organising contemporary events is the identification, monitoring and management of event impacts. In this chapter, we examine some of the main areas affected by events, along with the strategies that event managers can employ to balance event impacts.

BALANCING THE IMPACT OF EVENTS

Events have a range of both positive and negative impacts on their host communities and stakeholders (table 2.1, page 32). It is the task of the event manager to identify and predict these impacts, then manage them to achieve the best outcomes for all parties so the overall impact of the event is positive. To achieve this, the event manager must develop and maximise all foreseeable positive impacts, and counter potential negative impacts. Often, negative impacts can be addressed through awareness and intervention, so good planning is always critical. Ultimately, the success of the event depends on the event manager achieving this positive balance sheet and communicating it to a range of stakeholders.

Great emphasis is often placed on the financial impacts of events, partly because employers and governments need to meet budget goals and justify expenditure, and partly because such impacts are most readily assessed. However, government policies commonly acknowledge the 'triple bottom line' of social, economic and environmental goals/yardsticks in relation to events. Event managers should not lose sight of the full range of an event's impacts and the need to identify, describe and manage those impacts. It is also important to realise that different impacts require different means of assessment. Social and cultural benefits, for example, are vital contributors to the calculation of an event's overall impact, but describing them may require a narrative rather than a statistical approach. In this chapter, we discuss some of the complex factors that need to be taken into account when assessing the impacts of events.

■ **Table 2.1**
The impacts of events

IMPACTS OF EVENTS	POSITIVE IMPACTS	NEGATIVE IMPACTS
Social and cultural	• Shared experience • Revitalising of traditions • Building of community pride • Validation of community groups • Increased community participation • Introduction of new and challenging ideas • Expansion of cultural perspectives	• Community alienation • Manipulation of community • Negative community image • Bad behaviour • Substance abuse • Social dislocation • Loss of amenity
Physical and environmental	• Showcasing of the environment • Provision of models for best practice • Increased environmental awareness • Infrastructure legacy • Improved transport and communications • Urban transformation and renewal	• Environmental damage • Pollution • Destruction of heritage • Noise disturbance • Traffic congestion
Political	• International prestige • Improved profile • Promotion of investment • Social cohesion • Development of administrative skills	• Risk of event failure • Misallocation of funds • Lack of accountability • Propaganda • Loss of community ownership and control • Legitimation of ideology
Tourism and economic	• Destinational promotion and increased tourist visits • Extended length of stay • Higher yield • Increased tax revenue • Business opportunities • Commercial activity • Job creation	• Community resistance to tourism • Loss of authenticity • Damage to reputation • Exploitation • Inflated prices • Opportunity costs • Financial mismanagement • Financial loss

(**Source:** *Adapted from Hall 1989.*)

■ Social *and cultural impacts*

All events have a direct social and cultural impact on their participants and sometimes on their wider host communities, as outlined by Hall (1989) and Getz (1997). This impact may be as simple as a shared entertainment experience, as created by a sporting event or concert. Other impacts include increased pride — which results from some community events and the celebration of national days — and the validation of particular groups in the community. The program of the 2003 Greek Festival of Sydney reflects this advantage: 'This is a magnificent occasion for Australians of Greek origin to demonstrate pride in their culture, and to share the same with a multiplicity and diverse cultures that call Australia home' (Angelopoulos 2003).

Events also have the power to challenge the imagination and explore possibilities. A series of reconciliation marches around Australia in 2000 served to express community support for reconciliation with Aboriginal Australians, and to bring this issue powerfully to the attention of the media. In Sydney, the march took the unprecedented step of closing the Sydney Harbour Bridge, providing a powerful symbolic statement of bridging the Aboriginal and wider Australian communities. A further example is the Weipa Crocodile Festival in northern Queensland. This youth festival, bringing Aboriginal and white Australian youths together, has contributed to the reconciliation process and served as a model for similar festivals in Alice Springs and other outback areas (Jago et al. 2002).

Events can also contribute to the political debate and help to change history, as demonstrated by the watershed United Nations Conference on Environment and Development ('The Earth Summit') in Rio de Janeiro in 1992. Further, they can promote healing in the community, as demonstrated by events dedicated to the victims and survivors of the terrorist attack in New York on 11 September 2001, the Bali nightclub bombing in October 2002 and the Canberra bushfires in January 2003.

Research suggests local communities often value the 'feel good' aspects of hallmark events and are prepared to put up with temporary inconvenience and disruption because such events generate excitement and the long-term expectation of improved facilities and profile. Researchers, for example, identified the Australian Formula One Grand Prix in Adelaide as being popular among residents: 'The Grand Prix in 1985 set Adelaide alive . . . The spirit infected all of us, including large numbers of people who in "normal" times might be expected to be against the notion of this garish, noisy, polluting advertising circus' (Arnold et al. 1989, p. 187).

However, such events can have negative social impacts too. Arnold et al. (1989) identified 'the hoon effect' in relation to the 1985 Australian Formula One Grand Prix in Adelaide, when the number of road accident casualties in the five weeks around the event rose by 34 per cent compared with the number in the same period for the previous five years. Accounting for the rising trend of road accident casualties over those years, Arnold et al. calculated that about 15 per cent of these casualties were unexplained, and suggested these casualties could be due to people's off-track emulation of Grand Prix race driving.

The larger the event and the higher its profile, the greater is the potential for things to go wrong, thus generating negative impacts. Consider the collapse of the bridge at the entrance to the stadium for the Maccabiah Games in Israel in 1997, the tragic drownings during the Sydney to Hobart Yacht Race in 1998, and the death of a young rock fan in the mosh pit at the Big Day Out rock festival in 2001. Such events have far-reaching negative impacts, resulting not only in bad press but also damage or injury to participants, stakeholders and the host community.

Managing crowd behaviour

Major events can have unintended social consequences such as substance abuse, bad behaviour by crowds and an increase in criminal activity (Getz 1997). If not managed properly, these unintended consequences can hijack the agenda and determine the public perception of the event. Events as diverse as the Australasian Country Music Festival at Tamworth in New South Wales, the Australian Motorcycle Grand Prix at Phillip Island in Victoria and the Woodford Folk Festival in Queensland have had to develop strategies to handle alcohol-related bad crowd behaviour to protect their reputation and future.

Crowd behaviour can be modified with careful planning. Sometimes, this is an evolutionary process. The management of New Year's Eve in Sydney, for example, has led to a series of modifications and adjustments over successive years. In the early 1990s, teenage alcohol abuse resulted in bad crowd behaviour at Darling Harbour, including confrontations with police, injuries and arrests. The Darling Harbour Authority subsequently had its regulations changed to allow it to prevent alcohol from being brought to the venue. It also modified its program and marketing strategies to create the expectation of a family-oriented celebration. The result was a turnaround in crowd behaviour and a dramatic decrease in injuries and arrests. In the lead-up to the New Year's Eve of the new millennium, the celebrations were spread around different locations in the city, facilitating better crowd management and a reduction in behaviour problems. Other Australian events, such as the New Year's Eve celebrations at Bondi Beach and Byron Bay, have been similarly transformed. A similar trend is also apparent overseas, with initiatives such as the First Night Program of alcohol-free New Year's Eve celebrations, which began in Boston and has been adopted by a wide range of communities. As a result of better crowd management and improved strategies, global celebrations of the new millennium were largely reported as good spirited and peaceful.

Since the terrorist attack in New York on 11 September 2001, the threat of terrorism has resulted in increased security at major events worldwide. However, due to appropriate precautions, events such as the FIFA World Cup in South Korea and Japan in 2002 and the Rugby World Cup in Australia in 2003 were conducted safely without major incidents. Security for the Olympics was increased from 11 500 (including 4500 police officers) for the Sydney Games in 2000 to 45 000 (including 25 000 from the police force) for the Athens Games in 2004 (Kyriakopoulos and Benns 2004).

Community ownership and control of events

Events can also have wider effects on the social life and structure of communities. Traffic arrangements, for example, may restrict residents' access to their homes or businesses, as experienced for the Indy Grand Prix on the Gold Coast and the East Coast Blues and Roots Music Festival at Byron Bay. Other impacts may include a loss of amenities due to excessive noise or crowds, the resentment of inequitable distribution of costs and benefits, and the cost inflation of goods and services, which can upset housing markets and has the most severe impact on low-income groups, as outlined by Getz (1997). Communities should thus have a major say in the planning and management of events. However, Hall (1989) concludes that the role of communities is often marginalised and that governments often make the crucial decision of whether to host the event without adequate community consultation. Public participation then becomes a form of placation designed to legitimise the decisions of government and developers, rather than a full and open discussion of the advantages and disadvantages of hosting events.

It is thus all the more important for governments to be accountable, through the political process, for the allocation of resources to events. Hall (1992) maintains that political analysis is an important tool in regaining community control over hallmark events and ensuring the objectives of these events focus on maximising returns to the community. The furore over ticketing for the 2000 Sydney Olympic Games and the choice of venue locations for the 2003 Rugby World Cup matches indicate that the process of proper community consultation and participation remains a serious issue for governments in the staging of events.

■ Physical *and environmental impacts*

An event is an excellent way in which to showcase the unique characteristics of the host environment. Hall (1989) points out that selling the image of a hallmark event includes marketing the intrinsic properties of the destination. He quotes the use of images of Perth's beaches, the Swan River and historic Fremantle in advertisements for the America's Cup defence in 1987, and the emphasis on the creation of an aesthetically pleasing environment in the promotion of Sydney's Darling Harbour.

However, host environments may be extremely delicate, and great care should be taken to protect them. A major event may require an environmental impact assessment before council permission is granted for it to proceed. Even if a formal study is not required, the event manager should carefully consider the likely impact of the event on the environment. This impact will be fairly contained if the event is to be held in a suitable purpose-built venue — for example, a stadium, sportsground, showground or entertainment centre — but may be much greater if the event is to be held in a public space not ordinarily reserved for events — for example, a park, town square or street. Crowd movement and control, noise levels, access and parking will be important considerations. Other major issues may include wear on the natural and physical environment, heritage protection issues and disruption of the local community.

Effective communication and consultation with local authorities can often resolve some of these issues. In addition, careful management planning may be required to modify impacts. In Sydney, the Manly Jazz Festival worked for several years to progressively reduce the traffic impact of visitors to the festival, by developing a 'park and ride' system of fringe parking with shuttle buses to the event area. Many food and wine events have reduced their impact on the environment by using biodegradable containers and utensils instead of plastic, and by selling wine-tasting souvenir glasses that patrons can take home after the event. Many event managers are discovering that such measures make good financial as well as environmental sense.

In the staging of large events, the provision of infrastructure is often a costly budget component, but this expenditure usually results in an improved environment and facilities for the host community, and provides a strong incentive for the community to act as host. Brisbane profited from the transformation of the Expo 88 site into the South Bank leisure and entertainment precinct. Sydney's public space was enhanced by the redevelopment of derelict railway goods yards to create the Darling Harbour leisure precinct for Australia's Bicentenary in 1988. The Sydney Olympic Games in 2000 left a legacy of major state-of-the-art sporting venues and associated transport and communications facilities. The America's Cup in Auckland in 2000 and 2003 resulted in the transformation of the Auckland waterfront into an upmarket restaurant precinct. All these examples illustrate the lasting benefits that can result from the hosting of large-scale events.

Waste management and recycling

Governments are increasingly using public education programs and legislation to promote the recycling of waste materials and reduce the amount of waste going to landfill. Events are targeted as opportunities to demonstrate best practice models in waste management and to change public attitudes and habits. Resource NSW has developed a fully integrated event waste management, recycling and education program. This program is promoted through the seven steps to a waste-wise event (figure 2.1). Its website provides a list of recycling equipment, standard signage and companies that provide waste management services and environmentally friendly products, to assist the event manager in implementing the program. Resource NSW quotes research that shows that 89 per cent of people surveyed at special events in New South Wales consider recycling at events to be a very important issue (Resource NSW 2003).

For the event manager, incorporating a waste management plan into the overall event plan has become increasingly good policy. Community expectations and the health of the environment require that events demonstrate good waste management principles and provide models for recycling. The waste-wise event manager will reap not only economic benefits, but also the approval of an increasingly environmentally aware public.

Step 1 — commitment
Step 2 — event packaging
Step 3 — event equipment
Step 4 — management system
Step 5 — standard signage
Step 6 — communication and promotion
Step 7 — evaluation

(Source: *Resource NSW 2001.)*

■ **Political** *impacts*

Politics and politicians are an important part of the equation that is contemporary event management. Ever since the Roman emperors discovered the power of the circus to deflect criticism and shore up popularity, shrewd politicians have had an eye for events that will keep the population happy and themselves in power. No less an authority than Count Niccolo Machiavelli (1469), adviser to the Medicis in the sixteenth century, had this to say on the subject:

> ■ A prince must also show himself a lover of merit, give preferment to the able and honour those who excel in every art . . . Besides this, he ought, at convenient seasons of the year, to keep the people occupied with festivals and shows; and as every city is divided into guilds or into classes, he ought to pay attention to all these groups, mingle with them from time to time, and give them an example of his humanity and munificence, always upholding, however, the majesty of his dignity, which must never be allowed to fail in anything whatever. ■

The Royal House of Windsor took this advice to heart, providing some of the most popular events of the past century, with the Coronation of Queen Elizabeth II and the fairytale-like wedding of Prince Charles and Princess Diana. Australian Prime Minister Robert Menzies made good use of the public affection for the British royal family, with royal tours to Australia providing a boost to the popularity of his government. Successive Australian politicians have continued to use the spotlight offered by different events to build their personal profiles and gain political advantage. Former South Australian premier Don Dunstan used the Adelaide Festival to create an image of Adelaide as the 'Athens of the South' and of himself as a visionary and enlightened leader. Former mayor Sallyanne Atkinson used Brisbane's Expo 88 and successive Olympic bids to boost her mayoral profile. Her successor Jim Soorley used the successful Brisbane Riverfestival to advance his environmental regeneration agenda and reputation. Former New South Wales premier Neville Wran and colleague Laurie Brereton used the building of Darling Harbour to create an image of New South Wales as a go-ahead state, but critics at the time accused them of creating a monument to themselves. Former prime minister Bob Hawke bathed in the glory of Alan Bond's America's Cup victory in Fremantle. And, continuing in the grand tradition, former Victorian premier Jeff Kennett used a succession of events including the Australian Formula One Grand Prix, rugby's Bledisloe

Cup and the Presidents Cup golf tournament to create an image of himself as a winner — and New South Wales Premier Bob Carr as the loser — in the race for events. Prime Minister John Howard turned the Centenary of Federation celebrations to the benefit of his government by distributing grant funds through local federal members of Parliament.

Arnold et al. (1989, pp. 191–2) leave no doubt about the role of events in the political process.

> ■ Governments in power will continue to use hallmark events to punctuate the ends of their periods in office, to arouse nationalism, enthusiasm and finally, votes. They are cheaper than wars or the preparation for them. In this regard, hallmark events do not hide political realities, they are the political reality. ■

Governments around the world have realised the ability of events to raise the profile of politicians and the cities and states that they govern. Events attract visitors and thus create economic benefits and jobs. This potent mixture has prompted governments to become major players in bidding for, hosting and staging major events. This increasing involvement of governments in events has politicised the events landscape, as recognised by Hall (1989):

> ■ Politics are paramount in hallmark events. It is either naïve or dupli[citous] to pretend otherwise. Events alter the time frame in which planning occurs and they become opportunities to do something new and better than before. In this context, events may change or legitimate [sic] political priorities in the short term and political ideologies and socio-cultural reality in the longer term. Hallmark events represent the tournaments of old, fulfilling psychological and political needs through the winning of hosting over other locations and the winning of events themselves. Following a hallmark event some places will never be the same again, physically, economically, socially and, perhaps most importantly of all, politically. ■

Events have values beyond tangible and economic benefits. Humans are social animals, and celebrations play a key role in the wellbeing of the social structure. Events can engender social cohesion, confidence and pride: therein lies the source of their political power and influence, and the reason that they will always reflect and interact with their political circumstances and environments.

■ Tourism *and economic impacts*

A primary concern of an event entrepreneur or host organisation is whether an event is within budget and, hopefully, results in a surplus or profit. This is a simple matter of whether the income from sponsorship, merchandise and ticket sales exceeds the costs of conducting and marketing the event. However, from the perspectives of the host communities and governments, a wider range of economic impacts is often of equal or greater significance.

One of the most important impacts is the tourism revenue generated by an event. In addition to their spending at the event, external visitors are likely to spend money on travel, accommodation, goods and services in the host city or region. This expenditure can have a considerable impact as it circulates through the local economy. Effective tourism promotion can result in visitors to the event extending their length of stay and visiting other regional tourism destinations and attractions. In addition to the tourism generated during the event, events may attract media coverage and exposure that enhance the profile of the host town or city, resulting in improved long-term tourism image and visitation. Chapter 3 discusses these and other aspects of the tourism impact of events.

Business opportunities

Events can provide their host communities with a strong platform for showcasing their expertise, hosting potential investors and promoting new business opportunities. The media exposure generated by the success of an event can dramatically illustrate the capacity, innovation and achievements of event participants and/or the host community. Auckland maximised the economic benefits of staging the America's Cup defence in 2000 by integrating its marine industry components and stakeholders through MAREX (Marine Export Group), placing its marine industry at the centre of a range of exciting developments (Davies 1996).

During the Sydney Olympics, the New South Wales Government spent $3.6 million on a trade and investment drive coinciding with the event (Humphries 2000). This effort led to more than 60 business-related events, board meetings of international companies, briefings and trade presentations being held in Sydney at the time of the Olympics. Forty-six international chambers of commerce were briefed on business opportunities, and more than 500 world business leaders, Olympic sponsors and New South Wales corporate executives attended four promotional events. State Treasurer Michael Egan was quoted as saying, 'We'll be benefiting from the Games well after we think the benefits have worn off and in ways that will never show up in statistics' (Humphries 2000).

Little research has been done on analysing business development strategies for events and quantifying the amount of business that these strategies generate. More work needs to be done so event enhancement frameworks are better understood and their outcomes can be assessed.

Commercial activity

Whatever the generation of new business at the macro level, the suppliers of infrastructure, goods and services undoubtedly profit from the staging of major events. But do these benefits trickle down to traders and small business operators? A survey of 1000 tourism-related businesses was conducted in relation to the Rugby World Cup in Wales in 1999 (Anon. 2000). The accommodation sector fared best, with two-thirds of accommodation providers experiencing improvements in business performance, along with a 7.5 per cent increase in room rates in Cardiff and the south east of Wales. Around half of the food and drink outlets also reported increased performance; this sector reported making considerable investment in promotional activities and small-scale product development. In the retail sector, over half of survey respondents thought that the event had had a negative impact on their overall performance, despite improvements in average spend.

Muthaly et al. (2000) used a case study approach to examine the impact of the Atlanta Olympics on seven small businesses in Atlanta. The case study included:

- a wholesale restaurant equipment dealer, which expanded its existing business and current line of equipment, resulting in a 70–80 per cent increase in revenue as a result of the Games
- a one-person home rental business specifically started to provide bed-and-breakfast housing for Olympic visitors, which lost US$23 000 due to lack of any significant Games business
- a frozen lemonade stand franchise that employed up to 50 people at four fixed and three roving locations, which failed due to problems with inventory, staffing, unanticipated and unregulated competition, and lower than expected attendance at the Games
- an established beverage distributor, who became an approved Games vendor and reported increased profits through additional sales to usual customers and a firm policy of not extending credit to new customers
- a craft retail location at Stone Mountain Park, a major tourist attraction for Atlanta and the south east where some Olympic events were located. The owner lost about US$10 000 on a special line of Olympic theme dolls, sculptures and so on, as a result of added costs and a lack of customers.
- a UK-based currency service and foreign exchange business that established two locations downtown near the Olympic Park and two uptown near the retail and residential heart of the city. The principal felt that it was not a very successful business project, given the changing nature of the market (people using credit or debit cards in place of currency) and lack of communication with Olympic organisers.
- an established sporting goods retail store that reported increased sales of established lines and regular merchandise, but not of Olympic merchandise stocked to sell in front of the store. The owner reported considerable staffing difficulties due to poor transport planning and absenteeism as a result of the Games.

The study team concluded that large businesses such as Delta Airlines, local constructions companies, local law firms associated with the Olympics, and niche players that watched their risk carefully fared very well. However, for many small operators, dreams of big profits turned into heartache. Visitors did not come in anticipated numbers, and those who did come did not spend the amount of money expected. Olympic visitors proved to be sports mad and tight fisted, and uninterested in traditional tourist attractions.

From these and other studies, the anticipated benefits of major events to traders and small business operators appear to be sometimes exaggerated, with the results often being sporadic and uneven. Benefits also seem more likely to accrue to those businesses that are properly prepared and that manage and invest wisely in the opportunities provided by events. More research needs to be done in this field to identify appropriate strategies to enhance the benefits of events to small business.

Employment creation

By stimulating activity in the economy, expenditure on events can have a positive effect on employment. Employment multipliers measure how many full time equivalent job opportunities are supported in the community as a result of visitor expenditure. However, as Faulkner (1993) and others point out, it is easy to overestimate the number of jobs created by major events in the short term. Because the demand for additional services is short lived, employers tend to meet this demand by using their existing staff more rather than employing new staff members. Existing employees may be released from other duties to accommodate the temporary demand or requested to work overtime.

However, major events can generate substantial employment in the construction phase, as well as during the staging of the event. The America's Cup in Auckland in 2000 was estimated to generate 1470 new jobs in construction, accommodation, marine and related activities (Scott 2003). The 2000 Oktoberfest in Munich generated employment for an estimated 12 000 people through the 0.7 billion euro that 5.5 million visitors to the event spent over 16 days (Munich Tourist Office 2000, cited in Richards and Wilson 2002). The 2002 British Grand Prix at Silverstone was estimated to support 1150 full time equivalent jobs in the United Kingdom, including 400 full time equivalent jobs within 50 miles of the circuit (GHK Consulting 2004).

GOVERNMENT'S USE OF EVENTS AS ECONOMIC DEVELOPMENT STRATEGIES

The strong growth of the festival and special event sector is part of a general economic trend away from an industrial product base to a more service-based economy. Traditionally, communities and governments have staged events for their perceived social, cultural and/or sporting benefits and value. This situation began to change dramatically in the early 1980s when major events in many parts of the world began to be regarded as desirable commodities for their perceived ability to deliver economic benefits through the promotion of tourism, increased visitor expenditure and job creation.

Mules (1998) dates this change in attitude in Australia to around 1982–86, with the staging of the Commonwealth Games in Brisbane (1982), the Formula One Grand Prix in Adelaide (1985) and the America's Cup defence in Perth (1986–87). He notes that state governments began around this time to be aware of the economic significance of events, aided by studies such as that of the Formula One Grand Prix (Burns, Hatch & Mules, cited in Mules 1998), which established that the income generated by the event exceeded the cost to the South Australian Government of staging it.

As outlined in chapter 1, various state governments in Australia have pursued vigorous event strategies since the 1980s, building strong portfolios of annual events and aggressively bidding for the right for their state to host major one-off events. Apart from interstate rivalry and political kudos, what motivates and justifies this level of government involvement in what otherwise might be seen as largely commercial enterprises? According to Mules (1998), the answer lies in what he terms the 'spillover effects' of events. While many major events might make an operational loss, they produce benefits for related industry sectors such as travel, accommodation, restaurants, hirers and suppliers of equipment and so on. They may also produce long-term benefits such as destination promotion resulting in increased tourism spending. However, a single organisation cannot capture this wide range of benefits. Governments thus sometimes play a role in funding or underwriting events so these generalised benefits might be obtained.

ECONOMIC IMPACT STUDIES

In deciding what events should be funded and what levels of funding are appropriate, governments need to obtain a full picture of the events costs and the anticipated return on investment. To do so, they sometimes undertake economic impact studies, which seek to identify all of the expenditure involved in the staging of events, and to determine their impacts on the wider economy.

According to Faulkner (1993), the impacts of an event derive from three main sources:
1. expenditure by visitors from outside the region
2. capital expenditure on facilities required to conduct the event
3. expenditure incurred by event organisers and sponsors to stage the event.

However, this expenditure has flow-on effects that need to be taken into account in calculating the economic impact of an event. Money spent on a meal by a visitor to an event, for example, will flow on to businesses that supply the restaurant with food and beverage items. The money spent on the meal is direct expenditure, while the flow-on effect to suppliers is indirect expenditure. The event may also stimulate additional activity in the economy, resulting in increased wages and consumer spending. This is referred to as induced expenditure.

The aggregated impact on the economy of all of the expenditure is expressed as a multiplier ratio. Multipliers reflect the impact of the event expenditure as it ripples through the economy, and they vary according to the particular mix of industries in a given geographic location. The use of multipliers is controversial, and some studies prefer to concentrate on the direct expenditure of an event as being more reliable, although this does not give a true picture of the complex impact on the economy of the event expenditure.

Conducting economic impact studies that account for all of the myriad factors of the event expenditure and environment is quite complex and usually undertaken by specialist researchers with an economic background. However, a considerable body of literature is available to provide an insight for event managers into the process of conducting economic impact studies on events (see Burgan & Mules 2000; Crompton & McKay 1994; Giddings 1997; Hunn & Mangan 1999; Mules 1999; Mules & McDonald 1994).

The following is the Queensland Government's economic impact fact sheet for the 2003 Lexmark Indy 300 motor racing event held on Queensland's Gold Coast:

> The 2003 Lexmark Indy 300 generated a total economic impact of $50.43 million in Queensland (1999 — $42.09 million).
>
> ## Tourism
> - The 2003 attendance was the highest in the event's 13-year history, attracting 306 184 people over the four days.
> - A total of 159 096 visitor nights were generated in Queensland from the Lexmark Indy 300: 54 per cent of visitor nights were spent during the four days of the event, 23 per cent before the event and 23 per cent after the event.
> - The Lexmark Indy 300 was a catalyst for an extended stay in Queensland. Visitors from overseas spent an average of 7.3 nights in Queensland, substantially longer than the average length of stay by general overseas visitors (3.4 nights). Visitors from interstate spent an average of 6.3 nights in Queensland, an increase from the average length of stay by general tourists (4.7 nights).
>
> ## Economy
> - Spectators and event participants spent $42.63 million at the 2003 Lexmark Indy 300.
> - The accommodation, cafes and restaurants industry was the single greatest beneficiary, receiving an estimated 54 per cent of all spending. The retail trade industry received 23 per cent and the sport and recreation industry received 10 per cent of all spending in Queensland.
> - The economic value of the 2003 Lexmark Indy 300 was equivalent to 503 jobs in Queensland.
> - International Champ Car teams spent more than $1.7 million while in Queensland.
>
> ## Media exposure
> - The promotional value of the 2003 Lexmark Indy 300 was estimated at $15.50 million through international print and broadcast media.
> - Television coverage took the Gold Coast to an estimated 159 countries around the world. Network Ten's coverage of the 2003 Lexmark Indy 300 reached a peak audience of close to two million viewers in Australia on the Saturday and Sunday.
> - Approximately 750 print journalists, photographers and broadcast media attended from Australia and overseas.

(**Source:** *Based on Queensland Government 2004.*)

All events produce both positive and negative impacts, which it is the task of the event manager to assess and balance. Social and cultural impacts may involve a shared experience and may give rise to local pride, validation and/ or the widening of cultural horizons. However, social problems arising from events may result in social dislocation if not properly managed. Events are an excellent opportunity to showcase the physical characteristics of a destination, but event environments may be very delicate and care should be taken to safeguard and protect them. Governments have long recognised the political impacts which often include an increased profile and benefits to the host community. However, it is important that events fulfil the wider community agenda. Tourism and economic impacts include the expenditure of visitors to an event, the promotion of business opportunities, the creation of commercial activity and the generation of employment. Since the 1980s, governments in Australia have become increasingly aware of the potential tourism and economic benefits of events, and bid competitively for the right to host and stage events. In considering appropriate levels of funding for events, governments use economic impact studies to predict the likely impacts of events and then determine the wider outcomes.

Questions

1 Describe examples of events whose needs have been perceived to conflict with those of their host communities. As the event manager, how would you have resolved these conflicting needs?

2 Identify an event that you know has been marred by social problems or bad crowd behaviour. As the event manager, what would you have done to manage the situation and improve the outcomes of the event? In your answer, discuss both the planning of the event and possible on-the-spot responses.

3 Select a major event that has been held in your region and identify as many environmental impacts as you can. Evaluate whether the overall environmental impact on the host community was positive or negative. Recommend steps that could be taken to improve the balance.

4 Describe an event that you believe was not sufficiently responsive to community attitudes and values. What steps could the community take to improve the situation?

5 Select an event that you have been involved in as a participant or close observer. Identify as many impacts of the event as you can, both positive and negative, and then answer the following questions.

(a) Did the positive impacts outweigh the negative?

(b) What measures did the organisers have in place to maximise positive impacts and minimise negative impacts?

(c) As the event manager, what other steps could you have taken to balance the impacts and improve the outcomes of the event?

6   List and describe what you consider to be the main reasons that governments support events.

7   Obtain three event reports that have been compiled on events in your area or state. Compare and contrast these reports in terms of (a) the methods used to compile them and (b) how they have been used to communicate and promote the outcomes of the event.

Economic impact
of Floriade

Canberra is the home of the annual Floriade Festival — a floral festival that celebrates the end of winter and the arrival of the warmer weather of spring. It began
in 1988, the year of Australia's Bicentenary, and was a gift from the Australian
Government to the people who live and work in Canberra, the national capital.

Originally, the festival was intended as a 'one-off' event in the bicentennial year,
but it was very popular with local residents, and its month-long display of tulips
was an attraction to visitors. The Australian Capital Territory (ACT) Government
decided to run the event annually. To capitalise on its tourist potential, the event
was placed under the management of the ACT Government Tourism Authority
(currently known as the Australian Capital Tourism Corporation).

The event runs from mid-September to mid-October each year, and is held in
Commonwealth Park, which is federally owned and administered. Entry has
always been free, except for 1998–2000, when various charging mechanisms
were tried and eventually abandoned because they deterred patrons.

The floral display is installed in temporary garden beds each year and
removed, along with the garden beds, at the end of the event. This means the
event is very costly to stage, but has no gate revenue. The ACT Government considers that the resultant financial loss is justified in terms of the economic impact
of the event on the ACT economy.

Researchers from the University of Canberra have measured the economic
impact of the event each year from 1999 using a consistent method. The over-
riding rule of the method is that the economic impact is a function of the expenditure by visitors who came to Canberra as a result of the festival. Local residents
are omitted, as are visitors who were in Canberra for other reasons, such as holidays or visiting family. Festival patrons in Canberra primarily to attend the event
are often referred to as 'in-scope visitors'.

The study into economic impact uses a sample survey of attendees at Floriade
to estimate the number of in-scope visitors and their expenditure. In 2002, 776
patrons were surveyed out of a total of 164 784 patrons who attended Floriade
that year. The survey was conducted using trained field workers, who were
generally tourism students from the university. The 30-day duration of the festival
was divided into 120 blocks of time (of two hours each), and 10 of these blocks
were chosen at random to survey patrons.

Field workers approached patrons as they exited through one of the three gates.
Every sixth patron was approached, to spread out the sample and to keep it representative. The field workers conducted face-to-face interviews with the chosen
patrons, entering the responses onto a printed questionnaire. Data on the completed
questionnaires were subsequently keyed into a computer program for analysis.

Turnstiles were used at the entry gates to provide estimates of the total number of attendances. The number of people who attended the festival is different from the number of attendances, because some people attend more than once. The total attendance number was adjusted for the number of people who attended more than once, which was derived from the sample, to give the number of people attending. Data from the sample were then used to derive the number of people who came to Canberra primarily for Floriade as follows:

Total number of people attending (164 784)

Less Number of local residents (89 972)

Less Number of visitors for whom Floriade was not the prime reason for their visit to Canberra (37 032),

= Number of visitors who came to Canberra primarily for Floriade (37 780).

The table below shows the number of visitors who came to Canberra primarily for Floriade from 1999 to 2002. It also shows the average length of stay for visitors who spent at least one night in Canberra during their trip, plus the number of respondents in the sample who spent at least one night in Canberra. The year 2000 looks to be unusual in that it had the lowest number of in-scope visitors, plus the longest length of stay. It also had the lowest sample size (number of respondents) of overnight visitors, and small sample sizes sometimes cause greater errors of estimation. The estimates for 2000 should thus be treated with some caution.

■ *Visitors who came to Canberra primarily for Floriade, 1999–2002*

	1999	2000	2001	2002
In-scope visitor numbers	42 770	30 498	35 494	37 780
Average length of stay (nights)	1.9	2.8	1.8	1.5
Respondents who stayed overnight	246	65	88	92

The sample survey asked people for details of their expenditure while they were in Canberra for the festival. For this purpose, three distinct types of visitor were identified:

1. daytrippers from the surrounding region, who had no accommodation expenses
2. overnight visitors who stayed at least one night and arranged their own transport and accommodation
3. package visitors who were travelling on a package tour, some of whom undertook expenditure additional to the package cost.

(*continued*)

The largest category was the overnight visitor segment, both in terms of visitor numbers and aggregate expenditure, as shown in the following table for the 2002 survey.

■ *In-scope visitor numbers and aggregate expenditure, Floriade, 2002*

	VISITORS	AGGREGATE EXPENDITURE ($)
Daytrippers	10 805	390 768
Overnight visitors	23 650	4 826 067
Package tourists	3 325	653 200
Total	37 780	5 870 032

Survey data on expenditure each year is collected from respondents in standard categories (table below) that are easy for them to remember. The following table shows the total expenditure in each of the standard categories from the 2002 survey. As would be expected, much of the expenditure by visitors to Canberra was on accommodation and meals/beverages, which are traditional areas of tourist expenditure. This finding illustrates the link between tourism and the economic impact of events and festivals.

■ *In-scope expenditure, by category, Floriade, 2002*

CATEGORY	EXPENDITURE ($)
Accommodation	2 549 435
Meals and beverages	1 735 794
Transport	628 790
Merchandise	323 854
Other entertainment	115 541
Shopping	470 831
Other	45 787
Total	5 870 032

The final step in the economic impact study is to convert the expenditure shown in the above table into the impacts of this expenditure on income and employment in the ACT economy. This step is usually done using a detailed mathematical model of the economy. The 'income' refers to both wages and business income, and is measured using a concept known as gross state product (GSP) — the state/territory version of the well-known national concept, gross domestic product (GDP).

The following table shows the total in-scope visitor expenditure and the GSP impacts of Floriade on the ACT economy for 1999–2002.

■ *Economic impacts of Floriade, 1999–2002*

	1999	**2000**	**2001**	**2002**
In-scope expenditure ($ million)	7 509 778	9 638 467	6 599 063	5 870 032
Expenditure per person ($)	176	316	186	155
GSP ($ million)	6 811 026	8 629 113	4 681 318	6 375 401

After a peak in 2000, Floriade's economic impact on the Canberra economy has been falling. From 2000, visitor numbers have been rising, but visitors have been staying for a shorter time and, therefore, spending less when in Canberra. This trend should be a warning to Floriade organisers that they need to find ways of using the event to market Canberra's other tourist attractions, such as the Australian War Memorial, the National Gallery and the National Museum. If visitors to Canberra are aware that the city offers other tourist attractions, they are likely to stay longer in the city and spend more money, thereby increasing the economic impact.

Trevor Mules, Senior Lecturer in Tourism Economics,
Australian International Hotel School, Canberra

Questions

1 What expenditure is included in the economic impact of Floriade?

2 Floriade has attracted over 160 000 visitors, so how did the economic impact study collect expenditure information without having to interview all the visitors?

3 What are the three types of visitor identified in the Floriade study? How does the nature of their expenditure differ?

4 Explain how and why patrons to Floriade were surveyed to measure Floriade's economic impact. How was the survey information used to estimate the economic impact?

5 Floriade's economic impact seems to be decreasing. Suggest reasons for this fall and explain why it should worry the organisers. What should the organisers do in response?

6 Is it appropriate for taxpayers to pay for the costs of staging Floriade?

7 Why did the researchers exclude local Canberra residents from their economic impact calculations?

8 Why is the expenditure incurred in staging Floriade not included in the economic impact calculation along with in-scope visitor expenditure?

REFERENCES

Angelopoulos, G 2003, 'The Greek Festival of Sydney' program, p. 11.

Anon. 2000, *Rugby World Cup 1999 economic impact evaluation: summary report*, Segal Quince Wicksteed Limited and System Three, Edinburgh.

Arnold, A, Fischer, A, Hatch, J & Paix, B 1989, 'The Grand Prix, road accidents and the philosophy of hallmark events', in *The planning and evaluation of hallmark events*, eds GJ Syme, BJ Shaw, DM Fenton & WS Mueller, Avesbury, Aldershot.

Burgan, B & Mules, T 2000, 'Event analysis — understanding the divide between cost benefit and economic impact assessment', in *Events beyond 2000: setting the agenda — event evaluation, research and education conference proceedings*, eds J Allen, R Harris, LK Jago & AJ Veal, Australian Centre for Event Management, Sydney.

Crompton, JL & McKay, SL 1994, 'Measuring the impact of festivals and events: some myths, misapplications and ethical dilemmas', *Festival Management and Event Tourism*, vol. 2, no. 1, pp. 33–43.

Davies, J 1996, 'The buck stops where? The economic impact of staging major events', Paper presented to the Australian Events Conference, Canberra.

Faulkner, B 1993, *Evaluating the tourism impact of hallmark events*, Occasional paper no. 16, Bureau of Tourism Research, Canberra.

Getz, D 1997, *Event management and event tourism*, Cognizant Communication Corporation, New York.

GHK Consulting 2003, 'Economic impact of the British Grand Prix', www.ghkint.com/pub_pub13.htm (accessed 1 March 2004).

Giddings, C 1997, *Measuring the impact of festivals — guidelines for conducting an economic impact study*, National Centre for Culture and Recreation Studies, Australian Bureau of Statistics, Canberra.

Hall, CM 1989, 'Hallmark events and the planning process', in *The planning and evaluation of hallmark events*, eds GJ Syme, BJ Shaw, DM Fenton & WS Mueller, Avebury, Aldershot.

Hall, CM 1992, *Hallmark tourist events — impacts management and planning*, Belhaven Press, London.

Humphries, D 2000, 'Benefit to economy is unseen', *The Sydney Morning Herald*, 23 August, p. 8.

Hunn, C & Mangan, J 1999, 'Estimating the economic impact of tourism at the local, regional, state or territorial level, including consideration of the multiplier effect', in *Valuing tourism: methods and techniques*, eds K Corcoran, A Allcock, T Frost & L Johnson, Bureau of Tourism Research, Canberra.

Jago, L, Chalip, L, Brown, G, Mules, T & Ali, S 2002, 'The role of events in helping to brand a destination' in *Events and place making: proceedings of international research conference held in Sydney 2002*, eds L Jago, M Deery, R Harris, A Hede, & J Allen, Australian Centre for Event Management, Sydney.

Kyriakopoulos, V & Benns, M 2004, 'Passing the torch to Athens', *The Sun-Herald*, 22 February.

Machiavelli, N 1962 (1514), *The prince*, trans. L Ricci, Mentor Books, New York.

New South Wales Waste Boards 1999, Waste Wise Events, Waste Boards NSW, Sydney.

Mules, T 1998, 'Events tourism and economic development in Australia', in *Managing tourism in cities*, eds D Tyler, Y Guerrier & M Robertson, John Wiley & Sons, New York.

Mules, T 1999, 'Estimating the economic impact of an event on a local government area, region, state or territory', in *Valuing tourism: methods and techniques*, eds K Corcoran, A Allcock, T Frost & L Johnson, Bureau of Tourism Research, Canberra.

Mules, T & McDonald, S 1994, 'The economic impact of special events: the use of forecasts', *Festival Management and Event Tourism*, vol. 2, no. 1, pp. 45–53.

Muthaly, SK, Ratnatunga, J, Roberts, GB & Roberts, CD 2000, 'An event-based entrepreneurship case study of futuristic strategies for Sydney 2000 Olympics', in *Events beyond 2000: setting the agenda — event evaluation, research and education conference proceedings*, eds J Allen, R Harris, LK Jago & AJ Veal, Australian Centre for Event Management, Sydney.

Queensland Government 2004, http://statements.cabinet.qld.gov.au/cgi-bin/display-statement.pl?id=145&db=mediaas (accessed 1 March 2004).

Resource NSW 2001, '7 steps to a waste wise event', www.wastewise events.resource.nsw.gov.au/default.asp?dir=steps (accessed 1 March 2004).

Richards, G & Wilson, J 2002, 'The links between mega events and urban renewal: the case of the Manchester 2002 Commonwealth Games' in *Events and place making: proceedings of international research conference held in Sydney 2002*, eds L Jago, M Deery, R Harris, A Hede & J Allen, Australian Centre for Event Management, Sydney.

Scott, E 2003, 'On the waterfront', *Australian Leisure Management*, February–March 2003.

3

Event tourism *planning*

LEARNING OBJECTIVES

After studying this chapter, you should be able to:

- describe 'event tourism' and the destination approach to event tourism planning

- conduct an event tourism situational analysis to create a foundation for goal setting and strategic decision making

- describe the range of goals that a destination might seek to progress through an event tourism strategy

- list and describe organisations that might play a role in a destination's efforts at event tourism development

- describe generic strategy options available to organisations seeking to develop event tourism to a destination

- list and discuss approaches to the implementation and evaluation of event tourism strategies

- discuss the potential event tourism has to generate positive outcomes in small communities.

$\mathcal{I}$NTRODUCTION

This chapter will explore the relationship between events and tourism from the viewpoint of destinations (cities, towns, regions, states or countries) that are seeking to develop and implement strategies to increase visitation. The chapter begins with an overview of event tourism, before moving on to propose and discuss a strategic approach to event tourism planning. This approach involves: conduct of a detailed situational analysis; the creation of event tourism goals; the establishment of an organisational structure through which event tourism goals can be progressed; and the development, implementation and evaluation of an event tourism strategy. It is argued in this chapter that the value of this process lies in its capacity to generate a coordinated strategic approach to a destination's overall event tourism efforts. The final part of this chapter seeks to redress the tendency in dealing with event tourism to focus on cities, states and countries. It does this by briefly examining the significant, positive role that event tourism can play in the context of small communities.

$\mathcal{D}$EVELOPING DESTINATION-BASED EVENT TOURISM STRATEGIES

Government support at all levels has been integral to the expansion of event tourism. Not only have governments invested in the creation of specialist bodies charged with event tourism development, but many have also funded, or contributed significantly to, event-specific infrastructure, such as convention and exhibition centres and stadiums. The Asia Pacific region, for example, has experienced significant investment in business tourism infrastructure by national and provincial governments in recent years (Kelly 2003). The willingness of governments to support event tourism through policy initiatives and legislation is also increasingly evident. Once the Sydney 2000 Olympics bid was won, for example, the New South Wales Government moved quickly to pass legislation to create organising bodies, ensure Games security, and allow and expedite Olympic-related developments (New South Wales Government 2004). Such willingness, however, can sometimes create problems due to the public's lack of participation in decision making, as Waitt (2003) notes in connection with the Sydney Olympics.

Responsibility for progressing event tourism efforts varies from destination to destination. In smaller destinations, such as towns and regions, involvement may be limited to organisations such as tourism promotional bodies, local government and the local chamber of commerce. Larger destinations (cities, states, countries) are likely to have an expanded range of organisations involved in the event tourism area, including convention centres and visitor bureaus, tourism commissions/agencies, festival/public event bodies, major event agencies, government departments involved in areas such as sport and the arts, and event organising companies.

THE EVENT TOURISM STRATEGIC PLANNING PROCESS

A strategic approach to a destination's event tourism development efforts offers significant benefits. These benefits lie primarily in the areas of coordination and in the building of an event tourism capacity that represents the best strategic fit with the area's overall tourism efforts, and its current and projected business environment. This approach is presented in figure 3.1 as a series of sequential steps, each of which is discussed in this section.

The timeframe in which event tourism strategic plans operate will vary from destination to destination, but 5–15-year planning horizons are not uncommon. Events Tasmania, for example, employs a 10-year rolling events plan (Events Tasmania 2004), and EventScotland's major events strategy spans the period 2003–15 (see the case study on page 77).

■ **Figure 3.1**
Event tourism strategic planning process

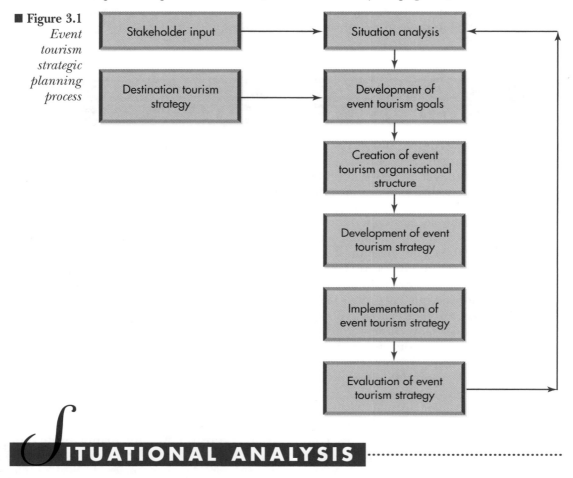

SITUATIONAL ANALYSIS

A detailed situational analysis should underpin the decisions made on what event tourism goals to set for a destination. This analysis should reflect the various perspectives of key stakeholders in the event area, such as tourism bodies, the destination's community, government agencies associated with areas such as the arts and sport, and major event organisers. In preparing the major events strategy for Scotland, for example, the consultancy company charged with this task (Objective Performance Limited) spent about 18 months engaged in research, including interviewing more than 80 individuals and organisations involved in major events in Scotland and overseas (Scottish Executive 2002).

A strengths, weaknesses, opportunities and threats (SWOT) analysis (chapter 5) is a useful way of assessing the situation that a destination faces in its efforts to develop event tourism. Figure 3.2 lists a range of factors that might feature in such an analysis undertaken as a precursor to developing a destination's event tourism strategy.

■ **Figure 3.2**
Possible factors for inclusion in a destination's event tourism SWOT analysis

Strengths/weaknesses

Existing stock of events

- Type
- Quality
- Uniqueness/competitive advantage
- Number
- Duration/timing (for example, whether most events are scheduled at a particular time of the year, such as summer, and whether this clustering is advantageous/disadvantageous from a tourism perspective)
- Current financial situation
- Image/reputation (particularly in visitor markets)
- Level of current demand from regional, intrastate, interstate and overseas visitor markets, and level of understanding of these markets.
- Economic, social and environmental impacts
- Existing links between events and the destination's tourism industry (for example, level of packaging evident and level of partnering with tourism industry marketing bodies)
- Stage of individual events in terms of their 'product' life cycle
- Evidence of long-term strategic planning

Venues/sites/facilities/supporting services

- Number, type, quality and capacity of venues/outdoor event sites
- Capacity of local suppliers (for example, equipment hire, food and beverage services) to support various types of events.
- Stock of supporting local tourism services (for example, accommodation suppliers, transport suppliers, tour operators)

Human resources

- Level/type of destination event venue/event management expertise
- Capacity to draw on volunteers to support event delivery
- Range/type of event-related training conducted in the area, or accessible to people from the area via means such as the Internet

(continued)

Stage of event sector development
- Existence of organisations such as industry associations, convention and visitors bureaus and major event agencies

Destination location relative to major tourist markets
- Travel time and costs
- Types and frequency of public transport to the area

Degree of political support
- Level of available funding for event tourism
- Potential for legislative support
- Location of a major event agency inside government (for example, in a number of Australian states, major event agencies are located in the Premier's department or departmental portfolio, which provides ready access to key decision makers)

Level of community support
- Community perspectives on economic outcomes (for example, whether the community perceives it will benefit economically from the events staged or whether they think most benefits will be 'exported' from the area)
- Level of anticipated local patronage for events (necessary to underpin the economics of many events)
- Level of willingness of the community to absorb short-term negatives, such as crowding and traffic congestion
- Willingness of a community to support events via volunteering, provision of home hosting services etc.

Extent and nature of existing relationships between events and the tourism industry
- Extent of event packaging evident
- Type/nature of links with tourism companies and organisations

Local weather patterns
- Rainy seasons or periods of extreme heat that may restrict the times in which events can be conducted

Opportunities/threats

Potential for partnering with selected organisations to progress one or more event tourism goals
- Possible partnering bodies:
  - Government departments
  - Cultural organisations
  - Tourism bodies
  - Chambers of commerce
  - Tourism businesses (to package events)
  - Environmental groups (to minimise impacts/maximise environmental outcomes)

Level and type of competition from other events in other destinations
- Direct competition from similar events
- Competition from dissimilar events conducted in the same time period

Market tastes/preferences for events
- Ability of an area to respond to market needs through existing and new events
- Impact on existing/planned events of changes in family structures, age of population, patterns of work/retirement, and attitudes to health etc.

Availability of external funds
- Capacity to attract government grants or loans
- Likelihood of attracting sponsorship

Potential to link events with overall destination branding efforts (for example, the Hunter Valley region of New South Wales uses events to reinforce its image as a producer of quality food and wine)

Local cultural/environmental attributes that have the potential to be leveraged for event purposes (for example, unique flora or fauna, a strong and vibrant indigenous culture, history, ethnicity, architecture, local agricultural pursuits)

Level/type of links between local/regional sporting/business/cultural bodies and their national or international associations (for example, strong links between a regional sporting body and its national association may facilitate successful bids for state/national championships in the sports concerned)

Capacity of destination to absorb event tourism impacts without negative environmental or community outcomes
- Perspectives of community groups, such as non-government environmental organisations, on events of various types and scale

General economic conditions
- Employment levels
- Interest rates
- Inflation
- Consumer confidence levels

Other
- Changes in weather patterns due to global warming
- Security and health issues (for example, terrorism, SARS)
- Political climate (for example, the extent to which events involving particular groups or nations will be supported by key stakeholders, such as state or national governments)

*D*EVELOPMENT OF EVENT TOURISM GOALS

The role event tourism is required to play in a destination's tourism development efforts will vary according to the overall tourism strategy that is being pursued. An understanding of this strategy is important as it provides, for example, the basis for establishing event tourism visitation targets, as well as insights into destination branding and positioning efforts that an event strategy may be required to support. While each destination's event tourism goals will differ, common considerations in setting such goals can be identified, and these are discussed below.

■ Leveraging *events for economic gain*

A key consideration in any event tourism strategy is the potential for events to bring 'new' money into a destination from outside visitors (chapter 2). A single large-scale event such as the America's Cup has the potential to contribute significantly to a destination's economy. When this event was held in Auckland, New Zealand, in 2000, Statistics New Zealand (cited in Barker, Page & Meyer 2002, p. 82) reported that 192 860 people arrived in February 2000 — up 14 per cent (23 780 arrivals) on the number in February 1999 — and that the increase might have been due to the yachting finals. Additionally, it was estimated that this event had a direct economic impact of NZ$172 million and an indirect impact of NZ$301 million for its host city (Barker, Page & Meyer 2002).

Even in developing countries, events can generate significant tourist demand (and therefore export income). In the Caribbean, for example, peaks in visitation in many countries often coincide with an event (Nurse 2003).

■ Geographic *dispersal of economic benefits flowing from tourism*

When the destinations seeking to engage in event tourism are large geographic entities, such as states or countries, it is not uncommon for them to use events as a means of encouraging travel to areas outside major tourism centres (see the EventScotland case study, page 77). In this way, the economic benefits from visitation are more widely spread.

■ Destination *branding*

A destination's 'brand' can be thought of as the overall impression, association or feeling that its name and associated symbols generate in the minds of consumers. Events are an opportunity to assist in creating, changing or reinforcing such brands. According to a study by Jago et al. (2003), such efforts depend greatly on local community support and on the cultural and strategic fit between the destination and the event(s) conducted there. This study also found, in the context of individual events, that event differentiation, the longevity/tradition associated with an event, cooperative planning by key players, and media support were central factors in the successful integration of individual events into a destination's overall branding efforts.

The Australasian Country Music Festival, Australia's largest country music event, is an excellent example of using an event for destination branding purposes. This event has been extensively leveraged to create a 'brand' for the town of Tamworth where, arguably, none existed before. The town is now firmly established as 'Australia's country music capital', a position it has sought to strengthen via a variety of means. These means have included developing a 'Hall of Renown' for country music artists, building a guitar-shaped tourist information centre and swimming pool, constructing a 20-metre high 'Golden Guitar' at one entrance to the town, establishing an interpretive centre that overviews the evolution of country music, and erecting memorials to country artists (Harris & Allen 2002).

Another example of 'identity' creation through events can be observed in the Scone district of New South Wales. This area brands itself as the 'Horse Capital' of Australia and conducts multiple events to reinforce this position, such as rodeos, horse races, long-distance charity rides, as well as its major event, the Scone Horse Festival.

Many other examples of branding through events can be identified. The general category of food and/or wine festivals, for example, perform this function for a number of destinations, reinforcing to the broader market the destination's status in connection with these products. Taste Washington, an annual food and wine festival in Washington State, is indicative of such events, stating its purpose as showcasing 'the bounty of the state's quality wine and food' (Washington Wine Commission 2004).

Another aspect of the link between events and destination branding is the use of events by tourism marketing bodies as integral parts of broad 'theme' years. Australia's Northern Territory, for example, declared 2002 the 'Year of the Outback'. A key component of this themed year was an event called Outback Central, conducted at the then newly opened Alice Springs Convention Centre (Australasian Special Events Magazine 2002). Events are also sometimes used as the basis for theme years, an example being the German National Tourist Board's year of trade fairs and conferences in 2003. The goal of this themed year, 'Germany — routes to success: trade fairs, congresses, conferences and more', was to consolidate and develop Germany's market position as an international destination for trade fairs, congresses and conferences (Germany National Tourist Board 2004).

■ Destination *marketing*

Associated with the issue of destination branding is the more general one of destination promotion. Destinations often use events to progress their overall tourism promotional efforts. Smith and Jenner (1998), for example, point to the dramatic rise in visitation to Atlanta, Georgia (a 78 per cent rise in overseas visitors and a 35 per cent rise in domestic visitors) over the three-year period following its announcement in 1990 as the site of the 1996 Olympics. They attribute this increase, in part, to the publicity that Atlanta was able to obtain as a result of hosting the Olympics. In the case of the Sydney 2000 Olympics, the Australian Tourist Commission (ATC) estimated an additional 1.7 million visits would result between 1997 and 2004, generating an additional $6.1 billion in foreign exchange earnings. It also considered that this event accelerated Australia's tourism marketing efforts by 10 years. This outcome was largely due to the additional $3.8 billion in media publicity obtained through ATC Olympic Games media relations activities, and the $300 million in exposure obtained through work with sponsors (Australasian Special Events Magazine 2001).

■ Creating *off-season demand for tourism industry services*

Events have the capacity to be scheduled in periods of low tourism demand, thereby evening out seasonal tourism flows. Skiing centres, for example, often use events as a means of generating demand during non-winter periods. Events can also be used as a means of extending the tourist season by conducting them just before or just after the high-season period.

■ Enhancing *visitor experiences*

Events add to the range of experiences a destination can offer, and thus add to its capacity to attract and hold visitors for longer periods of time (Getz 1997).

■ Catalyst *for expansion and/or improvement of infrastructure*

Events can provide a significant spur to both public and private investment in a destination. Many writers (for example, Carlsen & Millan 2002; Ritchie 2001; Selwood & Jones 2001; Hiller & Moylan 1999; Mules 1993) have highlighted the role that particularly large-scale events can play in urban renewal, and in the subsequent development of a destination's attractiveness and capacity as a tourist destination.

Investment by the private sector in restaurants and tourist accommodation, for example, is often central to this process, and may sometimes extend to the building of large-scale infrastructure items. The main stadium, Stadium Australia, for the Sydney 2000 Olympic Games, for example, was developed and is owned by private sector interests (Ogdon International Facilities Corporation 2004). Even at the level of small-scale community-based events, such as the Nymagee Outback Music Festival (see the event profile on page 74), significant positive changes to the physical aspects of a destination can result from the conduct of events designed to stimulate tourist visitation.

■ Progression *of a destination's social, cultural and/or environmental agenda*

A range of agendas may be pursued through the conduct of events — tourist visitation is one example. These other agendas may serve to condition how event tourism is approached, or may be independent of such considerations.

The pursuit of these broader outcomes can be observed in the context of the Manchester Commonwealth Games, for example. This event was leveraged by the city's council as a catalyst for educational, skill-building and health improvement programs, as well as a means of creating awareness and understanding of the various communities (from Commonwealth countries) that live in the Manchester area (Carlsen & Millan 2002). Environmental agendas can also be progressed through events. The Sydney 2000 Olympics sought to be labelled the 'Green Games'; among its many achievements in this regard was the clean-up of an area (Homebush Bay) that was highly contaminated with industrial waste. This area later became the main Olympic site (Harris & Huyskins 2002).

Whatever event tourism goals are set by a destination, specific benchmarks need to be established to assess progress towards those goals. Tasmania's major event agency (Events Tasmania), for example, states that it aims to increase its market share of event tourism from 5 per cent to 6 per cent by 2007. Additionally, it has quantified the number of events that it will facilitate as part of its efforts to achieve this objective; specifically, each year it aims to conduct:
- four to six events of state significance
- four to six major sporting events
- three to four regional events for each region
- six to 10 touring events
- 15–25 national championships (Events Tasmania 2004).

Other areas of a purely tourist nature, where goals might be set and progress measured, include tourist income generated from events, changes in length of tourist stays, use levels of tourism services (particularly accommodation), the extent of geographic spread of tourism flowing from the conduct of events, the volume of event-related media coverage received by a destination, and changes in destination market position/image flowing from the conduct of events.

CREATION OF AN EVENT TOURISM ORGANISATIONAL STRUCTURE

To progress a destination's event tourism goals, it is necessary to allocate responsibility for achieving these to one or more organisations. In the case of towns or regions, such responsibilities often lie with the same body charged with overall tourism development. In the case of cities, states or countries, multiple organisations may be involved, such as bodies responsible for festivals, business tourism, major events and overall tourism development (figure 3.3, page 62). In the Australian state of Victoria, for example, three significant organisations with major roles in event tourism development can be identified:
- *Tourism Victoria* (the State's tourism commission) aims to identify appropriate existing events and assist them in their efforts at tourism marketing and general business development (Tourism Victoria 2002).
- The *Victoria Major Events Corporation* acts to target and attract events that can provide substantial economic impact and/or international profile for Melbourne and Victoria (Australasian Special Events Magazine 2002).

- The *Melbourne Convention and Visitors Bureau* is concerned with 'increasing visitation and economic benefits for Melbourne and Victoria by maximising its potential in meetings, incentives, conventions and exhibitions' (Melbourne Convention and Visitors Bureau 2004).

In addition to these bodies, local and regional tourism bodies and some government departments (for example, Arts Victoria and Sport and Recreation Victoria) also play a role in event tourism development in that state.

■ **Figure 3.3** *Major event tourism organisations*

ORGANISATION TYPE	DESCRIPTION
Major event agencies	These bodies are commonly state or country based. Their roles vary depending on their charter. In some instances, they may be involved only in seeking to attract large-scale events through the bidding process (for example, Victoria Major Events Corporation). In other instances, they may also have responsibility for creating new events and developing existing events (see the EventScotland case study, page 77). Those agencies with a broader charter may also be charged with overall responsibility for facilitating the development of event tourism in a destination.
Government tourism organisations	These organisations, at local, regional, state and national levels, can perform a variety of event tourism development roles. In some cases, they may be responsible for developing and implementing a whole destination event tourism strategy. They may also provide a range of services designed to support and develop the sector, such as promotional assistance, grants, the maintenance of event calendars, and the provision of advice and assistance in a variety of areas (for example, marketing, liaising with government departments on behalf of events to obtain relevant permissions/licences etc.).
Specialist event agencies	These often government sponsored bodies act to develop and support specific event forms within a destination. Convention and visitors bureaus, for example, act to promote the development of destinations as locations for meetings, incentives, exhibitions, conventions and special events.

The existence of multiple bodies charged with event tourism development at a destination, creates the potential for a loss of focus on its overall event tourism goals, as well as a less coordinated approach to their achievement. For these reasons, there is a strong case for the creation of a single body, either within an existing organisation (see the event profile on Event Denmark, page 63), or in the form of a new organisation (see the case study on EventScotland, page 77), with a charter to coordinate, assist and, if necessary, 'push' organisations towards the achievement of broader whole-of-destination event tourism goals. In the absence of such a body, alternative mechanisms need to be developed to try to produce such an outcome. These mechanisms might include shared board memberships between key event tourism bodies, clearly defined organisational missions to prevent over-lapping efforts; regular 'round table' meetings between key organisations, and conditions on funding that require broader event tourism goals to be addressed. The State Government of New South Wales' requirement that the Sydney Convention and Visitors Bureau (SCVB) create a new division (the New South Wales Convention Bureau), to progress its goal of spreading the economic benefits of tourism into regional areas, is an example of this last point (Sydney Convention and Visitors Bureau 2002).

EVENT PROFILE

Event Denmark

At the end of 2003, the Danish Government announced five new steps designed to improve cooperation between business — including the tourism industry — and the nation's cultural life. Following on from this announcement, the Secretary of Culture (Mr Brian Mikkelsen) and the Secretary of Business and Economy (Mr Bendt Bendtsen) agreed on a plan designed to professionalise the development, management, marketing and evaluation of international events in Denmark. In support of seeking such an outcome, they claimed that:

■ The staging of many cultural and sports events is positive; it is profitable business, it supports the image of the region and the nation, and it is an asset for tourism, for the local society and commerce, as well as for the national economy (Blicher-Hansen 2003). ■

Many other countries (for example, the Netherlands, Scotland and Australia) had made similar observations and subsequently created specialist event agencies as a way of focusing efforts on driving visitation through these means.

Responsibility for progressing this plan fell to the national Danish Tourist Board (DTB), which subsequently developed a strategy embracing both the cultural and tourism aspects of events, and created a separate event division within the DTB called Event Denmark. In developing this strategy, the DTB acknowledged that international air travel would continue to grow despite terrorist acts. Additionally, it was believed that in Europe the number of short holiday breaks taken was likely to increase, fuelled in large measure by airline competition. Such competition was making a long weekend city break trip a possible and regular monthly 'habit'. The DTB also acknowledged, since many Europeans were already seasoned travellers, that the value of simply promoting a destination might no longer be enough to attract visitors for a second or subsequent time. Events, therefore, and their associated one-off uniqueness had a significant role to play in driving future repeat visitor

(continued)

growth. In particular, the DTB believed that events could create a 'personal' connection with people. This would be achieved through an association with an individual's cultural interests, whether a Magritte art exhibition in Paris, a unique production of Bizet's *Carmen i Sevilla* in Spain, or a performance of Hans Christian Andersen's fairytales in authentic surroundings in Denmark.

With these thoughts in mind, and with a desire to attract and develop more international events in Denmark, the DTB developed its event tourism strategy, giving responsibility for its implementation to the newly created Event Denmark. The following are the main aspects of this strategy:

- In the short term, generate a direct tourism effect — measured in terms of the number of visitors and their spending, level of immediate media exposure and awareness of the destination.
- In the medium term, support destination marketing in relation to the branding of Denmark. Branding themes that events could reinforce include the uniqueness of Danish culture (for example, music, ballet, food, design and architecture), sporting opportunities (for example, golf, football, sailing and cycling), historic traditions, and the uniqueness of the natural environment.
- In the longer term, enhance the overall profile of Denmark as a unique visitor destination to position the country as a 'must go' destination — one that is on the cutting edge in many areas and one that offers unique experiences.

In working through its strategy, the DTB sought to identify existing events that embraced its requirements. Key considerations were that such events needed to be:

- open to the public
- unique, not something that could easily be experienced elsewhere
- high quality in content
- appealing to an international audience
- strongly associated with Danish traditions and/or national values
- capable and open to marketing themselves internationally
- accessible via such means as online ticketing facilities
- able to use surplus tourism services (particularly accommodation) during periods of low seasonal demand
- managed in a professional manner
- designed to ensure that they were environmentally sustainable
- preferably conducted on an annual basis.

Once these key considerations were identified, Event Denmark would arrange for these events to be promoted to international markets in a variety of ways — for example, via inbound tour operators, specialised tour operators, overseas travel agents and international online event booking agencies. Additionally, Event Denmark would aid their promotional efforts in such markets by advising them on how to gain exposure on global event listing websites, and by conducting public relations efforts through the DTB's overseas tourist offices and Denmark's embassy network around the world.

While Event Denmark has just commenced operations, it is already obvious that by approaching event tourism development separately from tourism in general, the opportunity to leverage events for tourism purposes will be greatly enhanced.

(**Source:** *Based on Blicher-Hansen 2003.*)

DEVELOPMENT OF AN EVENT TOURISM STRATEGY

In terms of general strategic options available to a town, city, region, state or country's event tourism body, several possibilities can be identified. These strategies concern the development of existing events, bidding to attract existing (mobile) events, and the creation of new events. These three broad strategic options are not mutually exclusive — for example, event tourism bodies in any one destination may employ composite strategies involving two, or all three, of these options to achieve their destination's event tourism goals. Whatever strategy is selected, it needs to reflect the insights gained from the preceding situational analysis.

■ **Existing** *event development*

A range of possible approaches to using existing events to advance a destination's event tourism efforts can be identified. One option is to identify one or several events that have the capacity to be developed as major attractions for an area ('hallmark' events), with a view to using them as the foundation for image-building efforts. The previously cited example of the Tamworth Country and Western Music Festival is indicative of how events can be used in this way. A variant on this approach is to develop a single hallmark event that can then be supported by a range of similarly themed events. The Scone example discussed earlier (with its 'hallmark' Scone Horse Festival and associated smaller scale horse-based events) is reflective of such a strategy. It may also be possible to merge existing smaller events to create one or several larger events, or to incorporate smaller events into larger events to add to their uniqueness and subsequent tourism appeal. Yet another approach is to develop one or several hallmark events, while at the same time maintaining a mix of small-scale events scheduled throughout the year, as a means of generating year-long appeal for a destination.

■ Event *bidding*

Many events are mobile in the sense that they move regularly between different destinations. Some sporting events and many business events (for example, association/corporate conferences) fall into this category. Some types of event tourism organisations (namely many national or state-based major event agencies, and convention and visitors bureaus) have been specifically established for the purpose of attracting new events to a destination via the bidding process. Bodies of this nature need to be able to identify events of this type — a task that convention and visitor bureaus often undertake by maintaining representatives in other states and overseas, and by directly communicating with meeting, incentive, and exhibition planners. To attract such mobile events, it is necessary to prepare a formal bid (chapter 5) that makes a persuasive case as to why an event should be conducted in a specific destination. Before doing so, however, it is necessary to ensure a sound match exists between the event being sought and an area's capacity to host it. Regarding its bidding efforts, the Victoria Major Events Corporation (2004) notes:

> ■ A decision to bid to host an event is only made after an exhaustive assessment of the event's history and projected feasibility within Melbourne and Victoria. Such assessment includes consultation and cooperation with venues, sporting associations, local government, sponsors, the sporting public, media and various State Government Departments including Office of Premier and Cabinet, Tourism Victoria, Parks Victoria, Sport and Recreation Victoria and Business Victoria. ■

■ New *event creation*

New event creation should be based around the activities and themes identified in the situational analysis as providing substantial scope for the development of tourist markets. It should also be the case that new events, as Tourism Victoria (2002) points out, are capable of being integrated into the overall tourism product mix of a destination. Exactly what new events are created will vary with the strategic needs of each destination, with the range of generic options including active participant-based events, spectator-based sport events, religious events, events with environmental/cultural/heritage themes, music-based events, special interest events and business events. As with the development of existing events, event tourism organisations need to be mindful of the need to ensure new events are adequately resourced if they are to have the best chance of long-term survival. This being the case, it may be desirable for organisations involved in event tourism to limit their support to only a few new events.

■ General *considerations in event tourism strategy selection*

In making decisions about what event tourism strategy to pursue, it can be useful to think in terms of what 'portfolio' (or mix) of events (festivals, sporting competitions, business events etc.) is likely to deliver the required benefits for a destination from event tourism. A useful first step in this regard is to rate events (existing, new and events for which bids are proposed) — using available data and professional judgement — against established criteria. A simple 1 (low) to 5 (high) rating system (figure 3.4) could be employed for this purpose. If appropriate, a weighting could also be applied to each criterion, so the final numeric value associated with each event would be a product of the extent to which it was viewed as meeting each criterion, multiplied by the importance of that criterion.

■ **Figure 3.4**
Event rating scale

EVENT NAME	CRITERION 1	CRITERION 2	CRITERION 3	CRITERION 4	TOTAL
A	1	2	3	4	10
B	1	4	5	5	15
C	2	4	3	1	10

A useful approach to thinking about the 'mix' of events at a destination is to view them from a hierarchical perspective. Using this approach, events with high tourism value and the capacity to progress many of an event tourism body's goals would appear at the top, while those with lower tourism value and limited ability to progress the organisation's goals would be placed at the bottom. Such a hierarchy is commonly represented as a pyramid, as per the Events Tasmania hierarchical model of events (figure 3.5). Additionally, such models also provide insights into where 'gaps' may be in an area's current event portfolio. This model also notes the varying roles that Events Tasmania will play in different types of event.

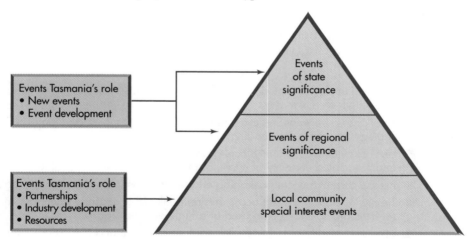

Support for events of state or regional significance includes funding programs, strategic planning and marketing, research and evaluation, targeted funds/grants, event experience design and event programming, resource leverage, and the facilitation of links. Support for local community special interest events includes regional event coordinators, forums and training, resources and website references and research.

■ **Figure 3.5** *Events Tasmania hierarchical model of events*   (**Source:** *Events Tasmania 2003, p. 4.*)

Once an event strategy has been selected, the next step is for the organisation(s) concerned to implement it by undertaking actions appropriate to its/their charter. This being the case, such actions may vary, from the provision of advice and marketing support up to the actual development and conduct of new events. The following section seeks to identify and broadly categorise the full range of actions that organisations directly involved in event tourism development might engage.

■ **Financial** *support*

Financial support may be provided in the form of grants, sponsorship and equity.

Grants

Grants are a common means of providing support for events that are deemed to have tourism potential. Tourism New South Wales, for example, operates a Regional Flagship Events program that provides $10 000 one-off grants or $20 000 a year for three years in a triennial funding arrangement (Tourism New South Wales 2004). Most other Australian states and territories operate similar systems. Queensland Events, for example, operates a granting system in partnership with local councils and regional tourist organisations (Queensland Events 2004). Some local councils have also moved to create event tourism grant schemes (for example, Richmond Valley Council in northern New South Wales). These grants are commonly based on a range of criteria, such as those in figure 3.6.

■ **Figure 3.6**
Common grant selection criteria employed by event tourism organisations

- Potential or demonstrated capacity to increase tourist visitation, yield per visitor and length of visitor stay
- Relationship between the event and area's overall tourism development strategy, including its branding efforts
- Level of evident community/local government/business/tourism industry support and associated capacity of event to grow and become self-funding
- Event's current tourism packaging efforts, or potential for tourism packaging
- Timing — does the event occur outside peak visitor seasons when tourism services are already being used at a high level?
- Level and quality of business, financial, operational and marketing planning in evidence
- Media value associated with the event
- Contribution to strategic social, cultural, environmental or economic outcomes sought by the destination
- Existence of processes designed to evaluate the event, particularly its tourism outcomes

Grants may also be provided by event tourism bodies in the form of seed money to allow new events to be established, or for specific purposes, such as the conduct of a feasibility study to determine the viability of a proposed event. Grants can also be used as a form of incentive to conduct an event in a specific destination. Events Tasmania, for example, operates a grants scheme that provides a per person payment to clubs and associations hosting events in that state for registered interstate/overseas visitors and accompanying guests. Through Sport and Recreation Tasmania (a government department), the State Government also provides funding support for organisations conducting national sporting championships when certain conditions are met (Events Tasmania 2004).

Sponsorship

Some event tourism organisations act to directly sponsor events as a way of financially assisting them, and/or as a way of leveraging the opportunity presented by the event to progress their destination branding efforts.

Equity

To facilitate the conduct of an event, a tourism event organisation may act to directly invest in it. The IndyCar race, for example — an event that takes place on the Gold Coast in Queensland in a traditionally off-peak period for tourism services — is operated by Indycar Australia. This company is jointly owned by the State of Queensland (through Queensland Events) and the private sector organisation International Management Group (IMG) (Queensland Events 2004b).

■ Ownership

Some event tourism bodies develop and produce events to stimulate visitation to their destination. They act in this way for a variety of reasons, including to ensure their charter is progressed without the need to rely on the private sector (which may be unwilling to take on the financial risk involved in event creation and delivery) and to overcome a lack of local event management expertise. Queensland Events, for example, operates a subsidiary company, Gold Coast Events Management Ltd, that owns and operates two events — the Gold Coast Airport Marathon and the Pan Pacific Masters Games (Queensland Events 2004b). Other event tourism bodies in Australia have also acted to establish and develop new events, including Events Tasmania, Australian Capital Territory Tourism and Northern Territory Major Events.

■ Bid *development and bid support services*

As noted, bidding is the major focus of a number of event tourism organisations. Such organisations act to research, develop and make bids, and/or work with bidding bodies (such as sporting or professional associations) to facilitate the making of a bid (including the creation of a bid committee).

Once a bid is won, however, the event tourism organisation commonly plays little, if any, further role other than perhaps assisting to stimulate event attendance or to create an organising committee.

■ Event *sector development services*

Event sector development services include research, training and education, and the establishment of partnerships and networks.

Research

Some tourism event organisations commission or undertake research on a range of event-related matters as a way of gaining information that will aid the development of individual events or the sector in general. Matters explored include trends in event visitor markets, developments in competitor destinations, visitor perceptions of the quality of event experiences (particularly those supported by the event organisation concerned), event sector stakeholder viewpoints, event economic impacts, and overall sector management practices. Regarding this last point, research can be insightful in assisting event agencies to develop programs designed to build the events sector. Evidence for this can be found in Goh's (2003) study, which highlighted weaknesses in this area in the context of Irish festivals, specifically:

- 47 per cent of festivals have no data on their audiences
- 59 per cent of festivals do not provide training for their volunteers
- 23 per cent of festivals have no presence on the world wide web
- 58 per cent of festivals have no strategic plan.

Training and education

To promote best practice and continuous improvement, and by doing so assist in creating events that are sustainable in the longer term, some event tourism organisations undertake — or commission outside bodies to undertake — training in areas such as event project management, event marketing and general industry best practice. Some also maintain a resource base (electronic or textual) on which event organisers can draw for educational/training purposes, as well as conducting industry events such as conferences.

Partnerships and networks

A range of opportunities exist for event tourism organisations to establish partnerships and networks both within the events sector and between the events sector and outside bodies. Forming links between individual events and other organisations that have the potential to enhance the attractiveness of events to visitor markets can be driven via the use of grants, for example. This can be done by explicitly favouring applications that demonstrate links with, for example, tourism bodies and cultural institutions, such as museums, heritage organisations, art galleries and community arts organisations. Other ways in which such links can be established include purposefully arranging formal and informal meetings and functions, involving members of the events industry, tourism organisations and the general business community. Once networks are established, they can serve a variety of purposes — for example, facilitating the sharing of information and expertise, expanding access to sponsorship opportunities and developing partnerships (both within and external to the event sector) that will assist in the development of tourist markets.

Event tourism organisations may also find they have much to gain by communicating their strategies to a range of public and private sector organisations, thus encouraging dialogue that may lead to the identification of opportunities to progress common agenda. Government departments associated with the arts, sport and state development, for example, may all see opportunities to further their goals through an association with one or more event tourism bodies.

■ Coordination

Event tourism bodies can play a range of coordination roles. These roles include developing an event calendar to reduce event clashes and providing a 'one-stop shop' at which event organisers can obtain relevant permissions and clarify government policies and procedures of relevance. Given that a range of government bodies may be involved in the delivery of any one event, event tourism organisations can also act to establish coordination and consultation protocols between different government units and agencies, as well as assisting events to 'navigate' their way through legislative and compliance issues.

■ Event/*destination promotion services*

To assist organisations (such as sporting bodies and professional associations) in their efforts to host specific events, event tourism organisations, depending on their charter, may provide a range of marketing collateral (figure 3.7). Such collateral may include brochure shells, giveaways, videos highlighting destination attractions and event facilities and services, and posters. Additionally, such organisations may seek to facilitate the conduct of events by, for example:

• providing information to organisations seeking to conduct events on a destination's event-related facilities and services
• hosting familiarisation tours and site visits by event organising committees
• assisting with the preparation of event programs and pre- and post-event tours
• acting as a liaison between government and civic authorities
• assisting in stimulating attendance at events via public relations activities and direct mail.

Tourism Australia, as part of its promotional role, seeks to 'position Australia as a unique, desirable and achievable destination for meetings, incentives, conventions and exhibitions' (Tourism Australia 2004). To progress this goal, Tourism Australia has developed promotional material for the business tourism industry and has acted in collaboration with the

Australian Association of Convention and Visitors Bureaus to create a body (Team Australia) to facilitate the collective planning and resourcing of selected promotional projects (Tourism Australia 2004).

■ Figure 3.7
Promotional
collateral —
Gold Coast
Convention
Bureau,
Queensland

Fact sheet: a three-page fold-out (six pages of content) containing generic information on the Gold Coast. Available in English, Japanese, Korean, Mandarin, German, French, Russian, Arabic, Italian and Spanish.
Tour shells: A3 page folding into A4 — perfect for conference programs, agendas, registration brochures etc.
Golf brochures: a 40-page brochure featuring the region's most spectacular golf courses and local golf tour operators
Holiday guides: a 100-page colour magazine detailing specific information on the Gold Coast, as well as product information — an ideal publication for delegate satchels
Videos: both in PAL and NTSC format, containing a three-minute motivational segment
CD-ROM: a CD-ROM containing a three-minute motivational segment and a nine-minute destinational segment, special events, images, brochures, editorials, maps, and web and email links

(**Source:** *Gold Coast Convention Bureau 2004.*)

■ Other

Other roles that event tourism organisations may play include: assisting in the development of business, marketing and risk management plans; providing advice on the negotiation of television rights and merchandising strategies; and lobbying on behalf of the sector on matters relating to new infrastructure development, for example.

EVALUATION OF AN EVENT TOURISM STRATEGY

Evaluation is fundamental to the success of any strategy. At the destination level, the broad goals that have been set for event tourism, and the objectives associated with those goals, will form the basis of any evaluation that takes place. The collection and interpretation of information is central to this process, with data on visitor flows associated with event tourism being of particular importance. In the context of business tourism in Australia, for example, data are available from a variety of sources, including Tourism Australia, state tourist commissions and the Bureau of Tourism Research. International bodies, such as the International Congress and Convention Association (ICCA) and the International Meetings Industry Association (IMIA), also conduct research that relates to Australia's comparative performance in this area. Tourism Australia (2004), for example, provides the following assessment (drawing largely on ICCA research) of Australia's recent business tourism performance.

In terms of meetings per country, Australia took a slight fall in the global rankings to 8th destination in 2003, after occupying 5th position in 2001. The USA was ranked number one, followed by Spain, the United Kingdom and Germany for the number of association meetings held in 2003.

In terms of market share, Europe remained number one in 2003 with 62 per cent of the market, compared to all other regions. There was a slight decrease in Australia's market share from 4.8 per cent in 2001 to 4 per cent in 2003.

Sydney took a slight fall in the rankings in 2003 to equal 14th destination (sharing with Dublin) in terms of total number of meetings per city, with 37 meetings, slipping from 8th position in 2001. Melbourne was ranked equal 24th (sharing with Glasgow) in 2003 with 31 meetings, slipping from equal 16th spot in 2001. After Sydney and Melbourne came Brisbane, ranked in equal 50th position with five other countries. Cairns dropped from 46th position in 2002 to equal 88th position in 2003 with nine other countries (including Adelaide).

The total number of participants attending international meetings in Australia between 1998 and 2003 is as follows:

- 1998: 62 322 participants
- 1999: 93 733 participants
- 2000: 111 278 participants
- 2001: 99 224 participants
- 2003: 109 084 participants.

In addition to whole-of-destination assessments of event tourism performance in the context of specific types of event, or events in general, each organisation involved in an area's event tourism development should have its own goals. To conform to the basic model of event tourism strategic planning used in this chapter, these goals should link directly to the destination's overall event tourism goals. Such individual assessments should also serve to 'build' towards an overall picture of a destination's event tourism performance, which can then be used to form the basis for future strategic decisions regarding event tourism development.

TOURISM EVENTS AND REGIONAL DEVELOPMENT

While the focus of discussion regarding event tourism is often on cities, states or countries, many regions and towns have acknowledged the benefits that can potentially flow from event tourism, and have actively sought to engage in it. The following event profile of Nymagee Outback Music Festival is a clear example of the capacity of events to bring significant positive change to small communities (in this case, Nymagee — an outback town in New South Wales) through expanded visitation. Local government in many regional areas is actively showing support for such efforts, being keen for communities to reap the economic and other benefits associated with events. Richmond Valley Council in northern New South Wales, for example, has recently established its own system of 'tourism event' grants, which are vetted by its tourism advisory committee (Richmond Valley Council 2004).

EVENT PROFILE

Nymagee Outback Music Festival

'*Nymagee*' is an Indigenous word for 'small plain surrounded by hills'. The village is in the centre of a triangle of three major towns: Cobar (100 kilometres north west), Nyngan (120 kilometres north east) and Condobolin (160 kilometres south east). In 2003, the town's population was 62 and that of the surrounding district was 160. Given the small size of the community, its survival is very much reliant on maintaining or building its population.

The local pub is home on most evenings to a mix of colourful characters, which can include graziers, shearers, wheat farmers, miners, local tradespeople, game hunters, musicians, geologists, journalists, politicians and a few urban escapees. A newspaper is rare, maybe once a week when the publican has just been to town. With little contact with the 'outside world', the community is generally left to shape its own destiny.

In 1998 the Nymagee community, which then numbered 35, met to discuss how to increase its population to ensure its future. One of the suggestions was to stage an outback music festival. This event, it was argued, could serve to raise the profile of the village and district and attract tourists and, ultimately, residents. The village subsequently decided to create such an event, although acknowledged that the logistics of staging it in a local paddock with no power in such a remote destination would be far from easy.

The first Nymagee Outback Music Festival was conducted in 1999. Visitors were accommodated in a temporary camping area on the event site, with bush 'pit' toilets acting to add to the 'outback' experience. It was held again in 2000 and 2002. The festival is a feast of culture in the country, combining live entertainment and arts with new and emerging local and visiting artists. In 2002 more than 100 musicians, including a number from overseas, performed 60 hours of concerts on four stages over three days. Additionally, the event included workshops and theatre. The majority of community members act as volunteers, assisting to set up the event and undertake operational and shut-down tasks. Some also exhibit and perform at the festival. A number of community groups from surrounding towns also assist with the delivery of the event.

In 1999 the festival drew 600 people; in 2000 attendance grew to 900. Despite the drought, the 2002 festival attracted over 1000 visitors to the village on the October long weekend, proving Nymagee's off-the-beaten-track location was no obstacle to visitors. Music lovers came from as far as Perth, Adelaide, Sydney, Melbourne, Japan, Vanuatu, Samoa and the Netherlands to enjoy the event.

The festival has provided a significant stimulus for tourism to the village and has resulted in a range of actions designed to enhance the visitor experience, including:

- beautification of the village
- tree planting
- improvements to the local park
- signage and mapping of historical points of interest and natural attractions
- development of tourist information material
- improving and signposting public amenities.

The festival has had a major impact on the tiny community of Nymagee. The population increased from 35 (in 1998) to 62 (in 2003). Construction of new houses and renovations are underway for the first time in decades. There has been a 60 per cent increase in annual tourism visitation, with visitors being drawn to the village by the arts and cultural image that the event has helped to generate. New residents attracted to the village are also establishing cottage industries – such as beekeeping and brush cutting – and by so doing have diversified the local economy away from its traditional farming and grazing base. Most importantly of all, however, the success of the event has brought with it a significant boost to community morale.

(**Source:** *Based on Dunne 2003.*)

$\mathcal{S}$UMMARY

For destinations ranging in size from small towns to countries, event tourism is increasingly becoming a key aspect of their overall tourism development efforts. In this chapter, a basic event tourism strategic planning model has been proposed that seeks to bring a measure of structure and discipline to this process. The first step in the model is a detailed situational analysis, which leads to the establishment of event tourism goals. These goals are then progressed through an organisational structure created for this purpose. Ideally, such a structure would involve the establishment of a single organisation with responsibility for the area, or the allocation of such responsibility to an existing body. In the absence of such a body, other options — such as regular meetings between key organisations in the area — can be used with similar intent. Once a structure is in place, strategic options need to be considered, and a strategy needs to be determined that is likely to involve multiple organisations. In the pursuit of this strategy, various tools and practices can be employed, including bidding, the provision of promotional and financial support, and activities designed to generally develop the event sector. How successful these practices are in progressing a destination's event tourism strategy and its associated goals needs to be assessed at both the destination level and the level of those organisations with a major input into the event tourism development process. Information gained from this process can then be used to refine future event tourism development efforts.

Questions

1. Discuss the value of having a clear understanding of a destination's overall tourism strategy before embarking on the process of creating an event tourism strategy.

2. List and discuss three goals that a destination may seek to progress through the development of an event tourism strategy.

3. What types of non-tourism goals might a destination seek to achieve by expanding its focus on event tourism?

4. In the absence of a single body with responsibility for directing a destination's event tourism efforts, what approaches might be used to ensure a coordinated response to this task?

5. Briefly discuss the three broad strategic options available to destinations seeking to expand visitation through the use of events.

6. What is meant by the term 'destination event portfolio'? What value does this concept have from an event tourism strategy perspective?

7. What types of action might bodies with a major involvement in event tourism consider taking to develop the event sector in their destination?

8. Briefly discuss how events can play a role in branding a destination.

9. Draw a basic event tourism strategic planning model. Briefly describe each step in this model.

10. Discuss the various forms that grants from event tourism bodies can take.

CASE STUDY ·································

EventScotland

In 2003, Scotland released a major events strategy titled 'Competing on an international stage', with a vision of becoming a leading events destination by 2015. The strategy included establishing a central body, EventScotland, to provide coordination and leadership in securing major events. The following extract explains the strategy's background and aims:

■ Introduction

We announced in *Programme for Government* in 2001 that the Executive would seek to develop a major events strategy for Scotland. This builds on the work that we have done to secure the Ryder Cup for Scotland in 2014 and our bid to host the European Football Championships in 2008 (Euro 2008).

Why develop a major events strategy?

Scotland is an event-rich country and these events serve to boost our international profile and image. World-class cultural and sporting events such as the Edinburgh Festivals or the Open Golf Championships (which we host on average at least every second year) are instantly associated with Scotland in many people's eyes. They demonstrate that we are a dynamic and modern country capable of making an impact — and delivering — on an international stage. They also serve to attract hundreds of thousands of visitors every year to our shores who come to experience events that are uniquely Scottish.

The staging of major sports events here also provides inspiration and ambition and encourages participation and competition at all levels. Governing bodies of sport and other sport organisations benefit from increased exposure and influence. Athletes, coaches, officials and volunteers benefit from preparation programmes and the competitions themselves. Our athletes have the opportunity to compete under home conditions in front of home support and young people in Scotland are inspired to participate and excel.

There are many organisations and agencies in both the public and private sectors responsible at present for delivering successful events in Scotland. Although each one can deliver success individually we have found overwhelming agreement with the view that, in order to fulfil our potential and compete on an international stage, Scotland must develop a co-ordinated and strategic approach to major events.

Proposals for Scotland's major events strategy

Based on (an) assessment of our current approach, we have identified the four key areas for action:

- building Scotland's international image by maximising the benefits of our existing successes and our 'icon' events, including the Edinburgh Festivals and the Open Golf

(*continued*)

- developing a portfolio of sporting and cultural events to underpin Scottish tourism and Scottish brand messages, to strengthen our sporting and cultural environments and to attract visitors to areas of Scotland with spare accommodation capacity, particularly outside traditional high season
- coordinating existing activity and exploring opportunities to enhance existing events being taken forward by public and private sector partners
- building a centre of knowledge and expertise on securing, promoting and delivering events to secure Scotland's reputation as a premier events destination by 2015.

EventScotland

In order to deliver these objectives, a new body will be established to give central coordination and leadership to the drive to secure major events for Scotland. Called EventScotland, this will be a tight organisation and its main task will be to work in partnership with public bodies, including those represented on the steering group and private sector events organisers, to deliver a portfolio of events in Scotland. This body would build on the success of existing events such as the Edinburgh Festivals and the Open Golf Championships and on the experience gained during the Ryder Cup and Euro 2008 bids, and it would seek out opportunities for hosting major events, working closely with other players. This new body will be small, flexible and arms length from [the] Government.

In detail, EventScotland's main tasks will be to:

(a) share information on the size, date and nature of existing and proposed events in Scotland. It will make available detailed information to partner organisations with an interest in events and provide information to the public through platforms such as visitscotland.com. As well as direct relationships with key players, an element of this function may include the establishment of a commercially secure 'extranet' available to partners.

The provision of a centrally held events calendar for Scotland is an essential prerequisite if we are to achieve our aim of becoming a foremost events destination by 2015. EventScotland will develop with partners the protocols necessary to ensure that this often commercially sensitive information can be gathered and shared appropriately to the benefit of all.

(b) assess, evaluate and determine which events EventScotland should support. This will include an economic, social and environmental appraisal of proposed events to determine whether they fit agreed priorities and how much — if any — EventScotland funding should be provided to it. EventScotland will work closely with public sector partners who already fund events to develop a common approach to event appraisal.

EventScotland will prioritise:
- events which highlight and capitalise on the unique visual appeal and landscape of Scotland
- events which showcase Scottish culture and sport
- events which Scotland can 'own', nurture, develop and (on occasion) export

- events which require little or no infrastructure additions, or which tie to planned infrastructure development
- events which underpin the priorities of the Scottish Executive and other public sector agencies involved in major event organisation
- events which have an intrinsic appeal to Scots
- events which highlight and promote the unique appeal and proposition of individual destinations (city, town or rural)
- events which focus on quiet times of the year
- events which offer a direct economic return on investment through tourism, promotion of Scottish business or other means
- events which stimulate a sense of pride in the local population
- events which are sustainable and which are accessible to a wide range of communities and groups
- events which can secure favourable broadcast and print media coverage in key tourism/investment markets
- events of an international, prestige and leading status
- events capable of generating new and/or complementary initiatives within the same sector at national, regional and grassroots levels
- events which offer commercial and showcase opportunities for Scottish businesses
- events which are available, achievable and affordable.

(c) stipulate conditions to govern use of the public money available to it. The role of EventScotland will be to add value to events rather than to replace or duplicate existing funding sources. It will require stringent evaluation of events to assess their success and it will develop these detailed criteria in conjunction with the other public sector organisations that already fund events. It will develop a methodology to ensure that these assessments and checks can happen quickly in order to maintain the commercial competitiveness of EventScotland.

(d) lead and support partners in securing new events for Scotland. This will involve identifying events available internationally which Scotland should bid for; building the appropriate partnerships to deliver successful bids; and interacting with event owners to bring these events to Scotland. Where appropriate, EventScotland will support other partners (local authorities, sports governing bodies or event organisers, for example) rather than lead a bid itself. This is some of the most commercially driven work which Event-Scotland would undertake, requiring it to put together quickly private/public sector funding or underwriting packages, contract hotel accommodation and sponsors and secure Ministerial endorsement where necessary.

(e) help to develop and improve existing events in order to maximise their benefits across the whole of Scotland. This again is commercially driven work involving, for example, identifying sponsors to work with existing event owners to extend their current activities, or working to develop satellite events in Scotland associated with existing successful events.

(continued)

(f) develop and maintain a rolling portfolio of events in line with strategic objectives (increasing visitor numbers in areas/times of spare capacity; promoting Scottish tourism/Scotland the brand key messages; developing events to address health, education, and closing the gap issues). This area of work will require in the first instance a close working relationship with the executive and other public sector partners in order to maintain a portfolio that closely reflects Executive objectives.

(g) develop a centre of knowledge and expertise to underpin and inform the above activity. It would learn from, codify and make available information about the funding, promotion and delivery of existing successful events. It would also learn from and make available information about the lessons learned from bidding for events including the Ryder Cup and Euro 2008.

(h) promote and communicate EventScotland as the hub of Scotland's major events strategy to partners, Ministers, the Scottish public and the international events audience.

(i) be accountable to Ministers and demonstrate an effective link to secure Ministerial endorsements as required. The clear and demonstrable support of Government is an essential element of a successful international events organisation (Scottish Executive 2002). ■

Questions

1 What was the rationale for the establishment of EventScotland by the Scottish Government?

2 Briefly describe the key roles that EventScotland is charged with performing.

3 Briefly discuss how EventScotland will determine which events it will support.

4 What differences (if any) do you see between the responsibilities of EventScotland and those of the other major event agency profiled in this chapter, Event Denmark?

REFERENCES

Australasian Special Events Magazine 2002, 'The impact of Victorian major events', August, www.specialevents.com.au (accessed 10 April 2004).

Australasian Special Events Magazine 2002, 'Year of the Outback 2002, centrepiece launched as unique conference venue', June, www.specialevents. com.au (accessed 10 April 2004).

Australasian Special Events Magazine 2001, 'Australian tourism recognised for olympic effort', May, www.specialevents.com.au (accessed 2 April 2004).

Australian Tourist Commission 2004, 'Business tourism fast facts', www.atc.australia.com/marketing.asp?art=2926 (accessed 2 April 2004).

Barker, M, Page, S & Meyer, D 2002, 'Evaluating the impact of the 2000 America's Cup on Auckland, New Zealand', *Event Management*, vol. 7, pp. 79–92.

Blicher-Hansen, L 2003, *Event Denmark strategy*, www.danskturisme.dk/web/netserv.nsf/dok/event-danmark (accessed 8 January 2004).

Carlsen, J & Millan, A 2002, 'The links between mega-events and urban development; the case of the Manchester 2002 Commonwealth Games' in *Proceedings of the events and place making conference*, eds L Jago, M Deery, R Harris, A Hede, J Allen, Australian Centre for Event Management, University of Technology, Sydney.

Dunne, J 2003, 'Nymagee case study', www.business.nsw.gov.au (accessed 2 April 2004).

Events Tasmania 2003, 'Strategic plan 2003–2008', www.eventstasmania.com (accessed 10 April 2004).

Events Tasmania 2004, 'National Event Grant Program', www.events tasmania.com (accessed 5 April 2004).

Germany National Tourist Board 2004, www.germany-extranet.net (accessed 3 April 2004).

Getz, D 1997, *Event management and event tourism*, Cognizant Communication, New York.

Goh, F 2003, 'Irish festivals, Irish life: the facts and how to use them', Presentation at the 2003 Irish Festivals Association Conference, www.aoife online.com. (accessed 28 March 2004).

Gold Coast Convention Bureau 2004, 'Collateral list', www.goldcoast conventions.com.au (accessed 2 April 2004).

Harris, R & Huyskens, M 2002, 'Public events: can they make a contribution to ecologically sustainable development?', www.business.uts.edu.au/acem/sustainability.html (accessed 30 March 2004).

Harris, R & Allen, J 2002, *Regional event management handbook*, Australian Centre for Event Management, University of Technology, Sydney.

Hiller, H & Moylan, D 1999, 'Mega-events and community obsolesence: redevelopment versus rehabilitation in Victoria Park East', *Canadian Journal of Urban Research*, vol. 8, no. 1, pp. 47–81.

Jago, L, Chalip, L, Brown, G, Mules, T & Ali, S 2003, 'Building events into destination branding: insights from experts', *Event Management*, vol. 8, pp. 3–14.

Kelly, M 2003, 'Feature article', *Venue Managers Association News*, 22 November.

Melbourne Convention and Visitors Bureau, 'About MCVB', www.mcvb.com.au (accessed 1 April 2004).

Mules, T 1993, 'A special event as part of an urban renewal strategy', *Festival Management and Event Tourism*, vol. 1, pp. 65–7.

New South Wales Government 2004, www.legislation.nsw.gov.au (accessed 10 April 2004).

Nurse, K 2003, 'Festival tourism in the Caribbean: an economic impact assessment', in *Proceedings of the fifth annual Caribbean conference on sustainable tourism development*, Caribbean Tourism Organisation.

Ogden International Facilities Corporation (Sydney), www.telstrastadium.com.au (accessed 1 April 2004).

Queensland Events 2004a, 'About us', www.qldevents.com.au (accessed 28 March 2004).

Queensland Events 2004b, 'Regional Events Development Program', www.qldevents.com.au (accessed 28 March 2004).

Ritchie, B 2000, 'Turning 16 days into 16 years through Olympic legacies', *Event Management*, vol. 6, pp. 155–165.

Richmond Valley Council 2004 'Tourism event funding application', Lismore, New South Wales.

Scottish Executive 2002, 'Scotland's major events strategy 2003–2015: competing on an international stage', www.scotland.gov.uk/publications (accessed 10 April 2004).

Selwood, J & Jones, R 1993, 'The Americas Cup in retrospect: the aftershock in Fremantle', in *Leisure and tourism: social and environmental change*, eds P Jonson, & G Cushman, Centre for Leisure and Tourism Studies, University of Technology, Sydney, pp. 656–60.

Smith, A & Jenner, P 1998, 'The impact of festivals and special events on tourism', *Travel and Tourism Analyst*, vol. 4, pp. 73–91.

Sydney Convention and Visitors Bureau 2002, *Annual report 2001–02*, Sydney.

Tourism New South Wales 2004, 'Regional Flagship Events Program', www.corporate.tourism.nsw.gov.au (accessed 4 April 2004).

Tourism Victoria 2002, 'Strategic plan 2002–2006', www.tourismvictoria.com.au (accessed April 2004).

Victorian Major Events Corporation, 'Methodology', www.vmec.com.au/miss/index.htm (accessed 10 April 2004).

Waitt, G 2003, 'Social impacts of the Sydney Olympics', *Annals of Tourism Research*, vol. 30, no. 1, pp. 194–215.

Washington Wine Commission 2004, 'Taste of Washington', www.tastewashington.org/seattle.cfm (accessed 10 April 2004).

2 EVENT
STRATEGY

Event strategy begins with the event concept. Detailed planning, inspirational leadership, sound human resource management and dynamic marketing are all key elements of successful event management. This part of the book examines the conceptualising and planning functions in some detail, and looks at the formation, leadership and training of event teams. It looks also at the event marketing process, and details strategic methods that event managers can employ to market their events competitively.

4 Conceptualising
the event

LEARNING OBJECTIVES

After studying this chapter, you should be able to:

■ identify the range of stakeholders in an event

■ describe and balance the overlapping and conflicting needs of stakeholders

■ describe the role of government, corporate and community sectors in events

■ discuss trends and issues in Australian society that affect events

■ understand the role of sponsorship in events

■ develop partnerships with sponsors and the media

■ identify the unique elements and resources of an event

■ understand the process of developing an event concept

■ apply the screening process to evaluate the feasibility of an event concept.

_I_NTRODUCTION

A crucial element in the creation of an event is the understanding of the event environment. The context in which the event is to take place will be a major determinant of its success. In order to understand this environment, the event manager must first identify the major players — the stakeholders and the people and organisations likely to be affected by it. The event manager must then examine the objectives of these major players — what each of them expects to gain from the event, and what forces acting on them are likely to affect their response to the event. Once this environment is understood, the event manager is then in the best position to marshal the creative elements of the event, and to shape and manage them to achieve the best outcomes for the event. This chapter examines the key stakeholders in events, and outlines some of the processes that event managers can use to produce creative and successful events.

_S_TAKEHOLDERS IN EVENTS

As discussed in the previous chapters, events have become professionalised and are increasingly attracting the involvement and support of governments and the corporate sector. One aspect of this growth is that events are now required to serve a multitude of agenda. It is no longer sufficient for an event to meet just the needs of its audience. It must also embrace a plethora of other requirements, including government objectives and regulations, media requirements, sponsors' needs and community expectations. People and organisations with a legitimate interest in the outcomes of an event are known as stakeholders. The successful event manager must be able to identify the range of stakeholders in an event and manage their individual needs, which will sometimes overlap and conflict (figure 4.1). As with event impacts, the event will be judged by its success in balancing the competing needs, expectations and interests of a diverse range of stakeholders. When questioned on the reasons for the success of the Sydney Olympic Games, the chief executive of SOCOG, Sandy Hollway, attributed this success to the effective coordination and management of a large and diverse range of stakeholders (Hollway 2002).

Mal Hemmerling (1997), architect of the Australian Formula One Grand Prix in Adelaide and former chief executive of SOCOG, describes the task of the contemporary event manager as follows:

■ So when asked the question 'what makes an event successful', there are now numerous shareholders that are key components of modern major events that are looking at a whole range of different measures of success. What may have been a simple measure for the event organiser of the past, which involved the bottom line, market share, and successful staging of the event are now only basic criteria as the measures by other investors are more aligned with increased tourism, economic activity, tax revenues, promotional success, sustained economic growth, television reach, audience profiles, customer focus, brand image, hospitality, new business opportunities and investment to name but a few. ■

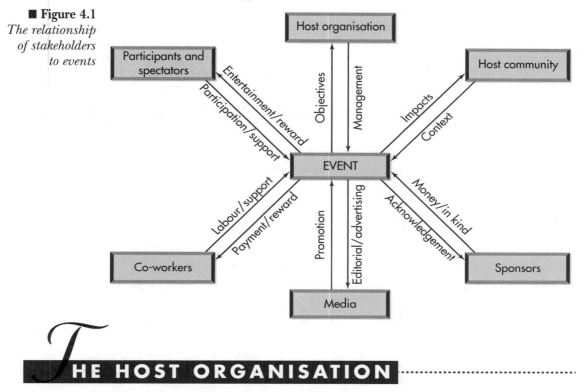

THE HOST ORGANISATION

Events have become so much a part of our cultural milieu that they can be generated by almost any part of the government, corporate and community sectors (table 4.1, page 88).

■ Government *sector*

Governments create events for a range of reasons, including the social, cultural, tourism and economic benefits generated by events. Some government departments have an events brief as part of their delivery of services — for example, state event corporations, ministries of arts, sport and recreation and ministries of racing. Other departments generate events as a means to achieve related objectives — departments of tourism to increase and extend tourist visits, departments of ethnic affairs to preserve cultures and encourage tolerance and diversity, and departments of economic development to assist industry and generate jobs. Many other departments are involved in one-off events to promote specific goods and services such as health promotions, Seniors Week, and Heritage Week. Such events may celebrate special days — for example, Australia Day, Anzac Day or World Environment Day. They are often characterised by free entry and wide accessibility, and form part of the public culture.

■ Corporate *sector*

The corporate sector is involved in events at a number of levels. Companies and corporations may sponsor events in order to promote their goods and services in the marketplace. They may partner government departments in the presentation of events that serve common or multiple agenda. Companies may also create their own events in order to launch new products, increase sales or enhance corporate image. These events, although they may still offer free entry, are often targeted at specific market segments rather than at the general public.

■ **Table 4.1**
Event typology

EVENT GENERATORS	TYPES OF EVENT
GOVERNMENT SECTOR Central government	Civic celebrations and commemorations — for example, Australia Day, Anzac Day
Event corporations	Major events — focus on sporting and cultural events
Public space authorities	Public entertainment, leisure and recreation events
Tourism	Festivals, special interest and lifestyle events, destinational promotions
Convention bureaus	Meetings, incentives, conventions, exhibitions
Arts	Arts festivals, cultural events, touring programs, themed art exhibitions
Ethnic affairs	Ethnic and multicultural events
Sport and recreation	Sporting events, hosting of state, national and international championships
Gaming and racing	Race meetings and racing carnivals
Economic development	Focus on events with industry development and job creation benefits
Local government	Community events, local festivals and fairs
CORPORATE SECTOR Companies and corporations	Promotions, product launches, image-building sponsorships, staff training and incentive events
Industry associations	Industry promotions, trade fairs, conferences
Entrepreneurs	Ticketed sporting events, concerts and exhibitions
Media	Media promotions — for example, concerts, fun runs, appeals
COMMUNITY SECTOR Clubs and societies	Special interest group events
Charities	Fundraising and profile-building events
Sports organisations	Local sporting events

Within the corporate sector, there are also entrepreneurs whose business is the staging or selling of events. These include sports or concert promoters who present ticketed events for profit, and conference organisers or industry associations who mount conferences or exhibitions for the trade or public — for example, wine shows, equipment exhibitions or medical conferences. Media organisations often become partners in events organised by other groups, but also stage events for their own promotional purposes or to create program content. Examples are radio stations promoting their identity through concerts, newspapers promoting fun runs, or television networks presenting Christmas carol programs live to air.

■ Community *sector*

Other events still emanate from the community sector, serving a wide variety of needs and interests. These may include local sporting events, service club fundraisers, car club gatherings, local art and craft shows — the spectrum is as wide as the field of human interest and endeavour. All of these sources combine to create the wonderful tapestry of events that fill our leisure time and enrich our lives.

■ Types *of host organisation*

Whether events emanate from the corporate, government or community sectors will determine the nature of the host organisation. If the host is from the corporate sector, it is likely to be a company, corporation or industry association. The event manager may be employed directly by the host organisation, or on a contract basis with the organisation as the client. If the host is from the government sector, the host organisation is likely to be a government or council department. Again the event manager may be a direct employee, or a contractor if the event is outsourced. If the host is from the community sector, the host organisation is more likely to be a club, society or committee, with a higher volunteer component in the organisation.

Whatever the host organisation, it is a key stakeholder in the event, and the event manager should seek to clarify its goals in staging the event. These goals will often be presented in a written brief as part of the event manager's job description or contract. Where they are not, it will be worthwhile spending some time to clarify these goals and put them in written form as a reference point for the organisation of the event, and a guideline for the evaluation of its eventual success.

THE HOST COMMUNITY

Event managers need to have a good grasp and understanding of the broad trends and forces acting on the wider community, as these will determine the operating environment of their events. The mood, needs and aspirations of the community will determine its receptiveness to event styles and fashions. Accurately gauging and interpreting these are basic factors in the conceptualising of successful events.

Among the current significant forces acting on the community are globalisation and technology, which are combining to make the world seem both smaller and more complex. These forces are impacting on almost every aspect of our lives, including events. Giddens (1990) defines globalisation as 'the intensification of worldwide social relations which link distinct localities in such a way that local happenings are shaped by events occurring many miles away and vice versa'.

This process is speeded up by technology and the media, which have the power to bring significant local events to a worldwide audience — overcoming the barriers of national boundaries and cultural differences. This is exemplified by the global television coverage of major sporting events. World championships and mega-events such as the Olympics and World Cup Soccer are beamed instantly to live audiences throughout the world, giving them previously unimagined coverage and immediacy.

As global networks increasingly bring the world into our lounge rooms, the question arises of how local cultures can maintain their own uniqueness and identity in the face of global homogenisation. International arts festivals increasingly draw from the same pool of touring companies to produce similar programs. Local festivals and celebrations must increasingly compete with international products and the raised expectations of audiences accustomed to streamlined television production. The challenge for many events is how to function in this increasingly global environment while expressing the uniqueness of local communities and addressing their specific interests and concerns.

Globalisation is also impacting on corporate events as companies increasingly plan their marketing strategies, including their event components, on a global level. This has resulted in some local Australian event companies being bought out by overseas companies in an attempt to create networks that can serve the international needs of their clients. This approach sometimes comes unstuck as different markets in, say, New York, Sydney and Hong Kong reflect different event needs and audience responses. However, the forces of globalisation are likely to lead to an increasing standardisation of the corporate event product and market.

Simultaneously, the all-pervasive Internet and advances in information technology are increasing the availability and technological sophistication of events. Basing his forecast on projections by leading futurists and trends in the event management industry, Goldblatt (2000, p. 8) predicts '24-hour, seven day per week event opportunities for guests who desire to forecast, attend, and review their participation in an event'. He also predicts that events will eventually become 'totally automated enabling event professionals to significantly expand the number of simultaneous events being produced using fewer human staff'. As a counter trend, Goldblatt also points out that 'with the advance of technology individuals are seeking more high touch experiences to balance the high tech influences in their lives. Events remain the single most effective means of providing a high touch experience'.

Event managers must be aware of these trends and learn to operate in the new global environment. Paradoxically, live events may increasingly become the means by which communities confirm their own sense of place, individuality and cultural uniqueness.

■ Involving *the host community*

In addition to the wider general community, events have a specific host community which impacts greatly on the success or failure of the event. This can be the geographical community where the event is located, or a community of interest from which the event draws its participants and spectators. Many researchers (Getz 1997; Goldblatt and Perry 2002; Jago et al. 2002) have recognised the importance of the host community being involved in and 'owning' the event, which in turn emits positive messages to visitors. Examples quoted by Jago et al. (2002) include the volunteers during the Sydney Olympics, whose community support contributed to a 'friendly' dimension of the event, and the local events that make up the Gold Coast's Indy Carnival during the lead-up to the Indy 300 race day, which create a local atmosphere that contributes to the destination's brand.

Many community members actively participate in events in their communities, and act as advocates on behalf of the event to potential participants. The Sydney Gay and Lesbian Mardi Gras and Nimbin's Mardi Gras are examples of events that are fuelled by social activists committed to the goals of the event. Local participation and ownership of events is perhaps most visible in the many local and regional events that continue to exist only because of the committed input of dedicated volunteers. The host community may also include residents, traders, lobby groups and public authorities such as council, transport, police, fire and ambulance brigades. The event manager should aim to identify and involve these representatives and to consult them in the planning of the event.

Councils may have certain requirements, such as parade and catering permits. Often police and councils will combine to form a 'one stop shop' for such matters as street closures, special access and parking arrangements.

If the event is large enough to impact significantly beyond the boundaries of the venue, a public authorities' briefing may identify innovative ways to minimise the impact and manage the situation. The Australia Day fireworks spectacular at Sydney's Darling Harbour, for example, regularly attracts 300 000 spectators, most of whom used to depart immediately after the end of the fireworks, causing an hour-long traffic jam on the surrounding freeways. By stepping down the entertainment in stages, working with point duty police and implementing one-way traffic in some areas, the delay was reduced to less than half that time.

Host communities have past experience of different events, and event managers can draw on this knowledge to ensure an event's success. In Sydney, public authorities consciously used major occasions such as Australia Day and New Year's Eve as practice runs for the Olympics, with event organisers, public transport and public authorities working together to trial operations and refine solutions.

In addition to formal contact with authorities, the event manager should be aware of the all-important local rumour mill that can often make or break the host community's attitude to the event.

Music festival organisers know only too well the power and impact of word of mouth on festival attendances. The success of rock festivals such as The Big Day Out and Livid in recent years has largely been driven by their reputations, making it imperative for the organisers to keep their programs current and in tune with their audiences. The Port Fairy Folk Festival in Victoria and the Woodford Folk Festival in Queensland both sell out with minimal expenditure on publicity, but only because their organisers jealously guard and protect the reputations of their festivals.

SPONSORS

In recent decades, there have been enormous increases in sponsorship, and a corresponding change in how events are perceived by sponsors. There has been a shift by many large companies from viewing sponsorship as primarily a public relations tool generating community goodwill, to regarding it as an important part of the marketing mix. Successful major events are now perceived as desirable properties, capable of increasing brand awareness and driving sales. They also provide important opportunities for relationship building through hosting partners and clients. Corporations invest large amounts in event sponsorship, and devote additional resources to supporting their sponsorships, to achieve corporate objectives and sales goals.

Sweaney (1997) defines commercial sponsorship as 'a high profile form of collaborative marketing between organisations which usually involves an investment in an event, facility, individual, team or competition, in return for access to an exploitable commercial potential'.

In order to attract sponsorships, event managers must offer tangible benefits to sponsors, and effective programs to deliver them. Large corporations such as Coca-Cola and Telstra receive hundreds of sponsorship applications each week, and only consider those events that have a close fit with corporate objectives and a demonstrable ability to deliver benefits.

■ Sponsors *as partners in events*

It is important for event managers to identify exactly what sponsors want from an event and what the event can deliver for them. Their needs may be different from those of the host organisation or the event manager. Attendance numbers at the event, for example, may not be as important to them as the media coverage that it generates. It may be important for their chief executive to officiate or to gain access to public officials in a relaxed atmosphere. They may be seeking mechanisms to drive sales, or want to strengthen client relationships through hosting activities. The event manager should take the opportunity to go beyond the formal sponsorship agreement and to treat the sponsors as partners in the event. Some of the best ideas for events can arise from such partnerships. Common agendas may be identified which support the sponsorship and deliver additional benefits to the event.

As part of their sponsorship of the Sydney Olympic Torch Relay in 2000, AMP created the 'Ignite the Dream' tour which travelled the entire Australian route of the relay, creating local celebrations in each town and city. AMP presented replicas of the Olympic cauldron to participating towns and used the torch relay to help reposition itself as a contemporary organisation with close community ties.

In 2002 Actew AGL was a sponsor of Celebrate Canberra. The company commissioned a giant birthday cake, and its staff cut and distributed the cake to the citizens of Canberra as their contribution to the celebrations (Ireland 2003). The same company sponsored a scarecrow competition for Floriade in Canberra in 2003, with members of the public invited to make and install scarecrows as part of the flower festival display. Prizes were awarded in categories of Best Business, Best Primary School, Best Secondary School, Best Charity and People's Choice (Floriade 2003).

The Sony Tropfest short film festival in 2004 offered New South Wales participants an opportunity to obtain a free DVD featuring films from the finalists in the competition by returning a coupon published in *The Sydney Morning Herald*. In addition to demonstrating the product capability of naming rights for sponsor Sony, this offer provided a valuable marketing opportunity for co-sponsor, *The Sydney Morning Herald* (The Sydney Morning Herald 2004 p. 33).

The role of sponsors in events, along with techniques for identifying, sourcing and managing sponsorships, is treated in more detail in chapter 8.

MEDIA

The expansion of the media, and the proliferation of delivery systems such as cable, satellite television and the Internet, have created a hunger for media product as never before. The global networking of media organisations, and the instant electronic transmission of media images and data, have made the global village a media reality. When television was introduced to Australia in time to cover the Melbourne Olympic Games in 1956, the world still relied largely on the physical transfer of film footage to disseminate the images of the Games interstate and overseas. Australia's Bicentennial celebrations in 1988 featured an Australia-wide multi-directional television link-up, which enabled Australians to experience the celebrations simultaneously from a diverse range of locations and perspectives, seeing themselves as a nation through the media as never before. The opening ceremony of the Winter Olympic Games in Nagano in 1998, featured a thousand-member world choir singing together from five different locations on five continents, including the forecourt of the Sydney Opera House. Global television networks followed New Year's Eve of the new millennium around the world, making the world seem smaller and more immediate. When the 2000 Olympics began, a simultaneous global audience estimated at two and a half billion people was able to watch the event tailored to their own national perspectives, with a variety of cameras covering every possible angle.

Sony Tropfest, which began with a small local audience at a Sydney coffee shop, was screened via satellite in 2004 to audiences in Sydney, Brisbane, Melbourne, Hobart, Canberra and Perth to a combined audience of over 120 000 (Sony Tropfest 2004).

This revolution in the media has in turn revolutionised events. Events now have a virtual existence in the media at least as powerful, sometimes more so, than in reality. The live audience for a sports event or concert may be dwarfed by the television audience. Indeed, the event may be created primarily for the consumption of the television audience. Events have much to gain from this development, including media sponsorships and the payment of media rights. Their value to commercial sponsors is greatly increased by their media coverage and profile. However, the media often directly affect the way events are conceptualised and presented, as in the case of One Day Cricket or Super League, and can have a profound effect on the relationship of the event with its live audience. So far, sports events have been the main winners (and losers) from this increased media attention.

The available media technology influences the way that live spectators experience an event. The wiring of the modern stadium allows for digital television and enables every spectator to have a unique seat with personalised communication services. Increasingly, spectators' viewing capabilities are technologically enhanced to parallel those of people watching at home.

Media interest in events continues to grow as their ability to provide saleable product and to attract commercial sponsors is realised. Sporting events, parades, spectacles, concerts and major public celebrations are areas of strong interest to the media, where the imperatives of television production are likely to influence the direction and marketing of events. The role of the media can vary from that of media sponsors to becoming full partners — or even producers — of the event.

Whatever the role of the media, it is important for the event manager to consider the needs of different media groups, and to consult with them as important stakeholders in the event. Once the media are treated as potential partners, they have much to offer the event. The good media representative, like the event manager, is in search of the good idea or unusual angle. Together they might just dream up the unique approach that increases the profile of the event and, in turn, provides value to the media organisation. The print media might agree to publish the event program as editorial or as a special insert, or might run a series of lead-in stories, competitions or special promotions in tandem with sponsors. Radio or television stations might provide an outside broadcast, or might involve their on-air presenters as comperes or special participants in the event. This integration of the event with the media provides greater reach and exposure to the event, and in turn gives the media organisation a branded association with the event.

CO-WORKERS

The event team that is assembled to implement the event represents another of the key stakeholders. For any event to be truly effective, the vision and philosophy of the event must be shared by all of the team, from key managers, talent and publicist, right through to the stage manager, crew, gatekeepers and cleaners. No matter how big or small, the event team is the face of the event, and each member a contributor to its success or failure.

Goldblatt (1997, p. 129) describes the role of the event manager in this process.

■ The most effective event managers are not merely managers, rather, they are dynamic leaders whose ability to motivate, inspire others, and achieve their goals are admired by their followers. The difference between management and leadership is perhaps best characterised by this simple but effective definition: *managers control problems, whereas leaders motivate others to find ways to achieve goals.* ■

Most people have experienced events which went well overall, but were marred by some annoying detail. There are different ways of addressing such problems, but team selection and management are always crucial factors in avoiding these problems. The Disney organisation, for example, has a system in which the roles of performer, cleaner and security etc. are merged into the concept of one team looking after the space. The roles tend to ride with the needs of the moment — when the parade comes through the theme park, it is all hands on deck. The daily bulletin issued to all staff members reminds them that customers may visit Disneyland only once in their lives, and their impressions will depend forever on what they experience that day. This is a very positive philosophy that can be applied to all events.

PARTICIPANTS AND SPECTATORS

Last but not least are the 'punters' on the day — the participants and spectators for whom the event is intended and who ultimately vote with their feet for the success or failure of the event. The event manager must be mindful of the needs of the audience. These include their physical needs, as well as their needs for comfort, safety and security. Over and above these basic requirements is the need to make the event special — to connect with the emotions. A skilled event manager strives to make events meaningful, magical and memorable. Hemmerling (1997) describes the criteria by which spectators judge an event:

■ Their main focus is on the content, location, substance and operation of the event itself. For them the ease with which they can see the event activities, the program content, their access to food and drinks, amenities, access and egress etc., are the keys to their enjoyment. Simple factors such as whether or not their team won or lost, or whether they had a good experience at the event will sometimes influence their success measures. Secondary issues, such as mixing with the stars of the show, social opportunities, corporate hospitality and capacity to move up the seating chain from general admission to premium seating are all part of the evaluation of spectator success. ∎

Current technologies can assist the event manager in involving and servicing event participants. The Internet now plays a major role in events, with participants using it to research the event before their arrival, keep track during an extended event and re-live the highlights of the event after they have departed. The 2003 Rugby World Cup website received 44.5 million 'hits' on the final day of the event (Rugby World Cup 2004). By understanding how psychographics and the event audience influence the event concept, event managers can tailor their events more adequately to meet the needs of participants. As discussed in greater detail in chapter 7, this understanding also helps to accurately direct the marketing efforts by using channels specific to the audience — for example, the marketing of Schoolies' Week on the Gold Coast through secondary schools in New South Wales, Victoria and Queensland.

CREATING THE EVENT CONCEPT

Goldblatt (1997) suggests the 'five Ws' as important questions to ask in creating the event concept:
1. *Why* is the event being held? There must be compelling reasons that confirm the importance and viability of holding the event.
2. *Who* will be the stakeholders in the event? These include internal stakeholders, such as the board of directors, committee, staff and audience or guests, and external stakeholders such as media and politicians.
3. *When* will the event be held? Is there sufficient time to research and plan the event? Does the timing suit the needs of the audience, and if the event is outdoors, does it take the likely climatic conditions into account?
4. *Where* will the event be staged? The choice of venue must represent the best compromise between the organisational needs of the event, audience comfort, accessibility and cost.
5. *What* is the event content or product? This must match the needs, wants, desires and expectations of the audience, and must synergise with the why, who, when and where of the event.

An important part of developing the event will be identifying unique elements and resources that can make the event special and contribute to its imagery and branding. Australia Day at Darling Harbour in 1993 had to be special, as an important International Olympic Committee delegation was scheduled to attend. It was the largest single delegation to visit Sydney and its purpose was to conduct a final inspection of the city, before the vote to decide the host city for the 2000 Olympics was held. The organisers identified the potential of Sydney Tower to be transformed by pyrotechnics into a giant Olympic torch. The idea was workshopped and incorporated into the event, creating a memorable image, which made the cover of *Time* magazine and played a part in convincing the delegation that Sydney was capable of staging a major celebration if awarded the Olympics.

■ Brainstorming

Once the parameters of the event have been set, it is desirable to *brainstorm* the concept of the event, letting the imagination soar and consulting as many stakeholders as possible. A good way to do this is to meet with them individually at first, establishing relationships and allowing each stakeholder to become comfortable with their role in the event. In these discussions ideas will arise, but the process should be acknowledged as exploratory and not yet seeking to reach fixed conclusions.

Once the diverse stakeholders are brought to the meeting table, the ideas will start to flow. This is a time to ignore restraints of practicality — of cost, scale or viability — that time will come. The task is to create and to dream, and no idea should be dismissed as too wild or impractical. The goal is to discover the right idea, the one that resonates so that everyone recognises it and is inspired by the challenge and the potential that it offers. This is where the skills of an event director come to the fore — the ability to draw out ideas, to synthesise content and eventually to engineer compromise. No matter how good an idea or how strong its support, eventually it must serve the objectives of the event and be deliverable within the available resources. With some good fortune, this idea may be identified in a single meeting, but most often the process will take several meetings and weeks or months of patience and hard work. But the results will be worthwhile if a strong vision for the event emerges, one that is shared and supported by all stakeholders, and which inspires confidence and commitment. This process is at the very heart of creative event planning and when it works well it is one of the joys of being in the business.

EVALUATING THE EVENT CONCEPT

The brainstorming process may occasionally result in a single exciting concept that matches the needs of the event. However, it is most likely that it will produce a range of possible concepts that will need to be carefully evaluated to select the best concept or, in some cases, to combine a number of distinct ideas into a single concept.

To determine the practicality and effectiveness of the chosen concept, it will be useful to undertake an evaluation of the event concept by what Shone and Parry (2001) describe as the 'screening process', also known as a feasibility study. This involves using marketing, operations and financial screens to determine the extent to which the event concept matches the needs of the event and the resources available to the event manager to implement it. The basic question is to what degree does the event concept serve the purpose or the overall objectives of the event? If the concept does not serve the required purpose, then no matter how attractive or exciting it may seem, it should be stored away and left, perhaps for another occasion.

■ The *marketing screen*

The first screen suggested by Shone and Parry is the marketing screen. This involves examining how the target audience of the event is likely to respond to the event concept and whether the concept will be inviting and attractive to its audience. To determine this, an environmental scanning process needs to be undertaken. This will help to determine whether the event concept resonates with current tastes and fashions and whether it is likely to be perceived as innovative and popular, or as ordinary and predictable. A good barometer will be the media response to the concept. If media representatives consider it to be of current interest, they are likely to become allies in the promotion of the event. If the media response is poor, then it will be difficult to promote interest and engage the audience.

For much of this assessment, event managers will need to rely on their own instincts and on testing the response of friends, co-workers and stakeholders to the concept. An alternative, particularly if a large investment is involved in the event, is to undertake some form of market research. This can be done within the resources of the event management company or by employing marketing professionals to conduct a market survey or focus group research. Such research may reveal not only the likely market acceptance of the concept, but also additional information, such as how much the target audience is prepared to pay for the event, or how the event concept may be adapted to meet market expectations or requirements.

A further factor in the environmental scan will be to examine the competition provided by other events in the market. This step will examine whether there are other events of a similar type or theme in a similar timeframe, or major events and public holidays that are likely to impact on the target market. An investigation of the competition through a 'What's on' in the city listing, tourism event calendars etc. will assist the event manager to identify and hopefully avoid, head-on collision and competition with other events.

■ The *operations screen*

The operations screen will consider the skills and resources needed to stage the event successfully, and whether the event manager has these skills and resources or can develop them or buy them in for the event. Specialised technical skills, for example, may be needed to implement the event concept. The event manager will need to consider whether event company staff members have these skills, or whether an external supplier needs to be engaged to provide them. Special licences, permits or insurance may be needed in order to implement the concept. If the event concept is highly innovative and challenging, the event manager may need to consider the degree of risk involved. It may be desirable to deliver an innovative event, but costly and embarrassing if the event is a failure because the skills and resources available to stage it are inadequate.

Another major consideration, as part of the operations screen, is staffing. This step will examine whether the event company has sufficient staff available with the right mix of skills and at the right time, place and cost to deliver the event effectively. If the event needs to rely heavily on volunteers, the operations screen will examine whether sufficient numbers are likely to be available, and whether the right motivation, training and induction procedures are in place.

■ The *financial screen*

The final screen suggested by Shone and Parry (2001) is the financial screen. This screen examines whether the event organisation has sufficient financial commitment, sponsorship and revenue to undertake the event. The first step in this process is to decide whether the event needs only to break even, which may be the case if it is being staged as a company promotional event, or whether it is required to make a profit for the host organisation.

The next step will be to undertake a 'ballpark' budget of the anticipated costs and income of the event. Breaking the event down into its component parts will allow an estimate to be formed of the costs for each component. A generous contingency should be included on the cost side of the ledger, as at this stage of the event there are bound to be costs that have been underestimated or not yet identified. Calculating the income may require deciding on the appropriate pricing strategy and identifying the 'breakeven' point of ticket sales. Other key revenue items to take into account may include potential government grants or subsidies, merchandising income and sponsorship support, both in cash and in kind. It is important not to overestimate the sponsorship potential, and professional advice or a preliminary approach to the market may be required in order to arrive at a realistic estimate.

Cash flow is an important aspect of the financial screen often overlooked by inexperienced event managers. It is important not only to have sufficient funds to cover the expenses of the event, but to have them available when they are required. If, for example, a large part of the revenue is likely to be from ticket sales on the day, then it may be necessary to chart out the anticipated expenditure flow of the event, and to consider whether credit arrangements need to be made.

Once the event concept has been screened and evaluated from the marketing, operations and financial aspects, the event manager is in a position to make an informed decision with regard to the conduct of the event. If the result is a 'go' decision, then the process of refining the event concept and developing the all-important event strategies and plans that are the subject of later chapters of this book can begin.

Goon Show comedian Spike Milligan was a well-known figure in the Woy Woy Peninsula of Gosford. During his lifetime, his generous involvement with local clubs and causes included his patronage of the Woy Woy Little Theatre Club, the Woy Woy Cricket Club and 2CCC Radio.

In 2002, Gosford City Council established the Spike Milligan Recognition Committee to investigate ways of commemorating his life. The committee decided on a festival with the following objectives:

1. Be funny!
2. Acknowledge Spike Milligan's art and life
3. Lift community spirit through Spike Milligan's humour
4. Foster creative talent of people of all ages in the area of comedy
5. Attract people to visit the Central Coast region of New South Wales.

Dates of 3–12 October 2003 were chosen for the festival, because these coincided with Mental Health Week and the staging of Rugby World Cup matches in Gosford, including the visit of the Irish Rugby Team. This was deemed appropriate, because Spike had supported mental health awareness due to his lifetime experience with depression, and had been a keen rugby fan. An additional bonus was the potential of the festival to attract and entertain visitors to the region during the high-profile period of the Rugby World Cup. Expressions of interest for involvement in the festival were called for, with the committee using its own contacts and Gosford City Council's database to invite community groups to contribute to the program according to their own interests and skills. This robust process of brainstorming and community involvement resulted in an innovative festival program, with the following highlights:

- a 'Walking Backwards to Woy Woy' Parade and Festival Day
- comedy shows in local clubs, including nationally recognised comedians such as Austen Tayshus, Steady Eddie, Libby Gore, Wil Anderson and Kevin Bloody Wilson
- an amateur comedy competition
- *Cosi!* — an Australian comedy on the theme of mental health
- a Kids Comedy Program, including writing workshops, story time and comedy performances
- 'Picasso According to Spike' — a comic art display
- 'Comic and Crazy Verse' — a competition and live performance
- 'Size 7 Socks from a Chicken's Laundry' – a comedy review
- 'The Puckoon Cup' — a cricket match
- 'An Evening with Spike Milligan' – 2CCC radio interviews with Desmond, Jane and Laura Milligan

- a tribute to Spike Milligan – an ABC Radio program
- the Stanley Awards gala dinner of the Australian Cartoonists' Society
- a Spike Milligan bushwalk organised by the National Parks and Wildlife Service
- recollections of Spike Milligan in Woy Woy, by the Brisbane Water Historical Society.

The festival attracted local, national and international attention, including coverage by the BBC World Service and newspapers in Dublin, Belfast and London. From this auspicious beginning, Spikefest is set to grow into a regional festival of national significance.

(**Source:** *Adapted from Bramble 2002.*)

SUMMARY

Events are required to serve a multitude of agenda, due to the increased involvement of governments and the corporate sector. The successful event manager must be able to identify and manage a diverse range of stakeholder expectations. Major stakeholders are the host organisation staging a particular event, and the host community, including the various public authorities whose support will be needed. Both sponsors and media are important partners, and can make important contributions to an event in support and resources beyond their formal sponsorship and media coverage. The vision and philosophy of the event should be shared by co-workers in the event team, and the contribution of each should be recognised and treated as important. Ultimately, it is the spectators and participants who decide the success or failure of an event, and it is crucial to engage their emotions.

Once the objectives of the event and the unique resources available to it have been identified, the next priority is to brainstorm ideas with stakeholders so that a shared vision for the event can be shaped and communicated. The screening process then needs to be applied to the chosen concept to determine whether it is achievable within the limited resources available to the event. No event is created by one person, and success will depend on a collective team effort.

Questions

1. Who are the most important stakeholders in an event, and why?

2. Give examples of different events staged by government, corporate and community groups in your region and discuss their reasons for putting on these events.

3. Name a major event that you have attended or in which you have been involved, and identify the prime stakeholders and their objectives.

4. Focusing on an event that you have experienced first-hand, list the benefits that the event could offer a sponsor or partner.

5. Using the same event example that you discussed in the last question, identify suitable media partners and outline how you would approach them to participate in the event.

6. What are the means by which an event creates an emotional relationship with its participants and spectators?

7. What events can you think of that demonstrate a unique vision or idea? What techniques have been used to express that vision or idea, and why do you consider them to be unique?

8. Imagine you are planning an event in the area where you live. What are its unique characteristics, and how might these be expressed in the event?

9. Using the event concept that you have developed in the last question, consider and list the skills and resources that will be necessary to implement the event.

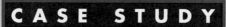

CASE STUDY ··

Edinburgh International
Book Festival — festival of ideas, journeying and imagining

Edinburgh's festivals are a vital part of Edinburgh's life, contributing major cultural, social and economic impacts as well as enhancing the city's civic profile. The economic impact of the festivals is well documented. A study by the then Scottish Tourist Board (Visit Scotland) in 1990 showed that £44 million of direct expenditure, £9 million of local income and 1300 full time equivalent jobs would not exist in Edinburgh and the Lothians if the festivals did not take place. In Scotland as a whole, direct expenditure measured £72 million, resulting in more than 3000 full time equivalent jobs (Scottish Tourist Board 1990). The multiplier effect on tourism businesses in the city is also significant, with hotel occupancy rates typically soaring to 80–90 per cent in the capital during the festival period.

Edinburgh is host to 15 diverse national and international festivals annually, as well as several community and participative festivals. These range from the prominent and internationally known Hogmanay and the Edinburgh International Festival (EIF) to lesser known but equally important festivals, such as The Harp Festival and the Scottish International Storytelling Festival. Together with its counterparts, the International, Jazz, Fringe and Film festivals, the Edinburgh International Book Festival forms what is now widely regarded as the biggest and best arts festival in the world during the summer months in Edinburgh.

Background

The book festival began in 1983 and is now a key event in the August festival season, celebrated annually in Scotland's capital city. Biennial at first, the book festival became a yearly celebration in 1997. Throughout its 20-year history, the festival has grown rapidly in size and scope to become the largest and most dynamic festival of its kind in the world. In its first year, the book festival played host to just 30 'Meet the author' events. Today, the festival programs over 600 events, which are enjoyed by people of all ages.

In 2001, Catherine Lockerbie, the book festival's fifth director, took the festival to a new level by developing a high-profile debates and discussions series that is now one of the festival's hallmarks. Each year, writers from all over the world gather to become part of this unique forum, in which audience and author meet to exchange thoughts and opinions on some of the world's most pressing issues. Catherine also comments on how there appears to be little tension between the commercial and artistic in terms of the programming: 'in fact, we have an

(continued)

experimental and willing audience, and they appear willing to buy tickets and books for relatively uncommercial authors'.

Running alongside the general program is the highly regarded Lloyds TSB Scotland Children's Programme, which has grown to become a leading showcase for children's writers and illustrators. Incorporating workshops, storytelling, panel discussions, author events and book signings, the Children's Programme is popular with both the public and schools alike and now ranks as the world's premier books and reading event for young people.

The festival also hosts a Schools Program and a Schools Gala day, exclusively for schools the day after the mainstream festival. This four-day program of author and arts events is the largest of its kind in the world, and is committed to enabling children to engage in 'the wonderful world of books ... with the focus firmly on participation, imagination and creation' (Karen Mountney, Children's Program Director). The event is nonprofit making, with a key aim being to improve access and contribute to education and lifelong learning for Scotland's school children. To encourage participation, the event is free for teachers and also provides a free bus fund bringing children to the festival from all over Scotland. Key events include the School Gala Day, when the book festival is open to schools only; the Outreach Program, which tours some of the authors to libraries in Scotland; and focused events for teachers, such as 'Improving children's writing skills' and 'Poetry in primary years'.

Since its inception, the book festival's home has been the beautiful and historic Charlotte Square Gardens, centrally located in Edinburgh's World Heritage listed Georgian New Town. Each year the gardens are transformed into a magical tented village, which welcomed 185 000 visitors in 2003.

The book festival is proud to run its own independent bookselling operation, with a strong publishers' presence. All proceeds from the sale of books are invested back into the running of the book festival, a not-for-profit charity organisation that annually raises 80 per cent of its own funds.

Festival operations

Compared with their peers in the United Kingdom and internationally, Edinburgh's festivals provide extremely good value to the city. Festivals with the turnover of Edinburgh's would expect to receive more in local subsidy. Internationally, public support accounts for approximately 42 per cent of the major European festivals budget, with smaller festivals receiving about 35 per cent (the Edinburgh International Book Festival receives 14.9 per cent). The book festival, however, is largely privately funded — sponsorship and development 26.7 per cent, book sales 22.9 per cent and box office 35.5 per cent, with key public funding bodies being the Scottish Arts Council and the City of Edinburgh Council (14.9 per cent). The book festival has developed a strong sponsor base, with the inaugural title sponsors being *The Herald/Sunday Herald*, five major sponsors and a series of smaller sponsors and supporters.

In terms of staff structure, the nine senior staff are full-time, year-round staff, and everyone else is on a temporary contract ranging from five months to three weeks. At peak times, up to 90 staff work on the festival, with 15 in the box office and 30 front of house. The festival has fought hard to retain its summer seasonal staff by paying them reasonably, offering discounts to the bookshop, catering and entrance to events, and instilling the feeling that they share ownership of the festival. Retention of staff offers the festival security and advancement, and increases the level of customer service at the event.

Target markets

Edinburgh residents, particularly those profiled as 'affluent city centre area' or 'well off town and city area', represent the largest group of visitors to the book festival (46 per cent). In 2003, 63 per cent of visitors were from Scotland, with the remainder from the United Kingdom and a small proportion (11 per cent) of international visitors. In terms of demographics, 35 per cent of visitors fall into the 35–54 age category, 24 per cent in the 25–34 age group, 22 per cent in the 55 years plus group and 20 per cent in the 16–24 age category.

Within the local segment, there are several key target markets: the Friends of the Book Festival, who, as well as being keen supporters and lovers of the festival, also have a strong fundraising remit; families, who are avid supporters of the Children's Festival; and schools throughout the region.

Key issues

Maximising quality and experience on site

A critical issue facing the book festival is managing capacity and visitor experiences on the site. The temporary nature of the site (which is erected yearly for the festival) can bring a host of problems, because all of the facilities have to be brought in and managed by the book festival. A key issue is obviously climate, because much of the site's ambiance is created through its outdoor nature and location. Extremely high rainfall in 2002 created problems of waterlogging and flooding. Thankfully, the main events were unaffected because they are held in huge staged tents, and 2003 experienced a return to sunshine.

Obviously, the site has fixed capacity. In 2003, it experienced visitor numbers of around 10 000 per day; although over half of the events were sold out, the book festival sold only 65 per cent of tickets. A further increase in numbers, therefore, would have an effect on the provision of facilities such as toilets and food and drink outlets.

Managing author and customer expectations

Critical to the success of the book festival is the event satisfaction of both authors and customers. Authors are invited to participate in the festival and pay a nominal and, surprisingly, equal fee. Key benefits to them include the exposure to their work that the festival brings, the opportunity to meet with their readers and sign books, and the access to international media who are present at the festival. Also, given the controversial nature of events such as 'East and West' and 'Imprisoned Writers', security and political issues arise from certain authors' presence. Due to sound relationships with the police and the presence of a security firm on site, there have been no disruptions to the festival.

(*continued*)

Customer expectations also have to be managed. Tickets could be bought online for the first time in 2003; with 22 per cent of tickets being sold via the book festival website, this was perceived to be a key improvement in ticket purchasing. Customer feedback is sought from the event in the form of a questionnaire at the information desks and invited email responses. Feedback from key stakeholders, such as the media and the sponsors, is also examined because they are invited to various corporate hospitality events throughout the duration of the festival.

Improving access

A key aim of the festival is to improve access. Recent research found that the 18–25-year-old market was the most under-represented; because this group would be the future lifeblood of the festival, research was undertaken in 2003 to examine strategies of how to increase the market share of this key segment.

Another issue is improving access to the festival for people from more deprived areas of Edinburgh. The Schools Programme is aiming to do this for the family market. The move in 2000 to abolish the entry fee and make the site accessible to all is also a step nearer to social inclusion. The presence of more commercial authors such as Candace Bushnell of 'Sex and the City' fame, alongside more radical thinkers such as Susan Sontag, is also instrumental in widening audience participation.

Collaborative working

Pooling and maximising resources has been seen as a critical way forward for Edinburgh's key festivals. Although informal networking and sharing of ideas and practices had commonly been practised, this was formalised in 2001 with the launch of the Edinburgh Festivals Strategy. The strategy recognised the need for a shared vision, which the City of Edinburgh Council, the various festivals and other interested parties could sign up to with a common plan of action. The Strategy Implementation Group holds responsibility for the implementation and monitoring of the Festivals Strategy Action Plan. The action plan is critical because it addresses recommendations, implementation partners, timescales and resource implications. Paul Gudgin, Director of the Edinburgh Festival Fringe, comments that 'it is helping to foster closer working relationships across many of their departments, and between all the festivals and a number of other key agencies' (Edinburgh Festival Fringe's 2002 annual report).

Cross-festival collaboration has resulted in improvements in the following areas:

- a joint festivals website — www.edinburghfestivals.co.uk
- the appointment of a tourism travel press officer for Edinburgh's summer festivals
- the production of a daily guide to the festivals, sponsored by *The Guardian* newspaper
- the production of an advocacy document for the festival
- multi-staffing of the festivals.

Conclusion

In 2003 the festival was the world's largest celebration of the written word, featuring more than 550 authors appearing at over 650 events, with contributors as diverse as Clive James, Irvine Welsh and Kate Adie. The book festival is increasingly perceived as a marketable commodity, and there are obvious tensions between artistic programming and commercialisation. However, the continued success of the book festival is evident and, as Catherine Lockerbie, Festival Director says, 'The book festival is bringing the rest of the world to us to engage in wider debate. A good thing'.

Jane Ali-Knight, Lecturer in Festival and Leisure Management, Napier University, Edinburgh, based on Edinburgh International Book Festival 2003

Questions

1 Tension between artistic programming and commercialisation is a critical problem for many festivals and events, particularly those with a strong community base. How can festival and event organisers put in place strategies to counteract this?

2 What kind of activities can the Edinburgh International Book Festival engage in to increase participation from the market segment aged 18–25 years?

3 How can customer experience be measured at a festival and event? Discuss three different techniques that can be used, outlining the strengths and weaknesses of each approach.

Underwater Fantasy

Underwater Fantasy was an incentive event for approximately 1900 employees of the Japanese door-to-door video distribution company KTC International. It was staged at the Sydney SuperDome on 29 December 2001 by Event Services Inc (ESI) of Tokyo, in association with local Australian companies. The Director of ESI, Lucky Morimoto, had seen documentation of a previous prize-winning event held at the Sydney SuperDome by Sydney event producer and designer Lena Malouf, and had also seen an underwater dive show in Perth, which sparked the concept for Underwater Fantasy.

After preliminary discussions, ESI appointed Lena Malouf Events Pty Ltd as executive producer and designer of the event. Glen Lehman of Lehman & Associates, a Sydney-based production company, was then appointed as the overall producer of the show. Other components of the event included Showcorp for sound, light and vision, the Sydney SuperDome, Theme Park Entertainment, the amphibious Aussie Duck, Laser Special Events and Mr Balloons.

Daily communication was established through ESI in Japan, whose computer system automatically translates from Japanese into English and vice versa.

Event objectives

The main objectives of the client were to:
- produce an event that transported the guests into an underwater fantasy, thus providing KTC Japan with the opportunity to showcase their company in Sydney
- reward the employees of KTC Japan who had shown loyalty and dedication, and who had excelled in their work.

These were complemented by objectives of the event organisers, which were to:
- exceed the client's expectation
- illustrate to the client that a world-class event could be staged outside Japan.

Creating the event theme

To create the theme and look of the underwater event, research was undertaken on colours, sea life and ocean embellishment, and then interpreted in theatrical terms through sets and props. The design used monochromatic harmony with accent colours to interpret the underwater theme. The effect was designed to delight the Japanese guests because of their love of sea life and beaches in Australia. The design aimed for a balance between form and function. The implementation of the themed work did not interfere with guests' walkways, entertainment activities or technical use.

The event

The guests arrived by bus to a waiting 40-piece brass band dressed in uniform and large signage welcoming them to the event. They were guided through to the pre-function area of the SuperDome, and the VIPs were directed to an upper lounge for cocktails. Décor and music here were minimal, because the interior of the venue was going to be the main highlight.

Guests entered the main function room through dramatic balloon tunnels. A beautiful visual effect was created by balloon artistry and lighting washes. Colourful foil fish, turtles, sharks and mini whales were suspended 8–18 feet above every second table in the function room. They wafted and moved gently (due to the air flow caused by the venue's air conditioning), not only filling the space, but providing the spectacle of a 'sea of fish' as guests ascended the stairs from the balloon tunnel. The 200 tabletops were styled at different levels, the settings including the embellishment of high-style sand, shells, weeds, glass bubbles, fish and other underwater themes.

The hand railing surrounding the floor area was decorated with more than 100 panels of blue, green, turquoise, salmon and pink 'coral', outlined by masses of fairy lights. Giant underwater scenic canvases flown in from Japan were hung on the stage. Guests were seated under a canopy of fabric and lasers. Amazement from the employees showed, with ooh's and aaah's heard throughout the room and the KTC executives announced the opening of the evening.

The roving entertainers then entertained the guests as the fish, mermaids and water head performers strolled through the room and among the tables. As the guests were finishing the first course, another wow factor was brought into play with the arrival of the amphibious vessel, the 'Aussie Duck'. This was doused with water to give the impression that it had just emerged from the ocean carrying all the divers. The divers exited from the duck and made their way over to a big black curtain, which then fell to provide the next wow factor — an enormous perspex dive tank. A dive show then took place, including everything from high dives to synchronised swimming, and concluding with a Houdini-style underwater escape.

The focus then shifted to the other side of the room, where the lights dimmed and a woman dressed in a suit of mirrors was suspended high above the guests. Lasers were fired at her and reflected across the room, much to the guests' delight. Presentations and prize giving followed, concluding with the entry of the Blacktown City Brass Band accompanied by the Jelly Beans, who played a rendition of the KTC company song. The president then made his closing remarks, followed shortly afterwards by the departure of the guests.

Challenges faced by the event

Production challenges and how they were resolved included:

- preparing the venue for 29 December — accomplished by arranging with venue management to work late on Christmas Eve and throughout Boxing Day.
- converting a sporting venue into a banquet hall for 1900 guests — achieved by having regular venue meetings, and maintaining constant and consistent communication.

(continued)

- overcoming language barriers — communication between the Australian producers and the Japanese client and a non-English speaking MC was achieved by having two separate talk-back radio systems: one for all the Australian crew and performers, and another for the Japanese producer and the stage manager. The Japanese producer also spoke English, so he became the conduit for communications between the event director and the Japanese MC, and also Japanese guests who made stage appearances. Because the guests were Japanese, special signage had to be created for access areas such as smoking, toilets and first aid. Some language barriers were experienced when trying to explain the stair system to access toilets and smoking areas, but these issues were overcome with a smile and a show of willingness to assist.
- supporting the dive tank — engineers were employed to design a structure to support the 40-tonne water tank.

Theme and design challenges and how they were resolved included:

- achieving lavish decoration of such a large space — sets and props were created to the given budget using the following elements:
  - shaped and painted plywood to create 150 pieces of 'coral'
  - shaped and painted light-weight foam for fish, suspended by a metal rod and fishing line to allow gentle movement, creating an animated and three-dimensional effect
  - 200 long chains of helium-filled balloons to create a bubble effect throughout the space above and around the guests
  - 10 000 fairy lights silhouetting the underwater shapes
  - lighting wash to bring the fish and coral to life.
- maintaining site lines — specially made steel stands were used as the containers for tabletop centrepieces to maintain site lines even though the tabletops varied in height and design. Sea embellishments and accessories were used to incorporate the bases with the overall design. The tabletops were designed and placed so the tall ones were at the back of the room, with the smaller ones towards the centre (so no sight lines were blocked).
- integrating the stage area — the stage backdrop provided the theme for the main focal point. However, similar coral shapes and fish were hung around the apron to carry the theme.

Entertainment challenges and how they were met included:

- coordinating the entertainers — Lena and Glen held meetings on a regular basis with Kathy Ferris, the entertainment agent, to control the huge number of entertainers. The company objectives and protocol gave her a clear understanding of where entertainment fitted into the proceedings. Performers included:
  - a 40-piece city brass band
  - six water head performers
  - eight divers
  - 10 members of the Studio One orchestra
  - a six-piece jazz ensemble
  - one laser lady
  - two mermaid site performers
  - four members of the Aussie Duck team
  - six walking fish site performers.

- finding a local vocal group to perform the company song — when the Japanese group of vocalists booked to perform the company song in Japanese were cancelled through unforseen circumstances, a local entertainment agent booked an Australian group called the Jelly Beans, who successfully mastered the company song in Japanese. Two of the Jelly Beans who had mastered the song then had to pull out of the event (due to their houses being under immediate threat from bushfires raging around the western suburbs of Sydney). It was impossible to secure replacement vocalists because considerable preparation was involved in mastering the Japanese song, but the remaining four Jelly Beans performed to the expectation of all concerned.
- tailoring performances to the Japanese-speaking audience — scripting changes were made to the dive show to reduce the amount of dialogue, and a far more slapstick approach was taken.

Distinctiveness of the event

The event was held in a sporting stadium or 'superdome'. This meant turning an international sporting arena into a state-of-the-art ballroom in the space of a few days. This was completed through precise planning of the teams, the theming, the coordination, the entertainment and a dedicated crew. The primary distinguishing feature of the event was the transformation created with theming of the overall look of the room. It took three days to set up, and prior to that, six months of planning, preparation and designing. The result was that guests took an extra 15 minutes filtering into the venue than was scheduled, and were in awe of the creative environment as they stood to admire the decorative work that had taken place.

It was unique to have the guests experience dinner in the surrounds of the Sydney Olympic Park. This allowed them to witness and experience the sites that so many had been privy to back home only from their television at the time of the Sydney Olympics.

Execution of the event

The success of the event was due to several key factors:
- The chain of command was established and maintained.
- The executive producer and producer remained in close communication.
- Changes were recorded, but paperwork flowed.
- Meetings were held weekly, bi-weekly and monthly.
- All the meetings were organised with full written agenda.
- Projects and tasks were listed, tackled and completed in bite-size pieces.
- All contractors were kept in the loop and notified of all changes.
- The client, Lucky Morimoto, was constantly updated, assuring confidence and security across the waters.

Lena Malouf, CSEP, Lena Malouf Events Pty Ltd, and
Glen Lehman, CSEP, Lehman & Associates

(continued)

Questions

1 From the case study, what issues arise for an Australian event company staging an event for a non-English speaking audience, and how might these be resolved?

2 Identify the 'five Ws' of the Underwater Fantasy event. What do you consider to be the prime 'wow' factor of the event?

3 Effective theming can add an additional dimension of attractiveness and impact to an event. Discuss this statement with reference to the Underwater Fantasy event.

REFERENCES

Bramble, C 2002, *Evaluation report on the Inaugural Spikefest*, unpublished report by Gosford City Council, Gosford, New South Wales.

Edinburgh International Book Festival 2003, 'About the book festival', www.edbookfest.co.uk/info (accessed 1 April 2004).

Floriade 2003, 'Australian Capital Territory Government and Australian capital tourism', www.floriadeaustralia.com (accessed 1 April 2004).

Getz, D 1997, *Event management and event tourism*, Cognizant Communication Corporation, New York.

Giddens, A 1990, *The consequences of modernity*, Polity Press, Cambridge.

Goldblatt, Dr JJ 1997, *Special events — best practices in modern event management*, Van Nostrand Reinhold, New York.

Goldblatt, Dr JJ 2000, 'A future for event management: the analysis of major trends impacting the emerging profession', in *Events beyond 2000: setting the agenda — event evaluation, research and education conference proceedings*, eds J Allen, R Harris, LK Jago & AJ Veal, Australian Centre for Event Management, University of Technology, Sydney.

Goldblatt, J & Perry, J 2002, 'Re-building the community with fire, water and music: the WaterFire phenomenon', in *Events and place making: proceedings of international research conference held in Sydney 2002*, eds L Jago, M Deery, R Harris, A Hede & J Allen, Australian Centre for Event Management, Sydney.

Gosford City Council 2002, Minutes from Community Services Meeting, Gosford, New South Wales.

Hemmerling, M 1997, 'What makes an event a success for a host city, sponsors and others?', Paper presented to The Big Event Tourism New South Wales Conference, Wollongong, New South Wales.

Hollway, S 2002, Keynote address delivered to Events and Place Making Conference, Australian Centre for Event Management, University of Technology, Sydney, 15–16 July.

Ireland, D 2003, Personal communication, 24 October 2003.

Jago, L, Chalip, L, Brown, G, Mules, T & Ali, S 2002, 'The role of events in helping to brand a destination', in *Events and place making: proceedings of international research conference held in Sydney 2002*, eds L Jago, M Deery, R Harris, A Hede & J Allen, Australian Centre for Event Management, Sydney.

Rugby World Cup 2003, www.rugbyworldcup.com/RugbyWorldCup/EN/ Tournament/News/sk+24+11+stats.htm (accessed 3 March 2004).

Shone, A & Parry, B 2001, *Successful event management — a practical handbook*, Continuum, London.

Sony Tropfest 2004, www.tropfest.com (accessed 25 February, 2004).

Sweaney, K 1997, 'Sponsorship trends' and 'Developing the Docklands', *Australian Leisure Management*, vol. 1, no. 3, pp. 18–19, and vol. 1, no. 5, p. 16, respectively.

The Sydney Morning Herald 2004, Advertisement: Free Sony Tropfest DVD, 23 February 2004.

5

The planning
function

LEARNING OBJECTIVES

After studying this chapter, you should be able to:

- discuss the significance of the planning process in achieving desired event outcomes

- discuss the strategic planning process as it applies to events

- describe selected organisational structures evident in the events area.

INTRODUCTION

This chapter provides an overview of the concept of planning as it applies to the conduct of events. It begins by discussing the centrality of planning to the overall success of an event and then moves on to describe the strategic event planning process. This process is identified as comprising a number of sequential and interrelated steps, each of which is briefly described here. Additionally, this chapter examines the range of organisational structures from which an event manager must select to support and implement their planning efforts.

WHAT IS PLANNING?

In its simplest form, the planning process consists of establishing where an organisation is at present, where it is best advised to go in the future, and the strategies or tactics needed to achieve that position. In other words, the planning process is concerned with end results and the means to achieve those results.

Perhaps the value of planning is best summed up by the words of the famous American general, Douglas MacArthur, who observed: 'Without a plan you're just a tourist.' MacArthur's comments allude to the value of planning in focusing an organisation (such as an event organising committee) on particular objectives and in the creation of defined pathways by which these objectives can be achieved. Central to the establishment of such pathways is an understanding of internal (for example, available resources) and external (for example, current economic conditions) factors that will condition any decisions that are made. Other benefits associated with the planning process include its capacity to:

• generate a range of potential alternative strategies for consideration
• identify and solve problems, reduce uncertainty about the future
• and assist an event to remain competitive (Hannagan 1998).

To engage productively in the planning process, an event manager needs to keep a range of matters in mind. Central among these matters are the need to monitor and evaluate progress, coordinate decisions in all areas so event objectives are progressed, and communicate with, inspire and motivate those responsible for carrying out the various elements of the plan. These matters are discussed in later chapters.

While the power of planning as a management tool is acknowledged, actually engaging in planning involves some measure of discipline on behalf of the event manager. As Sir John Harvey-Jones, a past chairman of ICI in the United Kingdom, notes: 'Planning is an unnatural process: it is much more fun to do nothing. The nicest thing about not planning is that failure comes as a complete surprise, rather than being preceded by a period of worry and depression'.

Event managers also need to be mindful that plans, as Hannagan (1998) and Thompson (1997) note, need to be adapted to changing circumstances. Additionally, they need to be conscious of not falling foul of planning 'pitfalls'. These include:

- overplanning and becoming obsessed with detail as opposed to overall strategic considerations
- viewing plans as one-off exercises rather than active documents to be regularly consulted and adapted
- seeing plans as conclusive rather than directional in nature (Johnson & Scholes 1999).

PLANNING FOR EVENTS

Where does the event planning process begin? The answer to this question depends on whether the event is being conducted for the first time or if it is a pre-existing event. In the case of a new event, the event manager may be required to first work through the broad concept of the event with key stakeholders and then undertake a feasibility study. If this study shows that the event is likely to meet certain key criteria (such as profitability), they would then move to develop a plan for its creation and delivery. In instances where an event is pre-existing and open to the bidding process (for example, a conference or sporting event), an initial decision needs to be made as to whether (after a preliminary investigation) it is worthwhile making a bid. If the answer is 'yes', a more detailed feasibility study might be conducted to identify such things as the costs and benefits associated with hosting it before preparing a formal bid. If a bid is prepared and it is successful, then detailed event planning would commence. The process associated with event planning in the context of new events and those attracted through the bidding process is shown in figure 5.1 (page 117). The event profile on page 118 provides insights into this process from a 'real world' perspective.

It should also be noted that event managers often find themselves in situations in which they are planning for recurring events such as annual festivals. In this situation, the steps in figure 5.1 (page 117) are not all relevant. In such instances, the event manager begins with an appraisal of the current situation faced by the event and also its previous plans. This process is likely to result in minor changes or refinements to existing vision statements, mission statements, goals, objectives and/or strategies, and the development of revised/new plans in areas such as marketing, human resources and finance. Also, on occasions, such reviews may result in major changes to the existing strategy and/or form of the event. Indeed, event managers need to keep in mind, as Mintzberg, Quinn and Voyer (1995) point out, the planning process tends to encourage incremental change, when what may be needed is a complete rethink of the current strategy.

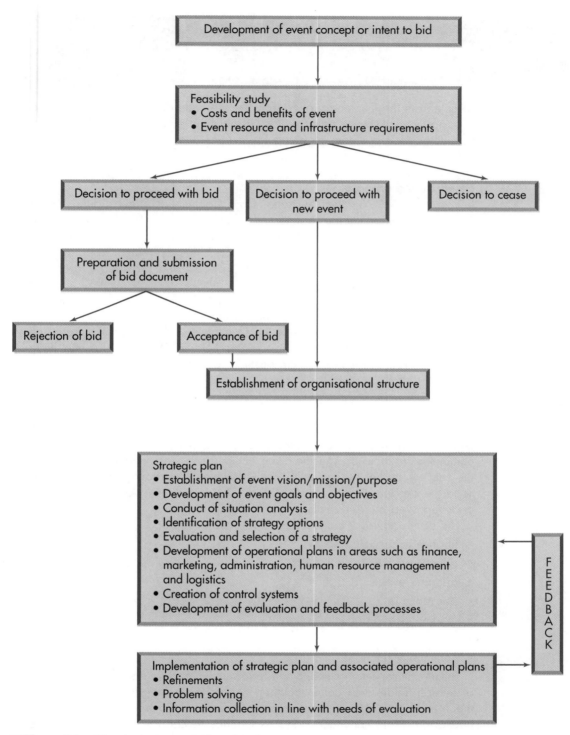

■ **Figure 5.1**   *The strategic event planning process*

(**Source:** *Based on Getz 1997, p. 76.*)

To celebrate the Centenary of Federation, the Federal Government formed a national council. Every state/territory established a Centenary of Federation committee to coordinate planning for a year-long, nationwide program of celebrations and commemorations.

Research and proposal

In February 1996, the Australia Day Council of New South Wales (ADCNSW) wrote to the Premier offering its expertise to the New South Wales Government in developing and implementing a program of activities to mark the centenary of Federation in 2001. The government responded by asking the ADCNSW to develop a full proposal and provided a grant for the necessary research required.

Over four months, the ADCNSW undertook 50 interviews with leaders in the community to seek their advice on the most appropriate way to celebrate the anniversary of the creation of the Commonwealth. In addition, research was conducted into the Federation events held in 1901 through the State Library of New South Wales, Film Australia and the National Film and Sound Archive.

Committee structure

The ADCNSW proposal to the State Government recommended that a state committee be created to oversee planning and the formation of advisory committees to focus on specific areas of operation. This model was based on the success of the existing ADCNSW structure. Importantly, it was to be a separate organisation to the ADCNSW. All appointees would be voluntary and approved by the Premier.

The seven advisory committees established covered:

- finance and sponsorship
- education, history and civics
- arts and events
- parade
- marketing and communications
- ceremonies
- community relations.

These advisory committees were made up of leaders from a broad range of related fields, who came together in a voluntary capacity to ensure that the New South Wales Centenary of Federation Committee (NSWCOFC) had appropriate knowledge and experience to call on when planning the event.

Determination of mission, aims and objectives

The proposal to the government included the suggested aims and objectives of the NSWCOFC. One of the clearest outcomes of the research and interview process was that the program for the centenary of Federation needed to be both a celebration of success and a commemoration of past challenges and mistakes. The aims and objectives were discussed and ratified by the NSWCOFC at its second meeting. The key aims were:

- provide genuine and extensive opportunities for the involvement of all the people of New South Wales and, in particular, for regional communities
- create inclusive, visionary and community-driven celebrations that are of lasting significance for future generations
- encourage community interest in the processes that led to the creation of the Commonwealth and what it has meant to the Australian nation
- implement programs, events, celebrations, legacies and educational initiatives for the community that have enduring and worthwhile results and benefits
- work together with indigenous and ethnic community groups and other community organisations and networks throughout New South Wales.

Each advisory committee also used these aims as a basis for establishing their own goals, programs and activities.

Federation Day

A clear example of how the organisational structure was critical to the success of the many events it conducted was Federation Day, 1 January 2001.

The three events on this day — the commemoration, parade and centennial ceremony — were all produced by the NSWCOFC. They attracted crowds of more than 580 000 people in Sydney, as well as a national television audience of over one million viewers.

While all parts of the organisation were involved in one way or another with these events, four advisory committees had the most significant roles. They were the ceremonies, parade, marketing and communications, and finance and sponsorship committees. These advisory committees determined strategies, made event programming decisions, were responsible for ongoing monitoring of activities against objectives, and provided feedback and advice to their relevant staff teams. Major decisions and recommendations were carried forward by the chairpeople of these committees to the NSWCOFC for approval.

Given the large scale of events on this day, the NSWCOFC had to monitor logistics and bring together teams on issues related to event development, such as traffic management plans and the preparation of various council approval applications. Representatives from all teams met monthly to discuss key issues, document overall strategies and ensure that team

(continued)

meetings with outside agencies, such as the New South Wales Police and the Roads and Traffic Authority, were coordinated across the organisation. In addition, the NSWCOFC actively participated in the ongoing government coordination process for all agencies involved in major events.

Cross-project teams were established to manage the planning in such areas as uniforms, accreditation, volunteers, and two-way communication systems and protocols. As part of the risk management strategy, all managers held meetings dedicated solely to Federation Day during the six weeks prior to 1 January 2001.

Michelle Morgan, Marketing and Communications Manager, ADCNSW

ELEMENTS OF THE STRATEGIC EVENT PLANNING PROCESS

■ Concept or *intent to bid*

In the context of new events, this stage involves making decisions (often in consultation with major stakeholder groups) concerning such matters as the type/form of the event (for example, festival, parade), duration, location/venue, timing, and key program elements that will serve to make the event unique or special. Once the event concept is sufficiently developed, it can then be subjected to more detailed analysis. (*Note*: Detailed discussion of developing event concepts can be found in chapter 4.) In instances where bidding is involved, events for which bids can be made need to be identified first.

Once this is done a preliminary assessment can be made as to their 'fit' with the capabilities of the event organising body and the hosting destination. Events deemed worthy of further investigation may then be the subject of more detailed scrutiny via a feasibility study.

■ Feasibility *study*

Before committing to an event, its organisers need to determine how feasible or otherwise it would be to conduct that event. There are many considerations that may be taken into account in conducting a feasibility study. These may include (depending on the event) likely budget requirements; managerial skill needs; venue capacities; host community and destination area impacts; availability of volunteers, sponsors and supporting services (for example, equipment hire firms); projected visitation/attendance; infrastructure requirements; availability of public/private sector financial support;

level of political support for the event; and the track record of the event in terms of matters such as profit. It should be noted that the level of detail and complexity associated with these studies will vary. An event such as the Olympic Games, for example, is likely to involve a more lengthy and detailed process than, say, a state sporting championship or an association conference.

■ Bid *preparation*

This step is required in instances where it is decided to bid for an existing event based on the outcomes of a feasibility study. The bidding process involves a number of steps, specifically:

- identifying resources that can be employed to support the event (for example, venues and government grants
- developing a critical path for the preparation and presentation of a bid document to the 'owners' of the event
- developing an understanding of the organisation conducting the event and the exact nature of the event itself
- identifying the key elements of past successful bids
- preparing a bid document
- presenting and/or submitting a bid to the 'owners' of the event, such as a sporting body
- lobbying in support of the bid.

Only when a bid is successful does formal strategic planning for the event commence.

■ Decision *to proceed or cease*

In the case of new events, the outcomes of the feasibility study will directly determine if and when the event will proceed. In the case of events involving a bid, this decision will depend on whether a bid is accepted or rejected.

■ Establishment *of organisational structure*

Following the decision to proceed with an event, an organisational structure will need to be created through which the event can be delivered.

Simple structures

As the name suggests, a simple structure has a low level of complexity. As figure 5.2 (page 122) illustrates, all decision making is centralised with the event manager, who has total control over all staff activities. This is the most common structure in small event management businesses as it is flexible, adaptable to changing circumstances, easy to understand, and has clear accountability — the manager is accountable for all the activities associated with the event. The flexibility of this structure commonly means staff are expected to be multi-skilled and perform various job functions. This can mean individual jobs are more satisfying, and produce higher levels of staff morale. However, this structure has some potential limitations. As staff do not have the opportunity to specialise they may not achieve a high level of expertise in any one area. Additionally, once an event organisation grows beyond a certain size, decision making can become very slow — or even non-existent — as a single executive has to make all decisions and carry out all the management functions. Also, if the manager has an autocratic style of management, staff can become demoralised when their expertise is not fully utilised. There is also an inherent risk in concentrating all event management information in one person — obviously, sickness at an inappropriate time could prove disastrous.

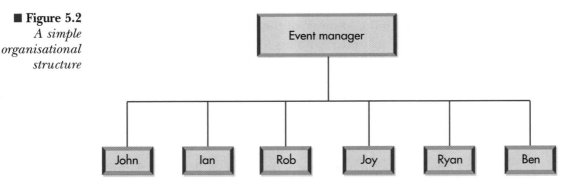

■ Figure 5.2
A simple organisational structure

Functional structures

As the name suggests, a functional structure departmentalises (that is, groups related tasks) in a way that encourages the specialisation of labour (paid/voluntary). Benefits of this form of structure are that individuals or groups (such as committees) can be given specific task areas, thus avoiding any overlap of responsibilities. Additionally, it is possible using this form of structure to easily add additional functional levels as the event requires them. In figure 5.3 an example of such a structure is given in the form of the Australian Open Tennis Championships. Potential limitations of this approach include problems of coordination due partly to a lack of understanding of other tasks, and conflict between functional areas as those doing the tasks attempt to defend what they see as their 'territory'. Various approaches can be used to prevent these problems arising. These approaches include employing multi-skilling strategies that require the rotation of staff through different functional areas, regular meetings between the managers/chairs of all functional areas, general staff meetings and communications (such as newsletters) that aim to keep those engaged on the event aware of matters associated with its current status (for example, budgetary situations or the passing of milestones). In chapter 6, we discuss activities that are essential elements of the leadership function of the event manager.

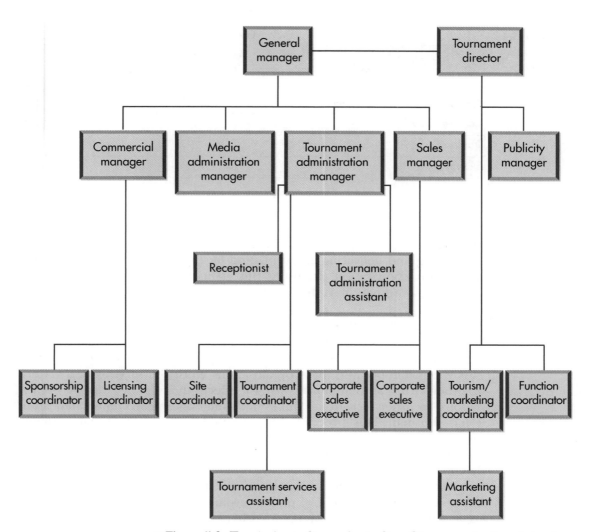

■ **Figure 5.3** *Tennis Australia — Australian Open organisational structure*

Program-based matrix structures

Another way of organising committees or groups into an organisational structure is treating the various aspects of an event program as separate (but related) entities. Organisers of a multi-venue sporting event, for example, may choose to have separate committees with responsibility for all tasks associated with event delivery at each location (figure 5.4, page 124). In order to do this, each committee/group leader would be required to manage a team of people with a comprehensive range of event-related skills. If this structure is employed, it is sound practice, as Getz (1997) notes, to have some tasks, such as security, communications and technical support, cut across all program areas to prevent duplication and enhance coordination.

■ Figure 5.4
Program-
based matrix
structure for a
hypothetical
multi-venue
sporting event

	Event manager		
	Venue teams (Each team would comprise people with a similar range of skills.)		
Support systems	Venue 1 team	Venue 2 team	Venue 3 team
Communications			
Transport			
Security			

A project-based matrix structure has several inherent advantages, including allowing groups/individuals to engage directly with the task (producing and delivering an event) and facilitating intergroup communication and cooperation. In using this structure, a high value must be placed on coordination so the event is presented as a unified whole.

Multi-organisational or network structures

Most specialist event management companies are relatively small in size (fewer than 20 people), yet many conduct quite large and complex events. This is possible because these organisations enlist the services of a variety of other firms and organisations. In effect, they create 'virtual organisations' in order to conduct the event, which disappear immediately after it has finished. This process is represented in figure 5.5, which shows various suppliers being enlisted by an event management firm to create a structure capable of creating and delivering an event. It should be noted that this process of growing an organisational structure quickly by contracting outside firms to perform specific functions is common in many forms of events, including public events such as festivals. Such an approach makes sense in situations where it is impractical to maintain a large standing staff when they can be used only for a limited period each year. Other advantages are that contracting specialist businesses with current expertise and experience on a need-only basis means there is no 'down time'. Budgeting can also be more exact because most costs are contracted and, therefore, known beforehand. This structure also allows for quick decisions because the core management group is made up of only a few people or one individual.

As with the other structures previously discussed, there are also possible disadvantages to be considered. These include issues associated with quality control and reliability of the contractors who are involved in performing tasks, and coordinating employees (from various other organisations) who lack a detailed understanding of the event. Nevertheless, the concept of the network structure is supported by contemporary management thinking on downsizing, sticking to core activities and outsourcing, and can be very effective for certain kinds of event.

■ **Figure 5.5** *A network structure*

DEVELOPING A STRATEGIC PLAN

Once it has been decided to proceed with an event, or a bid has been won, the event manager moves on to develop a strategic plan to guide their next stage of decision making.

The strategy process is about determining the current situation faced by an event (strategic awareness), the strategic options available to an event manager (strategic choices) and the mechanisms for implementing and evaluating/monitoring the chosen strategies (strategic implementation) (Thompson 1997, p. 51). The context in which this process takes place is that of the purpose/vision/mission of the event. Each of the elements of this process is discussed in turn in this section.

Purpose, vision and mission statements

At a minimum, a clear statement of purpose and vision should underpin every event. This statement in turn will be conditioned by the needs of the various stakeholder groups with an interest in the event. Such groups may include client organisations, the local community, government at various levels, potential attendees and participants, sponsors and volunteers.

In the case of many events, particularly those of a corporate or public relations nature, a considered statement as to its purpose is all that is really required to provide sufficient direction and focus.

An example of a statement is one developed for Brain Awareness Week, an annual international event conducted by the Dana Alliance (2004), a nonprofit organisation that seeks to provide information about the personal and public benefits of brain research:

■ Brain Awareness Week is an international effort organised by the Dana Alliance for Brain Initiatives to advance public awareness about the progress, promise, and benefits of brain research. ■

For events that are more complex in nature (such as large public events) and involve a number of stakeholder groups, it can be beneficial to reflect more deeply on the matter of purpose. It is evident that many events are now doing this and, as a result, are creating vision/mission statements to guide their development and conduct.

A vision statement can be separate from an event's mission, or the two may be combined. Vision statements usually describe what the event seeks to become and to achieve in the longer term (Thompson 1997, p. 141). They are also often brief, precise and motivational in nature. The Oregon Shakespeare Festival (2004), for example, states:

■ We envision the Oregon Shakespeare Festival as a creative environment where artists and audiences from around the world know they can explore opportunities for transformational experiences through the power of theatre. ■

Some events use more expansive vision statements, which are really a combination of both vision and mission. The Bunk Johnson/New Iberia Jazz, Arts & Heritage Festival, Louisiana, is one such example. Its vision is stated as:

■ The Bunk Johnson/New Iberia Jazz, Arts & Heritage Festival Inc. is a non profit corporation for advancement of scholarly research, collection and preservation of the visual and performing arts, crafts, oral traditions, culinary practices, history and cultures of the diverse people who reside along the Bayou Teche in south Louisiana. We are dedicated to sharing these gifts with others through an annual festival and encouraging special emphasis on the education of young people in the arts, music and heritage (Bunk Johnson/New Iberia Jazz, Arts & Heritage Festival 2004). ■

It should be noted that vision statements do not necessarily need to be written down (although it is often useful to do so), providing they are shared and understood by those involved with the event. It would be fair to say, for example, that while no formal vision statement existed at the time the Sydney Gay and Lesbian Mardi Gras began, those involved with it understood clearly that its long-term goal was about achieving equality and social acceptance.

A mission statement describes in the broadest terms the task that the event organisation has set for itself. If the event has also established a vision statement, then the mission needs to be viewed in terms of fulfilling this vision. Such statements, at their most advanced, seek to define an event's purpose, identify major beneficiaries and customer groups, indicate the broad nature of the event and state the overall operating philosophy of the organisation conducting it (for example, whether to be fully or partially self-funded). Several event mission statements that, to varying degrees, fulfil these criteria have been provided in table 5.1. In reviewing these, you should note that the mission statements for the Greek Orthodox Folk Dance Festival and Caribbean Days Festival perhaps best meet most of these criteria.

Once established, a mission statement acts as the basis upon which goals and objectives can be set and strategies established. They also serve to provide a shorthand means of conveying to staff (either paid or voluntary) an understanding of the event and what it is trying to achieve.

■ **Table 5.1** *Sample event mission statements*

EVENT	MISSION STATEMENT
Cherry Creek Arts Festival, Colorado	The mission of the Cherry Creek Arts Festival is to create access to a broad array of arts experiences, nurture the development and understanding of diverse art forms and cultures, and encourage the expanding depth and breadth of cultural life in Colorado (www.cherryarts.org/asp/users/ccainfo.asp).
Greek Orthodox Folk Dance Festival, San Francisco	The Greek Orthodox Folk Dance Festival Ministry is dedicated, through Orthodox Christian Fellowship and committed leadership, to promoting, encouraging and perpetuating Greek heritage and culture among individuals, families and communities expressed in folk dance, folk art, music and language (www.gofdf.org).
National Folk Festival, Canberra	The National Folk Festival will provide an annual celebration of Australian folk life, encompassing the quality of our creativity and the diverse cultural heritage of Australian communities by showcasing a fun-filled community event that features participation as an imperative (www.folkfestival.asn.au).
Caribbean Days Festival, North Vancouver	The mission of the Caribbean Days Festival is to create a self-sustaining and financially viable public event that will result, through its organisation in the awareness and continuity of the inherent value to all individuals, particularly youth, of the existing Caribbean and other cultures in Canada. The aim is to inspire individuals, through their personal involvement, to become active participants within the community at large (www.ttcsbc.com/cdf/mission.shtml).

Goals and objectives

Once an event's mission has been decided, the event manager must then move on to establish the event's goals and/or objectives. Goals are broad statements that seek to provide direction to those engaged in the organisation of the event, as seen in table 5.2 (page 129). Objectives in turn are used to quantify progress towards an event's goals and as such set performance benchmarks and allow event organisations to assess what aspects of their planning have succeeded or failed. It should be noted that the terms 'goals' and 'objectives' are often used interchangeably but they are really distinct concepts. It should also be noted that for some forms of event (particularly those of a corporate nature) the step of creating goals prior to establishing objectives is not usually necessary. The establishment of goals is useful when the event is complex in nature and involves a number of stakeholder groups. In such instances, they serve a useful role in building on the event's mission statement to provide direction and focus to the event organisers' activities.

Useful criteria that can be applied to the establishment of objectives are summed up by the acronym SMART, which refers to the fact that objectives should be:

- *specific:* focused on achieving an event goal (or, if no goals have been developed, its purpose)
- *measurable:* expressed in a way that is quantifiable
- *agreeable:* agreed on by those responsible for achieving them
- *realistic:* in terms of the event organisation having the human, financial and physical resources to achieve them
- *time specific:* to be achieved by a particular time.

Each event will obviously vary in terms of the objectives it establishes. Examples of such objectives are as follows:

- *Economic objectives*
  — Percentage return on monies invested or overall gross/net profit sought
  — Dollar value of sponsorship attracted
  — Percentage of income to be raised from fundraising activities
  — Percentage increase in market share (if the event is competing directly with other similar events)
- *Attendance/participation*
  — Total attendance/attendance by specific groups (for example, people from outside the area, specific age groups, professions)
  — Size of event in terms of stallholders/exhibitors/performers/attendees
  — Number of local versus outside artists
  — Percentage of an area's cultural groups represented in a program
  — Number of community groups involved with the event
- *Quality*
  — Percentage level of attendee/exhibitor/sponsor/volunteer satisfaction
  — Number of participants/speakers/performers of international reputation
  — Number of complaints from attendees/exhibitors/volunteers.
- *Awareness/knowledge/attitudes*
  — Percentage of attendees or others exposed to the event that have changed levels of awareness/knowledge as a result of the event
  — Percentage of attendees or others exposed to the event who have altered their attitudes as a result of it
- *Human resources*
  — Percentage of staff/volunteer turnover
  — Percentage of volunteers retained from previous year.

■ **Table 5.2** *Sample of event goals*

EVENT	GOALS
Northern Lights Festival Boreal (NLFB), Sudbury, Ontario	NLFB is committed to operating in a professional, fiscally responsible manner with the goal of financial self-sufficiency. NLFB is committed to reflecting the cultural diversity of Northern Ontario in its operations and programming. NLFB is committed to treating all performers and artists and their work professionally, with dignity, respect and fairness. NLFB is committed to developing, promoting and advocating for local artists and performers. NLFB is committed to developing, supporting and honouring the work of its volunteers, Board and staff. NLFB is committed to the accountability of the Board of Directors. NLFB is committed to developing, supporting and acknowledging the interests of its audiences. NLFB is committed to cultivating relationships with the community, other arts and cultural organisations, umbrella groups, sponsors and other community groups (www.nlfb.on.ca).
Greek Orthodox Folk Dance Festival, San Francisco	To establish and maintain an administrative body to achieve the purposes outlined in the mission statement. To provide leadership skills to perpetuate the Ministry through the practice of acquired leadership skills in the administration of this organisation. To bring people together in Orthodox Christian Fellowship and love, creating greater communion and stronger ties through interaction with fellow Orthodox Christians and promoting ethical and moral standards befitting the life of an Orthodox Christian. To promote, encourage and perpetuate Greek heritage and culture through outreach activities that inform others of the Ministry's events, opportunities and commitment to its purposes and goals (www.gofdf.org).

Situation analysis

A useful process that can be employed to gain a detailed understanding of an event's internal and external environment (or surroundings) is a strengths, weaknesses, opportunities and threats (SWOT) analysis. This process may involve referring to a range of existing information sources, including data collected previously on the event, census data and general reports on relevant matters such as trends in leisure behaviour. Additionally, it may be necessary to commission studies to fill information gaps, or to update event organisations on particular matters. A deeper understanding of the needs, wants, motives and perceptions of current or potential customer groups, for example, may be deemed necessary before changing an event in an effort to increase attendance.

The external environment consists of all those factors that surround the event and which can impact on its success. A thorough scanning of the full range of factors that make up the external environment should aid the event manager making decisions on such matters as target market(s) selection, programming, promotional messages, ticket pricing and when to conduct the event. Threats to the event (for example, proposed changes to legislation regarding outdoor consumption of alcohol) or the emergence of new competing events can also be identified through this process.

In this section, we examine the main components of concern in the external environment for event managers, along with some selected matters associated with each concern that have the potential to impact on events.

- *Political/legal* — the decisions made by all levels of government become laws or regulations that affect the way in which people live in a society. The laws regulating the consumption of food and alcoholic beverages, for example, have changed radically in Australia since the 1950s, making outdoor food and wine festivals possible.
- *Economic* — economic factors such as unemployment, inflation, interest rates, distribution of wealth and levels of wages and salaries can impact on the demand for events. Declining living standards in a particular region, for example, may require an event to reduce its ticket prices and seek alternative sources of revenue (for example, grants or sponsorship) to subsidise the event costs.
- *Social/cultural* — changes in a population's ethnic/religious make-up or leisure behaviour can act to influence event demand. These changes can provide opportunities (for example, a demand for multicultural events) or pose threats (for example, an increased tendency to engage in home-based leisure activities). Existing attitudes among a population towards a particular activity can also be a factor of interest to event managers. The love of sport possessed by many Sydneysiders, for example, was 'tapped' by the organisers of the Sydney 2000 Olympics, both to generate demand and to create a climate of tolerance for the various event preparation disruptions. The culture of a particular place can also provide a rich resource on which event managers can draw; for example, the architecture, traditions, beliefs, cuisine and artistic skills associated with a particular area can be embraced, selectively or collectively, by event managers.
- *Technological* — changes in equipment and machines have revolutionised the way people undertake tasks, including aspects of event management (chapter 13). One example is using the Internet to promote festivals, exhibitions and events. Entering the word 'festival' into an Internet search engine will produce links to a multitude of events on all parts of the globe. Another example is the use of the Internet as a vehicle for conducting events such as conferences. Internet sites that support event professionals, students and educators by providing information, directories, and resources online are also appearing (for example, domsresearch.com and www.acem.uts.edu.au).
- *Demographic* — the composition of society in terms of age, gender, education and occupation changes over time. A striking example is the entry of the baby boomers' generation (people born between 1945 and 1960) into middle age. The generation that gave the world rock'n'roll, blue jeans and relaxed sexual morals is, and will continue to be, a large market for event managers, and will always have very different needs to the preceding and succeeding generations.

- *Physical* — concern over such matters as pollution and waste generation within the broader community is affecting the way in which events are conducted. Many councils and waste boards actively encourage event organisers to 'green' their events (see www.wastewiseevents.wasteboards. nsw.gov.au). Another environmental consideration for event managers is the changing weather patterns caused by the impact of greenhouse gases. Such changes have the potential to impact on outdoor events, particularly when they are conducted.
- *Competitive* — other events that attract a similar audience need to be monitored. In this regard, comparisons relating to such matters as programs and pricing are useful. Events do not necessarily have to be similar in nature to attract a similar audience. A consumer exhibition organiser in a port city, for example, suffered a significant decline in demand for an event they had organised when a visiting aircraft carrier decided to conduct a public open day at the same time.

When the analysis of the external environment is complete, the next step in the strategic planning process is to undertake an internal analysis of the event organisation's physical, financial, informational and human resources in order to establish its strengths and weaknesses. Areas of strength or weakness associated with an event may include the level of management or creative expertise on which it can draw, the quality of its supplier relationships, ownership or access to appropriate venues and facilities (for example, stages and sound systems), the quality of event program elements, access to appropriate technology such as ticketing systems, the level of sophistication of the event management software systems in use, access to financial resources, the event reputation, the size of the volunteer base and the strength of links with potential sponsors.

Identification of strategy options

The environmental scanning process gathers crucial information that can be used by the event manager in selecting strategies to achieve the event's vision, mission or purpose. Strategies must use strengths, minimise weaknesses, avoid threats and take advantage of opportunities that have been identified. A SWOT analysis is a wasted effort if the material gathered by this analytic process is not used in strategy formulation.

Several generic strategies, which can be adopted by event managers, are summarised below.

Growth strategy

Many event managers have a fixation on event size and, as such, seek to make their events bigger than previous ones or larger than similar events. Bigger is often thought to be better, particularly by ambitious event managers. Growth can be expressed as more revenue, more event components, more participants or consumers, or a bigger share of the event market. It is worth pointing out that bigger is not necessarily better, as some event managers have discovered. An example of this is the Sydney Festival (a cultural festival that takes place each year in Sydney in January). It adopted a growth strategy by absorbing other events taking place in Sydney in January and calling them 'umbrella' events. Some critics observed that by doing this the festival lost its focus. A subsequent festival director responded by concentrating the festival around Sydney Harbour foreshore areas and decreasing the number of event components but increasing their quality.

It is important to recognise that an event does not necessarily have to grow in size for its participants to feel that it is better than its predecessors — this can be achieved by dedicating attention to quality activities, careful positioning and improved planning. However, a growth strategy may be appropriate if historical data suggest there is a growing demand for the type of event planned, or a financial imperative necessitates increasing revenue. The annual Woodford Folk Festival in Queensland, for example, expanded the focus of its program by including contemporary rock acts in an attempt to appeal to a market segment with a strong propensity to attend music events. Increased revenue gained in this way was directed at repaying the festival's debt.

Consolidation or stability strategy

In certain circumstances it may be appropriate to adopt a consolidation strategy — that is, maintaining attendance at a given level. Strong demand for tickets to the Port Fairy Folk Festival, an annual event in Victoria, for example, has allowed this event to sell tickets well in advance, cap attendance numbers and further enhance the quality of its program. By capping ticket sales in a climate of high demand, this event has also created a situation in which it has greater pricing freedom.

Retrenchment strategy

An environmental scan may suggest that an appropriate strategy is to reduce the scale of an event but add value to its existing components. This strategy can be applicable when the operating environment of an event changes. Retrenchment can seem a defeatist or negative strategy, particularly to long-standing members of an event committee, but it can be a necessary response to an unfavourable economic environment or major change in the sociocultural environment. The management of a community festival, for example, may decide to delete those festival elements that were poorly patronised and focus only on those that have proven to be popular with its target market. Likewise, exhibitions may delete an accompanying seminar program and focus on the core aspects of the exhibition.

Combination strategy

As the name suggests, a combination strategy includes elements from more than one of these generic strategies. An event manager could, for example, decide to cut back or even delete some aspects of an event that no longer appeal to their event target market(s), while concurrently growing other aspects.

Strategy evaluation and selection

Most management writers such as Thompson (1997) and Johnson and Scholes (1999) consider that strategic alternatives can be evaluated by using three main criteria:

1. *Appropriateness/suitability* — strategies and their component parts should be consistent. That is, strategies selected should complement each other and be consistent with the environment, resources, and values of the event organisation.

2. *Acceptability/desirability* — strategies should be capable of achieving the event's objectives. They should focus on what the environmental scan has identified as important and disregard the unimportant. Event companies should, however, be careful not to overlook potential risks involved in the strategy; for example, financial or environmental risk, or the risk of the required skills not being available in the organisation.

3. *Feasibility* — the proposed strategy should be feasible. It should work in practice, considering the resources available (for example, finance, human resource, time). The strategy should also meet key success factors (for example, quality, price, level of service).

Once again, it is important to stress that the strategies chosen must be congruent with the findings of the SWOT analysis, or the environmental scan becomes a waste of time and intellectual energy and results in inappropriate strategy selection.

Operational plans

Once the strategic thrust of the event has been agreed, the implementation of the plan can commence. This process can be carried out by means of a series of operational plans. This application of project management practices and techniques (chapter 12) is particularly useful at this point in the strategic planning process.

Operational plans will be needed for all areas central to the achievement of an event's objectives and the implementation of its strategy. Areas for operational planning will likely vary, therefore, across events. It would be common, however, for plans to be developed in areas such as budgeting, marketing, administration, staging, research and evaluation, risk management, sponsorship, environmental waste management, programming, transportation, merchandising and staffing (paid and volunteer).

Each area that develops operational plans will require a set of objectives that progress the overall event strategy; action plans and schedules; details of individuals responsible for carrying out the various aspects of the plan; monitoring and control systems, including a budget; and an allocation of resources (financial, human and supporting equipment/services).

Given that many festivals, exhibitions and events are not one-off, but occur at regular intervals — yearly, biennially or, in the case of some major sporting events, every four years — standing plans can be used in a number of operational areas. Standing plans are made up of policies, rules and standard procedures and serve to reduce decision-making time by ensuring similar situations are handled in a predetermined and consistent way.

Policies can be thought of as guidelines for decision making. An event may, for example, have a policy of only engaging caterers that meet particular criteria. These criteria might be based on licensing and insurance. Policies in turn are implemented by way of following established detailed instructions known as procedures. In the case of the previous example, procedures may require the person responsible for hiring caterers to inspect their licence and insurance certificates, check that they are current, and obtain copies for the event's records. Rules are statements governing conduct or action in a particular situation. An event may establish rules, for example, regarding what caterers can and cannot do with the waste they generate on site, or on what they can or cannot sell.

Control systems

Once operational plans are implemented, mechanisms are required to ensure that actions conform to plans. These mechanisms take the form of systems that allow performance to constantly be compared to objectives. Performance benchmarks (such as ticket sales over a given period) are particularly useful in this regard. Meetings and reports are generally central to the control process, as are budgets. Budgets allow actual costs and expenditure to be compared with those projected for the various operational areas. A detailed discussion of the control and budgeting processes appears in chapter 10.

Event evaluation and feedback

Evaluation is a neglected area of event planning; yet, it is only through evaluation that event managers can determine how successful or otherwise their efforts have been in achieving whatever objectives were set for the event. It is also through this means that feedback can be provided to stakeholders, problems and shortcomings of the planning process can be identified and improvements suggested if the event is to be repeated. Key considerations regarding evaluation from an event manager's perspective include when to evaluate, how to evaluate, and what to evaluate. The answers to these questions are provided in chapter 14.

■ Implementation *of strategic plan and associated operational plans*

Once implemented, a strategic plan and its associated operational plans are likely to require refinements to adapt them to changing circumstances. Additionally at this stage, information is collected to allow evaluation to occur.

*S*UMMARY ....

Planning is the basis for all successful events. To be successful, an event manager must gain a clear understanding of why the event exists (its vision/ mission/purpose), what it is trying to do and for whom (its goals and/or objectives), and also decide on the strategies needed to achieve these goals and/or objectives. Additionally, an appropriate organisational structure is needed to 'steer' these processes. In this regard, the event manager can select from a number of options, depending on the assessment of the advantages and disadvantages of each. Strategies, in turn, need to be implemented through a range of operational plans developed within the context of an overall event budget. These plans need to be monitored and adjusted as appropriate in the light of changing circumstances, and evaluated against the objectives set for them and the overall objectives of the event.

Questions

1. Briefly discuss the value of setting vision/mission/purpose statements for events.

2. Undertake an Internet search of a particular event type (for example, festivals), identify four events that have established mission statements and compare these to the criteria given in this chapter.

3. Conduct an interview with the manager of a particular event with a view to identifying the key external environmental factors that are impacting on their event.

4. When might an event employ a retrenchment strategy *or* a growth strategy? Can you identify any specific event where one of these strategies is in evidence?

5. Identify several events, determine if they have established objectives, and assess these against the SMART criteria discussed in this chapter.

6. Select an event with a functional organisation structure, and another with a network structure. Describe each of these structures, and discuss why you believe each event chose the organisational structure it did.

7. Explain the difference between a strategic plan and an operational plan.

8. Briefly discuss the difference between a policy and a procedure.

9. Explain why stakeholders are significant from the perspective of establishing vision and mission statements.

10. Critically examine the strategic planning process of a particular event in the light of the processes discussed in this chapter.

Sydney Theatre Company
Foundation Fundraising Party

Purpose of the event

The Sydney Theatre Company (STC) held its first fundraising party in 1995. The theme of that party was a (K)night of Medieval Mayhem. This first fundraising party attracted 1100 guests and became a landmark annual event for the STC. The success of the first event prompted the establishment of the STC Foundation, with the purpose of raising money specifically for the company and its research and development program. Since then, the STC has hosted various themed parties each year, except for 2000 because of the Olympics.

The producers aim to take the guests out of the everyday and into a theatrical interpretation of another time and place. The format of the night consists of drinks preceding a three-course dinner. Three major production numbers featuring choreographed song and dance surround the central fundraising activity of the night, the auction. The latter part of the evening is either live or club music depending on the party's theme. Shows are spectacular, with large numbers of performers (for Trocadero there were over 500) and many surprise elements. All STC Foundation events have been hailed as parties of the year with Trocadero named by *The Sydney Morning Herald* as one of the best parties of the decade.

Reason for fundraising

Research and development ensure the future of any theatre company. Without the ability to experiment and develop new projects, theatres are restricted to staging existing works or those developed by companies that are more affluent. Before the establishment of the STC Foundation, all research and development were funded by box office receipts. This resulted in the company's director having to either program a subscription series of safe choices to guarantee sufficient revenue, or limit research and development to an affordable minimum. Without guaranteed funding, development of long-term projects was not possible.

Organisation

As an established theatre company, the STC is in a unique position, having considerable resources in personnel skilled in every area of production, plus substantial staging materials, props and wardrobe. It also has the advantage of being able to broker deals with suppliers based on an ongoing connection with the Company.

However, the party must be scheduled into the STC's busy year to ensure staff availability and avoid clashes with main stage productions. So the STC's resources are not overloaded, freelance personnel are brought in to manage key areas. The final party production team is structured as follows:
• producers: STC

- director: STC
- technical director: STC
- box office and marketing: STC
- production manager: freelance
- design and choreography: freelance
- stage management: freelance
- sound, lighting, staging and catering: contract
- public relations: freelance
- security: contract.

All other crew and staff are drawn from the STC on either a paid or volunteer basis. There are two producers for STC events: Wayne Harrison, who directs the show, and Camilla Rountree, who manages the other organisational aspects and coordinates the entertainment and sponsorship.

Planning the timeline

February

- The theme for the party is chosen by the producers and presented to the foundation for a date to be chosen.
- Once the theme is adopted, creating the image for the party commences. This image must convey the mood of the event as well as lending itself to the design of an invitation, poster and program. It is, therefore, an important marketing tool.
- The producers engage the designer and choreographer and find a suitable venue. Once these three elements are in place, the entertainment can be planned.

April

The main organisation of the event begins.

- A meeting of the creative team is called, involving the choreographer, the designer and the producers. The director outlines his or her ideas and the first of many discussions takes place. Over the following months, the content of the show will change several times within the overall concept. This may be due to availability of artists, complications with staging, budget constraints or the advent of that most wonderful of things: 'a great idea'.
- A budget is drawn up, taking into account all projected costs at commercial rates, plus a contingency amount. Given that there is never sufficient money, sponsorships and deals are always necessary.
- The designer is given a broad outline of what will be needed to stage the event: the nature of the show, the number of guests, the number of corporate tables, whether a buffet or sit-down dinner is planned and any other specific requirements. The designer then draws up a floor plan to scale. This is the blueprint for the night and is used by every department. It will show seating arrangements, placement of performance areas and their dimensions, entrances, exits, catering and bar areas, and facilities such as toilets, taps, fire equipment and lighting grids. Without this plan, the party cannot progress to the next stage.

(*continued*)

May

- Work has commenced on sponsorships.
- Caterers have been contracted and briefed.
- Hiring companies have been given the dates.
- Details of the party are placed in EXSTCE, the STC magazine that is sent to the subscriber base of 20 000. This promotes advance bookings so the STC box office is briefed.

June

- Regular planning meetings commence, involving the creative team and the technical director. By this stage the producers are sourcing and booking artists for the show.

July

- All the printed material for the party has now been approved and is sent to the printers.
- Advertisements are placed in STC subscription series programs.

August

- Invitations are posted.
- The box office appoints an extra person to be responsible for processing bookings for the party.
- The publicists commence the job of creating media awareness of the party by sending out press releases.

September

- The production manager joins the team. From this point on he or she takes over the detail of staging, lighting, sound and catering needs. The production manager works closely with the STC technical director and the producers to coordinate work being carried out in-house being done by external contractors. Regular trips to the location are required to make sure every department is familiar with the venue.
- The designer finalises details for staging and the building of props, table lighting and the dressing of the room.

October

- The costume designer joins the team. Where original costumes are required, fabrics are bought and made up in the STC workrooms. Other clothes are sourced from various hiring and theatre companies. Costumes for waiters and ushers are organised. Artists are called in for fittings.
- A catering coordinator ensures all glassware, cutlery and crockery are suitable, quantities are correct, and everything is delivered on time and returned after the event to its source.
- Music tracks are prepared by a musical director. If a live band or orchestra is performing for a production number, music charts will have to be prepared for the musicians.
- The production manager prepares a preliminary running order for the show. This schedules every aspect of the night from the arrival of the guests to the last dance track. Sometimes at this point, problems arise with timing and logistics, and the running order has to change.

Three weeks prior
- Seating is finalised and tickets are posted to guests.
- All artists' contracts are finalised.
- A production assistant commences. It is the production assistant's job to send out delivery details for everything required for the event, to coordinate artists and prepare spreadsheets to be used for rehearsals and wardrobe checks.

Two weeks prior
- Rehearsals commence.
- The program for the night is finalised and printed.

Production week
Monday
- The riggers commence. Once they have finished, construction of the staging starts. Depending on the scale, this can take a day or more. Lighting and sound usually take about two days. Security personnel guard the venue at night.

Thursday
- The room is ready for a rough rehearsal.
- Plotting of the sound and lighting begins.
- Wardrobe is set up at the venue and fittings for extras are held.
- Cold rooms arrive and are switched on, ready for food and beverage delivery.

Friday
- Tables and chairs are set up.
- All catering requirements are delivered.
- Generators and 'porta-loos' are delivered as needed.
- Rehearsals take place with sound and lighting checks.

Saturday
- Tables are set.
- Dressing of the venue is completed.
- The caterers begin the on-site preparation of the food.
- Rehearsals run all day, so lunch is provided for the cast and crew.

On the night
- Everyone's on standby from one hour before the guests arrive.
- Last-minute checks take place, and then it is up to the professionalism of everyone involved to make sure the night runs smoothly.

Sunday
- Clean-up begins as soon as the last guest leaves.
- Staging, lighting and sound equipment is struck.
- Catering equipment is packed ready for collection.
- Tablecloths are bundled, and tables and chairs are stacked.
- Props and wardrobe are packed.

Monday
- Everything is collected and the venue is cleaned.

(continued)

Outcomes

The STC Foundation parties have been particularly successful both artistically and as fundraisers, bringing in over $200 000 per event.

Summary

To run a successful event there are five golden rules:

1. Plan well in advance.
2. Once you have chosen your theme, stick to it, but remain flexible enough to allow ideas to develop.
3. Employ people who are expert in their fields.
4. Learn what elements to prioritise; some things are more difficult to organise than you think.
5. For a fundraiser, remember your objective and be constantly on the alert for ways of doing things inexpensively but with style.

If you have a clear vision of what you want to achieve, are working with skilled people and have enough time, you can overcome many difficulties, even budget overruns. Budgets usually blow out in the last few days when unforeseen problems must be solved with money. With careful planning and enough time, most problems can be avoided. The last ingredient is always luck; added to a professional approach to event planning, things are usually right on the night.

Camilla Rountree, former producer, Foundation Events and
Wayne Harrison, former executive producer, Sydney Theatre Company

Questions

1 Write a purpose statement for the STC Foundation events.

2 Describe two key objectives for the event. In what ways do these correspond to the SMART principle?

3 Describe the strategies that the STC Foundation party uses to achieve its objectives.

4 Construct an organisational chart for the event.
   (a) What type of organisational structure does it demonstrate?
   (b) Why would this structure suit the requirements of this event?

5 Write a position description for the position of producer, foundation events in the event organisation.

6 Construct a policy document for the event that lists appropriate policies and procedures for producing the event.

7 Would you classify the process described in the case study as a single-use plan or a standing plan? Explain your answer.

REFERENCES

Beardwell, I & Holden, L 2001, *Human resource management: a contemporary perspective*, 3rd edn, Pearson Education, London.

Bunk Johnson/New Iberia Jazz, Arts & Heritage Festival 2004, 'Mission statement', www.bunkjohnson.org (accessed 19 April 2004).

Caribbean Days Festival, 'Mission statement', www.ttcsbc.com/cdf/mission.shtml (accessed 15 November 2003).

Catherwood, D & Van Kirk, R 1992, *The complete guide to special event management*, John Wiley & Sons, New York.

Cherry Creek Arts Festival, 'Mission statement', *www.cherryarts.org/asp/users/ccainfo.asp* (accessed 19 April 2004).

Cole, GA 1996, *Management: theory and practice*, 5th edn, Letts, London.

Cole, GA 1997, *Strategic management*, Letts, London.

Dana Alliance for Brain Initiatives 2004, 'Brain awareness week', www.dana.org/brainweek/ (accessed 19 April 2004).

Getz, D 1997, *Event management and event tourism*, Cognizant Communications, New York.

Greek Orthodox Folk Dance Festival, 'Mission statement', www.gofdf.org (accessed 19 April 2004).

Hanlon, C & Jago, L 2000, 'Pulsating sporting events', in *Events beyond 2000 — setting the agenda, proceedings of the conference on evaluation, research and education*, eds J Allen, R Harris, L K Jago & A J Veal, Australian Centre for Event Management, University of Technology, pp. 93–104.

Hannagan, T 1998, *Management concepts & practices*, 2nd edn, Financial Times/Pitman Publishing, London.

Heskett, J, Sasser, W & Schelesinger, L, 1997, *The service profit chain*, The Free Press, New York.

Johnson, G & Scholes, K 1999, *Exploring corporate strategy*, 5th edn, Prentice Hall Europe, Hemel Hempstead, England.

Keung, D 1998, *Management: a contemporary approach*, Pitman Publishing, London.

Mintzberg, H, Quinn, J & Voyer, J 1995, *The strategy process*, Prentice Hall, New Jersey.

Mullins, LJ 1999, *Management and organisational behaviour*, 5th edn, Financial Times/Pitman Publishing, London.

Northern Lights Festival Boreal, 'Mission statement', www.nlfb.on.ca (accessed 19 April 2004).

Oregon Shakespeare Festival 2004, 'Mission Statement — vision', www.orshakes.org/about/mission.html (accessed 19 April 2004).

Stoner, JAF, Freeman, RE & Gilbert Jr, DR 1995, *Management*, 6th edn, Prentice Hall, Englewood Cliffs, New Jersey.

Tennis Australia 1997, 'Australian Open organisational structure', Melbourne.

Thompson, JL 1997, *Strategic management: awareness and change*, 3rd edn, International Thompson Business Press, London.

6 Human resource
management and events

LEARNING OBJECTIVES

After studying this chapter, you should be able to:

- describe the human resource management challenges posed by events
- list and describe the key steps in the human resource planning process for events
- describe approaches to determining human resource needs for events
- list areas, in the context of events, where human resource policies and procedures might be required
- describe event staff and volunteer recruitment and selection processes
- describe approaches to training and professional development relevant in an event context
- discuss staff supervision and evaluation practices in which an event manager might engage
- describe practices associated with the termination, outplacement and re-enlistment of event staff and volunteers
- describe approaches that can be employed to motivate event staff and volunteers
- describe techniques that can be used for event staff and volunteer team building
- describe general legal considerations associated with human resource management in an event context.

$\mathcal{I}$NTRODUCTION

Effective planning and management of human resources is at the core of any successful event. Ensuring an event is adequately staffed with the right people, who are appropriately trained and motivated to meet its objectives, is fundamental to the event management process. This chapter seeks to provide an overview of the key aspects of human resource planning and management with which an event manager should be familiar. It begins by examining considerations associated with human resource management in the context of events. It then moves on to propose a model of the human resource management process for events and to discuss each of the major steps in this model. Selected theories associated with employee/volunteer motivation are then described, followed by a brief examination of techniques for staff and volunteer team building.

The final part of this chapter deals with legal considerations associated with human resource management. Issues associated with volunteer management receive significant coverage in this chapter, given the role volunteers play in the conduct of many types of event.

$\mathcal{C}$ONSIDERATIONS ASSOCIATED WITH HUMAN RESOURCE PLANNING FOR EVENTS

The context in which human resource planning takes place for events can be said to be unique for two major reasons. First, and perhaps most significantly, many events have a 'pulsating' organisational structure (Hanlon & Jago 2000; Hanlon & Cuskelly 2002). This means they grow in terms of personnel as the event approaches, but quickly contract when it ends. From a human resource perspective, this creates a number of challenges, including obtaining paid staff given the short-term nature of the employment offered; working to short timelines to hire and select staff, and to develop and implement staff training; and needing to shed staff quickly. Also, volunteers, as opposed to paid staff, often make up the bulk of people involved in delivering an event. In some instances, events are run entirely by volunteers. The challenges presented by this situation are many, and relate to such matters as sourcing volunteers, quality control, supervision, training and motivation. Later parts of this chapter suggest responses to these challenges.

$\mathcal{T}$HE HUMAN RESOURCE PLANNING PROCESS FOR EVENTS

Human resource planning for events should not be viewed simply in terms of a number of isolated tasks, but as a series of sequential interrelated processes and practices that take their lead from an event's vision/mission, objectives and strategy. If an event seeks to grow in size and attendance, for example, it will need a human resource strategy to support this growth through such means as increased staff recruitment (paid and/or volunteer) and expanded (and perhaps more sophisticated) training programs. If these supporting human resource management actions are not in place, problems such as high staff/volunteer turnover due to overwork, poor quality delivery and an associated declining marketplace image may result, jeopardising the event's future.

Events will obviously differ in terms of the level of sophistication they display in the human resources area, given factors such as their access to resources in terms of money and expertise. Contrast, for example, a local community festival that struggles to put together an organising committee and attract sufficient volunteers with a mega-event such as the Olympic Games. Nonetheless, it is appropriate that the 'ideal' situation is examined here — that is, the complete series of steps through which an event manager should proceed for human resource planning. By understanding these steps and their relationships to one another, event managers will give themselves the best chance of managing human resources in a way that will achieve their event's goals and objectives. As a way of introducing you to how this process can be applied to events, this chapter includes an event profile dealing with the successful volunteer program at the Sydney Olympic Games.

While a number of general models of the human resource management process can be identified, the one chosen to serve as the basis of discussion in this chapter is based on that proposed by Getz (1997). This model (figure 6.1) represents an attempt to display how this process works within an event context.

■ Figure 6.1
The human resource planning process for events

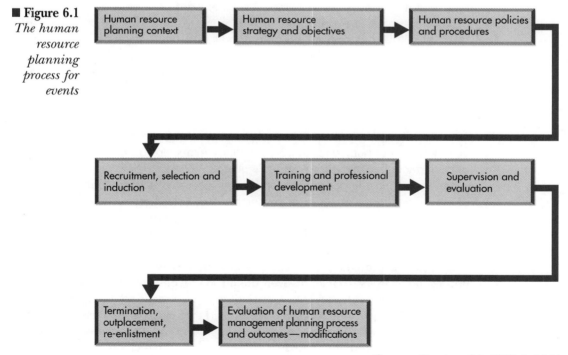

(**Source:** *Based on Getz 1997, p. 184.*)

Volunteers — never underestimate them. Always respect them and their 'power', always adopt the shared responsibility focus, always prepare them well, always expect the best from them, always give back to them as much as you expect from them, and always share ownership with them. Oh, and never ever take them for granted.

Volunteers are the backbone of many events, as well as being central to our society's service provision in areas such as welfare, recreation, the environment, the arts, and emergency services. Their 'visibility' and profile hit its peak in Australia in 2000 when the largest of all events was conducted in Sydney — the Olympic and Paralympic Games.

Remember them? Sixty-two thousand volunteers doing all sorts of specialist and non-specialist roles — who performed so magnificently that the President of the International Olympic Committee declared them (at the closing ceremony of the Olympic Games) 'the most wonderful and dedicated volunteers ever'. The ultimate rap, and so thoroughly deserved — not just for their five million hours of time but more importantly the quality of their efforts and the lasting images they created with visitors.

Positioning volunteers as an integral part of the games' workforce was critical to the success of the games. Whether paid or unpaid, all staff of the organising committee were part of one team — all dedicated to the same result of a fabulous and memorable games and one where people left our shores with great impressions of our country, city and people.

We embraced our volunteers, we trusted them, and we empowered them. But, with those rights came responsibilities — we had high expectations of them and there was never any shirking from that message. The volunteers wanted to be 'close' to the games, they wanted to later 'brag' about their role in making the games successful, they wanted to be busy and expected us to keep them busy and, importantly, they expected to be judged on their performance. Exactly what we also wanted.

The single most important reason for the success of the volunteer program at the games was the sense of ownership that volunteers were encouraged to take over the event. A little esoteric you might say but that single message drove their attitudes and their performance. Responsibility also accompanied that ownership. 'We may not represent our country again in so visible a way' was uppermost in their minds. Equally important was their attitude that they had to 'hang in there' with us even during the tougher times — they did.

What else made it work? A number of things — securing the right people (no, not every applicant got a job nor should that ever be the case), making sure each job was clearly defined and understood (yes, there were job descriptions and required skill sets in great volume), matching the volunteers to those jobs, intensive training (induction, job-specific and venue training) that promoted the need for high performance and customer service, good Aussie hospitality and having a sense of fun, detailed operational policies and procedures, and a comprehensive recognition and appreciation strategy. And finally, training of our paid staff in the management of volunteers was absolutely vital to effective management and job satisfaction for our volunteers (high retention rates were experienced at both events).

Sound easy? It wasn't. But gratifying and satisfying it surely was. Certainly, the program was not perfect, but the overall approach to volunteer management (as outlined here) was well conceived, and the fundamentals sound, leaving a lasting positive impression with our visitors and with the Australian community as a whole.

David Brettell, Program Manager, Venue Staffing and Volunteers,
Sydney Olympic and Paralympic Games 2000

■ **Human** *resource strategy and objectives*

This stage in the human resource management process for events involves a variety of activities, including establishing guiding strategies and objectives, determining staffing needs (paid and volunteer), and undertaking a job analysis and producing job descriptions and specifications. Each of these tasks is discussed in turn in this section.

Strategy

An event's human resource strategy seeks to support its overall mission and objectives. This link can be demonstrated by reference to the following examples that identify a few selected areas in which an organisation might set objectives and the subsequent focus on supporting human resource management objectives and activities:

- *cost containment* — improved staff/volunteer productivity, reduced absenteeism and decreased staff numbers
- *improved quality* — better recruitment and selection, expanded employee and volunteer training, increased staff and volunteer numbers, and improved financial rewards and volunteer benefits
- *improved organisational effectiveness* — better job design, changes to organisational structure and improved relations with employees and volunteers
- *enhanced performance regarding social and legal responsibilities* — improved compliance with relevant legislation, such as that relating to occupational health and safety, antidiscrimination and equal employment opportunity.

Whatever human resource management objectives are set for an event, they need to meet the SMART criteria discussed in chapter 5.

Staffing

Staffing is the main strategic decision area for event managers in the area of human resources, because without staff there is nothing really to 'strategise' about! Event managers need to make decisions concerning how many staff/volunteers are needed to deliver the event, what mix of skills/qualifications/experience is required, and when in the event planning process these staff and volunteers will be needed (for example, the event shutdown stage only). Getz (1997, p. 186) suggests one way of undertaking this task in the context of events, involving a three-stage process:

1. Identify all tasks associated with event creation, delivery and shutdown. Site-related tasks, for example, might include site design and layout, setting up fencing, erecting tents and stages, positioning/building toilets, and placing signs and waste containers.

2. Determine how many people are needed to complete the range of tasks associated with the conduct of the event. Do all the tasks have to be done in order, by the same work crew, or all at once by a larger crew? What level of supervision will be required? What tasks can be outsourced and what must be done by the event team? Will more staff than normal be required to perform tasks (such as security) as a result of some specific circumstance (such as a visit by a celebrity to the event)?

3. List the numbers of staff/volunteers and supervisors and the skills/experience/qualifications needed to form the 'ideal' workforce for the event.

The most difficult task in this process is step 2, particularly if the event is new. Armstrong (1999) claims that managerial judgement is by far the most common approach used in business to answer this question. Such an observation is also likely to apply to the world of events. That is, the event manager, or various functional managers if the event is large enough, calculates how many, and what type, of human resources are needed to meet their objectives. In doing so, they are likely to account for factors such as prior experience, demand forecasts for the event, the number of venues/sites involved, skill/expertise requirements, previous instances of similar (or the same) events, the degree of outsourcing possible, the availability of volunteers and strategies adopted by the event.

In the case of some tasks associated with the conduct of events, it is possible to estimate staffing needs by engaging in some basic arithmetic. The number of people who can pass through a turnstile per hour, for example, can be easily calculated by dividing the processing time for an individual into 60 minutes. Assume the figure generated in this way is 240 — that is, 240 people can be processed in an hour through one turnstile. Next, an estimate of event attendance (including peaks and troughs in arrivals) is required. Now assume total attendance for the event has been fairly consistent at 5000 over the past three years, with 80 per cent (4000) of people arriving between 9 am and 11 am. If this number of people is to be processed over a two-hour period, about eight turnstiles would need to be open (240 transactions per hour multiplied by two hours, divided by the number of attendees over this time, which is 4000). Based on these calculations, eight turnstile operators would be required for the first two hours; after this time, the number of operators could be dramatically decreased.

Job analysis

Job analysis is an important aspect of this stage of the human resource planning process. It involves defining a job in terms of specific tasks and responsibilities and identifying the abilities, skills and qualifications needed to perform that job successfully. According to Stone (2002), questions answered by this process include the following:

- What tasks should be grouped together to create a job or position?
- What should be looked for in individuals applying for identified jobs?
- What should an organisational structure look like and what inter-relationships between jobs should exist?
- What tasks should form the basis of performance appraisal for an individual in a specific job?
- What training and development programs are required to ensure staff/volunteers possess the needed skills/knowledge?

The level of sophistication evident in the application of the job analysis process differs between events. Some small-scale events that depend exclusively, or almost exclusively, on volunteers may simply attempt to match people to the tasks in which they have expressed an interest. Even under such circumstances, some consideration probably should be given to factors such as experience, skills and physical abilities.

Job descriptions

Job descriptions are another outcome of the job analysis process with which event managers need some measure of familiarity if they are to effectively match people (both employees and volunteers) to jobs. Specifically, a job description is a statement identifying why a job has come into existence, what the holder of the job will do, and under what conditions the job is to be conducted (Stone 2002).

Job descriptions commonly include the following information:

- *Job title and commitment required* — this information locates the paid or voluntary position within the organisation, indicates the functional area where the job is to be based (for example, marketing coordinator), and states the job duration/time commitment (for example, one year part-time contract involving two days a week).
- *Salary/rewards/incentives* associated with position — for paid positions, a salary, wage or hourly rate needs to be stated, along with any other rewards such as bonuses. In the case of voluntary positions, consideration should be given to identifying benefits such as free merchandise (for example, T-shirts and limited edition souvenir programs), free/discounted meals, free tickets and end-of-event parties, all of which can serve to increase interest in working at an event.
- *Job summary* — this brief statement describes the primary purpose of the job. The job summary for an event operations manager, for example, may read: 'Under the direction of the event director, prepare and implement

detailed operational plans in all areas associated with the successful delivery of the event'.

- *Duties and responsibilities* — this information lists major tasks and responsibilities associated with the job. It should not be overly detailed, identifying only those duties/responsibilities that are central to the performance of the job. Additionally, it is useful to express these in terms of the most important outcomes of the work. For an event operations manager, for example, one key responsibility expressed in outcome terms would be the preparation of plans encompassing all operational dimensions of the event, such as site set-up and breakdown, security, parking, waste management, staging and risk management.

- *Relationships* with other positions within and outside the event organisation — what positions report to the job? (An event operations manager, for example, may have all site staff/volunteers associated with security, parking, staging, waste management, utilities and so on reporting to him/her.) To what position(s) does the job report? (An event operations manager may report only to the event director/manager.) What outside organisations will the position need to liaise with to satisfactorily perform the job? (An event operations manager may need to liaise with, for example, local councils, police, roads and traffic authorities, and local emergency service providers.)

- *Know-how/skills/knowledge/experience/qualifications/personal attributes* required by the position — in some instances, particularly with basic jobs, training may quickly overcome most deficiencies in these areas. However, for more complex jobs (voluntary or paid), such as those of a managerial or supervisory nature, individuals may need to possess experience, skills or knowledge before applying. Often, a distinction is drawn between these elements, with some being essential while others are desirable. Specific qualifications may also be required. Increasingly, job advertisements for event managers, for example, are listing formal qualifications in event management as desirable. Personal attributes — such as the ability to work as part of a team, to be creative, to work to deadlines and to represent the event positively to stakeholder groups — may also be relevant considerations.

- *Authority* vested in the position — what decisions can be made without reference to a superior? What expenditure limits are on decision making?

- *Performance standards* associated with the position — criteria will be required by which performance in the position will be assessed. While such standards apply more to paid staff than to voluntary positions, they should still be considered for the latter. This is particularly the case if volunteers hold significant management or supervisory positions where substandard performance could jeopardise one or more aspects of the event. If duties and responsibilities have been written in output terms, then these can be used as the basis of evaluation.

- *Trade union/association membership* required with position

- *Special circumstances* associated with the position — does the job require heavy, sustained lifting, for example?

- *Problem solving* — what types of problem will commonly be encountered on the job? Will they be routine and repetitive problems or complex and varied issues?

While job descriptions for paid positions often involve most, if not all, the information noted previously, voluntary positions are often described in far more general terms. This is because they often (but not always) involve fairly basic tasks. This is evident from figure 6.2, which provides job descriptions for several voluntary positions at the Summer Solstice Folk Music, Dance and Storytelling Festival in California.

■ **Figure 6.2**
Summer Solstice Folk Music, Dance and Storytelling Festival — selected volunteer job descriptions

FESTIVAL SET-UP AND TEAR-DOWN	DESCRIPTION
Arts and Crafts Row Set-up AND tear-down	You will help vendors and craftspeople carry their merchandise from their cars to their booths, using a dolly. You MUST work both morning and evening parts of this job! This is an active outdoor job that requires lifting and carrying.
Banners Set-up AND tear-down	This is VERY hard work, but fun! You will be working outdoors in teams to hang the fabric banners that decorate the festival. Some teams will need one person who can climb ladders. You MUST work both a Thursday OR Friday set-up shift AND the Sunday tear-down shift.
Festival signs Set-up AND tear-down	This is active outdoor work, but not as heavy as banner set-up. You will be helping put up and take down information signs on the festival grounds. You MUST work both a set-up shift AND the Sunday tear-down.
Festival site Set-up AND tear-down	You will be setting up the festival workshop areas. This job entails a lot of moving chairs and desks around! It's an active physical job, partly indoors and partly outdoors. You MUST work both the Friday set-up shift AND the Sunday tear-down.
Legacy quilt Set-up AND tear-down	You will be setting up the legacy quilt and structure. This job entails constructing a wooden structure using bolts and hanging quilts. It's an active physical job outdoors. You MUST work both the Friday set-up shift AND the Sunday tear-down.
Parking lot Set-up AND tear-down	You will be helping layout and stake the parking lots. This is active outdoor work. You MUST also work tear-down on Sunday afternoon.
Street signs Set-up AND tear-down	Teams of two will follow maps and drive around the Calabasas area, putting up direction signs. On Sunday, you will take down the same signs you put up. You MUST work both the Friday set-up shift AND the Sunday tear-down. You MUST have an available car to use.

(**Source:** *California Traditional Music Society 2004.*)

Job specification

A job specification is derived from the job description and seeks to identify the experience, qualifications, skills, abilities, knowledge and personal characteristics needed to perform a given job. (Crompton, Morrissey and Nankervis 2002) In essence, it identifies the types of people who should be recruited and how they should be appraised. The essential and desirable criteria shown in figure 6.3 provide an example of how job specifications are used in the recruitment process.

■ **Figure 6.3**
Job advertisement for an event manager

EVENTS MANAGER, Clerk. Grade 7/8, Royal Botanic Gardens, Sydney. Pos. no. R8G 9716. Total remuneration package valued to $72 534 p.a. (salary $65 731–$59 382). Responsible for managing community and commercial use of Gardens' lands, including special events and venue hire. **Essential:** Demonstrated extensive experience in events management or related industry. Excellent oral and written communication skills. Demonstrated customer service, negotiation, team and interpersonal skills. Well-developed administrative, planning, staff and financial management skills. Ability to manage competing demands for land use. Computer skills in word processing, spreadsheets and venue booking systems. Current driver's licence. Ability to implement EEO, OH&S policies and practices. **Desirable:** Database skills. An understanding of the role of a botanic garden. Tertiary qualifications in events management or a related field. Membership of ISES. Inquiries: Joe Smith (02) 9231 8111.

■ Policies *and procedures*

Policies and procedures are needed to provide the framework in which the remaining tasks in the human resource planning process take place: recruitment and selection; training and professional development; supervision and evaluation; termination, outplacement, reemployment; and evaluation. According to Stone (2002, p. 25), policies and practices serve to:

• reassure all staff that they will be treated fairly — for example, seniority will be the determining factor in requests by volunteers to fill job vacancies
• help managers make quick and consistent decisions — for example, rather than a manager having to think about the process of terminating the employment of a staff member or volunteer, they can simply follow the process already prescribed
• give managers the confidence to resolve problems and defend their positions — for example, an event manager who declines to consider an application from a brother of an existing employee may point to a policy on employing relatives of existing personnel if there is a dispute.

Human resource practices and procedures for events are often conditioned or determined by those public or private sector organisations with ultimate authority for them. A local council responsible for conducting an annual festival, for example, would probably already have in place a range of policies and procedures regarding the use of volunteers. These policies and procedures would then be applied to the event. Additionally, a range of laws influence the degree of freedom that the management of an event has in the human resource area. Laws regarding occupational health and safety, holiday and long service leave, discrimination, dismissal and compensation all need to become integrated into the practices and policies that an event adopts.

If an event manager goes to the time and effort to develop policies and procedures, he or she also needs to ensure these are communicated to all staff and applied. Additionally, resources need to be allocated to this area so the 'paperwork' generated by those policies and procedures can be stored, accessed and updated/modified as required. Such paperwork may include various policy/procedure manuals and staff records such as performance evaluations and employment contracts.

Again, the larger (in terms of number of staff and volunteers) and more sophisticated (in terms of management) the event, the more likely it is that the event managers would have thought more deeply about policy and procedure concerns. Nonetheless, even smaller events will benefit in terms of the quality of their overall human resources management if some attempt is made to set basic policies and procedures to guide actions.

■ Recruitment, *selection and induction*

The recruitment of paid and volunteer employees is essentially about attracting the 'right' potential candidates to the 'right' job openings. Successful recruitment is based on how well previous stages in the human resource planning process have been conducted, and involves determining where qualified applicants can be found and how they can be attracted to the event organisation. It is a two-way process, in that the event is looking to meet its human resource needs at the same time as potential applicants are trying to assess whether they meet the job requirements, wish to apply for the position and perceive value in joining the organisation. Figure 6.4 (page 154) represents the recruitment, selection and induction process in diagrammatic form.

How event managers approach the recruitment process depends on the financial resources they have available to them. With large events, a budget is likely to be set aside for this purpose, designed to cover costs such as recruitment agency fees, advertising, the travel expenses of non-local applicants and search fees for executive placement companies. The reality for most events, however — particularly those relying heavily on volunteers — is that they will have few resources to allocate to the recruitment process. Nonetheless, they can still successfully engage in this process by:

• *using stakeholders* (for example, local councils, community groups, sponsors and event suppliers) to communicate the event's staffing needs (volunteer and paid) to their respective networks. McCurley and Lynch (1998), in the context of volunteers, call this approach 'concentric circle recruitment' because it involves starting with the groups of people who are already connected to the event or organisation and working outwards. It is based on the premise that volunteers are recruited by someone they know — for example, friends or family, clients or colleagues, staff, employers, neighbours or acquaintances such as members from the same clubs and societies.

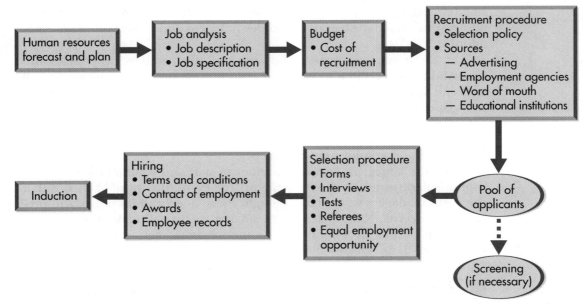

■ Figure 6.4 *The recruitment, selection and induction process for paid and voluntary employees*
(**Source:** *Based on Clark 1992.*)

- *writing sponsorship agreements* in a way that requires the sponsor, as part of their agreement with the event, to provide temporary workers with particular skills, such as marketing staff
- *identifying and liaising with potential sources of volunteers/casual staff*, including universities and colleges (projects and work placements/internships may be specially created for these groups, particularly if they are studying festival, exhibition and event management or a related area such as film), job centres, religious groups, service clubs (such as Lions and Rotary), community service programs, senior citizen centres and retirement homes, chambers of commerce, and community centres. The International Festival and Events Association maintains an internship 'bank' on its website (www.ifea.com/education/intern.asp).
- *determining the make-up* (for example, age, sex, occupations) and motivations of existing volunteers, and using this information as the basis of further targeted recruitment
- *gaining the assistance of local and specialist media* (for example, radio, television, newspapers, specialist magazines) in communicating the event's human resource needs. This process is greatly assisted if one or more media organisations are in some way (such as through sponsorship) associated with the event.
- *targeting specific individuals within a community who have specialist skills* to sit on boards or undertake specific tasks, such as those tasks associated with the legal and accounting aspects of conducting an event
- *registering with volunteer agencies*. In Australia, these agencies include Volunteering NSW/ACT/South Australia/Queensland/Tasmania.

- *conducting social functions* at which, for example, existing volunteers or staff might be encouraged to bring potential candidates, or to which particular groups/targeted individuals are invited.

Once an appropriate pool of applicants has been identified, the next step is to select from among them those applicants that best fit the identified available positions. It is important to approach this process systematically, employing appropriate tools, to avoid the costs (financial and otherwise) that come from poor selection (increased training time, high turnover of staff/volunteers, absenteeism, job dissatisfaction and poor performance).

A useful starting point in the selection process is the selection policy. This policy should have been developed earlier in the policy and procedures stage of the human resource planning process. In constructing such a policy, thought needs to be given to:

- how the event organisation intends to comply with equal employment opportunity legislation
- approaches to measuring the suitability of candidates — for example, simple rating scales based on set criteria
- sourcing people — for example, will the event organisation promote from within where possible?
- the decision makers — that is, who will have the final decision on who to engage?
- selection techniques — for example, will tests be employed? Will decisions be made after one interview or several?
- the organisation's business objectives — for example, do the candidates selected have the qualities and qualifications to progress the event's objectives?

The application process will vary based on the needs of the position, the number of applications anticipated and the resources of the event organisation. In cases where a large number of applications are anticipated, it may be appropriate to consider screening applicants by telephone by asking a few key questions central to the position's requirements — for example, do you have a qualification in event management? Those individuals who answer these questions appropriately can then be sent an application. In the case of volunteers, applicants for positions in small-scale events may be asked to simply send in a brief note indicating what skills/qualifications they have, any relevant experience and the tasks they would be interested in doing. For larger events, volunteers may be asked to complete a registration form such as that developed by the National Folk Festival in Australia (figure 6.5, page 156).

However basic, application forms for paid employees generally seek information on educational qualifications, previous employment and other details deemed relevant to the position by the applicant. The names and contact details of referees who can supply written and/or verbal references are also normally required. Additionally, a curriculum vitae (CV) is generally appended to these forms. Once received, applications allow unsuitable applicants to be culled; those applicants thought to be suitable for short-listing can be invited to attend an interview. Volunteers may simply be notified that they have been accepted and asked to attend a briefing session.

APPLICATION TO VOLUNTEER 2004

You can mail, fax or email this form to the Festival Office.
Mail to: National Folk Festival, PO Box 156, CIVIC SQUARE, ACT 2608
Fax: (02) 6247 0906 email: volunteer@folkfestival.asn.au

Office Use Only
Master/Vol ID No:_____
1st Pref:_____

National Folk Festival

Applications are accepted from December 2003 until positions fill. The majority of positions will be filled by 27 February 2004 and volunteers notified of their rosters by 12 March 2004. You officially become a volunteer once you have been ROSTERED.

TELL US ABOUT YOU: (in confidence)

Surname: _____
First Name: _____ Title:_____
Date of birth: ____/____/____ Age:_____ Gender: ☐ Female ☐ Male

Please complete all details legibly. If you are a veteran volunteer, we need to check our records against this form for changes. Please make sure our records are correct by filling in all details.

Address: _____
Suburb/Town: _____ State: _____ Postcode: _____
Phone: (h) _____ (w) _____ (m) _____
Email: _____
Emergency Contact: _____ Phone: _____
Special Requirements (eg. wheelchair access): _____

WHEN ARE YOU AVAILABLE? (Please circle the APRIL 2004 dates you plan to be available to us)

☐ SETUP   ☐ FESTIVA

| Mon 5th | Tue 6th | Wed 7th | Thu 8th | Fri 9th | Sat 10th | S 11 |

FOR NEW VOLUNTEERS TO THE FESTIVAL:
SKILLS:
Do you have any of the following skills/experience/qualifications

☐ Current First Aid Certificate
☐ Childcare
☐ Cash Handling
☐ Customer Service
☐ Basic Admin
☐ Telephone Skills
☐ Marketing
☐ Management & Team Supervision Skills
☐ Computing:
  ☐ - Database
  ☐ - Web page
  ☐ - Desktop Publish-

ing
☐ Art/Craft Skills
☐ SecurityTraining/Expe
☐ Trade Qualifications
  ☐ - Carpen
  ☐ - Joiner
  ☐ - Electric
  ☐ - Welder
  ☐ - Plumbe
☐ Handyman Skills
☐ Ticketed Plant Oper
☐ Bus/Truck/Forklift Li
☐ Sound Systems
☐ Training

Comments: _____

Please complete pag

FOR RETURN (VETERAN) VOLUNTEERS:
Skills: Have you added any skills, qualifications or licences that could help?

☐ Current First Aid Certificate   Please specify:_____
☐ Security Licence/Experience   _____
☐ Trade Qualifications   _____

VOLUNTEERING HISTORY
Which years? ☐1993 ☐1994 ☐1995 ☐1996 ☐1997 ☐1998 ☐1999 ☐2000 ☐2001 ☐2002 ☐2003
Previous work areas:__ _____
Area you worked in 2003: _____ Request same team this year? ☐ Yes ☐ No
If NO, any particular reason?_____

WHAT YOU'D LIKE TO DO
Please nominate ONLY three preferences in order (1,2,3) ..from below
DURING FESTIVAL (Thursday night 8 April through to Monday 12 April):

1. Service Teams
__ Guinness Bar
__ Session Bar
__ Wine Bar
__ Bar Cashier
__ Childcare
__ Data Entry
__ Festival Office
__ Mural/Art Activities
__ Shop
__ Surveys
__ Ticket Office
__ Treasury

2. Volunteer Teams
__ Volunteer Centre
__ Volunteer Healing
__ Volunteer Kitchen
__ Volunteer Reception
__ Volunteer Reserve
3. Site Teams
__ Camping/Gates
__ Communications
__ Firewood
__ Lost Property
__ Mug Jugglers
__ On-site Minibus Drivers

__ Parking
__ Site Decoration
__ Site Stewards (Security)
__ Stores
__ Waste & Recycling
4. Performer Teams
__ Blackboard Crews
__ Instrument Lockup
__ Kids Festival
__ Performer Reception
__ Performer Transport
__ Stage Management

BEFORE FESTIVAL:
__ Bar Setup
__ Camping/Gates
__ Construction
__ Construction Cook

__ Masterclass Assistant
__ Setup Office
__ Setup General
__ Stores/Tool Town

AFTER FESTIVAL:
__ Cleanup
__ Deconstruction
__ Office Packdown /Move
__ Stores/Tool Town

CORE VOLUNTEERS

The festival places trust in around 900 volunteers turning up as agreed and working their rostered 16 hours over the festival to make all areas work smoothly.

Do you wish to be considered for Core Volunteer Work? ☐Yes ☐No

Conditions of becoming a Core Volunteer.

I agree to abide by the Code of Conduct and to complete 16 hours of volunteer work DURING the 2003 Festival, as rostered. (This does not include training sessions in the lead up to the festival). In exchange I will receive a free season pass to the Festival, including camping, and access to volunteer facilities and benefits such as subsidised meals from the volunteer kitchen.

I understand that if I do not fulfil my part of the agreement (ie. collect my free pass but do not turn up to work my allocated shifts) I will be billed for a season ticket to the Festival. In the event of accident, misadventure or illness I will contact the Festival as early as circumstances allow so that a replacement may be found.

If offered a Core Volunteer position, I agree to abide by the above conditions.

Signed: _____ Date: ____/____/____

■ **Figure 6.5** *National Folk Festival volunteer registration form*
(**Source:** *National Folk Festival 2004.*)

When selecting among applicants, Robertson and Makin (1986) (cited in Beardwell & Holden 2001) suggest taking into account the following factors:

- The use of *past behaviour* can be employed to predict future behaviour. That is, the manner in which a person completed a task in the past is the best predictor of the way that person will complete a task in the future. Biographical data (obtained from the curriculum vitae or application form), references and supervisor/peer group ratings are commonly the major sources of such information.
- A range of techniques can be used to assess *present behaviour*, including:
  - tests, which may be designed to measure aptitude, intelligence, personality and basic core skill levels (for example, typing speeds)
  - interviews (see later discussion)
  - assessment centres, which conduct a series of tests, exercises and feedback sessions over a one- to five-day period to assess individual strengths and weakness
  - portfolios/examples of work, which are used to indicate the quality/ type of recent job-related outputs. An applicant for the position of a set designer for a theatrical event, for example, may be asked to supply photographs of his or her previous work.
- If appropriate, interview information can be supplemented with observations from simulations to predict *future behaviour*. If the position is for a sponsorship manager, for example, applicants can be asked to develop a sponsorship proposal and demonstrate how they would present this proposal to a potential sponsor. Another common approach, according to Noe et al. (2002), is to ask managerial applicants to respond to memos that typify problems they are likely to encounter.

Interviews are likely to be the most common means of selection used by event organisations, so it is worthwhile spending some time looking at how best to employ this approach.

Interviews

According to Noe et al. (2002), research clearly indicates that the interviewing process should be undertaken using a structured approach so all relevant information can be covered and candidates can be directly compared. Mullins (1999) suggests using a checklist of key matters to be covered in the interviews. A sample checklist for a paid position associated with an event is shown in figure 6.6 (page 158). Checklists should also be used if interviews are to be conducted for volunteers. Answers might be sought to questions regarding the relationship between the volunteer's background/experience and the position(s) sought, reasons for seeking to become involved with the event, the level of understanding about the demands/requirements of the position(s) (such as time and training), and whether applicants have a physical or medical condition that may have an impact on the types of position for which they can be considered (keeping equal employment opportunity legislation in mind).

Applicant responses flowing from the interview process need to be assessed in some way against the key criteria for the position. One common means of doing this is a rating scale (for example, 1 to 5). When viewed collectively, the ratings given to individual items lead to an overall assessment of the applicant in terms of how he or she fits with the job, the event organisation and its future directions.

Interviews may be conducted on a one-on-one basis or via a panel of two or more interviewers. The latter has some advantages in that it assists in overcoming any idiosyncratic biases that individual interviewers might have, allows all interviewers to evaluate the applicant at the same time and on the same questions and answers, and facilitates the discussion of the pros and cons of individual applicants.

INTERVIEWER'S CHECKLIST

Position title: _____ Candidate's name: _____ Date: _____

Interviewees: _____

Interview
1. Qualifications held
2. Employment history
3. Extent to which applicant meets essential criteria for the position
4. Extent to which applicant meets desirable criteria for the position
5. Organisational fit
    (a) To what extent will the position result in personal satisfaction for the applicant?
    (b) To what extent does the applicant identify with the organisation's values and culture?
    (c) Can the applicant's remuneration expectations be met?

Assessment
Summary rating of applicant based on the above criteria. A simple scale of 'all, most, some, none' may be used for criteria 3 and 4. Additionally, some relevant summary comments may be made on each applicant.

Action
Follow-up action to be taken with applicant — for example:
■ Advise if successful/unsuccessful.
■ Place on eligibility list.
■ Check references.
■ Arrange pre-employment medical check.

■ **Figure 6.6** *Sample interviewer's checklist*

Once the preferred applicant has been identified, the next step is to make a formal offer of appointment, by mail or otherwise. In the case of paid event staff, the short-term nature of many events means any offer of employment is for a specific contracted period. The employment contract generally states what activities are to be performed, salary/wage levels, and the rights and obligations of the employer and employee (figure 6.7, page 159). In the case of volunteers, a simple letter of appointment, accompanied by details regarding the position may be all that is necessary. It is also appropriate to consider supplying volunteers with a statement about their rights and those of the event organisation regarding their involvement in the event (figure 6.8, page 159). Once an offer has been made and accepted, unsuccessful applicants should be informed as soon as possible.

■ Figure 6.7
General components of an employment contract

- A statement of job titles and duties
- The date of employment commencement
- Rate of pay, allowances, overtime, method and timing of payment
- Hours of work including breaks
- Holiday arrangements/entitlement
- Sickness procedure (including sick pay, notification of illness)
- Length of notice due to and from the employee
- Grievance procedure
- Disciplinary procedure
- Work rules
- Arrangements for terminating employment
- Arrangements for union membership (if applicable)
- Special terms relating to confidentiality, rights to patents and designs, exclusivity of service, and restrictions on trade after termination of employment (for example, cannot work for a direct competitor within six months)
- Employer's right to vary terms and conditions subject to proper notification

■ Figure 6.8
Rights and responsibilities of volunteers and voluntary organisations

Both the volunteer and the organisation have responsibilities to each other. The volunteer contracts to perform a specific job and the organisation contracts to provide the volunteer with a worthwhile and rewarding experience. In return, each has the right to some basic expectations of the other.

Volunteers have the right to:
- be treated as co-workers. This includes job descriptions, equal employment opportunity, occupational health and safety, anti-discrimination legislation and organisational grievance processes.
- be asked for their permission before any job-related reference, police or prohibited person checks are conducted
- a task or job worthwhile to them, for no more than 16 hours a week on a regular basis
- know the purpose and 'ground rules' of the organisation
- appropriate orientation and training for the job
- be kept informed of organisation changes and the reasons for such changes
- a place to work and suitable tools
- reimbursement of agreed expenses
- be heard and make suggestions
- personal accident insurance in place of workers compensation insurance
- a verbal reference or statement of service, if appropriate.

Organisations have the right to:
- receive as much effort and service from a volunteer worker as a paid worker, even on a short-term basis
- select the best volunteer for the job by interviewing and screening all applicants. This might include reference and police checks and, where appropriate, prohibited person checks for roles that involve working directly with children.
- expect volunteers to adhere to their job descriptions/outlines and the organisation's code of practice
- expect volunteers to undertake training provided for them and observe safety rules
- make the decision regarding the best placement of a volunteer
- express opinions about poor volunteer effort in a diplomatic way
- expect loyalty to the organisation and only constructive criticism
- expect clear and open communication from the volunteer
- negotiate work assignments
- release volunteers under certain circumstances.

(**Source:** *School of Volunteer Management 2001.*)

Induction

Once appointees (paid or voluntary) commence with an event organisation, a structured induction program designed to begin the process of 'bonding' the individual to the event organisation needs to be conducted. Getz (1997, p. 189) suggests a range of actions be taken as part of an effective induction program:

- Provide basic information about the event (mission, objectives, stakeholders, budget, locations, program details).
- Conduct tours of venues, suppliers, offices and any other relevant locations.
- Make introductions to other staff and volunteers.
- Give an introduction to the organisational culture, history and working arrangements.
- Overview training programs.

In addition to these actions, it is sound practice to discuss the job description with the individual to ensure he or she has a clear understanding of matters such as responsibilities, performance expectations, approaches to performance evaluation, and reporting relationships. At this time other matters associated with the terms and conditions of employment should also be discussed/reiterated, including probationary periods, grievance procedures, absenteeism, sickness, dress code, security, holiday/leave benefits, superannuation, salary and overtime rates, and other benefits such as car parking and meals. One means of ensuring mutual understanding of these matters is to have the staff member/volunteer read and sign their position description. Figure 6.9 gives an example of a position description that could be used for this purpose for volunteers.

The induction process can also be facilitated by the development of an induction kit for distribution to each new staff member or volunteer. Such a kit might contain:

- an annual report
- a message from the organising committee chairperson/chief executive officer welcoming staff and volunteers
- a statement of event mission/vision, goals and objectives
- an organisational chart
- a name badge
- a staff list (including contact details)
- a uniform (whether a T-shirt or something more formal)
- a list of sponsors
- a list of stakeholders
- any other appropriate items — for example, occupational, health and safety information.

A central outcome of the induction process should be a group of volunteers and staff who are committed to the event, enthusiastic and knowledgeable about their role in it, and aware of what part their job plays in the totality of the event.

■ **Figure 6.9**
*Example
of a job
description
and contract
for a
volunteer*

Job title: _____

Supervisor: _____

Location: _____

Objective (Why is this job necessary? What will it accomplish?):

_____

Responsibilities (What specifically will the volunteer do?):

_____

Qualifications (What special skills, education, or age group is necessary to do this job?): _____

Training provided: _____

Benefits (parking, transportation, uniforms, food and beverage, expenses):

_____

Trial period (probation, if required): _____

References required (yes or no): _____

Any other information: _____

Date: _____

Signature of volunteer (to be added at time of mutual agreement):

_____

Signature of supervisor: _____

(**Source:** *Bradner 1997, p. 75.*)

■ Training *and professional development*

According to Stone (1998), training and professional development are both concerned with changing the behaviour and job performance of staff and volunteers. Training focuses on providing specific job skills/knowledge that will allow people to perform a job or to improve their performance in it. Professional development, on the other hand, is concerned with the acquisition of new skills, knowledge and attitudes that will prepare individuals for future job responsibilities.

Both training and professional development are significant in driving the success of an event, acting to underpin its effective delivery. For small and mid-sized events, much training is on-the-job, with existing staff and experienced volunteers acting as advice givers. This approach, while cheap and largely effective, has limitations. The major one is that it is not often preceded by an assessment of the event's precise training needs and how best to meet them within resource limitations.

A formal approach to training needs assessment serves to determine whether training taking place is adequate and whether any training needs are not being met. Additionally, such an assessment generates suggestions about how to improve training provided by the event. These suggestions might include those noted on page 162.

- Sending, or requesting stakeholder/government support to send, staff/volunteers on training programs dealing with specific areas or identified training needs (for example, risk management, event marketing and sponsorship)
- Identifying individuals associated with the event who would be willing to volunteer to conduct training sessions
- Commissioning consultants/external bodies to undertake specific training
- Encouraging staff/volunteers to undertake event-specific training programs (now provided by some public and private colleges, universities and event industry associations) in return for certain benefits (for example, higher salaries, appointment to positions of greater responsibility/satisfaction)

When trying to identify what training is required to facilitate the effective delivery of an event, the central consideration is to determine the gap between the current performance of staff and volunteers and their desired performance. This can be achieved by:

- performance appraisals of existing staff/volunteers (what training staff identify as being required to make them more effective)
- analysis of job requirements (what skills the job description identifies)
- survey of personnel (what skills staff state they need).

■ Figure 6.10
Training program offered by the Australia Centre for Event Management, University of Technology, Sydney

EXECUTIVE CERTIFICATE IN EVENT MANAGEMENT

This course may be conducted in-house and/or customised to your requirements.

Recent years have seen the emergence of a vibrant Australian events industry. This large and growing industry creates significant demand for professionals trained in the management of events. This course provides a strong basis for the overall management of events, both public (for example, festivals, parades, celebrations, sporting events) and corporate (for example, exhibitions, product launches, private functions).

The course comprises two parts: event management and marketing (three days) and event operations (four days). Tutorials and assignment work is carried out between these two sessions, with ongoing support from presenters. Guest presenters from industry add to the practical edge this course provides.

You gain
- a comprehensive range of skills and practical tools, encompassing all aspects of event management and operations
- graded certificate
- excellent networking opportunities with industry participants and past graduates.

(**Source:** *University of Technology, Sydney 2004.*)

■ Supervision *and evaluation*

As a general rule, the bigger and more complex the event, the greater the need is for staff/volunteers to perform a supervisory function. This function may be exercised through a variety of means, including having would-be supervisors understudy an existing supervisor, developing a mentoring system or encouraging staff to undertake appropriate professional development programs.

One of the key tasks of supervisors and managers is that of performance appraisal. This task involves evaluating performance, communicating that evaluation and establishing a plan for improvement. The ultimate outcomes of this process are a better event and more competent staff and volunteers. Stone (2002) proposes a dynamic performance appraisal program (figure 6.11) based on goal establishment, performance feedback and performance improvement.

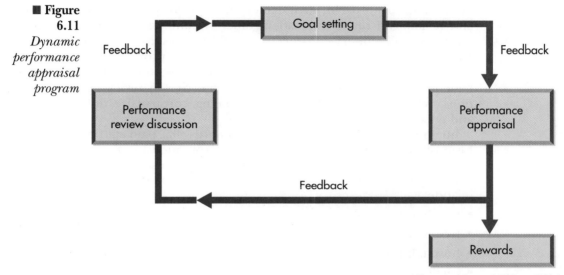

■ **Figure 6.11**
Dynamic performance appraisal program

(**Source:** *Stone 2002, p. 291.*)

According to Stone (2002), goals should be mutually arrived at by a supervisor and a volunteer or staff member. These goals, while specific to the particular job, are likely to relate to matters such as technical skills and knowledge, problem solving/creativity, planning and organising, interpersonal skills, decision making, commitment to quality and safety, the achievement of designated results, attitudes and personality traits, reliability/punctuality, and professional development. It is important that measurements of progress towards goals are established, otherwise there is little point in setting goals in the first place. A person charged with overseeing waste management for an event, for example, may be assessed in terms of the percentage of material recycled from the event, levels of contamination in waste, the percentage of attendees (as determined by survey) that understood directions regarding the placement of waste in containers, and the level of complaints regarding matters such as full bins. Other areas for assessment might include those associated with personal development (enrolment and completion of a specific course), interpersonal relationships (opinions of supervisors/co-workers) and problem solving/creativity (approaches employed to respond to the unexpected).

Performance, in terms of progress towards the established goals, can be assessed in a variety of ways, including performance scales. According to Wood et al. (2001), irrespective of what assessment measures are used, responses to the following questions must underpin any efforts in this area: what does the job require? What does the employee/volunteer need to do to perform effectively in this position? What evidence from how work is undertaken would indicate effective performance? What does the assessment of evidence of performance indicate about future actions required?

Once an appraisal has been conducted, there should be a follow-up review discussion in which the supervisor/manager and the staff member/volunteer mutually review job responsibilities, examine how these responsibilities have been performed, explore how performance can be improved, and review and revise the staff members/volunteers short-term and long-term goals. The interview process should be a positive experience for both parties. To this end, it is worthwhile considering providing training to the managers/supervisors involved in this process so they adhere to certain basic practices such as preparing for the interview by reviewing job descriptions, reviewing previous assessments, being constructive not destructive, and encouraging discussion.

Integral to the appraisal system are rewards that paid staff receive in the form of salaries, bonuses, profit sharing, promotion to other jobs or other events, and benefits such as cars and equipment use (for example, laptop computers). Options also exist to reward volunteers for their efforts. These include:

- training in new skills
- free merchandise (for example, clothing, badges, event posters)
- hospitality in the form of opening and closing parties, free meals/drinks
- certificates of appreciation
- opportunities to meet with celebrities, sporting stars and other VIPs
- promotion to more interesting volunteer positions
- public acknowledgement through the media and at the event
- free tickets to the event.

The 'flip side' to rewards — that is, discipline — also requires managerial consideration. It is useful to have in place specific policies and practices that reflect the seriousness of different behaviour/actions, and these should be communicated to all staff (paid and voluntary). These policies and practices are likely to begin with some form of admonishment and end with dismissal. Many of the approaches to disciplining paid employees (such as removing access to overtime) are not applicable to volunteers. Instead, approaches that may be applied to volunteers include re-assignment, withholding of rewards/benefits and suspension from holding a position as a volunteer.

■ Termination, *outplacement and re-enlistment*

Whether employing staff on contract or as permanent employees, event managers are occasionally faced with the need to terminate the services of an individual. This action may be necessary in instances where an employee breaches the employment contract (for example, repeatedly arriving at the workplace intoxicated) or continually exhibits unsatisfactory performance. This need may also arise when economic or commercial circumstances of the organisation conducting the event require it to shed staff (such as when there is insufficient revenue due to poor ticket sales).

Various legal issues surrounding termination need to be understood by those involved in event management. In Australia, these issues relate to unfair or unlawful dismissal, and are spelt out in the *Workplace Relations Act 1996* (Cwlth). Essentially, employers are required to give employees an opportunity to defend themselves against allegations associated with their conduct; in cases of unsatisfactory performance, they must warn and counsel the employee before terminating his or her service. These requirements do not apply to contracted or casual employees, or to staff on probation. A need can also arise to dismiss volunteers; for this purpose, Getz (1997) suggests a variety of approaches. These include making all volunteer appointments for fixed terms (with volunteers needing to re-apply and be subjected to screening each time the event is conducted) and using job descriptions and performance appraisals to underpin appropriate action.

Outplacement is the process of assisting terminated employees (or indeed volunteers), or even those who choose to leave the event organisation voluntarily, to find other employment. By performing this function the event organisation is providing a benefit to employees for past service, as well as maintaining and enhancing its image as a responsible employer. In the case of an event organising company that decides to downsize, as many did after the 2000 Sydney Olympic Games, this process could lead to staff being aided to take up positions with, for example, corporations operating their own event divisions or large events that maintain a full-time staff year round. Even volunteers who are no longer needed can be helped into other positions by being put in contact with volunteer agencies or other events.

With recurring events, such as annual festivals, opportunities often exist to re-enlist for paid or voluntary positions. Many staff from the Sydney Olympic Games, for example, took up positions within the organisation responsible for the Athens Olympics. To maintain contact with potential volunteers and past staff between events, a variety of approaches can be employed, including newsletters (see, for example, the National Folk Festival website, www.folkfestival.asn.au/Pages/volunteers.html), social events, the offer of benefits for re-enlistment, and personal contact by telephone between events.

Event managers should also keep in mind that staff will often leave of their own accord. The involvement of such staff in exit interviews can provide valuable information that could be used to finetune one or more aspects of an event's human resource management process. A study of volunteers at a jazz festival (Elstad 2003), for example, found the main reasons (in order) that volunteers quit were: (1) their overall workload, (2) a lack of appreciation of their contribution, (3) problems with how the festival was organised, (4) disagreement with changing goals or ideology, (5) wanting more free time for other activities, (6) a lack of a 'sense of community' among volunteers, (7) family responsibilities, (8) the festival becoming too large, (9) the inability to make decisions regarding their own position, (10) a dislike for some of their responsibilities, (11) lack of remuneration and (12) moving out of the festival's geographic area.

■ Evaluation *of process and outcomes*

As with all management processes, a periodic review is necessary to determine how well, or otherwise, the process is working. To conduct such a review, it is necessary to obtain feedback from relevant supervisory/management staff, organising committee members, and paid and voluntary staff. The California Traditional Music Society, for example, uses a questionnaire to obtain feedback from volunteers (figure 6.12). A specific time should then be set aside, perhaps as part of a larger review of the event, to examine the extent to which the human resources management process as a whole (and its various elements) achieved the original objectives. Once the review is complete, revisions can be made to the process for subsequent events.

MOTIVATING STAFF AND VOLUNTEERS

Motivation is a key, if implicit, component of the human resource management process. It is what commits people to a course of action, enthuses and energises them, and enables them to achieve goals, whether the goals are their own or their organisation's. The ability to motivate other staff members is a fundamental component of the event manager's repertoire of skills. Without appropriate motivation, paid employees and volunteers can lack enthusiasm for achieving the event's corporate goals and delivering quality service, or can show a lack of concern for the welfare of their co-workers or event participants.

In the context of volunteers, pure altruism (an unselfish regard for, or devotion to, the welfare of others) may be an important motive for seeking to assist in the delivery of events. Although this proposition is supported by Flashman and Quick (1985), the great bulk of work done on motivation stresses that people, while they may assert they are acting for altruistic reasons, are actually motivated by a combination of external and internal factors, most of which have little to do with altruism. As Moore (1985, p. 1) points out, 'volunteers clearly expect to obtain some reward for their participation and performance'.

Researchers from a variety of disciplines have done much work over many years on what motivates people, particularly in the workplace. Perhaps the most relevant and useful of these studies within the context of festivals and events are content theories and process theories.

Name: _____   Job: _____

CTMS VOLUNTEER SURVEY — 2003

As in past years, we ask that you help by responding to these questions about your volunteer duties, so that we can continue to improve your entire volunteer experience. Please fill out this questionnaire and mail it back to CTMS in the return envelope provided. If you have any further comments or suggestions, please feel free to write or type your comments separately. Thanks again, and we look forward to seeing you again next year!

The Volunteer Coordination Committee

What shift(s) did you work?

Did you clearly understand, before the festival, what you were supposed to do, what **time** you were expected to work, and **where** you were going to work?

Was the printed training information you received at the training meetings thorough and complete? What would you change or add to it?

Do you think there were enough volunteers assigned to your job? Were you kept so busy that you could not do your job properly?

Do you think there were too many volunteers assigned to the same job as you were? Were you bored?

Was your job too difficult or strenuous for you in any way? Please explain.

Was there an extremely busy time during your shift? When was it? Do you feel you needed more help during this time?

Was there an extremely quiet time during your shift? When was it?

Did you run into any difficulties or situations that you didn't expect or didn't know how to handle? What were they? What did you do?

Is there anything you think CTMS should have provided or advised you to bring with you that would have made your job easier, more comfortable, or more efficient?

Were you able to get away during your shift to use a restroom if you needed one? If you were alone at your position, did someone come around and offer to relieve you temporarily so you could use a restroom?

Were there any problems that you were aware of that need correction for next year?

Would you volunteer for next year? If not, why not?

Thank you very much for completing and returning this questionnaire. Please write any comments specific to your volunteer job on a sheet of paper. Please write any other comments relative to the festival in general on a separate sheet of paper. Return both to CTMS, 4401 Trancas Place, Tarzana, CA 91356-5399.

(**Source:** *California Traditional Music Society 2003.*)

■ Content *theories*

Content theories concentrate on what things initially motivate people to act in a certain way. As Mullins (1999, p. 415) points out, they 'are concerned with identifying people's needs and their relative strengths, and the goals they pursue in order to satisfy these needs'. Figure 6.13 represents the essential nature of theories of this type.

■ **Figure 6.13**
The basis of content theories of motivation

(**Source:** *Peach and Murrell 1995.)*

Content theories assert that a person has a need — a feeling of deprivation — which then drives the person towards an action that can satisfy that need. Maslow's (1954) hierarchy of needs, illustrated in figure 6.14 (page 169), popularised the idea that needs are the basis of motivation.

In essence, Maslow's theory proposes that lower order needs must be satisfied before people are motivated to satisfy the next, higher need. That is, people who are trying to satisfy physiological needs of hunger and thirst have no interest in satisfying the need for safety until their physiological needs are satisfied. The first three needs are perceived as deficiencies; they must be satisfied to fulfil a lack of something. In contrast, satisfaction of the two higher needs is necessary for an individual to grow emotionally and psychologically.

Although little empirical evidence exists to support Maslow's theory, it can give insights into the needs people may be seeking to fulfil through employment. Some research, for example, indicates a tendency for higher level needs to dominate as individuals move up the managerial hierarchy.

Another researcher who falls within the ambit of content theory is Hertzberg (1968). He argues that some elements, which he calls hygiene factors, do not of themselves motivate or satisfy people. Among these factors are pay levels, policies and procedures, working conditions and job security. However, the absence or perceived reduction in these items can stimulate hostility or dissatisfaction towards an organisation. Hertzberg further argues that other factors, which he calls motivators, of themselves lead to goal-directed behaviour. These elements include achievement, recognition and interesting work. Hertzberg's theory is illustrated in figure 6.15.

■ Figure 6.14
Maslow's hierarchy of needs

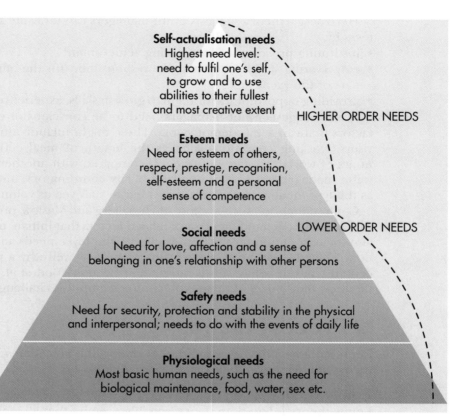

Self-actualisation needs
Highest need level:
need to fulfil one's self,
to grow and to use
abilities to their fullest
and most creative extent

HIGHER ORDER NEEDS

Esteem needs
Need for esteem of others,
respect, prestige, recognition,
self-esteem and a personal
sense of competence

LOWER ORDER NEEDS

Social needs
Need for love, affection and a sense of
belonging in one's relationship with other persons

Safety needs
Need for security, protection and stability in the physical
and interpersonal; needs to do with the events of daily life

Physiological needs
Most basic human needs, such as the need for
biological maintenance, food, water, sex etc.

(**Source:** *Wood et al. 2004.*)

■ Figure 6.15
Hertzberg's two-factor theory of motivation

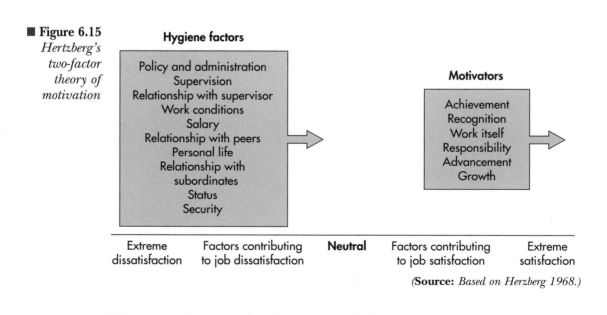

Hygiene factors

Policy and administration
Supervision
Relationship with supervisor
Work conditions
Salary
Relationship with peers
Personal life
Relationship with
subordinates
Status
Security

Motivators

Achievement
Recognition
Work itself
Responsibility
Advancement
Growth

| Extreme dissatisfaction | Factors contributing to job dissatisfaction | **Neutral** | Factors contributing to job satisfaction | Extreme satisfaction |

(**Source:** *Based on Herzberg 1968.*)

Hertzberg's theory suggests event managers can motivate staff and volunteers by:

- instituting processes of recognising achievement
- empowering staff so they can take responsibility for the outcomes of their part of the event
- providing opportunities for them to grow in skills, experience and expertise.

It also suggests event managers need to be conscious of certain hygiene factors that can act as demotivators. These might include attitudes of supervisors, working conditions such as the length of meal/coffee breaks and hours of work, the status of one job compared with another (for example, waste management officer versus publicity coordinator), and policies such as the type/quality of uniforms provided to staff versus volunteers.

Content theories, such as those of Hertzberg and Maslow, provide managers with some understanding of work-related factors that initiate motivation; they also focus attention on the importance of employee needs and their satisfaction. They do not, however, explain particularly well why a person chooses certain types of behaviour to satisfy their needs (Wood et al. 2004). Process theories, the subject of the next section, take up this challenge.

■ Process *theories*

Representative of process theories of motivation are Adams's (1965) equity theory and Vroom's (1964) expectancy theory.

Equity theory

Equity theory is based on the reasonable premise that all employees (or, for that matter, volunteers) expect to be treated fairly. This being the case, if one employee or volunteer perceives a discrepancy in the outcomes that he or she receives (for example, pay or type of work allocated) compared with those of other employees or volunteers, that employee or volunteer will be motivated to do more (or less) work (Wood et al. 2004). This situation is represented in the equation below:

$$\frac{\text{Individual rewards}}{\text{Individual inputs}} \quad \overset{comparison}{\longleftrightarrow} \quad \frac{\text{Others' rewards}}{\text{Others' inputs}}$$

What an employee or volunteer perceives as fair in terms of compensation (monetary or non-monetary) is subjective. The best way of maintaining an awareness of what an individual is thinking in this regard is to develop and maintain open lines of communication. If inequity is perceived and goes unnoticed, a number of outcomes are possible, including:

- a reduction in effort
- pressure to increase remuneration
- exit from the organisation.

Expectancy theory

Expectancy theory holds that an individual's motivation to act in a particular way comes from a belief that a particular outcome will result from doing something (expectancy). This outcome will result in a reward (instrumentality). The rewards for accomplishing this outcome are sufficient to justify the effort put into doing it (valence). Motivation, under this theory, can therefore be expressed as:

$$\text{Motivation} = \text{Expectancy} \times \text{Instrumentality} \times \text{Valence}.$$

This being the case, whenever one of the elements in this equation approaches zero, the motivational value of a particular decision is dramatically reduced. Event managers need to be aware of this and, therefore, try to maximise all three motivational components. In other words, there must be a clear payoff if employees and volunteers are to perform at a high level. To understand what this payoff needs to be for each staff member and volunteer is difficult; however, the chances of doing so are greatly increased if lines of communication are kept open and if a genuine effort is made to understand each individual.

As an example of how expectancy theory works, take the situation of people who decide to work on their local community festival. They may have certain expectations:

- an *expectation* that by working on the event they will gain certain new skills
- an *expectation* that these new skills in turn will enhance their future employability, thus creating an *instrumentality*
- an *expectation* that the jobs for which they will be able to apply with these new skills are ones that they would find extremely rewarding, adding a strong degree of *value* to the circumstances.

If all three factors are strongly positive, then motivation will be high. It is from this theoretical framework that Peach and Murrell (1995, pp. 238–9) derive their reward and recognition techniques, which are shown in figure 6.16.

■ **Figure 6.16**
Reward and recognition techniques

REWARD SYSTEMS THAT WORK	RECOGNITION TECHNIQUES
Rewards that integrate the needs of the individual and the organisation in a win–win understanding	Carefully constructed systems that are built on the motives and needs of volunteers — individualised need recognition for each person
Rewards based on deep appreciation of the individual as a unique person	Recognition integrated into task performance, where clear performance objectives are established
Rewards based on job content, not conditions — rewards intrinsic to the job work best	Corporate growth and development objectives that become opportunities for recognition
Assignment of tasks that can be performed effectively, leading to intrinsic need satisfaction	Longevity and special contributions recognised frequently, not just every 10 years
Consistent reward policies that build a sense of trust that effort will receive the proper reward	Recognition grounded deeply on the core values of the organisation — what is recognised to help as a role model
Rewards that can be shared by teams so winning is a collective and collaborative experience	

(**Source:** *Peach and Murrell 1995.*)

TECHNIQUES FOR EFFECTIVE STAFF AND VOLUNTEER TEAM BUILDING

As noted at the outset of the chapter, event organisations often come together quickly and exist for short periods. This being the case, one of the greatest challenges faced by an event manager is creating a sense of 'team' with a strong desire to progress the event's objectives. In the context of volunteers, Nancy McDuff (1995, pp. 208–10), an internationally recognised authority on volunteer programs, proposes a 14-element formula for effective team building and maintenance:

1. *Teams are a manageable size.* Most effective teams are between two and 25 people, with the majority fewer than 10.
2. *People are appropriately selected to serve on a team.* Care and attention is paid to selecting people with the right combination of skills, personality, communication styles and ability to perform, thereby improving the chances of the team being successful.
3. *Team leaders are trained.* Leaders who find it difficult to delegate and want to do everything themselves make poor leaders. Try to ensure team leaders have training in supervision skills.
4. *Teams are trained to execute their tasks.* It is unrealistic to expect teams to perform effectively without appropriate training. The training should include the team's role in the activity and how that role contributes to the activity's overall success.
5. *Volunteers and staff are supported by the organisation.* Teams must feel that the administration is there to support their endeavours, not to hinder them.
6. *Teams have objectives.* The purpose of the team is spelt out in measurable objectives. Having a plan to achieve those objectives helps build trust.
7. *Volunteers and staff trust and support one another.* People trust each other when they share positive experiences. When each team is aware of the organisation's objectives and how its role helps to achieve those objectives, it trusts co-workers and supports their efforts.
8. *Communication between volunteers and the event organisation is both vertical and horizontal.* Communication, which means sending 'meanings' and understandings between people, is a process involving an active and continuous use of active listening, the use of feedback to clarify meaning, the reading of body language, and the use of symbols that communicate meaning. Communication travels in all directions — up and down the reporting line, and between teams and work groups. Working together is facilitated by good communication.
9. *The organisational structure promotes communication between volunteers and staff.* The organisation's structure, policies and operating programs permit and encourage all members of the organisation to communicate with their co-workers, their managers and members of other

departments. This help builds an atmosphere of cooperation and harmony in the pursuit of common objectives.

10. *Volunteers and staff have real responsibility.* A currently fashionable concept of management is 'empowerment'. This means giving staff authority to make decisions about their work and its outcomes. Let us look at the example of a group of volunteers having the somewhat mundane task of making sandwiches. If they are empowered with the authority to decide what sandwiches to make, how to make them and where to sell them, their enthusiasm for the task will probably be enhanced and there will be a corresponding improvement in outcomes.

11. *Volunteers and staff have fun while accomplishing tasks.* Managers should strive to engender an atmosphere of humour, fun and affection among co-workers within the culture of the organisation. Such actions as ceremonies to acknowledge exemplary contributions to the event, wrap-up parties and load-in celebrations can facilitate this atmosphere.

12. *There is recognition of the contributions of volunteers and staff.* Paid staff should express formal and informal appreciation of the work of volunteers, and volunteers should publicly recognise and appreciate the work of the paid staff. This mutual appreciation should be consistent, public and visible.

13. *Volunteers and staff celebrate their success.* Spontaneous celebrations with food, drink, friendship and frivolity should be encouraged by management of the event, to celebrate achievement of objectives. The event manager should allocate a budgeted amount for these occasions.

14. *The entire organisation promotes and encourages the wellbeing of volunteer teams.* Everyone in the organisation sees himself or herself as part of a partnership and actively promotes such relationships.

Once teams are in place and operating effectively, the event manager should monitor their performance and productivity by observing their activities and maintaining appropriate communication with team leaders and members. If deficiencies are noticed during the monitoring procedure, then appropriate action can be taken in terms of training, team structure changes or the refinement of operating procedures in a climate of mutual trust.

*L*EGAL OBLIGATIONS

Event managers need to be mindful of laws and statutes that have an impact on the employee and employer relationship, some of which have previously been noted in this chapter. Areas covered by these laws and statutes include occupational health and safety, discrimination, employee dismissal, salaries/wages, and working conditions (for example, holiday and long service leave, superannuation and workers compensation). To obtain current information on these matters in the Australian context, event managers should consider contacting the following organisations:

• Worksafe Australia (for occupational health and safety matters)
• the Human Rights and Equal Opportunity Commission (for discrimination matters)

- the Australian Industrial Relations Commission (for dismissal matters)
- state/territory departments of industrial relations (for matters relating to wages and working conditions).

Event managers should also remember there are common law requirements regarding the duties of parties to an employment relationship. In the context of volunteers, common law precedents provide rights to damages if negligence can be shown on behalf of an event organiser.

$\mathcal{S}$UMMARY

Event managers should approach the task of human resource management not as a series of separate activities but as an integrated process involving a number of steps, taking the event organisation's mission, strategies and goals as their starting points. These steps have been identified in this chapter as: (1) the human resource strategy and objectives; (2) policies and procedures; (3) recruitment; (4) training and professional development; (5) supervision and evaluation; (6) termination, outplacement and re-enlistment; and (7) evaluation and feedback. These steps have application to the employment of both paid and volunteer staff, as well as to events of varying size and type. This chapter has also dealt with the issue of motivation, examining two broad theoretical perspectives on the matter, process and content theories. The final sections of this chapter dealt with mechanisms for developing task teams to conduct events, and with the legal considerations associated with human resource management.

Questions

1. Interview the organiser of an event of your choice and ask him or her what legal/statutory requirements have an impact on human resource management processes and practices.

2. In the context of a specific event, identify the policies and procedures regarding human resource management. Collect examples of forms and other material that support them.

3. Develop a job specification for the position of event manager for a special event of your choice.

4. List the questions that you would ask a candidate during an interview for the position given in question 3.

5. Undertake a job analysis for an event of your choice.

6. Identify all voluntary positions involved in the event examined in question 5. Write brief job descriptions for each position.

7 Propose an induction and training program for the event identified in question 5.

8 Critically review one stage in the human resource management process (as proposed in this chapter) employed by an event of your choice.

9 Discuss general approaches that you might employ to motivate the volunteer staff associated with an event. Which of these approaches would be most appropriate for an event such as the one you examined in question 8?

10 Construct a post-event evaluation questionnaire for volunteers involved in the event identified in question 5.

CASE STUDY ....

Cherry Creek Arts Festival
volunteer program

The Cherry Creek Arts Festival is Colorado's signature cultural event and one of America's most competitive outdoor juried arts festivals. The festival offers the opportunity for visitors to meet and talk with exhibiting artists, sample fine cuisine, visit special exhibits and create their own works of art.

Since its commencement in 1990, the Cherry Creek Arts Festival has made use of the services of more than 12 000 volunteers, who collectively have invested more than 200 000 hours of their time. The success of the festival's volunteer program has resulted from its focus on retention, recruitment, benefits and training, each of which is briefly discussed in this case study.

Retention
The festival encourages volunteers to remain 'connected' to the event throughout the year by involving them in a range of activities associated with preparing for the event, such as mail-outs, the design and implementation of arts and crafts projects, and weekly pre-event administrative and operational activities. A monthly emailed newsletter also updates volunteers on matters of interest, including programming, special announcements, staff changes and important dates. Special offers by event sponsors available only to volunteers are also conveyed via the newsletter.

Volunteers need to see there is room for upward movement in connection with their involvement with the event. To achieve this, the festival ensures each of the 20 committees (all of which are chaired by volunteers) have at least two assistant chairs. Assistant chairs must have at least two years' experience on the committee, and chairs must have had at least one year's experience as an assistant.

To ensure volunteers are effectively managed, a volunteer coordination committee has been created. This committee monitors volunteer food/beverage services, ensures volunteers are in the right place at the right time, and generally seeks to ensure the 600-odd volunteers are looked after.

The current level of volunteer retention is 71 per cent.

Recruitment
While efforts at volunteer retention have been very successful, there is still the need to replace approximately 30 per cent of volunteers each year. A volunteer information and registration form is emailed to a wide variety of businesses, organisations and groups each year. This document also includes testimonials from past volunteers, such as the following from Howard Smartt, a volunteer in 2002.

■ Last year's Arts Festival was a 72-hour high for me. It was a win–win situation where I got to contribute to my community and discover new talents I didn't know I had. I've signed up for this year's event and encourage others to volunteer too because it's so much fun to interact with the artists, visitors and other volunteers. ■

A 'Get involved with art' volunteer recruitment postcard is mailed six weeks before the event. Details regarding the volunteer program are included in the festival's annual newspaper supplement, which is published the weekend before the event. There are also public service announcements on radio and television. Website registration makes the process of becoming involved easier.

Benefits

Benefits do not have to be big and expensive, but they do have to be frequent and sincere. The words 'thank you' cannot be said enough. Beyond words, a volunteer program must provide for all the volunteers' on-site needs. Although this may seem to be a daunting task, it becomes manageable with the partnership of local businesses — for example, in 2003:

- A working relationship was established with Whole Foods to provide 400 meals per day for each of the three event days for the volunteer team. This company also sold meals to event patrons, donating 5 per cent of its total sales on two days of the event to the festival.
- Local business Peaberry Coffee set up a coffee station for volunteers, supplying them with coffee, tea and pastries (morning only) on each day of the event.
- Pasta chain restaurant Noodles & Company sponsored more than 800 meals for volunteers leading up to and after the event.
- Eldorado Springs Natural Water provided bottles of cold water throughout the event, while Pepsi provided a fountain at volunteer 'headquarters' and Coors provided kegs of beer for the post-event 'thank you' party.

In addition to providing for the food and beverage needs of volunteers, the festival offers a discount on all event merchandise and a complimentary T-shirt.

Training

Volunteers are the frontline of the festival, so their performance is a key criterion by which patrons evaluate the festival. Event training is conducted for two groups: new volunteers (two hours) and returning volunteers (one hour). Once their training is completed, volunteers are required to spend time with the committees to which they have been allocated, to familiarise themselves with the committee's role and their respective tasks.

A training handbook for volunteers has been prepared and is distributed to all volunteers (new and returning) when they attend their respective training sessions. This document contains important information, including the telephone numbers and names of committee chairs and key event staff, volunteer parking details, dress requirements, an event map, performance schedules, event rules and regulations, a sponsor listing and tips for making the event fun and safe for patrons.

(continued)

Volunteer committee chairs meet on a monthly basis, beginning six months before the festival. These meetings are designed to allow the 'team' responsible for the event to bond and to become familiar with the full time staff member who will be assisting them.

Recognition

Recognition must be frequent, meaningful and from the heart to maintain and grow a volunteer program. Although T-shirts, food and beverages are nice, they are not enough to keep volunteers coming back year after year. The recognition tools that the festival employs are:

- 'thank you' notes to each volunteer who assists pre-, post- and during the event
- in many of the communications sent out to various stakeholders, formal acknowledgement of the important role performed by volunteers
- gifts of appreciation to volunteer chairs
- a volunteer 'thank you' party at the completion of the event
- a committee chair 'wrap up' dinner two weeks after the event
- publication of a complete listing of volunteer names in a full-page advertisement two weeks after the event.

Results

The results of a volunteer program can be measured in terms of shifts worked, total volunteer hours and wage equivalents. For the 2003 festival, 3692 volunteer shifts (or 23 998 volunteer hours) were worked, equivalent to US$123 589.70 of labour (calculated at minimum wage).

But to really measure the success of a volunteer program, one needs to talk to the volunteers. The following comment from one of the 2003 event volunteers, Myra Keeble, is indicative of many others that were received:

■ Talk about organised! From the moment I clicked on the Volunteer Opportunities field of the Cherry Creek Arts Festival website, to making my final goodbyes to my fellow festival colleagues, I felt like I was involved in a team effort to help create a wonderful festival. The details involved in producing a festival like CCAF are daunting, but the pre-festival volunteer coordination efforts, including team selection, Thursday night work parties, online scheduling, orientation sessions, the publication of a volunteer handbook, and crew leadership communication all helped to make the event run smoothly. My role at the festival was small, but it still felt rewarding and fun. ■

Questions

1 How does the Cherry Creek Arts Festival measure the success of its volunteer program?

2 What role does recognition play in the success of the events volunteer program?

3 Can you suggest any additional means by which the event could improve its already impressive retention statistics?

4 What functions does a volunteer training manual (such as the one discussed in this case) perform?

REFERENCES

Adams, JS 1965, 'Inequity in social exchange', in *Advances in experimental social psychology*, ed. L Berkowitz, Academic Press, New York.

Armstrong, M 1999, *A handbook of human resource management practice*, 7th edn, Kogan Page, London.

Beardwell, I & Holden, L 2001, *Human resource management: a contemporary perspective*, 3rd edn, Pearson Education, London.

Bradner, J 1997, 'Recruitment, orientation, retention', in *The volunteer management handbook*, ed. T Connors, John Wiley & Sons, New York.

California Traditional Music Society 2003, 'CTMS volunteer survey — 2003', www.ctmsfolkmusic.org/pdf/festival/2003/Solstice/Volsurvey.pdf (accessed 27 April 2004).

California Traditional Music Society 2004, 'Festival volunteer job descriptions', www.ctmsfolkmusic.org/volunteer/festival/JobDescriptions.asp (accessed 20 April 2004).

Clark, R 1992, *Australian human resources management*, McGraw Hill, Sydney.

Crompton, R, Morrissey, B & Nankervis, A 2002, *Effective recruitment and selection practices*, 3rd edn, CCH Australia, Sydney.

Elstad, B 2003, 'Continuance commitment and reasons to quit: a study of volunteers at a jazz festival', *Event Management*, vol. 8, pp. 99–108.

Flashman R & Quick, S 1985, 'Altruism is not dead: a specific analysis of volunteer motivation', in *Motivating volunteers*, ed. L Moore, Vancouver Volunteer Centre, Vancouver.

Getz, D 1997, *Event management and event tourism*, Cognizant Communication Corporation, New York.

Hanlon, C & Cuskelly, G 2002, 'Pulsating major sport event organisations: a framework for inducting managerial personnel', *Event Management*, vol. 7, pp. 231–43.

Hanlon, C & Jago, L 2000, 'Pulsating sporting events', *Events beyond 2000 — setting the agenda*, Proceedings of the Conference on Evaluation, Research and Education, eds J Allen, R Harris, LK Jago & AJ Veal, Australian Centre for Event Management, Sydney, pp. 93–104.

Hertzberg, F 1968, 'One more time: how do you motivate employees?', *Harvard Business Review*, vol. 46, no. 1 pp. 361–7.

Maslow, A 1954, *Motivation and personality*, Harper & Row, New York.

McCurley, S & Lynch, R 1998, *Essential volunteer management*, 2nd edn, Directory of Social Change, London.

McDuff, N 1995, 'Episodic volunteering', in *The volunteer management handbook*, ed. T Connors, John Wiley & Sons, New York.

Moore, L 1985, *Motivating volunteers*, Vancouver Volunteer Centre, Vancouver.

Mullins, LJ 1999, *Management and organisational behaviour*, 5th edn, Financial Times/Pitman Publishing, London.

Noe, R, Hollenbeck, J, Gerhart, B & Wright, P 2003, *Resource management*, 4th edn, McGraw Hill, New York.

Peach, E & Murrell, K 1995 'Reward and recognition systems for volunteers', in *The volunteer management handbook*, ed. T Connors, John Wiley & Sons, New York.

School of Volunteer Management 2001, *Rights and responsibilities of volunteers and voluntary organisations*, Pamphlet, Sydney.

Stone, R 2002, *Human resource management*, 4th edn, John Wiley & Sons Australia, Brisbane.

University of Technology Sydney 2004, 'Executive Certificate in Event Management', www.shortcourses.uts.edu.au/code/coursedetails.php?&sc_code=ECEM (accessed 20 April 2004).

Vroom, V 1964, *Work and motivation*, John Wiley & Sons, New York.

Wood, J, Chapman, J, Fromholtz, M, Morrison, V, Wallace, J, Zeffane, R, Schermerhorn, J, Hunt, J & Osborn, R 2004, *Organisational behaviour: a global perspective*, 3rd edn, John Wiley & Sons Australia, Brisbane.

Robyn Stokes

CHAPTER 7

Strategic
marketing of events

LEARNING OBJECTIVES

After studying this chapter, you should be able to:

■ describe how strategic marketing can be applied to festivals and special events

■ understand the consumer decision process for festival and events

■ apply the principles of services marketing in creating strategies for event and festivals

■ plan the event 'service–product' experience, including its programming and packaging

■ develop event pricing strategies or other entry options

■ create strategies for place/distribution, physical setting and event processes that respond to consumer needs

■ establish relationships with event consumers and stakeholders through integrated marketing communication strategies.

INTRODUCTION

This chapter examines a strategic approach to festival and event marketing, and how the event manager carries out all of the marketing activities necessary to achieve the event's objectives, as set out in the strategic plan. To begin, it is useful to explore the concept of marketing as an event management function.

WHAT IS MARKETING?

In simple terms, marketing is concerned with satisfying consumer needs and wants by exchanging goods, services or ideas for something of value. More often, we are not just purchasing products, we are buying experiences (as we do with events and festivals) or adopting new ideas — for example, participation in extreme sports or new theatre forms. We might offer our dollars in exchange for a concert experience, but for some types of marketing exchanges — for example, community festivals — we could simply offer a coin donation.

Kotler, Bowen and Makens (1999, p. 20) suggest that marketing is 'human activity directed at satisfying needs and wants through the exchange process'. In effect, marketing has evolved well beyond early views of the marketing concept (McCarthy & Perreault 1987) as being the meeting of customer needs through decisions about the four Ps — product, place, price and promotion.

While it is agreed that the consumer is the primary focus of marketing, changes over time have dramatically reshaped the marketing function. These include:

- growth in the number and diversity of services (including events) that require different marketing approaches from those for goods
- recognition of the unique marketing requirements of not-for-profit organisations (typical of many festivals)
- the increasing importance of stakeholders — for example, the community, government, investors/sponsors, media and others who can be as influential as consumers can be in affecting the success and survival of an organisation
- advances in technology such as the Internet, the linking of computers with telecommunications, and other innovations that affect the marketing of services, including events
- internationalisation, which has created global opportunities to enter new markets — for example, the touring and staging of events in offshore locations.

As a result of these changes, marketers of events and festivals have the benefit of new knowledge in services marketing, stakeholder and relationship management, and e-marketing to help shape their strategies.

Increasingly, this knowledge helps the event or festival marketer to perform the marketing role defined by Hall (1997, p. 136) as:

> ■ . . . that function of event management that can keep in touch with the event's participants and visitors (consumers), read their needs and motivations, develop products that meet these needs, and build a communication program which expresses the event's purpose and objectives. ■

The following list shows the marketing activities that an event marketing manager may undertake to produce a successful festival or special event:

- Analyse the needs of the target market to establish the design of the event experience and the way in which it will be delivered.
- Predict how many people will attend the event and the times that different groups or market segments will attend.
- Research any competitive events that could satisfy similar needs, to devise a unique selling proposition.
- Estimate the price or value that visitors are willing to exchange to attend an event — for example, ticket price or donation.
- Decide on marketing communication, including the media mix and messages that will reach the audiences of the event.
- Consider how the choice and design of venue(s) and the methods of ticket distribution fit with the needs of attendees.
- Establish the success of the event in achieving its marketing objectives.

All of these activities, vital for a successful event, are part of the marketing function. This chapter explores how event marketing managers seek insights into consumers of their festival/event and the event marketing environment before developing their marketing strategies and plans. We discuss ways in which event managers can apply theories of strategic marketing, including services marketing and relationship management to develop their event marketing approach.

■ The *need for marketing*

Some critics of marketing argue that some cultural festivals and events should not be concerned with target markets and satisfying market needs, but should simply focus on innovation, creativity and the dissemination of new art forms. The argument is that consumers' needs are based on what they know, so consumers are less likely to embrace innovative or avant-garde cultural experiences. Dickman (1997, p. 685) highlights the reluctance of some administrators 'to even use the word [marketing], believing that it suggested "selling out" artistic principles in favour of finding the lowest common denominator'.

Erroneously, this view assumes that marketers, by adopting a consumer focus, respond only to the expressed needs of event visitors. In reality, sound marketing research can unveil the latent needs of consumers that only innovative events can satisfy. Often, a distrust of marketing is based on a misunderstanding of marketing principles and techniques. This attitude can be self-defeating for the following reasons:

- The use of marketing principles gives event managers a framework for decision making that should result in events that reflect innovation and creativity, but cater for market segments that seek novelty or the excitement of something new.
- Sponsoring bodies need reassurance that their sponsorship is linking their brand with their target markets. Sound marketing practices give marketers the ability to convince sponsors that a festival or event is the right marketing investment.
- All three levels of government (local, state and national) financially assist many festivals and events. Governments usually fund only those events whose management can demonstrate some expertise in marketing planning and management.
- Event stakeholders, such as the community, environmentalists and indigenous leaders, as well as consumers, are critical in today's societal marketing approach. A societal marketing approach (Kotler, Bowen & Makens 1999) emphasises the importance of society's wellbeing alongside satisfaction of the needs and wants of event or festival markets.
- Consumers, particularly those who reside in major cities, have an enormous range of leisure activities on which to spend their disposable income. This means a festival or special event, as a leisure activity, will attract only those who expect to satisfy at least one of their perceived needs.

All festivals and events, therefore, can benefit from understanding marketing principles and having some experience in applying those principles to satisfy the identified needs of a target market. Failure to understand the role of marketing, including its societal perspective, can lead to dissatisfied consumers and a weak relationship with stakeholders who strongly influence an event's long-term survival.

■ Events *as 'service experiences'*

The marketing concept is just as applicable to a leisure service such as an event as it is to any other product. We are exposed to many well-known brand names in leisure services that have been marketing success stories, and some of these are special events — for example, the Moscow Circus, the Edinburgh Tattoo, the Melbourne Cup and Sydney's Gay and Lesbian Mardi Gras.

Events as services differ from products in a number of ways. What is different about services is that we must experience them to consume them — the delivery and consumption of an event are *inseparable*, happening simultaneously in most cases. Given this immediacy of service consumption, the way in which an event is experienced can vary daily or each year the event or festival is staged. The challenge for event managers and marketers is to try to manage these *variations in quality*. Because people are central to the delivery of most services (including the staff or vendors at an event, as well as its visitors), managing the quality of an event experience depends on managing its human delivery and the behaviour of its consumers — that is, people who attend an event affect the level of enjoyment of other visitors.

Other key differences of services like events are that they are *intangible* and, unlike a product, cannot be *owned* — that is, we don't take the experience home with us. While a skateboard has *search qualities* (we can examine it for its shape, texture and colour), events or festivals have only *experiential qualities*. There is nothing tangible for us to pick up, touch, feel or try before purchasing tickets or after the event (other than event merchandise or mementos). Event marketers add some tangibility via promotional posters, event programs or compact discs of the artists' work, but the primary purchase is an intangible experience. The marketer has the challenge, therefore, of providing potential visitors with advance clues about the nature of the event experience.

It is generally agreed that the intangibility of services makes them much harder to evaluate than goods, and this is also true for events. Many special events also have some *credence qualities* — characteristics that we, as consumers, don't have enough knowledge or experience to understand or evaluate. For certain types of event, real-time interpretation (subtitles at the opera or expert commentary at a sports game) and post-purchase interpretation (views expressed by commentators or critics) enhance the consumer's experience.

For marketers, a further challenge is the *perishability* of the event experience — for example, seats unsold at today's football game or tonight's concert will not be available for sale again. While we can store an unsold product on the shelf, we cannot store today's unused opportunities for festival attendance until tomorrow or another date. Events are delivered in real time. If the weather is poor on the day of the festival, unsold tickets cannot be retrieved, and food and beverage sales for that day are lost. This means event demand and supply must be well understood, so seating, food and beverage, and other vital supplies to an event are not wasted.

The five key characteristics of services discussed here — inseparability, variations in quality, intangibility, lack of ownership and perishability — each have implications for an event's services marketing mix discussed later in this chapter.

■ The *nexus of event marketing and management*

Given the differences between services and goods, there is a need to understand the tight links between an event's marketing, its people management (human skills and expertise) and its operations management (for example, site layout, ticketing, queuing, sound and lighting, and other functions). While chapters 6, 13 and 14 explore those topics, it is important to grasp just how closely the events marketer needs to work with other managers to ensure consumer needs and expectations are fully met.

When we attend an event, our entire experience can be enhanced by the spectacle of stage design or lighting, special sound effects or ways in which the venue is designed to bring the performance to the audience. Our experience can also be marred by poor acoustics or incorrect advice from venue staff about parking or entry to the event. In their study of theatre event satisfaction, Hede, Jago and Deery (2003) used an expert panel to identify event attributes that consumers evaluate — for example, vision from the seats, theatre ambience, quality of the acting and singing, costumes and service at the theatre. It is important, therefore, to create a synergy between marketing, human resource and operations management — a relationship called the services trinity (figure 7.1).

■ **Figure 7.1**
*The event
services
trinity*

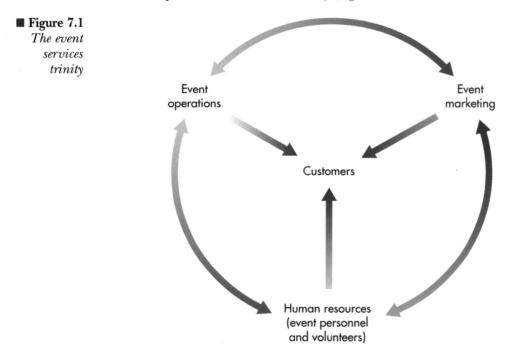

Event
operations

Event
marketing

Customers

Human resources
(event personnel
and volunteers)

■ **The** *role of strategic marketing*

Before describing the strategic marketing process, it is useful to think about what 'strategy' means. In the world of business and in event management and marketing, strategy can be interpreted as how an organisation (or event) marshals and uses its resources to achieve its business objectives, within its everchanging political, economic, socio-cultural and technological environment. Chapter 5 on event planning outlined this process. In this chapter, the strategy process is linked to the marketing function to show the framework in which event managers develop marketing objectives and strategies to satisfy consumer needs.

Some key points about strategy are that it is:

- *longer term, rather than short term* — once a marketing strategy is decided, it can be wasteful of resources and disruptive to an event to change the strategic direction. Careful thought is required before deciding on what marketing strategies to use to achieve event objectives.

- *not another word for tactics* — strategy is the broad overall direction that an event takes to achieve its objectives, while tactics are the detailed manoeuvres or programs that carry out the strategy. Tactics can be changed as market conditions change, but the overall direction — the strategy — remains constant (at least for the planning period).

- *based on careful analysis of internal resources and external environments* — it is not a hasty reaction to changes in the market.

- *essential to survival* — well-considered marketing strategies enable event managers to achieve the objectives of their event.

While the logic of deciding on a long-term strategy appears sound, festivals and events, like other organisations, vary in the extent to which their strategies are deliberate or emergent processes (Mintzberg 1994). In particular, festivals that begin their life as community celebrations run by local volunteers are less likely to have a deliberate strategy process. It is unlikely that the Birdsville Races in outback Queensland, for example, commenced with a formal marketing vision and process that led to the strong brand image that the event enjoys today. It can be wrong, therefore, to assume failure will result from implicit (rather than explicit) strategies or those that simply emerge from the hundreds of decisions made by organisers in staging an event. However, a holistic vision of an event's direction and the fit between the marketing strategy and vision is a desirable starting point. The following definition reflects the essence of the strategy concept for the practising events marketer: 'Strategic event marketing is the process by which an event organisation aligns business and marketing objectives and the environments in which they occur, with marketing activities that fulfil the needs of event consumers'.

Based on this definition, the starting points for any strategic marketing process should be the long-term objective(s) and mission or vision of the event organisers. Figure 7.2 shows the forces that influence these platforms of the strategic marketing process.

■ **Figure 7.2**
Constructing the mission

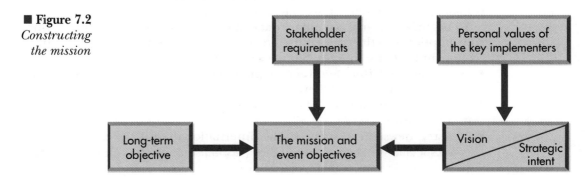

As shown in the figure, both the stakeholders of the event and the personal values of its organisers are critical influences. The mission of the Woodford Folk Festival, now internationally recognised for its success, mirrors that of its founding body, the Queensland Folk Federation. This mission is to 'stimulate, facilitate and foster the preservation and promotion of folk culture for the common good'.

The vision and values of the Queensland Folk Festival and the festival's director, Bill Hauritz, have had a profound effect on all aspects of the Woodford festival, including its marketing. Other events present more of an event-focused mission — for example, Brisbane's Out of the Box Festival of Early Childhood offers a festival to enrich the cultural lives of children, their communities and the city of Brisbane. Some events and festivals also state the philosophical principles that underpin their mission and guide event management and marketing. Out of the Box organisers express philosophies that recognise children as cultural contributors, children's individuality and diversity, and children's aesthetic learning and care. In effect, an event's philosophies and mission statement are an important foundation for determining the strategic marketing approach that best reflects the interests of its stakeholders and achieves its marketing objectives.

Stages in the strategic marketing process for events include: research and analysis of the macro-environment, including the competitive, political, economic, social and technological (C-PEST) forces; research into the psychology of event consumers; segmentation, targeting and positioning (STP); the setting of marketing objectives; and decision making about generic marketing strategies and the event's services marketing mix. Figure 7.3 (page 189) shows a recommended framework for developing the event marketing strategy.

$\mathcal{E}$VENT MARKETING RESEARCH

Before the marketing strategy is developed, research is usually conducted at: (1) the macro level, to understand external forces affecting the event and its markets, and (2) the micro level, to gain insight into the event's existing and potential consumers and any strategies previously used by the organisers. A range of event marketing information can be obtained from primary and secondary sources to guide the strategy process.

To begin, a search of secondary data on macro-level trends affecting leisure consumption and the competitive environment for events can be drawn from on-line and off-line sources. Some useful information sources are:
- government statistics and reports (national and state statistics on the consumption of festivals and events, arts and sport)
- media coverage (about the events sector and particular events or festivals in the region)
- industry newsletters such as the international *Special Events Magazine* (www.specialevents.com) and the *Australasian Special Events Magazine* (www.specialevents.com.au/magazine)

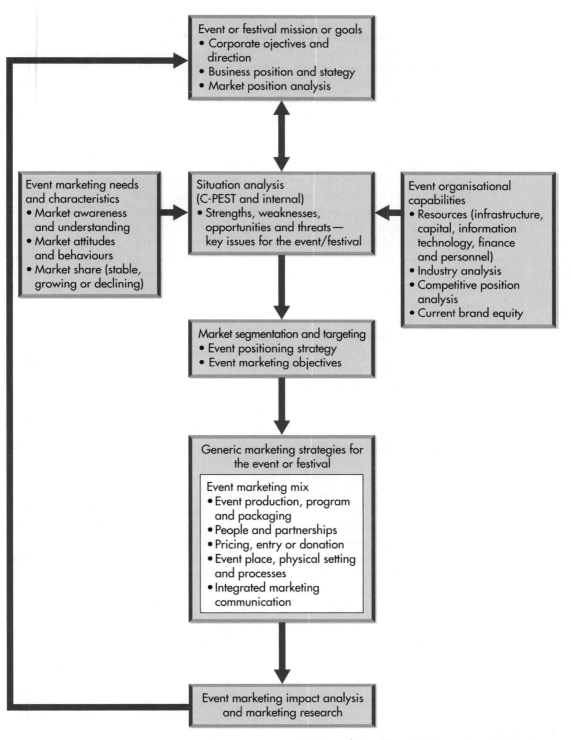

■ **Figure 7.3** *The strategic event marketing process*

- historical and current data from other events, festivals and event organisers. A content analysis of the websites of festivals, events and event production agencies can be a valuable research technique. Accolade Event Management, which directed the ceremonies of the Rugby World Cup 2003, is one of many event producers whose website offers a window to new and innovative event types (www.accolade.net.au).

A greater depth of understanding of macro-level issues such as event funding and the sponsorship environment, the seasonal saturation of events, the potential for oversupply of particular types of event, and new technologies for event delivery can also be obtained through depth interviews with opinion leaders — for example, longstanding event directors or producers, public sector event agencies and academics.

At the micro level, event marketers can use a mix of research techniques to gain insights into consumer segmentation and targeting. Past event reports that show vendor participation, event visitation, situational issues influencing past attendance and event satisfaction are desired resources, but not always available. Often, established members of the event organising body (including volunteers) become a rich source of informal advice about the event's consumption trends. More specific insights into existing event consumers can be reliably obtained from a mix of qualitative research (either depth interviews or a series of focus groups with eight to 10 people in each of the different segments of the market) and quantitative research (on-site intercept surveys or post-event research). For intercept surveys that are commonly undertaken at entry or exit points of the event, a randomly selected sample of at least 200 attendees (Getz 1997) is recommended. In this context, 'random' means all event customers have an equal chance of being selected for the survey. As customers exit the event, for example, every tenth customer could be asked to participate.

Data related to the visitors' demographics, motives, satisfaction and intention to revisit the event are generally sought. The data analysis can be manually performed for a small-scale survey that seeks only descriptive data about event consumers. However, a statistical software package such as SPSS offers a deeper understanding of relationships between variables such as attendance motives and satisfaction. However, do not succumb to paralysis through analysis. Market research is an aid to competent event marketing, it does not replace it.

■ Analysing *event environments*

Strategic marketing is a planning tool that emphasises thorough analyses. The marketer's own sense of judgement is not enough to make good strategic decisions (Rao & Steckel 1998). Astute marketing decisions emerge from a thorough analysis of competitor activities, the political, economic, socio-cultural and technological environments (C-PEST) in which the event occurs, and an analysis of the event organisation's internal resources.

The re-branding of Sydney's Royal Easter Show

The Royal Agricultural Society of New South Wales has produced Sydney's Royal Easter Show for over 120 years. In 1998, the show moved from its traditional venue at the Sydney Showgrounds at Moore Park, an inner city suburb of Sydney, to a custom-built site at Homebush in the geographic centre of Sydney, where it attracted a record crowd of 1.26 million, higher than the previous record crowd of 1.23 million set in 1947. The Moore Park site became the site of Fox Studios and its associated leisure precinct.

It took more than 50 years and a move to a site that became a venue for the Sydney Olympics 2000 for the attendance record to be broken. This is an obvious symptom of an event product not adapting to socio-cultural and demographic environmental changes. The rural population of New South Wales has been in relative decline since the 1940s, with a concurrent increase in the urban population, which led to a decline in interest in the traditional show activities of agricultural produce displays and show bags.

To counter this declining interest, the show was re-branded in 2000 as the 'Great Australian Muster', to give it a fresh identity and reinforce it as a uniquely Australian event.

The elements that now make up the show include: *Celebrate Australia*, which is a celebration of Australia's bush heritage featuring bush skills put to the test in a Stockmen's Challenge; an International Rodeo Challenge; *The Man from Snowy River*, which is an action-packed re-enactment of the famous poem by Banjo Patterson; the *Hell West and Crooked Outback Stunt Show*, which is a high-energy, action-packed 30-minute show of stunts featuring fights, falls, fire, music and explosions; and the International Test Wood Chopping competition. These elements convey to the ever-growing urban population of Sydney their image of an idealised rural life where the pioneers of Australia battle the physical environment to produce the rugged Australian of myth and legend.

Event marketing is concerned with identifying consumer needs and then satisfying them within the boundaries of the organisation's mission. The marketers of the Royal Easter Show realised that the socio-cultural and demographic environments of Australia have changed, so they altered their product (a leisure experience) to reflect these changes.

The C-PEST analysis

Figure 7.4 depicts each of the analyses contained in the C-PEST framework. Note that the global entertainment environment is included because changes in the world of artistic or sporting endeavour need careful monitoring by event and festival managers. Such trend analyses are done for a good reason: to establish opportunities and threats for the festival/event and its management. Using this process, organisers can shape marketing strategies to capitalise on emerging entertainment opportunities and neutralise threats.

■ **Figure 7.4**
*Components
of the
environment
analysis*

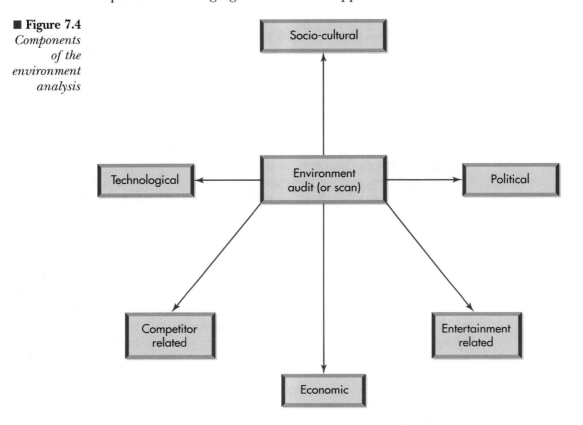

In conducting environmental analyses, it is easy to become overwhelmed by potential influences on the effective marketing of the event or festival. Stick to what is most critical to the event or festival in developing its marketing strategy in the current environment. To illustrate the C-PEST framework, the situation of the Sydney Festival is considered. Now more than 25 years old, the Sydney Festival is a three-week celebration of dance, theatre, visual arts, opera and music, which energises the city's business district each year.

Competitive analysis
In describing competitor analysis and strategy, Porter's (1990) seminal work identified four elements that affect competition within an industry (figure 7.5). This analytical tool is used to understand both industry-level and company-level competition, and it can also guide festival and event managers in their marketing decision making.

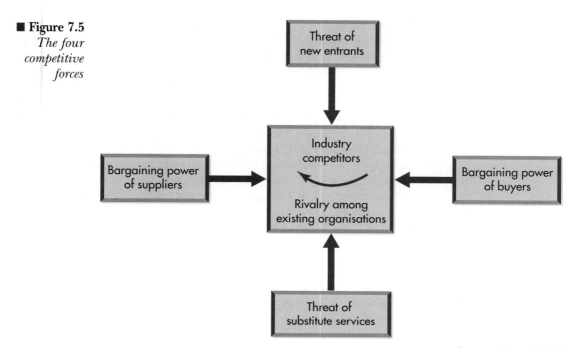

■ **Figure 7.5**
*The four
competitive
forces*

(**Source:** *Porter 1990.*)

To begin, festival or event *suppliers* include the venues, artists and physical resources (such as lighting and staging) needed to produce a show. Unless other artistic festivals occurring at the same time depend on these suppliers, no major difficulties usually emerge with event supply. However, given that the mission of the Sydney Festival is to provide the best of Australian and world talent for its audience, the organisers will liaise with suppliers of highly valued artists who have the power to increase talent costs or specify the conditions under which the artists will perform. Here, a relational strategy of building long-term alliances with agents and other festivals is important to ensure a continuity of supply at reasonable prices. This relational strategy could also be applied in forging close ties with venues such as the Sydney Opera House, so the best venues for the festival's events are available and affordable. While some event suppliers such as venues and entertainment agents can wield considerable power, relationship marketing strategies help to address this power imbalance.

Because the *buyers* of the Sydney Festival are large in number, little power is concentrated in their hands. Their only power is their price sensitivity to the festival's offerings. Given the festival's mission of providing the best international entertainment, an end result could be higher ticket prices. If consumers decide a particular offering does not give value for money, and they stay away in droves, the festival organisers and sponsors could suffer embarrassment and a loss of dollars. Consequently, the role of the marketer is to carefully identify (through experience and market research) the price level at which this sensitivity could arise.

A threat of *new entrants* exists if there is some potential for market share to be lost to another festival offering similar experiences. Australian history is littered with festivals that no longer exist. Sydney's Waratah Festival, for example, was once a festival highlight for Australia's biggest city. Now, it is a fading memory of Sydney's older residents. If there are few barriers to new entrants, this can be a real threat to the festival's viability. However, festivals such as the Sydney Festival depend on government and other sponsors for much of their funding, so the barriers to entry are quite high. These entry barriers remain high while major sponsors (including state government and corporate partners) are satisfied with the results of the festival — that is, so long as the funding agencies' objectives are met and the organisers' strategy for sponsorship management (chapter 8) ensures their business results are achieved.

The notion of substitutes for an event or festival is based on the marketing premise that consumers are purchasing not a service, but a package of benefits — in this case, an array of stimulating entertainment. If a substitute experience provides entertainment that is more satisfying or just as satisfying in the same timeframe at a lower cost, then the threat of substitution becomes very real. A commonly cited strategy to avoid this threat is to offer a unique event experience to a well-defined target market that is not readily substituted. For the Sydney Festival, the scale and sophistication of festival programming mean the festival would not be easily or quickly replaced by another event on the city's calendar. Yet, the ongoing proliferation of events and festivals, and the 'copy catting' that typifies services (including events), is a growing challenge for event marketers. 'Me too' events occurring on a smaller scale at other times of the year may have little short-term effect on attendance. However, a gradual dilution of the existing event's unique selling proposition (the aspect that best distinguishes it in the marketplace) is one potential outcome of new entrants with similar event offerings.

Political environment

All three levels of government can be active players in producing and sponsoring events and offering event development grants. For the Sydney Festival, both the New South Wales Government and Sydney City Council have played an active role in sponsorship and venue supply. Strategies to maintain this involvement are necessary, especially if a change of government occurs. As well as identifying the nature of government support, organisers need to take steps to understand new legislation or changes in the regulatory environment that affect event delivery — for example, rising public liability costs and regulations related to racing, gaming, lotteries and so on.

Economic environment

Some issues that have an impact on event marketing strategies are the buoyancy of the economy, foreign exchange rates, interest rates, employment rates, growth in household incomes, and the government's fiscal policy. The value of the Australian dollar compared to the currency of other nations, for example, can raise or lower the cost of attracting foreign artists to the

Sydney Festival. Methods of combating economic challenges that affect the festival's mission are subject to continual review.

Socio-cultural environment

Factors of a social or cultural nature that affect event marketing strategies include the size and variety of cultural/subcultural groups in the event's target market; changes in lifestyle, including work–leisure patterns; changing demography; changes in entertainment demand; and changes in education levels and household structures. Organisers of the Sydney Festival might observe that women aged 18–30 years are more outwardly mobile, less tied to child rearing than ever before, and have more time and income to participate in events. A slightly higher proportion of females than males has been shown among attendees at various festivals — for example, the BMW Wine Marlborough Festival, New Zealand's largest and most famous festival, has consistently attracted more females than males, with a 60/40 split in 2003 (Hall & Mitchell 2004). A concentration of women in the workforce and increased travel by retirees have also contributed to a declining volunteer base for events and festivals (Cordingly 1999).

Technological environment

Changes in technology present both opportunities and challenges for event organisers. In particular, the use of the world wide web, email marketing (including e-newsletters) and a mix of on-line and off-line event participation is now prevalent. The event website serves as a diverse branding tool for festivals and events, with opportunities for consumer interaction with event performers/players, up-to-the-minute event results and replays, and on-line recognition of event sponsors. For the Sydney Festival, organisers used web pages to show sneak previews of the 2005 events, promote major sponsors, advise on festival policies for receiving new submissions to its program, and provide current news about event personnel. In analysing the technological environment, event marketers should evaluate the advantages and disadvantages of all forms of technology. Direct marketing via SMS messaging on mobile phones, for example, has become a popular event marketing tool, both before and during events (see the case on John Farnham's The Last Time Tour in chapter 8). For those events with few resources and no permanent staff, the ability to build and maintain an effective website and stay abreast of new technology can be daunting. Yet, the failure to update a festival website on a regular basis or respond to on-line enquiries in a timely fashion can devalue the brand in the eyes of event visitors and sponsors. Marketers analysing their technological environment should note any opportunities for low-cost, technical support that could be available to their event or festival.

Entertainment environment

Entertainment is characterised by constant change as new ways of expression are developed, whether through new artistic forms or new types of sporting endeavour. The festival or event director generally tries to offer new experiences to consumers, to balance the familiar and novel event components. Trend analysis in the entertainment environment can be done via desk research and travel to centres of artistic innovation or places where emerging sports are practised (certainly a fun part of the job). While most events and festival organisers do not take an annual 'ideas tour' to exotic places to construct their marketing plan, they actively observe entertainment trends all year around. A good understanding of event innovations is also gained from reading professional and popular journals, networking with industry colleagues and travelling to trade fairs and exhibitions. Again, a key purpose of this analysis is to align the event's marketing strategies with opportunities and strengths, and to minimise the impacts of any threats and weaknesses.

Internal resource analysis

Another vital step in developing the marketing strategy is the assessment of the event's internal resources. Classic economists categorise the resources available to an entrepreneur as land, labour and capital. In event or festival organisations, the resources are human resources, physical resources and financial resources.

Human resources

The event strategist analyses the number and type of staff and volunteers available, the particular skill sets required to produce the event, the costs of employing people, and innovative ways in which people can contribute to the event's success. An analysis of the Sydney Festival would show that the festival's directors have been individuals with a high profile since the festival's inception. As a result, a lynchpin of the marketing communication strategy is the use of the director as the public face of the festival who features strongly in media releases and interviews. Promoting a festival through its senior producers/directors and organised word-of-mouth by staff and volunteers also minimises the cost of an event's marketing communication campaign. The Woodford Folk Festival is an example of a festival that has capitalised almost entirely on word-of-mouth marketing through its volunteers to build a loyal body of event goers.

Physical resources

For an event, physical resources can include ownership of a venue (although this is rare). More often, they include computer hardware and software, desktop publishing equipment, access to venues at competitive rates and the use of conference rooms in buildings of some significance. The use of event management software capable of supplying timely data on all aspects of the festival would be a physical resource strength. A far less tangible resource is the festival's brand equity (that is, public awareness and attitudes towards the event, built over a longer period). It is fair to assume community goodwill towards the Sydney Festival has become a valued resource.

Financial resources

Without access to suitable finance, no event marketing strategy can be put into place. Current access to funds or a demonstrated ability to acquire capital is an obvious strength for any event. This access includes the ongoing involvement of government and corporate sponsorship funds. With the direct involvement of the state government, the patronage of the Governor, the inclusion of the Sydney City Council on the festival board, and its corporate sponsors, the Sydney Festival enjoys a stable resource base. Adequate financial resources or backing for events and festivals often simultaneously depends on the strengths of its partnerships (a key reason for this element featuring in the event marketing mix).

The SWOT analysis

Once the C-PEST and the internal resource audit are completed, an analysis of strengths, weaknesses, opportunities, threats (SWOT) can be conducted. This summary of the critical issues identified through the C-PEST and internal resources analyses (Tribe 1997) enables the event marketer to marry opportunities and strengths, improve weaknesses, negate threats and, just as importantly, have a sound basis for establishing marketing objectives and strategies for the event. This task is made easier if all the data collected are summarised into no more than 10 bullet points for each section of the SWOT analysis.

■ The *event consumer's decision-making process*

Understanding the consumer decision-making process for events and festivals is aided by the following PIECE acronym:

- *problem recognition* — the difference between someone's existing state and their desired state relative to leisure consumption
- *information search* — an internal and/or external search; limited or extensive search processes for leisure (including event) solutions
- *evaluation and selection* of leisure alternatives
- *choosing whether to attend* an event and which optional purchases to make at the event or festival
- *evaluation* of the post-event experience.

Reflecting this PIECE process, the consumer identifies a need that may be satisfied by attending an event or other leisure experience, searches for information about such an experience in different media (the entertainment section of newspapers, the radio, magazines, friends and relatives), and then evaluates the alternatives available. Most of us then examine how the leisure experience compares with a list of the attributes we most desire. As event goers, we may want to improve our family ties, so we attend a local community festival that all members of our family can enjoy. Alternatively, we may be looking for a novel or innovative event to satisfy our curiosity. After experiencing (or 'consuming') the event, we re-evaluate the experience for its quality of service and its capacity to satisfy our needs.

Problem recognition

For would-be event or festival consumers, problem recognition means a difference exists between what they would like to experience and what they have to satisfy that need (Neal, Quester & Hawkins 2002). The central starting point for this problem recognition is the existence of one or more needs that may be satisfied by attending a festival or event. Events and festivals fulfil physiological needs (exercise, relaxation, sexual engagement), interpersonal needs (social interaction) and/or personal needs (enhanced knowledge, new experiences, fulfilment of fantasies) (Getz 1991, 1997). How quickly we decide whether to attend an event partly depends on our event purchase involvement — that is, our level of interest in the purchase process, once it has been triggered (Neal, Quester & Hawkins 2002). Some events are spontaneous, low-involvement decisions, such as when we visit a local park on the weekend, notice a small, cultural festival in progress, and wander over to join in. In contrast, attending events such as the Olympic Games in Beijing in 2008 or visiting the United Kingdom to watch Wimbledon's tennis championship are high-involvement decisions.

Information search

In looking for information, most consumers try to determine (1) the relevant criteria on which to base their decision — the nature of event performers, the location, other attractions in the area, the ticket price and so on — and (2) the extent to which the event will satisfy their needs. As they compare different leisure experiences, event consumers engage in both external and internal searches for information.

External influences

Among the *external* influences on the potential event goer are various social factors. These factors are described below in the context of event participation:

- *Family and household influences,* such as the desires of children, often influence the leisure behaviour of parents. The need for family cohesion and building familial ties is a strong leisure motivator for many people. It explains the enormous numbers of children and exhausted parents who congregate at the show bag pavilion of agricultural shows around Australia. Many festivals focus on children's entertainment for this reason.
- *Reference groups* are those groups that influence the behaviour of individuals. Groups in close contact with individuals (peers, family, colleagues and neighbours) are called primary reference groups. Those who have less frequent contact are called secondary reference groups. Most people tend to seek the approval of members of their reference groups. If attendance at a particular festival is perceived to be acceptable and desirable, then group members are more likely to attend. Showing examples of a typical reference group (for example, a nuclear family or a group of young people) enjoying themselves at a festival can be a persuasive communication strategy when those groups represent the festival's target market.

- *Opinion formers or opinion leaders* are those people within any group whose views about events and leisure experiences are sought and widely accepted. These opinion leaders are often media, theatrical or sports personalities (including critics and commentators) who are highly rewarded for their endorsement of products and leisure services. Often, the views of critics and commentators have a strong impact on attendance in sport and the arts.

  The adoption of new leisure services tends to follow a normal distribution curve. Innovators (generally opinion leaders within a group) are the first to try the experience. Early adopters, who are a little more careful about adopting the innovation, follow them and act as opinion leaders for the majority. Laggards are the last to try something new; some may be loyal attendees of very mature events or events that are close to decline. It is logical that the marketing of new festivals or events begins by targeting the opinion formers or innovators within the market.

- *Culture* includes the 'knowledge, beliefs, art, morals, laws, customs and any other capabilities and habits acquired as a member of society' (Neal, Quester & Hawkins 2002, p. 22). Australia is an example of a culturally diverse country in which Indigenous people and various ethnic groups with different patterns of living co-exist. Our culture can affect our buying habits, leisure needs, attitudes and values.

  Culture has a profound influence on the design, marketing and consumption of events and festivals. In effect, events are simultaneously a celebration and a consumption experience that reflect our way of life. A growth of interest in events as diverse as Brisbane's Chinese Autumn Moon Festival, the Panyiri (Greek) Festival and the Laura Aboriginal Dance and Cultural Festival in north Queensland demonstrate the influence of, and interest in, culture.

An external search involving reference groups or other sources becomes especially important when event or festival attendance requires an extended decision-making process. Going to the Olympic Games, for example, is a high-involvement, extended decision, and event goers will seek advice from websites, travel agents and other sources. Participating in some cultural events, such as the Laura Aboriginal Dance and Cultural Festival, could involve extended decision making because it requires travelling to an isolated township. The Laura festival is alcohol free, and visitors must respect the Ang-gnarra Festival Grounds, which are traditional Bora grounds where Aboriginal people have congregated for thousands of years.

Internal influences

A range of *internal influences* also affect consumer decision making about events. These influences include *perception* (how we select and process information), *learning and memory, motives, personality traits* and *consumer attitudes*. If, for example, we have an existing preference (attitude) that steers us towards a classical music event, then we could deliberately select information about competing leisure activities. Similarly, if we have information stored in our memory that helps to resolve a need (a mental picture of spectacular fireworks at Brisbane's Riverfire), then that event could quickly become the single, most satisfactory solution to our entertainment needs on a given weekend in Brisbane.

Personality, or an individual's characteristic traits that affect behaviour, is another influence on event or festival decisions (Stanton, Miller & Layton 1994). People can be introverted/extroverted, shy/self-confident, aggressive/retiring and dynamic/sluggish. Although the effects of personality on consumer choice are difficult to measure, we can assume that festivals that celebrate adventure or sporting prowess will attract participants with 'outgoing' personalities. An awareness of particular personality characteristics among event consumers can help marketers to finetune their strategies.

Among all of the internal influences, 'in developed economies, most consumer behaviour is guided by psychological motives' (Neal, Quester & Hawkins 2001, p. 19). A body of empirical research on motives for event and festival attendance has emerged since the 1990s. Three theories of event motives, as summarised by Axelsen and Arcodia (2004), are:

1. the *needs achievement hierarchy* — a theory based on Maslow's original hierarchy, whereby motives change as each level of need — from the physiological through to self-actualisation — is satisfied
2. *'push' and 'pull' motives* — a theory that push factors (for example, escapism or curiosity) propel us towards an event, while pull factors (for example, aspects of events, such as wine and gourmet food) draw us to an event
3. *intrinsic motives* for leisure — a theory related to 'push' and 'pull' motives that we seek change from routine (escape) and intrinsic personal and interpersonal rewards from visiting/travelling to other environments. Examples of these rewards might be the increased sense of endurance and friendships formed during a historic horse riding event (as described by Mannell & Iso-Ahola 1987).

A set of common motives (or need satisfiers) for attending festivals has been cited in a wide range of studies (see, for example, Backman et al. 1995; Crompton & McKay 1997; Uysal, Gahan & Martin 1993). A summary of motives for festival attendance that consistently emerge are:

- *socialisation or external interaction* — meeting new people, being with friends and socialising in a known group
- *family togetherness* — seeking the opportunity to be with friends and relatives and doing things together to create greater family cohesion
- *escape from everyday life, as well as recovering equilibrium* — getting away from the usual demands of life, having a change from daily routine and recovering from life's stresses
- *learning about or exploring other cultures* — gaining knowledge about different cultural practices and celebrations
- *excitement/thrills* — doing something because it is stimulating and exciting
- *event novelty/ability to regress* — experiencing new and different things and/or attending a festival that is unique.

The above list tends to reflect the earlier three theories of event motives (Axelsen & Arcodia 2004). These motives have been found in most festival studies and also among visitors to events and exhibitions. Both special event and gallery visitors during the Asia–Pacific Triennial Art Exhibition (staged at the Queensland Art Gallery every three years), for example, seek social interaction, novelty and relaxation through their attendance (Axelsen & Arcodia 2004). The order of importance given to different attendance motives appears to vary according to the type of festival or event. Visitors to a specialised festival, such as a hot air balloon festival, have been shown to be highly motivated by a desire to socialise with people sharing the same interest (Mohr et al. 1993), while people attending a community festival have been shown to be motivated by 'escape' from day-to-day life (Uysal, Gahan & Martin 1993).

Evaluating alternatives and making event choices

It is fair to assume that consumers rarely weigh up whether they will attend more than one or two events on a given day. Instead, they are likely to choose between an event/festival and the cinema, a private party or an entirely different leisure activity. For everyday products and services, evaluative criteria are often *price*, *brand image* and the *contents* of the market offer.

Services such as events that we have not previously attended are quite hard to evaluate, and we experience some uncertainty due to the financial, social, psychological, sensory, performance and time-related risks involved (Lovelock, Patterson & Walker 2001). Even if a festival has free entry, we may have travel costs, child care and other costs involved. Socially, we may think about the types of people we will encounter at an event, and the psychological costs and benefits of those encounters. We also evaluate the time that it will take to attend the event, and sensory risks such as our ability to see the stage or hear the music with clarity. The choice of whether to attend sports events can be linked to the stadium atmosphere, layout and facilities, rather than team performance. Robertson and Pope (1999) found the atmosphere, the live action, stadium cleanliness and ease of getting seating were quite influential in the decision to attend Brisbane Lions (AFL) games.

Any number of values may be applied in making different event consumption choices. Functional values, such as our perception of an event's price–quality relationship and ease of access, may dominate. Alternatively, emotional values may be more influential (the likely effects of a festival experience on our mood). Other conditional values for a festival may be whether there is convenient transport, good quality classical music or nearby accommodation that suits our tastes.

Post-event evaluation

Once we have attended an event, we start to compare what we expected with what we experienced. Consumer expectations arise from a combination of marketing communications planned by the event or festival organiser, word of mouth from friends and family, previous experience with this or similar events, and the event's brand image. The exercise of comparing consumer's expectations with actual experiences of services is now commonplace. However, even when markets are tightly segmented into a group of people with a common characteristic, members of the same group can have different perceptions of the benefits they receive. Two close friends may attend Byron Bay's Splendour in the Grass event: one may rate all of the event services very highly, yet the other may not be as enthusiastic, despite having experienced the same service. The relationship between event goers' satisfaction, their perceptions of service quality and their intentions to revisit is very important to marketers who want to build a loyal visitor market.

■ Event *satisfaction, service quality, repeat visits*

Because leisure services are intangible, inseparable, variable and perishable, defining service quality is difficult. From the viewpoint of a festival or event consumer, quality service occurs when expectations of the event match perceptions of the service experienced. Understanding perceived service quality is thus a primary goal of marketers. Both existing and potential attendees can have a perception of event quality (formed from experience of the event, word of mouth and/or other marketing communication). However, perceptions of the event itself are based on the *technical* (performance outcomes) and *functional* (process related) qualities of the experience (Gronroos 1990). Other external factors — for example, wet weather and personal factors such as an argument with a partner during the event — also affect consumer perceptions.

Because it is harder to evaluate 'technical' quality (such as the musical performance at the festival), much of the focus in measuring perceived service quality is on functional aspects, or ways in which service is delivered. For this reason, the five main dimensions of service quality in the commonly used SERVQUAL questionnaire (Parasuraman, Zeithaml & Berry 1988) mostly reflect functional service aspects:

1. *assurance* — staff and/or volunteers give the appearance of being knowledgeable, helpful and courteous, and event consumers are assured of their wellbeing
2. *empathy* — the event staff and/or volunteers seem to understand the consumers' needs and deliver caring attention
3. *responsiveness* — the staff and volunteers are responsive to the needs of the consumer
4. *reliability* — everything happens at the event in the way the marketing communication has promised
5. *tangibles* — the physical appearance of the event equipment, artists' costume/presentation and the physical setting meet visitor expectations.

Using these five dimensions, the SERVQUAL questionnaire measures the difference between visitor expectations and perceptions of a festival or event. When the visitors' perceptions of their event experience match or exceed their expectations, a quality experience has been delivered, and the outcome is satisfied attendees who could decide to go the event next time it is held.

Event satisfaction is related to perceived service quality, but it is experience dependent. Satisfaction can be measured only among existing visitors to the event. Not every customer will be satisfied all the time. To maintain a competitive position, however, the event marketer should aim to achieve more than a basic level of satisfaction. A sense of delight or extreme satisfaction among event visitors is the ideal outcome (Lovelock, Patterson & Walker 2001). To this end, one objective in an event's strategic marketing should involve visitor satisfaction — for example, '95 per cent of event participants will give a satisfied or higher rating of the event'. Figure 7.6 shows how consumer dissatisfaction can occur based on some perceived gap in festival or event quality.

■ **Figure 7.6**
Quality —
the fit
between
customer
expectations
and
perceptions

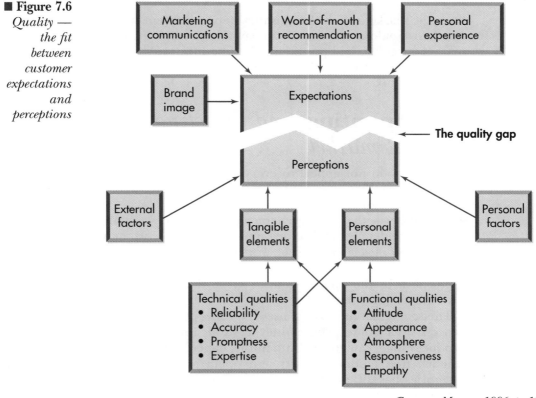

(**Source:** *Morgan 1996, p. 159.*)

Given the difficulty in understanding consumer expectations (with there being no clear set of expectations for each service setting), it is often argued that a 'perceptions only' measure of satisfaction (one that excludes expectations) is more useful. For festivals, various writers suggest consumer 'perceptions' are better indicators of the link between quality, visitor satisfaction and intentions to revisit (see, for example, Baker & Crompton 2000; Thrane 2002). Because musical performance has been highlighted as an important determinant of quality at a festival (Saleh & Ryan, 1993; Thrane 2000), the use of the SERVQUAL approach alone is probably not the marketer's best approach to research. Thrane (2000), however, also notes that aspects of quality measured by SERVQUAL do contribute to jazz festival patrons' satisfaction and intentions to revisit. A research instrument that adequately investigates both festival 'performance' and 'process' should be considered, therefore, in evaluating festival and event marketing strategies.

STEPS IN THE STRATEGIC MARKETING PROCESS

Strategic marketing involves distinct steps that event managers must understand to create a successful strategy. These steps include segmenting the market, targeting and positioning, setting measurable marketing objectives, choosing generic marketing strategies, and designing an effective marketing mix.

■ Segmenting *and targeting the event market*

Most events do not appeal to everybody, so it is essential to identify those consumer segments whose needs most closely match the event experience. The market segments chosen should be:

- *measurable* — that is, the characteristics of the segment (socioeconomic status, gender, age and so on) must be accessible to the event marketer
- *substantial enough in size* to be worth targeting
- *accessible* by normal marketing communication channels
- *actionable* by the event organiser, given the marketing budget and other resources (Morgan 1996).

The segmentation process uses the concept of the buyer decision-making process as a guide. The Sydney Festival, for example, has an extensive product range, categorised into music, dance, visual arts, family, theatre and cinema, free outdoor activity and opera/musical theatre. Each of these categories has different offerings, appealing to the buyer behaviour of different submarkets. The visual arts category alone features about 12 different offerings. By thinking about the potential visitors to the visual arts exhibits, the festival organisers can develop a mental snapshot of the overall target market for the visual arts category and events within it. Actual segmentation of the markets could be based on geography, demography (including the visitors' lifecycle phase) and/or behaviour (lifestyles, benefits sought and attendance profile — that is, first timers or repeat visitors).

Geographic segmentation based on the place of residence of event visitors is a commonly used method. Many community festivals are dominated by local visitors or daytrippers from the immediate state or region. The McLaren Vale Sea and Vine Festival in South Australia drew 89 per cent of its audience from South Australia in 2000, with only small proportions from interstate (8 per cent) and overseas (3 per cent). For this reason, managers of community festivals often decide to focus on local residents as their major geographic segment. A key determinant of geographic segmentation is the potential 'drawing power' of the event as a tourist attraction. An event such as a capital city agricultural show (for example, the Ekka in Brisbane or The Great Australian Muster in Sydney) has drawing power for a statewide geographic market, but only a minor interstate market. Although many event organisers have visions of creating tourist demand, few events develop the brand equity and 'pull' characteristics to succeed as independent tourist attractions. Many more events could succeed in attracting tourists if organisers improved their skills in packaging and marketing the event alongside other regional tourist experiences. If an event demonstrates its ability to draw external markets — for example, Sydney's Gay and Lesbian Mardi Gras — then the potential geographic spread could be:

- local residents of the area
- day visitors from outside the immediate area
- intrastate domestic tourists
- interstate domestic tourists
- international inbound tourists.

Demographic segmentation relies on the characteristics of people, such as age, gender, occupation, income, education and cultural group. The life-cycle phase of visitors is a further means of demographic segmentation, as is a socioeconomic scale based on occupation (usually the major income generator in family units). Table 7.1 details this scale in an event context.

■ **Table 7.1** *A classification of socioeconomic market segments for events*

GROUP	SOCIO-ECONOMIC GROUP	OCCUPATIONAL EXAMPLES	TYPES OF EVENT GROUP IS LIKELY TO ATTEND	APPROXIMATE SHARE OF POPULATION (%)
A	Upper middle class	Higher managerial or administrative, professional: lawyers, doctors, dentists, captains of industry, senior public servants, senior military officers, professors	Cultural events such as fundraisers for the opera, classical music festivals	3
B	Middle class	Intermediate managerial, administrative or professional: university lecturers, head teachers, pharmacists, middle managers, journalists, architects	Cultural events (but purchasing cheaper seats), food and beverage festivals, historical festivals, arts and crafts festivals, community festivals	15 *(continued)*

GROUP	SOCIO-ECONOMIC GROUP	OCCUPATIONAL EXAMPLES	TYPES OF EVENT GROUP IS LIKELY TO ATTEND	APPROXIMATE SHARE OF POPULATION (%)
C	Lower middle class	Supervisory, clerical, junior managerial or administrative: clerks, sales representatives, nurses, teachers, shop managers	Most popular cultural events, some sporting events, community festivals	24
D	Skilled working class	Skilled blue collar workers: builders, fitters, waterside workers, police constables, self-employed tradespersons	Motor vehicle festivals, sporting events, community festivals	28
E	Working class	Semiskilled and unskilled workers: builder's labourers, factory workers, cleaners, delivery drivers	Some sporting festivals, ethnic festivals	17
F	Social security	Those at the lowest level of subsistence: pensioners, casual and part-time workers	Very little, except occasionally free community events	13

(**Source:** *Adapted from Morgan 1996.*)

Media buyers in advertising agencies first used these classifications because they tend to be quite good predictors of reading and viewing habits. In general, As and Bs read broadsheet newspapers such as the *Sydney Morning Herald* and the *Age* in Melbourne, whereas Cs, Ds, and Es read the tabloid press, such as the *Daily Telegraph* and the *Herald Sun*. However, these classifications are not always an accurate guide to income, because many Cs earn considerable incomes. The essential difference between As, Bs, Cs and the other categories is in the level of education. For directors of festivals and events that include cultural elements, their target market is usually an educated one (frequently post-year 12 education or above).

Other demographic variables are gender and age. The group aged 35+ years is a growing market segment, among whom food and wine festivals have become a popular leisure experience (with women marginally out-numbering men). Targeting the media-savvy, Generation X market (18–34 years old), which is not at all homogenous (singles, couples with and without children), requires a different approach. Depending on the event, several different generations may be targeted, with event program elements designed to cater for each age segment. Brisbane's Riverfestival is a good example of a festival that targets a diverse demographic. The festival's events target preschool and older children (RiverEd and Riverkidz), the Generation X segment (RiverConcert) and baby boomers (RiverSymphony and RiverFeast). Some events, such as the Riverfire fireworks show, attract all demographic segments.

Marketers sometimes employ a combination of age and lifestyle segmentation. 'Full nesters' are the target market for events that feature entertainment for both children and adults, whereas 'AB empty nesters' are the perfect market for cultural festivals featuring quality food and drink, and arias from well-loved operas. However, care should be taken not to resort to age stereotypes. Many baby boomers are fit, active and interested in all types of culture (popular and contemporary, as well as high culture festivals such as classical music or theatre). It could be argued that the most successful community festivals are those that include all age groups, rather than focusing on just one age group.

Psychographic segmentation, or dividing a market according to its lifestyle and values, is another useful planning technique. The Roy Morgan Research Centre's research of Australian values and lifestyles has segmented consumers based on shared values and attitudes — for example, visible achievers, those who are socially aware and young optimists (Stanton, Miller & Layton 1994). However, like personality segmentation, psychographic market segmentation has serious limitations for an event marketer. It is difficult to accurately measure the size of lifestyle segments in a quantitative manner. Nevertheless, this type of segmentation offers a better understanding of the types of experience that different 'lifestyle' groups seek from their leisure experience.

■ Positioning *the event*

How to position an event in the mindset of the market is an important strategic decision. Positioning represents the way in which the event is defined by consumers, or 'the place it occupies in consumers' minds relative to competing offerings' (Kotler et al. 2001, p. 256). Event positioning can be achieved in at least 10 different ways:

1. *the existing reputation or image of the event* — for example, the Olympic Games and other longstanding events such as the Edinburgh Tattoo
2. *the charisma of a director or leader* — for example, the Sydney Festival's director
3. *a focus on event programming* — for example, Ten Days on the Island in Tasmania, which is a festival programmed and positioned around the 'island' concept
4. *a focus on performers* — for example, major sports (such as the football and golf) and theatre that highlight the players/peformers
5. *an emphasis on location or facilities* — for example, Wimbledon, which is now synonymous with world-standard tennis

6. *event users* — for example, Queensland's Out of the Box Festival of Early Childhood
7. *price or quality* — for example, a free civic concert series versus an operatic performance by the world's three best tenors
8. *the purpose or application of the event* — for example, health awareness of SIDs or diabetes, or celebrations such as Australia's Centenary of Federation
9. *the event category or 'product' class* — for example, fashion events, food and wine festivals, and concerts
10. *multiple attributes* — for example, the RAQ Fashion Festival, which is positioned on its designers, reputation and image, as well as its purpose of bringing new fashion designers into the public eye.

Once decisions have been made about the event's segmentation, targeting and positioning, a platform is available to decide on event marketing objectives, strategies and tactics.

■ Developing *event marketing objectives*

Any successful development of a marketing plan is based on sound marketing objectives. Cravens, Merriless and Walker (2000, p. 272) make this important point: 'For marketing to be a beneficial business discipline, its expected results must be defined and measurable'. Hypothetical examples of marketing objectives for an event such as the Sydney Festival might be to:

• increase box office receipts in 2006 by 10 per cent
• increase the percentage of seats sold in all ticketed events to 80 per cent in 2006
• retain 90 per cent of sponsors for 2006
• increase publicity generated in print and electronic media by a further 10 per cent from 2006.

It is important to stress again how marketing objectives, like all objectives, must be measurable and not expressed in vague terms that make measurement impossible. While many managers are tempted to state general aims rather than set objectives (making it harder to be accountable for whether event objectives have been achieved), this temptation must be resisted. Clearly defined and measurable objectives give the marketer the *ends*, while strategies and their supporting tactics are the *means* to those ends.

The dimensions of the marketing objective have an impact on the choice of strategies. Consider the hypothetical objective for the Sydney Festival of increasing box office receipts by 10 per cent in 2006. This increase is a substantial amount, much higher than the inflation rate, which implies that a business objective of the festival is to grow substantially each year to satisfy the entertainment and cultural demands of a more diverse audience base. The objective and the strategies to achieve it are chosen, therefore, only after careful analysis of the market needs, organisational capabilities and opportunities.

■ Choosing *generic marketing strategies for events*

Before events marketers begin the more precise task of deciding on marketing elements such as the program, the ticket price and other variables, they should reflect on their overall strategies for the event's future. Is there a plan to grow or expand the event and/or its markets? Or is there a plan to consolidate the current program and further penetrate existing markets? Any number of strategic options is available to the event/festival, depending on its resources, its competition and its objectives. (Chapter 5 explained a range of these strategies.)

Here, we discuss the application of Porter's (1990) generic strategies and the potential use of strategies of growth, integration and diversification (Kotler, Bowen & Makens 1999) as they affect events marketing. First, Porter (1990) suggests most organisations have a choice of strategies of *differentiation, focus* or *cost leadership.* For the events marketer, decisions on these strategies are based on whether the aim is for the event to hold a leadership position in a region or city's leisure market or to have a narrower, yet well-defined market scope. Brisbane's Riverfestival appears to have established a leadership position, with brand equity in diverse market segments and some economies of scale and efficiency in its management (including its branding and communication strategies). In contrast, the Australian Gospel Music Festival draws a more specialised audience with a focus strategy, servicing a particular segment — that is, Christian music lovers — with a high-quality performance. A differentiation strategy means creating something that is perceived to be quite unique across the event/ festival sector. Interesting examples of events that employ this strategy are the Black Stump Camel Races in western Queensland and Leyburn's Sprint around the Houses near Brisbane.

Other marketing strategy options arise from the overall event strategies of intensive *growth, integration* and *diversification.* Perhaps the most commonly cited tool in deciding on growth strategies is the product–market matrix (Ansoff 1957, cited in Kotler, Bowen & Makens 1999) shown in figure 7.7.

■ **Figure 7.7**
Ansoff's product– market matrix

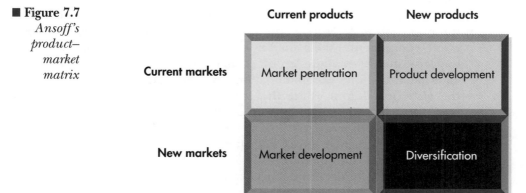

(**Source:** *Ansoff 1957.*)

An event that has a well-designed program, but is not yet drawing large numbers, could consider a market penetration strategy — that is, concentrating on attracting more people from the same target market. If organisers consider that the event could reach a different target market without changing its program, a market development strategy could be used. Finally, if consumer satisfaction studies show the event is not satisfying its current visitor needs, new and different program elements could be needed. The arena spectacular, Outback Thunder, staged during the Brisbane Ekka represents a good example of a new event being used to better satisfy the needs of contemporary visitors.

Integration strategies also present marketing opportunities for events. An event producer may decide to formally integrate with a venue provider (a festival that goes under the wing of a cultural centre) or integrate with other events or festivals. It has been suggested that integration strategies have become more common in recent years among those events unable to cover excessive public liability fees. However, integration is also an opportunistic strategy: finding an event that complements the existing program and brings new partnerships to a larger festival can be very attractive.

Diversification strategies can lead the marketer to add new events or support services to its stable of entertainment, or go into complementary businesses. A festival may develop an innovative range of merchandise for its existing market or it may market its software for visitor relationship management to other festivals. Such strategic options represent an important framework for deciding on the event's marketing mix, which is discussed next.

■ Selecting *the event's 'services marketing' mix*

Variations on the marketing mix have been made since the original four Ps of marketing were proposed (McCarthy 1971). This chapter uses an adaptation of Getz's (1997) event marketing mix to present nine closely related components of events marketing. While each element is of considerable strategic importance, it is relatively easy to group them, as shown below:

- the event *product experience* (the core service), its *programming* (different event components, their quality or style) and its *packaging* (a mix of opportunities within the event or marketing of the event with other external attractions, accommodation and transport)
- the *place* (location(s) where the event is held and its tickets are distributed), its *physical setting* (the venue layout relative to consumer needs) and on-site event *processes* (queuing and so on)
- *people* (cast, audience, hosts and guests) and *partnerships* (stakeholders such as sponsors and media)
- *price*, or the exchange of value to experience the event
- *integrated marketing communication* (media and messages employed to build relationships with the event markets and audiences) (Getz 1997).

PLANNING EVENT 'PRODUCT' EXPERIENCES

Festivals and events, as service product experiences, contain three elements (Lovelock, Patterson & Walker 2001):

1. the *core* service and benefits that the customer experiences — for example, performing arts or sports event
2. the *tangible 'expected'* product — for example, the venue and seating, pricing, essential services and access
3. the *augmented* product or additional features that differentiate an event from its competitors — for example, its artists, service quality, the type of visitors, different modes of transport, and merchandise.

As suggested earlier, an important characteristic of the marketing of leisure services is that people are also part of the product. In other words, much of the visitors' satisfaction comes from their interactions with other people attending the event. This means event marketers need to ensure (1) visitor segments within their audience are compatible and (2) there is an ease of interaction among people on-site.

■ Developing *the event*

The 'product' of an event is the set of intangible leisure experiences and tangible goods designed to satisfy the needs of the event market. The development of an event or festival can be easily modelled on the processes used to plan, create and deliver services (figure 7.8, page 212).

The product life cycle concept suggests most events travel through the stages of introduction, growth and maturity to eventual decline or rejuvenation in a new form. Although there is no predictable pattern of life cycle transition for most products and services, we can find many examples of events that appear to have experienced all life cycle phases. Attendance at Australia Day festivals, for example, has waxed and waned as the 'product' has been changed to reflect changing community needs. Once, only hundreds attended the celebrations staged for this day; now, with a rejuvenation of the Australia Day celebration 'product', attendances are again healthy. To avoid the decline, event managers need to closely monitor public acceptance of the content of their event product, to ensure it is still congruent with the leisure needs of contemporary society.

The creation of new service experiences usually ranges from major service innovations through to simple changes in the style of service delivery (Lovelock, Patterson & Walker 2001). These are evident in the event and festival sector:

- *Major 'event' innovations* — new events or festivals for previously undefined markets. Extreme sports events may represent one such innovation that emerged in the 1990s. However, major 'event' innovations are extremely hard to identify in an already crowded and innovative events sector, in which a wide variety of events serve existing, rather than new, leisure segments.

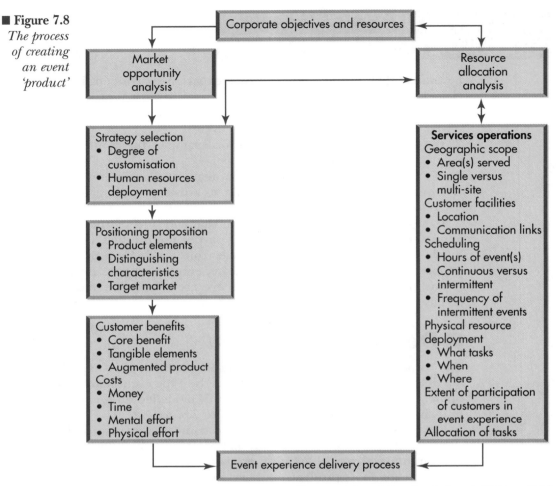

■ **Figure 7.8**
The process of creating an event 'product'

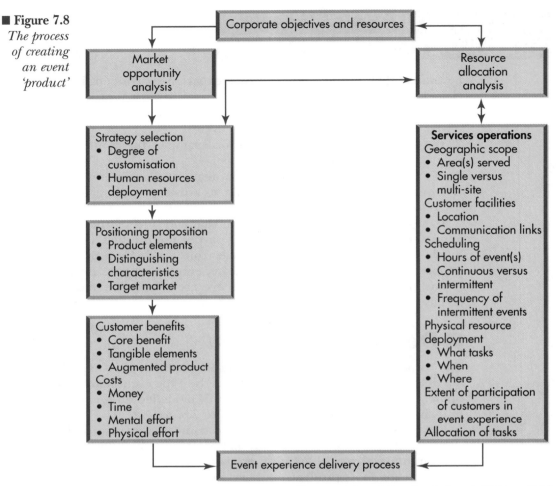

Corporate objectives and resources

Market opportunity analysis

Resource allocation analysis

Strategy selection
• Degree of customisation
• Human resources deployment

Services operations
Geographic scope
• Area(s) served
• Single versus multi-site
Customer facilities
• Location
• Communication links
Scheduling
• Hours of event(s)
• Continuous versus intermittent
• Frequency of intermittent events
Physical resource deployment
• What tasks
• When
• Where
Extent of participation of customers in event experience
Allocation of tasks

Positioning proposition
• Product elements
• Distinguishing characteristics
• Target market

Customer benefits
• Core benefit
• Tangible elements
• Augmented product
Costs
• Money
• Time
• Mental effort
• Physical effort

Event experience delivery process

(**Source:** *Adapted from Lovelock et al, 2004, p. 222.*)

- *Major process innovations* — use of new processes to deliver events in new ways with added consumer benefits. The Internet has played a central role in innovating event delivery — for example, Queensland's cyber dance millennium event for youth gave teenagers a chance to attend and/or log on to a dance event to celebrate the turn of the century.
- *Product (event) line extensions* — additions to the current event programs of existing events or festivals. This form of product development is very common. RiverEd, for example, is an environmental event initiative of the Riverfestival for school children, which extends the festival's event program to include year-round happenings in schools.
- *Process (event delivery) extensions* — adjustments to the way in which existing events or festivals are delivered. The use of Internet ticketing agencies and on-line booking of festival space by food and beverage vendors, for example, have enhanced event delivery processes.

- *Supplementary service innovations* — extra services that build on the event or festival experience. Examples are on-site childcare facilities, automatic teller machines and public telephones at event sites.
- *Service improvements* — modest changes that improve the event performance or the way in which it is delivered. Examples are a fashion festival featuring the work of a wider array of designers, and more outlets being provided for ticket purchase.
- *Style changes* — simple forms of product development for an event. Examples are improved seating arrangements, a new festival logo and better costumes.

For any event, the decision to undertake any of the 'product' development strategies proposed must be based on market research. Although it is not possible to pre-test events as market offerings, new concepts or style changes (such as a new festival logo) are readily tested in the target market using qualitative research techniques such as focus groups. Some form of event concept testing is desirable before major changes are made.

■ Programming *the event*

A critical aspect of the event product that is not widely discussed is the development of an attractive event program. For event managers, it is important to have an event portfolio that reflects (1) the mission, (2) the desired level of quality that satisfies artistic and market criteria, and (3) the revenue or profit objectives of event managers. The nature and range of market segments, and the ability to create thematic links between program elements are further considerations. Often, organisers need to balance the personal or artistic vision of event directors with the realities of market success criteria and the costs involved. The event program may also reflect media broadcasting requirements, the availability of desired performers or players, and the practicalities of staging the event concept. In addition, the event manager must consider the programming of competing events, the event's life cycle phase (for example, more mature events may require some innovative programming to survive) and the duration of the event.

An excellent example of event programming is the 2003 Ten Days on the Island festival created by Australian artistic director Robyn Archer. This festival gained its thematic cohesion by capitalising on Tasmania's island status and linking each event to an island theme — for example Papua New Guinea, Madagascar and Sicily. Reflecting on their event programming experience at a Dublin discussion forum (Theatre Shop Conference 2002), Archer and several other producers pointed to at least four key elements in programming success:

1. *The need for a distinguishing core concept in the program* — what is it that you're presenting that actually has meaning to the audience? The Stompem Ground event in Broome, Western Australia celebrates Aboriginal musicians and bands who are out of the mainstream, many of

whom are brilliant but unknown. Its program is of great import in providing a platform for new and existing Aboriginal artists.

2. *The need to marry the event program with its physical environment or site* — what kinds of performances will really be spectacular in this setting? What kinds of performers and stage structures (existing and created) will shine in this environment? The Festival of Perth enhanced its 2002 program by staging musical events in the historic streets of nearby Fremantle and presenting a unique sculptural event on the Nullarbor Plain.

3. *The role and operational approach of the artistic director/producer* — the producers are both program gatekeepers (selecting event participants from proposals submitted by performers) and poachers (travelling around to pick the best performers, just as sports clubs send out their talent scouts).

4. *Established criteria for program content* — criteria include the compatibility of performers to a festival's market, the history of this type of performance at other events, and a performance's technical quality. Some producers of bigger festivals have a rule about (1) how many times an overseas act has performed within the country, and (2) a desired ratio of innovation and tradition in their event portfolio.

Programming is both an art and a science. The event manager considers the artistic or sport-related criteria that an event should achieve, as well as its marketing criteria. However, as with all successful entertainment, an intangible 'wow' factor also differentiates the truly successful event program.

■ Packaging *the event*

Packaging is perhaps one of the most underdeveloped elements of the event marketing mix. Avenues for packaging include the opportunity to package different types of entertainment, food and beverage, and merchandise as a single market offer (a service bundle), and the opportunity to package the event with accommodation, transport and other attractions in the nearby region. Many festivals fail to tap into packaging opportunities that can be an effective means of better positioning the festival in its current markets and attracting tourists. In contrast, motor racing events such as the Gold Coast Indy and the Clipsal 500 in Adelaide draw interstate and overseas tourists, demonstrating some sophistication with packaging. Close ties between the Clipsal 500 and the South Australian Tourism Commission (SATC) were evident in SATC's 2004 packages, which included return economy class airfares from other Australian cities, four nights' accommodation and a four-day grandstand ticket to the event. The ability to package an event goes back to its 'drawing power' discussed earlier. However, in the performing arts and sport, special package deals for existing subscribers or members represent another viable marketing use for the package concept.

PEOPLE AND PARTNERSHIPS

The principles of relationship marketing and management of key stakeholders and consumers now pervade the marketing literature. Many festivals and events start their lives on the basis of 'relationships and goodwill' between a dedicated group of people, so it is not unusual to find that successful events have solid partnerships and strong links with loyal supporters (attendees, volunteers, government and corporate representatives). For many festivals, a 'sense of sharing a common vision' often pervades the atmosphere, with a loose alliance between the types of people who run the festival and those who enjoy it. With large-scale events, it is hard to create that same sense of belonging, but strategies dedicated to building relationships with volunteers, sponsors and visitors are common. Partnerships are critical in attracting the resources to plan, manage and evaluate the event's marketing strategies.

The people of interest are not just event staff and volunteers (chapter 6) and event attendees, but also the wider residential community. Community consultation and relationship building should be marketing concerns for an event from its inception. While organisers of the Gold Coast Indy worked to overcome negative reactions by local residents, Melbourne's Formula One Grand Prix is an example of an event that retains a long-standing group of protestors. From a brand equity perspective, events need ambassadors internally and externally to fully capitalise on their competitive potential.

PRICING, FREE ENTRY OR DONATION

Given the diversity of leisure experiences offered to consumers, price can be a key influence on event demand. Contrasts in pricing strategy exist according to the type of event and its target markets. A mass-market event such as an agricultural show must keep its price at a level of affordability for its customers — middle income, middle Australia. On the other hand, a fundraising event for the Sydney Theatre Company can ask a much higher price because its target market is much smaller (AB segments who are company subscribers), with the ability to pay for a high-price, high-quality experience. A high price can also project quality (or 'value for money') to potential consumers and influence their decision to purchase.

While many special events are ticketed, a large number of festivals do not charge an entrance fee, and some simply seek a gold coin donation. However, a 'free' event still presents costs to the consumer and costs to the producer. Other key influences on ticket price or entry fees are competing opportunities and perceived value. The concept of 'net value' or the sum of all perceived benefits (gross value) minus the sum of all the perceived costs (monetary and otherwise) is useful for event marketers. The greater the positive difference between perceived benefits and costs, the greater the net value to the consumer.

With the Sydney Theatre Company fundraiser, potential consumers compare the perceived benefits — dinner, drinks, entertainment, parking, opportunities to socialise, prestige and the novelty of an unusual night out — with the perceived costs. These costs could include money, time, the physical effort involved in getting to the venue, psychic costs (related to social interaction) and sensory costs (such as going out on a rainy night). If the organiser has adequately positioned the event and communicated its benefits, the target market is likely to perceive a positive net value and purchase tickets.

In establishing the pricing strategy for an event, an organiser will account for two cost categories:

1. *fixed costs* — those costs that do not vary with the volume of visitors (for example, venue rental, interest charged on loans, lighting and power costs, the cost of volunteers' uniforms, and artists' fees)

2. *variable costs* — those costs that vary with the number of visitors to the event (for example, the cost of plastic wine glasses at a festival, catering costs at a product launch, and the cost of staff needed to serve attendees).

As well as analysing the above costs, the event manager should investigate the price of competing leisure experiences. If a similar leisure experience has a price of x, the choices are:

1. match and charge the price x

2. adopt a cost leadership strategy and charge $x - 25$ per cent, or

3. adopt a differentiation strategy and use a price of $x + 50$ per cent, and use marketing communications to promote the value of the event.

Pricing strategies used to achieve event objectives may be revenue oriented, operations oriented or market based. A revenue-oriented strategy is designed to maximise revenue by charging the highest price that the target market will pay. The Sydney Theatre Company's fundraiser is an example of a revenue-oriented pricing strategy. An operations-oriented pricing strategy seeks to balance supply and demand by introducing cheaper prices for times of low demand and higher prices at times of higher demand. Agricultural shows often use an operations-oriented pricing strategy. Finally, a market-oriented strategy uses differential pricing, which may be linked to alternate event packages. A clear link between packaging and pricing exists where a three-day music festival charges one price for those who participate for all three days (the fanatics), a day price to capture the first-timers or 'dabblers', and another price to see the headline act and enjoy a gourmet dinner package.

Key questions that the event marketer must resolve in determining the pricing strategy relate to both pricing levels and methods of payment. Figure 7.9 summarises the decisions to be made by the marketer, along with some of the strategic options available.

How much should be charged?
- What costs must be covered?
- How sensitive are customers to different prices?
- What are leisure competitors' prices?
- What levels of discounts to selected target markets are appropriate?
- Should psychological pricing (for example, $10.95 instead of $11) be used?

What should be the basis of pricing?
- Should each element be billed separately?
- Should one admission fee be charged?
- Should consumers be charged for resources consumed?
- Should a single price for a bundled package be charged?

Who shall collect payment?
- The event organisation?
- A ticketing intermediary?

Where should payment be made?
- At the event?
- At a ticketing organisation?
- At the customer's home? Using the Internet or telephone?

When should payment be made?
- When tickets are given out?
- On the day of the event?

How should payment be made?
- Cash — exact change?
- Credit card?
- Electronic funds transfer at point of sale (EFTPOS)?
- Token donation?

(**Source:** *Adapted from Lovelock, Patterson & Walker 2004, p. 256.*)

EVENT 'PLACE', PHYSICAL SETTING AND PROCESSES

'Place' refers to both the site where the event takes place (the venue) and the place at which consumers can purchase their tickets. Other decisions with marketing implications are (1) the design of the event setting, and (2) the processes used to deliver and experience the event.

The choice of a single venue or multiple sites for sports or cultural events should be made in the context of the event's overall strategy — for example, a strategy of market penetration or expansion. Increasingly, event marketers are recognising that market expansion can be achieved by taking their events to new locations. In 2003, the Queensland Conservatorium Symphony Orchestra staged a two-hour performance for an enthralled crowd at the Isis Downs shearing shed in western Queensland — an example of an innovative use of 'place' to add to an event's sense of 'occasion'.

The physical setting, as noted in the discussion of programming, is crucial to the satisfaction of the event consumer. Most services marketers include it as a key element in the marketing mix, alongside processes of service delivery. As a result, you are encouraged to review the consumer implications of all facets of event design (chapters 13 and 14) to ensure you fully understand them.

In deciding the most appropriate place(s) for ticket distribution, organisers may question whether to use a ticketing agency. Ticketing agencies widen the distribution network, ease the consumer's purchase process and speed up the entry of customers to a venue. While they also facilitate credit card purchases and telephone bookings, charges are incurred by both the event organiser and the customer. The benefits of using a ticket agency depend on the type of event, the availability of other ticket distribution options (such as the box office of a small theatre company and/or direct mail), the willingness of the target market to pay for a ticketing service, and the service's relative affordability.

Selling tickets via a ticketing agency or another distribution network such as the Internet has some advantages for the event producer. Ticket sales can be monitored, and the data collected can guide decisions on the level of marketing communication expenditure needed to attract the targeted visitor numbers. The security problems inherent in accepting cash at the door or gate are also alleviated. Because customers pay in advance, the cash flow to the event producer occurs well before the staging of the event, with obvious financial advantages for the event organiser.

The use of the Internet as a distribution medium for events is now widespread, with the key advantages of on-line ticket sales being:

- *speed* — consumers can purchase tickets without leaving their home, queuing or waiting for a phone operator to become available
- *consumer ease* — consumers can view the different experiences offered by the event or festival in their own time, selecting the events or shows that best suit their pocket and time constraints
- *revenue* — ticket revenue comes from the buyer's credit card, which facilitates security and ease of collection
- *up-to-date technology* — more and more consumers expect leisure services to be available for purchase on the Internet. An on-line presence is critical in establishing an event or festival brand.

The Melbourne International Comedy Festival, a multi-venue, multi-show festival, is one of many events that employ on-line ticket distribution. The festival uses a ticketing agency, Ticketmaster7.com, which also manages Comedy Festival box office, on-line and telephone purchase of tickets. This festival's organisers have adopted creative pricing strategies that link with the booking process, such as the Laugh Pack in 2004: consumers booking through Ticketmaster7 who paid for three different shows at the same time qualified for a Laugh Pack price. Events and festivals rarely have their own on-line booking system that can accept bookings and credit card details electronically at no charge to the consumer. However, advances in technology are likely to result in increased efficiencies in on-line distribution over time.

Apart from ticketing, other operational processes have an immediate impact on the experience of event consumers. Visitors evaluate security checks on entry to the event, queuing for food, and the speed of access to services such as automatic teller machines and toilets. While later chapters address many of these event 'processes', the marketing implications of a smooth integration of 'front stage' and 'backstage' happenings at an event cannot be underestimated. The physical environment and processes that happen in that physical space directly contribute to the event's brand image — for example, mosh pits and crowd surfing at youth concerts are a logistical issue with significant implications for these events' ongoing market acceptance.

*I*NTEGRATED MARKETING COMMUNICATION FOR EVENTS

Where 'promotion' was once the primary term for the communication element in the marketing mix, the use of 'integrated marketing communication' (IMC) has all but overtaken it. With diverse changes in media technology, market expectations and competition, the traditional idea of promoting 'to' a market has been replaced by the need to form relationships 'with' the market. Integrated marketing communication 'considers all sources of contact that a consumer has [with the event] as potential delivery channels for messages and, makes use of all communication methods that are relevant to consumers' (Shimp 2003, p. 8). The platform for creating IMC strategies for events and festivals is knowledge about the visitors –– the consumer database that allows the event to establish a dialogue with the event's consumers. How an event manages its consumer relationships drives its brand value (Duncan 2002). When we think about an event brand such as the Sydney Gay and Lesbian Mardi Gras, we think of 'an integrated bundle of information and experiences that distinguish [it]' (Duncan 2002, p. 13) from competing leisure experiences. Figure 7.10 (page 220) offers an insight into the IMC process for an event, and the range of traditional and non-traditional media that create brand relationships.

Branding for an event is much more than a physical identity such as the five interlocking rings of the Olympics. The Olympics brand is based on perceptions, how we relate to that event and what it promises, as well as the physical logo and symbols (for example, the Olympic torch). However, clever use of the brand helps the event manager to make an intangible phenomenon more tangible for event consumers.

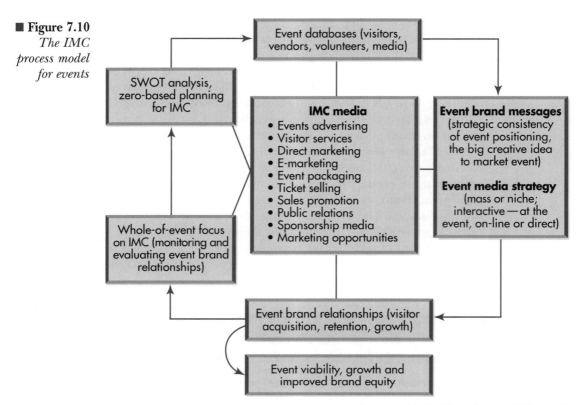

■ **Figure 7.10**
The IMC process model for events

Event databases (visitors, vendors, volunteers, media)

SWOT analysis, zero-based planning for IMC

IMC media
- Events advertising
- Visitor services
- Direct marketing
- E-marketing
- Event packaging
- Ticket selling
- Sales promotion
- Public relations
- Sponsorship media
- Marketing opportunities

Event brand messages (strategic consistency of event positioning, the big creative idea to market event)

Event media strategy (mass or niche; interactive — at the event, on-line or direct)

Whole-of-event focus on IMC (monitoring and evaluating event brand relationships)

Event brand relationships (visitor acquisition, retention, growth)

Event viability, growth and improved brand equity

(**Source:** *Adapted from Duncan 2002, p. 9.*)

In developing an IMC strategy, an organiser should understand four sources of brand messages (Duncan 2002):

1. *planned messages* (media releases, personal selling by the box office and/or ticket agency, advertising, e-newsletters, website)
2. *unplanned messages* (unexpected positive or negative impressions formed by word of mouth, media coverage, complaints)
3. *product messages* (implied messages of decisions about the event — program, pricing, venue)
4. *service messages* (the nature of contact with festival or event staff or volunteers, the quality of event transport, other support services).

Given these message types, the event brand is shaped by more than its planned promotional tools; instead, there are many influences on the brand, some of which are more controllable than others.

Mirroring the strategy process, the development of an IMC plan hinges on an effective SWOT analysis, plus consumer and stakeholder research. The information from the analysis and research provides the platform for deciding whether objectives and strategies for the IMC campaign should be informational, transformational (attitudinal), behavioural or relational in their focus. Figure 7.11 shows how these different approaches correspond with the 'think, feel, do' model of consumer behaviour.

■ **Figure 7.11**
*Event
message
objectives
and
strategies*

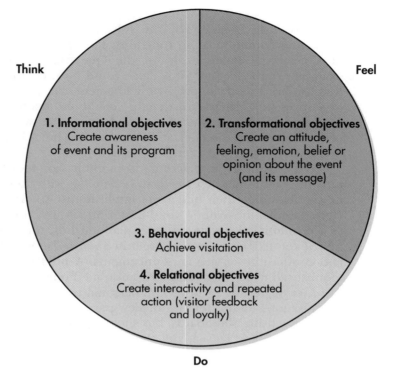

Think

Feel

1. Informational objectives
Create awareness
of event and its program

2. Transformational objectives
Create an attitude,
feeling, emotion, belief or
opinion about the event
(and its message)

3. Behavioural objectives
Achieve visitation

4. Relational objectives
Create interactivity and repeated
action (visitor feedback
and loyalty)

Do

(**Source:** *Adapted from Duncan 2002, p. 320.*)

Importantly, consumers do not react to marketing messages in any set order — they may feel, then act (local festival attendance) and later think about the experience, or they may go through a sequential processing of 'think, feel and act' (such as a decision to visit France to attend the next Rugby World Cup). It is important to consider these different decision-making patterns of market segments when deciding how to set out the objectives of a campaign.

The IMC strategy reflects the thrust of the chosen objectives and uses both *message* and *media* strategies to fulfil them. To illustrate, the Queensland Reds rugby union team may have a behavioural objective of 'achieving a 10 per cent increase in attendance at home games at the Ballymore oval in 2006'. Their message strategy would be developed with reference to the psychological appeal — for example, motivators such as the responsibility of locals to support the home side, and the atmosphere and nostalgia attached to Ballymore as a rugby venue. Planning the IMC campaign requires 'one voice, one look' (Duncan 2002) — that is, all direct marketing, advertising, publicity and event packaging must convey the same message and look in its communication. At a national level, the Australian Rugby Union successfully achieved 'one voice, one look' with its True Colours campaign for the Rugby World Cup 2003.

For the Queensland Reds, the media strategy involves choosing how the mix of planned advertising, e-marketing, publicity and/or other media will be used to best convey the message about home game attendance. As shown in figure 7.10 (page 220), the IMC mix can include a wide range of marketing communication functions. Public relations may involve the use of a celebrity spokesperson in the Queensland Reds campaign — for example, rugby legend John Eales could be used to boost interest in the Reds. A direct mail campaign and an e-newsletter to a database of corporate executives (a key market for rugby) could also feature John Eales and give further strategic consistency to the campaign. Sales promotion in the form of a competition directed at Brisbane's AB households in select suburbs might also bolster the attendees at rugby games.

Given the numerous marketing communication tools to include in an IMC mix, the event marketer needs to be familiar with their strengths and weaknesses, including their budgetary implications. An event with a mass market (for example, the Sydney Royal Easter Show) may use television advertising as a promotional device, whereas planned IMC for a community festival is more likely to concentrate on organised word of mouth, local media publicity and community service announcements. A brief review of the more commonly used marketing communication mediums is offered here.

Advertising is any form of non-personal promotion paid for by the event organisation. Radio, television, newspapers, magazines, the Internet, outdoor advertising (billboards, bus shelters and toilets) and mobile platforms such as buses and taxis are all channels for advertising. For most events and festivals, the expense of mainstream media (capital city television, newspapers and radio) cannot be justified. Media partnerships (such as Riverfestival's sponsorship by Channel 9) can help to resolve this issue. However, the creative process of producing the messages can also be expensive, especially if done by an advertising agency. In creating advertising campaigns for events and festivals, it is vital to:
- provide tangible clues to counteract the intangible nature of the event — that is, show the artistic event or sports players in action, the event logo, the spectacle of the fireworks
- seek continuity over time by using recognisable symbols, spokespersons, trademarks or music — for example, football codes often use the tunes of famous artists, such as 'We are the champions' by Queen
- promise what is possible to foster realistic expectations — for example, show real-time action (It is necessary to take care with promises about ticket availability because they can become contentious.)
- make the service more tangible and recognisable by showing members of the target market enjoying the event — for example, the roar and spectacle of a grand final crowd at the football is very persuasive.

Public relations is used to build mutually beneficial relationships with stakeholders and consumers. It uses a wide range of tools, including publicity, special events, community consultation, e-publications and traditional newsletters. While all activities incur costs, media publicity is often favoured by festival organisers because it provides unpaid space in the media that reaches the event's market. An advantage to festival and event directors is that people generally enjoy reading about the sport, the arts and entertainment. However, marketers must be aware that the media will use a story only if it has news value (a unique angle or item of information of interest to readers, viewers or listeners). Journalists also carefully assess the structure and style of media releases, and the credibility of their source.

Sales promotion consists of those activities that use incentives or discounts to increase sales or attendance. Examples of sales promotion are family days at city shows or exhibitions, offering group discounts or a free ticket for one child. Alternatively, consumers may be offered free merchandise (T-shirts and posters) when purchasing several tickets or more.

Direct marketing communicates one-on-one with existing festival or event goers via mail, the telephone or the Internet. It relies on organisers developing a list of people who previously attended the event and obtaining knowledge about their demographic profile and preferences. Incentives for consumers to provide information may include entry in a competition and the receipt of next year's event program. Organisers can purchase lists of potential event consumers from direct marketing agencies. However, a key consideration in collecting information to build a database is the need to gain consumer permission and to respect consumer privacy. An understanding of current regulations about direct marketing (including the use of e-newsletters) is now mandatory.

Many event directors find it difficult to determine a marketing communication budget. They sometimes use guides such as a percentage of ticket sales (5–10 per cent), what competitors appear to be spending or what was spent last year. However, zero-based budgeting is the best approach, whereby the marketer works from a zero base to cost out the best mix of IMC strategies and tactics to achieve the set objectives. A marketing objective of selling 10 000 tickets could flow on to an IMC objective of educating a potential market of 100 000 people about the benefits of the event. A mix of advertising, direct marketing (on-line and off-line) and publicity might be considered. Yet, the IMC campaign cost must be realistic for that event or festival. In-kind support by website designers, graphic artists and printers, plus sponsored media space (television, newspapers and/or radio), can reduce a festival or event's financial outlay. However, for most events, the need to prioritise IMC strategies and tactics to trim down the financial outlay is inevitable. Wherever possible, the IMC strategies that move the event closer to a behavioural result must be preserved.

Summary

A common misconception of many in the festival and event area is that marketing means nothing more than 'event promotion'. As this chapter has shown, marketing is a structured and coherent way of thinking about managing an event or festival to achieve objectives related to market/stakeholder awareness, event attendance, satisfaction and either profits or increased understanding of a cause.

The core of event marketing is the focus on existing and potential leisure consumers — in this case, the event attendee. Successful marketing flows from a complete understanding of these consumers — who they are, where they live and the leisure needs they seek to satisfy. This understanding comes from primary and secondary market research and two-way communication with event stakeholders and consumers. From this knowledge, organisers can develop strategies and tactics that span the event product (including its programming and packaging), its place (venues, the physical setting and ticket outlets), its delivery processes, its people and partnerships, and integrated marketing communication.

Questions

1. Identify the five key characteristics of services. Offer examples of each characteristic in the event or festival context.

2. Discuss some technological challenges that have an impact on the marketing success of events managers.

3. Outline five key motives for festival attendance.

4. Identify the key steps in the consumer decision process. Offer examples of how each step affects the event consumer.

5. What considerations (other than monetary costs) influence decisions on pricing an event?

6. What are the four key criteria for successful programming identified by event producers?

7. Provide examples of three forms of product development in the event or festival context.

8. Why is the term 'promotion' less relevant than 'integrated marketing communication' (IMC) for events marketers?

Brisbane's Ekka —
repositioning and growing a hallmark event

Brisbane's annual Ekka is a hallmark event attracting about half a million people to the RNA Showgrounds over its 10 days and adding more than $100 million to Brisbane's economy each year. The Royal National Agricultural and Industrial Association of Queensland (RNA) is responsible for organising the Ekka (or, as it is officially called, the Royal Queensland Show). The RNA's main business is to provide entertainment to Queensland, particularly Brisbane, residents. The RNA relies on ticket sales for most of its revenue, and the business growth objective for the Ekka is to increase visitor attendances each year by targeting repeat visitors (those who attend every year) and casual visitors (those who attend at least every three years). Visitor numbers also affect the Ekka's ability to maintain revenue from advertising and sponsorship. The Ekka's working relationships with its sponsors involve both cash and contra deals, and represent a key strength that has provided important marketing benefits for the Ekka.

Recent data show a national decrease in attendance at agricultural shows, including the Ekka. While Ekka 2001 attracted approximately 680 000 visitors, Ekka 2002 attracted around 480 000 visitors. Ekka 2002, carpark leasing and investment activities resulted in a loss of $2.2 million to the RNA.

The Ekka 'event concept' and its brand recognition
The Ekka is an established brand name, widely recognised by Queenslanders. In the consumer's mind, the Ekka brings the country to the city for a celebration of the 'best of the best' of Queensland. The uniqueness or market differentiation of the Ekka is its overall 'service experience', which involves farm animals, wood-chopping, agricultural exhibits, art and craft, horse events, fashion parades, fireworks, sideshow alley, show bags and more. The Ekka is also the only show that judges and showcases the best of Queensland's agricultural, pastoral, horticultural and industrial industries. Competitors in these fields compete for prestigious awards and recognition.

The Ekka's target markets
The Ekka has always targeted a broad cross-section of the Queensland population, but research has shown that the appeal of agricultural shows is limited to a specific target market that must be captured to sustain and grow future Ekkas. The greatest market segment (about 36 per cent of respondents to the Ekka 2002 market research) comprises families with children aged under 14 years. Senior citizens are the second largest group (23 per cent of attendees). (The box

(continued)

below shows a snapshot of the Ekka's market research from 2002.) These findings underpinned the decision for the Ekka 2003 marketing strategy to treat families with young children as the primary target market and senior citizens as the secondary target market.

■ Seventy-three per cent of attendees were Brisbane residents (down 5 per cent from 2001), 10 per cent were Gold or Sunshine Coast residents (down 2 per cent from the Sunshine Coast), 10 per cent lived in other areas of Queensland (down 1 per cent) and 4 per cent were from interstate.

■ Forty-four per cent were male and 56 per cent were female.

■ Fourteen per cent of respondents earn $80 000 or more, and 14 per cent earned less than $20 000.

■ Twenty per cent of respondents visited every year, 70 per cent visited at least every three years, and 9 per cent said Ekka 2002 was their first visit.

■ Seventy per cent of respondents' groups spent at least $100 at Ekka 2002, with 35 per cent spending $100–200. The most significant differences in spending among target segments involved senior citizens, who were the most likely to have spent less than $100 in their group and the least likely to have spent $200 or more.

■ Reasons for attending Ekka 2002 were as follows: for the kids' benefits (32 per cent); to see the exhibits, displays and shows (19 per cent); tradition/never miss it (16 per cent); the Ekka is enjoyable/fun (14 per cent); for friends/family (13 per cent); working there (4 per cent); show bags (3 per cent); something to do/an outing/look around (3 per cent); events/entertainment (2 per cent); free tickets (2 per cent); the rural aspect (2 per cent); to see changes (2 per cent); and other (9 per cent).

Findings of the Ekka Attendees Survey 2002

Loyal visitors see the Ekka as an annual tradition. Many attendees visited the Ekka as a child and now visit with their family and grandchildren. An indicator of the potential for growth in Ekka attendance is Brisbane's status as one of the fastest growing cities in Australia. With a population of approximately 1.5 million people, Bisbane also had the second highest percentage of children aged 0–4 years (6.8 per cent, or 101 362 people) in 2001 and the second highest percentage of people aged 15–24 years of all Australian capital cities after Canberra (15.4 per cent or 229 523 people).

Issues highlighted for treatment by Ekka's marketing management

Over 2001–02, the personnel involved in Ekka's marketing management identified the following key issues:

• the need to focus the marketing strategy on the particular needs of one or two clearly defined visitor segments rather than targeting everyone

• the need to overcome the perception that the Ekka was repetitive, predictable and lacking in innovation. People generally felt the Ekka did not provide a unique experience.

• the need to further promote the Ekka and ensure promotion was commenced well in advance of the event

- the need to refurbish buildings and other infrastructure to entice visitors to the show
- the need to offer better value for money. Admission prices were perceived as expensive, given they did not include many activities. This was the most disliked aspect of the Ekka. Cheaper specialist shows, such as home and garden shows, were seen to be eroding the Ekka's attendance. Overall, consumers felt that some of those specialist shows gave better value for money, were not as crowded, and offered something of interest without expensive diversions. In addition, different types of competitor in Australia's amusement, leisure and recreation industries were constantly adopting new strategies that could capture the Ekka's market.
- the need to recognise the potential for suppliers to exit the show due to declining visitor numbers, which would further affect the Ekka's ability to provide a unique service experience for attendees
- the need to reposition the Ekka to accommodate changes in consumer attitudes and wants. A negative mindset towards agricultural events may present a palpable threat for the Ekka's marketers.

Following on from the issues to be addressed, the Ekka 2003 marketing management strategy identified the following key success factors:

- *Target children aged 7–14 years to attract families.* The event is known for family-friendly entertainment and products, and there is an expectation of family interaction. A focus on children, who have significant influence on family spending, meant that visitor attendance at 2003 was likely to increase. Communication methods used by the marketers needed to account for children's media preferences and habits, including the introduction of a simplified, interactive children's Ekka website and promotional incentives for attending. Opportunities for social interaction were introduced to the website, including e-cards, downloadable screen savers, colouring-in competitions and games. The more time children spent on the website, the more familiar they would become with the Ekka brand. This familiarity would provide children with information and incentives about the Ekka, and stimulate their interest in experiencing it.
- *Provide stimulating 'product' experiences for children.* A goal was to highlight the Ekka as a great place to visit in the minds of children, along the lines of the experience provided by the Cartoon Network pay-TV channel. The Cartoon Network uses 'on the ground' events as part of its marketing mix — for example, hosting events such as the Looney Tunes Kids Games in Melbourne, which brought the Cartoon Network's brand 'beyond the television'. The Ekka wanted to capture that kind of stimulation in some of its product offerings.
- *Deliver on the marketing promises.* Other Ekka 2003 opportunities and challenges included:
  - developing pricing strategies and ticketing options to allow visitors to choose the offer that best represented value for money for them
  - addressing problems identified at Ekka 2002, at which many parents were unhappy that the area traditionally used for children's rides was occupied by youth activities such as Extreme Games and Planet X, the number of children's rides had decreased, and the rides were in the sun

(*continued*)

— improving products and introducing new experiences

— using the Internet to target children aged 7–14 years and to gather primary data on children for use in developing future marketing strategies.

Ekka 2003 marketing program and outcomes

Ekka 2003 used an aggressive integrated marketing communications (IMC) program that addressed the aims and objectives stated in the event's 2003 action plan. The marketing strategy focused on the key success factors discussed earlier. Its aims and outcomes were as follows:

- *Positioning the Ekka as a fun family event* through a new slogan ('Smile. It's Showtime!'), new creative concepts (the 'Ekka animals') and an innovative and family-friendly entertainment program. In 2002, the focus was purely on promoting the principal main arena entertainment. The 'Ekka animals' — a llama, cow, horse and pig with human smiles — were used in various media.

- *Developing an active marketing program that addressed all Ekka target markets.* An IMC program involved the use of print, radio, television, outdoor media, public relations activities and an extensive promotional program. The mix of these mediums extended Ekka's reach, guaranteeing exposure in many areas of Queensland.

- *Increasing visitor attendance, including paying visitor attendance.* Marketing activities, including ticketing strategies to pre-sell tickets, were effective in increasing visitor attendance. Pre-sold tickets were up 88 per cent from pre-sold tickets for Ekka 2002, and total attendance increased by 6 per cent. Paying visitor attendance also increased by 6 per cent (above expectations of 5 per cent).

- *Attracting more children aged 7–14 years.* Children represented 15 per cent of total paying visitors at Ekka 2002, which resulted in $553 993 in revenue to the RNA. Among attendees at Ekka 2003, 22 per cent were children, resulting in $853 150 in revenue. The Ekka continued to attract its core segment of families: 23 per cent of survey respondents were members of a 'family with most children aged 14 and older' and 22 per cent were 'family with most children aged 5 to less than 14 years'. Ekka 2003 attracted people who attended with their partner (48 per cent), their children (30 per cent) and other family members (27 per cent). The results thus reinforced that the Ekka is truly a family event. There was also an increase in the number of single people living alone or in shared accommodation who attended Ekka 2003 (23 per cent), compared with Ekka 2002.

- *Reinforcing perceptions of the Ekka as a value-for-money event.* Ekka 2003 was not highly regarded for its value for money. Satisfaction with the Ekka admission price was lower than in 2002.

- *Increasing the likelihood of return visits to Ekka 2004.* Market research showed that visitor satisfaction levels with entertainment, atmosphere and excitement for Ekka 2003 (rated 8.4 on a 10-point scale) were higher than for Ekka 2002 (rated 7.8). There was also greater satisfaction with staff, event location and access, exhibits and the shows staged in the main arena. Market research showed a greater likelihood of respondents at Ekka 2003 attending the Ekka in the future, compared with respondents at Ekka 2002. Ekka 2003 attracted a large proportion of people (46 per cent of respondents) who did not attend Ekka 2002 and also first-time visitors to the show (8 per cent of respondents).

- *Achieving visitor revenue of $3.3 million.* Budgeted visitor revenue exceeded $3.3 million.
- *Maintaining marketing expenditure at $430 000.* The marketing expenditure was maintained below the budget of $430 000. This did not include the budgeted $40 000 for printing of the Ekka showguide. The total marketing and printing budget for Ekka 2003 was $470 000, while the total expenditure was $436 557, equating to a saving of $33 443.
- *Holding the entertainment expenditure at $855 000.* The entertainment expenditure budget for Ekka 2003 was maintained at $855 000.
- *Creating theme days during the Ekka 10-day period.* The last day of Ekka was themed 'Seniors Day' and hosted the official launch of Seniors Week, along with entertainment targeted specifically at older people. On this last day, the admission price for seniors was lowered to $10 instead of the concession rate of $14.

Overall, Ekka 2003 was a much more successful event than Ekka 2002. It attracted large volumes of positive media attention before and during the show. The introduction of a new theme ('Smile. It's Showtime!') and an innovative and friendly entertainment program, supported by an extensive integrated marketing communications program (and mostly great weather), contributed to the enjoyable service experience at the show.

Bill Proud, Managing Director, The Marketing Centre

Questions

1 The marketing for the Ekka 2003 led to increases in attendance figures and gate revenue, achieving profitable results. What other marketing strategies and actions could have been used to ensure a turnaround in profit and attendances?

2 The marketing strategy clearly targeted children aged 7–14 years and seniors (55+ years). Was this the correct segmentation strategy or could a more targeted approach have been undertaken? Why?

3 A range of different stakeholders are involved in the RNA and important to the success of the event. Do you think the strategies discussed addressed all of the needs of the different stakeholder groups of this event? How could they be improved in this sense?

4 The Ekka receives a high level of publicity and exposure. Consider a range of ways in which the event organisers could build further innovation into their integrated marketing communication strategies to appeal to the target markets.

5 Perceptions of the Ekka's pricing continue to be a problem for the event organisers. Offer some thoughts on how the organisers could develop new pricing/ticketing options for the Ekka.

REFERENCES

Accolade Event Management, www.accolade.net.au (accessed April 2004).

Ansoff, I 1957, 'Strategies for diversification', *Harvard Business Review*, September–October, pp. 113–24.

Axelsen, M & Arcodia, C 2004, 'Motivations for attending the Asia–Pacific Triennial Art Exhibition', Paper presented at the 14th International Research Conference of the Council for Australian University Tourism and Hospitality Education, 10–13 February, Brisbane.

Backman, KF, Backman, SJ, Muzaffer, U & Sunshine, K 1995, 'Event tourism: an examination of motivations and activities', *Festival Management and Event Tourism*, vol. 3, no. 1, pp. 26–34.

Baker, DA & Crompton, JL 2000, 'Quality, satisfaction, and behavioural intentions', *Annals of Tourism Research*, vol. 27, no. 3, pp. 785–804.

Cordingly, S 1999, *Managing volunteers*, Volunteers Australia, www.fuel4arts.com.au (accessed 3 March 2004).

Cravens, D, Merrilees, B & Walker, R 2000, *Strategic marketing management for the Pacific region*, McGraw-Hill, Sydney.

Crompton, J & McKay, S 1997, 'Motives of visitors attending festival events', *Annals of Tourism Research*, vol. 24, no. 2, pp. 425–39.

Dickman, S 1997, 'Issues in arts marketing', in *Making it happen: the cultural and entertainment industries handbook*, ed. R Rentchler, Centre for Professional Development, Melbourne.

Duncan, T 2002, *IMC: using advertising and promotion to build brands*, McGraw-Hill Irwin, New York.

Getz, D 1991, *Festivals, special events and tourism*, Van Nostrand Reinhold, New York.

Getz, D 1997, *Event management and event tourism*, Cognizant Communications, New York.

Gronroos, C 1990, *Services marketing and management*, Lexington Books, Lexington, Massachusetts.

Hall, CM 1997, *Hallmark tourist events: impacts, management and planning*, John Wiley & Sons, Chichester, England.

Hall, CM & Mitchell, R 2004, 'BMW Wine Marlborough 2003: a profile of visitors to New Zealand's oldest wine festival', Paper presented at the 14th International Research Conference of the Council for Australian University Tourism and Hospitality Education, 10–13 February, Brisbane.

Hede, A-M, Jago, L & Deery, M 2003, 'Satisfaction-based cluster analysis of theatre event attendees: preliminary results', Paper presented at the 13th International Research Conference of the Council for Australian University Tourism and Hospitality Education, 5–8 February, Coffs Harbour, New South Wales.

Kotler, P, Bowen, J & Makens, J 1999, *Marketing for hospitality and tourism*, 2nd edn, Prentice Hall International, Upper Sadler River, New Jersey.

Lovelock, C, Patterson, P & Walker, R 2004, *Services marketing*, 3rd edn, Pearson Australia Education, Sydney.

Mannell, R & Iso-Ahola, S 1987, 'Psychological nature of leisure and tourism experience', *Annals of Tourism Research*, vol. 14, no. 3, pp. 314–29.

McCarthy, E & Perreault, W 1987, *Basic marketing*, Irwin, Homewood, Illinois.

McCarthy, EJ 1971, *Basic marketing: a managerial approach*, Irwin, Homewood, Illinois.

Melbourne International Comedy Festival, www.comedyfestival.com.au (accessed April 2004).

Mintzberg, H 1994, *The rise and fall of strategic planning*, Prentice Hall, New York.

Mohr, K, Backman, K, Gahan, L & Backman, S 1993, 'An investigation of festival motivations and event satisfaction by visitor type', *Festival Management and Event Tourism*, vol. 1, pp. 89–97.

Morgan, M 1996, *Marketing for leisure and tourism*, Prentice Hall, London.

Neal, C, Quester, P & Hawkins, H 2002, *Consumer behaviour*, 3rd edn, McGraw-Hill, Sydney.

Out of the Box Festival of Early Childhood (Brisbane), www.ootb.qpat.com.au (accessed April 2004).

Parasuraman, A, Zeithaml, V & Berry L 1988 'SERVQUAL: a multiple-item scale for measuring consumers' perceptions of service quality', *Journal of Retailing*, vol. 64, no. 1, pp. 22–37.

Porter, M 1990, *Competitive advantage of nations*, Free Press, New York.

Rao, V & Steckel, J 1998, *Analysis for strategic marketing*, Addison-Wesley, Reading, Massachusetts.

Robertson, D & Pope, N 1999, 'Product bundling and causes of attendance and non-attendance in live professional sport: a case study of the Brisbane Broncos and the Brisbane Lions', *The Cyberjournal of Sports Marketing*, vol. 3.

Saleh, F & Ryan, C 1993, 'Jazz and knitwear: factors that attract tourists to festivals', *Tourism Management*, August, pp. 289–97.

Shimp, T 2003, *Advertising, promotion and supplemental aspects of integrated marketing communication*, 6th edn, Thomson, Ohio.

Stanton, W, Miller, K & Layton, R 1994, *Fundamentals of marketing*, 3rd edn, McGraw-Hill, Sydney.

Sydney Festival, www.sydneyfestival.org.au (accessed April 2004).

Theatre Shop Conference 2002, 'Panel discussion: programming criteria used by international festivals', www.fuel4arts.com (accessed April 2004).

Thrane, C 2002, 'Music quality, satisfaction and behavioural intentions within a jazz festival context', *Event Management: an International Journal*, vol. 7, no. 3, pp. 143–50.

Tribe, J 1997, *Corporate strategy for tourism*, ITB Press, London.

Uysal, M, Gahan, L & Martin, B 1993, 'An examination of event motivations', *Festival Management and Event Tourism*, vol. 1, pp. 5–10.

Woodford Folk Festival, www.woodfordfolkfestival.com.au (accessed April 2004).

Robyn Stokes

CHAPTER

8

Sponsorship
of events

LEARNING OBJECTIVES

After studying this chapter, you should be able to:

- understand the use of sponsorship in the context of festivals and events

- discuss trends that have led to the growth of sponsorship as a marketing communication medium in the private and public sectors

- recognise the benefits that event managers can attract from reciprocal partnerships with sponsors

- identify the key sponsorship benefits sought by events and sponsoring bodies

- discuss the importance of sponsorship 'leveraging'

- understand the need for sponsorship policies to guide decision making by events and their sponsors

- outline the sequential stages in developing and implementing an event sponsorship strategy

- develop strategies and tactics to manage event–sponsor relationships and achieve positive and enduring relationships with sponsors.

INTRODUCTION

Sponsorship, either provided as cash or in-kind support such as products or services (often called 'contra'), is central to the revenue and resources of new and continuing events. Event managers and marketers are usually actively engaged in tasks such as identifying potential sponsors, preparing sponsorship proposals and managing their ongoing relationships with sponsors. This chapter begins with a discussion of the role and growth of sponsorship as a marketing communication medium. It also explores the benefits that events and their sponsors seek, before explaining the policies, strategies and actions needed for successful event and festival sponsorship.

WHAT IS SPONSORSHIP?

Sponsorship has become a critical element in the integrated marketing communication mix (discussed in chapter 7) of many private and public sector organisations. Among the different types of marketing communication (for example, public relations, advertising, personal selling, sales promotions and direct marketing), sponsorship is said to be one of the most powerful mediums now used to communicate and form relationships with stakeholders and markets (Grey & Skildum-Reid 2003). Globally, expenditure on event sponsorship is escalating each year — from $23.16 million in 1999 (Sponsorship Research International 2000) to an estimated $26.2 billion in 2003 (Business Line 2003). Overall sponsorship spending in Australia and New Zealand each year is estimated to be around $870 million (Grey & Skildum-Reid 2003, p. xiv). Importantly, most spending estimates only take into account the sponsorship purchase itself, but it is generally accepted that many sponsors will spend at least equal to the cost of the event property itself on leveraging or maximising investment impacts. (Meenaghan 2001a).

Although sponsorship may be attached to social causes and broadcast media such as television programs as well as special events (de Pelsmacker, Geuens and Van den Bergh 2004), just about every public event is now sponsored in some way (Kover 2001). With the emphasis now on 'connecting with' rather than 'talking at' the marketplace, event and festival sponsorship can be an ideal way for marketers to create brand interaction with consumers and stakeholders. The Toyota Gympie Muster, for example, engages country music-loving consumers in Queensland with a well-known motor vehicle brand. In contrast, the Australian Pipeline Trust (APT) has sponsored Flying Fruit Circus tours into outback Australia to build good relationships with Aboriginal and mining communities and other relevant stakeholders where its pipelines are laid (Australian Business Arts Foundation 2004).

In simple terms, sponsorship is the purchase (either with cash or in-kind support) of exploitable rights and marketing benefits (tangible and intangible) that arise from direct involvement with a personality/player, special event, program, club or agency. The following definition also explains the concept:

■ Sponsorship — an investment in sport, community or government activities, the arts, a cause, individual, or broadcast which yields a commercial return for the sponsor. The investment can be made in financial, material, or human terms (Smart Marketing Street Wise Workshops 2001). ■

Importantly, sponsorship is a strategic marketing investment, not a donation (philanthropy) or a grant (a one-off type of assistance) which means events and festivals must view sponsorships as working business partnerships. Most sponsors are investors who expect to see a direct impact on their brand equity (enhanced awareness and imagery) as well as increased sales and profits. In the case of public sector sponsors, some kind of social marketing result is usually sought (for example, a greater awareness of water conservation or the dangers of drink driving). Heineken sought brand exclusivity for its beer and increased sales through its Rugby World Cup 2003 sponsorship, while Victoria's Transport Accident Commission (TAC) has boosted the awareness of road safety in regional areas by sponsoring Wangaratta's Jazz Festival (Australian Business Arts Foundation 2004).

While long-term cash sponsors are highly sought after by events and festivals, a mix of private sector cash and in-kind sponsorship, plus government grants, can be vital for emerging festivals. Noise 2003, an Australian youth media art festival profiling creative works across radio, television, print and online media drew $2 million in revenue from three revenue streams: the federal government, in-kind and cash sponsors (Longridge 2004). According to Longridge (2004, p. 1) event managers say: 'In-kind support is essential for us. You can't buy airtime on Triple J, Radio National, Classic FM, ABC TV, SBS Radio etc. This in-kind support provides vital media channels to reach large audiences.' Hence, creating a successful event or gaining festival sponsorship means establishing a reciprocal relationship between the organisation providing the sponsorship (corporate, media and/or government) and the event. However, it also means an emotional connection must be made with those consumers targeted by both the event and its sponsors. This three-way relationship which underpins the success of sponsorship is illustrated in figure 8.1 (page 236).

APT's sponsorship of the Flying Fruit Circus is a good example of the interplay between the event itself, its sponsors and the needs of the target market. The event organiser created 'Stepping Stones in Circus Dust' which involved performances and workshops in schools — the end result for the sponsor's target market was a dramatic increase in school attendance by Aboriginal children (Australian Business Arts Foundation 2004). This type of sponsorship illustrates how a mutually beneficial relationship can emerge when an event initiates opportunities that closely fit the sponsor's corporate or marketing objectives (Geldard & Sinclair 2004). The chapter now discusses a number of trends, including the need for more innovative and flexible marketing media, which underpin the rising popularity of sponsorship.

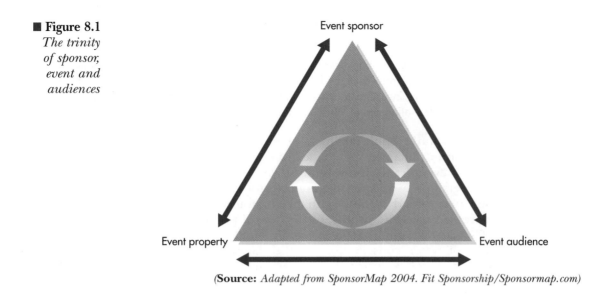

■ Figure 8.1
The trinity of sponsor, event and audiences

Event sponsor

Event property

Event audience

(**Source:** *Adapted from SponsorMap 2004. Fit Sponsorship/Sponsormap.com*)

TRENDS INFLUENCING THE GROWTH OF SPONSORSHIP

The worldwide interest in sponsorship as a form of integrated marketing communication stems from a range of sociocultural and business (including marketing and media) trends. Firstly, a growth in the popularity of events and festivals as leisure experiences has parallelled recognition that festivals and events offer unique social environments (at the event and on-line) to tap into niche markets. Creative sponsorship can reach consumers in environments when they are having 'a good time' and so they are more likely to accept a well-considered marketing message. It is no surprise that marketers are keen to tap into the kind of loyalty that festival-goers display — such as enduring primitive hygiene and severe sleep deprivation to see their favourite bands live (*New Media Age* 2003). There is also evidence that committed and loyal fans of a musical group or sport will attach themselves to those brands that support their interest; for example, Uncle Tobys, Billabong and Toyota are companies that have gained significant brand equity from Australian sports sponsorships. Similarly, Virgin Mobile, as a major festival sponsor in the United Kingdom, considers that 'festivals offer a fantastic opportunity for brands to get close to consumers when they are excited and passionate. It's by harnessing that passion and adding to that experience that you benefit' (*New Media Age* 2003). While sports have dominated events sponsorships accounting for 75–80 per cent of sponsorship expenditure (Harrison 2004), evidence suggests that the corporate sector is seeking a greater balance of investment across the arts and sport. Despite Heineken's extensive involvement with the Rugby World Cup and the

Australian Open Tennis, it was reported in late 2003 that the company was shifting its global focus towards cultural events (Pearce 2003). Most large brands now use a sponsorship mix within a wide-ranging brand marketing strategy. Telstra, for example, has attached its brand name to the National Rugby League competition and Telstra Stadium, but also the Business Women's Awards and Bangarra Dance Theatre (Harrison 2004).

Other influential trends on sponsorship are evident in the arenas of business, marketing and media. Companies expanding into international markets have harnessed the value of event sponsorship to create brand awareness in their new markets. Sports sponsorship has become a multi-billion dollar business in Asia with companies, such as Samsung, becoming global brands and leveraging investment in global sports. Samsung, for example, made a $4.6 million sponsorship investment in a historic, one day cricket contest between India and Pakistan (*Media* 2004).

The growth of sponsorship can also be attributed to changes in marketing itself — with the shift away from simple transactions to relationships (Gronroos 1994). New trends in marketing communication media give event sponsors the chance to interact directly with their markets to create a brand relationship. Simultaneous brand exposure can be achieved through a range of on-site communication and alternative media. Sponsors are getting extra exposure, for example, as a result of live streaming events onto the Internet, text messages, sponsorship of live sites away from the event and giant screens at festivals that display text and photo messages from the crowd responding to billboard ads. Events such as the V Festival and the Rip Curl Newquay Boardmasters Festival in England use Jumbo-trons (giant text screens) and posters inviting text responses for instant-win opportunities such as VIP access to the backstage area and free product samples (*New Media Age* 2003).

Sponsorship is also gaining leadership in most marketers' 'tool kits' because consumers are more cynical about traditional advertising — sponsorship is perceived to give 'more bang for the sponsor's buck'. When sponsorship is perceived to be a commercial activity with some benefit to society, consumers view advertising as being more manipulative with far less social value (Meenaghan 2001b). The involvement in traditional media by marketers has also shifted as a result of:

- the rising costs of media space and the reduced effectiveness of advertising — many of us now simultaneously use multiple media, such as television, Internet, mobiles, text messaging etc. (Duncan 2002)

- a growth in the overall number of media outlets (including pay TV channels, radio stations, specialist magazines, direct mail pieces, and the Internet) with media advertising becoming extremely cluttered (De Pelsmacker, Geuens & Van den Bergh 2004; Duncan 2002)

- the expansion of pay TV channels (satellite and cable) and their subsequent need for program material. Events, especially sport events, have thus had more opportunity to be televised, enhancing exposure opportunities available to event sponsors (Lieberman 2002).

- the globalisation and commercialisation of sport (Hinch & Higham 2004) as both amateur and professional sports offer more opportunities for organisations to engage in sponsorship of events that have huge television audiences
- a proliferation of brands, products and services offered by fewer manufacturers/providers (Duncan 2002). Companies, therefore, choose to improve their distributors' relationships with event-related entertainment and hospitality.

Sponsorship, especially through events and festivals, has been able to exploit these trends because it communicates in experiential environments, rather than one-way, persuasive media. Yet some events are also becoming cluttered with the diverse brands of multiple sponsors. As a result, sponsors must work closely with event organisers to achieve 'cut-through' with their own brands. Research by MEC MediaLab across 20 countries suggests that over 40 per cent of respondents believe sports events have become too heavily sponsored (*Media* 2004). In this context, the event manager's task of making strategic decisions about an event's portfolio of sponsors (discussed later in this chapter) will become even more critical as sponsorship matures as a marketing medium.

Economic fluctuations will also continue to influence the sponsorship environment. The ratio of events and individuals seeking sponsorship to the overall sponsorship dollars available in Australia's corporate sector challenges the event manager's access to new, 'large dollar' partnerships. A number of other potential influences on the event manager's ability to attract sponsorship (De Pelsmacker, Geuens & Van den Bergh 2004) that should be considered are:

- the changing expenditure patterns among marketers; for example, increased interest in radio and television program sponsorship (Dolphin 2003) and cause-related projects
- an increased diversity in the types of industries, firms and agencies using sponsorship (ranging from local florist shops to national financial institutions)
- a demand for more sophisticated (and innovative) sponsorships, tailored to a sponsor's needs, which produce a behavioural result (sponsorships that 'make the phones ring')
- the growing attachment of sponsors to events with broadcast coverage — events that are not televised or streamed to the audience via other channels are less attractive to corporate sponsors because the sponsors receive less exposure.

All of these environmental trends underline the need for event managers to ensure their preliminary research and SWOT analysis (chapter 7) includes a comprehensive analysis of the sponsorship environment. Part of ensuring the success of the event's sponsorship strategy is knowing the range of benefits that will attract sponsor partners — not just the benefits to be accrued by the event or festival.

SPONSORSHIP BENEFITS FOR EVENTS AND SPONSORS

Sponsorships are pursued by events and festivals and purchased by corporations, media and government based on a thorough assessment of the benefits to be derived. Event managers must therefore obtain a good understanding of the full suite of potential benefits that a sponsorship will bring to their event/festival and their sponsors so they can customise their strategies. Figure 8.2 shows the relationship between events/festivals in terms of the benefits exchanged by each of the sponsorship partners.

■ **Figure 8.2**
Mutual benefits sought by events and sponsors

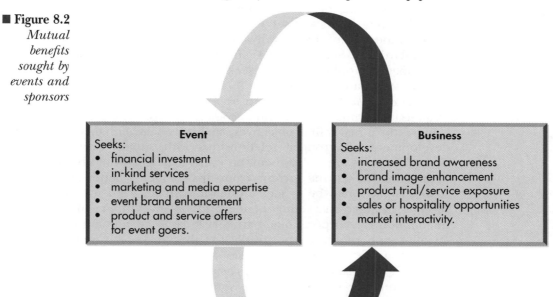

Event

Seeks:
- financial investment
- in-kind services
- marketing and media expertise
- event brand enhancement
- product and service offers for event goers.

Business

Seeks:
- increased brand awareness
- brand image enhancement
- product trial/service exposure
- sales or hospitality opportunities
- market interactivity.

Before embarking on a sponsorship strategy, the event manager should consider the sponsor-partnering benefits for the event and whether the event or festival is 'sponsorship ready'.

■ How *events can benefit if they are 'sponsorship ready'*

For many events and festivals, sponsorship (through cash and/or contra) brings a valuable opportunity for long-term business partnerships that not only grow the event, but also the audience numbers of a particular art form or sport. In Australia, Uncle Tobys sponsorship of the successful iron man event not only improved the brand equity of the event and sport, but it became a platform for Uncle Tobys to take 'ownership' of the sports audience. Despite ending its sponsorship of the iron man event a couple of years earlier, in 2003, the health food snack and cereal group was ranked as the most recognised sports sponsor in the country (Cummins 2003). For the event or festival, sponsorship is therefore much more than a means of boosting revenues. Wider objectives for having sponsor partners at an event could include sustaining an art form or developing a new sport (for example, whipboxing was recently pioneered in Queensland), achieving issues-related objectives such as a sustainable environment or ensuring the survival of not-for-profit agencies; for example, the Royal Flying Doctor Service.

Despite the obvious advantages of sponsorship, not all events and festivals understand the management implications of attracting business partners. Many event managers assume sponsorship is an appropriate source of income for their event and set about seeking to obtain it — later running into difficulties — not the least of which is being unable to attract any sponsors. Geldard and Sinclair (2004) identify a number of questions that an event manager should ask before seeking sponsorship as a revenue stream. These questions are as follows:

- *Does the event have sufficient rights or benefits that can be offered to sponsors?* Organisations must be able to recognise the potential of the event to achieve their marketing objectives, such as image enhancement or the development of stronger relationships with suppliers/buyers. If the desired benefits are not present, an event manager would be wasting his or her time in seeking income from this source. A better alternative in some instances may be to seek a donation which, by its nature, does not require strategic marketing benefits to be given in return. It is not uncommon for corporations, particularly large corporations, to provide an allocation of funds specifically for this purpose. Commonly, these funds are made available to events of a community or charitable nature.

- *Are the event's stakeholders likely to approve of commercial sponsorship?* It is not hard to imagine situations where some members of a particular association or the potential event audience might view commercial sponsorship negatively. A conservation body seeking sponsorship for its annual conference, for example, could find that its membership is against commercial involvement and at best, extremely selective about the companies with whom they will associate. In effect, broad support among the event's internal stakeholders is essential for sponsorship to be successful.

- *Are there some companies that are simply not suitable as sponsors?* Event managers need to identify organisations that are inappropriate as sponsorship partners. A charity event aimed at raising funds for a children's hospital or another health-related cause, for example, is unlikely to accept sponsorship from breweries or tobacco companies.

- *Does the event have the resources to market and manage sponsorship?* A considerable amount of time and effort is required to research, develop and market sponsorships to potential sponsor targets. Furthermore, sponsors must be 'serviced' after the contract is finalised, which means the event manager needs to ensure all promises made in the proposal are fulfilled. This involves allocating staff and other resources to building and sustaining the sponsor relationship.

■ Sponsors' *benefits — links with the consumer response*

An appreciation of the consumer effects of sponsorship helps to understand the engagement of corporate and government bodies with events and festivals. Knowledge and familiarity with a corporate or product brand, as well as attitudinal and behavioural effects have been linked with event sponsorship. The sponsor's investment assisting a sport or art form is believed to create goodwill among attendees, which in turn influences their attitude and behaviour towards the sponsor's brand (Meenaghan 2001a).

Although there is still a great deal of research to be conducted on sponsorship effects (most data has been gathered by private firms), it appears that sponsorship does stimulate goodwill (a positive attitude) which in turn influences consumer relationships with sponsors' brands. According to Meenaghan (2001a, p. 102), the goodwill is generated for sponsors at three levels: the generic level (consumer feelings about their engagement in sponsorship as an activity), the category level (within sports audiences or arts) and at the individual activity level (fans of an AFL team such as the Sydney Swans develop goodwill towards QBE as a team sponsor). Clearly, goodwill effects are achieved intensely for sponsors at an event category level (art or sport) and the individual event/activity level. Underlining the importance of fan/audience involvement with an event category in getting a sponsorship result, Performance Research (2001) has reported that over half of those with an interest in the arts said that they would almost always buy a product that sponsored cultural events (Dolphin 2003). Figure 8.3 (adapted from Meenaghan 2001a) shows how sponsorship effects narrow at an individual event/activity level. It also demonstrates how the intensity of goodwill towards the sponsor moves in parallel with the intensity of fan or event consumer involvement.

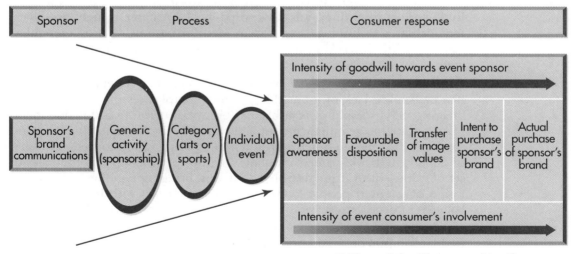

■ **Figure 8.3**   *The sponsorship effects process*
(**Source:** *Adapted from Meenaghan 2001, p. 115.*)

Clearly, some additional benefits can be gained from leveraging a sponsorship in target markets with higher levels of event knowledge — 'involved' or 'highly active' event consumers are more likely to make an effort to process a sponsor's message (Roy & Cornwell 2004). The more actively engaged a person is with what is being sponsored, the stronger the carry-over effect and the link between the sponsor's brand and the event (De Pelsmacker, Geuens & Van den Bergh 2004). This is a good reason why many companies try to sponsor festivals or events that have loyal and dedicated audiences.

The translation of a passion for the event itself into customer gratitude/goodwill and a commitment (SponsorMap 2004) to use the sponsor's services or products is of interest to all existing and would-be sponsors. Emphasis is placed on consumers being in a positive environment at events as sponsoring brands are perceived in a favourable light. However, products that gain a stronger link to the event and its audience are often those that are demonstrated creatively in some way during the event (Cornwell, Roy & Steinard 2001). For the 2003 Melbourne Fringe Festival, Slurpee developed a lime version of its drink to link in with Fringe's lime green marketing theme — the coloured drink added a fun dimension, but was also a simple way for the brand to obtain an instant impact in the Fringe Festival audience (Harrison 2004).

Based on consumer behaviour theories, various writers (De Pelsmacker, Geuens & Van den Bergh 2004; Geldard & Sinclair 2002, Meenaghan 2001b) highlight an array of marketing benefits of event and festival sponsorship gained by corporate sponsors. These benefits include the following:

- *Access to specific niche/target markets* — a conference of medical specialists in a particular field, for example, might provide a significant opportunity for manufacturers of particular drugs/medical equipment to gain access to a large number of potential buyers/decision makers at one time and in one place. The 2003 World Congress on World Physics and Biomedical Engineering in Sydney was sponsored by LAP Laser, which produces medical laser technology, and Varian Medical Systems — two companies with a distinct interest in reaching the medical specialists attending this congress.

- *Corporate brand image creation/enhancement* — for major service providers like banks, the lack of a tangible product complicates the task of brand imaging. Sponsorship of festivals and events is therefore a valuable form of corporate image enhancement, illustrated by the National Bank's sponsorship of Cirque du Soleil's production, *Quidam* which toured Australia in 2004. The bank's stated rationale for the sponsorship was the shared set of values with Cirque de Soleil — that is, bringing together a disparate range of talented people 'to work as one team, act with integrity, show balance in decisions, strive for excellence' (National Bank 2004).

- *Building brand awareness for an organisation and its services/products* — Kellogg's has been a national rugby league sponsor in Australia and has sought awareness of its Nutri-Grain brand through the Kellogg's Nutri-Grain Cup schoolboys championship. Direct branding on the football, the company's grassroots involvement in junior development clinics and the players' appearances at schools were used to build brand awareness in a key target market for Nutri-Grain cereal (Australian Sponsorship Marketing Association 2001).

- *Influencing consumer attitudes about a product or service brand* — some companies use sponsorship as a strategy to change consumer perceptions about a longstanding brand. Suncorp's Rugby World Cup sponsorship goal was to build credibility for the bank's GIO brand outside its home state of Queensland (Ferguson 2004). Consumer surprise about the link between an older brand such as GIO and the Rugby World Cup was welcomed by Suncorp as the first step towards repositioning GIO in the mindset of consumers in Australia's southern states.

- *Associating a product or service with a particular lifestyle* — makers of alcoholic beverages, for example, often sponsor or directly support youth-oriented events, such as rock music festivals, to develop an association between their product and a demographic that is young, fun seeking and keen to experiment. Bacardi Martini toured the 2003 summer festival circuit in the United Kingdom with BBar, a marquee that held up to 1000 people and featured 65 DJs and a small army of cocktail mixers. The aim was to create a memorable experience that tied in with Bacardi's brand values — an association with the party spirit (Wallis 2003).

- *Improving relationships with distribution channel members* — a corporation may be seeking to develop stronger relationships with agents or firms that currently distribute its products or to establish new distribution outlets. Rugby World Cup 2003, for example, paved the way for Bundaberg Rum to achieve overseas distribution of its product. During the World Cup, Suncorp also used its sponsorship to enhance relationships with its brokers in commercial lending. 'We did a series of fun incentives for brokers to increase their monthly sales targets which we linked to touch points of Rugby World Cup...at the first level of sales, they got a football pump, at the next level, they got a real football, with the ultimate incentive being the chance to fly to a game with hotel accommodation for four friends.' (pers. comm. with T Ferguson, Sponsorship Manager, Suncorp, 10 March 2004)

- *Achieving product sales and merchandising opportunities* — for companies with a product (rather than an intangible service), high sales targets can be set for an exclusive in-game presence at sporting events — for example, Heineken at the Rugby World Cup — or through having exclusive rights in their product category at a festival. Yellow Glen, for example, has targeted various Australian food and wine festivals for additional champagne sales. The ability to give away branded merchandise such as water bottles, jerseys and umbrellas to extend brand exposure is also valued.

- *Demonstrating product attributes* — many festivals and events are primarily used by sponsors to demonstrate new products or technology. Through its sponsorship of events such as the Edinburgh Festival and Brisbane's International Film Festival, the mobile phone distributor Nokia has showcased the functionality of its handsets and educated people about new technologies such as MMS. Similarly, the telecommunications giant Orange uses its sponsorship of the Glastonbury festival in the United Kingdom, to offer free recharge points, provide e-top-ups and phone cards and to get people to experiment with technology like text alerts — 'We're not there to primarily sell' (Wallis 2003).

- *Providing employee rewards and recognition* — organisations often perceive the sponsorship of a sporting or cultural event as a way of giving their employees access to a corporate box and/or tickets to reward or motivate them. The National Bank's sponsorship of Cirque du Soleil in 2004, for example, might have provided an opportunity for the bank to directly reward its staff for their team work achievements — one of the values noted by the bank in sponsoring the touring production (National Bank 2004).

- *Creating goodwill and a climate of consent for an organisation's activities* — companies as diverse as mining organisations, energy providers, banks and pharmaceutical manufacturers all support charity events to create an image in the community of being good corporate citizens. The Sigma company (Sigma 2004) has directly supported Red Nose Day, Daffodil Day and a charity bike ride in 2002 to raise funds to find a cure for leukaemia through its Guardian and Amcal pharmacies in Australia.

- *Entertaining key clients with corporate hospitality* — corporate hospitality is an important drawcard for sponsors, especially those with business-to-business clients: 'There is nothing quite like strawberries and cream washed down with chilled champagne at the Wimbledon Tennis Championships to woo potential business' (Ellery 2004). Where working relationships are quite intense, corporate hospitality events can break down the barriers and create social bonds that forge a better relationship between suppliers and clients.

In looking at the many benefits derived by sponsors, it should also be remembered that public sector bodies (for example, local councils, state government departments, authorities/commissions and agencies) heavily engage in sponsorship. Many of the benefits illustrated in the corporate context are equally applicable to them. Most public sector agencies now employ marketing strategies to generate awareness of their products/services or issues and to influence community behaviour (for example, safe driving or water conservation). For this reason, the Brisbane City Council and other agencies such as Healthy Waterways and Brisbane Water are active partners in the city's Riverfestival event.

As noted in chapters 2 and 4, local, state or federal governments will normally support events through sponsorships, grants or contributions towards constructing the infrastructure needed to stage events because of the community benefits they bring. Events and festivals can also stimulate economic development in an area (for example, the Australasian Country Music Festival in Tamworth, New South Wales), create a greater sense of identity or cohesion and enhance the facilities available to local residents. To attract sponsorship, event organisers must think about how they can provide at least several of the benefits identified here.

■ Sponsorship *leveraging — adding value to the investment*

To fully capitalise on a sponsorship investment, most corporate and government agencies develop a leveraging strategy or a range of marketing activities that extend the sponsorship benefits well beyond the event or festival's promised offer. The 2003 Sponsorship Decision Makers Survey found that more than 50 per cent of Australian sponsors are now spending at a ratio of around 2 : 1 on leveraging their sponsorships (Sponsorship Insights and the Australian Sponsorship Marketing Association 2003). The average spend of Australian sponsors on leveraging is slightly higher than their counterparts in the USA. Nevertheless, Adidas as an official sponsor of the FIFA 2002 World Cup reportedly budgeted around $88 million to exploit their sponsorship with the cost of official sponsorships being somewhere between $20–28 million (Pickett 2002).

For Suncorp's Rugby World Cup (RWC) 2003 sponsorship, the leveraging ratio was closer to 3:1, but Suncorp achieved quantifiable results with enhanced brand equity (awareness and favourability) and sales (Ferguson 2004). As part of its overall sponsorship package, Suncorp invested in broadcast sponsorship for the first time, which included exposure through a 15-second in-game commercial, sponsorship of GIO Player of the Match, and opening and closing billboards. The success of RWC sponsorship paved the way for Suncorp's four-year sponsorship of the Wallabies team. Alongside state government public relations, it also served to reverse the previously low recognition and name use of Suncorp Stadium (built on the site of Lang Park) in the Brisbane media and marketplace. (Following RWC 2003, a much improved 95 per cent media recognition and use of the name was evident.)

A number of factors contributed to Suncorp's successful leveraging of RWC sponsorship. These included:

- a careful analysis of the match between the event property and the sponsor's market — Suncorp established that the rugby audience was both their existing and aspirational audience (a good basis for a leverage investment).

- a dedicated internal marketing strategy — RWC was a property that needed to be adopted by all business areas within the company. Marketing and sales personnel were briefed on how the RWC could be leveraged with a 50/50 buy-in between the sponsorship unit and a business unit on specific marketing activities. Staff were also directly engaged with the sponsorship.

- an intensive consumer branding campaign themed on the RWC — for example, television campaigns, outdoor advertising in transit hubs, branch office imagery, live sites at Brisbane's South Bank and in regional towns with extensive branding and giveaways, direct mail offers, website incentives and merchandise prizes, and the use of rugby ambassadors such as Nick Farr Jones on Suncorp's recorded telephone messages).

- a dedicated business-to-business marketing campaign centred on 31 corporate hospitality events staged throughout Australia either in the stadiums or close to the stadiums where RWC games were held — Suncorp's business banking managers each injected funds from their budgets towards the corporate entertainment of clients, and all managers achieved measurable results in sales and referrals.

For Suncorp, like most other event and festival sponsors, effective leveraging relies on establishing multiple opportunities for consumers to engage with their brand and their personnel (on-site, off-site and on-line). One of these opportunities can be the chance for consumers to interact with the event's players or performers. Player interaction was one of the benefits sought by Suncorp in its Wallabies contract. Suncorp's sponsorship manager, Terri Ferguson (2004), says the company has developed the rugby ambassador program 'because we found out through our research that the Wallabies were loved, but people couldn't get near them. We wanted to use our benefits to bring the consumer closer'. Rugby 'fan days' at Suncorp Stadium further build this interactivity and consumer exposure to the company's stadium branding.

When sponsors already have a high level of corporate brand awareness, leveraging is best focused on activities that achieve two-way communication with the market — for example, business-to-business customer hospitality or specific consumer offers (either during the event or on-line). The need for sponsors to offer event consumers something they cannot obtain elsewhere is gaining importance. Beverage marketer Red Bull, for example, has set up a branded skate ramp at festivals in the United Kingdom, while the Walls company created a unique ice-cream beach to engage visitors at the 2003 V Festival in England (Wallis 2003). In effect, the need to think of leveraging strategies that achieve 'cut-through' to a media savvy market without irritating them is the sponsor's challenge (and also the event marketer's concern in order to add value for their sponsors).

THE VALUE OF SPONSORSHIP POLICY

Just as most corporate and government agencies will establish a sponsorship policy to drive their decision making, Grey and Skildum-Reid (2003) strongly recommend that all events seeking sponsorship design a policy to guide their actions. They suggest that a sponsorship policy should state:
- the event's history of sponsorship and their approach to it, including some definition of what constitutes sponsorship versus grants and donations
- the event's objectives, processes and procedures for seeking sponsorship
- the rules for entering into sponsorship and the kinds of companies that will be excluded. It could be stated, for example, that no sponsorships are to be accepted from companies or individuals who are party to significant tendering processes for the event or companies with values that may be

contrary to those of the event. A rationale for not including certain types of potential sponsors is useful as a later reference for event management. Most policies will also indicate that sponsorships must be finalised through written agreements.

- the uniform approach adopted in seeking sponsorship, including whether all proposals are to follow a particular format and whether each sponsorship is required to have a management plan developed for it (see later discussion)
- the levels of accountability and responsibility, such as whether all sponsorships are to be signed off and overseen by a designated person
- the time at which the policy will be subject to review and evaluation.

For most events and festivals, involving the senior management of the event as well as staff and lead volunteers in the drafting of the sponsorship policy is a wise idea. Having a sense of ownership of the sponsorship policy becomes important if there are conflicts or disputes over decisions about sponsors. For larger events and festivals, the policy would also be presented to and approved by a board of directors.

STAGES IN DEVELOPING THE EVENT SPONSORSHIP STRATEGY

Although you should already have an overall marketing strategy and plan for your event or festival (see chapter 7), developing an event sponsorship strategy is a more defined task. Remember that it will have an interactive relationship with the event's marketing strategy because, whether it is venue design, ticketing, integrated marketing communications or even the program itself, you will need to be creative about how you can integrate the sponsor's brand with your own marketing plans. The NRL team, the Brisbane Broncos, has achieved sponsorship success by applying a strategy-making formula that is similar to Grey and Skildum-Reid's process (2004). For the Brisbane Broncos, this involves:

- building information on the Broncos' audience — for example, television and game-day demographics, psychographics and buying patterns
- reviewing the potential of the Broncos marketing plan to maximise sponsor value
- building a list of potential sponsors based on the Broncos' asset register (everything that they are able to sell as part of their sponsorship offer)
- planning and implementing the sponsorship approach (including the sponsorship proposal, follow-up and negotiation)
- having a well-considered action plan to service the Broncos sponsors (about 30 different organisations spanning major/media sponsors, corporate sponsors and support sponsors) (Allsop 2004).

As noted in chapter 7, having a strategy means knowing the direction in which you are headed, which also applies to your event's sponsorship. For event managers, this involves thinking about event/festival visitors and the types of synergy they might have with corporate brands. It also involves thinking about the attributes and values of the event and companies that might share those values, and about the mix of sponsors who together might create a close-knit sponsor family, and brainstorming the kinds of partnerships that will grow the event.

■ Profiling *the event audience*

As a first step in creating your strategy, consider again the target markets of your event or festival. By adopting the market segmentation strategies outlined in chapter 7, you will have a sound basis for matching potential sponsors to the consumers who frequent your event. Like all forms of integrated marketing communication, event sponsorship is most successful as a marketing medium when there is a solid database that profiles existing visitors and members/subscribers and their preferences. Sponsors will look for a reliable picture of the event audience to 'buy' the potential brand links you propose to develop, and to justify their investment.

In the case of Suncorp, research after the RWC 2003 showed that consumers saw some of the Wallabies' and Suncorp's brand values as one and the same — such research can be a critical platform for a high-dollar sponsorship. However, even for smaller events and festivals, steps to identify the market and demonstrate a fit between the event and sponsors' markets must be taken. This may be a more straightforward task for smaller festivals where links can be logically made with small to medium brands in their local market (Harrison 2004). To obtain detailed market information to assist with sponsorship planning, some of the research tools noted in chapter 7 (for example, on-site surveys and focus groups) can be especially useful.

■ Creating *the event's asset register*

Where the assets of a regional festival may be relatively easy to identify, the inventory of assets available to an NRL team like the Brisbane Broncos, or even a televised festival, are much more extensive. Despite the variation in the size and scope of different events and festivals, some common assets include the agreement to purchase product/services from a sponsor (for example, alcohol, transport, food), event naming rights, exclusivity (the capacity to lock out competition within a brand category), business and sponsor networking opportunities, merchandising rights, media exposure, including advertising opportunities during the event, venue signage, joint advertising with sponsors, the capacity to demonstrate product or technology at the event, corporate hospitality services and a volume of tickets for the sponsor's use.

In building their asset register, the Brisbane Broncos take steps to group their assets (for example, in-game media exposure, player apparel), record the quantities and current availability of those assets (for example, 15 seconds of remaining in-game advertising) and build the sale value and cost of sales into the pricing of their marketable assets (Allsop 2004). An overall asset register serves to tabulate the profits (the value minus the cost) for every individual sponsorship.

For a smaller event or festival, the process will be much less complex. Where the Broncos could have a list of 100 saleable assets or more (over a series of games), a local festival staged annually has an inventory that is much easier to manage. Yet, with a little creativity, the festival or event marketer can also create new assets. Apart from identifying assets like signage not previously used for branding within the festival (for example, brand exposure at the front of a concert stage), some tailor-made assets for sponsors can be devised. The Brisbane Broncos, for example, created a competition in conjunction with their sponsor, Harvey Norman (homewares/furniture), which centred on an in-store promotion in south east Queensland stores — the prize was the then Broncos captain, Gordon Tallis, sitting on the winner's sofa. This availability of the team's lead player for a sponsor leveraging activity was an extension of the asset register.

It is fair to assume that many small- to medium-sized events and festivals with few sponsorship management staff will have untapped resources. However, in identifying and expanding the event's asset register, careful consideration must also be given to the time and personnel needed to effectively manage and market those assets.

■ **Building** *the event sponsorship portfolio*

In designing a sponsorship strategy, event managers will usually work out how a portfolio of sponsors can be established, given the bundles of festival or event assets that are available for purchase. Geldard and Sinclair (2004) identify strategies for this, such as sole sponsorship, hierarchical packages (for example, tiers of gold, silver, bronze), a pyramid structure (whereby each sponsor level below the principal sponsor jointly spends the amount invested by the top sponsor with proportional benefits), a level playing field (all sponsors negotiate and leverage their own benefits) and an ad hoc approach.

Although sole sponsorship of a regional festival may have the advantage of 'keeping it simple', the festival's survival is threatened if the sole sponsor is lost. For this reason, many events and festivals with a limited array of assets choose the tiered approach (different levels of dollar investment for set benefit packages). However, as Grey and Skildum-Reid (2004, p. 97) point out, 'most events/festivals end up formulating their packages so that all of the levels get access to the best benefits, with the lower levels simply getting less of the supporting benefits'. For this reason, many events, including the Brisbane Broncos, now tailor their asset packages for each sponsor using only broad categories, such as major/media, corporate and support sponsors.

Using this approach, the sponsors are usually grouped according to their *type* (for example, naming rights, presenting sponsorship of a section, event, entry, team or particular day, preferred suppliers etc.) and their *exclusivity* (among sponsors at any level, among sponsors at or below a given level, as a supplier or seller at the event or within event-driven marketing collateral)

(Grey & Skildum-Reid 2004). The purchase of other event assets such as merchandising rights, licenses and endorsements, hospitality, signage and database access by sponsors, to name just a few, serve to further differentiate the event sponsor packages.

The use of tailor-made sponsorship packages is recommended for a number of reasons (Welsh 2003):

- Packaged event properties are rarely a perfect fit for potential sponsors — most are either too broad or too narrow in their consumer reach and the rights available may be either more or less than the sponsor wants.
- Sponsors are often seeking more control over their sponsorship and its potential leveraging than packaged strategies offer — the simple transactional nature of buyer-seller arrangements is being replaced by partnerships and in some cases, the sponsor clearly has leadership in driving the relationship.
- Poor sponsorship packaging by events and festivals can lead to a greater instance of *ambush marketing* in certain industry/product categories (for example, banking and finance) or attempts by non-sponsoring companies to capitalise on an event's image and prestige by implying that they are sponsors (IEG Network 1997).
- Multiple layers of sponsorship introduced by events are causing some confusion — as the different sponsorship categories become more prolific, there is more potential for a loss of control by event organisers and sponsor conflicts (Shani & Sandler 1998).

In light of these challenges, the appeal of determining sponsor partnerships on a case by case basis (with all sponsors informed of this practice) is growing. Noise 2003, the youth media arts festival mentioned earlier in the chapter, is just one of many events shifting towards tailor-made sponsorships. The general manager of Noise, Sharon Longridge, says, 'We don't adopt the typical sponsorship models with gold, silver and bronze partners ... for us, this area falls into a vital part of the festival — partnerships.' (Longridge 2004) In 2003 the event had around 80 different partnerships, each built on the principle of reciprocity, rather than the traditional 'package' purchase.

■ Matching *event assets with potential sponsors*

Once the approach to building the sponsorship portfolio is determined, the business of identifying the right sponsor(s) begins. As noted, a first criterion is to find those organisations that want access to the same audience (or a significant component of it), or who have a specific problem that the event may assist in solving. Sponsorship managers for events use various research techniques to identify potential sponsors. By keeping track of business developments through industry associations, business and financial media and the web, a great deal of information can be gathered on the marketing direction of firms to guide sponsorship targeting. Which organisations are looking to enter new markets in your state or region? Which companies appear to have attributes and values that match those of your event/festival? The National Bank's partnership with Cirque du Soleil, which was based on values of applauding talent and teamwork, showed some creativity in this regard. For the Brisbane Broncos, a shared attribute of being market leaders was cited as a reason for their Coca-Cola partnership (Allsop 2004).

The event manager should also actively identify any government agencies or firms that are seeking to reposition themselves, regain market acceptance or introduce new products or services. Once identified, and depending on the nature of the event, such organisations can become a sponsorship target. An organiser of a garden festival, for example, may notice that a horticultural company has just launched a new range of fertilisers. This development could be a sponsorship opportunity if the company can be convinced that the event draws the right consumer audience to increase awareness and sales of its new product line.

Event managers can also obtain insights into potential sponsors by reading their annual reports or viewing their websites. These sources often provide a good picture of the broad strategies the organisation is pursuing. They also indicate the types of sponsorship they already have in place and whether they have any specific requirements for sponsorships (figure 8.4, page 253). Another means of finding potential sponsors is to simply identify who has sponsored similar events or festivals in the past. This can be done by examining programs/promotional material/websites of these other events, or directly contacting the event organisers (many festivals and events now see the value in some productive networking and information sharing).

Finally, it is unlikely that you will be looking for all of your sponsors simultaneously, unless you are managing a brand new event. Therefore, the existing sponsors of the event or festival can be a very useful source of referral to other potential sponsors. This method of finding sponsors can be highly successful because the existing sponsor is presenting their company as a satisfied partner of the event in 'opening the door' and endorsing the event as a sponsorship property.

Once potential sponsors are identified, a more detailed examination of their business and marketing objectives and the types of asset that will meet their needs can be completed. Additional information that might be sought includes the types of event the organisation is willing to sponsor, whether the organisation is tied to particular causes (for example, charities) and the time in their planning cycle when they allocate their sponsorship budget (sponsorship proposals should be submitted to them some months before this time). Information such as this last item is likely to require direct enquiry to the company's marketing personnel.

■ The *sponsorship approach*

Once the potential sponsor(s) have been listed, the next challenge for the event manager is to determine the marketing or management person who will be the sponsorship decision-maker within the targeted company. In small companies, this person is likely to be the chief executive officer (CEO) or managing director. In companies of moderate size, the marketing or public relations manager may make such decisions, while in large corporations a dedicated sponsorship section could exist within the marketing, public relations or corporate affairs areas, as exists for Telstra, Australia Post, Toyota and other major sponsors of Australian events.

Before developing any written proposal, it is customary to write a brief introductory letter to profile your event and the sponsorship opportunity. However, some sponsorship managers make direct contact by email or telephone, especially if they have been referred by another sponsor or have some informal rapport with the company's personnel (which may be the case for a sports sponsorship property such as Brisbane Broncos or an arts property such as the Sydney Festival). There are definite benefits in becoming acquainted with the company before preparing a proposal, simply because you need to fully understand their product/brand attributes, their business objectives, their competition, how they use their current sponsorships and the ways in which sponsorship proposals need to be structured to satisfy their needs. If you can develop some preliminary rapport with those deciding on the value of your proposed partnership, you will have a better grasp of why they may be interested in sponsoring the event/festival and how the proposal should be written to attract their investment. However, the ability to personally discuss your interest in a partnership may depend on the company's policy about written or verbal communication in the first instance.

The most successful sponsorship approach is one where the event has put a lot of effort into planning before approaching the sponsor (much like going for a job). Certainly, you should start to think about how you can marry the event with the company's culture and explore some innovative ways in which to address the company's marketing objectives before you commence your final proposal (Harris 2004).

Preparing and presenting sponsorship proposals

A formal proposal document is commonly how sponsorship is negotiated and partnerships are formed. In broad terms, Geldard and Sinclair (2004) suggest that the sponsorship proposal should address the following questions:

- What is the organisation being asked to sponsor?
- What will the organisation receive for its sponsorship?
- What is it going to cost?

The length and level of detail a proposal uses to answer these questions depends on the value and cost of the sponsor partnership. However, a comprehensive treatment of these areas would mean the proposal would include:

- an overview of the event, including (as applicable) its mission/goals, history, location, current and past sponsors, program/duration, staff, past or anticipated level of media coverage, past or predicted attendance levels, and actual or predicted attendee profile (for example, age, income, sex, occupation)

- the sponsorship package on offer and its associated cost. In pricing the sponsorship, it should be remembered that marketers have a range of alternative marketing media such as advertising, direct marketing and other tools that could achieve similar outcomes (depending on the sponsor's marketing objectives).
- the proposed duration of the sponsorship agreement
- the strategic fit between the proposal and the business and marketing needs of the organisation. Discussion here will be based on research conducted using the sources noted earlier.
- the event's contact details for the company's response and follow-up negotiation.

Many large corporations, to assist sponsorship seekers, have developed specific proposal guidelines or criteria. In figure 8.4, an example of these guidelines is provided. You will also note from this example that this company, Country Energy, requires a lead time of at least 60 days. This is less than the usual timeframe required by potential sponsors. Most sponsors require at least a 12-month timeframe to maximise their sponsorship and around two years for a major sponsorship — for example, a Rugby World Cup. Sponsorships for events scheduled less than six months from the time of the initial approach have far less opportunity to be successfully leveraged by marketing personnel.

To help Country Energy evaluate a sponsorship request, a proposal should include/cover relevant points from the list in figure 8.4.

■ **Figure 8.4**
Country Energy's sponsorship criteria

Event details
- A concise description of the event or activity
- Event objectives
- The geographic location, as well as local, state or national extensions
- A brief background of the applicant, listing experience, mission statement and long term goals for the organisation or event
- Staffing of the event/organisation
- Date and times of the event or activity
- Other critical deadlines
- How you will judge the success of your event

Financial details
- How much money is requested?
- How will it be spent?
- Are there other sponsors involved? If so, who?
- Will you be seeking other sponsors?

Target audience
- How many people will be present at the event (for example, attendance)?
- How many people will be participating in the event (for example, the number of volunteers, committee etc.)?
- Who are the target audiences for your event (for example, age, gender, employment status etc.)?

(continued)

Publicity
- How will the event be promoted (for example, television, radio, print)?
- What, if any, media coverage do you expect? Is this an aim?
- What are the benefits for Country Energy in sponsoring this event? Can you offer exclusivity or signage opportunities to Country Energy?

History of the event or activity
- Has the event been conducted in the past?
- If yes, how did you evaluate it and what were the results?
- Examples/copies of promotional items, publicity, advertising from previous events

The future
- Do you intend repeating this event?
- Is there potential for Country Energy to be involved in the future?

Assessment of applications
- Applicants will be advised in writing of the outcome of their proposal.
- It should be noted Country Energy receives many applications for sponsorship and is unable to fund all those requests. Sponsorships will be selected on the basis of criteria offering strong community links and participation.

Submission of applications
- Read our sponsorship selection criteria.
- Complete our sponsorship application form.
- Applications must be made in writing and provide at least 60 days lead time.

(**Source:** *Country Energy 2004.*)

From the points discussed, it is possible to gain an insight into what makes a successful proposal. However, the failure rate with sponsorship proposals suggests that much more needs to be understood by events managers about their preparation. According to Ukman (1995), there are six attributes of a successful proposal:

1. *Sell benefits, not features* — many proposals describe the features of the event, such as the artistic merit of the festival, rather than the event's marketing assets and sponsor benefits. Sponsors buy marketing communication platforms so that they can reach their stakeholders and market(s) to form relationships or sell products/services.

2. *Address the sponsor's needs, not those of the event* — many proposals emphasise the event's need for money, rather than the sponsor's needs such as market access, corporate hospitality or a better understanding of a new brand. Remember, event sponsorships should be seen as partnerships, not a means to patch holes in the event budget (Harrison 2004).

3. *Tailor the proposal to the business category* — as noted, each of the event's assets will have a different level of importance to each potential sponsor. An insurance company, for example, might be interested in an event's database, while a soft drink marketer is likely to be more concerned with on-site sales opportunities. A tailored strategy should be worked out based on some research and head-to-head discussions among event personnel before laying out the sponsorship document.

4. *Include promotional extensions* — the two major sources of sponsor benefits are addressed here. First, there are the assets being purchased; for example, identification in marketing collateral and on-site signage that come with the deal and only require action on the part of the event manager. The second set of benefits emerges from the sponsor's event leveraging discussed earlier — for example, trade, retail and sales extensions. Particular leveraging activities might include competitions, redemption offers (for example, free ticket offers for the customers of a sponsor's wholesalers) and hospitality. It is not enough to give sponsors a checklist of the direct benefits of the assets being purchased — a proposal should include the 'exploitation or leveraging menu' showing them how to leverage their investment.

5. *Minimise risk* — risk can be reduced through indicating some guaranteed marketing activities (including media space) in the package, listing reputable co-sponsors and showing the steps that will be taken to minimise the risk of ambush marketing by other companies. A clear indication of how the event/festival will service the sponsorship should also be given prominence in the proposal.

6. *Include added value* — the proposal should be presented in terms of its total impact on achieving results for the sponsor, rather than focusing on one aspect such as media. Generally, sponsors will be looking for an array of those benefits highlighted earlier in the chapter — how the sponsorship will build relationships internally with staff, ways in which it will facilitate networking with other sponsors or potential business partners, and how it can build sales among consumer and business audiences.

Given that many of the organisations targeted by events as potential sponsors receive large numbers of proposals each week, an effort should be made to ensure the proposal provides sufficient information on which a decision can be made. If the organisation has published guidelines for sponsorship seekers to follow, it should be evident from the contents page and a quick scan of the proposal that these matters have been addressed. Some attempt to make a proposal stand out can also be useful. A food and wine festival might print a brief version of the proposal on a good bottle of wine, for example, as well as submitting the fuller version. But be aware that glossy, printed proposals and presentations are usually not well accepted, because they do not suggest that the event is offering a customised partnership (Grey & Skildum-Reid 2003).

Time is increasingly crucial in business. If a proposal is too long, has not been based on sound research, does not contain adequate information or it leaves out key elements (such as event contact details), the chances of the proposal being discarded are high. As a general rule, the length of a sponsorship proposal should be commensurate with the amount of money sought and must be as succinct as possible. If the dollar value of the sponsorship is substantial and the proposal is over five pages (more than 10 pages could be too long), an executive summary should give a snapshot of its key elements along with a contents page.

Undertaking the sponsorship screening process

Commonly, organisations apply a screening process to sponsorship proposals as they seek to determine which relevant benefits are present. An understanding of this screening process is useful to the event manager as it assists in crafting sponsorship proposals. The framework for understanding the screening process developed by Crompton (1993) remains one of the most comprehensive developed to date. The framework adopts the acronym CEDAREEE to identify the major elements of the sponsorship screening process employed by corporations. The acronym is derived from:

- **C**ustomer audience
- **E**xposure potential
- **D**istribution channel audience
- **A**dvantage over competitors
- **R**esource investment involvement required
- **E**vent's characteristics
- **E**vent organisation's reputation
- **E**ntertainment and hospitality opportunities.

These criteria are expanded in figure 8.5.

■ **Figure 8.5**
Screening criteria used by businesses to determine sponsorship

1. **Customer audience**
   - Is the demographic, attitude and lifestyle profile of the target audience congruent with the product's target market?
   - What is the on-site audience?
   - Is sponsorship of this event the best way to communicate the product/service to this target audience?

2. **Exposure potential**
   - What is the inherent news value of the event?
   - What extended print and broadcast coverage of the sponsorship is likely?
   - Will the extended coverage be local, regional or national? Is the geographical scope of this media audience consistent with the product's sales area?
   - Can the event be tied into other media advertising?
   - Can the company's products/services be sold at the event?
   - What is the life of the event?
   - Are banners and signage included in the sponsorship? How many and what size? Will they be visible during television broadcasts?
   - Will the product's name and logo be identified on promotional material for the activity?
   - Event posters — how many?
   - Press releases — how many?
   - Point-of-sale displays — how many?
   - Television advertisements — how many and on what stations?
   - Radio advertisements — how many and on what stations?
   - Print advertisements — how many and in what print media?
   - Internet advertisements (on the event website, banner advertisements) — how many and on what sites?
   - Where will the product name appear in the event program? Front or back cover? Number and site of program advertisements? How many programs?

- Will the product's name be mentioned on the public address system? How many times?
- Can the sponsor have display booths? Where will they be located? Will they be visible during television broadcasts?

3. **Distribution channel audience**
   - Are the sponsorship's advantages apparent to wholesalers, retailers or franchisers? Will they participate in promotions associated with the sponsorship?

4. **Advantages over competitors**
   - Is the event unique or otherwise distinctive?
   - Has the event previously had sponsors? If so, how successful has it been in delivering the desired benefits to them? Is it strongly associated with other sponsors? Will clutter be a problem?
   - Does the event need co-sponsors? Are other sponsors of the event compatible with the company's product? Does the company want to be associated with them? Will the product stand out and be recognised among them?
   - If there is co-sponsorship, will the product have category and advertising exclusivity?
   - Will competitors have access to signage, hospitality or event advertising? Will competition be allowed to sell the product on site?
   - If the company does not sponsor it, will the competitor? Is that a concern?

5. **Resource investment involvement required**
   - How much is the total sponsorship cost, including such items as related promotional investment, staff time and administrative and implementation effort?
   - Will the sponsorship investment be unwieldy and difficult to manage?
   - What are the levels of barter, in-kind and cash investment?
   - Does the event guarantee a minimum level of benefits to the company?

6. **Event's characteristics**
   - What is the perceived stature of the event? Is it the best of its kind? Will involvement with it enhance the product's image?
   - Does it have a 'clean' image? Is there any chance that it will be controversial?
   - Does it have continuity or is it a one-off?

7. **Event organisation's reputation**
   - Does the organisation have a proven track record in staging this or other events?
   - Does it have the expertise to help the product achieve its sponsorship goals?
   - Does the organisation have a reputation and an image with which the company desires to be associated?
   - Does it have a history of honouring its obligations?
   - Has the company worked with this organisation before? Was it a positive experience?
   - Does it have undisputed control and authority over the activities it sanctions?
   - How close to its forecasts has the organisation been in delivering benefits to its sponsors?
   - How responsive is the organisation's staff to sponsors' requests? Are they readily accessible?
   - Is there insurance and what are the company's potential liabilities?

(continued)

8. **Entertainment and hospitality opportunities**
   - Are there opportunities for direct sales of product and related merchandise, or for inducing product trial?
   - Will celebrities be available to serve as spokespeople for the product? Will they make personal appearances on its behalf at the event, in other markets, or in the media? At what cost?
   - Are tickets to the event included in the sponsorship? How many? Which sessions? Where are the seats located?
   - Will there be access to VIP hospitality areas for the company's guests? How many will be authorised? Will celebrities appear?
   - Will there be clinics, parties or playing opportunities at which the company's guests will be able to interact with the celebrities?

(**Source:** *Adapted from Crompton 1993.*)

Not all of these criteria are used in the assessment of each sponsorship proposal, or by every company, as a different range of desired outcomes or benefits will be specified. The required inclusions in sponsorship proposals such as those shown earlier for Country Energy, usually provide a good indication of the criteria that will be used to assess the sponsorship proposal.

An organisation that has received a sponsorship proposal will act in several possible ways. After scanning the proposal, its management and/or marketing personnel may:

- dispose of it
- request further information
- seek to negotiate in an attempt to have the sponsorship offering improved to meet its needs
- accept the proposal as presented (it is more likely though that some adaptations will occur through negotiation).

Once sent, it is sound practice to follow up sponsorship proposals within a reasonable period (for example, two weeks afterwards) to determine their status (for example, yet to be considered, under review or rejected). On occasions, the proposed sponsorship package may be of interest to the organisation, but they may wish to 'customise' it further. If this is the case, both the event and potential sponsor can negotiate to move the sponsorship towards a more mutually beneficial offer. Event managers should have a clear understanding of the minimum payment they are prepared to accept for the event assets on offer — to what extent can the event move in its negotiations to create a 'win-win' situation (particularly if multiple sponsors are being sought)? At this stage, it is vitally important not to undervalue the event's assets — a sponsorship sold below its potential market value will eventually need a price correction, which creates tension with event partners.

Event organisers also need to consider the time, effort and dollars that they devote to seeking sponsorship in determining their final 'price'. Harrison (2004, p. 8) suggests that 'the amount of money, or its equivalent value to you, that you raise in sponsorship should be (at least) double the amount that it has cost you to get it, otherwise you are going backwards'. When it is clear that both the event and sponsor have a sponsorship arrangement that offers the best possible outcomes for both partners, it is then usual for a written contract to be developed.

Negotiating event sponsorship contracts

It is sound business practice to commit the sponsorship agreement to paper to avoid misunderstandings about the event assets and benefits being offered, their costs, payment terms and the responsibilities of both parties. Where the contract was once just a reference for event organisers and sponsors, in the case of major sponsorship deals, the contract now establishes the ground rules for the ongoing working relationship between the sponsorship partners. Chapter 10 offers some more general guidelines about event contracts. With large-scale events, the document can be a 'saviour' for high-ticket sponsors, ensuring the ticketing obligations of the event organiser are met and that category exclusivity for the sponsor is protected to discourage ambushers. Closer event-sponsor relationships may technically be easier to establish in smaller-scale events and festivals, but the business practicalities of having a contract (approved by the lawyers of both parties) makes a lot of sense. If a prolonged period of negotiation is needed for a sponsorship (this is usual for a very large event sponsorship property), having a legal letter of agreement to confirm that the sponsorship will go ahead is important.

To help plan the content of an event sponsorship contract, various sponsorship agreement pro formas are available, which can help draft the document for discussion with the sponsor and legal advisors. Grey and Skildum-Reid (2003) offer excellent support materials of this nature in their toolkit. The content of contracts would usually include: the objectives and responsibilities of both parties, benefits to be obtained by the event and the sponsor, termination conditions, ambush marketing protection, details of media, branding and leveraging, the promised exclusivity, marketing and sponsor servicing and insurance and indemnity requirements. For small events and festivals, the scope and depth of the contract will be reduced (and the cost of legal advice is a key consideration), but often some in-kind (contra) support from a legal service can be obtained by a local community festival.

MANAGING AND 'SERVICING' SPONSORSHIPS

Once sponsorship has been secured, it must be effectively managed in order to ensure the benefits that were promised are delivered. Indeed, this is usually a requirement that is spelt out in some depth in sponsorship contracts for large events. However, a sponsorship management plan is critical for events and festivals of all types. This allows the event to show the steps it is taking to satisfy the sponsor's marketing needs listed in the sponsorship agreement and to build a quality relationship with its sponsors.

Servicing sponsors can involve everything from maintaining harmonious relationships between a sponsor's staff and people within the event/festival to ensuring sponsor's signage is kept in pristine condition. Some festivals and events also tailor their servicing approach to the sponsor's needs. Sharon Longridge (2004, p. 5) from Noise 2003 says, 'We devise the most effective ways to manage each partner/sponsor as opposed to a one size fits all approach. Some are more informal and a monthly chat is the best approach, others require the ultra professional treatment and formal project updates are appropriate.' However, there should be no doubt about the level of servicing that a sponsor likes or expects if your front-end negotiations have been well managed. Allsop (2004) from the Brisbane Broncos suggests that at least 10 per cent (but preferably up to 50 per cent) of the sponsorship revenue should be set aside for actively servicing the sponsorship, and this management budget needs to be spent wisely.

■ Communication, *commitment and trust between partners*

Great relationships between events and sponsors (like any other relationship) are built on a strong foundation of communication, commitment and trust. Smooth working relationships are going to have a strong impact on the sponsor's decision to renew their contract (Aguilar-Manjarrez, Thwaites & Maule 1997). Research has also shown a link between having a market orientation (a customer-focused approach to doing business) and building commitment, satisfaction and trust between the sponsor partners (Farrelly & Quester 2003). It appears that sponsors who don't see their event partner as being particularly 'market/consumer-oriented' often engage in less joint marketing activities with that event. As a result, it is important to establish effective communication with sponsors so that they see the event as a serious marketer who will look for joint leveraging opportunities. Both the sponsor and the event need to have a reasonably equal input to how the sponsorship can be 'tapped', to achieve its full potential. Perceptions by the sponsor of an equitable contribution to the relationship could lead it to look for a more customer-oriented event (Farrelly & Quester 2003) in its next sponsorship round.

A number of suggestions and actions (based on Geldard & Sinclair 2004) can be adopted to ensure positive and enduring relations are developed with sponsors:
• *One contact* — one person from the event organisation needs to be appointed as the contact point for the sponsor. That person must be readily available (a mobile phone helps), have the authority to make decisions regarding the event and be able to forge harmonious relationships with the sponsor's staff.

- *Understand the sponsor* — a method of maintaining harmonious relationships is to get to know the sponsor's organisation, its staff, its products and its marketing strategies. By doing this, it becomes easier to understand the needs of the sponsor and how those needs can be satisfied.

- *Motivate an event organisation's staff about the sponsorship* — keeping staff informed of the sponsorship contract, the objectives of the sponsorship and how the sponsor's needs are to be satisfied will help ensure the sponsorship will work smoothly and to the benefit of both parties.

- *Use of celebrities associated with the event* — if the event includes the use of artistic, sporting or theatrical celebrities, ensure sponsors have an opportunity to meet them in a social setting. Most people enjoy immensely the opportunity to tell anecdotes about their brush with the famous!

- *Acknowledge the sponsor at every opportunity* — use all available media to acknowledge the sponsor's assistance. Media that can be used include the public address system at a local festival, newsletters, media releases, the annual report and staff briefings.

- *Sponsorship launch* — have a sponsorship launch to tell the target market about the organisations and agencies that will sponsor the event or festival. The style of the launch depends on the type of sponsorship and the creativity of the event director. Finding an innovative angle to draw media coverage is valuable.

- *Media monitoring* — monitor the media for all stories and commentary about the event or festival that include mention of the sponsor (a media monitoring firm may be contracted to perform this task). This shows the sponsor that the event takes a serious interest in the sponsorship and is alert to the benefits the sponsor is receiving.

- *Principal sponsor* — if the event has many sponsors, ensure the logo of the principal sponsor (that is, the sponsor who has paid the most) is seen on everything to do with the event, including stationery, uniforms, flags, newsletters, stages and so on. Usually, this requirement will be spelt out in legal agreements, but it is important to add value for the principal sponsor wherever it is possible.

- *Naming rights* — if the event has given naming rights to a sponsor, it has an obligation to ensure these rights are used in all communications employed by the event organisation. This includes making every endeavour to ensure the media are aware of, and adhere to, the sponsored name of the event. Sometimes this is difficult, but it must be attempted so the event holds up its side of the deal.

- *Professionalism* — even though volunteers manage many events, this does not mean that staff can act like amateurs. Sponsors expect to be treated efficiently and effectively, with their reasonable demands met in a speedy manner. Sponsorship is a partnership and loyalty to that partnership is often repaid with an ongoing investment.

- *Undersell and overdeliver* — do not promise what cannot be delivered. Be cautious in formulating your proposal and then ensure the expectations raised by the sponsorship agreement are met and, ideally, exceeded.

There is plenty of evidence of events who have found innovative ways to 'go that extra mile' with their sponsorship relationships. Noise 2003 seconded its radio producer to media partner Triple J so it used the station's media facilities, but it also gained a part time producer who created quality content for broadcast (Longridge 2004). An artistic director of the Melbourne Festival once visited the workplace of one of the sponsors to talk about the creative processes and how these processes could assist the company and its staff with product development and organisational change (Harrison 2004). Often, it takes only a little imagination to think of ways in which to prove to sponsors that the event or festival is an active business and marketing partner.

■ Management *action plans to 'service' sponsors*

In addition to the sponsorship contract, it is useful to prepare a sponsorship management plan. At its most basic, this *action plan* should identify what objectives the sponsorship will achieve for the sponsor, the benefits that have been promised, costs associated with providing specified benefits, review and evaluation approaches and the timeline for activities that need to be conducted to deliver on the sponsorship. These planning elements are discussed below.

Objectives associated with any given event sponsorship will be tailored to the needs of that partnership, but they should be realistic and measurable (as advised in chapter 7). The sponsor's key objective in the TAC (Transport Accident Commission) Wangaratta Jazz Festival, for example, was to create awareness of the message 'If you drink, then drive, you're a bloody idiot.' (Australian Business Arts Foundation 2004) The sponsor also had some sub-objectives related to forging community relationships. The event organiser, together with the sponsor, set out some specific performance measures in the event's management plan for later evaluation. Such measures included the minimum number of promotional spots on television and radio featuring recognition of the TAC and its social marketing message.

Stakeholders affected by the sponsorship also need to be addressed in the management plan — these groups would include attendees, members of the broader community in which the event is taking place, staff of the sponsoring organisation and media. All *benefits and associated actions* need to be clearly identified, along with the target group(s) to be reached and *costs* (financial or otherwise) that are associated with them. These costs might include signage manufacture and erection, supporting advertisements, promotional material, prize money, sponsor hospitality costs, professional fees, labour costs associated with hosting sponsors on-site, tickets, postage and preparation of an evaluation report. A budget needs to present all costs and show those costs in the context of the overall value of the sponsorship. For the Brisbane Broncos (discussed earlier), this information is also recorded in their asset register, where the profit (the value less costs) is calculated for every individual sponsorship (Allsop 2004). Figure 8.6 provides a checklist of items to be included in a sponsorship budget (see chapter 10 for more information on preparing budgets). It should also be remembered that sponsorship (both in-kind and cash) attracts GST, and this tax must be factored into any bottom line calculations.

(see chapter 10 for more information on preparing budgets)

■ **Figure 8.6**
A checklist of items to be included in a sponsorship budget

Items that will incur cash outlays or person cost ($), hours to support the sponsorship
- ❑ Event programs
- ❑ Additional printing
- ❑ Signage production
- ❑ Signage erection
- ❑ Support advertising
- ❑ Hospitality — food and beverage
- ❑ Telephone, Internet and fax
- ❑ Public relations support
- ❑ Tickets for sponsors
- ❑ VIP parking passes
- ❑ Cost of selling sponsorship (staff time at $ per hour)
- ❑ Cost of servicing sponsorship (staff time at $ per hour)
- ❑ Legal costs
- ❑ Travel costs
- ❑ Taxis and other transport
- ❑ Evaluation research/report
- ❑ Media monitoring

Total costs

Profit margin

Minimum sponsorship sale price

A list of the *actions* necessary to fulfil the sponsorship should be made, specifying what is to be done and who is responsible. Mapping out all of the management and marketing activities on a spreadsheet or other form of graphic display can be a useful exercise.

An *evaluation and review* process needs to be built into the sponsorship management plan. The review process should be ongoing and act to identify and address any problems that could affect sponsorship outcomes. Evaluation is concerned with providing a clear understanding of how the sponsorship performed against the objectives that were set for it. Evaluation seeks to answer questions such as: Did the promised media coverage eventuate? Did the attendee profile of the event reflect the market profile described in the sponsorship proposal? What was the overall quality of the sponsorship's delivery and management? Evaluation also gives the partners the chance to finetune the sponsorship arrangements, so both parties are well placed to renew the partnership.

In general terms, the development of the sponsorship business plan can be a creative and rewarding task that simply serves to communicate to the sponsor that its investment is being managed professionally.

MEASURING AND EVALUATING THE SPONSORSHIP

A shared responsibility of the event or festival and its sponsor is the measurement of the overall impact of the partnership. There are two components to measurement and evaluation: first, the evaluation of the effectiveness of the partnership and how the sponsor and event have contributed to it and, second, the measurement of the consumer-related marketing objectives set by the sponsor. While most events seek some feedback from their sponsors about the effectiveness of their sponsorship management, much more effort needs to be devoted to measuring the consumer effects of sponsorship. Many events have limited budgets for conducting sophisticated market research (and should consider some of the techniques suggested in chapter 7), but many sponsors also do surprisingly little research to determine whether their investment in an event was warranted in terms of value for money. The 2003 Australian Sponsorship Decision-Making Survey found that more than 50 per cent of participating companies did not currently undertake any measurement of their sponsorships (Sponsorship Insights and the Australian Sponsorship Marketing Association 2003). This contrasts with advertising campaigns where pre- and post-testing of consumer effects is commonplace.

Some of the factors that complicate the measurement of sponsorship are that brand marketers often use a number of media, including sponsorship, to create brand relationships and there are often carry-over effects of previous media and marketing expenditure on brand awareness and image (De Pelsmacker, Geuens & Van den Bergh 2004). Of particular importance in sponsorship measurement is the use of audience research that measures unaided and aided recognition of the event sponsor's name (sponsor awareness), attitudes towards the sponsor and any actions/behaviours that the sponsorship has caused in its target audience (this could be a signed contract on an important deal for a business-to-business bank client or a driver who has reduced their driving speed as a result of the sponsor's event messages).

While there is a need for more formal research (and publicly available findings) about the effects of sponsorship, it is clear that some sponsors of high-dollar event properties are becoming very rigorous about their measurement of the value of sponsorship. The following event profile details Suncorp's approach in evaluating its sponsorship of the 2003 Rugby World Cup.

Overall, it is clear that there is a marked contrast in the effort and expenditure devoted to measuring sponsorship effects across different events and festivals and among sponsors themselves. What is clear is that marketing budgets and sponsorship expenditure are subject to tighter scrutiny as competition for funds increases — it is timely, therefore, for all events and festivals and sponsorship managers (who also compete for dollars in their companies) to review their measurement tools.

Suncorp conducted brand recall surveys, attitude tracking and focus groups in their Queensland and interstate markets to understand the consumer response to their sponsorship of the 2003 Rugby World Cup. From May to December 2003, the company interviewed 100 people per month asking them to name the RWC sponsors. Commuters at Wynyard station in Sydney were involved in exit surveys to track attitudes towards the GIO sub-brand and the effectiveness of an outdoor campaign. Studies were also conducted to understand brand awareness and whether goodwill continued after the event.

As a preface to the Wallabies sponsorship, Suncorp also used focus groups during the RWC's quarter finals among customers and non-customers, rugby fanatics and non-fanatics to find out what they thought about the Suncorp and GIO brands and also what they thought about the Wallabies team. (The timing of this research before the Wallabies made it into the finals was important to avoid bias.) This was the sponsor's way of discovering that there was a strong fit between the perceived brand values of Suncorp and the Wallabies team. Media tracking was also used to assess the value of Suncorp's expenditure which determined a media value of between $4 and $5 million in unpaid media space during the RWC sponsorship.

T Ferguson, Sponsorship Manager, Suncorp 2004

SUMMARY

Sponsorship has increasingly become a mainstream component of the marketing communication media of many corporations and public sector organisations. Influences on sponsorship growth worldwide can be found in the business and marketing environment and in the diversity of consumer and stakeholder benefits that sponsorships create.

From an event's perspective, sponsorship often (but not always) represents a significant potential revenue stream. Yet, sponsorships are fast becoming business partnerships that offer resources beyond money. To succeed in the sponsorship stakes, event organisers must thoughtfully develop policies and strategies, providing a clear framework for both events/festivals and sponsors to decide on the value and suitability of potential partnerships. Having an inventory of the event or festival assets available for sale is an important starting point for those seeking sponsorship.

The sponsorship approach should be based on comprehensive research at the front end before a formal proposal is written and submitted to potential sponsors. Event managers need to embrace the full range of benefits that organisations seek through their sponsorship, and formalise and manage their agreements so that commitments made to sponsors are met. This chapter has provided critical insights into how to manage communication with sponsors as the event's business partners, how to maximise joint marketing opportunities and how to gain the long-term trust and commitment of sponsoring firms and agencies.

Questions

1 What is the difference between looking at event sponsorships as transactions versus business relationships?

2 Identify at least five trends that explain the expanded use of sponsorship as a marketing medium.

3 Identify a public sector organisation that is sponsoring one or more events and contact the person responsible for sponsorship. Ask them what they are trying to achieve through their sponsorship strategy and how they assess the outcomes.

4 Name an event or festival for which sponsorship may be inappropriate and discuss why you have formed this conclusion.

5 Obtain several non-current sponsorship proposals from event organisers/corporate sponsorship managers. Critically evaluate the content and presentation of these documents in the light of what you have read in this chapter.

6 Identify a festival or event of interest to you and state the steps that you would follow in identifying potential sponsors for this event.

7 Investigate a specific recurring event with a view to identifying the potential assets and benefits it might be able to offer sponsors. Are all of these assets currently being offered to sponsors? If not, what reasons could exist for these assets being untapped?

8 Select an event and contact its organisers with a view to determining whether they have developed sponsorship policies or sponsorship business plans. Establish why they have, or have not, done so. If they have developed one or both of these documents, investigate how the content was decided.

Telstra's sponsorship of
John Farnham's
'The Last Time Tour'

Telstra was the naming rights sponsor of Australian pop icon John Farnham's The Last Time Tour, which was known either as:

• Telstra presents John Farnham the Last Time, or
• Telstra CDMA* presents John Farnham the Last Time.

Telstra had previously had a lengthy association with John Farnham and his manager, Glenn Wheatley, through using them in an advertising campaign for Telstra Mobile products and The Last Time Tour offered Telstra the opportunity to further consolidate that association.

Sponsorship objectives

The following sponsorship objectives were set for Telstra's sponsorship of the John Farnham concert tour. A comprehensive sponsorship plan was written during the negotiation period, which included activities that would deliver each of these objectives:

• increase use of SMS (Short Messaging Service)
• increase use of WAP (Wireless Application Program)
• demonstrate mobility
• generate awareness of Telstra's sponsorship
• generate customer goodwill
• reward existing customers through sponsorships
• positively impact and involve staff
• link Telstra to a cause/charity.

Sponsor overview

Two of Telstra's business units used the benefits offered by this major national tour, with Telstra Mobile using the benefits offered by the metropolitan concerts and Telstra Countrywide using those offered by the country concerts.

Telstra is Australia's major provider of telecommunications services. Telstra's vision is to be a world-class, full-service, integrated telecommunications company helping Australian and Asia–Pacific customers and communities prosper through their access to innovative communications services and multimedia products. Telstra Country Wide (TCW) exists to provide better communications services to regional Australians and to increase Telstra's business performance in regional Australia. Telstra has a long history of supporting and leveraging major sponsored events in Australia. The company has a comprehensive sponsorship policy and strategy, and generally integrates sponsorships into its mainstream marketing activities very effectively.

*CDMA = Collision Detection Multiple Access

(continued)

Contract negotiations/discussion

The contract negotiations were detailed and protracted, and eventually a third party was brought in by Telstra to conclude the contract negotiations. Given the existing relationship between John Farnham, Glenn Wheatley and Telstra, the purchase price was reduced for Telstra. Market value for this sponsorship was a seven-figure sum.

Benefits offered to the sponsor

The most obvious benefit was the ability to use the Australia-wide tour that encompassed all capital cities and many major country towns, offering extensive national exposure and numerous opportunities for Telstra area managers to entertain their major clients, or potential clients at a high quality, highly desired event.

Other major benefits included:

- use of branding and imagery (that is, the right to associate with tour imagery in advertising and promotions)
- naming rights to both the metropolitan and regional tour
- signage at all concerts, launch and promotional events associated with the tour
- full-page advert in the program
- 20 'A' reserve tickets for each concert
- 20 programs at each concert
- 10 CDs at each concert
- priority ticketing for Telstra customers via Telstra.com
- branding on all media and communications
- category exclusivity (telecommunications)
- cross promotions with Channel 7
- exclusivity during programs on channels Seven and Prime
- right to develop tour icon and ring tone
- in-venue SMS promotion
- right to webcast
- autograph session competitions at every venue
- signage on tour vehicles.

Sponsorship costing

The costing of the sponsorship was split up into four sections: (1) the cost of the negotiation and pre-planning phase, (2) the purchase price of the sponsor-ship, (3) costs relating to running the metropolitan phase of the tour (Telstra Mobiles), and (4) the cost of running the country phase of the tour (TCW).

Activities undertaken to support the sponsorship

Activities to support the sponsorship included: local radio competitions in the lead-in to each concert, offering concert tickets and signed CDs; banners and signage placed at each venue by tour staff; and brochures placed on each seat, explaining how to use the SMS feature on a mobile phone.

An SMS competition was run at each venue, offering the opportunity to meet John Farnham backstage after the concert, have a photograph taken with him and receive an autographed CD. This was promoted both by brochure (either on seats or handed to concert goers as they came through the gates) and by pre-recorded voiceovers by Glenn Wheatley prior to the concert. At the interval, a voiceover reminded concert goers to turn on their mobile phone to check whether they had won.

Staff involvement

Telstra staff were offered staff discounts for group bookings. Staff were also able to purchase tickets via the Internet prior to general sale of tickets. Telstra management in each region that the concert visited were able to invite their most important customers and prospective customers along. Each concert offered 20 tickets, 20 programs and 10 John Farnham CDs. The area general manager was able to participate in the distribution of winners' CDs at the in-venue competition and, in some instances, took part in the winners' meet-and-greet session with John Farnham.

Evaluation

The sponsorship was evaluated by external consultants at both mid-term and the conclusion of the tour. (Evaluation of all implementation activities was undertaken.)

A combination of *output* and *outcome* measures were examined, wherever possible using existing (recent) research, thereby reducing the cost of the evaluation phase of this sponsorship. (Outputs are the items traditionally measured, which include the provision of contracted benefits such as signage, media, and hospitality, whereas outcomes are measures of the sponsorship's effect on the target's decisions and attitudes towards the company.)

Evaluation was undertaken of the following aspects of the sponsorship:

- whether an appropriate return on investment was returned to Telstra via this sponsorship
- whether a quantitative measurement of outputs was generated, including media coverage, venue/event signage, publicity, reach and frequency
- whether there was an increase of Telstra CDMA and its messages, products and services among those exposed to the sponsorship versus those that were not
- the consumer perceptions of Telstra's image and involvement in the sponsorship
- an assessment of sponsorship effectiveness against the pre-set objectives
- the delivery of contracted benefits
- an assessment of the effectiveness of sponsorship of this event as opposed to other promotional opportunities available.

Research/evaluation material included:

- audience research undertaken at concerts (including a balance of gender and age groups). This research took the form of face-to-face interviews at randomly selected concerts.
- media analysis received from the event management company, Talentworks. All material received was reviewed by the evaluators.
- raw information/documents received from both Telstra and Talentworks
- comparison with comparable properties undertaken by The Sponsorship Unit (TSU). Material was sourced from TSU's in-house library.

(continued)

At the end of the concert tour, all of Telstra's planned sponsorship objectives (for Telstra Mobile and TCW) had been achieved in the regions visited by the tour.

- SMS use generated by the in-venue competition had exceeded objectives, with up to 38 per cent of the audience participating in the promotion. (Remember, many of these people would have been entering as part of a couple, so this was an extremely good result.) At the end of the tour (both regional and metropolitan), almost one in two concert goers had entered the in-venue SMS competition, resulting in over 100 000 SMS messages being sent.
- A radio station SMS competition was conducted with the major FM or AM station in each market in the three weeks before the concert (providing the audience with a chance to win one of six double passes to the John Farnham concert and a copy of 'The Last Time' CD). Although the competition generated around 10 000 entries, this number was lower than expected.
- Nine per cent of those who entered the SMS competition had never previously used the SMS feature on their phones.
- Eighty-one per cent of regional concert attendees and 76 per cent of metropolitan attendees were able to identify Telstra as a sponsor of the concert. (The next closest sponsor in awareness terms jumped from 1 per cent awareness to 11 per cent awareness after a free product giveaway.) In industry terms, this is an excellent result.
- Fifty-seven per cent of regional audiences and 51 per cent of metropolitan audiences stated that they either agreed or agreed strongly with the statement 'When I see a company sponsoring the John Farnham Concert Tour, I feel good about that company'. This is a very good result, with a common benchmark for this measure being around 18–23 per cent.
- Seventeen per cent of all tickets to the tour (regional and metropolitan) were booked via Telstra.com before the general release of tickets. This meant that Telstra customers had the first choice of tickets. An offer of tickets being made to Telstra customers via SMS to their mobiles did not go ahead due to Telstra policy precluding such advertising.
- The hospitality (used by area managers to entertain high-value customers or prospective customers) was very well received and resulted in an estimated eight figure sum in new and retained sales that have been directly attributed to the opportunity to entertain at the concert. This entertainment was used in line with Telstra's hospitality guidelines, with strict staff/guest ratios being observed.

Edward Geldard, General Manager, The Sponsorship Unit Pty Ltd,
and Laurel Sinclair, Managing Director, The Sponsorship Unit Pty Ltd

Questions

1 Discuss how well Telstra's evaluation of its concept sponsorship reflects the sponsorship effects process shown in figure 8.3 (page 241).

2 Select five key benefits of event sponsorship (pages 242–4) and briefly explain how Telstra achieved those benefits from its tour sponsorship.

3 Using Ansoff's product–market matrix (page 209), discuss the growth strategies that Telstra appeared to achieve from its tour sponsorship. In your discussion, use examples from the above case study.

REFERENCES

Aguilar-Manjarrez, R, Thwaites, D & Maule, J 1997, 'Modelling sports sponsorship selection decisions', *Asia-Australia Marketing Journal*, vol. 5, no. 1, pp. 9–20.

Allsop, K 2004, 'How the Broncos "do" sponsorship', Presentation at Queensland University of Technology, 19 April 2004.

Anonymous 2003, 'Event sponsorship's fastest growing marketing medium (global sponsorships are expected to reach $26.2 billion in 2003)', *Business Line*, 21 August (accessed via Factiva database 2 May 2004).

Australian Business Arts Foundation 2004, 'Business arts partnerships', February, www.fuel4arts.com (accessed 2 May 2004).

Australian Sponsorship Marketing Association 2001, 'Sponsorship case study: a closer look at the AFR 2001 National Sponsorship Awards Sponsorship Strategy Category Winner — Kellogg's Australia', *ASMA Sponsorship Report*, September, p. 4.

Cornwell, T, Roy, D & Steinard II, E 2001, 'Exploring managers' perceptions of the impact of sponsorship on brand equity', *Journal of Advertising*, vol. 30, no. 2, summer, pp. 41–51.

Country Energy 2004, 'Sponsorship public guidelines', www.countryenergy.com.au (accessed 1 May 2004).

Crompton, J 1993, 'Understanding a business organisation's approach to entering a sponsorship partnership', *Festival Management and Event Tourism*, vol. 1, pp. 98–109.

Cummins, C 2003, 'Business — marketing and advertising — Uncle Tobys tops poll as sporty brand', *Sydney Morning Herald*, 22 May.

De Pelsmacker, P, Geuens, M & Van den Bergh, J 2004, *Marketing communications — a European perspective*, 2nd edn, Prentice Hall Financial Times, Harlow, Essex.

Dolphin, R 2003, 'Sponsorship: perspectives on its strategic role', *Corporate Communications: an International Journal*, vol. 8, no. 3, pp. 173–186.

Duncan, T 2002, *IMC: Using advertising and promotion to build brands*, McGraw-Hill Irwin, Boston.

Ellery, S 2004, 'Hospitality — summer attractions', *PR Week*, 5 March (accessed via Factiva Database 2 May 2004).

Farrelly, F & Quester, P 2003, 'The effects of market orientation on trust and commitment — the case of the sponsorship business to business relationship', *European Journal of Marketing*, vol. 37, no. 3/4, pp. 530–53.

Ferguson, T 2004, Suncorp Sponsorship Manager, personal communication, 10 March.

Geldard, E & Sinclair, L 2004, *The sponsorship manual*, 2nd edn, The Sponsorship Unit, Melbourne.

Grey, AM & Skildum-Reid, K 2003, *The sponsorship seeker's toolkit*, 2nd edn, McGraw-Hill, Sydney.

Gronroos, C 1994, 'From marketing mix to relationship marketing: towards a paradigm shift in marketing', *Asia-Australia Marketing Journal*, vol. 2, no. 1, 9–29.

Harrison, P 2004, 'Sponsorship — cutting through the hype', The Australia Council for the Arts, February www.fuel4arts.com.

Hinch, T & Higham, J 2004, 'Sport tourism development', in *Aspects of Tourism*, Channel View Publications, Clevedon, UK.

IEG Network 1997, 'Glossary ambush marketing, www.sponsorship.com/forum/glossary.html (accessed April 2004).

Kover, AJ 2001, 'The sponsorship issue', *Journal of Advertising Research*, February, p. 5.

Lieberman, A with Esgate, P 2002, *The entertainment marketing revolution*, Prentice Hall Financial Times, Upper Saddler River, New Jersey.

Longridge, L 2004, 'Festival fund raising: noise', *Noise and the Australian Arts Council*, February, www.fuel4arts.com (accessed April 2004).

Media 2004, 'Game, set and client match', 9 April (accessed via Factiva database, May 2004).

Meenaghan, T 2001a, 'Understanding sponsorship effects', *Psychology and Marketing*, vol. 18, no. 2, pp. 95–122.

Meenaghan, T 2001b, 'Sponsorship and advertising: a comparison of consumer perceptions', *Psychology and Marketing*, vol. 18, no. 2, pp. 191–215.

National Bank 2004, 'Cirque du Soleil — our shared values', www.national.com.au/Community (accessed 3 May 2004).

New Media Age 2003, 'Festivals — joining the throng', 31 July (accessed via Factiva database May 2004).

Pearce, L 2003, 'Open seeks new sponsor after Heineken decision', *The Age*, 31 December.

Performance Research 2001, *Independent studies*, Henley on Thames, England.

Pickett, B 2002, 'As Cingular Ads parody, not all sponsorships fit the brand-building bill', National Hotel Executive, September, www.prophet.com/knowledge/articles/archive1.html (accessed April 2004).

Roy, D & Cornwell, TB 2004, 'The effects of consumer knowledge on responses to event sponsorships', *Psychology and Marketing*, vol. 21, no. 3, pp. 185–207.

Shani, D & Sandler, D 1998, 'Ambush marketing: is confusion to blame for the flickering of the flame?', *Psychology and Marketing*, vol. 15, no. 4, pp. 367–383.

Sigma 2004, 'People and community', www.sigmaco.com.au (accessed 2 May 2004).

Smart Marketing Street Wise Workshops 2001, www.smsw.com/contacti.htm (accessed 25 April 2001).

SponsorMap 2004, www.sponsormap.com.au/sponsormap.html (accessed 3 May 2004).

Sponsorship Research International 2000, *World-wide sponsorship market values*, London.

Sponsorships Insights and the Australian Sponsorship Marketing Association 2003, 'Trends in sponsorship management: revelations from the 2003 Australian Sponsorship Decision-Making Survey', www.asma.com.au (accessed 1 May 2004).

Ukman, L 1995, 'Successful proposals', www.sponsorship.com/forum/success.html (accessed 25 April 2001).

Wallis, N 2003, 'Analysis — festivals find their place in the sun', *Marketing Event*, 11 November.

Welsh, J 2003, 'Reinventing sponsorship', www.poolonline.com, no. 2, spring, pp. 1–2.

3 EVENT MANAGEMENT

This part of the book looks at the systems that event managers can use to put the event plan into action. The chapter on project management looks at how to integrate the various event plans. The following chapter looks at controlling events and, in particular how the budget process can be used as a controlling mechanism in the implementation of an event. The chapter on legal and risk management describes the legal factors that event managers need to be aware of, and how to identify, minimise and manage the risks inherent in an event. This section also looks at the staging of events, and the evaluation and reporting process.

9

Project *management for events*

LEARNING OBJECTIVES

After studying this chapter, you should be able to:

- discuss project management as an approach to the management of festivals and events

- describe the phases of event management

- discuss the knowledge areas involved in conducting an event using project management techniques

- describe the project manager's place in the event management structure and the competencies they require

- use the fundamental techniques of project management

- comment on the limitations of the project management approach in event management.

INTRODUCTION

The production of a festival or event is a project. There are many advantages in using project management techniques to manage the event or festival. Project management oversees the initiation, planning and implementation of the event, in addition to monitoring the event and the shutdown. It aims to integrate management plans from different knowledge areas into a cohesive, workable plan for the entire project.

In this chapter, we will examine how the project manager fits into the event management structure. There are specific tools and techniques used by project managers and we overview the most common of these. We will then examine how evaluation of a project can build on the project management knowledge base to improve future project performance. We also look at some limitations of the project management approach to event management.

PROJECT MANAGEMENT

According to the leading textbooks on project management, world business is moving towards the accomplishment of business objectives through separate projects. Gray and Larson (2000, p. 3), quoting *Fortune Magazine* and the *Wall Street Journal*, call it 'the wave of the future'. Due to the changing nature of modern business, products and services now have to be managed as projects as a response to this change. A product in the modern world is continually evolving. Software upgrades are an example of this, and they create an environment that is constantly evolving.

O'Toole and Mikolaitis (2002), in their text on corporate event project management, note that the expansion of the event industry is a result of this change. New events are needed to launch products: new conferences and seminars are needed to educate the market and new festivals are needed to reposition towns and regions in the marketplace as the national economy changes. Government departments are not immune from this. The Australian Taxation Office, for example, organised a number of events to explain the Goods and Services Tax to the public and tax agents.

As project management is used to manage these developments, the event industry appreciates that these techniques can be successfully employed in events. Events and festivals can be seen as a response to a constantly changing business and cultural environment and as projects — they can import increasingly pervasive management methodology.

What is a project? Gray and Larson (2000, p. 4) provide a succinct definition:

■ a project is a complex nonroutine one-time effort limited by time, budget, resources and performance specifications designed to meet customer needs. ■

According to this definition, special events and festivals are projects. The project produces an asset such as a building, film, software system or even a man on the moon — or a special event or festival. The asset is the ultimate deliverable of the project. The management is the planning, organising, leading and controlling of the project.

The project management of events concentrates on the management process to create the event, not just what happens at the event. Many texts and articles confuse the event with its management. The event is the deliverable of a management process. A bridge, for example, is the deliverable of a series of processes called engineering and construction. The event may take place over a period of hours or days. The event management process may take place over many months or years. Project management is a system that describes the work before the event actually starts, the event and finally the shutdown of the event.

Project management is called the 'overlay' as it integrates all the tasks of management. Event management is made up of a number of management areas, including planning, leading, marketing, design, control and budgeting, risk management, logistics, staging and evaluation. Each of the areas continuously affect each other over the event life cycle. Project management can be regarded as integrating all of these disciplines; thus it covers all the different areas of management and integrates them so they all work towards the event objectives.

O'Toole and Mikolaitis (2002, p. 23) describe the advantages of using project management for events:

1. It is a systematic approach that can be improved with every event. Project management describes the management system. Once something is described it can be improved. If it remains hidden there is nothing to improve.

2. It avoids the risk that the event's success relies on one person. By having a system with documentation, filing and manuals, as well as clear communication and teams, the event is understood by anyone with the right experience.

3. It uses a common terminology and therefore facilitates clear, timely communication.

4. It ensures accountability to the stakeholders. Stakeholder management is a fundamental knowledge area of project management.

5. It makes the management of the event apparent. Too often the management is hidden by the importance of the event.

6. It helps train staff. Project management provides a framework for step-by-step training of staff.

7. It is used in all other areas of management, not just events. The management methodology used for the event can be transferred to any project. Once the event is over, the staff will find they have learned a useful transferable skill.

8. It is common to other businesses. Many of the event stakeholders will already be familiar with the terminology.

Points 4 and 5 are related to the event itself being mistaken for the management. Clear and timely accountability to numerous event stakeholders is a requirement for event managers. The accountability cannot wait until the event is delivered. Stakeholders, such as the police, sponsors and government may want a series of reports on the progress of the management. It is too late to find out that the management company was incompetent during the event. Clients are demanding a work in progress (WIP) report. A project management system has this reporting facility as a part of the methodology.

Project management comprises basic concepts that are not necessarily found in ongoing management. As described in Gray and Larson's (2000) definition of a project, it has a specific completion date, budget and product. This product or deliverable cannot be improved except by commencing on another project. Unlike ongoing management, such as a company continually producing a product and adapting it, a project has to produce the best product the first time. There is no time for improvement. In the words of the music industry 'you are only as good as your last gig'. The management of the project passes through phases. The management has to be aware of the knowledge areas and the way they change over the project life cycle. The following event profile examines how project management was used to manage the media requirements for the 2003 Rugby World Cup.

EVENT PROFILE

Packing down with the world's journalists

Project management is not always about high-rise property developments: it can be about event management, or even about managing the media requirements for an event.

The biggest sporting event in 2003, the Rugby World Cup, is being held in Australia. It is one of the largest sporting events the country has hosted, and Bovis Lend Lease has been engaged to manage one aspect of its staging — the logistics of media coverage.

Bovis's brief is to develop media facilities and press centres at all World Cup venues to accommodate an anticipated 500 local and international media representatives. The company will convert an existing building in Sydney's historic Rocks district into the headquarters for the client — the International Rugby Board — for the duration of the tournament. This building will also be the main media facility and will include an auditorium for major tournament announcements, interviews and press conferences. Project director for the Rugby World Cup project, Tim Urquhart, says the skill of project management can be applied equally to an event or to a property development, because at the end of the day both are simply projects. 'An event is a little less tangible than property, but it has a definitive end date.

As such, its phases are very different from a property development,' Urquhart says. He says the first, crucial phase is to agree with the client about what must be put in place. 'In this early phase, the brief and budget must be defined; the client often has no idea about how much is to be spent.'

The Rugby World Cup will be held in 11 venues in 10 cities across Australia, although Bovis did not have to find the venues. Urquhart says, 'Australia already has great football venues. But we had to audit them, looking at additional requirements over and above their everyday use. In the first match, we anticipate 15 broadcast organisations will be involved in the venue plus 100 press agencies. Almost every country has its own representation, and we are building temporary press sub-centres. In essence, we are providing temporary facilities and buildings, which will be required over and above how the venue is normally used. This includes a lot more technology and cabling. As a comparison, there will be hundreds more members of the press and broadcasters than at the Bledisloe Cup.'

As many as 55 000 visitors are due in Australia for the 2003 Rugby World Cup, which will be held in October and November in Sydney, Gosford, Wollongong, Brisbane, Townsville, Melbourne, Canberra, Perth, Adelaide and Launceston. Twenty nations will compete, divided into four pools of five teams, for a total of 48 matches. The temporary media accommodation will be constructed by staff drawn from Bovis' regional offices throughout Australia. Urquhart anticipates that about 30 to 40 workers will be required and he explains: 'We were able to offer on-the-spot staff, as we have a physical presence in most locations. We have to be flexible about the process so that we can change things as we go along. Even in the building phase, planned for September, we will still be making changes. But that is inherent in the event industry and (is) what makes it so different from the building industry. Press and broadcasters may change their minds, depending on which teams progress through to the finals,' he says.

How much did all this cost? 'Money is difficult to talk about: it does not equate to the costs of a normal building project but to management time,' Urquhart says. To win this contract, Bovis approached the Australian Rugby Union about two years ago, drawing their attention to Bovis' core expertise. It was involved with the Atlanta 1996 Olympics and Sydney 2000 Olympics. It has also provided consulting services for the 2006 Melbourne Commonwealth Games and the 2008 Beijing Olympics, as well as to several cities preparing to bid for 2012 Olympics.

(**Source:** *Robertson 2003.*)

A project will pass through a series of phases or stages. Figure 9.1 illustrates these phases.

■ **Figure 9.1**
The phases of project management
(**Source:** EPMS 2004.)

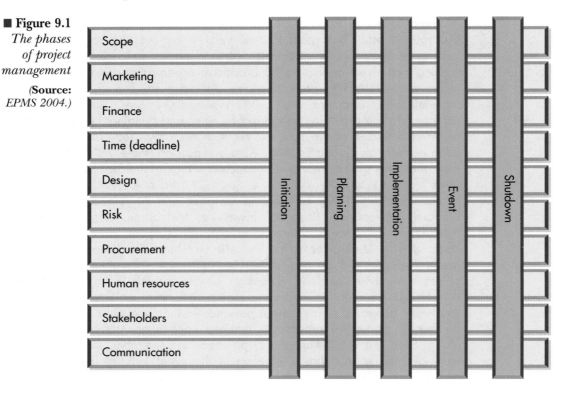

A project phase is a series of related tasks, performed over a period of time and under a particular configuration of management to produce a major deliverable. The end of a phase is often characterised by a major decision to begin the next phase. There are a number of different views on project phases. Some texts on project management for software development describe up to seven phases. Civil engineering texts have four phases of project management described in the *Guide to the project management body of knowledge 2000*. Event and festival management is accurately portrayed as having five phases. The phase approach to describing the management is purely descriptive — as with any description, it approximates reality. The aim is to provide clarity to the confusing tasks involved in event management. Some project phases overlap — planning and implementation can take place at the same time in different areas of management. The promotion schedule, for example, may be happening at the same time as aspects of the program are being redesigned. This chaos, however, does have a pattern and the five-phase approach is a useful tool to help the reader to understand it.

■ Initiation

The first phase of initiation is characterised by the idea of the event being developed and setting the objectives. It may be a vague idea, for example, that a town should organise a heritage festival or a promoter decides to organise a rainforest concert. As well as this event concept, the initiation phase may include a feasibility study. The project feasibility study will report on the viability of the event and the management required to deliver it. It may include site and date suggestions, possible sponsors and supporters, a draft budget, possible risks, required management for the event and event logistics. The feasibility study may incorporate a number of alternative configurations of the event, so that the sponsor or client can choose the best options that will suit them. The initiation phase interfaces and overlaps with the process of conceptualising the event as discussed in chapter 4 and with the strategic planning process as set out in chapter 5. The project objectives will relate to the objectives of the host in sponsoring the event.

The business case for the project is often used as a form of feasibility study. It describes the reason for the event in terms of the return on investment to the host community or company. The end of the initiation phase is characterised by a 'go/no-go' decision — whether to proceed with the event or not.

■ Planning

The second phase is the project planning. Planning is characterised by working out what is needed and how it will fit together. Chapter 5 discusses this phase in detail from a strategic point of view. Each of the knowledge areas on the left side of figure 9.1 will produce a separate plan. A major role of project management is to integrate all these plans; that is, to make sure they all work together. For this reason the plans are often called baseline plans. They are regarded as a starting point rather than a finished plan. Once the plans have been formulated they need to be implemented.

■ Implementation

Implementation is the third phase. The characteristics of this phase in project managing events are:
- the application of all the plans, such as hiring staff, sending out requests for tender, confirming contractors and carrying out the promotional schedule
- monitoring and controlling — testing the plans and confirming how relevant they are as the organising progresses
- making decisions based on the comparison between the plans and reality
- work in progress reporting to the key stakeholders
- active risk management.

The beginning of this phase is a time of high activity with meetings to discuss specific issues, decisions to be made and communication between various parties. The management may need to visit the planning phase when there are major changes and the plans need to be revised. At this time, the team has to be focused on the project scope and ensure all the plans are compatible with each other and with the overall objectives of the event.

In traditional project management, this third phase is the final phase and involves handover of the deliverable. Events are not a tangible asset that can be handed over in the same way as a building. For this reason, it is wise to add an extra phase into the project phases and call this 'the event'.

■ The *event*

Unlike civil engineering project management, the project event manager is working during the deliverable; that is, the event. Although this is not seen as a separate phase by traditional texts on project management, it fits into the definition above. During the event, the tasks and responsibilities tend to roll on regardless of what the management wants to have happen. The staff numbers during the event, including volunteers, may increase dramatically. The short time period, attendance of the major stakeholders, the audience and the participants, means that the management cannot rely on the same management techniques used during the lead-up to the event. This is recognised in all events, when the operations manager, artistic director or the stage manager takes over the running of the event. In the theatre, at an agreed time before the show, the stage manager is regarded as the ultimate authority. At a certain time before the event the management team will move into 'operations mode', which might mean getting out of the office and into their costumes for the event. The monitoring and controlling at this point will be devolved to other teams and the management will run the event by looking for errors and making on-the-spot decisions. The tools and techniques used by management during this phase are found in chapter 13 on staging.

■ Shutdown

The event manager will be responsible for the shutdown of the event. It is the last phase and requires a separate series of tasks and responsibilities. Management will be scaled down and return to their pre-event formation. Chapter 12 describes the processes use in event shutdown. This phase includes the on-site shutdown and the management closure. The shutdown plans will be created during the planning phase, and the shutdown ideally is the implementation of these plans. However, in an industry beset by major changes, the shutdown will rarely go exactly to plan. Monitoring and decision making from management will be needed. The shutdown phase can take the event from a seeming success to a failure if the management does not make the right decisions at this time. Shutdown includes preparation for the next event. On-site, this includes packing for the next event; off-site, the management will be archiving the documents and assessing their management. It is during this phase that the success of the management system is evaluated and the baseline plans or templates created for future events.

In summary, the best way to describe the event management process from a project management perspective is in terms of five phases: initiation, planning, implementation, the event and shutdown. These phases comprise the life cycle of the project. Each of the phases will require different management techniques and tools. Different areas of knowledge will be used. During the event, the event management team will be monitoring the event for any changes, rather than initiating any major new actions.

KNOWLEDGE AREAS

The management of any festival or special event will be concerned with the areas illustrated on the left side of figure 9.1 (page 282). The relative importance of each of these management areas will change and evolve over the phases. From this figure, the event itself is seen as a small part of the whole management process.

As mentioned in the planning section, management will produce a number of deliverables in each of these knowledge areas. In the finance area, for example, management will produce a financial plan and a budget. The marketing area will produce a marketing plan and a promotion plan. The design area will produce the site plan and the actual event program. These deliverables are used throughout the management process to organise the event. They focus the staff in each individual area and become the documentation of the event. The areas correspond to the departments of an ongoing business organisation. The project management approach seeks to integrate the plans from each separate knowledge area into a cohesive, workable plan for the project.

PMBoK 2000™ (the *Project management body of knowledge*) lists nine areas of knowledge for traditional project management areas: scope, cost, time, integration, procurement, quality, human resources, communication, and risk. Event management is slightly different. It will also be concerned with marketing and designing the event. In the construction industry, the project manager would rarely be involved in designing the building, finding the money to build it or making decisions on the building's marketability. These are major concerns for the special event and festival manager. These areas of project management knowledge can be explained as follows:

- *Scope* encompasses all the work, including all the plans, and is defined further in this chapter. The scope, therefore, helps to integrate the many plans. Controlling the scope is a fundamental responsibility of the project manager.
- *Marketing* is a combination of processes that help define the event and, therefore, the scope of the event. Marketing is described in chapter 7. Marketing the asset is not a traditional separate function of project

management; however, some of the modern texts on civil engineering and software projects are teaching aspects of marketing. As described in chapter 10, marketing may be regarded as a feed-forward control mechanism for events and as a risk management tool to minimise uncertainty.

- *Finance* would be called 'cost' in traditional project management. In some industries, the project management would not be concerned with the source of funds. However, in events and festivals, the funding — or revenue — is often a basic responsibility of the event or festival management. These issues are dealt with in chapters 7, 8 and 10.
- *Time management* in the form of schedules and milestones is primary to all project management. For events and festivals the deadline takes on a higher significance. Project management has developed numerous techniques to manage time.
- *Design* and creation of the asset is found in the project management of software and product development. The event or festival may be changing design right up until the day it starts. Event project management, therefore, must incorporate design under its integration of the event planning. Chapters 4 and 13 describe the processes involved in event design. Within the design area of knowledge resides the PMBoK heading of 'quality'.
- *Risk management* is seen as one of the knowledge areas of project management. Although it is a recent phenomenon in event management, managing risk is a fundamental function of project management. It covers all the other areas of management, is constantly undertaken and produces up-to-date reports, which is why it has been adapted for the project management of many events. Projects do not see risk management as an arduous exercise. It is regarded as a way to improve the quality of the project and the deliverable. Chapter 11 describes event risk management in detail.
- *Procurement* includes the sourcing and managing of supplies and the management of contracts. This is described in chapter 11. It is closely linked to sponsorship, finance and risk management.
- *Human resources* could be seen as a part of procurement, but the special conditions of dealing with people, such as team building and leadership, are indispensable to all projects, and so human resources is considered a separate area of knowledge. Chapter 6 describes this aspect in relation to events in detail.
- *Stakeholder management* is an important responsibility of the event manager. Some large public events will have more than 70 stakeholders; therefore, it is an important area of management for the event team. Finding and servicing sponsors is one of the areas of stakeholder management. Sponsorship was examined in detail in chapter 8.
- *Communication* includes external communication with the stakeholders and internal communication with the event team. It changes as event organising progresses. The external communication is linked to marketing and stakeholder management. On-site communication is linked to the staging and logistics of events as described in chapters 12 and 13.

■ Role *of the project manager*

Project management can be seen as a collection of skills and knowledge that allows the integration of various contractors to deliver the project. The old term for a project manager was a contract manager. What is the role of the event manager, given that this is also his or her job? There are three solutions to this problem:

1. Expand the skill base of the event manager to include project management.
2. Reduce the responsibilities of the event manager and hire a project manager.
3. Train existing project managers in events management.

Each of these solutions is being undertaken for different events and festivals. Event managers are being trained in project management at a variety of courses around the world. Project management is now a core subject in these courses. Figure 9.1 (page 282) illustrates all the areas of responsibility of the event manager trained in project management. Solution 2 is found in public events where the event management is split between the event director and the producer in charge of the creative aspects of the event, and the event project manager is in charge of the contracts, communication, compliance and other management areas. The event producer and event project manager have equal status in the organisation and report to the client. Originally, for large events, the roles would have been event director and operations or logistics manager; however, the operations manager could not take on the responsibilities of legal compliance, management integration and accountability, hence the pressure to create a new position of event project manager. In figure 9.1, the event director would be mostly concerned with the event design.

Solution 3 is used for very large events such as the Olympics and Grand Prix. The large project management companies, such as APP and GHD are involved in events as diverse as the Asian Games and the Sydney Royal Easter Show. In this case, the event is planned and controlled by the project management company who hire an event director as a contractor. In figure 9.1, the project company is responsible for all the areas of management. Their primary task is the integration and contract management. Most of the areas, such as marketing and finance, would be outsourced.

■ Key *competencies of a project manager in events*

Education providers and project managers' employers are moving towards a competency approach to training and employment. Project managers employed by events and festivals are expected to prove their skills in the application of project management to events. This is often expressed in terms of key performance indicators, competency levels or education benchmarking.

An informal survey of recent project management job descriptions for events and festivals has these competencies or skills as essential to the position:

- develop and work in a team and provide leadership
- successfully define tasks and deliver on time and to quality
- integrate the project plan with the strategic, marketing and artistic plan of the event
- undertake risk management according to the standards of the industry
- use financial controls, indicators and reports effectively
- develop a procurement plan and manage contracts
- demonstrate high level communication skills in presentation and negotiation
- liaise and manage a wide range of external stakeholders, including public and private organisations
- produce management progress reports for senior management and clients, including project evaluation and project closure
- possess knowledge of the event and similar events in this field
- have the ability to employ and assess project software and management systems related to events.

Other areas that may come under the responsibilities of the event project manager are:

- site design and management
- defining client requirements
- sponsorship management
- event concept development.

The three areas of event management often missing from the project management areas of responsibility are: the event concept creation, sponsorship development and marketing. In the more traditional application of project management, the finance of the project and the design of the asset are not in the domain of the project manager. In civil engineering, for example, the client will provide the finance and the architect will provide the asset design. However, these are increasingly becoming the roles of project management. Software project management will have a large influence on the design of the product; therefore, an event project manager may be required to expand their competencies to include design, marketing and finance.

Most universities offer courses on project management. University of Sydney, for example, as part of their project management course on-line, offer a module in event project management; University of Technology, Sydney, and Victoria University include project management in their events courses. The National Competency Standards in Australia for event management include competencies in project management. Any private college or TAFE courses that use these standards will include project management.

PROJECT MANAGEMENT TECHNIQUES

Numerous techniques have evolved in project management through live testing in areas as diverse as information technology, product development and engineering. Many techniques originally come from other disciplines such as operations, research and logistics. Most of these techniques are useful to event management. The scope and work breakdown structure are used to delineate the event and provide a management framework for planning and control. The techniques are not used in isolation and they form a process or a series of tasks that overlap. The process is outlined as a cascade model in figure 9.2. The description of project management as a linear process is only an approximation, as each stage of the process will influence the early stages.

■ **Figure 9.2**
Project management cascade

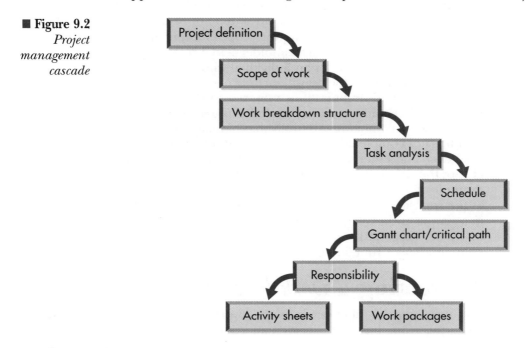

■ **Defining** *the project and scope of work*

The indispensable technique in project management is defining the project and, therefore, defining the scope. Misunderstandings over what is involved in the management of an event are common. Most project management literature stresses that the time spent on clearly defining a project in the initiation phase is time well spent. What is involved in the management? Who will do what? What will be the responsibilities of the client and the event company? These are some of the questions that assist project definition. Note that project definition is not the same as defining the event. A simple event may still be a complex project.

The scope — or scope of work — refers to the amount of work required to get the event up and running and then to shut it down; it is all the work. To define the scope is to gain an understanding of the event and its management. Often the event is described in terms of what is happening at the event. The scope definition captures the work necessary to deliver the event, as well as what is going on at the event.

The scope definition may be contained in the brief from the client or primary event sponsor; however, the client brief may be too simple and eventually lead to misunderstandings. Often the brief will only describe the deliverable, that is, the event and the work required to create it will be hidden. This has been a common problem in project management and the clarity and detail of the brief is identified as essential in the initiation period. For this reason, the event brief may be clarified by an addition of a statement of work (SOW). O'Toole and Mikolaitis (2002) describe the statement of work as 'a document that sets out the event objectives, lists the stakeholders, draft budget, scope, schedule and an outline of responsibilities'.

An important part of defining the scope is listing and understanding the requirements of the event stakeholders. In project management, a stakeholder is an organisation or an individual who has an interest in the project. Under this definition, the list will include negative stakeholders, such as competing events and organisations opposed to the event. The primary stakeholders will include sponsors and the organising committee. Secondary stakeholders include organisations that have an interest in the event if some action is not completed, or an unexpected incident occurs. For many events the Police and Emergency Services are secondary stakeholders. The deliverable of the stakeholder analysis is the stakeholder management plan. A good example of a stakeholder management plan in events is the sponsorship plan, as the sponsors are key stakeholders in events. The number of stakeholders in a simple event is large when compared to other projects. For this reason, figure 9.3 (page 291) and figure 9.1 (page 282) show stakeholder management as a major function of the event project manager.

■ Creating *a work breakdown structure*

The next step in the cascade is the 'work breakdown structure' (WBS). Once the scope has been decided and defined, it needs to be categorised, documented and communicated. The creation of the WBS is a technique that focuses management on the work required to deliver the event. The creation of a visual display of all the work that needs to be done can assist the staff in understanding the scope of the work.

To deliver the event there will be an extensive number of tasks that have to be completed. These tasks can be complex and a long list of them may not be very helpful. A way to get this under control is to 'aggregate' the tasks under headings. All the tasks concerning the venue, for example, could be grouped under the heading 'venue' or 'on-site'. The tasks that concern finding the money and working out the cost could be listed under the heading 'finance'. Deciding on task groups and headings should be completed during the initiation phase or at the beginning of the planning phase.

Alternatively, another way to describe task grouping is breaking down all the work required to deliver the event into manageable units. These management units will require common resources and skills. As O'Toole and Mikolaitis (2002) point out, the work breakdown structure often parallels the folder system used on the computer or in the filing cabinet. For a public festival, the work breakdown structure may parallel the sub-committees' set up to organise the event. A festival may have four systems: committee, file folders, email folders and paper folders. It makes sense to have them all integrated under the names of the headings in the work breakdown structure. The committee, the paper folder, the email folder and the file folder should all be called 'venue', for example. It is a simple procedure to standardise the names of folders, but often overlooked. A local festival, for example, may have the following sub-committees: finance, marketing (or promotion), legal or risk, human resources (such as volunteers) and administration.

Note that each of these correspond to the knowledge areas illustrated in figure 9.1 (page 282). This is an example of the work breakdown structure where the sub-committees represent the work needed to organise the event.

Once the work breakdown structure is created it can be used for the next stage in planning the event. Figure 9.3 illustrates the plans and documents that can be created from the WBS. These plans and documents are often called the deliverables. They are proof that the tasks have been carried out and they are used by other areas of event management; that is, they are delivered to the event management team.

■ **Figure 9.3**
Plans and documents created from the work breakdown structure (WBS)

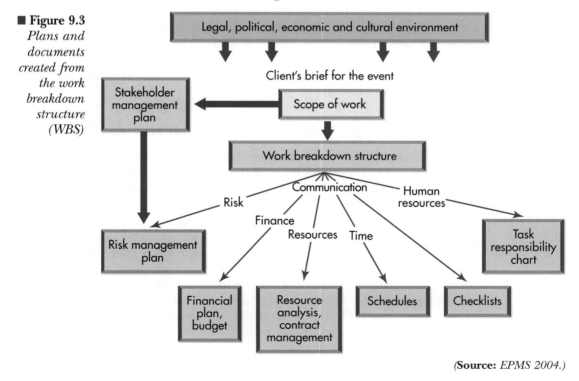

(**Source:** *EPMS 2004.*)

■ Analysing *the resources*

The resource list is developed from the WBS. The WBS is fundamental to resource analysis. The resources may be services, such as security, or goods, such as tents and chairs. Resources may also be a mixture of both, such as catering and sound. Resource analysis allows the event management to decide on what services and goods are:

- outsourced to suppliers
- sourced from the client or sponsor
- specially created or constructed for the event.

These are major decisions as they will impact on the budget. The resources may be grouped together and given to the one supplier. In project management this is called creating a work package. On large events, the supplier may need to submit a tender to supply these goods or services. An example of this is the supply of sound. From the WBS it appears that sound equipment will be needed in various areas of the event, including the different stages and the entrance. These requirements are grouped together and given to a number of sound companies to supply a quote for the work.

One of the outputs or deliverables of the resource analysis is a list of suppliers. This deliverable is the input into the contract management process. Chapter 11 on risk management explains this process in detail.

Perhaps the most important output of the resource analysis will be the human resource plan. This plan will be linked to the tasks and responsibilities described in the next section. In project management, the tasks are matched to the skills found in the pool of human resources available for the project. This process is outlined in chapter 6. A straightforward measurement of hours required for the event and the cost per hour can give the overall cost of this resource; however, many events use volunteers. A cost-benefit analysis of volunteers is difficult, as there are so many intangible benefits and hidden costs.

■ Identifying *tasks and responsibilities*

The decomposition of event management into the WBS may identify all the tasks that need to be completed to deliver the event; however, this is highly unlikely as there are myriad tasks for even the simplest of events. One only has to think of the many tasks involved in organising a wedding. The WBS will classify the tasks in manageable units. Each manageable unit will have groups of tasks associated with it. A WBS, for example, may have 'promotion' as a heading. Promoting the event will include the tasks of identifying the media, contacting the media, creating a schedule, creating a press release and many more. Each task has to be completed by a certain time and by a person or group of people, hence the task analysis is the beginning of assigning responsibilities. Chapter 6 on human resources goes into this area in more detail.

In project management practice it is common to map the WBS on the organisational structure. Each organisational unit corresponds to an area of the WBS. The management structure of a community event, for example, will be made up of a number of sub-committees. Each will have a clearly defined group of tasks assigned to it. An output of this process, often called task analysis, is the task responsibility chart or document. On this document are the tasks listed, who is responsible or what company, when the tasks should be completed and how the completion of tasks will be communicated. A task/responsibility list can also be put together at the end of meetings. Sometimes these are called action lists. Project managers prefer a task/responsibility list to the minutes of the meeting, because they are a 'call to action'. They are direct and the task is not hidden in other information, which is not relevant to the required actions.

■ Scheduling

Project management can be loosely defined as planning the who, what, where and when. The schedule represents the when. Almost all events have a fixed date or a deadline. Completed tasks take on an importance not found in other types of management. The schedule is a vital control tool allowing the project to progress. A mistake in scheduling can have a widespread affect to the other areas of management — leading to blowouts in costs, thereby compromising quality. The deadline is so important that most event managers work back from the date of the event. The schedule can be clearly represented by a Gantt chart.

Gantt chart

Gantt charts are bar charts named in honour of the management science theorist Henry Gantt who applied task analysis and scheduling to the construction of navy ships. The Gantt chart is simple to create and its ability to impart knowledge quickly and clearly has made it a popular tool in project management. The steps in creating a Gantt chart are described as follows:

- *Tasks* — break down the work involved in the area of event management into manageable tasks or activities. One of the tasks, for example, of the security team for the event is the erection of the perimeter fence around the site. This can be further broken down into the arrival of the fencing material, the arrival of volunteers and equipment, and the preparation of the ground. As discussed above, this work is usually done as part of identifying tasks and responsibilities.

- *Timelines* — set the time scale for each task. Factors to consider are the starting and completion times. Other considerations in constructing a time scale are availability, hiring costs, possible delivery and pick-up times and costs. A major factor in the arrival time and day of large tents, for example, is their hiring costs. These costs can depend on the day of the week on which they arrive, rather than the amount of time they are hired for. Note that the schedule for many aspects of the event management will work back from the date of the event.

- *Priority* — set the priority of the task. What other tasks need to be completed before this task can start? Completing this priority list will create a hierarchy of tasks and identify the critical tasks.

- *Grid* — draw a grid with the days leading up to the event across the top and a list of the tasks down the left-hand side of the grid. A horizontal bar corresponding to each task is drawn across the grid. The task of preparing the ground for the fencing, for example, depends on the arrival of materials and labour at a certain time and takes one day to complete. The starting time will be when the prior tasks are completed and the length of the timeline will be one day. The horizontal bars, or timelines, are often colour coded so each task may be easily recognised when the chart is completed for all activities.
- *Milestones* — as the chart is used for monitoring the progress of the event, tasks that are of particular importance are designated as milestones and marked on the chart. The completion of the security fence, for example, is a milestone as it acts as a trigger for many of the other event preparation activities.

Figure 9.4 shows an example of a simplified Gantt chart. This chart is common to most small regional festivals.

■ **Figure 9.4**
Simplified Gantt chart of a small festival

Tasks	F	S	S	M	T	W	T	F	S	S	M	T	W	T	F	S	S
Clear and prepare site		■	■	■	■						opening night				◇		
Generators arrive						■											
Lighting on site								■	■	■	■	■	■				
Tents arrive									■	■	■						
Stages arrive and set up											■	■	■				
Site security														■	■	■	
Sound system arrives															■		

◇ **Milestone:** start of festival

In his work on the human factors in project management, Dinsmore (1998) stressed that this display of project tasks and timelines has a high communication value to an event. It forestalls unnecessary explanations to the staff and sponsors and gives a visual representation of the event. Timelines are used in all events, regardless of their size. The on-time arrival of goods and services even at a small event can add significant value.

The advantages of a Gantt chart are that:
- it visually summarises the project or event schedule
- it is an effective communication and control tool (particularly with volunteers)
- it can point out problem areas or clashes of scheduling
- it is readily adaptable to all event areas
- it provides a summary of the history of the event.

For the Gantt chart to be an effective tool, the tasks must be arranged and estimated in the most practical and logical sequence. Underestimating the time needed (length of the timeline) can give rise to cost blow-out and render any scheduling ineffective. As Lock (1988, p. 89) points out:

■ Extended schedules produced in this way are an ideal breeding ground for budgetary excesses according to Professor Parkinson's best-known law, where work is apt to expand to fill the time available. ■

Network analysis: critical path

One important aspect of any project is the relationship of tasks to each other. This can be difficult to show on a chart. With larger events, the Gantt chart can become very complex, and areas where there is a clash of scheduling may be obscured by the detail of bars and colours. A vital part of event management is giving tasks a priority.

Assigning a priority to a task is essential as the event must be delivered on time. The arrival and set-up of the main stage at an event, for example, is more important than finding an extra extension cord. However, on a Gantt chart all of the listed tasks are given equal importance (or weight). The network analysis tool was developed to overcome these problems.

Network analysis was created and developed during defence force projects in the USA and United Kingdom in the 1950s and now has widespread use in many project-based industries. The basis of network analysis is its critical path analysis, which uses circles to represent programmed events and arrows to illustrate the flow of activities, thus the precedence of programmed tasks is established and the diagram can be used to analyse a series of sub-tasks. The most efficient scheduling can be derived from the diagram; this is known as the critical path. Figure 9.5 (page 296) illustrates a network derived from the Gantt chart shown in figure 9.4 (page 294). The critical path is shown as an arrow. This means if the generator did not arrive on time, everything along the critical path would be directly affected. The lights would not be put up and, without evening light or electricity to run the pneumatic hammers, the tents could not be erected. Without the protective cover of the tents, the stage could not be constructed and so the sound system could not be set up. The critical path is indeed critical.

There are a number of software packages available to help create the Gantt chart and critical path. These are project management programs, which are usually used in the construction industry. Unfortunately, most of these packages are based on a variable completion time or completion within a certain time. In the event industry, the completion time (that is, when the event is on) is the most important factor and every task has to relate to this time. The event manager cannot ask for an extension of the time to complete all of the tasks. Time charts and networks are very useful as a control and communication tool; however, like all project management techniques, they have their limitations. Graham, Goldblatt and Delpy (1995) describe how the Los Angeles Olympic Organising Committee gave up on the critical path chart as it became too unwieldy. There were 600 milestones. Rather than assisting with the communication and planning, it only created confusion. The solution was for the committee to return to a more traditional method of weekly meetings.

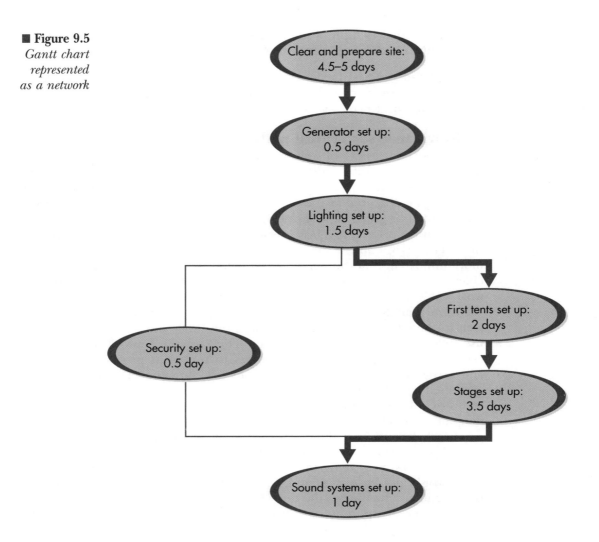

Clear and prepare site:
4.5–5 days

Generator set up:
0.5 days

Lighting set up:
1.5 days

First tents set up:
2 days

Security set up:
0.5 day

Stages set up:
3.5 days

Sound systems set up:
1 day

■ **Responsibilities** — *from documents to deliverables*

In managing a large event, the staff will be made up of various teams, volunteers and sub-contractors. If they are together only for a single event, they may not have a history of working together. This unfamiliarity with each other may lead to confusion in communication. There must be a way of communicating to the management team and stakeholders when tasks are completed, without creating unnecessary data information. The concept of deliverables is one way to control this complexity. The event itself is the major deliverable of all the tasks that make up the event management. A deliverable within the management of the event is the map of the site showing the layout of the event. To create this map the person responsible has to complete the design of the event and consider its logistics; therefore, the map is one of the outputs of the design process. The map is then delivered to other members of the event management team for use in her or his areas. A contract with a supplier is also a deliverable. It is proof that the negotiations have been completed. The deliverable of time planning is the schedule. As seen from these examples, the deliverables are often documents or files. They are developed by one group and passed on to another. After the event, these documents are also used to evaluate the management and may be used to prove the competence of the management. Figure 9.3 (page 291) shows some of the event documentation. Some project management theory suggests that the project should identify all the deliverables and work backwards from these to discover the tasks necessary to create them. This working back from the deliverables allows the construction of the project's WBS.

The event documents can be compiled into an event manual. The manual can then be used for future events, as these documents may be used as templates.

The deliverables include:

1. WBS — a deliverable of the planning scope
2. task responsibility chart — a result of analysing all the tasks that need to be completed and assigning them to the relevant people
3. checklists — an indispensable tool for the event manager (these are created across all areas of the event)
4. schedules — these range from the Gantt charts to production schedules used on the day of the event
5. resource analysis — list all resources required and the contracts needed
6. financial plan and budget — an output of the financial planning process
7. stakeholder management plan — includes the sponsorship plan and the various communication plans, such as the promotion plan, as well as the reporting plan for the secondary stakeholders; for example, the local police
8. risk management plan — a deliverable of the risk management. It may take the form of a risk register and a procedure for updating the register.

The deliverables from points two to eight emanate from the WBS and they help to refine the WBS. There are other documents used in events, including the contact list and site of venue layout map.

■ Payback *period and return on investment*

A term that is increasingly used in the event industry is the return on investment (ROI). It is a financial measure of the return to the event's key stakeholders as a result of its outcomes. The effects of the event can be multiple and include an increase in sales, community goodwill, increase in tourism, and a change of behaviour. These outcomes should relate to the event objectives — a reason that the objectives should be measurable. In project management, it is expressed as the payback period. The payback period is the length of time needed to pay all the costs of the event. After the payback period, the consequences of the event produce a surplus. A music concert payback period may occur during or before the concert, as the ticket sales will cover the event costs. The payback period for a local car rally may be measured in years after the event. There are a number of payback problems found only in events (and not other project-based industries). To establish the payback period, the real costs of the event have to be estimated. Some events, such as those that have in-kind sponsorship or use volunteers, will have difficulty achieving this. The benefits of many events are intangible and difficult to measure in financial terms; however, there are economic tools to assist this process. The most common tool for measuring the intangible benefit of community wellbeing, is to establish the consumer surplus. The consumer surplus is the amount that the attendee would have paid to attend the event. Using this tool the cost/benefit of an event can be estimated and therefore so can the payback period.

■ **Work**-*in-progress report and earned value*

The client or major sponsor of an event cannot afford to wait until the event to know if it will be success. Often, they require a report on how well the management is doing. This form of report is called a WIP, or work in progress. Using a project management methodology means that these reports are easily generated. The Gantt chart should give the client an idea of how the tasks are going. Earned value is a project technique that places a value on the percentage of the task completed. If the $10 000 promotion campaign for the event is 50 per cent complete at a certain date, for example, it is said to have an earned value of $5000.

Part of the WIP report is the risk register outlined in chapter 11. The register describes the risks that have been identified and the actions taken to treat them. The register is a 'live' document. The WIP report is one of the control mechanisms for event management. Further discussion of control issues is found in chapter 10.

PROJECT EVALUATION

The evaluation of an event is generally concerned with its impact and level of success. Chapter 14 goes into this matter in detail. Project evaluation concerns the evaluation of the management of the event. The term that is common in other areas of project management is the acronym 'PEIR':

project evaluation, implementation and review. This evaluation process is performed after the project is completed.

One of the attractions of using a project management system is that it enables this type of evaluation and subsequent improvement in management. By setting up a WBS the management can assess the tasks, responsibilities, schedules and risk management systems and improve upon them.

Project evaluation includes comparing the actual progress of the project against the project plan. As a result, the evaluation can suggest areas for improvement in the management. This is different to evaluating the event. It may be part of an event evaluation process; however, it is often forgotten. Figure 9.6 (page 300) illustrates the project management system used by various events. One essential part of this system is the evaluation and archiving. Whereas PEIR occurs after the project is complete, the event plan, archive and review system is a description of the whole project management system from an evaluation point of view. Understanding the way a management system is evaluated creates a system that can be evaluated. The evaluation in this case is evaluating the validity of the system itself. As EPARS — the event, plan, archive and review system — in figure 9.6 illustrates, one event is used as the baseline plan for the next event.

Event project evaluation includes:
• comparing the task descriptions and planned timelines with their actual performance
• assessing the ability of the system to respond to change; that is, its flexibility
• evaluating the timeliness of reports
• assessing the effectiveness of management decisions
• comparing planned milestones with the reality.

Each of these areas should indicate a fault or success in the management system. This feedback system can be used for each event to improve the management of the events. In this way, the event or festival is far more than a temporary and intangible affair. It is a way to improve the management of events in general. The event or festival can be regarded as a test of the management system.

An interesting offshoot of using such a system as EPARS, is that events can be used as a training model. By having a repeatable and improvable management system, a local festival can be used to train people in the skills of project management. Without a describable management system, the skill learned by working on a project cannot be assessed and, therefore, certified. Certification is basic to proving competency. This issue is taken further in chapter 15. A number of countries, such as South Africa, are assessing this as a way to train their unemployed youth in business and organisational skills.

The work of Janet Landey and her company, Party Design, in Johannesburg is revolutionising the role of events in a developing country. As part of the government's policy of Black Economic Empowerment, her company trains the unemployed through work at events. Even the cleaners become part of the entertainment at the events. Party Design assists in setting up event companies in places like Soweto and in the townships.

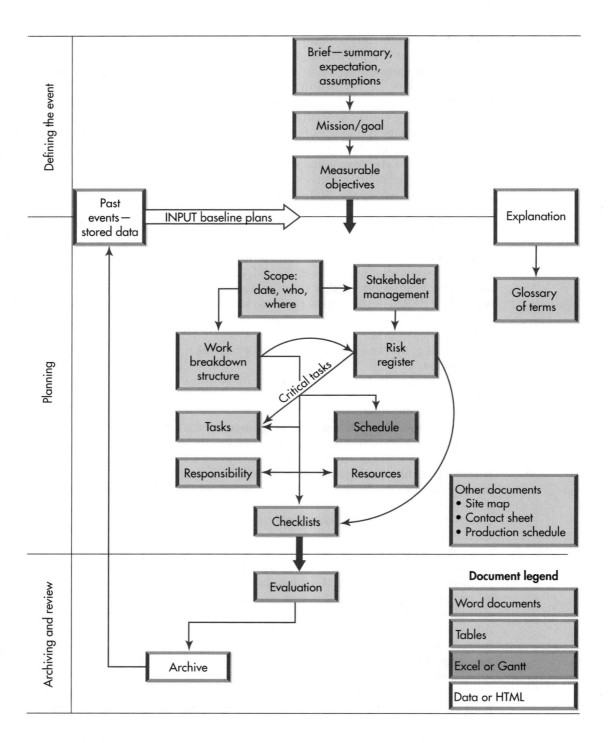

■ **Figure 9.6** *The event plan, archive and review system*
(**Source:** *EPMS 2004.*)

PROJECT MANAGEMENT SYSTEMS AND SOFTWARE

As project management is an integrated system, it appears to be easily translated into a software system. There are a number of project management software systems available to assist the practising project manager. Whether any of these can be directly and simply applied to events is a point for further discussion. Much of the project management software is excellent for planning the event management, as it imposes a discipline on the event team and demands a common language. Each of the systems is similar but due to the fluid nature of event management is limited in its usefulness. The 'Kepner-tregoe' and 'Prince 2' are two examples of highly developed and tested project management systems. The event plan, archive and review system, shown in figure 9.6 (page 300), is a visual display of the project management system used to structure the management of the event and, at the same time, assist in knowledge management. By creating templates the company or organisation can save this information to be fed back into the next event. EPARS represents the adaptation of the traditional project management process, as illustrated in figure 9.2 (page 289), to the event environment. The inclusion of the stakeholder management as a basic function of event management, is an example of this. EPARS includes the use of checklists in the event management process. Checklists are used continually by event managers as they are easy to create and change.

Of the software systems, the most popular for event management is Microsoft Project. It is easy to buy and is readily set up. It can construct a Gantt chart quickly and is a useful tool for explaining the event to clients. The progress of the event management can be quickly ascertained by the percentage of tasks completed. The limitations of any project management software application to event management is a result of the variability of events themselves. Changes happen all the time. Venue changes, airline cancellations, different performers, more finance, new sponsors and new opportunities to promote the event are just some of the common changes in the event environment. In particular, a special event — that is, one not attempted before — will have a new configuration of suppliers and supplies. In such a situation, using current project management software to manage the event will be inadequate.

Using software for events is limited by its ability to work in a complex, changing and uncertain environment. Most event software currently employed is found in the more predictable and stable parts of the event industry; repeat exhibitions, conferences, meetings and seminars have a wide choice of software — special events and festivals do not have this software choice.

An important aspect of the project management process is that it is scalable. It can be applied to small events or large festivals. It can also be applied to any one area of an event, such as the promotion, or to the whole of the event. Chapter 13 on staging an event shows the tools associated with this. These correspond to the outputs of the project management process.

The production schedule is a combination of task/schedule and responsibility documents. Project management software may be successfully applied to a part of the event; for example, a predictable section of the event, or a promotion schedule.

*L*IMITATIONS OF THE PROJECT MANAGEMENT APPROACH TO EVENT MANAGEMENT

The limitations of the direct application of traditional project management have been analysed by O'Toole (2000) and Shone (2001). Traditional project management depends on a solid definition of the asset during the initiation phase and on a stable management environment. All the management tasks can then be measured against the defined asset. Festivals and special events are not as clearly defined. Often they become more defined as the management of the project progresses, new marketing information comes to hand, and new promotion ideas and programming openings arise. A large part of event managing is taking advantage of new opportunities, which can mean that events can radically change, right up until the morning of the event. Project management, therefore, has to be flexible. Increased documentation, plans, written procedures and rules can easily lead to a management inertia unsuitable to this industry. It can destroy the core characteristic of special events and diminish the 'wow factor', the surprise, the vibe, or the theatre of events — essentially what makes the event 'special'. One solution to this problem used by major events (described in the previous section) is to appoint an artistic director and an event project manager. The former represents the innovative and creative aspects of the event content, while the project manager looks after the management responsibilities. Other areas that limit the use of project management are:

1. *Using volunteers* — the work of the volunteers is difficult to quantify and yet, as shown in chapter 6, they are vital to the success of many festivals. To measure key success factors is an imperative task in a traditional project management system.
2. *Stakeholders number* — more stakeholders mean more objectives the event has to meet. Given that some stakeholders will change during the lead-up to the event, there is a more uncertainty in these objectives. This leads to a fluid management environment, with the event company continually keeping an eye on any change to the stakeholders. When this is combined with the intangible outcomes of an event, clearly defining stakeholder requirements can be almost impossible. In one sense, each individual audience member may have an array of expectations.
3. *Marketing* — the ability to respond to market changes is a fundamental principle of marketing. This is in opposition to a management system that relies on the definition of the deliverable to stay the same. In project

management, thinking about marketing can be regarded as a risk management strategy. The aim of marketing from this point of view is to increase the predicability of management. Using marketing tools such as consumer decision profiling, marketing segmentation, promotion and optimising the market mix can reduce uncertainty.

4. *Finance* — finance may be found right up to the day of the event, during the event and after it is over. Extra sponsors may 'come on board', more tickets may be sold, or, for example, the auction may be a great success. This is another area of uncertainty that makes project planning difficult. Most project management theory assumes a fixed and defined source of funds, therefore, it tends to concentrate on the control of costs.

5. *Event design* — many events are supposed to have a large element of surprise — called the 'wow factor'. This is not an easy element to quantify or describe. At many events and festivals the right 'wow' can be the difference between success and failure. Traditional project management depends on the asset or deliverable being defined during the initiation phase. The surprise aspect of the event is often difficult, if not impossible, to describe. For some events, describing the 'wow' or surprise may lessen its value. It would be similar to describing the plot of a 'whodunnit' mystery before reading the book.

6. *Infrastructure and resources* — usually of a temporary nature. Events and festivals can have notoriously short timelines. Other projects may take years to complete, whereas the event project may be over in a month. Short-term logistics, temporary structures and short-term contracts do not allow the luxury of detailed analysis that is recommended by many project management books. Overall, the event management is under the cloud of the deadline. Every aspect of the management, therefore, must be continually assessed according to its effect on the deadline.

SUMMARY

An event or a festival has all the characteristics of a project. The traditional tools of project management can assist the event team integrating all the areas of management. Each of these areas of management produces deliverables. The deliverables are the result of a number of tasks (proof of good management) and are communicated to the event team. Project management can supply management structure of the event. It concentrates on this management, whereas the event itself is often the focus of event studies. Event managers can benefit by using techniques such as scope definition, WBS, scheduling and critical path analysis. The WBS describes the work and generates other plans, such as the tasks, resource analysis and the risk register. By using project management, the event manager can easily produce the progress reports on the management. It provides a professional methodology and the language of modern business, that can be adapted to the event management environment. As events grow in scope, the project management becomes the most important aspect of the management. In such cases, an event project manager will be appointed. The event project manager's role is to integrate all the event plans and produce an accountable management system. Although project management is increasingly seen as a solution to compliance and management accountability, it has its limitations. These arise from the intangible nature of the event and the ever-changing event environment.

Questions

1 Construct a work breakdown structure for these events:
   (a) a rock concert
   (b) a wedding
   (c) a regional festival
   (d) an award ceremony.

2 Construct a schedule of key tasks for the events listed in question 1.

3 List the milestones for the events listed in question 1.

4 What are examples of tasks that can clash? What techniques can be put in place to recognise these clashes in time to enable the event management to fix them?

5 List the types of events and their characteristics that would suit the project management approach.

CASE STUDY

The Forum Group

The Forum Group is a medium-sized event management company, employing 12 full time staff and three contract staff. Based in Sydney, the company runs a variety of events, from small executive meetings to Christmas parties, product launches and large conferences. The Forum Group prides itself on its professional and project management approach to organising events, and the systems and processes it has developed to support this approach. The company has much experience in running information technology-focused events. This case study focuses on a large IT user conference, a format for an event that The Forum Group has run for a few different clients over the years. The event is usually annual and the format attracts more than 1000 delegates. Total participants including sponsor organisations, staff and speakers add up to more than 1500 people. The event is usually in a major Australian city and has multiple concurrent sessions, keynote sessions, a large exhibition, gala evenings, hands-on workshops, 'ask the experts' areas and many spin-off smaller events that leverage the main event. The event has a main organising committee made up of both Forum Group personnel and client staff, and an extended team made up of support staff and agencies.

Objectives

This format of event usually has a number of objectives that the client would like to achieve. Areas that objectives would be developed around, for example, include:

- number of delegates
- profile of delegates
- sales
- lead generation
- strengthening partner relationships
- increased employee morale
- product or company awareness
- strengthening customer relations
- encouraging product implementation and use
- enabling delegate and partner networking
- customer education
- press coverage
- marketing campaign messages.

Scope of work

Often the event is run every year, so the bulk of the scope of work is already known and built on from previous years' material. An event brief is formalised to outline the event name, preferred date and venue, event owner and executive sponsor at the client site, organising committee participants, agenda outline,

(continued)

audience target, budget and objectives. Other details that may be outlined include style of the event, any targeted keynote speakers, any major product launches or messages that need to be incorporated into the format and any history on past events that may be relevant. A meeting is arranged to go through the brief and discuss each area with the main organising committee to see if any further details can be provided, to ensure all parties involved understand the main concepts and to build on the brief with any further ideas at the time. Often the debrief notes of the previous event (if there was one) are used to inject new ideas and future improvements.

From this high-level outline of the project, a project plan is produced by The Forum Group to scope the tasks, resources and deadlines required in order to achieve the desired outcomes.

Tailoring the master plan

Given that The Forum Group staff have multiple years' experience in running events of this nature, a master plan for this type of event has been developed that includes all possible tasks that may be incorporated. This plan is a working document that is updated with input from previous events and is therefore very comprehensive. Tasks are also included that may not be required, but they serve to prompt discussion and add possible new ideas to the committee in the planning process. Plans are also tailored to clients to incorporate their specific requirements.

The master plan includes milestones, header tasks and detailed tasks under each area of the event management requirements. Task heading examples include:

- Venue
- Management
- Finance
- Registration
- Agenda
- Speakers
- Social program
- Marketing
- Press
- Exhibition and sponsorship
- Design and printing
- Travel
- Staging and production
- Technical
- On-site
- Post event.

On each line item for each task, detail is kept for the completion deadline of that task, who is responsible for seeing that the task is completed, notes to assist in managing that task and sometimes a link to a relevant document that may be required in executing that task. There is also a column to show the completion status of that task. The way these items are recorded varies slightly depending on whether we are using a Microsoft Excel or Microsoft Project master project plan template.

The draft master plan becomes the working document. A copy of the plan is given to the overall owner of the event at the client site, and relevant parts of the plan are distributed to other team members to guide their involvement. This plan forms the basis for managing work to be done and committee meeting agenda, and is updated as new tasks are added to the scope of work. The event owner at The Forum Group regularly updates the plan to show completed tasks, and may even 'drip feed' parts of the plan to other staff members as tasks are required to be done (rather than always distributing the whole plan, which can be quite overwhelming for an event of this size).

Tasks that are not necessarily the main responsibility of staff at The Forum Group are still on the plan, so progress can be checked. A complete project management approach, therefore, can be adopted so one key person is aware of the total project progress.

Teams are developed that will focus on specific areas of the event, such as technical requirements, client staffing and the client's product booth display. There are team leaders to make management and communication easier for the project owner. Given that for these types of events there is often a large client commitment on resources and time, it also helps the staff at The Forum Group to get comprehensive support in order to disseminate the information that needs to be passed on.

Software and communication tools

The Forum Group has run this event with two different major software project management tools and a variety of supporting software and communication tools. Microsoft Word is used extensively for documents, faxes, meeting minutes, and runsheets. Microsoft Outlook/Instant Messenger is used extensively to keep in touch with committees, distribute documents, plan meetings, schedule appointments in calendars and also to instant-message people for quick responses when required. Microsoft Excel is used mainly for budget master documents and also sometimes for sorting data. It can also be used for project planning if Microsoft Project is not the client's preferred option. Microsoft Project is a sophisticated project master plan used by clients and management teams or when Sharepoint sites are used. It allows The Forum Group to build on the spreadsheet and incorporate more advanced reporting, as well as using features such as linked documents. Sharepoint sites are used to post the main planning information such as project plan, budgets and key documents so the committee can always view the latest versions of documents. This saves on distribution time.

Web registration tools are also used to allow delegate registration via the web. The tool is often custom-made by the client and linked to their main or event website, and is built to integrate with the main delegate management software if there is a separate system being used (as is often the case when delegate payments are involved). Events (Amlink) Software is the system The Forum Group uses to pull in delegate registration details from the client's web registration tool which enables the management of delegate information, invoicing and financial reporting to be completed. It is also used for attendee reports, data downloads for badge processing, email contact with delegates and maintaining profiles on delegates. Adobe Illustrator is used to build documents, such as the exhibition and sponsor prospectus, so it can be easily sent out as a graphic, yet small, file (and cannot be changed by recipients).

Reporting progress

Throughout the planning timeline, reports are produced to help keep contributors on track and also to assist if required; for example, in highlighting any red flags or generally getting an extended audience involved in the progress of the event. Different audiences require different reports. Often detailed task reports of the complete plan are regularly given to the main client owner, sub-projects (for
(continued)

approximately a month in advance) are given to other committee members, high-level reports on milestone progress are given to executive sponsors of the events, as well as any tasks that may be running behind deadline or that require more resources than originally planned.

Other aspects are tracked too, such as actual hours for tasks compared to projected hours and any reasons attributed to this variance. On the financial side, the master budget is updated regularly to show variances once actual quotes are received and to show changes if briefs are altered, and also final charges. The budget is used initially as a tool to help guide expenditure and set delegate registration fees and required recoveries from exhibition and sponsorship revenue. After that it becomes a tool to show whether the bottom line is on track and, if not, ways that it could be brought into line.

On-site and the post event review
The master project plan shows major on-site tasks and build dates that need to be achieved. Nearer the event, these tasks are taken and combined with other documents, such as the final event orders required to produce a very detailed on-site run sheet. The run sheet covers all aspects that have been highlighted in the planning process, and can show subsets of the event so it can be distributed to staff members that only need to see those parts. The run sheet can be sorted by room to help the venue, and also by time to help those in charge of ensuring the event runs smoothly. As the event runs, any unforeseen red flags or notes, on any last minute tasks can be recorded and considered earlier in future planning.

Post-event review meetings are held with staff, the main committee, sponsors, attendees, suppliers — in fact an effort is made to either chat to or formally survey all major stakeholder groups. The results of these findings are discussed in a post-event committee review. Any ideas or future improvements are then translated into tasks that can be fed back in to the master project plan for future events.

Amanda Trotman, The Forum Group 2004

Questions

1 Reviewing the event objectives, how would each of these be measured?

2 Discuss the role of defining the scope of work in this case study.

3 Describe the function of the master plan in terms of the creation of plans and as a control document. List the plans and use a diagram to illustrate the functions.

Project managing
The Dream

On the GamesForce 2000 T-shirts adorning the (debatably) more fashionable staff buzzing around Sydney 2000 headquarters was the slogan, 'Delivering The Dream'.

The successful delivery of this dream (the Olympic and Paralympic Games) to the customers and project stakeholders such as the competing athletes, the International Olympic Committee (IOC), national organising committees, spectators, media and the great Australian public depended totally on the seamless integration and project management of the 'big five' Sydney 2000 organisations: the Sydney Organising Committee for the Olympic Games (SOCOG) (including sponsors and service providers), Sydney Olympic Broadcast Organisation (SOBO), Olympic Coordination Authority (OCA), Olympic Roads and Transport Authority (ORTA) and Olympic Security Command Centre (OSCC).

SOCOG's Project Management division had the central responsibility for understanding, scoping, integrating, recording and reporting the sub-projects of all four key organisations to the SOCOG Board and executive sub-groups, plus the IOC Executive Board and IOC Coordination Commission. In essence they had the responsibility for coordinating the master project — project managing *The Dream*.

Getting across the Games

Understanding the relationships (or dependencies) between organisational sub-projects demands a willingness to work away from your desk; this is essential for building relationships. Initially, many of the venue teams with which I interacted showed a reluctance to share key information and project direction, naturally triggering my suspicion. I felt like a private detective hired by SOCOG to report venue management shortfalls and critical issues (which was not wholly true!) and not their achievements.

The difficulty in translating micro-level detail into macro-level reporting is in maintaining the meaningfulness of summarised information, without misrepresenting the accountable party. For instance, a summary bar may roll up 20 activities — 15 may have been achieved by the deadline, and five may be either pending completion or require an extension of time. The summarised status on completion is 75 per cent — in work management terms it may be 99.9 per cent — with five signatures required from a single source on five outstanding documents!

It became increasingly important to maintain a regular presence within the venue teams — to be proactive, but not too obtrusive. The key to gaining trust was to provide a range of services that benefited the venue teams (for example, providing user-defined reports, chasing problematic program areas on their behalf, sharing information) — in essence, becoming a part time extension of their team.

(*continued*)

To give you an understanding of the complexity of the SOCOG project management task, you only have to look at the key statistics pertaining to SOCOG's organisational breakdown structure, which are listed below.

- Six 'groups' — for example, games coordination
- Nineteen 'divisions' — for example, project management and special tasks
- Eighty-four 'programs' — for example, project management
- Thirty competition venues
- Five major non-competition venues
- Three villages — Olympic, Media and Technical Officials
- Training venues, hotels, arts festivals and so on
- A Games-time workforce of 110 000 (paid, volunteers and contractors)

The sheer size of the multi-organisational Sydney 2000 with its multiple projects and multiple dependencies made managing and reporting the status of the master project at varying (hierarchical) levels extremely challenging.

Thoughts into action

There was no blueprint for the Olympic Games (as for many other unique events) and, although when I joined SOCOG we had on board many people who had experienced the highs and lows of Olympic Games, World Cups and other large events, the need to speed up the 'conceptual' phase and turn thoughts into structured directives and future actions became the immediate objective.

Working hand-in-hand with operational integration program area project management, the concept of the 'Games coordination timeline' was devised to communicate the importance of project managing the events while continually focusing Sydney 2000 on the delivery of the two final stages of the Games project delivery.

The strategy behind the two-stage approach was to bring the Games closer in the minds of the organisation ('only two stages to go!') and make the achievement of these stages more tangible to the responsible delivering parties.

The two stages of the Games coordination timeline can be seen in the following table.

■ *The two stages of the Games coordination timeline*

STAGE	NAME	DATES	FOCUS
One	Venue project plan	01-01-99–31-01-00	'How we're going to get there', off-site activity planning, documentation and approvals
Two	Day-by-day plan	01-08-00–31-11-00	'What we're going to do when we get there', on-site activity installation, training, rehearsal, operation space-specific — CPA

'Venuisation' — building the team

The promotion of the Games coordination timeline was strategically launched in line with Sydney 2000's arguably most important organisational restructuring. This organisational metamorphosis was referred to as *venuisation*.

Venuisation, in basic terms, is the shift of organisational focus from program-based delivery to venue-based delivery. The venue structure was created, multi-organisational venue teams began to develop, and Sydney 2000 organisations began to interact with each other on a day-to-day, face-to-face basis in a singular office environment.

Venuisation immediately began to improve communications between formerly remote organisations, and instil an empathy in each organisation's individual agendum, an empathy which was previously either unrecognised or, in some cases, not acknowledged.

Project managing the event managers

In my humble and biased opinion SOCOG recruited well. The knowledge, professionalism and dedication of the Games workforce was quite astounding.

However, in many organisations positive personal attributes do not always guarantee the possession of project management focus and skills. A good event operations manager, for example, may not necessarily make a good event project manager.

The key management issues SOCOG project management had to successfully overcome with the implementation of the Games coordination timeline are briefly outlined in the following table.

■ *Key management issues*

ISSUE	DEFINITION	SOLUTION	OUTCOME
Technofear	Fear of the autonomous use of SOCOG's adopted project management software — Primavera P3	Use of a spreadsheet approach — deemed more user-friendly. Facilitated by P3's email-friendly post office system. Centrally managed by SOCOG project management.	Excellent response record to deadlines imposed by the monthly project management cycle; clarity and ownership of information; online ownership and updates
Empathy	Lack of understanding of the dependencies inherent in the delivery of the venue-based project	Pilot project developed before global release — evolution of the 'pilot' communicated to the venue teams.	Consistency in information reported: — level of content — activity descriptions — project structure
Multiple definitions	Key words and project phases that meant different things to different people	Joint OCA and SOCOG definitions of overlay, logistics and operations phases developed by project management/OCA, adopted by Sydney 2000 organisations.	Clear and global understanding of delivery phases, dependencies and project documentation; improved understanding of project management principles
Adoption	Lack of/fear of ownership of the plan — fear of incriminations through transparency and subsequent elevation of information	Venue readiness meetings organised on a monthly basis as part of the project management cycle — chaired by the venue manager. Plan owned by the team.	Venue team ownership of information

(*continued*)

Another 'positive' problem SOCOG project management had to overcome in establishing the Games coordination timeline was Sydney 2000's focus on test events. Although a distraction from developing the plans, the lessons learnt and the essential team building gained through working on these high-profile, international-standard events added a greater integrity to the information being reported for the Games.

Managing the software

SOCOG consciously adopted Primavera P3 software as its primary project management tool for controlling the delivery of the Olympic and Paralympic Games. P3 is a high-end software application which is more than capable of managing multiple projects with multi-level sub-projects. By comparison with its off-the-shelf competitors it has an advanced suite of standard functions, including EVR (earned value report), user-defined reporting, post office and remote data entry.

For an experienced project manager, this tool has the flexibility and 'grunt' to generate scenarios and reports reliably and speedily. SOCOG, for example, has extracted information from the core day-by-day project plan to generate the logistics 'bump in' and the site management 'overlay transition' schedules, setting the parameters for program area task-level activity.

In my opinion, another plus for P3 is the fact that it is a code-driven application, which encourages the project manager to scope the project and sub-projects prior to developing the plan. The work breakdown structure becomes the framework and control mechanism for the project, as shown in the following table.

■ The Games work breakdown structure

LEVEL	CODE-FIELD	DESCRIPTION
1	Master project (1)	The Games coordination timeline
2	Project (2)	Venue project plan and day-by-day plan
3	Event (2)	The Olympic Games and the Paralympic Games
4	Precinct (4)	Geographical areas — for example, Sydney West
5	Venue (30)	Specific venues allocated to precincts — for example, Sydney International Equestrian Centre, Sydney West
6	Space (multiple)	Specific (predominantly) room locations within the venue
7	Cluster (multiple)	Logistical delivery and resupply area within the venue — cluster of spaces
8	Activity/task	Action description
9	Responsibility	Notification of who is delivering the action and who is receiving the action
10	Reporting	Activities tagged to user-defined reports

The drawbacks for P3 as an event project management tool are few, as long as the event manager understands the software and project management principles that drive the creation of the work breakdown structure, coding structure and interdependencies.

For medium-level projects P3 might be considered a bit expensive (about $7000 off the shelf), but if you believe Primavera is the way to go there is an offspring of the parent product called Suretrak which has most of the 'whistles and bells' without the sting in the pocket.

You do not have to manage all aspects of a project or multiple projects through a single software application. SOCOG project management did not fully utilise the P3 suite. For instance, cost planning and analysis and resource levelling is owned by the venue manager but controlled via a quantity surveyor/finance manager and venue staffing manager respectively. The quantity surveyor uses specially developed in-house software, and the venue staffing manager uses an off-the-shelf spreadsheet package.

Project managing a 'medium-size' event

Many of the principles discussed in this paper can be applied to a medium-sized event. Whatever the scope and budget of your project I would encourage you to do the following:

- Adopt a two-stage (off-site and on-site) focus.
- Project manage space-specific, on-site activities using CPA.
- Use mid-range PM software, such as Primavera Suretrak or MS Project.
- Be proactive — work away from your desk.
- Regular PCGs are essential — the key players are the event manager, quantity surveyor/finance/commercial manager, architect and local government agencies.
- Establish common project terminology.
- Develop your deployment and recruitment plans early — evolve the plan.
- Use the project plan in a positive way, highlight achievements and incorporate key performance indicators.
- If inexperienced or constrained by time, use the services of an experienced project management consultant to set up and administer the project.

Neil Timmins, Manager, Programming and Planning,
Sydney Olympic Park Common Domain

Questions

1 Identify the key management issues in these events. Define the issues, provide a solution and describe the outcome for:
    (a) an Australian overseas trade exhibition in the Philippines, including a festival of Australian culture.
    (b) an international agricultural exhibition in Brisbane
    (c) the Pan-Indian Ocean Music Festival in Kalgoorlie
    (d) a world trade conference in Melbourne.

(continued)

2 Construct a lexicon of event terms that may cause confusion at events. This would include terms such as bump-in, shutdown, set-up and staging.

3 Why did the Olympics organisation structure change from program-based to venue-based? Was there an alternative way to organise the Olympics?

4 Why did the author use the term 'autonomous' in describing the fear of software?

5 Compare the use of software by the Sydney Festival and the Sydney Olympics. Why didn't the Olympics use the program set up by the Sydney Festival?

6 Discuss the constraints of webcasting the Olympics. Some of these will be technical, political and financial.

REFERENCES

Dinsmore, PC 1998, *Human factors in project management*, AMACOM, New York.

Graham, S, Goldblatt, J & Delpy, L 1995, *The ultimate guide to sports event management and marketing*, Richard Irwin, Chicago.

Gray, C & Larson, E 2000, *Project management: the managerial process*, McGraw-Hill International, Boston.

Lock, D 1988, *Project management*, Gower Press, Aldershot, England.

O'Toole, W 2000, 'Towards the integration of event management best practice by the project management process', in *Events 2000: conference proceedings of 'Events beyond 2000: setting the agenda'*, Sydney.

O'Toole, W 2004, *Event project management system* (EPMS 2004), CD-ROM, www.epms.net, Sydney.

O'Toole, W & Mikolaitis, PJ 2002, *Corporate event project management*, John Wiley & Sons, New York.

Project Management Institute 2000, *Guide to the project management body of knowledge 2000*, Philadelphia.

Robertson, B 2003, 'Packing down with the world's journalists', *Australian Financial Review*, 23 August, www.afr.com/articles/2003/08/26/1061663787807. html (accessed 12 February 2004).

Shone, A with Parry, B 2001, *Successful event management*, Continuum, London.

10 Control
and budgets

LEARNING OBJECTIVES

After studying this chapter, you should be able to:

■ understand the use of control by management

■ identify the control systems used in special events and festivals

■ analyse the factors that create successful control mechanisms

■ identify the key elements of budgetary control and explain the relationship between them

■ understand the advantages and shortcomings of using a budget.

INTRODUCTION

After planning the festival or event, the central function of management is controlling. Without a management system, such as project management, control becomes impossible. This chapter, therefore, should be read in conjunction with chapter 9. This chapter introduces the various methods that the festival or event management can use to recognise that the event is going to plan and respond to any changes. The event budget is perhaps the most important control plan. This chapter then outlines tips on increasing revenue and decreasing expenditure.

WHAT IS CONTROL?

Control consists of making sure what happens in an organisation is what is supposed to happen. The control of an event can range from the event manager simply walking around the site and discussing daily progress with staff, to implementing and monitoring a detailed plan of responsibilities, reports and budgets. The word 'control' comes from the Latin *contrarotulare*, meaning 'against the roll'; in ancient Rome, it meant comparing something to the official records, which were kept on paper cylinders or rolls. In modern times, the word has retained some of this meaning, and the control of any business activity involves comparing the progress of all key functions against a management plan to ensure that projected outcomes are met.

Event planning can be effective only if the execution of the plan is carefully controlled. To do this, it is necessary to develop proper control mechanisms. These are methods which are designed to keep a project on course and return it to plan if it wanders. Control affects every aspect of the management of events, including:

• project management
• logistics
• human resources
• administration,

and its basic nature remains the same in every area.

The nature of control is described by Beniger (1986), who identified two complementary activities:

1. *Information processing* — this is necessary for all planning. When it is goal-directed, it allows the continual comparison of an organisation's stated goals against reality.
2. *Reciprocal communication, or feedback* — there must be a constant interchange between the controller and the areas being controlled.

These two activities depend on an effective communication system.

This chapter explores control in the context of festivals and special events. It will demonstrate that the choice of workable control mechanisms is central to the success of an event, and discuss budgets, which are the main control system used in event management.

ELEMENTS AND CATEGORIES OF CONTROL

The process of control involves establishing standards of performance and ensuring that they are realised. This can be a complex process, but consists of three main steps:

1. *Establishing standards of performance* — these can come from several sources, including standard practices within the event management industry; guidelines supplied by the board of management of the event; specific requirements of the client and sponsors; and audience or guest expectations. Standards must be measurable.

2. *Identifying deviations from standards of performance* — this is done by measuring current performance and comparing it with the established standards. Since the event budget is expressed in measurable terms, it provides an important method of highlighting areas that are straying from the plan and which require attention.

3. *Correcting deviations* — any performance that does not meet the established standards must be corrected. This can entail the use of many types of problem-solving strategies, including renegotiating contracts and delegating.

These three steps are also called the control cycle (Burke 1993) and are central to the successful delivery of an event. Such a cycle would be applied with varying frequency, depending on the size and complexity of the event itself.

Generally, events are characterised by two types of controls: operational and organisational. Operational controls are used for the day-to-day running the event. Organisational controls relate to the overall objectives of the event organisation; for example, whether the event is profitable and satisfies the client's brief. Hicks (1976) suggests a further category of controls according to when they are applied:

• *Predictive control* tries to anticipate and identify problems before they occur. Predicting cash flows for an event is an important area because expenses are not concurrent with income. Venue hire, for example, is usually paid in advance of the event. Similarly, for an event with a small budget, briefing a lawyer is another example of predictive control. Some companies, for instance, may be less likely to pay promised fees to a small company than they would to a larger, more powerful company. Also, the organisers of a small one-off event are not in a position to threaten a defaulting company with withdrawal of further work opportunities. In these and similar situations, a swift letter from a solicitor who has been briefed beforehand can often hasten payment. Another term for predictive controls is *feedforward*.

• *Concurrent control* measures deviation from the standards as they occur. The event manager's informal question of 'How's it going?' falls into this category. The monitoring of food stalls during an event, for instance, is essential to ensure health and safety regulations are being followed. It may be difficult to predict just how a food provider will deviate from the guidelines. (At one festival, for example, tea and coffee urns were placed against a canvas dividing wall. On the other side, a children's play group was in operation.)

- *Historic controls* are mostly organisational controls and can include analysis of major deviations from an event plan so the next event runs more closely to plan. Such controls review the concluded event and are concerned with the question, 'How were objectives met?'

To compare actual and planned progress in managing an event, points of comparison are necessary. These include the following:

- *Benchmarks* are identifiable points in the organisation of the event where a high standard is achieved. Benchmarks emphasise quality and best practice. Catering of a high standard, for example, could be a benchmark for a corporate party. Attaining a benchmark is often a cause for celebration by the event company.

- *Milestones*, or key dates, are intermediate achievement dates that stand as guideposts for monitoring an event's progress. They mark particularly critical completion times. The arrival of the headline performers at the venue, for example, is a critical time, and the submission date of a grant proposal is a key date. A milestone trend chart is a graphic illustration of the milestones and includes whether they have been met or delayed. It is a sophisticated technique used for large events. By tracking the milestones, a trend may be discovered. If all the milestones are late, for example, it may indicate a problem with the management. Schedule slippage is another term for this.

- *Identification of deliverables* is a method used by project management, as set out in chapter 9. A deliverable is the tangible result of one of the areas of project management. This tangible result may be documents such as a report, a contract, a site map or a contact list. To use the budget as an example, the budget is a document that is a result of planning the event finance. It enables staff to be focused on the job of creating the budget and is proof that the task of financial planning has been completed. The budget is then passed on to other areas of the event management. Therefore the deliverable encapsulates a part of the management and is proof that it has been performed. A more obvious deliverable would be the arrival of sound equipment at an event. Using this system, the event manager identifies all the deliverables from the work breakdown structure (WBS). These are given dates for completion and used to control the progress of the event management.

Event control can be expensive in terms of time and money. Its cost and effectiveness depend on the choice of the control mechanisms that make up the control system. Control mechanisms must be:

- *meaningful and efficient* — they should be directed only at those areas that contribute to the success of the event. These significant areas have to be identified in advance and addressed in the event plan. A limited amount of time is available for measuring and comparing — this process must be streamlined so it does not become an end in itself.

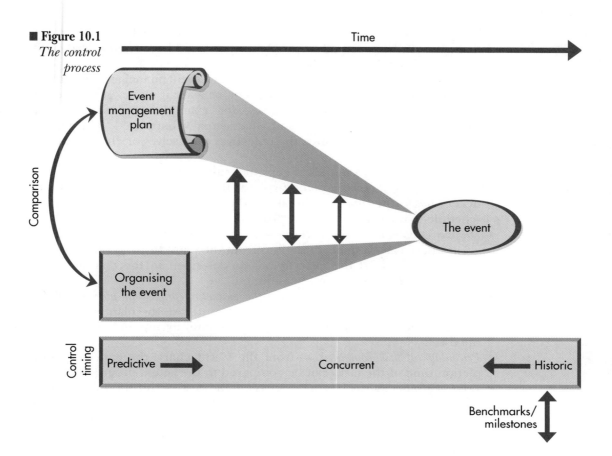

Figure 10.1
The control process

- *simple* — controls should not be more complicated than necessary. Their aim is practical as they have to be communicated to many levels within an event. An excessively complicated system of controls can alienate a broadly-based festival committee.
- *relevant* — controls must be prepared to match each area of event management and they should be distributed to those who have the responsibility of carrying them out. There is no point in the publicity section, for example, having data that concern the budget of the performers.
- *timely and flexible* — deviations from the plan should be identified early and addressed before they develop further. Concurrent controls should allow sufficient time to correct any gaps with the plan. Flexibility is essential, as the controls may need to respond to revision of the event plan up until the last moment. Sometimes, milestones must be moved to accommodate changes in the event. A benchmark may be an attendance of 1000 people, for example, but if only 800 chairs were delivered, it is no longer a best practice benchmark and must be dropped so it does not create a logistical problem.
- *able to suggest action* — the most useful control mechanisms provide corrective actions to be taken when members of the event team find a gap between the plan and reality. Without these suggestions for action,

inexperienced staff or volunteers can become confused and the festival manager can be swamped by problems that could have been solved easily by others, if guidance had been provided.

When deviations or gaps are identified, the event manager can make a reasoned choice — either to close the gap, or leave it alone and revise the plan. Historic organisational controls, for example, may show a gap between the festival objectives and what actually happened. The festival manager can choose to change the objectives themselves or change aspects of the event instead.

The following are examples of gaps that can be measured:

- *Ticket sales targets versus actual sales* — for the entrepreneur, the amount of ticket sales is the 'make or break' of the event. Any deviations from the schedule may cause a cash flow problem.
- *Supplier compliance versus contracts* — in the fluid situation of setting up an event, there can be many deviations from the plan. In particular, the supplier may not send the exact goods as described in the contract. This needs to be anticipated and pre-empted.
- *The 'buzz' or event awareness versus the marketing/promotion plan* — if the promotion of the event is not creating any interest, the plan may have to change. The level of press coverage or community support may indicate the 'buzz'.
- *Percentage of task completed* — from the Gantt chart, the expected completion time of the tasks can be compared to the actual progress.
- *Level of sponsor support versus sponsorship objectives* — the sponsorship may be lagging behind the initial expectations of the event company. This may be a result of changes within the sponsor's business, a situation that could result in a lack of funds or support as the event draws near.
- *Actual logistics versus the operation plan* — a small deviation from the plan can create major problems throughout the event. If the delivery trucks to an exhibition arrive at the wrong docks, for example, the delay and confusion can be magnified in a short time.
- *Entertainment versus crowd response* — if the crowd are not responding as expected then it may be time for quick managerial action.

CONTROL METHODS

Some of the control methods used in events are very straightforward, while others are complex and require a high level of financial reporting skills. However, they all have the same aim: to highlight areas that have strayed from the plan so that management can take appropriate action.

■ Reports *and meetings*

Reports that evaluate the progress of an event are perhaps the most common control method. The reports are presented at management or committee meetings. The frequency of these meetings will depend on the proximity of the event date. Many event management companies hold weekly meetings with reports from the teams (or sub-committees) and individuals responsible for particular areas. The meetings are run using standard meeting rules, such as those described in Renton (1994), with a time for sub-committee reports. The aim of these reports is to assist the meeting in making decisions.

Typically, an annual community festival would have monthly meetings throughout the year leading up to the event, and increase these to weekly meetings two months before the festival is scheduled to begin. The Broome Shinju Matsuri Festival of the Pearl, for example, has weekly meetings that alternate between the festival committee and those of the general community (which discuss major decisions by the festival committee). In this way, the public has some control over the planning of the festival. At the committee meetings, the sub-committees dealing with publicity, sponsorship, entertainment, youth and community relations report their actions. The reports expose any gaps so the event coordinator can take action to close them. This is also called management by exception because it assumes everything is flowing well, that routine matters are handled by the sub-committee, and that the event coordinator need step in only when significant deviations from the plan demand it.

Project status report

The status report is a 'snapshot' of the progress of the project. These are described in chapter 9 under the heading of 'Work in progress (WIP) reports'. The WIP is the common term used for a project status report in the event industry. The headings often found in a WIP report for a large or complex event include:

- WBS — areas filled in according to their progress
- funds committed — the commitment of funds may be informal (such as by verbal agreement) but will have an effect on the amount of funds available
- risk register — a list of the risks and the status of their treatment
- variances or exceptions — any changes to the original plans.

■ Delegation *and self-control*

The use of sub-committees at a festival is an example of delegating activities to specialist groups. Part of the responsibility of each sub-committee is to solve problems before they occur. Since it is impossible for the event manager to monitor all the areas of an event, this method is valuable because it allows delegated groups to control their own areas of specialisation. However, the sub-committee must confine its actions to its own event area and the event manager must be aware of possible problems arising across different sub-committees. Solving a problem in the entertainment part of an event, for example, could give rise to problems in the sponsorship areas.

■ Quality

There are various systems to control the quality of an event and the event company itself. In particular, quality control depends on:
- gaining and responding to customer feedback
- the role played by event personnel in delivering quality service.

Integrating the practical aspects of controlling quality with the overall strategy of an event is called total quality management (TQM). TQM seeks to create an event company that continually improves the quality of its services. In other words:
- feedback
- change and improvement

are integral to the company's structure and operations.

Various techniques of TQM are used by event companies. One technique is finding and rewarding quality champions — volunteer programs often have awards for quality service at an event. Different professional organisations, such as the International Special Events Society (ISES) and the International Festivals and Events Association (IFEA), share the same aim: to strive to improve the quality of festivals and events. They do this by disseminating information and administering a system of event evaluation and awards for quality.

■ The *break-even chart*

This simple graphic tool can highlight control problems by finding the intersection of costs and revenue. Figure 10.2 shows a simple but effective break-even chart for an event that is dependent on ticket sales. A Neil Cameron Fire Event (Cameron 1993), for example, would have fixed costs of stage, pyrotechnics and administration. But the greater the attendance, the larger the cost of security, seating, cleaning, toilets and so forth. However, at one point the revenue from ticket sales exceeds the costs. At this point — the break-even point — the event starts making a profit.

■ Figure 10.2
The break-even chart

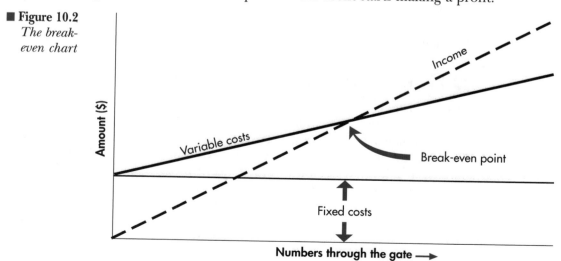

If a fixed cost such as venue hire is increased, the extra number of people needed 'through the door' can quickly be calculated. How would the organisers attract those extra people to the event? One means might be increased promotion.

■ Ratio *analysis*

There are several ratios that can be used to identify any problems in the management of an event. They can also be used for predictive control as in the earlier example. Their main function is as indicators of the health of the event organisation. In particular the ratio of:

$$\frac{\text{Current assets}}{\text{Current liabilities}}$$

indicates the financial strength of the organisation. However, calculation of assets can be difficult, since special events by their nature have few current assets except those intangible qualities: goodwill and experience. In a similar way to a film production company, an event company may be formed to create and manage a one-off festival for which every asset is hired for the duration of the event.

Return on investment is a significant ratio for any sponsors or investors in an event. This is expressed as:

$$\frac{\text{Net revenue}}{\text{Investment}}$$

The revenue for a sponsor may be expressed in advertising dollars. Print press exposure, for example, can be measured by column centimetres and approximated to the equivalent cost in advertising. This ratio is most often used for events that are staged solely for financial gain. An entrepreneur of a major concert performance must demonstrate a favourable return on investment to potential investors to secure financial backing.

Other ratios can provide valuable data. As Brody and Goodman (1988) explain in their discussion of fundraising events, the ratio between net and gross profit is important in deciding the efficiency of an event for fundraising, and provides a means to compare one event to another. This ratio is called the percentage of profit or the profit margin. Another useful ratio is free publicity to paid advertising, particularly for concert promoters.

By performing a series of appropriate ratio analyses, an event management company can obtain a clear picture of the viability of the organisation and identify areas requiring more stringent control.

■ Management *system*

Perhaps the most thorough way of developing control methods is to establish a management system. Project management is such a system that is suitable to events and festivals. A system is similar to the blueprint in designing a house. It enables the house to be built so that all the parts fit together and tells the builder if there are any discrepancies. The WBS, combined with the schedule and task/responsibility list, is the blueprint for the event. Without this blueprint the event manager will not know if there are any problems until it is too late. The system will sort out the important problems needing immediate attention from the minor problems. It establishes a management environment in which it recognises that each area of the event management mutually influences the other areas. Using a project management system means a thorough contracting process is employed. The contract, with its penalties and rewards, is often the critical part of the control system.

■ Management *incentives and staff rewards*

The management of an event can be financially tied to its success. Staff bonuses and rewards are a common control method in other industries. In the music industry, for example, staff bonuses are common for large concerts if they are successful. Keeping the event restricted to the budget is another common reason for rewarding the management of an event. Chapter 6 describes these different reward systems under the heading of 'Staff motivation'.

THE BUDGET

A budget can be described as a quantified statement of plans (in other words, the plan is expressed in numerical terms). The budget process includes costing and estimating income and allocating financial resources. An event budget is used to compare actual costs and revenues with projected costs and revenues. In particular, maximum expenditure for each area of the event's operation is estimated. To achieve this efficiently, a budget can take many forms. It may be, for example, broken into sub-budgets that apply to specific areas of a complex or large event such as the staging, logistics, merchandising and human resources. Budgets are of particular importance to the management of events because most aspects of the event incur costs requiring payment before the revenue is obtained. Cash flow needs special attention. Most funding or sponsorship bodies need to see a budget of the proposed event before they will commit their resources. This second part of the chapter expands on these points and provides an example to illustrate them.

A number of examples, including an event by Scouts Australia, will illustrate the form of an event budget and its use.

■ Constructing the budget

Two types of budget process can be used in event management. The line-item budget, as the name suggests, focuses on each cost and revenue item of the total event, and the program budget is constructed for a specific program element (Getz 1997). An example of the latter is a budget devised for a festival that concerns only the activities of one of the performance areas or stages. Such a budget effectively isolates this area of the event from the general festival finance. In this way, individual budgets can be used to compare all the performance areas or stages. The line items are performers' fees and so on.

The creation of a budget has the advantage of forcing management to establish a financial plan for the event and to allocate resources accordingly. It imposes a necessary financial discipline, regardless of how informally an event may be organised. In a similar way to the Gantt chart, it can be used for review long after the event is over.

Preparing a budget is illustrated by figure 10.4 (page 328). The process begins by establishing the economic environment of the event. The economics of the region and the nation (and even world economics) may impinge on the event and significantly change the budget. An example of this is the effect of the fall in the value of the Australian dollar on the major arts festivals. Within a week the cost of the entertainment imported for the festivals rose by over 10 per cent. To determine the economic environment, it is useful to ask the following questions: What similar events can be used as a guide? Will changes in the local or state economy affect the budget in any way? If it involves international performers or hiring equipment from overseas, will there be a change in the currency exchange rates? These, and many more questions, need to be answered before constructing a budget that will result in reasonable projections of costs and revenue.

The next step is to obtain the guidelines from the client, sponsors or event committee. A client may request, for instance, that only a certain percentage of their sponsorship be allocated to entertainment, with the rest to be allocated to hospitality. Guidelines must fit with the overall objectives of the event and may require constructing sub-budgets or program budgets. This is both an *instructive phase* — in that the committee, for example, will instruct the event manager on the content of the budget — and a *consultative phase,* because the event manager would ask the advice of other event specialists and the subcontractors.

The third step is to identify, categorise and estimate the cost areas and revenue sources. The categories become the line items in the budget. A sample of the categories is given in table 10.1 (page 326). This is a summary, or a first-level budget, of the cost and revenue areas. The next level down expands each of these line items and is shown in tables 10.2 (page 331) and 10.3 (page 335). The use of a computer-generated spreadsheet enables a number of levels in the budget to be created on separate sheets and linked to the first-level budget. Cost items take up the most room on a budget and are described in the following pages.

INCOME	AMOUNT	EXPENDITURE	AMOUNT
Grants		Administration	
Donations		Publicity	
Sponsorship		Venue costs	
Ticket sales		Equipment	
Fees		Salaries	
Special programs		Insurance	
Concessions		Permits	
TOTAL		Security	
		Accounting	
		Cleaning	
		Travel	
		Accommodation	
		Documentation	
		Hospitality	
		Community groups	
		Volunteers	
		Contingencies	
		TOTAL	

Once the costs and possible revenue sources and amounts are estimated, a *draft budget* is prepared and submitted for approval to the controlling committee. This may be, for example, the finance sub-committee of a large festival. The draft budget is also used in grant submissions and sponsorships. The federal government funding bodies, including the Australia Council and Festivals Australia, have budget guidelines and printed forms that need to be completed and included in the grant application. Figure 10.3 shows a software program from Arts Victoria to assist festivals in their budgeting.

■ **Figure 10.3**
Festival
expenditure
template
(**Source:** *Arts*
Victoria's
Festivals DIY
Kit.)

Festival expenditure | Menu | | Save |

Press to go to different sections
⬇ **Performers**   ☐
⬇ **Visual arts**   ☐
⬇ **Facilities/equipment**   ☐
⬇ **Operating expenses**   ☐
⬇ **Festival salaries**   ☐
⬇ **Travel costs**   ☐
⬇ **Administration**   ☐

Press to recalculate the total   ☐

Performers

Actual	Estimate		$	% External
⦿	○	Performers' fees	☐	☐
⦿	○	Music/stage director's fee	☐	☐
⦿	○	Other—performers	☐	☐
Top of page		*Press to recalculate the total*	☐	

Operating expenses

Actual	Estimate		$	% External
⦿	○	Marketing—publicist	☐	☐
○	⦿	Marketing—advertising	☐	☐
⦿	○	Marketing—printing	☐	☐
○	⦿	Marketing—other	☐	☐
○	⦿	Documentation	☐	☐
⦿	○	Materials	☐	☐
⦿	○	Royalties, prizes	☐	☐
○	⦿	Other—operating expenses	☐	☐
Top of page		*Press to recalculate the total*	☐	

Festival salaries

Actual	Estimate		$	% External
⦿	○	Festival director's fees	☐	☐
○	⦿	Coordinators	☐	☐
⦿	○	Administration	☐	☐
○	⦿	Other—festival salaries	☐	☐
Top of page		*Press to recalculate the total*	☐	

The final step involves preparation of the budget and financial ratios that can indicate deviations from the initial plan. An operating business has a variety of budgets, including capital expenditure, sales, overheads and production. Most special events will require only an operation budget or cash budget.

Note the similarity between the classification system used for the budget and the WBS described in chapter 9 ('Project management'). The WBS is often used as a basis of a budget. The costs of the lower levels are added to give the overall costs — called 'rolling up'. This means many aspects of the event can be coded. A simple coding system can be used to link the WBS, the budget, the task sheets and risk analysis — for example, the artwork (A) and the publicity (P) can use the code PA. This can be cross-referenced to the company, person who is responsible, possible risks or the amount budgeted.

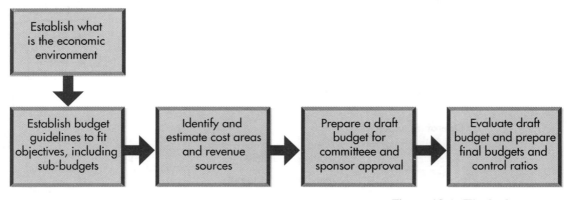

■ **Figure 10.4** *The budget process*

■ Cash flow

The special nature of events and festivals requires close attention to the flow of cash. Goldblatt (1997), Getz (1997), and Catherwood and Van Kirk (1992) all emphasise the importance of the control of cash to an event. Goldblatt (1997) stresses that it is imperative for the goodwill of suppliers. Without prompt payment the event company faces immediate difficulties. Payment terms and conditions have to be fully and equitably negotiated. These payment terms can ruin an event if they are not given careful consideration beforehand. To obtain the best terms from a supplier Goldblatt suggests the following:

• Learn as much as possible about the suppliers and subcontractors and the nature of their business. Do they own the equipment? What are the normal payment terms in their business? Artists, for instance, expect to be paid immediately, whereas some information technology suppliers will wait for 60 days.
• Be flexible with what can be offered in exchange — including sponsorship.

- Try to negotiate a contract that stipulates a small deposit before the event and full payment after it is over.
- Suggest a line of credit, with payment at a set time in the future.
- Closely control the purchasing.
- Ensure all purchases are made through a purchase order that is authorised by the event manager or the appropriate finance personnel. A purchase order is a written record of the agreement to supply a product at a pre-arranged price. All suppliers, contractors and event staff should be informed that no purchase can be made without an authorised form. This ensures spending is confined to what is permitted by the budget.
- Obtain a full description of the product or service and the quantities required.
- Itemise the price to a per unit cost.
- Calculate any taxes or extra charges.
- Determine payment terms.
- Clarify delivery details.
- Consider imposing penalties if the product or service delivered is not as described.

As figure 10.5 shows, the ability of an event coordinator to effect any change diminishes rapidly as the event draws closer. The supply of goods and services may, of necessity, take place close to or on the actual date of the event. This does not allow organisers the luxury of reminding a supplier of the terms set out in the purchase order. Without a full written description of the goods, the event manager is open to all kinds of exploitation by suppliers and, because the event may be on that day, there may be no choice but to accept delivery.

■ Figure 10.5
Control, cost and time

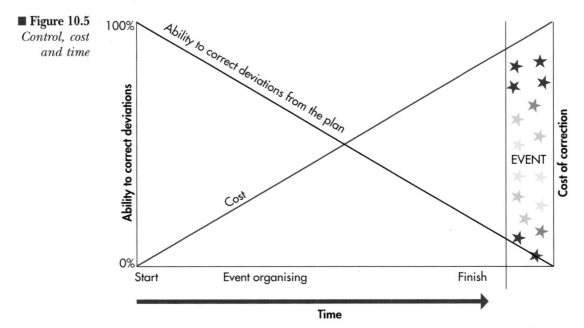

(**Source:** *Burke 1993.*)

When considering cash flow, ticketing strategy advantages of events such as the Port Fairy Folk Festival are obvious. As tickets are sold months before the event, the management is able to concentrate on other areas of planning. A similar advantage is obtained by event companies that specialise in the corporate area — generally, they are paid up-front. This allows the event manager or producer the freedom to negotiate terms and conditions with the suppliers without having to worry about the cash flow. A cash flow timing chart similar to the Gantt chart is often helpful in planning events. This shows the names of the suppliers and their payment requirements. It includes deposit dates, payment stages, payment on purchase, monthly fixed cost payments and 30-, 60- or 90-day credit payments.

■ Costing

The cash flow at an event is heavily dependent on the cost of goods and services. These are estimated for the construction of the budget. The prediction, categorisation and allocation of costs is called the costing. In relation to the break-even chart (figure 10.2, page 322), two types of costs have been identified. These are described in the following text.

Fixed costs or overheads are costs associated with the event that occur regardless of how many people come to the event. They include the unchanging expenses concerned with the operation of the event management company; for example, rent, staff salaries, telephone and other office expenses. At a large festival these expenses may include rates, land tax and interest on loans. When deciding on a budget, these costs should be apportioned reasonably to the various event areas. This process is called absorption of the overheads by the cost centres. Cost centres, for example, include entertainment, catering, staging or travel. If the fixed costs are incorrectly absorbed the cost centre will be wrongly described. For a correct financial picture of a future event, the overheads have to be reasonably spread to all areas. The aim of an event company is to reduce the fixed costs without affecting the quality of the event.

Variable costs are expenses that pertain solely to the event and are directly related to the number of people who attend the event. Food and beverage costs are linked directly to the number of people attending an event. If more people attend an event more tickets need to be printed, more staff may need to be hired and certainly more food provided.

This division of costs is not as clear-cut in the event industry as in other industries. It is sometimes clearer instead to talk in terms of direct costs (the costs directly associated with the event, whether variable or fixed) and overheads (costs associated with the running of the event company). In this case, the direct costs are the major costs — and the aim of the event company is to control these costs. Table 10.2 lists the detailed budgeted costs of a one-off event.

The advantage of a budget in table 10.2 is that it can be used as a template for future events. The use of computers allows the festival organiser to create a generic budget and apply it to each event. The items not needed are simply deleted.

		$			$
Administration	Office rental			Communication	
	Fax/photocopy			First aid	
	Computers			Tents	
	Printers			Tables and chairs	
	Telephone			Wind breaks	
	Stationery			Generators	
	Postage			Technicians	
	Office staff			Parking needs	
	SUBTOTAL			Uniforms	
Publicity	Artwork			SUBTOTAL	
	Printing		Salaries	Coordinator	
	Poster and leaflet distribution			Artists	
	Press kit			Labourers	
	Press ads			Consultants	
	Radio ads			Other	
	Programs			SUBTOTAL	
	SUBTOTAL		Insurance	Public liability	
Venue	Hire			Workers compensation	
	Preparation			Rain	
	SUBTOTAL			Other	
Equipment	Stage			SUBTOTAL	
	Sound		Permits	Liquor	
	Lights			Food	
	Transport			Council	
	Personnel			Parking	
	Toilets			Childcare	
	Extra equipment			SUBTOTAL	

(continued)

		$			$
Security	Security check		Documentation	Photo/video	
	Equipment			SUBTOTAL	
	Personnel		Hospitality	Tent	
	SUBTOTAL			Food	
Accounting	Cash and cheque			Beverage	
	Audit			Personnel	
	SUBTOTAL			Invitations	
Cleaning	Before			SUBTOTAL	
	During		Community	Donations	
	After			SUBTOTAL	
	SUBTOTAL		Volunteers	Food and drink	
Travel	Artists			Party	
	Freight			Awards and prizes	
	SUBTOTAL			SUBTOTAL	
Accommodation			Contingencies		
	SUBTOTAL			SUBTOTAL	

Catherwood and van Kirk (1992) divide the costs of an event into four main categories:

1. *operational or production costs*, including hiring of event staff, construction, insurance and administration
2. *venue/site rental*
3. *promotion* — advertising, public relations, sales promotion
4. *talent* — costs associated with the entertainment.

To obtain the correct cost of each of the elements contained in the budget categories (sometimes called cost centres) there is a common costing process involved. The steps are described below:

- *Conceptual estimate* or 'ballpark figure' — this would be used in the conceptual development stage of the event to give management an idea of what costs are involved. Generally, this would have an accuracy of +/− 25 per cent.
- *Feasibility study* — this includes comparing costs in similar events. The cost of headline speakers, for example, varies according to their popularity and type of career. Asking other event managers about current speaker fees gives the event producer a basis for negotiating a fair price and a more realistic budget estimation.

- *Quote or definitive estimate* — this is the cost quote in reply to the tender. The larger festivals will put many of the elements of the event out to tender, including sound, lights and security. A near-correct estimate can be made on this basis. For small events, the quote may be obtained by phoning a selection of suppliers and comparing the costs. However, it is rarely the case that the costs are comparable, as there are so many unusual features or special conditions. Once an event company has built up a relationship with a supplier, it tends to stay with that supplier.

■ Tips on reducing costs

With careful and imaginative planning, costs can be reduced in a number of areas. They are discussed below:

- *Publicity* — an innovative event may need a large publicity budget that is based on revenue from ticket sales. The event manager's aim should be to reduce this wherever possible. Established festivals may need very little publicity as 'word of mouth' will do all the necessary work. The annual Woodford Folk Festival with a budget of $2.3 million spends very little on publicity because it has built up a strong reputation with its target audience. The more innovative the event then the greater is the possibility for free publicity. The Tropicana Festival of Short Films in Sydney, for example, gains enormous free publicity as it attracts film stars to the event.
- *Equipment and supplies* — suppliers of products to events have down times during the year when their products may be hired cheaply. In particular, theatrical productions at the end of their run are a ready source of decoration and scenery. Annual events like the Sydney Gay and Lesbian Mardi Gras often have equipment in storage that can be hired.
- *In-kind gifts* — many organisations will assist events to achieve cross-promotional advantages. Entertainment can be inexpensive if there is a chance that an organisation can promote a performance or product at the event. For instance, at the Macquarie Marshes concert, the boutique wine company Bloodwood agreed to supply their wine freely to the pre-event party for the media and friends, in exchange for the rights to sell their product at the concert.
- *Hiring charges* — the hire costs of large infrastructure components, such as tents and generators and headline acts can be reduced by offering work at other festivals and events. The large cultural festivals around Australia, for example, including the Melbourne International Festival and the Adelaide Festival of the Arts, can offer a festival circuit to any overseas performer. Costs are amortised over all the festivals.
- *Priorities cost centres* — at some time it will be necessary to cut costs. You will need to anticipate the effect on the overall event if one area is significantly changed or eliminated. In project management this is called sensitivity analysis (Burke 1993). Estimates are made of the effect of cost changes on the event and the cost centres are placed in a priority list according to the significance of the effect. A sensitivity analysis, for example, could be applied to the effect of imposing a charge on a

program that was previously free. While this could significantly increase revenue, it may produce a negative effect in sponsorship and audience satisfaction, which may well be translated into the reduction of revenue.

- *Volunteers* — costs can be reduced by using volunteers instead of paid staff. It is important that all the skills of the volunteers are fully utilised. These skills should be continually under review as new skills may be required as the event planning progresses. For charitable functions, volunteers will often absorb many of the costs as tax deductible donations.

■ Revenue

Anticipating potential sources of revenue should be given as much attention as projecting expenses. The source of the revenue will often define the type of event, the event objectives and the planning. A company product launch has only one source of revenue — the client. Company staff parties, for example, are paid for by the client with no other source of revenue. The budget then has only one entry on the left-hand side. A major festival, on the other hand, has to find and service a variety of revenue sources such as sponsors and participants. This constitutes a major part of festival planning.

Revenue can come from the following sources:
- ticket sales — most common in entrepreneurial events
- sponsorship — common in cultural and sports events
- merchandising
- advertising
- 'in-kind' arrangements
- broadcast rights — an increasingly important source of revenue in sport events
- grants — federal, state and local government
- fundraising — common in community events
- the client — the major source for corporate events.

Table 10.3 (page 335) features an expanded list of revenue sources. For many events, admission fees and ticket prices need careful consideration. The revenue they generate will impact on the cash flow and the break-even point. The ticket price can be decided by one or more of three methods:

1. *Covering costs* — all the costs are estimated and added to the projected profit. To give the ticket price, this figure is then divided by the expected number of people that will attend the event. The method is quick, simple and based on knowing the break-even point. It gives a 'rule of thumb' figure that can be used as a starting point for further investigations in setting the price.
2. *Market demand* — the ticket price is decided by the prevailing ticket prices for similar or competing events. In other words, it is the 'going rate' for an event. Concert ticket prices are decided in this way. In deciding on the ticket price, consider elasticity of demand. For instance, if the ticket price is increased slightly will this affect the number of tickets sold?
3. *Perceived value* — the event may have special features that preclude a price comparison to other events. For an innovative event, for example,

the ticket price must be carefully considered. By its nature this kind of event has no comparison. There can be variations in the ticket price for different entertainment packages at the event (at many multi-venued events the ticket will include admission only to certain events), for extra hospitality or for special seating. Knowing how to grade the tickets is an important skill in maximising revenue. There are market segments that will not tolerate differences in pricing, whereas others expect it. It can be a culturally-based decision and may be part of the design of the event.

■ Table 10.3
Revenue sources — second level

INCOME		$	INCOME		$
Grants	Local		Ticket sales	Box office	
	State			Retail outlets	
	Federal			Admissions	
	Arts			SUBTOTAL	
	Other		Merchandise	T-shirts	
	SUBTOTAL			Programs	
Donations	Foundations			Posters	
	Other			Badges	
	SUBTOTAL			Videos	
Sponsorship	In-kind			SUBTOTAL	
	Cash		Fees	Stalls	
	SUBTOTAL			Licences	
Individual contributions				Broadcast	
	SUBTOTAL			SUBTOTAL	
Special programs	Raffle		Advert sales	Program	
	Auction			Event site	
	Games			SUBTOTAL	
	SUBTOTAL		Concessions		
				SUBTOTAL	

■ Tips for increasing projected income

Ticket scaling

There are many ticketing strategies that strive to obtain the best value from ticket sales. The most common strategy is to vary the pricing, according to seat position, number of tickets sold and time of sale. Early-bird discounts and subscriptions series are two examples of the latter. Another strategy involves creating a special category of attendees. This could include patrons, special clubs, 'friends of the event', people for whom the theme of the event has a special meaning or those who have attended many similar events in the past. For a higher ticket price, for example, patrons are offered extra hospitality, such as a separate viewing area, valet parking and a cocktail party.

In-kind support and bartering

One way to increase income is to scrutinise the event cost centres for areas that could be covered by an exchange with the supplier or bartering. The advertising can be expanded for an event, for example, with a program of 'give-aways'. These are free tickets to the event given away through the press. Due to the amount of goodwill surrounding a fund-raising event, bartering should be explored as a method of obtaining supplies. Bartering may have significant tax implications. It should not be undertaken without close scrutiny of this risk.

Merchandising

The staging of an event offers many opportunities for merchandising. The first consideration is 'Does the sale of goods enhance the theme of the event?'. The problems of cash flow at an event, as stated earlier in this chapter, can give the sale of goods an unrealistic high priority in event management. It is easy to cheapen a 'boutique' special event with the sale of 'trinkets'. However, the attendees may want to buy a souvenir. A large choir performing at a one-off spectacular event, for example, may welcome the opportunity to sell a video of their performance. This could be arranged with the choir beforehand and result in a guaranteed income. As a spin-off, the video could be incorporated into promotional material for use by the event management in bidding for future events.

Broadcast rights

An increasingly important source of revenue, particularly in sporting events, is the payment for the right to broadcast. A live television broadcast of an event is a lucrative area for potential — but it comes at a price. The broadcast, rather than the needs and expectations of the live audience, becomes master of the event. Often the live audience becomes merely one element in the televising process. At the ARIA (Australian Record Industry Association) Awards the audience includes 'fillers' — people who fill any empty seats so that the camera will always show a capacity audience.

If the entire event is recorded by high-quality video equipment, future broadcast rights should also be investigated. For instance, in many countries there is a constant demand for worthwhile content for pay television (cable or satellite). At the time of writing, Internet broadcast is in its infancy. There have been a number of music and image broadcasts but they are limited by the size of the bandwidth. There can be no doubt that this will become an important medium for the event industry.

Sponsorship leverage

Leverage is the current term for using event sponsorship to gain further support from other sponsors. Very few companies or organisations want to be the first to sponsor a one-off event. However, once the event has one sponsor's support, sufficient credibility is gained to enable an approach to other sponsors. Gaining the support of a major newspaper or radio station, for example, allows the event manager to approach other sponsors. The sponsors realise that they can obtain free publicity.

Special features

When an event is linked to a large population base, there are many opportunities for generating income. Raffles, for example, are frequently used to raise income. At a concert dance in England, all patrons brought along a prize for a raffle to be drawn on the night. Everyone received a ticket in the raffle as part of the entry fee to the event. The prizes ranged from old ties to overseas air tickets. Every person received a prize and the raffle became part of the entertainment of the evening.

Holding an auction at an event is also an entertaining way to increase income. Prior to the Broome Fringe Festival (held in June 1998), the event manager organised an innovative auction. The items auctioned included haircuts, 'slave for a day', body work and massages. The sale of players' jerseys, complete with the mud stains, after a major football match has also proved a lucrative way of raising revenue.

■ Reporting

The importance of general reporting on the progress of event planning has already been described in this chapter. The budget report is a means of highlighting problems and suggesting solutions. It is an effective form of communication to the event committee and staff, and should be readily understood. It is important that appropriate action is taken in response to the report's suggestions. Figure 10.6 is a list of guidelines for a straightforward report.

■ **Figure 10.6**
*Reporting
guidelines*

- The report should relate directly to the event management area to which it is addressed.
- It should not contain extraneous information that can only obscure its function. Brevity and clarity are key objectives.
- The figures in the report must be of the same magnitude and they should be comparable.
- The report should describe how to take remedial action if there is a significant problem.

The most common problem in an event is the cost 'blow out'. Special event planners often encounter unforeseen circumstances that can cost dearly. The subcontractor who supplies the sound system, for example, can go bankrupt; the replacement subcontractor may prove far more expensive. One of the unwritten laws of project management is that the closer the project is to completion, the more expensive any changes become. Appropriate remedial action may be to use cheaper catering services or to find extra funding. This could take the form of a raffle to cover the extra costs. Figure 10.5 (page 329) graphically shows how the cost of any changes to the organisation of an event escalate as the event date nears.

A major problem associated with a budget, particularly for special events, may involve blind adherence to it (Hicks 1976). It is a tool of control and not an end in itself. The elegance of a well laid-out budget and its mathematical certainty can obscure the fact that it should be a slave to the event objectives, not its master. A budget is based on reasonable projections made within an economic framework. Small changes in the framework can cause large changes in the event's finances. For instance, extra sponsorship may be found if the right products are added to the event portfolio. A complicated, highly-detailed budget may consume far more time than is necessary to make the event a success.

Time is a crucial factor in special event management. Keeping rigidly within budgetary standards can take up too much time and energy of the event management, thus limiting time available for other areas.

Finally, a budget that is constructed by the event management may be imposed on staff without adequate consultation. This can lead to losing valuable specialist staff if they find themselves having to work to unreasonable budgetary standards. In particular, an innovative event requires the creative input of all the staff and subcontractors. At these events, informal financial control using a draft budget is often far more conducive to quality work than strict budgetary control.

It needs to be remembered that a budget is only an approximation of reality, and not reality itself. It will need to be adjusted as the event changes and new information comes to hand. However, it is a vital part of the control mechanism for events.

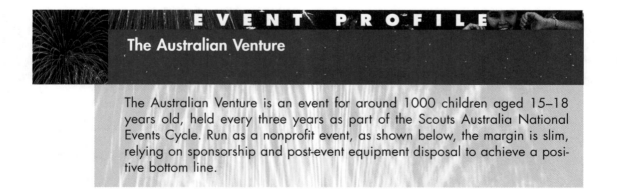

EVENT PROFILE

The Australian Venture

The Australian Venture is an event for around 1000 children aged 15–18 years old, held every three years as part of the Scouts Australia National Events Cycle. Run as a nonprofit event, as shown below, the margin is slim, relying on sponsorship and post-event equipment disposal to achieve a positive bottom line.

Scouts Australia
AV2006 — 13th Australian Venture January 2006
Preliminary budget
Income and expenditure

Budget income and expenditure summary for Australian Venture 2006

Item	No.	Per head	Amount
Income			
Participant fees — venturers	1000	$600.00	$600 000.00
Participant fees — leaders	100	$500.00	$ 50 000.00
Participant fees — support staff	200	$300.00	$ 60 000.00
Participant fees — day workers	100	$ 50.00	$ 5 000.00
Saleable items recoup			$ 9 000.00
Sponsorship			$ 20 000.00
		Total income summary:	$744 000.00

	Budget
Expenses	
Operations	$140 000.00
Activities	$180 000.00
Administration	$ 60 000.00
Accommodation and catering	$258 500.00
Marketing	$ 49 000.00
Sites and services	$ 34 000.00
Total expenditure summary:	$721 500.00
Surplus/(Deficit)	$ 22 500.00

The budget was initially developed by department heads putting in requests. The event director then had to combine budgets from each department, eliminating duplicated costs (for example, the marketing department had included catering for functions, which the catering department had also covered in their budget) and cutting some budgets dramatically to achieve the participation fee goal.

As the previous event had been considered expensive by participants, the goal for this event was to reduce the fee compared to the previous event; the base fee is $200 less at $600, although the aim was $50. The final $50 reduction was unachievable as set event policies decreed a 10 per cent contingency fee and another 5 per cent in specific fees, such as a support fund for international participants.

The sponsorship total may be considered low for this type of event; however, this is intentional due to another event policy. Any profits from the event that are a prescribed budget line are distributed post-event in a specific manner. Any profits not forecast are kept by the organising state. It is also not advisable for us to rely on sponsorship in the budget phase — if the sponsorship figure is not achieved, then there will be a budget deficit.

Patrick Johnson, Promotions Manager, 13th Australian Venture

There is little point expending effort in creating a plan for an event if there is no way to closely monitor it. The event plan is a prerequisite for success. The control mechanisms to keep the project aligned to the plan need to be well thought out and easily understood by the management team. When the event strays from the plan there needs to be ways to bring it back into line or to change the plan.

An estimate of the costs and revenues of an event is called the budget and it acts as the master control of an event. With a well-reasoned budget in place, all sections of an event know their spending limits and can focus on working together. The cash flow of an event needs special considerations. When is the cash coming in? Moreover, when does it need to go out? An event that does not have control mechanisms, including a well-planned budget, is not going to satisfy its stakeholders. Not only will it fail, but organisers will never know the reason for its failure. A sound budget gives management a solid foundation on which to build a successful event.

Questions

1. Can the use of control and monitoring overwhelm the creative aspects of event management?

2. List the milestones for management of a fun run event of 10 000 people.

3. What are other gaps that can be measured to indicate a deviation from the event plan?

4. The budget is often perceived as the most important part of event management. What are the limitations of running an event by the budget? Do many events such as the arts festivals always come in under budget? What can lead to drastic changes in the budget?

5. Identify the cost centres and revenue sources for:
   (a) a celebrity poetry reading for a charity
   (b) a rural car auction with antique cars
   (c) a corporate Christmas party
   (d) a hot air balloon festival.

6. Staging, logistics, risk management and project management all have their techniques for monitoring and controlling. Compare them. Can they all come under the method used in risk management?

7. Why is cash flow of such importance to event management? Can an event be run on credit?

CASE STUDY ·····················

New Year's Eve, Sydney

New Year's Eve in Sydney's city centre is an event that attracts millions of members of the general public to the city harbour foreshores. There are many landowners or venue managers in these areas around the Sydney harbour. In the past 20 years, these stakeholders have developed many strategies to manage the one to two million people that arrive in the city for the big night.

There was little or no additional infrastructure or 'managed access areas' 20 years ago. There were some extra trains and buses to bring people to and from the city (to discourage drink driving), but it was up to the public to find a good vantage point to see the stunning fireworks displays that have been a Sydney New Year's Eve tradition.

People positioning themselves to view the fireworks led to major overcrowding issues among the more popular areas such as the foreshore. The overcrowding caused subsequent problems, such as:

- damage to trees
- injuries among the general public
- damage to property such as fences and vehicles
- disruption to traffic as crowds spilled onto the road
- litter problems where bins were overfilled and detritus was left along the roads and pavements.

The following initiatives were devised by the major landowners to control the crowds accessing the area:

- The City of Sydney, who ran the fireworks event, relieved pressure in the city by firing the pyrotechnics from a number of barges on the harbour. This meant the foreshore 10 kilometres away became an attractive vantage point.
- The Sydney Opera House erected barricading when the site managers deemed the venue was full. In later years, experiencing New Year's Eve on the Opera House forecourt became a ticketed event. The general public could either apply for tickets via a public lottery system or buy tickets to see a concert, opera or play inside the Opera House.
- The Royal Botanic Gardens (which normally close at sunset) simply shut to the general public a few hours before sunset and only allowed entry to ticketed party-goers to their own event.

Since the mid-1990s, the concept of 'managed access' has spread to all areas of the Sydney Harbour foreshores, including Darling Harbour and The Rocks. These involve compulsory bag searches on all the major pedestrian accessways that lead to popular vantage points. These were initiated as a result of the large amount of glass-cut injuries sustained by wearers of open shoes. However, there is now an added benefit of limiting the amount of alcohol (in plastic only) a person can bring into the controlled areas.

(*continued*)

The event

The Roads and Traffic Authority (RTA) is the owner and manager of the Cahill Expressway. The expressway is always closed for New Year's Eve because the only feeder road to it (the Sydney Harbour Bridge eastern lanes) is closed on New Year's Eve for the fireworks detonation, an annual event at 9 pm and midnight.

Since the practice of closing the Cahill Expressway commenced, the general public quickly comprehended the benefits of an empty freeway that had prime views of the fireworks; within several years, the crowds became unmanageable. Complaints of missiles being thrown from the freeway onto the ferry terminal and misbehaviour by intoxicated party-goers were recorded. It made sense for the RTA to manage its land more efficiently on New Year's Eve. It decided, therefore, to provide tickets to the public by a lottery system. This was run from late November on the RTA website and also over the counter at RTA outlets.

The four-lane expressway stretches for approximately 2 kilometres beyond the final traffic of the southern end of the Sydney Harbour Bridge. To locals, this is past the southern pylons of the bridge to the Conservatorium of Music. (The road runs right over the top of Circular Quay railway station and the Circular Quay ferry terminal.) The prime viewing area that runs over the railway station is approximately 700 metres long and three car lanes wide. (The fourth lane is fenced off for emergency vehicle access.) There is a further 700 metres with a hindered view of the bridge, but a good view of the sky for the fireworks display.

The main entry and bag search point for the public is at the marquee located in front of the Conservatorium. The public can enter through this marquee, eight at a time, and people queue to 100 metres back. The bag search area comprises eight guards, eight trestle tables and four ticket collection staff. If patrons inadvertently bring alcohol in glass bottles, it is confiscated and returned to them on their departure. The total capacity of the venue is a comfortable 5000 persons — less than one person per square metre in the prime viewing area and more space in the restricted viewing area. Patrons usually bring a blanket to spread on the tarmac until the fireworks begin, and have a picnic. Many patrons have prams, most have picnic hampers but there is plenty of room to move.

Facts

- The road was closed at midday.
- Tickets handouts commenced at 1620 hours.
- Gates for 2100 hours session opened at 1800 hours.
- Gates for midnight session opened at 2205 hours.
- The road was re-opened when cleaning concluded at the Conservatorium at 0335 hours.

Because there are two separate fireworks shows — one at 9 pm and one at midnight — the patrons must exit at the end of the 9 pm session and re-enter for the midnight session 30 minutes later. This enables a full cleaning of the site to occur, including a pump-out of the 40 portaloos.

A list of providers and their provisions follows on the next page.

On-site security
- 60 security officers from midday to 3 am

On-site
- 42 portaflush loos
- two accessible loos
- street signage
- 9 metre × 15 metre marquee for entry area
- eight trestle tables
- four portaflood devices
- 50 KVA generators

ATF
- 1500 metres of security fencing from entry area to the Sydney Harbour Bridge
  Plant hire:
- four × VMS units with eight-frame messaging; distribution of 200 metres
- 30 two-way Motorola radios
- 30 batteries
- three × six-bay charger units
- five covert ear pieces
- five lightweight headsets
  Public address:
- 30 speakers on stands to relay the simulcast
- one radio microphone for announcements on the expressway
- one radio microphone for announcements at the entry point

Cleanevent
- four dumpsters
- cleaning staff
- a street sweeping machine (two runs)

Other
- Royal Volunteer Coastguard Patrol — charity group
- food and beverage to the general public as a fundraising opportunity

The process of managed access has grown in an organic way throughout Sydney. It has developed as much or as little as the landowners or venue managers have demanded. Darling Harbour, which could hold several million pedestrians, does not deny any public access because it is not as susceptible as other foreshore areas to overcrowding. However, the Sydney Harbour Foreshore Authority manages the entry points and conducts bag searches.

Janet Eades, event manager

Questions

1 Control, risk management and logistics form the basis of this case study. Identify each of the issues in these areas. How do they relate to each other?

2 Discuss bag searching at venue entry as a control technique. What other aspects of control are treated by such a search? What are the risks?

3 Identify the predictive, concurrent and historic controls in this case study.

REFERENCES

Beniger, J 1986, *The control revolution*, Harvard University Press, Cambridge.

Bennett, R 1994, *Managing: activities and resources*, 2nd edn, Kogan Page Limited, London.

Brody, R & Goodman, M 1988, *Fund-raising events: strategies and programs for success*, Human Sciences Press Inc., New York.

Burke, R 1993, *Project management: planning and control*, 2nd edn, John Wiley & Sons, New York.

Catherwood, D & Van Kirk, R 1992, *The complete guide to special event management*, John Wiley & Sons, New York.

Getz, D 1997, *Event management and event tourism*, Cognizant Communications, New York.

Goldblatt, J 1997, *Special events: best practices in modern event management*, 2nd edn, Van Nostrand Reinhold, New York.

Hicks, H & Gullet, C 1976, *The management of organisations*, McGraw-Hill Kogakusha Ltd, Tokyo.

Renton, N 1994, *Guide for meetings and organisations: volume 2, meetings*, 6th edn, The Law Book Company Ltd, Sydney.

FURTHER READING

Cameron, N 1993, *Fire on the water*, Currency Press, Paddington, Australia.

11
Risk
management and
legal issues

LEARNING OBJECTIVES

After studying this chapter, you should be able to:

■ define risk and its relationship to the management of festivals and special events

■ understand the role of risk management in the event management process

■ use the tools of risk identification

■ construct a risk management plan

■ explain the central role of event ownership in event administration

■ identify the necessary contracts for events and their components

■ understand the variety of rules and regulations governing events

■ describe the process of gaining insurance.

INTRODUCTION

A working definition of event risk is any future incident that will negatively influence the event. Note that this risk is not solely at the event itself. In many texts on events, risk is taken to mean safety risk or financial risk, but this definition ignores problems in other areas of event management that may harmfully influence the success of the event. Fraud, for example, is a risk that has surfaced at many events. Misrepresentation of the event by marketing or overpromotion is another risk. Each of these risks may result in safety and financial troubles at the event. Risk management can be defined as the process of identifying these problems, assessing them and dealing with them. Fortunately, risk management may also uncover opportunities. In the past, this may have been done in an informal manner; however, the current management environment demands that the process be formalised. The event team must be able to show that risk management is being employed throughout the project. This chapter outlines the process of risk management. The process is made up of understanding the context of risk, risk identification, evaluation and control. This process can be applied to all the areas of event management. The second section of the chapter describes the legal issues. Some of these issues are complex, involving permits, licences and state and federal legislation. They often differ in each state and for each council. One of the fundamental concepts common to all states is the duty of care, and this is defined later in the chapter. Contracts are essential to all event management, and the process of contract management is also described in this chapter. Many of the event risks are transferred to a third party via an insurance contract.

In this chapter, two areas of event management often included in the risk area are considered in detail: legal compliance and contract management.

RISK MANAGEMENT PROCESS

Special events are particularly susceptible to risks. Risk, in the event context, may be formally defined as the likelihood of the special event or festival not fulfilling its objectives. A unique venue, large crowds, new staff and volunteers, movement of equipment and general excitement are all a recipe for potential hazards. The event manager who ignores advice on risk prevention is courting disaster and foreshortening his or her career in the event industry. The sensible assessment of potential hazards and preventive action is a part of the overall risk management.

Risk is not necessarily harmful. One reason, among many, that an event company wins the job of organising an event is that competing companies perceive the event to be too risky. The successful company can manage all the risks with its current resources. Risk is the basis of the entrepreneur's business. Without risk, there can be no competitive advantage. Without the appearance of risk, there can be no tightrope walking or extreme games.

Part of what makes an event special is the uncertainty — it has not been done before.

The Australia New Zealand Risk Management Standard (AS/NZS 4360: 1999) defines risk management thus:

> ■ Risk management is the term applied to a logical and systematic method of establishing the context, identifying, analysing, evaluating, treating, monitoring and communicating risks associated with any activity, function or process in a way that will enable organisations to minimise losses and maximise opportunities. Risk management is as much about identifying opportunities as avoiding or mitigating losses. ■

Every part of event management has potential risks. Berlonghi (1990) categorises the main areas of risk as follows:

- *Administration*: the organisational structure and office layout should minimise risk to employees.
- *Marketing and public relations*: the promotion section must be aware of the need for risk management. By their nature, marketeers are optimistic about the consequences of their actions and tend to ignore potential risks.
- *Health and safety*: a large part of risk management concerns this area. Loss prevention plans and safety control plans are an important part of any risk management strategy. The risks associated with food concession hygiene and sanitation require specific attention.
- *Crowd management*: risk management of crowd flow, alcohol sales and noise control (see chapter 12 on logistics).
- *Security*: the security plan for an event involves careful risk management thinking.
- *Transport*: deliveries, parking and public transport contain many potential hazards that need to be addressed.

A good risk management strategy will also cover any other operational areas that are crucial to the event and that may need special security and safety precautions, such as ticket sales and other cash points and communications.

In chapter 9, the areas of event project management are introduced and risk is one of those areas, but it is not an isolated area. The risk management process cuts right across all the other areas. In any one of the areas of knowledge and management, the risks must be identified and pre-empted, and their management fully integrated into the event plan. By using a project management approach to the event, risk management becomes an underlying process that is employed continuously in every area of the management.

■ Understanding *context*

The context of risk management includes the type of event, the management structure, the stakeholder analysis and the general risk environment. Throwing white powder, for example, was considered a major danger at events a few years ago due to the publicity about the anthrax scare. The white powder incidents were logged each week around Australia — these were hoaxes. However, an incident could cause a stampede if any crowd member thought it was anthrax. Today, throwing white powder might not rate a mention in the press. Terrorism is a major concern for some events. While the attacks on the World Trade Center and Pentagon in 2001 increased the perceived threat in countries previously thought safe from terrorism, it must be remembered that terrorism at events has been a concern since the Munich Olympics. It is an ongoing concern in many countries. The 2001 attacks in the USA increased the public perception in western countries of this risk. Some nations deal with terrorism as part of their day-to-day security. Large events, as they attract global media interest, can be a terrorism target. The conclusion is that the surrounding environment has to be taken into account in the risk management process. The organisation culture of the client and the event company are also part of the context to be considered. Some companies or organisations are highly risk averse and would prefer a predictable event that has been tried and tested for many years. These clients prefer the 'franchised' event. A large part of the risk will originate with or involve the stakeholders. A comprehensive stakeholder analysis is a prerequisite for thorough risk management. The stakeholders may also provide the support to deal with the risks. The legislation on duty of care and public liability are further examples of the event environment that will impinge on the risk management process. The financial risk is an example of an everchanging context. The currency exchange rate, the financial state of the sponsors, fraud and the demands of the shareholders are some of the external developments that can affect the financial viability of the event. A comprehensive risk assessment cannot be performed without understanding the context of the event, the risk environment and the stakeholder's requirements. One must remember this context is changing and therefore needs to be reassessed as the event management progresses.

■ Identifying *risks*

The next stage in the process is identifying the risks. Pre-empting problems requires skill, experience and knowledge. Something that appears safe to some of the event staff may contain hidden dangers. A sponsor's sign at an event may look securely mounted when examined by the marketing manager, but it will require the specialist knowledge of the stagehands to ensure it is secure. As the event manager cannot be an expert in every field, it is best to pool the experience of all the event staff and volunteers by convening a risk assessment meeting. A meeting should aim to gather risk management expertise. For large or complex events, an event risk consultant may be hired. The meeting is also an opportunity to train and motivate event staff in the awareness, minimisation and control of risks.

Identification techniques
Several techniques assist in identifying risks:
- *Work breakdown structure* — breaking down the work necessary to create an event into manageable parts can greatly assist in the identification of risks.

It provides a visual scheme as well as the categorisation of the event into units associated with specific skills and resources. An example of the work breakdown structure (WBS) is found in chapter 9. Isolating the event areas in this way gives a clear picture of the possible problems. One of the areas of the WBS for an award night, for example, is the work associated with the Master of Ceremonies (MC). The author has posed this question at many event workshops: 'What could go wrong with the MC?'. Some of the problems identified by event managers' experience include: being inebriated, not turning up, leaving early, not reading the script, using inappropriate language, having a scruffy appearance, believing they are the main act, being unable to use a microphone and insulting the sponsor. This does not imply that these are common problems; however, an event manager would be foolish to ignore the experience of others. The construction of a work breakdown structure assists another area of management — the creation of the risk management plan — and thus illustrates the importance of the project management system to event management. Although the work breakdown structure is a necessary tool for risk management, it may not reveal the problems that result in a combination of risks. A problem with the ticketing of an event, for example, may not be severe on its own. If it is combined with the withdrawal of a major sponsor, the result may require the event to be cancelled.

- *Test events* — large sporting events often run smaller events to test the facilities, equipment and other resources. The Olympics test events were effectively used to iron out any problems before the main event. A test is a self-funded rehearsal. The pre-conference cocktail party, for example, is used to test some aspects of the conference. Many music festivals will run an opening concert on the night before the first day of the festival, as a means of testing the equipment.
- *Internal/external* — to assist risk analysis it is useful to have a classification system according to the origin of the risk. Internal risks arise in the event planning and implementation stage. They may also result from the inexperience of the event company. These risks are generally within the abilities of the event company to manage. External risks arise from outside the event organisation and may need a different control strategy. This technique focuses on mitigating the impact of the risk — dealing with the consequences. The impact of a star soccer player cancelling, for example, may be minimised by allowing free entry to the event. For this reason, the SWOT analysis is a risk identification technique. The strengths and weaknesses correspond to internal risks, and the opportunities and threats correspond to the external risks.
- *Fault diagram* — risks can also be discovered by looking at their impact and working backwards to the possible cause. This is called a result-to-cause method. A lack of ticket sales at an event, for example, would be a terrible result. The fault diagram method would go back from this risk through the various event aspects to postulate its cause. The list of causes is then used to manage the risk.
- *Incident report* — almost all large public events have an incident report document. These may be included in the event manual and are to be

filled out by the event staff when there is an incident. The incident data can then be used by agencies to give an event risk profile. The ambulance service has such data on medical incidents for events. By giving the ambulance service key characteristics of an event, such as audience number, alcohol availability, age group and type of event activity they can predict the type of medical incidents most likely to occur.

- *Contingency plan* — an outcome of the risk analysis may be a detailed plan of viable alternative integrated actions. The contingency plan contains the response to the impact of a risk and involves a decision procedure, chain of command and a set of related actions. An example of contingency planning was the response to the Y2K (turn of the millennium) threat. On the south coast of NSW, for example, the New Year's Eve events required an emergency plan. If the Y2K adversely affected the computer system at the local Navy airfield, the emergency services would be called to the navy base. This could pose a major problem for any event in the local area, particularly as at that time of year there is a high fire danger in the region.

- *Scenario development and tabletop exercises* — the use of a 'what if' session can uncover many risks. A scenario of problems is given to the event team and interested stakeholders. They work through the problems and present their responses. This is collated and discussed. These tabletop exercises are surprisingly effective. One tabletop exercise used the scenario of an expected fireworks display not happening at a major New Year's Eve event. All the agencies around the table then responded, describing the consequences as they saw it and their contingency plans. The problems included disappointed crowds, a rush for the public transport and other crowd management issues. Would the event company be able to announce to the crowd of 500 000 what had happened? The fireworks went off as planned in the following year. Two years later, however, the fireworks did not occur. A number of the agencies such as police, emergency service and railways were able to use their contingency plans. Major sponsors and government clients may send an event company a number of scenarios and ask for their response. This is a way of testing the competence of the event management.

- *Consultation* — part of each state's occupational health and safety code is the concept of consultation. The event management team is required to consult with the various suppliers on their safety plans for the event. It is slightly different for different regions; however, consultation can also be used to strengthen the risk identification and analysis. Suppliers have a wealth of information on what can go wrong. Consultation does not imply just asking questions, the event manager must provide relevant information so that the other party can give a considered opinion. This opinion must be taken into account in the planning of the event and risk management.

An essential aspect of risk identification is a way to accurately describe them. The risk for an outdoor event is not 'weather'. A beautiful fine day is still 'weather'. Heat or rain may be the risk descriptor. However, this is still not accurate enough. Extreme heat or rain before the event is getting closer to describing the actual risk. The process of describing the risk accurately also enables the event team to think the risk through.

■ Evaluating *the risk*

It is obvious that there are an infinite number of things that can go wrong and a finite number that can go right. Identifying risk can open a Pandora's box of issues. Risk assessment meetings often reveal the 'prophets of doom' who can bring an overly pessimistic approach to the planning process. This is itself a risk that must be anticipated. The event team must have a method of organising the risks so they can be methodically managed. Once the risks are accurately described, they should be mapped according to:

- the likelihood of them occurring (for example, on a five-point scale from rare to almost certain)
- the consequence if they do occur (for example, on a five-point scale from insignificant to catastrophic).

An accurate way of describing the risks is essential to clear communication. At a recent risk meeting, for example, the risk of providing *incorrect information to the media* was identified as 'likely' and the consequence was 'moderate' to 'major'. It was assessed as needing attention and requiring a solution. At another meeting it was found that the decision to possibly cancel the event was being left to the event's general manager (GM). However, during the event, the GM would be in a high security area with politicians, and difficult to contact. The risk of *GM impossible to contact* was rated 'certain' and 'catastrophic'. The solution was simple: have security clearance for a 'runner' to be able to communicate between the event team and the GM.

A risk meeting with the staff and volunteers is often the only way to uncover many risks. It is important that the meeting be well chaired and focused, since the time needed for risk assessment must always be weighed against the limited time available for the overall event planning. An effective risk assessment meeting will produce a comprehensive and realistic analysis of the potential risks in a risk register. The risk register is the document output of the risk management process and is further explained in the documentation section later in this chapter.

■ Control

After the risks have been evaluated, the event management team needs to create mechanisms to control any problem that can arise. The decisions include:

- changing the likelihood that a problem will occur — this can include avoiding the problem by not proceeding with that aspect of the event. A recent water-ski event, for example, was unable to obtain insurance. The management identified the part of the event that was high risk and cancelled it. This enabled the event to go ahead with the necessary level of insurance.
- changing the consequence if the problem does occur — such as contingency planning and disaster plans
- accepting the risk
- transferring the risk to another party.

Insurance is an example of changing the consequence by transferring the risk and accepting a smaller risk. The risk that is now accepted is:

- the insurance contract will be honoured (for example, the insurance company could go bankrupt)
- the event makes enough money to pay for the insurance.

The risk management process can be defined, therefore, as transferring the risks to a part of the event management that has the resources (including skills, experience and knowledge) to handle it. This is an important point because the risk is rarely, if ever, completely eliminated, except by cancelling the event. Once a risk has been identified and a solution planned, its likelihood of occurring and its consequences are reduced.

In his comprehensive manual on risk management for events, Berlonghi (1990) suggests the following risk control strategies:

- *Cancel and avoid the risk* — if the risk is too great it may be necessary to cancel all or part of the event. Outdoor concerts that are part of a larger event are often cancelled if there is rain. The major risk is not audience discomfort, but the danger of electrocution.
- *Diminish the risk* — risks that cannot be avoided need to be minimised. To eliminate all possible security risks at an event, for example, may require every patron to be searched. This solution is obviously unworkable at a majority of events and, instead, a risk minimisation strategy will need to be developed — for example, installing metal detectors or stationing security guards in a more visible position.
- *Reduce the severity of risks that do eventuate* — a major part of safety planning is preparing quick and efficient responses to foreseeable problems. Training staff in elementary first aid can reduce the severity of an accident. The event manager cannot eliminate natural disasters but can prepare a plan to contain the effects.
- *Devise back-ups and alternatives* — when something goes wrong, the situation can be saved by having an alternative plan in place. In case the juggler does not turn up to a children's party, for example, the host can organise party games to entertain the children. On a larger scale, back-up generators are a must at big outdoor events in case of a major power failure.
- *Distribute the risk* — if the risk can be spread across different areas, its impact will be reduced if something does go wrong. One such strategy is to widely spread the cash-taking areas, such as ticket booths, so that any theft is contained and does not threaten the complete event income. This does not eliminate the risk, it transfers it to an area that can be managed by the event company — such as security and supervision. Having a variety of sponsors is another way to distribute risk. If one sponsor pulls out, the others can be approached to increase their involvement.
- *Transfer the risk* — risk can be transferred to other groups responsible for an event's components. Subcontractors may be required to share the liability of an event. Their contracts generally contain a clause to the effect that they are responsible for the safety of their equipment and the actions of their staff during the event. In Australia, most performing groups are required to have public liability insurance before they can take part in an event.

■ Mitigating *actions*

The following examples of mitigating actions are based on recommendations of the USA Emergency Management Institute.

At every event, people will leave some items unattended. Event officials must decide beforehand how to handle unattended packages and have a written plan for all personnel to follow. The issues to consider include: Who will respond? Are dogs trained to identify explosives available? Will the area be evacuated?

Concealment areas are areas where persons may hide or where someone may hide packages or other weapons. The best way to avoid problems in these areas is to map the event venue and identify the areas that could be used as hiding spots. Venue staff can assist in this matter.

Venue and security personnel should work together to conduct a security sweep of the venue. A few areas to address in advance are: How often is security going to go through the event site? What are they looking for? How do they handle incidents? Who is going to do the sweep? Once a sweep of the area has been done the area must be secured.

Each of these mitigating actions, in addition to Berlonghi's strategies, can be reduced to the management of two risk dimensions: likelihood and consequence. A back-up generator is an example of reducing the *consequence* of a blackout. Checking the capacity of the electricity supply is an example of reducing the *likelihood* of a power failure.

Risk communication

Effective risk communication includes the following:

- *Understanding the terminology of risk* — the risk needs to be accurately described and understood by all the event staff and volunteers.
- *Open communication channels* — it is a well-known problem at events that staff are hesitant to tell event management that a task has not been completed. If they identify problems there must be a way that this can be communicated to the event management in a timely manner. The State Emergency Service use a system of team leaders. Part of the leaders' roles is to collect this data.
- *Informal methods of communication* — management theorists, such as Peter Drucker (1973), stress how important these informal methods are to the success of a company. This is true for events. The dinners, chats over coffee or just a friendly talk can greatly assist the communication process. Walking the site is a time-honoured way to find out what is going on.

The formal process of communicating risk includes the distribution of the risk plan. It is the output or deliverable of the risk management process. The plan contains a list of identified risks, their assessment, the plan of action, who is responsible and the timeline for implementation. In the fluid event management environment, a fixed plan may be quickly out of date. A risk management plan of a parade, for example, will have to be revised if there are any additions to the parade, such as horses. For this reason, it is recommended by most project management texts that a live risk register be established. The risk register is a plan that is constantly updated and revised. As new risks are identified they are added to the register. The register has a number of functions:

1. It is a live management tool.
2. It can be used to track risks so they are not forgotten.
3. It is proof of actions for a work-in-progress report.
4. It can be used after the event to help prove competent management.
5. It can be used for the next event to assist risk identification and planning.
6. It can have various levels of access to allow staff and senior management a role in risk management.
7. It can communicate the main issues, simply and clearly.

A live risk register can be put on the intranet or Internet, and is therefore accessible to all members of the event team. At any time, it can be printed off and placed in a report to the various stakeholders. The risk register thus provides a snapshot for the event management process.

■ Specific *event risks*

Many of the risks that are specific to the event industry happen at the event itself. Issues with crowd movement are an obvious area of risk. The consequences of a crowd-related incident can lead to duty of care and criminal liability issues, so they are a high priority in the event manager's mind. However, the risks at the event may be a result of ignoring the risks before the event. For this reason, the risk management must be tracked across all areas of event management. Many of the risks at the event can be tracked back to a lack of time in management. The lack of time is, in reality, an inability to scope the event management. The conclusion is that a systematic method must be used. Due to the temporary nature of events, there are numerous risks. Using volunteers at events, for example, can result in many kinds of risks. Some of the risks listed at a recent workshop relating to volunteers include: don't listen, don't turn up, complain and form subgroups that 'white ant', can't control, no accountability and deplete the asset. The latter refers to a problem with repeat events, when the volunteers are set in their ways and the event needs to change. The discussion is not exhaustive. It highlights some of the areas specific to events.

Crowd management

The two terms often confused are crowd control and crowd management. As Abbot (2000, p. 105) points out:

> ■ Crowd management and crowd control are two distinct but interrelated concepts. The former includes the facilitation, employment and movement of crowds, while the latter relates to the steps taken once the crowd has lost control. ■

The concept of crowd management is an example of pre-empting problems at the event by preparing the risk management before the event. Many crowd control issues arise from inadequate risk management by the event company. However, there can still be unforeseen risks with crowds.

There are many factors that impinge on the smooth management of crowds at an event. The first risk is correctly estimating the number of people who will attend the event. No matter how the site is designed, too many attendees can put enormous strain on the event resources. Even at free events, too few attendees can significantly affect the event objectives. The launch of the Paralympic mascots in the Sydney Domain attracted an audience of only 500 when the site was designed for thousands. It gave a spacious look to the event site. Crowd risk management is also a function of the audience type and the audience's standard of behaviour. A family event will have different priorities in risk management compared with a rock festival. The expectations of the crowd can be managed with the right kind of information sent out before the event. Crowd management for large events has become a specialist field of study, and there are a number of consultancies in this area. The crowd control issues are amply illustrated by the incidents at the large outdoor events such as the Big Day Out and the Haj. An excellent resource on the study of crowds is found at www.crowdsafe.com.

Alcohol and drugs

Events can range from a family picnic with the audience sipping wine while watching a show to a New Year's Eve mass gathering of youths and the heavy consumption of alcohol. Under the law, both events are treated the same. The Responsible Service of Alcohol provision in many countries is a method of reducing the likelihood of this risk. Some annual events have been cancelled due to the behaviour problems that arise from selling alcohol. The alcohol risk management procedures can permeate every aspect of some events, including limiting ticket sales, closing hotels early, increasing security and roping off areas.

For the New Year's Eve celebrations at Darling Harbour, the management also identified the major risks resulting from broken glass. In the past, the site needed a large and expensive clean-up after the event, and the safety issue was paramount. After consultation with all the stakeholders, their risk management procedure included:

• erecting a perimeter fence around the site
• allowing alcohol only in licensed premises
• having an alcohol-free and glass-free policy for all public areas
• rearranging the entertainment to appeal to families and senior citizens
• publicising the new policy in all advertisements.

A worthy mention is the risk of drugs at events. Many modern events, in particular rave parties, involve risks arising from the drug use. Emergency and first aid services are faced with the quandary of treating the problem and reporting the incident to police. Some rave or dance parties are secret — which is part of the allure — and first-aid services have to decide whether to inform the police of these parties and, therefore, risk the possibility of not being contracted again by the organisers. Another risk related to drug use is the presence of syringes and their safe handling by staff.

Communication

The risks involved in communication are varied as it concerns the event organisation and reporting any risks. Setting up a computer and filing system for the event office can prevent future problems. Easy access to relevant information is vital to good risk management. A standard, yet customised, reporting procedure can also reduce the risk of ineffective communication. Communication can include: how the public is informed of the event, signage and keeping the attendees informed when they are at the event site. The event manual is an excellent communication device for the procedures, protocol and general event information for staff and volunteers. There can be a risk of too much data obscuring the important information; therefore, it needs to be highly focused.

Environment

The risk to the environment posed by modern businesses is of increasing concern to the general community. There are dangerous risks such as pollution, spills and effluent leakage and the more indirect risks minimised by waste recycling, water and energy conservation. The impacts and therefore the priorities for their control will vary over the event project life cycle.

Emergency

An awareness of the nearest emergency services and their working requirements is mandatory for the event management. The reason for using outside emergency services is that the situation is beyond the capabilities of the event staff and needs specialist attention. It is important to understand the chain of command when emergency services arrive. They can be outside the control of the event management staff, who would act purely in an advisory capacity. They may be called in by any attendee at an event.

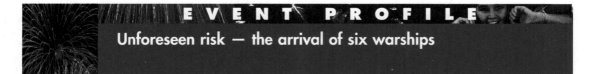

EVENT PROFILE

Unforeseen risk — the arrival of six warships

One of the more unusual events in the world was the exchange of East Timor from United Nations control to a newly elected government and the celebrations of independence that accompanied this event. It marked the formation of a new country. It occurred on 20 May 2002 and involved representatives of more than 80 countries. The major stakeholders were the people of East Timor, the United Nations and the United Nations Peace Keeping Forces, international media, neighbouring countries (including Indonesia and Australia and their militaries), the Independence forces and the anti-independence forces in East Timor, representatives from the USA, the Catholic Church, and the new East Timor government.

The risk management for such an event with a short timeframe, high uncertainty and sudden changes had to be performed through multiple meetings and leadership decisions. As there had been an insurgency war between the independence movement and the Indonesian military, it was a surprise when the President of Indonesia, Megawati Sukarnoputri, agreed to attend the celebrations. The Indonesian military wanted to ensure their president had adequate security. Three days before the celebrations the military sent six warships into the area. The warships were visible from the island and, for some East Timorese people, were an ominous reminder of the protracted war. This was a major unforeseen risk. First, the president would be present and, second, the Indonesian military would want to be involved in this celebration of independence from their rule.

According to a report at the time, Jose Ramos Horta (the East Timorese Foreign Minister) said the conclusion from several separate security surveys — conducted by the United Nations, as well as the British, American and Australian intelligence services — was that the risk to visiting delegations during the independence celebrations was 'extremely low'. As a result, he said, 'We did not feel that an advance team comprising six warships was needed to provide security to a head of state'.

Fortunately, a combination of United Nations and East Timor assurances and an agreement to reduce the Indonesian military presence to armoured vehicles and helicopters saved the situation. The last warship left Dili harbour 24 hours before the event. The president's visit went well and the new nation was launched.

■ Review

Evaluating the successes and failures of the risk control strategy is central to the planning of future events. The event company must be a 'learning organisation'. The analysis of, and response to, feedback is essential to this process.

*L*EGAL ISSUES

Underpinning all aspects of an event are the legal issues. The actual laws relating to events and their management are different for each state and country. As events grow in number and importance to the economy, there will be more laws relating to them. There are some common principles. This chapter now introduces the concepts of event ownership and the crucial duty of care of the event management. The contract is the documentation of the relationship between the event and the various stakeholders. It is important, therefore, that event and festival management be familiar with the key terms used in the contract.

A key question in event administration is 'Who owns the event?'. The legal owner of an event could be the event coordinator, the committee, a separate legal entity or the sponsors. It is important to recognise that the ownership of the event entails legal responsibility and, therefore, liability. The members of an organising committee can be personally held responsible for the event. This is often expressed as 'jointly and severally liable'. The structure of the event administration must reflect this, and the status of various personnel, such as the event coordinator, the subcontractors and other stakeholders, must be clearly established at the outset. Likewise, sponsorship agreements will often have a clause as to the sponsor's liability and, therefore, the extent of their ownership of the event. All such issues need to be carefully addressed by the initial agreements and contracts.

The organising committee for a nonprofit event can become a legal entity by forming an incorporated association. Such an association can enter into contracts and own property. The act of incorporating, under the relevant association incorporation Act in each state, means that the members have limited liability when the association incurs debts. It does not grant them complete exemption from all liability such as negligence. By law, an association must have a constitution or a list of rules. Such documents state the procedures and powers of the association, including auditing and accounting matters, the powers of the governing body and winding-up procedures. In many cases, community and local festival events do not form a separate incorporated association as they are able to function under the legal umbrella of another body, such as a local council. This gives the event organising committee considerable legal protection as well as access to administrative support. For a one-off event, this administrative support can save time and resources, because the administrative infrastructure, such as a fax machine, phone lines, secretarial help and legal and accounting advice, is already established.

Establishing an appropriate legal structure for an event management company is an exercise in liability minimisation. Several structures are possible for an event company, which could operate as a sole trader, partnership or a company limited by liability. Each of these legal structures has different liability implications. Legal advice may be required to determine the most appropriate structure for a particular circumstance.

CONTRACTS

A contract is an agreement between two or more parties that sets out their obligations and is enforceable by law. It describes the exchange to be made between the parties. A contract can be a written or an oral agreement. In the world of event management, an oral contract is of little use if problems occur in the future; therefore, it is appropriate to put all contractual agreements in writing. This may frequently take the form of a simple letter of agreement, not more than a page in length (figure 11.1). However, when large amounts of money and important responsibilities are involved, a formal contract is necessary.

As Goldblatt (1997) explains, a typical event industry contract will contain:
- the names of the contracting parties, their details and their trading names
- details of the service or product that is offered (for example, equipment, entertainment, use of land and expert advice)
- the terms of exchange for such service or product
- the signature of both parties indicating understanding of the terms of exchange and agreement to the conditions of the contract.

■ **Figure 11.1**
An example of a letter of agreement

Festival copy (sign and return)

Date:
To:

PERFORMER AGREEMENT

This agreement is between the Folk Federation of South Australia Inc (hereafter referred to as the Festival) and _____ (hereafter referred to as the Performer).

The Festival and Performer(s) agree that:

1. **Performances:** The Festival engages the Performer(s) for the following days and times to perform at the 1998 Victor Harbor Folk Festival):
   (See Timetable attached)

   and the Performer(s) accept the said engagement.

2. **Payment:** Provided that the Performer(s) fulfil the obligations set out in the agreement, the Festival shall pay the Performer(s) an agreed fee of
   $ _____ .

3. **Time of payment:** Payment will be made *by cheque* within 10 days of the Festival (unless otherwise arranged).
   Cheque to be made out to: _____ name of person/company

4. **Other commitments:** to the Performer(s) include the following: *(n/a denotes not applicable)*
   Number of passes to performers: _____
   Travel: _____
   Transit: _____
   Accommodation: _____

5. **Travel arrangements** made by the Festival are final and the cost of any changes not agreed to during the negotiations of this contract shall be borne by the Performer(s).

   (continued)

6. **Outside performances:** The Performer(s) shall inform the Festival of any other engagements taken during the period 2–5 October within 50 km of the Victor Harbour Folk Festival.

7. **Cancellation:** If any performances by the Performer(s) are cancelled or prevented for any reason, including but not limited to, public calamity, strike, lockout, Act of God or due to reasons beyond the control of the Festival, the Festival shall not be liable to the Performer(s) for fees, costs, expenses or damages of any kind.

8. **Publicity:** The Performer(s) agree to allow *short* takes of their performances to be photographed, recorded or video taped by the Festival or by Festival approved media to assist in promotion of the Festival and Performer(s) may obtain copies of such recordings or photography at their own expense. The Performer(s) shall provide the Festival as requested with the necessary materials required to adequately promote the Festival and the Performer. This may take the shape of recordings, photographs, biography and appearances or media interviews subject to availability of such materials.

9. **Deductions:** The Festival shall have the right to deduct or withhold from the Performer(s) any amounts required to be deducted by law. The Festival does not take responsibility for the payment of any taxes and any amounts payable under superannuation guarantee legislation relating to the artists' income from this engagement.

10. **Merchandise:** The artist agrees that any merchandise items offered for sale by the artist at the Festival shall be sold solely through the Festival shop operated on behalf of the Festival. The artist further agrees that a 15 per cent commission will be deducted from the reconciled gross sales.

11. **All notices:** regarding this agreement shall be in writing and served by mail, email, telegram, or facsimile addressed to the parties at their respective addresses.

12. **In the event of a dispute:** this agreement shall be governed by and construed in accordance with the laws of the province of South Australia.

13. **Alterations:** This agreement may not be changed without consent of both parties; however, the Festival shall have the power to make changes to Performer(s) program times under special circumstances.

Please sign **BOTH** copies of this agreement and **RETURN ONE** to the Festival office.
* A signed copy of this contract is required for issue of cheque to the Performer(s).

Signed for the Festival   _____ 1998

Signed for the Performer(s)   _____ 1998

To make this mutual obligation perfectly clear to all parties, the contract would set out all key elements. These would consist of: financial terms (including a payment schedule), a cancellation clause, delivery time, the rights and obligations of each party and an exact description of the goods and services being exchanged.

Event management companies may need a wide range of contracts to facilitate their operation. Some of these are shown in figure 11.2.

■ **Figure 11.2**
Contracts required by an event management company

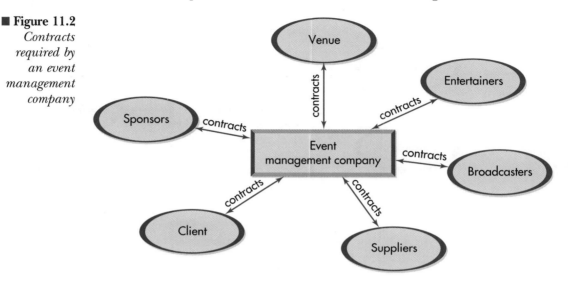

An event of medium size would require a set of formal contracts covering:

- the event company or coordinator and the client
- the entertainers
- the venue
- the suppliers (for example, security, audiovisual and caterers)
- the sponsor(s).

For smaller events, these details may be arranged by letters of agreement.

■ Contract *management*

It is surprising that so little is written on event contracts. Like other projects, contracts are the bedrock of the management. Originally, project management was called contract management. The process of managing the contracts is illustrated in figure 11.3 (page 362). A common mistake by inexperienced event management companies is to assume that once the contract is set up it does not require reviewing. Event contracts need to be reviewed. Changing conditions, a common feature of event management, can lead to many contract problems. In some areas of an event, particularly large sporting events, contracts are frequently renegotiated. They can be described as 'an agreement frozen in time'. For this reason they provide a certainty in management.

Different contracts have different 'styles' and the event manager must be familiar with them. Some of these contracts are discussed in the following text.

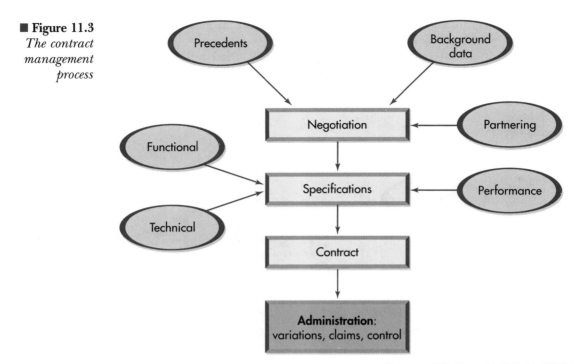

(**Source:** *O'Toole and Mikolaitis 2002.*)

■ Entertainment

A common feature of entertainment contracts is the 'rider'. This is an attachment to the contract, usually on a separate piece of paper. Hiring a headline performer may necessitate signing a 20- to 30-page contract. The contract often contains a clause requiring the event company to provide the goods and services contained in the rider, as well as the performance fee. The rider can list such things as food, extra accommodation, transport and set-up assistance. The event company ignores this at its peril. The rider can be used by the entertainer's agent as a way of increasing the fee in real terms, which can have serious consequences for the budget of an event. A university student union that employs a well-known rock group at a minimal fee for a charity function, for example, would find its objectives greatly damaged by a rider stipulating the reimbursement of food, accommodation and transport costs for 30 people.

Another important clause in any entertainment contract is exclusivity. A headline act, for example, may be the major attraction for an event. If the act is also performing nearby this could easily detract from the uniqueness of the event. A clause to prevent this is inserted into the contract. It indicates that the performer cannot perform within a specified geographic area during the event or for a certain number of days prior to and after the event. The intricacies of entertainment contracts led many texts to suggest that event managers obtain legal advice about contracts when planning a celebrity concert.

The contract must contain a clause that stipulates that the signatories have the right to sign on behalf of the contracting parties. An entertainment group may be represented by a number of agents. The agents therefore must have written proof that they exclusively represent the group for the event.

■ Venue

The venue contract will have specialist clauses, including indemnifying the venue against damages, personnel requirements and the provision of security staff. The contract can also contain these elements:

- *security deposit*: an amount, generally a percentage of the hiring fee, to be used for any additional work such as cleaning and repairs that result from the event
- *cancellation*: outlining the penalty for cancellation of the event and whether the hirer will receive a refund if the venue is re-hired at that time
- *access*: including the timing of the opening and closing of the doors, and actual use of the entrance ways
- *late conclusion*: the penalty for the event going over time
- *house seats*: the free tickets reserved for venue management
- *additions or alterations*: possible changes to the internal structures of the venue
- *signage*: the signs of any sponsors and other advertising. (Venue management approval may be required for all promotional material.)

When hiring a venue, it is important to ascertain exactly what is included in the fee. Just because there were chairs and tables in the photograph of the venue, for example, does not mean that they are included in the hiring cost.

■ Sponsor

The contract with the sponsor would cover issues relating to quality representation of the sponsor such as trademarks and signage, exclusivity and the right of refusal for further sponsorship. It may specify that the sponsor's logo be included on all promotional material, or that the sponsor has the right to monitor the quality of the promotional material. Geldard and Sinclair (1996) advise that the level of sponsor exclusivity during an event will need to be reflected in the contract between the event committee and the sponsor. Possible sponsor levels are: sole sponsor, principal sponsor, major or minor sponsor and supplier. The contract would also describe hospitality rights, such as the number of complimentary tickets supplied to the sponsor.

■ Broadcast

Broadcast contracts can be very complex due to the large amounts of money involved in broadcasting and the production of related merchandise, such as videos and sound recordings. The important clauses in a broadcast contract address the following key components:

- *Territory or region* — the broadcast area (local, state or international) must be defined. If the attached schedule shows the region as 'world', the event company must be fully aware of the rights it is bestowing on the broadcaster and their value.

- *Guarantees* — the most important is the one stating that the event company has the rights to sign for the whole event. Some local councils, for example, require that an extra fee be paid for broadcasting from their area. Also, performers' copyright can preclude any broadcast without written permission from their record and publishing companies. Comedy acts and motivational speakers are particularly sensitive about broadcasts and recordings.

- *Sponsorship* — this area can present problems when different levels of sponsorship are involved. Sometimes the rights of the event sponsor and the broadcaster's sponsors can clash.

- *Repeats, extracts and sublicences* — these determine the allowable number of broadcast repeats, whether the broadcaster is authorised to edit or take extracts from the broadcast and how such material can be used. The event company may sign with one broadcaster, only to find that the rights to cover the event have been sold on for a much larger figure to another broadcaster. In addition, a sub-licence clause may annul many of the other clauses in the contract. The sub-licensor may be able to use its own sponsors, which is problematic if they are in direct competition with the event sponsors.

- *Merchandising* — the contract may contain a clause that mentions the rights to own products originating from the broadcast. The ownership and sale of such recordings can be a major revenue source for an event. A clause recently introduced in these sorts of contracts concerns future delivery systems. Multimedia uses, such as CD-ROMs, cable television and the Internet, are all relatively recent and new communications technologies continue to be developed. It is easy to sign away the future rights of an event when the contract contains terms that are unknown to the event company. It is wise to seek out specialist legal advice.

- *Access* — the physical access requirements of broadcasting must be part of the staging and logistic plan of the event. A broadcaster can easily disrupt an event by demanding to interview performers and celebrities. It is important to specify how much access the broadcaster can have to the stars.

- *Credits* — this establishes, at the outset, the people and elements that will be listed in the titles and credits.

The broadcaster can offer all kinds of assistance to the event company. It has an interest in making the event presentable for television and will often help decorate the site. The level of assistance will depend on its stake in the event.

CONSTRUCTING A CONTRACT

The process of constructing a contract is shown in figure 11.4, and comprises five main steps: intention, negotiation, initial acceptance, agreement on terms and signing. This process can be facilitated if the event management has standard contracts, where the name of the supplier and any special conditions can be inserted. This saves the event company going through unfamiliar contracts from sponsors, suppliers and entertainers, which can be very time consuming.

■ Figure 11.4
The process of constructing a contract

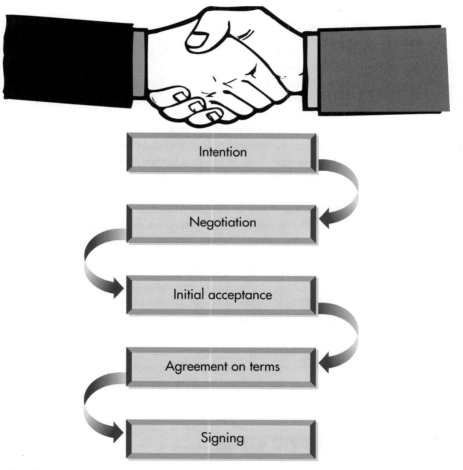

- Intention
- Negotiation
- Initial acceptance
- Agreement on terms
- Signing

For large events and more complex contracts a 'heads of agreement' is sent after the negotiations are completed. This is a summary of any important specific points, listing the precise service or product that is being provided. The contract can be renegotiated or terminated with the agreement of all parties. The final contract should contain a clause that allows both parties to go to arbitration in the event of a disagreement.

TRADEMARKS AND LOGOS

Another kind of ownership issue for event management is the ownership of trademarks and logos. Recently, a federal court order was granted to the Sydney Organising Committee for the Olympic Games preventing another party from using an image that was deemed too similar to their own logo. This illustrates the importance of event symbol ownership.

The event company must also be aware of the risks of misrepresenting its event. There is a danger, when promoting an event, of exaggerating its benefits. Descriptions of the product must always be accurate, as disgruntled consumers may take legal action to gain punitive damages when they feel that advertising for an event has made false claims. The Trade Practices Act can be used to argue such cases:

■ Part V of the *Trade Practices Act 1974* (Cwlth) prohibits 'unfair practices' within the marketplace and has, in certain instances, been effectively used to protect those involved in events marketing.

The sections most often relied on are section 52, which prohibits 'misleading or deceptive' conduct, and sections 53(c) and (d) which concern representations made by a corporation that it has, or its goods and services have, sponsorship approval or affiliation that it in fact does not have.

These sections are of obvious benefit to individuals and associations alike as they provide the means by which effective action can be taken against those who wish to associate themselves with an event when they have no right to do so.

Section 52 states 'a corporation shall not, in trade or commerce, engage in conduct that is misleading or deceptive or is likely to mislead or deceive.' Section 52 has often been used to restrain the unauthorised use of 'personalities' in advertising and marketing strategies. An instance where section 52 was used to protect the rights of a sporting personality in an advertising and market campaign was in the case of World Series Cricket Pty Ltd v Parish (1977) 17 ALR 181. A claim was made alleging a breach of section 52 of the Trade Practices Act in relation to the holding of an event. In this case, it was the first year that World Series Cricket was to be held. The Australian Cricket Board commenced proceedings because the Board claimed that the public would be misled through the various advertisements in believing that the particular event has been endorsed by the Board. The claim was upheld (Fewell 1995). ■

DUTY OF CARE

A fundamental legal principle is taking all reasonable care to avoid acts or omissions that could injure a 'neighbour'. This is called duty of care and is covered by an area of law known as torts. A tort is a breach of duty owed to other people and imposed by law and, in this, it differs from the duties arising from contracts, which are agreed between contracting parties. Unlike criminal law, which is concerned with deterrence and punishment, the law of torts is concerned with compensation. An outline of the duty of care from the National Occupational Health and Safety Commission is described in figure 11.5.

For event management, duty of care means taking actions that will prevent any foreseeable risk of injury to the people who are directly affected by, or involved in, the event. This would include event staff, volunteers, performers, the audience or spectators and the public in the surrounding areas.

Duty of care requires everything 'reasonably practicable' to be done to protect the health and safety of others at the workplace. This duty is placed on:
■ all employers
■ their employees
■ any others who have an influence on the hazards in a workplace.

The latter includes contractors and those who design, manufacture, import, supply or install plant, equipment or materials used in the workplace.

'Reasonably practicable' means that the requirements of the law vary with the degree of risk in a particular activity or environment which must be balanced against the time, trouble and cost of taking measures to control the risk. It allows the duty holder to choose the most efficient means for controlling a particular risk from the range of feasible possibilities preferably in accordance with the 'hierarchy of control'.

This qualification allows those responsible to meet their duty of care at the lowest cost. It also requires changes in technology and knowledge to be incorporated but only as and when it is efficient to do so. The duty holder must show that it was not reasonably practicable to do more than what was done or that they have taken 'reasonable precautions and exercised due diligence'.

(**Source:** *National Occupational Health and Safety Commission 1995.*)

In late 2002, an event manager was successfully prosecuted under s.145 of the Crimes Act (Criminal Nuisance) in New Zealand in relation to a tragic death at the 100-kilometre cycle event in the Christchurch region. The Act states:

■ Everyone commits criminal nuisance who does any unlawful act or omits to discharge any legal duty, such act or omission being one which he or she knew would endanger the lives, safety or health of the public, or the life, safety or health of an individual. ■

*I*NSURANCE

Central to any strategy of liability minimisation is obtaining the correct insurance. The Community Festival Handbook (1991) contains helpful suggestions regarding insurance. These include the following:
• Allow enough time to investigate and arrange the correct insurance. This may include asking for quotes and professional advice. Finding the right insurance broker is the first priority.
• Make sure the event committee or company is fully covered for the whole time — that is, from the first meeting.

- Request all suppliers of products and services show they have liability cover.
- Be prepared to give the insurance broker all information concerning the event and the companies involved. They may require a list of possible hazards, such as pyrotechnics.
- Be prepared to record the details of any damage or injury. Photographs and videos are helpful.
- Keep all records, as a claimant has six years to formulate a claim.
- Do not accept the transfer of liability of the suppliers to the event management.
- Check what is included and excluded in the insurance document. Rain insurance, for example, is specific about the amount and time of the rain. Are the event volunteers covered by the insurance?
- Are there any additional stakeholders insured? These are companies or individuals that are covered by the insurance but are not the named insured. The sponsors and the venue, for example, may benefit from the insurance policy.

There are many kinds of event insurance. These include weather insurance; personal accident insurance for the volunteer workers; property insurance, including money; workers' compensation insurance; public liability; directors' and officers' liability. The choice of the particular insurance cover is dictated by the risk management strategy developed by event management.

The phenomenal increase in premiums in all insurance areas has been a shock to the industry. Some events have been cancelled. A number of strategies have been implemented to manage this situation:

- *Bulk buying* — a number of events and event companies have pooled their insurance premiums and approached the insurance brokers with a large pool of funds.
- *Analysing the activities of the event into levels of risk* — the high premium may be the result of one aspect of the event. By changing or eliminating this from the event program it may reduce the event risk seen by the insurance company.
- *Creating a comprehensive risk management procedure* — many events that previously ignored risk management have turned to the formal risk management process. This is one positive outcome of the insurance issue. The risk management plan becomes a document used to communicate with the insurance company. Given the experience of insurance companies, it is wise to seek their input on this document.
- *Capping liability* — some state governments have enacted levels of payouts for damages sustained at an event. This allows the insurance company to predict their payments and, therefore, assess the premiums.
- *Holding harmless clauses or forfeiting the right to sue* — the attendee signs a contract to the effect that they are voluntarily assuming the risk inherent in the event activity. This requires legal advice as there has not been a test case at the time of writing.
- *Insuring offshore* — some events have gone overseas for insurance. This may be a difficulty as the insurance company will be subject to the law of their country, not Australian law.

REGULATIONS, LICENCES AND PERMITS

There are long lists of regulations that need to be satisfied when staging a simple event. The bigger and more innovative the event, the larger the number of regulations. The correct procedure in one state may be completely different in another. The principal rule is to carry out careful research, including investigating similar events in the same area and seeking advice on what permits and licences are necessary to allow an event to proceed.

It is always the responsibility of an event company to find out and comply with all pertinent rules and regulations. A street parade through Sydney, for example, can come under a wide range of government authorities. The Paddington Festival Parade along Oxford Street required a series of long meetings with the two local councils, police and traffic authorities. The event itself was over in two hours. In Victoria, a special licence is required to erect tents over a certain size. This includes tents that are used for only one night. Local noise regulations can change within the same city within the jurisdiction of different councils. Not only that, but event management must pay particular attention to workplace health and safety regulations.

Figure 11.6 describes some of the permits, licences, insurances and regulations with which a community festival taking place on the south coast of Victoria must comply. An event manager may need to seek legal advice to ensure all relevant regulations are taken into account.

■ **Figure 11.6**

Legal requirements for the Port Fairy Folk Festival

Insurance
(a) Public liability insurance of $10 000 000; excess $500; property damage claims only
(b) Personal accident insurance covering 700 volunteers:
   ■ $800 — weekly benefits
   ■ $60 000 — death benefits
   The policy also covers the committee, charitable and school organisations that provide the food stalls.
(c) Occasionally, special insurance is taken out to cover tents with specific risks — for example, the Circus Oz tent.
(d) Car parks are covered against damage to vehicles.
(e) Insurance against theft, fire and other damage to the equipment owned by the festival committee. Equipment includes storage sheds, staging, electrical equipment, tables and chairs.

Legislation to be aware of
1. Liquor licensing for alcohol
2. Health — food vans, smoking and toilets
3. Victorian building regulations — tent construction and people in the arena. Tent construction workers must be licensed.
4. Country Fire Authority — fire reels, hoses and extinguishers

(continued)

5. Licences governing security personnel
6. Police Act — vehicle access along streets, crowd control
7. (a) Local Government Act — leasing of municipal property
   (b) By-laws of the Moyne Shire Council — drinking alcohol in the streets, fence erection, signage, street closure, planning permits and craft stall permits
8. Banking Act — control of finances
9. Insurance legislation
10. Residential tenancies and caravan parks legislation — accommodation of performers, ticket holders and guests
11. Associations Incorporation Act, governing the organising committee
12. General contract law — agreements with performers, printing and agreement with the Australasian Performing Rights Association (APRA)
13. Environmental Protection Authority (EPA) — noise levels

(**Source:** *Bruce Leishman, of Tait Leishman Taylor Lawyers.*)

Permits and licences allow special activities during an event such as the handling of food, pyrotechnics, the sale of liquor and road closures. They can even cover the performances. The Australasian Performing Rights Association (APRA) issues licences for the performance of its members' works. APRA functions as a collection society, monitoring and collecting royalties on behalf of its members (music composers and their publishers). So when an event company decides to set fireworks to music, it is not just a matter of hiring a band.

Many regulations, permits and licences change with each local government area and state and new regulations and reinterpretations of the old rules are proclaimed regularly. The National Occupational Health and Safety Commission constantly reviews and publishes its codes. In 2002, it released a 10-year plan to improve the occupational health and safety compliance nationwide. Also, workers compensation regulations are different in each state. The Public Halls Act is administered by local councils, and often its interpretation will vary from council to council. Local councils are also responsible for issuing entertainment licences and open air permits for events. Even event accounting may need permits, and an event company must register a business name before opening a bank account.

This complex area needs the close attention of event management. Companies must undertake detailed research into all regulations affecting their event and should allocate time to deal with the results of that research. Government agencies can take a long time to respond to requests. It is imperative, therefore, to begin seeking any permits and licences early and to factor delays and difficulties with obtaining them into the timeframe of the event planning process.

 **UMMARY** ••

Risk management is a modern, formal process of identifying and managing risk. It is one of the functions of any event management and the process should be part of the event's everyday organisation. There are risks that are specific to events, and to particular events. To correctly identify these risks, knowledge of the unique risks is essential. The risk is more than risks at the event itself. The output of this process is a live risk register that shows the risks and their management schedule. As part of this risk strategy, the management has to understand their legal requirements. They have a duty of care to all involved in an event. Any reasonably foreseen risks have to be eliminated or minimised. Liability minimisation is part of this strategy. This includes: identifying the ownership of the event, careful structuring of the event management, taking out insurance and adhering to all rules and regulations pertaining to the event. Specific legal issues of concern to the event management team include contracting, trademarks and trade practices. Legal matters can be complex and can differ from state to state. It is recommended that any event company seeks legal advice when unsure of these matters.

Questions

1 List the risks to a regional festival arising from these areas:
   (a) local organising committee
   (b) sponsorship
   (c) volunteers
   (d) council politics
   (e) participants in the parade
   (f) computers
   (g) experience of organising group.

2 List the areas covered by the contract between the event company and supplier of audiovisuals.

3 In the example of East Timor handover celebrations, what other risks can you identify? How can you prepare for unforeseen risks?

4 Event management has been described as 'just solving problems'. Can risk management replace all the other methods of management, such as marketing, logistics and project management, to create an event?

5 Contrast the risks involved in staging an outdoor concert and those involved in producing an indoor food fair. What risk management strategy could be used to reduce or eliminate these risks?

6 What actions can be taken to reduce the cost of overall liability insurance? Should the event company be insured for patrons to be covered after they leave the event?

7 Investigate what licences and permits are needed for a street party.

Federation Day 2001

Federation Day, 1 January 2001, marked the centenary of the inauguration of the Commonwealth of Australia, when six colonies came together as a nation. The major Federation Day events — Journey of a Nation (The Federation Parade) and The Centennial Ceremony, both staged in Sydney, launched a year-long program of Centenary of Federation celebrations across Australia.

The Federation Parade was unlike any event ever seen in Australia. It represented a journey through a series of themes relevant to Australia, celebrating and acknowledging the nation's significant and momentous achievements and challenges over 100 years. A fly-past of historic aircraft preceded the parade, which featured giant floats, horses, and 6500 participants representing every state and territory, regional communities, performing artists, marching bands, volunteer organisations, sporting bodies, young people, Indigenous peoples, ethnic groups, charities, churches and community organisations. The parade was watched by a crowd of more than 500 000, and another one million are estimated to have watched the live television broadcast.

The Centennial Ceremony combined spectacular pageantry and Australia's eminent performing artists with official addresses from the nation's leaders in a unique and moving commemoration of nationhood. The ceremony involved more than 400 performers and was attended by more than 85 000 spectators. The event was also broadcast live to a national television audience in excess of one million people.

The NSW Centenary of Federation Committee developed a comprehensive risk management strategy for Federation Day events which was integrated into every aspect of the event planning, from administration to marketing, as well as on the day of the events. The NSW Centenary of Federation team grew rapidly in the lead up to Federation Day, at its peak exceeding 400 staff.

The unique circumstances of Federation Day increased the degree of risk involved in staging the events. Some factors included:

- anticipated large audiences (in excess of 600 000)
- unique elements of the events — for example, parade floats, staging design and untried locations
- complex technology
- large numbers of volunteers with limited experience
- significant VIP involvement
- national media broadcasts and high levels of media interest in events
- the large number of partnership and stakeholder agencies involved — for example, NSW Police, the Roads and Traffic Authority, the City of Sydney, community organisations and sponsors.

The risk management process was practical and simple, aimed at involving all staff in the identification, evaluation and minimisation of risks. Staff were already doing a form of risk management in their planning of high quality events; however, there was no consistent risk management process across the organisation, and no risk management documentation.

The first step for the NSW Centenary of Federation Committee was to develop a risk management plan and a number of supporting documents to assist in implementing the process. The first risk identified was that the busy staff needed to take time out to learn about the formal risk management process. The committee decided the best way to do this was to devote a day to a workshop and hire an outside facilitator. The workshop, held in August 2000, was based on the Australian New Zealand Standard on Risk Management (AS/NZ 4360). After the rationale for risk management was outlined, a step-by-step process for identifying, evaluating and controlling risks associated with major events was presented.

Participants then formed small groups with representatives from various areas of the organisation (ensuring their experience was pooled) to identify potential risks across a range of areas (both internal and external), including event content, operations, sponsorship, marketing, public relations, finance and administration. The 'fault tree' approach was used, whereby a possible 'bad outcome' was given and groups worked back to suggest possible causes. Each group then gave a report on their findings. In subsequent meetings, scenarios (for example, overcrowding at the venue) were also used to identify risks and strategies to minimise these.

It became clear that risk identification can come from anyone involved in the event — event manager, volunteer, accountant, sponsor, supplier etc. It was important to make it easy for all members of the organisation to identify and share their information. This process of eliciting information from stakeholders and using a systematic approach to the documentation was the first step in becoming a risk resilient organisation.

The Committee realised that risk management is not just a formal process. It is very human and requires a personal commitment by the staff. The manager of a recent high-profile event, which had ended in disaster, was invited to speak to the staff. The event manager's account of his experience and the lessons he had learned helped to reinforce the importance of following a risk management process and ensuring proper documentation.

Once risks were identified, they were evaluated in order of importance. Each risk was given a priority based on the likelihood of its occurrence and the severity of the consequences. Supporting documents were provided to assist staff in evaluating the level of risk, enabling a comprehensive and realistic analysis of all potential risks. Some of the key risk factors identified included:
• impact of the preceding New Year's Eve events
• information technology, equipment or communications failure
• budget blow-out
• poor internal communication between teams
• poorly informed volunteers and crew
• negative media coverage
• overcrowding or crowd-crush

(continued)

- inadequate or incorrect information in the media
- adverse weather
- parade float breakdown
- damage to venues
- late changes to program
- major traffic or transport delays
- sponsor dissatisfaction.

Strategies for controlling each of the risks were then developed. A Federation Day risk management plan was developed, outlining the events and the identified risks, the key risk factors and concerns, and the strategies for dealing with these. It was necessary to revisit the plan a number of times in the weeks leading up to the events to identify any new risks and/or ensure planned strategies remained appropriate.

The risk management plan was supported by several key documents, including a crisis communications plan, crowd management plan and emergency plan for each event. Booklets were also given to all event staff, including volunteers, on Federation Day to record any incidents or issues that may have occurred.

The risk management process developed by the NSW Centenary of Federation Committee proved very effective in minimising the risks associated with the major Federation Day events. Significantly, the process was integrated into the planning of other Centenary of Federation programs and events and it became a model for other event organisations. When viewed from this perspective, the initiative produced results well beyond the Federation Day events.

Jo Hatton, NSW Centenary of Federation Committee

Questions

1 What were the unique features of this event and how did this contribute to the risk assessment?

2 Draw the risk management process in a step-by-step diagram. Describe how this was applied to the Federation Day event.

3 The case study mentioned the informal processes — describe them and explain why they are important.

REFERENCES

Abbot, J 2000, 'The importance of proper crowd management and crowd control in the special events industry', in *Events beyond 2000: setting the agenda, Proceedings of conference on event evaluation, research and education*, eds J Allen, R Harris, LK Jago & AJ Veal, Australian Centre for Event Management, Sydney.

Berlonghi, A 1990, *Special event risk management manual*, Bookmasters, Mansfield, Ohio.

Drucker, P 1973, *Management*, Harper and Row, New York.

Federal Emergency Management Agency 2000, *Special events contingency planning job aid manual*, Emergency Management Institute, Canberra.

Geldard, E & Sinclair, L 1996, *The sponsorship manual*, The Sponsorship Unit, Olinda, Victoria.

Goldblatt, J 1997, *Special events: best practices in modern event management*, 2nd edn, Van Nostrand Reinhold, New Jersey.

O'Toole, W & Mikolaitis, P 2002, *Corporate event project management*, John Wiley & Sons, New York.

Neighbourhood Arts Unit 1991, *Community festival handbook*, City of Melbourne, Melbourne.

Standards Australia 1999, AS/NZS 4360, Australian New Zealand Risk Management Standard, Canberra.

12
Logistics

LEARNING OBJECTIVES

After studying this chapter, you should be able to:

- define logistics management and describe its evolution
- understand the concept of logistics management and its place in event management
- construct a logistics plan for the supply of customers, event products and event facilities
- use event logistics techniques and tools.

INTRODUCTION

This chapter adapts the science of business and military logistics to events. The management of an event is divided into supply, setting up and running the event on site, and the shutdown process of the event. Communication, flow and supply are the three elements of event logistics treated in this chapter. Various checklists that can assist in the management of event logistics are outlined.

WHAT ARE LOGISTICS?

'One of the hardest tasks, for logisticians and nonlogisticians alike, is to look at a list and spot what's not there' (Pagonis 1992, p. 73). Placing the word 'logistics' into its historical context provides an understanding of its use in present event management. Logistics stems from the Greek word *logistikos*, 'skilled in calculating'. The ancient Romans used the term for the administration of their armies. The term evolved to refer to the practical art of the relocation of armies. Given the complexity of modern warfare, logistics became a science that included speed of operations, communications and maintenance of the armed forces. After World War II, modern businesses applied the experience and theory of logistics as they faced similar problems with transport and supply to those faced by the military.

The efficient movement of products has become a specialised study in the management discipline. Within large companies, especially international companies, a section can be devoted to coordinating the logistics requirements of each department. Logistics have become a discipline in their own right. This has led to consolidation into a separate independent function in companies, often called integrated logistics management. Coyle, Bardi and Langley (1988) describe logistics as the planning, implementing and control of the flow and storage of products, and the related information from production to the point of consumption, according to consumer requirements.

The value of a company's product or services can be improved by the efficient coordination of logistics in the company. Gilmour (1993) argues that logistics in Australia, due to the special conditions and widespread distribution of customers, services and products, takes on an importance not found in many other countries. He emphasises that the logistic practices developed in the USA and Europe are not good enough for Australian conditions, and that Australia, to be competitive in world markets, needs to pay attention to overcoming the disadvantages and challenges of its vast geographic distances.

For a complete understanding of event logistics, this chapter is divided into sections dealing with the tasks of event logistics and the role of the logistics manager.

THE ELEMENTS OF EVENT LOGISTICS

The elements of event logistics can be organised into the logistics system shown in figure 12.1. This system is used to organise the logistic elements of an event.

Whereas most logistics theory concerns the supply of products to customers, event logistics includes the efficient supply of the customer to the product, and the supply of facilities to and from the event site. In this sense, it has more in common with military logistics than modern business logistics. Business logistics are an ongoing activity and part of the continual management of a company. Military and event logistics often concern a specific project or campaign rather than continuing management. There is a defined preparation, lead-up, execution and shutdown. As well, issues such as inventory control and warehousing that are the basis of business logistics are not as important to a one-off event.

■ **Figure 12.1**
Elements of the logistics system

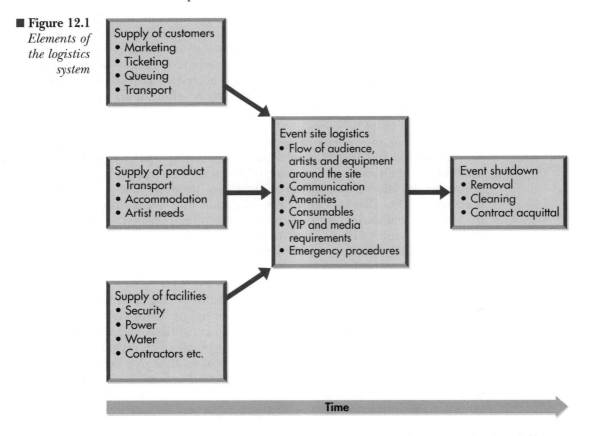

The areas of importance to event logistics can be categorised as follows:
- *Supply* — this is divided into the three areas of customer, product and facilities. Supply also includes the procurement of the goods and services.

- *Transport* — in Australia, as pointed out by Gilmour (1993), the transport of goods and services can be a major cost to an event and requires special consideration.
- *Linking* — logistics are part of the overall planning of an event and are linked to all other areas. With large multi-venue events, the logistics become so complex that an operations or logistics manager is often appointed. The logistics manager functions as part of the overall network management structure outlined in this chapter.
- *Flow control* — this refers to the flow of products, services and customers during the event.
- *Information networks* — the efficient flow of information during the event is generally a result of efficient planning of the information network. This concept is expanded in the section about on-site logistics.

All these areas need to be considered when creating a logistics plan. Even for small events, such as a wedding or a small product launch, a logistics plan must be incorporated in the overall event plan. For these types of event, logistics come under the title 'staging', which is described in chapter 13.

Given that the major elements of logistics are supply and movement, logistics play a large role in some types of event, including:
- events that have a large international component, such as major conferences, sporting events and overseas corporate incentive programs
- complex events in foreign countries, such as trade exhibitions and conferences
- events that occur in remote locations and need most of the supporting resources transported to the site
- exhibitions of large or complex products, such as mining or agricultural exhibitions
- events that are moving, such as travelling exhibitions and races.

■ Supply of *the customer*

The customers of an event are those who pay for it. They can be the audience (concerts and festivals), spectators (sport), and the sponsors or clients (corporate events). The customers have expectations, which include logistical aspects, that have to be met for a successful outcome. The way in which the event is promoted will particularly influence their expectations.

■ Links with *marketing and promotion*

The supply of customers is ultimately the responsibility of marketing activities. The numbers, geographic spread and expectations of the customers affect the logistics planning. The targeting of specialist markets or widespread publicity of an event will require a logistics plan with very different priorities. The transport requirements of the customers vary according to the distance travelled — for example, the majority of the audience of the Port Fairy Folk Festival drives from Melbourne, so vehicle access and parking are a priority at the festival site. The Womadelaide festival in Adelaide, with its nationwide publicity campaign, has a large interstate audience. This offers opportunities for special negotiations with the airlines and hotels.

If the publicity of an event is spread nationwide, the logistics will be different from those of a product launch that concerns only the staff and customers of a company. In this way, the logistics are closely linked to the marketing of an event.

■ Ticketing

Ticketing is important to events whose primary income is from the entrance fee. Most corporate events, including office parties and product launches, and many public events are free. However, for other events, such as sports events, the extent of ticket sales can determine success or failure (Graham, Goldblatt & Delpy 1995). Ticket distribution is regarded as the first major decision in event logistics.

The pricing and printing of the tickets is generally not a logistics area; however, ticket distribution, collection and security are of concern. In Australia, tickets for events can be sold through distributors such as Ticketek for a fee, or they can be sold by mail. The Port Fairy Folk Festival sells all its tickets at least four months in advance. Selling tickets at the gate gives rise to security problems in the collection, accounting and depositing of funds. The ticket collectors need training to deal with the public, and to move the public efficiently through the entrance. The honesty of the staff may also be a security concern. Larger venues use an admission loss-prevention plan to minimise the possibility of theft.

It is not unusual in Australia to sell tickets through retail outlets. For the Macquarie Marsh Project, an environmental concert in the wetlands of central New South Wales, the organiser used local tourism information centres as a distribution channel to sell tickets. Inventory control and cash receipts are two areas that require special attention when using retail outlets for ticket distribution. Numbering of the tickets and individual letters of agreement with each outlet are the most efficient methods of control. The letter of agreement would include the range of ticket numbers, the level of the tickets (discount or full price) and the method of payment. Depending on the size of the event, the ticketing can be crucial to the event's success and can take up a significant amount of the event director's time. Figure 12.2 is a checklist of the logistics of ticketing an event.

An innovative method of ticketing for festivals is to use the hospital-style wristbands called crowd control bands. These are colour coded to indicate the level of the ticket — a day ticket, a weekend ticket or a special performer's ticket. The use of these wristbands introduces a visual method of control during a large event, because the sale of food and drinks is allowed only if the wristband is shown. In this way, the food vendors become part of the security for the event.

The Internet is increasingly used for the distribution of tickets for large events, concerts and conferences. This use of the Internet illustrates the linking of logistics and marketing. Originally, events were marketed via this medium through advertisements on a website. The introduction of encrypted data enabled an increase in the privacy and security of on-line payment methods and ticket sales. The website collaborates with the existing ticketing system and also can be connected to travel agencies.

■ **Figure 12.2**
*Ticketing —
logistics
checklist*

Does the artwork on the ticket contain the following?
❑ Number of the ticket
❑ Name of the event
❑ Date and time of the event
❑ Price and level of the ticket (discount, complimentary, full price, early bird)
❑ Seating number or designated area (Ticket colouring can be used to show seating area.)
❑ Disclaimer (In particular, this should list the responsibilities of the event promoter.)
❑ Event information, such as a map, warnings and what to bring
❑ Artwork so the ticket could be used as a souvenir (Part of the ticket could be kept by the patron.)
❑ Contact details for information
❑ Security considerations, such as holograms to prevent copying

Printing schedule
❑ When will the tickets be ready?
❑ Will the tickets be delivered or do they have to be collected?
❑ If there is an error or a large demand for the tickets, will there be time for more to be printed?

Distribution
❑ What outlets will be used — retail, Ticketek (or similar), the Internet, mail or at the gate?
❑ Has a letter of agreement with all distributors, setting out terms and conditions, been signed?
❑ What method of payment will be used (by both the ticket buyer to the distributor and in the final reconciliation) — credit card, cash, direct deposit?
❑ Are schedule of payment and reconciliation forms available?
❑ Does the schedule of communications referring to ticket sales indicate sales progress and whether more tickets are needed?

Collection of tickets
❑ How will the tickets be collected at the gate and transferred to a pass-out?
❑ How experienced are the personnel and how many will there be? When will they arrive and leave?
❑ Is a separate table for complimentary tickets needed at the ticket collection site?
❑ What security arrangements are in place for cash and personnel?
❑ How will the tickets be disposed of?

Reconciliation of number of tickets with revenue received
❑ What method of reconciliation will be used? Is an accountant being used?
❑ Is the reconciliation ongoing, at the conclusion of the event, or at the end of the month?
❑ Has a separate account been set up just for the event to assist the accountancy procedure?

■ Queuing

Often, the first experience of a customer at an event is queuing for tickets or parking. Once inside the event, customers may be confronted with queues for food, toilets and seating. An important aspect of queue theory is the 'perceived waiting time'. This is the subjective time that the customers feel they have waited. There are many rules of thumb about diminishing the customers' perceived waiting time. In the catering industry, an informal rule is one food or beverage line for every 75 to 100 people. Figure 12.3 lists some factors to consider in the logistics of queuing.

■ **Figure 12.3**
Queuing —
factors to
consider

- How many queues and possible bottlenecks will there be?
- Has an adequate number of personnel greeters, crowd controllers, ticket collectors and security staff been allocated?
- Is signage (including the estimated waiting time) in place?
- When will the queues form? Will they form at once or over a period of time?
- How can the perceived waiting time be reduced (for example, queue entertainers)?
- What first aid, access and emergency procedures are in place?
- Are the lighting and sun and rain protection adequate?
- Are crowd-friendly barricades and partitions in place?

At the Atlanta Olympics, the perceived waiting time at the entrance queues was diminished by the use of entertainers. Exit queuing can be the last experience for the customer at an event and needs the close attention of the event manager. At Darling Harbour's New Year's Eve celebrations in Sydney, the authorities use 'staggered entertainment' to spread the exit time of the crowds.

The oversupply of customers at a commercial event can give rise to security and public safety problems that should be anticipated in the logistics plan. Only pre-sale tickets will indicate the exact number of the expected audience. When tickets are sold at the entrance to an event, the logistics plan has to include the possibility of too many people turning up on the day. Oversubscription may be pleasing for the event promoter, but can produce the logistical nightmare of what to do with the excess crowd.

■ Customer *transport*

Transport to a site is often the first physical commitment by the audience to an event. The method and timing of arrival — public or private transport — is important to the overall logistics plan. The terms used by event managers are 'dump', when the audience arrives almost at once, and 'trickle', when event goers arrive and leave over a longer period. Each of these needs a different logistics strategy. The first impression of the event by the audience can influence all subsequent experiences at the event. For this reason, it is the most visible side of logistics for customers. In their work on sports events, Graham, Goldblatt and Delpy (1995) comment on the importance of spectator arrivals and departures. They stress that arrival and departure are a part of the event hospitality experience. The first and last impression of an event will be the parking facility and the traffic control.

The organisation of transport for conferences takes on a special importance. In a handbook for conference organisers by *CIM Rostrum* (vol. 32), the linking of transport and the selection of the venue is emphasised. The selection of the conference venue or site has to account for the availability and cost of transport to and from the site. As well, the transport to other facilities has to be considered. A venue that involves a 'long haul' will increase the overall costs of a conference or event, as well as adding to the organisational confusion. CIM further points out that lengthy travel can make the conference seem less attractive to the delegates and, therefore, have an impact on delegate numbers.

For large events, festivals and parades, further logistics elements are introduced to the transport of the customer to the event. In particular, permission (council, main roads departments, police) and road closures need to be part of the logistics plan. Figure 12.4 (page 384) lists the elements of customer transport that need to be considered for an event.

An innovative way of solving many logistics problems (parking and so on) and enhancing the audience experience was used by the organisers of the Australian Music Festival in Glen Innes, New South Wales. The festival took place at the old Glen Innes railway station, and the audience arrived by steam train with the performers. By the time the passengers arrived from Central Station (Sydney) on the Great Northern train, the festival experience had already begun.

The Glen Innes festival also demonstrates how the transport arrangements for the customer (audience) can be linked to the transport of the product (musicians). This can be taken much further and include sponsorship deals with transport companies. In particular, the transport of equipment can be offset against the large number of tickets required to transport the audience. Australian domestic airlines often negotiate a discount for excess baggage charges incurred by performers if the event account is large enough.

The lack of transport facilities can be used as part of the event experience. As Nick Rigby, Head Ranger at Cape Byron, New South Wales, describes:

■ For our inaugural environmental heritage concert at the Pass we did not allow cars near the site as it would have spoilt the feeling of the evening. The audience had to park a kilometre away and walk along the beach to the Pass. This little journey was part of the environmental experience. We had volunteers steering people in the right direction and welcoming them to Cape Byron. It was quite a sight, over a thousand adults and children strolling along the beach with their picnic 'Eskies' and blankets. ■

❑ Have the relevant authorities (for example, the local council, the police and the Department of Main Roads) been contacted for information and permission?

❑ What public transport is available? Are timetables available?

❑ Has a backup transport system been organised (in case the original transport system fails)?

❑ Is the taxi service adequate and has it been informed of the event? (Informing the local taxi service is also a way of promoting the event.)

❑ What quality is the access area? Do weight and load restrictions apply? Are there other special conditions that must be considered (for example, underground sprinkler systems under the access area)?

❑ Is there adequate provision for private buses (including an area large enough for their turning circle), driver hospitality and parking?

❑ Is there a parking area and will it be staffed by trained personnel?

❑ Is a towing and emergency service available if required?

❑ Has transport to and from the drop-off point been organised (for example, from the parking station to the site or venue entrance and back to the parking station)?

❑ At what rate are customers estimated to arrive (dump or trickle)?

❑ Is there adequate access and are there parking facilities for disabled customers?

■ Supply of product — *product portfolio*

Any event can be seen as the presentation of a product. Most events have a variety of products and services — a product portfolio — that help to create the event experience for the customer. The individual logistics requirements of the various products need to be integrated into a logistics plan.

For a large festival, the product portfolio may include more than 200 performing groups from around Australia and overseas. For a small conference, the product may be a speaker and video material. The product can also include the venue facilities, which is why the term 'the event experience' is used to cover all aspects of the customers' experience. It can include, for example, the audience itself and just catching up with friends, in which case the people become part of the product portfolio.

■ Transport

If the product portfolio includes products coming from overseas, the logistics problems can include issues such as carnet and customs clearance. A carnet is a licence issued by Customs that allows the movement of goods across an international border. A performing artist group coming into Australia is required to have clearance for all its equipment, and needs to pay any taxes on goods that may be sold at the event, such as videos or compact discs.

A large account with an airline can allow the event manager an area of negotiation. An airline company may grant savings, discounts, free seats or free excess baggage in exchange for being the 'preferred airline' of the event.

The artistic director should forward the transport requirements for the performers to the logistics manager well before the event. This illustrates the linking of the functional areas of a large event.

Importing groups from overseas or interstate provides the logistics manager with an opportunity to communicate with these groups. The 'meet and greet' at the airport and the journey to the site can be used to familiarise the talent with the event. The artist's event or festival kit may include a site map, rehearsal times, accommodation details, the dressing room location, equipment storage and transport home details, for example.

■ Accommodation

The accommodation requirements of the artists (such as performers, keynote speakers or competitors) must be treated separately from the accommodation of the audience. The aim of the event manager is to get the best out of the 'product'. Given that entertainers are there to work, their accommodation has to be treated as a way of increasing the value of the investment in entertainment. Substandard accommodation and long trips to the site are certain ways of reducing this value. Often, these requirements are not stated and need to be anticipated by the logistics manager.

■ Artists' needs *on site*

A range of artists' needs must be catered for, including transport on site, storage and movement of equipment, stage and backstage facilities, food and drink (often contained in the contract rider), sound and lights. All these have a logistics element, but are described in detail in chapter 13.

As with accommodation, an efficient event manager will anticipate the on-site needs of the artists. Often, this can only be learned from experience. The manager needs to be sensitive to requirements that are culturally based, such as food, dressing rooms (separate) and appropriate staff to assist the performer.

SUPPLY OF FACILITIES

The supply of the infrastructure to an event site introduces many of the concepts of business logistics. The storage of consumables (food and drink) and equipment, and the maintenance of equipment become particularly

■ Figure 12.5 *Woodford Folk Festival order sheet*

VENUES	Hoecker	Marquee	Shade	Backstage	Floors	Site office	Stage size	Extensions
Big top		160' × 110'		12' × 12'			9.6 × 4.8 × 0.9 m	(2) PA wings 3.6 × 2.4 m
Concert	20 × 30 m			12' × 12'			9.4 × 4.8 × 0.6 m	
Folkloric theatre	20 × 30 m			6 × 9 m 3 × 6 m	6 × 9 m 3 × 6 m		9.6 × 4.8 × 0.6 m	Foldback risers at 0.45 m
Forum	15 × 20 m						5 × 4 × 0.45 m	
Blues	20 × 20 m			24' × 24'			8.4 × 4.8 × 0.6 m	
Dance	15 × 20 m				12 × 9.6 m		7.2 × 4.8 × 0.6 m	
Murri	10 × 20 m						8.4 × 4.8 × 0.6 m	
Children's festival Workshop Cafe		40' × 60' 24' × 36'	(2) 13 × 15 m	12' × 12' (7) 12' × 12'	 4 × 4 m		6 × 4.8 × 0.3 m	
Cooroboree ground			13 × 18 m	12' × 12'				
Talking circle				12' × 12'				
Visual arts				(12) 4 × 4 m TT (2 sides each)	3.6 × 3.6 m	Penny to organise		
Greenhouse		48' × 60'					5.6 × 3.6 × 0.45 m	
Fire event		(3) 36' × 36'	8 × 10 m			2.4 × 4.8 m 2.4 × 3.6 m		
Amphitheatre	20 × 15 m			5 × 10 m 12' × 24'	18 × 13 m			
Troubadour		40' × 60'					4.8 × 2.4 × 0.3 m	
The Wok House							5.4 × 3.6 × 0.3 m	
Bim Bamboo!!								
Lantern factory		36' × 36'						

FACILITIES

Administration		36' × 36'				2.4 × 6 m A/C		
Signology		15' × 15'						
Green room		(2) 30' × 36'						
Street theatre		(2) 12' × 12'						
Sponsors' lounge	10 × 10 m				10 × 10 m			
Front gate	5 × 10 m					2.4 × 4.8 m A/C		
Camping gate	6 × 6 m					JS caravan		
Welcome tent		4 × 4 m TT						
Organisers' green room	10 × 15 m							
Treasury						3.4 × 6 m A/C		
Cashiers						2.4 × 4.8 m A/C		
Security						2.4 × 4.8 m A/C		

BARS

Guinness		48' × 60'		10 × 10 m		2.4 × 4.8 m	4.8 × 3.6 × 0.3 m	
Session		48' × 48'						
Carnival		(2) 30' × 36'						
The Club		48' × 60'					5.4 × 3.6 × 0.4 m	
The Cafe		30' × 36'	8 × 10 m					
Blues		(2) 30' × 36'						

MURRI CAMP

Kitchen		30' × 36'	8 × 10 m					
Accommodation		(3) 6 × 9 m			(3) 6 × 9 m			
		(3) 6 × 9 m			(3) 6 × 3 m			

TOTALS

Steps	Chrs	8'T	3' Rnd	6' Rnd	Cold room	Cool cube	Tubs	Electricity	Plumbing	Pickets	Hessian	Extras
4 — 450 mm	1100	4										
1 — 600 mm	500	3										
1 — 600 mm	350	2										
	40	3	6									small fridge small urn
1 — 450 mm	300	2										
1 — 800 mm	350	2										
	150	2										
1 — 600 mm	250	2										
	150	2										4 tiered seats/2 fans
	60	12										4 × 4 m sandpit
	48	4	12		small fridge							12 hay bales
		1										
	100	40						1 switchboard	1 tap			
	200	4										
	30	10										
	10	4										
	20	4	3									fridge
	140	6	15	2								
		2								60 (20 × 4'3"s)	80 m	
	12	6										
	20	15										
	2	2										
	40	60										
	12	2						caravan		6	30 m	2 floods in punchbowl
	20		6									fridge
	10	10										
	5	4										
	4	4										
	100	15										
	10	8										
	4	3										
	200	4	20	2	1	1	6					
	120	4	20		1	1	6					
	120	3	20		1	1						
	200	4	20		1	1	6					
	120	3	20		1	1	4					
	150	4	25		2	1	6					
	120	3	20		1 (small)	1	4					gas BBQ
												gas rings
	150	4	25		2	1	6					
	3847	**256**	**167**	**4**	**7**	**6**	**28**					
ORDER	5000	280	180									

significant. For a small event taking place over an evening, the venue supplies most of the facilities. The catering, toilets and power, for example, can all be part of the hiring of the venue.

Larger festivals or more innovative events require the sourcing of many of the facilities. Some of these facilities are discussed in detail in chapter 13. An inaugural outdoor festival needs to source almost all the facilities. To find the best information about the availability and cost of facilities, the event manager should look for a project in the area that required similar facilities. Earth moving equipment, toilets, generators, fencing and security, for example, are also used by construction and mining companies. Some facilities can be sourced through film production companies. Many of the other facilities travel with festivals. Large tents and sound systems need to be booked in advance.

Figure 12.5 (see page 386) is an order sheet listing some of the facilities used for the Woodford Folk Festival in southern Queensland. Note the need for steps and the number of site offices.

Innovative events, like a company-themed Christmas party in an abandoned car park, require a long lead time to source the facilities. It may take months to source unusual and rare props and venues, for example. These lead times can significantly affect the way in which the event is scheduled.

ON-SITE LOGISTICS

The site of an event may vary from an old woolshed for a bush dance to an underground car park for a Christmas party, to a 50-hectare site for a festival. Logistics considerations during the event become more complex with the size of the event. The flow of materials and people around the site and communication networks become the most important area of logistics.

■ Flow

With larger festivals and events, the movement of the audience, volunteers, artists and equipment can take a larger part of the time and effort of the logistics manager than does the lead-up to the event. This is especially so when the site is complex or multi-venued and there is a large audience. During the lead-up to an event, subcontractors can take care of many elements of the logistics. The movement of the electricity generators to the site, for example, is the responsibility of the hire company. However, once the facilities are on site, the logistics manager is responsible for their positioning, movement and operation.

Something is being moved around on most events sites. The logistics must take into account the potential for flow of equipment and people during an emergency.

The access roads through a large festival and during the event have to accommodate:

- artist and equipment transport
- garbage removal
- emergency fire and first-aid access and checking
- stall set-up, continual supply and removal
- security
- food and drink supplies
- staging equipment set-up, maintenance and removal
- site communication.

As illustrated by figure 12.6, even during a straightforward event, many factors of the traffic flow must be considered. The performers for an event need transport from their accommodation to the stage. Often, the performers go via the equipment storage area to the rehearsal rooms, then to the stage. At the conclusion of the performance, the performers return their equipment to storage, then retire for a well-earned rest in the green room. For a community festival with four stages, this to-ing and fro-ing can be quite complex.

At the same time as the performers are transported around the site, the media, audience and VIPs are on the move. Figure 12.6 does not show the movement of the food vendors' suppliers, water, security, ambulances and many more. When any one of the major venues empties, there is further movement around the site by the audience. This results in peak flow times when it may be impossible to move anything around the venue except the audience. These peaks and lows have to be anticipated in the overall event plan.

■ **Figure 12.6**
Some traffic patterns to consider when planning an event

1. Performers' accommodation⟶ equipment storage area⟶ rehearsal area⟶ stage⟶ equipment storage area⟶ social (green room)
2. Media accommodation⟶ media centre⟶ stages⟶ social area
3. VIP accommodation⟶ stages⟶ special requests
4. Audience pick-up points⟶ specific venue

Each event contains surprising factors in traffic flow. For the Easter Show, which was formerly held at the Sydney Showground, the narrow gate that allowed entrance to the performers was also the gate that was used for the various animals. Each day of the two-week show had a queue that contained a mix of school orchestras, dancers, bands, sound equipment, Brahman bulls, sheep trucks, camels and horses moving in both directions. This flow was coordinated by one gatekeeper.

■ Communication

On-site communication for the staff at a small event can be via the mobile phone or the loud hailer of the event manager. Given the complexity of larger events, however, the logistics plan must contain an on-site communications plot. The Woodford site communications plot (figure 12.7, page 390) shows the complexity of communications at a festival that attracts 90 000 admissions.

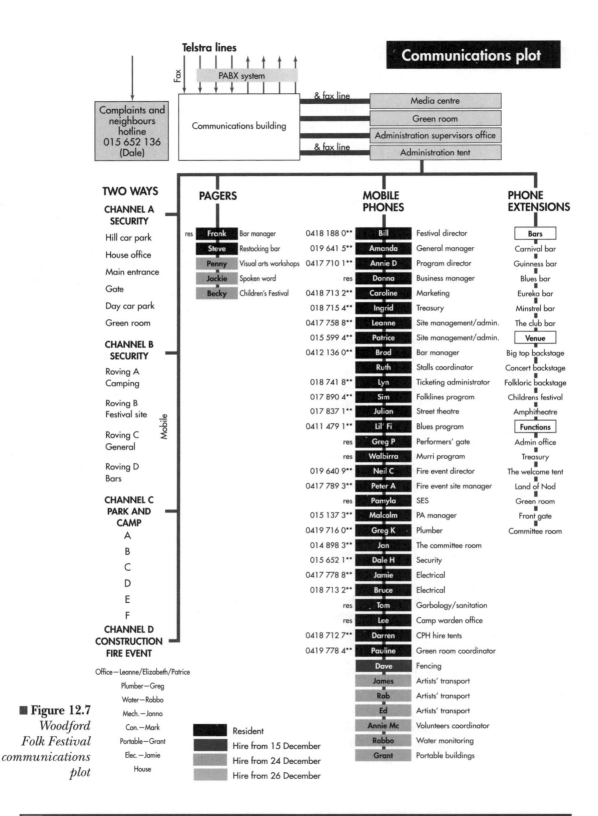

Telstra lines

Fax

PABX system

& fax line → Media centre

Complaints and neighbours hotline 015 652 136 (Dale)

Communications building → Green room

Administration supervisors office

& fax line → Administration tent

TWO WAYS | **PAGERS** | **MOBILE PHONES** | **PHONE EXTENSIONS**

CHANNEL A SECURITY

Hill car park
House office
Main entrance
Gate
Day car park
Green room

CHANNEL B SECURITY

Roving A Camping
Roving B Festival site
Roving C General
Roving D Bars

CHANNEL C PARK AND CAMP

A
B
C
D
E
F

CHANNEL D CONSTRUCTION FIRE EVENT

Office—Leanne/Elizabeth/Patrice
Plumber—Greg
Water—Robbo
Mech.—Jonno
Con.—Mark
Portable—Grant
Elec.—Jamie
House

Mobile

PAGERS

res | Frank | Bar manager
 | Steve | Restocking bar
 | Penny | Visual arts workshops
 | Jackie | Spoken word
 | Becky | Children's Festival

MOBILE PHONES

0418 188 0** | Bill | Festival director
019 641 5** | Amanda | General manager
0417 710 1** | Annie D | Program director
res | Donna | Business manager
0418 713 2** | Caroline | Marketing
018 715 4** | Ingrid | Treasury
0417 758 8** | Leanne | Site management/admin.
015 599 4** | Patrice | Site management/admin.
0412 136 0** | Brad | Bar manager
 | Ruth | Stalls coordinator
018 741 8** | Lyn | Ticketing administrator
017 890 4** | Sim | Folklines program
017 837 1** | Julian | Street theatre
0411 479 1** | Lil' Fi | Blues program
res | Greg P | Performers' gate
res | Walbirra | Murri program
019 640 9** | Neil C | Fire event director
0417 789 3** | Peter A | Fire event site manager
res | Pamyla | SES
015 137 3** | Malcolm | PA manager
0419 716 0** | Greg K | Plumber
014 898 3** | Jan | The committee room
015 652 1** | Dale H | Security
0417 778 8** | Jamie | Electrical
018 713 2** | Bruce | Electrical
res | Tom | Garbology/sanitation
res | Lee | Camp warden office
0418 712 7** | Darren | CPH hire tents
0419 778 4** | Pauline | Green room coordinator
 | Dave | Fencing
 | James | Artists' transport
 | Rob | Artists' transport
 | Ed | Artists' transport
 | Annie Mc | Volunteers coordinator
 | Robbo | Water monitoring
 | Grant | Portable buildings

PHONE EXTENSIONS

Bars
Carnival bar
Guinness bar
Blues bar
Eureka bar
Minstrel bar
The club bar

Venue
Big top backstage
Concert backstage
Folkloric backstage
Childrens festival
Amphitheatre

Functions
Admin office
Treasury
The welcome tent
Land of Nod
Green room
Front gate
Committee room

Resident
Hire from 15 December
Hire from 24 December
Hire from 26 December

■ **Figure 12.7**
Woodford Folk Festival communications plot

The communications plot includes fax, two-way radios, pagers, mobile phones and landline extensions. The Woodford communications plot also contains the title of each manager, as well as the complaints and neighbours' hotline.

The communication of information during an event has to work seamlessly with the other functions of event management. In particular, the immediacy of the information is important. The information has to be highly targeted and timely enough for people to act on it. This immediacy of information is unique to events because they must meet a deadline and generally involve large numbers of people. For this reason, event management tends to involve a variety of communication methods and devices, including:

- *two-way radios* — very common at large events, where the channels are reserved for emergency and police
- *mobile phones and text messages* — although limited by capacity, possibly becoming overloaded in an emergency. For this reason, some large venues acquire additional coverage.
- *signage* — a common form of communication. Its placement and clarity are important issues (dealt with later in this chapter).
- *runners* — people whose job it is to physically take the information to the receiver. Runners are indispensable if there is a power failure. Some large public events have bicycles ready for this purpose.
- *news sheets* — paper news sheets used to inform the exhibitors of daily program changes and updates on the attendee numbers and types
- *loud hailer* — surprisingly useful devices at some events such as parades
- *a sound system* — useful for announcements. The event team should know how to use it correctly.
- *flags* — often used at sports events such as car racing
- *visual and audio cues* — used to communicate the start or finish of an action. Whistles, horns, flashing lights can all be used in this way. Artistic lighting can be used to move an audience around a venue.
- *closed circuit television and web cams* — used in venues such exhibition and entertainment centres
- *short-range FM radios* — used to broadcast information during the event
- *WiFi and Bluetooth* — two recent technologies that are employed at some conferences and exhibitions to send and receive information
- *bulletin boards* — a humble and often effective way of contacting the volunteers and performers on site.

The movement around the event site or venue of equipment, suppliers and people — that is, the logistics during the event — needs an efficient communication system. For this reason, events often have levels of redundancy or backups for any one type of communication. The test of good communication planning is a power failure or emergency when the system will stop or be overloaded, and the event management team will be swamped with decisions to be made. Communication planning has to account for such a situation, so it must be a fundamental part of the project management and undergo a thorough risk assessment.

On-site signage is an important part of communicating to the attendees of an event. It may be as simple as messages on a whiteboard in the volunteers' dining area, or it may involve large on-site maps showing the public the locations of facilities. Two important issues of on-site signage are position and clarity. A direction sign that is obscured by sponsors' messages, for example, diminishes its value to the event.

For large events, the signage may need a detailed plan. The issues to consider are:

- overall site placement of signs — at decision points, at danger spots, so they are integrated into the event
- the types of sign needed, such as directional, statutory (legal and warning signs), operational, facility and sponsor
- the sign literacy of the attendees — what sort of signs are they used to reading?
- the placement of signs — entrance, down the road, height
- the supply of signs, their physical maintenance and their removal
- the credibility of the signs — if a facility is moved, then the signs may need to be changed.

The most effective way of communicating with the audience at an event is to have the necessary information in the program. Figure 12.8 shows information for the audience for a small festival in northern New South Wales.

~Festival Information~

Staying at the festival Limited on-site camping is available at a flat rate of $10 per person. N.B. this fee is not for profit, it's to cover the costs of providing facilities.

Other accommodation There are three caravan parks in Lismore, delightful rural cabins, B&Bs, hotels, motels and backpacker accommodation. You can book your stay in or around Lismore through the Lismore Tourist Information Centre (no booking charge). Please tell them you are coming to the festival.

People with disabilities Facilities are provided for people with disabilities. If you have special needs please contact us first and we will do our best to help you.

Volunteers Our heartfelt thanks to all the wonderful folk who have given their time and energy to create this very special event.

This festival is run entirely by volunteers, who appreciate a helping hand! If you can put in a couple of hours to help it would be great, just check in at the festival office.

Festival workers put in even more time. If you would like to help with setting up or clean-up, etc., please call us.

The bars The festival is a licensed event, run strictly according to licensing regulations! Under 18s and anyone who seems intoxicated will not be served. No BYO. Photo ID required.

First aid The Red Cross will be on site throughout the festival.

Car parking We welcome back the **Tuncester Bush Fire Brigade** to take care of the car park.

(Donations to these two essential voluntary services would be appreciated.)

Lost and found care for children and things — located in the club house.

Tickets Please bring your ticket to exchange for a wristband which must be worn throughout the festival. Spot checks will happen!

We suggest you bring your own mug for soft drinks, etc. to save on disposables. Sunscreen and hats are strongly recommended and you may need a jumper for the cool spring nights.

The Lismore Folk Trust Inc.

A not-for-profit organisation run solely by volunteers, the Trust produces this annual festival, the Lismore Lantern Festival and other events throughout the year. Membership entitles you to concessions at all Folk Trust events, newsletters (vacancy for an editor!) and is essential support for the festival. You can find out more about the Trust, and how to join, at the festival office.

Proudly supporting Summerland House, Alstonville

■ **Figure 12.8** *Festival information from the Northern Rivers Folk Festival program*

■ **Amenities and** *solid waste management*

For large festivals and events, the logistics site map always includes the layout of the amenities. Figure 12.9 is an example of a large festival logistics site map that shows the layout of amenities.

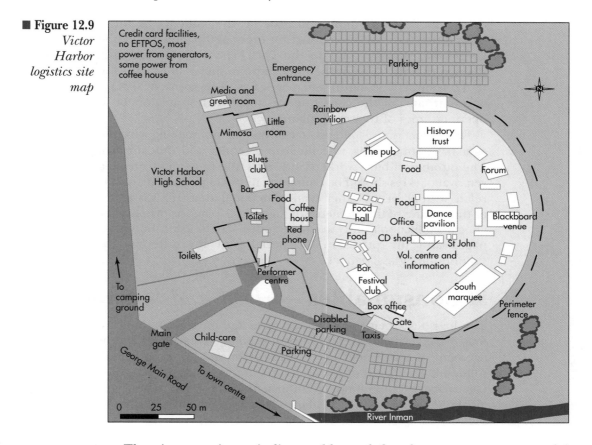

■ **Figure 12.9**
*Victor
Harbor
logistics site
map*

The site map is an indispensable tool for the event manager and is described in more detail later in this chapter. The schedules for the maintenance and cleaning of the amenities are part of the plan. For smaller events, these areas may be the responsibility of the venue management and part of the hiring contract.

Responsibility for cleaning the site and restoring it to its original condition is of particular importance to an event manager, because it is generally tied to the nature of the event. An event in Sydney's Royal Botanic Gardens attracted a huge audience to a delicate area. The mere movement of the audience severely damaged the grass and resulted in the Gardens administration being suspicious of any further events in the area. If a national park is used as the site for an event, a review of environmental factors (REF) is mandatory. The REF is a list of criteria that the activity must meet to be permitted under various Acts and Regulations. These include the *National Parks and Wildlife*

Act 1974 (NSW), the *Endangered Fauna (Interim Protection) Act 1991* (NSW) and the *Threatened Species Conservation Act 1995* (NSW). As well, the REF has to contain descriptions of the implications of the activity, the impact on the existing environment and land use, and the activity's significance to the local Aboriginal community.

Well-maintained toilets, particularly their number, accessibility and cleanliness, can be a very important issue for the audience. A rule of thumb for community festivals is one toilet for every 150 people (Neighbourhood Arts Unit 1991). Respondents to the Port Fairy Folk Festival audience survey stressed that the state of the toilets was an important factor for return visits to the festival. The logistics manager has to be aware of 'peak flows' during an event, and of the consequences for vehicle transport of waste and the opening times of treatment plants.

The collection of solid waste can range from making sure the venue manager has enough bins, to calling for a tender and subcontracting the work. The number of bins, workers and shifts, the timelines for collection and the removal of skips should be contained in the logistics plan, because they interrelate with all of the other event functional areas. This is a further example of the linking of the elements of logistics. A plan for primary recycling (recycling at collection point) would include both the education of the public (signage) and the provision of special bins for different types of waste (aluminium, glass, paper).

■ Consumables — *food and beverage*

The logistics aspects of food and beverage on a large, multi-venue site primarily concern storage and distribution. Food stalls may be under the management of a stall manager because state and local regulations need to be followed. The needs of the operators of food stalls, including transport, gas, electricity and plumbing, are then sent to the logistics manager. The sale of alcoholic beverages particularly can present the logistics manager with security issues.

At a wine and food fair, the 'consumables' are the attraction. The collection of cash is often solved by the use of pre-sale tickets that are exchanged for food and wine samples. The tickets are bought at one place on the site, which reduces possible problems with security, cash collection and accounting.

Figure 12.10 lists some of the main factors to consider when including food and beverage outlets at an event. As well as feeding and watering the public, catering logistics include the requirements of the staff, volunteers and performers. The catering area for the staff and performers, often called the green room, provides an opportunity to disseminate information to the event staff. At the Northern Rivers Folk Festival, a strategically placed, large whiteboard in the green room was used to communicate with volunteers.

Last, but not least, is the catering for sponsors and VIPs. This generally requires a separate plan to that for the general catering. In some festivals, a hospitality tent is set aside for special guests. This aspect of events is covered in chapter 13.

- Have local and state liquor licences been granted?
- What selection criteria for stall applicants (including the design of the stall and menu requirements) will be used?
- What infrastructure will be needed (including plumbing, electrical and gas)?
- Does the contract include provisions for health regulations, gas supplies, insurance and workers compensation?
- What position on the site will the stalls occupy?
- Have arrival, set-up, breakdown and leaving times been set?
- What cleaning arrangements have been made?
- Do stallholders understand the need for ongoing inspections, such as health, electricity, plumbing, garbage (including liquids) disposal and gas inspections?
- Are there any special security needs for which organisers must cater?
- How and when will payment for the stalls be made?
- Will the stallholders provide in-kind support for the event (including catering for VIPs, media and performers)?
- Are all staff trained in the responsible service of alcohol?

■ VIP and *media requirements*

The effect on event logistics by media coverage of the event cannot be over-estimated. Even direct radio broadcasts can disrupt the live performance of a show, both in the setting up and the actual broadcast. The recording or broadcasting of speeches or music often requires separate microphones or a line from the mixing desk, and these arrangements cannot be left until just before the performance. Television cameras require special lighting, which often shines directly into the eyes of the audience. The movement of a production crew and television power requirements can be distracting to a live performance, and need to be assessed before the event.

Media organisations work on very short timelines and may upset the well-planned tempo of the event. However, the rewards in terms of promotion and even finance are so large that the media logistics can take precedence over most other aspects of the event. These decisions are often made by the event manager in consultation with event promotors and sponsors. This is an area that illustrates the need for flexible negotiations and assessment by the logistics manager.

The requirements of VIPs can include special security arrangements. Again, it is a matter of weighing up the benefits of having VIPs with the amount of extra resources that are needed. This, however, is not the logistics manager's area of concern; the event manager or event committee should deal with it. Once the VIPs have been invited, their needs have to take precedence over the public's.

■ Emergency *procedures*

Emergency procedures at an event can range from staff qualified in first aid, to using the St John Ambulance service, to the compilation of a comprehensive disaster plan. The location of first aid should be indicated on the site map, and all the event staff should be aware of this location. Large events require an emergency access road that has to be kept clear. These issues are so important that a local council may immediately close down an event that does not comply with the regulations for emergencies.

Festivals in the countryside can be at the mercy of natural disasters, including fires, storms and floods. Figure 12.11 shows just one page of the disaster plan of the Woodford Folk Festival 1997.

■ **Figure 12.11**
Extract from the Woodford Folk Festival 1997 disaster plan

Authority
This plan is written under the authority of the *State Counter Disaster Organisation Act 1974–78*.

Aim
The aim of this plan is to set out the policies and procedure to be followed by State Emergency Service personnel in times of major incidents, disasters or emergencies that may occur during the Woodford Folk Festival.

In matters where this document is silent, then the Caboolture Shire Disaster Plan will come into effect and be enacted.

Objectives
To establish the general guidelines to be followed for all incidents and/or emergencies
To set the guidelines to be followed in the event of a fire
To set the guidelines to be followed in the event of a multicasualty incident
To set the guidelines to be followed in the event of a lost person
To set the guidelines to be followed in the event of a flood in the festival site
To set the guidelines to be followed in the event of a severe storm causing damage
To set the general guidelines to be followed for any other event that may occur

Command and control
The control organisation for emergencies and searches is the Queensland Police Service.

The control organisation for fire incidents is the Queensland Fire and Rescue Service.

The control organisation for medical and multicasualty incidents is the Queensland Ambulance Service.

The support and management organisation for the above is the Queensland State Emergency Service.

The control organisation for storm damage operations is the Queensland State Emergency Service.

The Maleny State Emergency Service Group activities at the Woodford Folk Festival are overseen by the training officer and are conducted as training.

In the event of an incident or emergency occurring, the Maleny training officer or delegate must be informed immediately, regardless of the time of day.

The on-site emergency procedures are an example of the two functions of event management — risk and logistics — working together to formulate a plan. Overall, they come under the project plan. They are now mandatory for many events, as illustrated by figure 12.12, which an excerpt from *Event management: planning guide for event managers in Victoria.*

■ Figure 12.12
An example of an emergency response plan

The event must have a formal, written emergency response plan, which should be developed with [Australian] standards. The plan should be provided to all event organisers, key stakeholders, police and emergency service personnel. The plan should:
- detail arrangements for on-site emergencies not requiring outside help
- specify arrangements to request further police and other emergency services assistance
- specify arrangements to hand over control to police and emergency services as required
- identify personnel who can authorise evacuation
- identify how the event will be interrupted
- provide a grid plan of the venue and all services
- identify access and evacuation routes
- identify evacuation areas for performers, employees and patrons
- establish an emergency control centre, which has back-up power and lighting
- provide details of coded messages to alert and stand down emergency service and security personnel
- identify the role event staff will take in supporting civilian services
- identify meeting points for emergency services
- identify triage and ambulance loading areas
- include details of hospitals prepared for a major incident
- identify access and egress routes, and the security of these routes
- provide details of a temporary mortuary facility.

Note: In any major incident, for the purposes of the law, the venue is considered a crime scene and thus under total control of the police.

(**Source:** *Government of Victoria 2004.*)

Considerations for creating the plan include: under whose authority is the plan being prepared? And what are the plan's aims and objectives? The the emergency plan will influence the design of the site, particularly for large public events. Local councils require emergency access to all parts of the event, and the access route must be the correct width for an emergency vehicle and kept clear at all times. A mistake in this area can result in the event being closed immediately.

Emergencies can occur at any time during the event, and the planning has an effect on the evacuation procedures. These procedures should be different:

• while the audience is arriving, before they have entered the venue or site. The logistics involved are concerned with stopping the inflow.
• while some of the audience is already in the venue and others are arriving. This is a complex period of two directions of flow: people who are arriving and haven't heard that the event has been cancelled, and those who are eager to leave.
• during the event, when most of the audience is on-site.

The disaster plan stresses the lines of authority and necessary procedures. These procedures include the partial evacuation of the festival site in the event of a disaster (particularly prolonged heavy rain). It notes that rescuers should concentrate on personnel in immediate danger when conducting an evacuation.

SHUTDOWN

As Pagonis (1992) points out, military logistics is divided into three phases:
1. deployment
2. combat
3. redeployment.

Redeployment often takes the most effort and time. The amount of time and effort spent on the shutdown of an event are in direct proportion to the size of the event and its uniqueness. Repeated events, like many of the festivals mentioned in this chapter, have their shutdown schedule refined over many years. Shutdown can run quickly and smoothly. All the sub-contractors know exactly how to get their equipment out, and where they are placed in the order of removal. The event manager of a small event may only have to sweep the floor and turn off the lights.

Most difficulties arise in inaugural events, large events and multi-venued events. In these cases, logistics can be as important after the event as at any other time, and the need for planning is most apparent. As illustrated in figure 12.13 (page 400), the management of event shutdown involves many elements. In project management terminology, this is called the asset handover and project closure. In event management, the most forgotten part is the closure of the project. The tools of project management can be used to manage the shutdown process. The shutdown plan should include a work breakdown structure, a task/responsibility list and a schedule with a critical path, and be subject to risk analysis. It forms part of the overall event project plan.

The on-site issues initially involve the crowd. Whether for a sporting event, a conference or a concert, not much major work can be done until the crowd leaves. However, some tasks can be started, such as packing one stage while the crowd's attention is elsewhere. Crowd management at this time is vital because the event management is responsible for the crowd's safety as people leave the venue and make their way home. It is wise to include this issue in the risk management plan. If some members of the crowd want to 'party on', it is smart to plan this activity well ahead of time. Some of the local discos and hotels may welcome the increase in patrons, if told beforehand.

The site may look empty after the event, but the experienced event manager knows that the work has only just begun. The equipment needs to be collected, repaired and stored, or immediately returned to its owners. Small equipment such as hand-held radios are easily lost, so many events have a sign-on/sign-off policy for these items. With large crowds, you can almost guarantee there will be an assortment of lost items. A member of staff needs to walk the site to check whether anything has been left behind — called the 'idiot check' in the music industry. At this point, the event manager realises the value of a torch!

As the site is being shut down, it may also be prepared for the next event. This is a consideration for all the other resources. The equipment may be packed away so it can be easily found and used for the next event. Shutdown thus has a further element: preparation for the next event. Extensive site clean-up is also often required, as detailed in the following 'event profile'.

EVENT PROFILE

Clean-up

For the organisers of Sydney's annual Gay and Lesbian Mardi Gras, site clean-up is a major task. Hundreds of thousands of people line the streets to watch the mardi gras parade each February, requiring significant crowd control measures and leaving a lot of rubbish behind when they leave.

Rubbish removal, particularly the removal of broken glass, is a significant problem. A study after the 2000 mardi gras found that one small section of the roadway took more than two hours to clean. To make matters worse, some local residents put their own household rubbish out on the street, including old fridges and lounge suites, believing that a general council clean-up was in progress and that it was a good opportunity to get rid of unwanted items. One year, more than 15 000 plastic milk crates were collected, requiring significant labour and time, and three semi-trailers. Given the size of the crowds, crowd control barriers are used extensively. The collection of the barriers after the event is a major shutdown exercise, requiring 16 trucks and 63 staff in a closely controlled operation. The clean-up staff are carefully coached on how to deal with the public. The intoxicated nature of many people in the crowd is just one of the problems.

Dennis Wheeler, Event project management system (CD-ROM)

The shutdown of an event is the prime security time. The mix of vehicles, movement of equipment and general feeling of relaxation provides a cover for theft. The smooth flow of traffic leaving an event at its conclusion must also be considered. Towing services and the police may need to be contacted.

Very large events may require the sale of facilities and equipment at a post-event auction. Some events in Australia find that it is more cost-effective to buy or make the necessary equipment and sell it after the event. Finally, it is often left to the person in charge of logistics to organise the final thank-you party for the volunteers and staff.

Back at the event office, there will be at least a few weeks of project closure. This will include acquitting all the contracts, paying the bills and collecting all the records of the event, media clippings and any incident report sheets. These records will assist when all the reports have to be prepared and any funding is acquitted.

Although the next step may not be the responsibility of the person in charge of logistics, the event logistics manager will have an important role. The event is not over until the management of the event has been assessed (chapter 9). The logistics plan is part of the overall event project plan, so has to be assessed for its effectiveness. It cannot be assessed unless there are written documents or files to compare against the reality of the event logistics. It will be difficult, if not impossible, to suggest real improvements for the next event without these. Too often, in the rush to the next event, the logistics problems are forgotten. The event management produces not just the event, but also a way in which to manage the event.

Checklists are an example of a logistics management system. They represent the micro-management of the event. In the past, many events would have discarded these checklists after the event, yet the checklist is a portable tool — for example, the ticket checklist is common to all events, so it can easily be adapted to a checklist for invitations to a charity event. Checklists should be assessed after the event, along with the rest of the management system.

■ **Figure 12.13**
Event shutdown checklist

Crowd dispersal
- ❏ Exits/transport
- ❏ Safety
- ❏ Related to programming
- ❏ The dump and staggered entertainment

Equipment
- ❏ Bump-out schedule, including correct exits and loading docks
- ❏ Shutdown equipment using specialist staff (for example, computers)
- ❏ Clean and repair
- ❏ Store — number boxes and display contents list
- ❏ Sell or auction
- ❏ Small equipment and sign-off
- ❏ Schedule for dismantling barricades

Entertainment
- ❏ Farewell appropriately
- ❏ Payments — cash
- ❏ Thank-you letters/awards/ recommendations

Human resources
- ❏ The big 'thank you'
- ❏ Final payments
- ❏ Debrief and next year
- ❏ Reports
- ❏ Celebration party

Liability
- ❏ Records
- ❏ Descriptions
- ❏ Photo
- ❏ Video

On-site/staging area
- ❏ Cleaning
- ❏ Back to normal
- ❏ Environmental assessment
- ❏ Lost and found
- ❏ Idiot check
- ❏ Site/venue hand-over

Contractors
- ❏ Contract acquittal
- ❏ Thank-you

Finance
- ❏ Pay the bills.
- ❏ Finalise and audit accounts — best done as soon after the event as possible (the following day or week).
- ❏ Thank donor and sponsors.

Marketing and promotion
- ❏ Collection of media clippings/video news
- ❏ Reviews of the event — use a service?
- ❏ Market research on community reaction

Sponsors and grants
- ❏ Acquit grants and complete reports — don't be placed on the D list of funding bodies!
- ❏ Meet sponsors and enthuse for next time.

Government and politics
- ❏ Thanks to services
- ❏ Reports to council and other government organisations

Client
- ❏ Glossy report, video, photos
- ❏ Wrap-up and suggestions for next time

TECHNIQUES OF LOGISTICS MANAGEMENT

The tools used in business and military logistics can be successfully adapted to event logistics. Because an event takes place at a specific time and specific place, the tools of scheduling and mapping are used. The dynamic nature of events and the way that the functional areas are so closely linked mean a small change in one area can result in crucial changes throughout the event. The incorrect placement of an electric generator, for example, can lead to a mushrooming of problems. If the initial problem is not foreseen or immediately solved, it can grow to affect the whole event. This gives initial negotiations and ongoing assessment a special significance in event logistics. The logistics manager needs to be skilled in identifying possible problem areas and needs to know what is *not* on the list.

We will now consider the role of logistics managers and their relation to the other functional areas and managers of an event.

■ The event *logistics manager*

As mentioned throughout this chapter, the logistics manager has to be a procurer, negotiator, equipment and maintenance manager, personnel manager, map maker, project manager and party organiser. For a small event, logistics can be the direct responsibility of the event manager. Logistics become a separate area if the event is large and complex. Multi-venued and multi-day events usually require a separate logistics manager position.

Part of the role of the logistics manager is to efficiently link all areas of the event. Figure 12.14 shows the lines of communication between the logistics manager and other managers for a large, complex, multi-venued event. It is a network diagram because, although the event manager or director has ultimate authority, decision-making authority is usually devolved to the submanagers who work at the same level of authority and responsibility as the event manager.

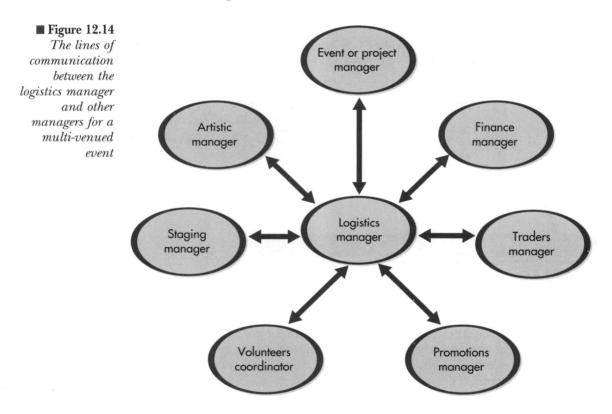

The information required by the logistics manager from the other festival managers is shown in table 12.1. Clear communication between managers in this network is also partly the responsibility of the logistics manager. Many of the tools and techniques of the logistics manager are discussed in chapter 9.

POSITION	GENERAL ROLE	INFORMATION SENT TO LOGISTICS MANAGER
Artistic director	Selection of, and negotiation with, artists	Travel, accommodation, staging and equipment requirements
Staging manager	Selection of, and negotiation with, subcontractors	Sound, lights and backstage requirements and programming times
Finance director	Overseeing of budgets and contracts	How and when funds will be approved and released, and the payment schedule
Volunteers coordinator	Recruitment and management of volunteers	Volunteers selected and their requirements (for example, parking, free tickets)
Promotions manager	Promotion during the event	Requirements of the media and VIPs
Traders manager	Selection of suitable traders	Requirements of the traders (for example, positioning, theming, electricity, water, licence agreements)

Figure 12.15 shows an example of a job advertisement for an event logistics manager.

■ **Figure 12.15**
A job advertisement for an event logistics manager

Position description

Title	**International Youth Parliament 2004 Logistics Officer**
Category	**Category 6**
Section	**Public Policy & Outreach**
Unit	**International Youth Parliament**
Responsible to	**International Youth Parliament 2004 Sitting Coordinator**
Location	**Sydney**
Employment Basis	**Contract to end of August 2004 subject to probationary period**
Hours	**Full time**
Annual salary	

Scope of position

The International Youth Parliament 2004 Logistics Officer works closely with the International Youth Parliament 2004 Sitting Coordinator to ensure that all logistics for the second sitting of the International Youth Parliament, running 5–12 July, 2004, are arranged in advance and that the event runs smoothly. The International Youth Parliament 2004 Logistics Officer is required to attend the full event and will be expected to live on-site for the duration. It is expected that there will be approximately 250 international participants aged between 18 and 25 in attendance.

(continued)

1. Responsibilities

1.1 Organise all logistics for second sitting of the International Youth Parliament including arrangement of venues, catering, simultaneous translators, IT and AV requirements and compliance with insurance requirements.

1.2 Organise all travel, meals and accommodation for delegates, workshop facilitators and keynote speakers within Australia.

1.3 Liaise with the venue manager (at St Joseph's College) to develop a participants' code of behaviour and ensure that it is adhered to during the event.

1.4 Assist delegates with travel arrangements to Australia, particularly ensuring all international visitors obtain the necessary visas to enter Australia.

1.5 Organise all equipment required for the event and ensure that it is fully functional.

1.6 Manage timelines, timetables and scheduling for the event and ensure that it is fully functional.

1.7 Manage timelines, timetables and scheduling for the event and associated activities.

1.8 Ensure that all participants have access to clear and accurate information regarding expectations and activities at all times.

1.9 Ensure the comfort of delegates and speakers during their stay, including arrangement of translators, dietary, cultural and religious requirements and entertainment.

1.10 Work with the International Youth Parliament Fundraiser to secure in-kind sponsorship and donations.

1.11 Support the marketing of the International Youth Parliament, including arrangement of promotional events and delegate meetings with sponsors and community organisations, ensuring appropriate signage and marketing opportunities for sponsors.

1.12 Other related tasks as required by the International Youth Parliament 2004 Sitting Coordinator

2. Budget

2.1 Assist with the development and monitoring of expenditure budget.

3. Policy

3.1 Implement organisational policy in area of delegation.

4. Human resources

4.1 This position has no responsibility for the supervision of staff but does assist in the coordination of volunteers.

4.2 Required to undertake job responsibilities in a manner consistent with EEO/ AA policy

4.3 Required to undertake job responsibilities in a manner consistent with OH&S policies and procedures

5. Knowledge and experience

5.1 Experience organising large conferences and events

5.2 Knowledge of cultural and religious requirements for international delegates

5.3 Experience pursuing and acquiring in-kind sponsorships

5.4 Computer literacy, particularly MS Office and email use

5.5 Knowledge of international social justice and development issues (desirable)

6.   Skills and personal attributes

6.1   Essential skills — skills of a high order are required in the following areas:
- Event management, timetabling and production
- Project management
- Time management and organisational skills
- Exceptional written and verbal communication/interpersonal skills
- Public speaking and presentation
- Ability to manage and work to tight deadlines and with limited budgets

6.2   Personal attributes
- Ability to think analytically
- Ability to follow procedures
- Attention to detail
- High levels of energy and motivation
- Ability to inspire and motivate others
- Must possess a current valid drivers licence and have access to a reliable vehicle for work purposes
- Ability to work flexible hours, including some evenings and weekends
- Understanding of, and commitment to, adhere to EEO/AA policies

■ Site or *venue map*

A map of the event site or venue is a necessary communication tool for the logistics manager. For small events, even a simple map can be an effective tool that obviates the need for explanations and can quickly identify possible problem areas. The map for larger festivals can be an aerial photograph with the logistic features drawn on it. For smaller events, it may be a sketch map that shows only the necessary information to the customer. The first questions to ask are 'what is the map for?' and 'who will be reading it?'. A logistics site map contains very different information from that on the site map used for promotional purposes. The map needs to filter information that is of no interest to the logistics plan. Monmonier (1996, p. 25), in his highly respected work on mapping, summarises this concept:

> ■ A good map tells a multitude of little white lies; it suppresses truth to help the user see what needs to be seen. Reality is three-dimensional, rich in detail, and far too factual to allow a complete yet uncluttered two-dimensional scale model. Indeed, a map that did not generalize would be useless. But the value of a map depends on how well its generalized geometry and generalized content reflect a chosen aspect of reality. ■

The three basic features of maps — scale, projection and the key (showing the symbols used) — have to be adapted to their target audience. Volunteers and subcontractors, for example, must be able to clearly read and understand it. The communication value of the site map also depends on where it is displayed. Some festivals draw the map on the back of the ticket or program.

The checklist for items to be included on a site map can be very detailed. Figure 12.16 (page 406) shows a standard checklist of the logistics site map for a small festival.

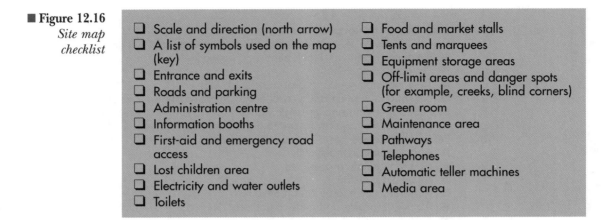

❏ Scale and direction (north arrow)
❏ A list of symbols used on the map (key)
❏ Entrance and exits
❏ Roads and parking
❏ Administration centre
❏ Information booths
❏ First-aid and emergency road access
❏ Lost children area
❏ Electricity and water outlets
❏ Toilets

❏ Food and market stalls
❏ Tents and marquees
❏ Equipment storage areas
❏ Off-limit areas and danger spots (for example, creeks, blind corners)
❏ Green room
❏ Maintenance area
❏ Pathways
❏ Telephones
❏ Automatic teller machines
❏ Media area

For a recent event in outback New South Wales, a sketch map on the ticket showed how to find the site, parking and the location of facilities. Next to the map was a list detailing the behaviour expected of event participants. The festival site map shown in figure 12.9 (page 393) would be used by volunteers, staff, performers and all other personnel at the event. The promotional map for the audience, on the other hand, would be in colour and display points of interest to the public.

For corporate events, a simple map of the venue at the entrance, showing the location of seating, toilets, food areas and the bar, can relieve the staff of having to answer a lot of questions!

NEGOTIATION AND ASSESSMENT

No matter what the size of the event, mutual agreement on supply and conditions is vital. In particular, the special but changing nature of one-off events requires the logistics manager to master the techniques of dynamic negotiation. In his work on negotiation and contracts, Marsh (1984, p. 1) defines negotiation as:

■ a dynamic process of adjustment by which two parties, each with their own objectives, confer together to reach a mutually satisfying agreement on a matter of common interest. ■

Logistical considerations need to be covered by the initial negotiations with subcontractors. Agreement on delivery and removal times are an indispensable part of the timelines, because they form the parameters of the critical path.

The management of special events in Australia is a dynamic industry. The special nature of many events means initial negotiations cannot cover many aspects. Decisions and agreements thus need to be continually reassessed. Both parties to the agreement have to realise that the agreement needs to be flexible. However, all possible problems have to be considered at the beginning, and there are logistics tools to enable this to happen.

Having prepared the schedules and site map, an important tool to use is what Pagonis (1992, p. 194) describes as the skull session:

> ■ Before implementing a particular plan, I usually try to bring together all of the involved parties for a collective dry run. The group includes representatives from all appropriate areas of the command, and the goal of the skull sessions is to identify and talk through all the unknown elements of the situation. We explore all possible problems that could emerge, and then try to come up with concrete solutions to those problems. Skull sessions reduce uncertainty, reinforce the interconnection of the different areas of specialisation, encourage collaborative problem solving, and raise the level of awareness as to possible disconnects [sic] in the theatre. ■

Goldblatt (1997) calls this gap analysis. Gap analysis is studying the plan to identify gaps that could lead to a weakening in the implementation of the logistics plan. Goldblatt (1997) recommends using a critical friend to review the plan to look for gaps in logical thinking.

The identification of risk areas, gaps and 'what ifs' is important in the creation of a contingency plan. At the Woodford Folk Festival, which takes place in the hottest months of the year in Queensland, the supply of water was identified as a priority area, and a contingency plan was thus created for a viable alternative. This included having water carts on call and making sure the nearest water pipe was available to the general public.

*C*ONTROL OF EVENTS LOGISTICS

The monitoring of the logistics plan is a vital part of the overall control of an event. An important part of the plan is the identification of milestones — times by which crucial tasks have to be completed. The Gantt chart (chapter 9) can be used to compare projected performance with actual performance by recording performance times on the chart as the tasks occur. It is a simple monitoring device.

The aim of the logistics manager is to create a plan to enable the logistics to flow without the need for active control. The use of qualified subcontractors with experience in events is the only way in which to make this happen. This is where the annual festival, with its established relationship with suppliers, has an advantage over the one-off, innovative event. The objective of the director of the Port Fairy Folk Festival, for example, was to enjoy the festival without having to intervene in any on-site problems!

EVALUATION OF LOGISTICS

The ultimate evaluation of the logistics plan is the success of the event and the easy flow of event supply and operations. However, the festival committee, the event director and/or the sponsors may require a more detailed evaluation. The main question to ask is whether the logistics met their objectives. If the objectives as set out in the plan are measurable, then this task is relatively straightforward. If the objectives require a qualitative approach, then the evaluation can become imprecise and open to many interpretations.

An evaluation enables the logistics manager to identify problem areas, thus enabling improvement and adding value to the next event. Techniques used in evaluation are:
- quantitative — a comparison of performance against measurable objectives (sometimes called benchmarking)
- qualitative — discussion with stakeholders.

The term 'logistics audit' is used for a systematic and thorough analysis of the event logistics. Part of the audit concerns the expectations of the audience and whether they were satisfied.

For very large events, the evaluation of the logistics may be contained in the overall evaluation that is put out to tender. In 1997, the Australian Department of Foreign Affairs and Trade launched a multidimensional promotion of Australia in India. It included a series of events throughout India, ranging from trade shows to cultural activities. The logistical problems of such a varied event spread over a large area in a foreign country with a huge population are many. The evaluation report on this promotion (Buchan Communications Group 1997) was mostly concerned with the business outcomes, but large sections were concerned with the logistics. The participants evaluated areas such as travel, communication and accommodation. Other areas of logistics were 'evaluated' by the fact that they were unseen by the participants and, therefore, deemed a success. As a result of the security measures put in place, for example, there were no terrorist activities during the promotion. (The day after the promotion finished, a train was blown up.)

THE LOGISTICS PLAN

Whether the event is a school class reunion or a multi-venued festival, a written logistics plan needs to be part of the communication within the event. It could range from a one-page contact list with approximate arrival times, to a bound folder covering all areas. The folder for a large event would contain:
- a general contact list
- a site map
- schedules, including timelines and bar charts

- the emergency plan
- subcontractor details, including all time constraints
- on-site contacts, including security and volunteers
- evaluation sheets (sample questionnaires).

All of these elements have been described and discussed in this chapter. They can make up the event manual that is used to stage the event. The manual needs to be a concise document because it may need to be used in an emergency. An operation manual may be used only once, but it has to be able to withstand the rigours of the event. Some organisations, particularly in the exhibition industry, have a generic manual on their intranet that can be adapted for all their events in any part of the world.

Although we emphasise the importance of planning, over-planning can be a significant risk, particularly with the special event, because there is often a need to respond and take opportunities when they arise. Artistry and innovation can easily be hampered by a purely mechanical approach to event creation. As pointed out in the Marine Corps doctrinal publication no. 4, *Logistics* (1997):

■ To deal with disorder, the logistics system must strive for balance. On the one hand, it must estimate requirements and distribute resources based on plans and projections; otherwise the needed support will never be available where and when it is required. On the other, a system that blindly follows schedules and procedures rapidly loses touch with operational realities and inhibits rather than enables effective action. ■

*S*UMMARY

Military logistics is as old as civilisation itself. Business logistics is a recent science. Event logistics has the advantage of building on these areas, using the tools of both and continually improving on them as the event industry in Australia grows.

The event logistics system can be broken down into the procuring and supply of customers, products and facilities. Once on-site, the logistics system concerns the flow around the site, communication and requirements of the event. At the conclusion of the event, logistics relate to breaking down structures, cleaning and managing the evacuation of the site or venue.

For small events, logistics may be the responsibility of the event manager. However, for larger events, a logistics manager may be appointed. His or her role within the overall event management was described earlier, and their relationship with other managers is vital. The logistics of an event need to be treated as any other area of management and have in-built evaluation and ongoing control. All of these elements are placed in a plan that is a part of the overall event plan.

Logistics is an invisible part of events. It enables customers to focus completely on the event without being distracted by unnecessary problems. It becomes visible only when it is looked for or when there is a problem. It enables the paying customer, the public, the client or the sponsor to realise and even exceed their expectations.

Questions

1. What areas of logistics need to be contained in initial agreements with the event suppliers?

2. Set out an emergency plan for a small event.

3. List the logistics tasks for (a) a street parade, (b) a product launch and (c) a company party.

4. Create a list of types of event. For each type of event, rate the significance of logistics.

Sydney Marathon
Festival

Frontiers Group Australasia engaged APP Events in 2002 and 2003 to provide the event management resources for the planning, approvals, logistics, stakeholder liaison, volunteer management and implementation of the Sydney Marathon Festival, the only legacy event from the Sydney Olympics. The Sydney Marathon Festival in 2003 incorporated:

- the Flora Sydney Marathon
- the Flora/*Sunday Telegraph* Half Marathon
- the *Sunday Telegraph* 10-kilometre Bridge Run
- the 2-kilometre Kids Run for Health.

The event is the only community road race that closes the Sydney Harbour Bridge, with the marathon, half marathon and 10-kilometre runs all crossing the world-famous landmark. The 2003 event was held on Sunday 14 September, with the marathon and half marathon finishing at Sydney Olympic Park (also the venue of the kids' run), while the 10-kilometre run finished at the Sydney Opera House. The post-race recovery, celebrations and presentations were held at both Sydney Olympic Park and the Royal Botanic Gardens.

Overall, participant numbers reached an event high, with an increase of approximately 28 per cent on 2002 figures. Some 1666 competitors entered the marathon, with 2668 in the half marathon and 8515 in the 10-kilometre bridge run. There was representation from over 28 countries, which contributed over 600 international competitors, including 333 from Japan.

The 2002 and 2003 events were deemed to be a great success by key stakeholders and government agencies, as well as the thousands of participants who tested their athletic ability on the day. The event is now set to enhance its NSW Government hallmark status well into the future.

Logistics plays a vital role in the delivery of such a major event. Detailed below are the key logistical considerations during planning of this event.

The event venues

The Flora Sydney Marathon has one astounding difference from your 'average' event venue — that is, 42.2 kilometres of 'event venue', excluding the start and finish areas. The 2003 marathon started at North Sydney Oval and finished at Sydney Olympic Park, running through the central business district, including crossing over the Sydney Harbour and Anzac bridges. A key element of logistics for an event of this scale is the organisation of road closures. Closures began in the early hours of the morning, with areas such as the Harbour Bridge being re-opened in record time in 2003. Given that the Flora Sydney Marathon is the only

(*continued*)

community run that closes the Harbour Bridge, the organisers had to consider logistical organisation, public awareness strategies and effective organisation in consultation with the Roads and Traffic Authority, the police, State Emergency Services (SES) and other key service groups. This consultation involves detailed planning sessions that result in the design and production of over 300 individual traffic control points that make up the traffic management plan. In 2003, a public awareness strategy was implemented before the event, to create a profile of the event among the general public, highlighting road closures and how their areas would be affected. This service to the community was implemented through mass letterbox drops and media coverage.

Communications

Radio communications and emergency procedures play a vital role in the overall flow of the event. In 2003, event organisers and key volunteers received an event-day radio, which enabled effective communication along the 42.2-kilometre course. Radios were a key logistical tool for the marathon because finish venue managers needed to know the exact time the race started and when the runners were 20 kilometres and 40 kilometres away, to ensure no surprises. The radio network consisted of four base stations located at the Police Operations Centre (POC), where all transmission were received. All key organisers were present in the POC, including the police, St John Ambulance, NSW Ambulance and the SES.

Event bump-in and bump-out

The procurement manager, operations manager and venue managers for the 2003 event jointly organised event bump-in and bump-out at each venue. From liaison with suppliers and contractors, an exact schedule was devised. Once times and dates were finalised, a bump-in run sheet was produced and distributed to suppliers, contractors and venues. The event operations guide also included event day run sheets, detailing arrival times of equipment, staff, suppliers and competitors. Infrastructure bump-in details were devised in Excel spreadsheets and organised into venues and course zones, which enabled event organisers to identify any clashes or areas for concern. Bump-in commenced on the Saturday before the event day for all venues, with the remaining set-up occurring early on the event day; for some event staff, this meant being on site from 3 am Sunday morning to 6 pm Sunday night.

Risk management

APP Events created and implemented a risk management plan for the Sydney Marathon Festival. This plan extensively fulfilled the following functions:
• identifying what, why and how risks arise as a basis for further analysis
• analysing risks in terms of likelihood and consequence
• prioritising risks to identify management priorities
• developing preventative and/or response measures involving administrative, operational and training aspects
• establishing a system to monitor and review the performance of the process, and changes that might affect it
• communications — aiding the operations plan on the day of the event.

By creating and implementing this risk management plan, AAP Events identified all potential logistical problems and implemented strategies to prevent such problems from occurring.

Operations

A key logistical tool for the 2003 Sydney Marathon was the official operations guide. The guide contained all key information, including run sheets, course maps, venue layout plans, radio instructions, key contacts, emergency procedures and incident reporting cards. It supplied event organisers, contractors and volunteers with critical operational information and procedures, ensuring a higher level of education and awareness. Event day radios were directly linked to the POC, where key event organisers and stakeholders were located. The POC had the ability to contact emergency services directly to enable fast and effective service for an injured athlete. The POC was the marathon's 'big brother' facility; cameras and radios enabled the centre to see and hear all, which meant any logistical concerns could be addressed and overcome swiftly.

Event timing

Timing coordination in the 2003 Sydney Marathon played a key role in the overall effectiveness of event logistics. In a official race event such as the marathon, every minute is of vital importance. If the race starts 10 minutes late, then roads re-open 10 minutes later, causing disruption to the whole city. During the 2003 10-kilometre bridge run, a problem occurred as a direct result of failure to adhere to event timing logistics. An independent company was contracted for the clothing bag logistics on event day, and given extensive information regarding timing procedures to ensure athlete clothing bags reached the finish in the shortest time possible. The company had a few short minutes to cross the road closures and drive to the finish line. Due to this company supplying two trucks instead of the agreed four trucks on event day, the trucks took more time to pack and they failed to reach the road closure on time. Due to this timing failure, 8500 athletes at the 10-kilometre finish were stranded, waiting over an hour for their belongings contained within the trucks. The contractor involved was at a loss to know why a staff member had acted contrary to the agreed operational plan for event day, and subsequently apologised to event organisers and competitors.

Environmental impact

Another key concern on the 2003 event day was a problem that event organisers could not prevent — gale-force winds. Environmental impact was considered within the risk management planned, and strategies to combat such problems were devised. Unfortunately, the major implication of these winds was that athletes had a more arduous task, running against the wind. Finishing times were thus approximately 10 minutes slower than in 2002. A review was planned on wind loads for some of the infrastructure, to ensure more effective means of restraining movement would be provided for the next year's event.

(continued)

Debrief procedures and stakeholder liaison

Post-event formal debrief processes were conducted to finalise all logistical details in 2003. Debrief meetings were held with the client and key stakeholders. For the marathon, the key stakeholders consisted of all groups who played a significant role in the running of the event, including:

- the event owners — Athletics Australia and Frontiers Group Australasia
- government bodies — the Central Sydney Operations Group (CSOG), the NSW Police, the Road Transport Authority and medical groups
- venue councils and authorities — the North Sydney Council, Centennial Parklands, the Royal Botanical Gardens, the Sydney Opera House and the Sydney Olympic Park Authority (SOPA)
- contractors — equipment and logistics suppliers
- volunteers — a strong volunteer workforce of 620 volunteers on event day.

From this debrief procedure, APP Events produced a detailed report, which included a list of recommendations for the 2004 event. This was part of the ongoing refinement process to ensure progressive improvement of the hallmark event in Sydney. From the report, a summary was given to the New South Wales Government to ensure confirmation of future support. (For further information on APP Events, please refer to the company's website www.app.com.au.)

APP Events

Questions

1 List the stakeholders involved in this event.

2 Using figure 12.1 (page 378), divide the supply side of this event's logistics into attendees, participants and facilities.

3 List five of the risks to the event and possible minimisation strategies for each.

4 How could the event manager have foreseen the transport problem?

5 What aspects of event logistics would have to change to accommodate an increase of 28 per cent in the number of event participants?

6 Discuss the relationship between project management (as outlined in chapter 9) and logistics management.

7 Analyse this event in the categories of logistics: supply, transport, linking, flow control and information network.

REFERENCES

Buchan Communications Group 1997, *Australia–India new horizons evaluation report*, Department of Foreign Affairs and Trade, Canberra.

Catherwood, DW & Van Kirk, RL 1992, *The complete guide to special events management*, John Wiley & Sons, New York.

CIM Rostrum n.d., 'The comprehensive convention planner's manual', vol. 32, Rank Publishing Company, Sydney.

Coyle, JJ, Bardi, EJ & Langley Jnr, CJ 1988, *The management of business logistics*, 4th edn, West Publishing, St Paul.

Dinsmore, PC 1990, *Human factors in project management*, AMACOM, New York.

Gilmour, P 1993, *Logistics management: an Australian framework*, Addison Wesley Longman, Melbourne.

Goldblatt, J 1997, *Special events: best practices in modern event management*, 2nd edn, Van Nostrand Reinhold, New Jersey.

Government of Victoria 2004, *Event management: planning guide for event managers in Victoria*, Melbourne.

Graham, S, Goldblatt, J & Delpy, L 1995, *The ultimate guide to sports event management and marketing*, Richard Irwin, Chicago.

Lock, D 1988, *Project management*, Gower Press, Aldershot, England.

Marine Corps 1997, *Logistics*, Doctrinal publication no. 4, www.doctrine.quantico.usmc.mil/mcdp/mcdp4.html.

Marsh, PDV 1984, *Contract negotiation handbook*, 2nd edn, Gower Press, Aldershot, England.

Monmonier, M 1996, *How to lie with maps*, 2nd edn, University of Chicago Press, Chicago.

Neighbourhood Arts Unit 1991, *Community festival handbook*, City of Melbourne, Melbourne.

O'Toole, WJ 2003, *Event project management system*, CD-ROM, www.epms.net.

Pagonis, Lt General WG 1992, *Moving mountains: lessons in leadership and logistics from the Gulf War*, Harvard Business School Press, Boston.

Queensland Folk Federation Incorporated 1997, *Operational and site management plan 1997*, Brisbane.

Staging *events*

LEARNING OBJECTIVES

After studying this chapter, you should be able to:

- analyse the staging of an event according to its constituent elements

- demonstrate how these elements relate to each other and to the theme of the event

- understand the safety elements of each aspect of staging

- identify the relative importance of the staging elements for different types of event

- use the tools of staging.

The term 'staging' originates from the presentation of plays at the theatre. It refers to bringing together all the elements of a theatrical production for its presentation on a stage. Most events that use this term take place at a single venue and require organisation similar to that of a theatrical production. However, whereas a play can take place over a season, a special event may take place in one night. Examples of this type of event are product launches, company parties and celebrations, awards ceremonies, conference events, concerts, large weddings, corporate dinners, and opening and closing events.

Staging can also refer to the organisation of a venue within a much larger festival. A large festival may have performance areas positioned around a site. Each of these venues may have a range of events with a distinct theme. At the Sydney Royal Easter Show, there are a number of performance areas, each with its own style. Because it is part of a much larger event, one performance area or event has to fit in with the overall planning of the complete event and with the festival programming and logistics. However, each performance area is to some extent its own kingdom, with its own micro-logistics, management, staff and individual character. One stage of Sydney's Royal Easter Show had the theme 'world music and dance', for example. The venue had its own event director, stage manager, and light and sound technicians. Although it was part of the overall theme of the Royal Easter Show, it was allowed a certain amount of autonomy by the show entertainment director.

The main concerns of staging are as follows:
• theming and event design
• programming
• choice of venue
• audience and guests
• stage
• power, lights and sound
• audiovisuals and special effects
• catering
• performers
• crew
• hospitality
• the production schedule
• recording the event
• contingencies.

This chapter analyses the staging of an event according to these elements. It demonstrates how these elements revolve around a central event theme. The type of event will determine how important each of these elements is to the others. However, common to the staging of different events are the tools: the stage plan, the contact and responsibility list, and the production schedule.

THEMING AND EVENT DESIGN

When staging an event, the major artistic and creative decision to be made is that of determining the theme. The theme of an event differentiates it from other events. In the corporate area, the client may determine the theme of the event. The client holding a corporate party or product launch may want, for example, medieval Europe as the theme, or Australiana, complete with native animals and bush band. Outside the corporate area, the theme for one of the stages at a festival may be blues music, debating or a children's circus. Whatever the nature of the event, once the theme is established, the elements of the event must be designed to fit in with the theme. This is straightforward when it comes to deciding on the entertainment and catering. With the medieval corporate party, the entertainment may include jongleurs and jugglers, and the catering may be spit roasts and wine. However, audiovisuals may need a lot of thought to enhance the theme; the sound and lights must complement the entertainment or they may not fit in with the period theme. Figure 13.1 is a breakdown of the elements of staging, and it emphasises the central role of the theme of the event.

■ **Figure 13.1**
The elements of staging revolve around the theme

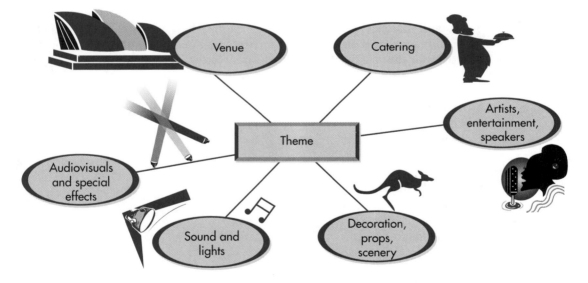

The director of the Port Fairy Folk Festival expresses the importance of staging in the following way:

■ A great concert experience begins with the excitement built by the advertised program and venue facilities. The audience must be given reasonable comfort and have their expectations met. You must deliver the advertised act, at the advertised place and time and leave them wanting more. This means that the staging will look good, preferably great, the sound production and lighting will be of high quality, the overall presentation will be dignified and professional. ■

On 2 February 2004, the Ballarat Botanical Gardens hosted a dedication ceremony for the official opening of the Australian Ex-Prisoners of War Memorial, which was designed to commemorate Australians who were held prisoners during the Boer War, world wars I and II, and the Korean War.

The memorial contains more than 35 000 names and is designed as a place of national honour, remembrance and healing for all Australians. The theme for the event was to pay special tribute to the men and women who had been held captive as prisoners of war. It was about honouring, recognising and reflecting on the contribution these people made to Australia, with the memorial being a mark of respect from a grateful nation.

The audience consisted of 6200 invited guests, including ex-prisoners of war, widows, families, friends, representatives from defence and service organisations, politicians, dignitaries and donors. Official guests were provided with a seat. A further 3000 to 4000 people from around Australia attended and either brought their own seats or stood for the service. The majority of the audience were seniors, but many ex-prisoners of war were represented by their children and grandchildren.

The ceremony consisted of speeches from the Governor-General, the Mayor of the City of Ballarat, the Minister for Veterans Affairs (representing the Prime Minister), the Premier of Victoria, the National President of the Australian Ex-Prisoners of War Association, the Chair of the Memorial Appeal Committee and the major donor, Tattersalls. The Chief of the Defence Force performed the official opening, and defence force chaplains conducted the dedication and consecration. All key dignitaries were invited to place wreaths on the memorial, the Roulettes made flyovers, and various readings were done, including one by a secondary school student to represent the youth of Australia. The service went for 90 minutes and was situated at the memorial site in an outdoor setting. The Australian Army Band Melbourne and the Welsh Male Choir provided music. Both were experienced in performing at military-style events. Defence force cadets were involved in various tasks, including ushering guests to their seats, greeting guests, and an involvement in the actual ceremony. The size and content of wreaths and their placement on the memorial during the ceremony had to be done in order of precedence. Both political and military protocols had to be observed throughout the ceremony.

The program content, the site design and the presentation were built around the most important VIPs of the day: the ex-prisoners of war. The staging was simple and minimalist, with significant effort being put into ensuring the focus of the day was the memorial rather than the event

(continued)

infrastructure. The staging for the speakers, band and choir was designed to blend with the site, rather than be the focus. The stage height was selected on the basis of visibility by the audience, ease of access by the speakers, and fit with the memorial site. While the performers would have preferred a covered stage, it would have detracted from the site, so other sun protection mechanisms were put into place. The speakers' stage contained the Australian and Victorian flags, plants that were considered to be compatible with the site, and professional podiums that showed no signage.

The audio system was designed to ensure not only those seated could hear the service, but also the guests surrounding the official seating section. Hearing the service was vitally important to the audience, so additional resources were allocated to obtaining the best possible sound system. Silenced generators to power the sound, catering and food vendors were used. The sound system selected blended as much as possible with the environment, rather than standing out as a feature.

No signage was allowed on site, and a special effort was made to ensure the site was safe for all of those attending. This effort included barricading off areas that might have been a trip hazard and ensuring cadets were available to assist guests to and from the seats. Cadets were perceived to be more fitting with the theme, rather than the usual ushers. The 6200 seats provided for invited guests were all white (at considerable expense and effort, but worthwhile in terms of fitting with the theme). The aisle widths were slightly wider than usual to allow wheelchairs, walking frames and access by ambulance officers. The first-aid and medical support for the event had to be visible yet not obtrusive. Free water was provided as a part of the risk management plan. There was minimal site decoration to ensure the memorial was the key focus. Plants were used primarily to minimise trip hazards on the site.

The road directly behind the memorial was closed to ensure vehicles were not travelling during the ceremony, and parking areas were allocated to ensure vehicles did not detract from the venue. VIPs, including ex-prisoners of war, were allocated parking nearest to the memorial site, with other guests having available free shuttle buses to transport them from the carpark to the memorial site.

The invitations, the program for the service, and the letterhead were designed to fit the theme. The style, colour, font size and content accounted for the key audience for the event, so the artwork was symbolic, formal and respectful.

While the occasion was serious and sombre, it was also an opportunity to celebrate the fact that ex-prisoners of war now have a memorial in remembrance and recognition. Speakers were thus asked to show appreciation for the sacrifices and to celebrate the lives of the men and women who served.

After the official opening, a reunion luncheon for ex-prisoners of war was conducted on site for 1650 people. Attendance included ex-prisoners of war, widows and invited dignitaries. The lunch venue had to fit with the theme, so a 45 metre × 30 metre white marquee was erected on site. The set-out (placement of tables, chairs, food, beverages and decorations), the menu and the speeches were designed to ensure those present had the maximum opportunity to circulate. The luncheon was finger food (practical rather than lavish). There was some pressure to have a more lavish luncheon (additional decorations and a sit-down meal), but this was resisted to ensure the reunion theme of the event was maintained.

A number of food vendors were brought to the site for those not invited to the luncheon. The food and beverage served was relatively simple, and vendors were selected on their presentation and type of food. While a number of 'showground-style' vendors applied, these were not selected because they did not fit the theme of the event.

The media strategy focused on ensuring the media had an understanding of the purpose of the memorial and the theme of the opening. Media were required to be accredited and were provided with background information on the memorial and the opening. Specific information was provided on the theme of the opening, rather than assuming the media would pick it up on the day. Media personnel were asked to respect the occasion, treat it as a service similar to Anzac Day, and operate within the parameters set out in the media kit.

The site of the event was the memorial venue, located in the Botanical Gardens. All infrastructure (stages, seating, sound, power, toilets, catering and marquees) had to be brought to the venue. The brief to providers contained details on the event and the sense of occasion, and attention was paid to ensuring the services had the right 'look' for the occasion.

Tracey Hull, Events Ballarat

PROGRAMMING

The program of the event is the flow of the performers, speakers, catering and the other elements of the event over time. It is the schedule of performance. As with all the elements of staging, programming is both an art and a science. The program of the event depends on:

- the expectations of the audience
- the constraints of the venue and infrastructure
- the culture of the client and main sponsors
- the availability of elements of the staging, and their relationship to each other
- the logistics.

It is similar to the order in a street parade — the timeline or schedule of the program is set out in a linear fashion. Far from this being a simple example, a parade is multifaceted, and there is little the event manager can do to change it once it starts moving. Consider the music: the brass band cannot be performing near the highland pipe band; they perform at slightly different beats. An event program also has a rhythm all of its own. The mix of entertainment, catering and speeches has to be well thought out so the event builds and the audience has times of intensity and times of rest. A new year's eve program, for example, gradually lifts the audience to the moment before midnight.

A large festival's program is a complex of activities. Many festivals use a form of a Gantt chart to map the various attractions and to help the audience navigate the event program. If the event is broadcast, the event program may have to be in sync with the television programming. This is a major consideration for sport events.

In the words of Colin Slater of the event company Sing Australia (in the Australian Capital Territory), 'The program on the night must begin by establishing the atmosphere ... You don't want to boss the audience — give them time to settle in. Then we get the MC to introduce the night so the purpose of the event is clearly known by all. Also, I like to involve the audience before they eat to get them all to loosen up and relax. The night should start bright and happy and have its plateaus, so it is not full-on all night. Program it to finish on an absolute high whether they are dancing or clapping or singing'.

CHOICE OF VENUE

The choice of venue is a crucial decision that will ultimately determine many of the elements of staging. Figure 13.2 lists the major factors in the choice of a venue. The venue may be an obvious part of the theme of the event. A corporate party that takes place in a zoo is using the venue as part of the event experience. However, many events take place within 'four walls and a roof', the venue being chosen for other factors. It can be regarded as an empty canvas on which the event is 'painted'. Cameron (1993), in his work on community theatre, describes the events he has staged in disused factories, forests and stages floating on water. He describes how the event manager can use the atmosphere and natural beauty of open-air performances. In these situations, the traditional roles of stage manager and event manager become blurred. When the audience and the performers mix together, and where they and the venue become the entertainment package, the delineation between stage and auditorium is no longer appropriate.

A special event that uses a purpose-built venue, such as an entertainment centre, will find that much of the infrastructure will be in place. However, because so many factors in an event depend on the venue or site, an inspection is absolutely necessary. For conference events, *Rostrum* (vol. 32) suggests the event manager attends a function at the venue and tests the facilities. It recommends placing a long-distance telephone call, trying the food and staying in the approved accommodation.

- Matching the venue with the theme of the event
- Matching the size of the venue to the size of the event
- Venue configuration, including sight lines and seating configuration
- History of events at that venue, including the venue's reputation
- Availability
- What the venue can provide
- Transport to, from and around the venue; parking
- Access for audience, equipment, performers, VIPs, staff and the disabled
- Toilets and other amenities
- Catering equipment and preferred caterers
- Power (amount available and outlets) and lights
- Communication, including telephone
- Climate, including microclimate and ventilation
- Emergency plans and exits

Two documents that are a good starting point for making an informed choice about the venue are the venue map and the list of facilities. However, *CIM Rostrum* (vol. 32) recommends that the event manager meet the venue management before commiting to hire the venue. The principal purpose of this meeting is to check the accuracy of the two documents, because the map, the list of facilities and the photographs can be out of date or aimed at promoting the venue rather than imparting detailed information. The photograph of the venue, for example, may be taken with a wide-angle lens so all the facilities are included. Such a photograph may not give a realistic view of the site if it is being used for event design.

As with many aspects of supplier selection, the Internet has had a significant effect on venue choice. Using a search engine is often the first action in the investigation of a suitable venue. Some websites display a choice of venues once certain information (such as size of audience, approximate location and type of event) has been entered. The major hotels, conventions and exhibition centres, universities and purpose-built venues have websites to enable the matching of event requirements to venue characteristics. However, this method has the same limitations as those of using photos and brochures to assess a venue. The websites are a tool for selling the venue, not a technical description. In addition, many suitable venues may not have an Internet presence. An Internet search will show only venues that expect to host events. If the event is truly special, the event venue may be part of that theme. A car park or a rainforest, for example, will not appear in a search for event venues.

AUDIENCE AND GUESTS

The larger issues of audience (customer) logistics have been described in chapter 12. The event staging considerations concerning the audience are:

- position of entrances and exits
- arrival times — dump or trickle
- seating and sight lines
- facilities.

Goldblatt (1997) emphasises the importance of the entrance and reception area of an event in establishing the event theme, and suggests the organiser should look at it from the guest's point of view. It is in this area that appropriate signage and meeting and greeting become important to the flow of 'traffic' and to the wellbeing of the guests. An example of a carefully planned entrance area was at a recent Woodford Folk Festival, where the children's area was entered through the mouth of a large papier-mâché dragon.

Once the guests have entered the event area, problems can occur that are specific to the type of event. In the case of conferences, audiences immediately head for the back rows. Interestingly, Graham, Goldblatt and Delpy (1995, p. 65) mention the opposite problem occurs at sports events, where the front rows are rushed as soon as the gates open. The solution, therefore, is in the type of admission — for example, organisers can adopt reserved seating methods, using ticket numbers or roped-off sections and a designated seating plan. The style of seating can be chosen to suit the event; theatre, classroom and banquet-type seating are three examples. Ultimately, the seating plan has to consider:

- the type of seating — fixed or movable
- the size of the audience
- the method of audience arrival
- safety factors, including emergency exits and fire regulations
- the placement and size of the aisles
- sight lines to the performances, speakers or audiovisual displays
- disabled access
- catering needs.

The facilities provided for the guests will depend on the type of event. Referring to figure 13.3 (page 425), the corporate event will focus on particular audience facilities as they relate to hospitality and catering, whereas a festival event will concentrate on audience facilities as they relate to entertainment. There are no chairs, for example, for the audience in some of the Port Fairy Folk Festival performance areas, but the nature of the festival means spectators are happy to bring their own chairs or sit on the ground. At the other end of the spectrum, the 1998 Australian Petroleum Production and Exploration Association Conference Dinner, organised by Sing Australia in the Great Hall at Parliament House, Canberra, had high-quality furnishings and facilities.

THE STAGE

A stage at an event is rarely the same as a theatrical stage complete with proscenium arch and auditorium. It can range from the back of a truck to a barge in a harbour. In event management, the term 'stage' can be applied to the general staging area and not just to a purpose-built stage. However, all stages require a stage map called the stage plan. The stage plan is simply a bird's-eye view of the performance area, showing the infrastructure, such as lighting fixtures, entrances, exits and power outlets. The stage plan is one of the staging tools (figure 13.10, page 440) and a communication device that enables the event to run smoothly. For large events, the stage plan is drawn in different ways for different people, and supplied on a 'need-to-know basis'. A stage plan for the lighting technician, for example, would look different from the plan for the performers. The master stage plan contains all these different plans, each drawn on a separate layer of transparent paper. Other plans used in event design are the front elevation and side elevation. In contrast to the bird's-eye view of the stage plan, these plans show the staging area as a ground-level view from the front and side respectively. They assist in establishing the audience's sight lines — that is, the audience's view of the staging area and performers.

A large stage plan was used for a conference of the Société Internationale d'Urologie in Sydney. The 3000 guests were treated to three streams of entertainment that reflected modern Australia: 'multicultural', including a lion dance and middle eastern dancers; 'land and sea', including a large sailing boat and Aboriginal and Australiana entertainers; and 'cities', with fashion parades and modern dancers.

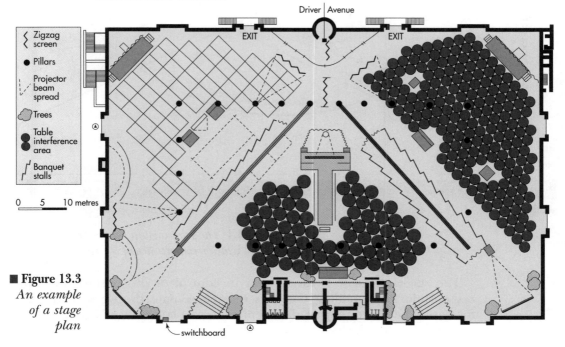

Figure 13.3
An example of a stage plan

Roger Foley, of Fogg Production, the creator of the Australian Multicultural Show, described the stage plan:

■ The stage plan is 100 per cent accurate. I went to the building's architects to get an exact drawing and we used that as the master stage plan. The accuracy of having all the building's peculiarities on a plan allowed all the subcontractors to anticipate any problems in setting up. [There were] 1-metre markings on the building's circumference. All these little things enabled the whole show, including 13 stages and 21 food stalls, to be set up and bumped out in 24 hours. A stage plan for each of the individual stages was created by enlarging that section from the master plan and filling in the necessary information. ■

When the staging of an event includes a large catering component, the stage plan is referred to as the venue layout or floor plan. This is the case in many corporate and conference events, for which hospitality and catering become a major part of the staging. Figure 13.4 illustrates how the focus on the staging elements changes according to the style of event.

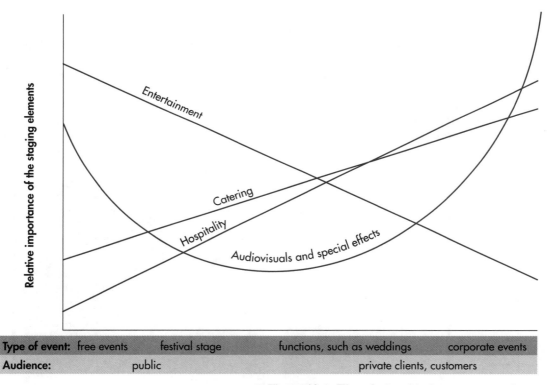

■ **Figure 13.4** *The relationship between types of event and the relative importance of the staging elements*

The stage manager is the person in control of the performance and responsible for signalling the cues that coordinate the work of the performers. The scheduling of the event on a particular stage is generally the responsibility of the event manager. The stage manager makes sure this happens according to the plan. The public face of the event may be called the master of ceremonies (MC) or compere. The compere and the stage manager work closely together to ensure all goes according to the plan. The compere may also make public announcements, such as those about lost children and program changes.

The combination of electric wiring, hot lights, special effects and the fast movement of performers and staff in a small space that is perhaps 2 metres above ground level makes the risk management of the staging area particularly important. At the event, stage safety is generally the responsibility of the stage manager. Figure 13.5 lists key safety considerations.

■ **Figure 13.5**
Factors to consider in stage safety

- There must be a well-constructed stage done professionally by a company with adequate insurance.
- There must be clear, well-lit access points to the stage.
- All protrusions and steps should be secured and clearly marked.
- Equipment and boxes should be placed out of the way and well marked.
- There should be work lights that provide white lighting before and after the event.
- All electric cabling must be secured and tagged.
- A first-aid kit and other emergency equipment should be at hand.
- There must be clear guidelines on who is in charge during an emergency.
- A list of all relevant contact numbers should be made.

The director of the Port Fairy Folk Festival gives this advice for stage managers:

■ Make sure you anticipate the many little things that can ruin an otherwise great concert experience. Watch out for distracting buzzes or cracks in the sound (e.g. from powerful fridges); settle out-of-control children or noisy audiences; ensure all small stage requirements are there (e.g. chair, stool, table, water); ensure you have competent MCs who are well prepared; stop delays before they start. ■

The backstage area is a private room or tent near the performance area, and is set aside for the performers and staff. It provides the crew with a place to relax and the performers with a place to prepare for the performance and wind down afterwards. It can be used for storage of equipment and for communication between the stage manager and performers, and it is where the food and drink are kept.

POWER

Staging of any event involves large numbers of people. To service this crowd, electricity is indispensable. It should never be taken for granted. Factors that need to be considered concerning power are listed on the following page.

- The type of power — three phase or single phase
- The amount of power needed, particularly at peak times
- emergency power
- The position and number of power outlets
- The types of lead and the distance from the power source to the device
- The correct wiring of the venue, because old venues are often improperly earthed
- The incoming equipment's volt/amp rating
- Safety factors, including the covering of leads and the possibility of electricity earth leakage as a result of rain
- Local and state regulations regarding power.

*L*IGHTS

Lighting at a venue has two functions. Pragmatically, lights allow everyone to see what is happening; artistically, they are integral to the design of the event. The general venue or site lighting is important in that it allows all other aspects of staging to take place. For this reason, it is usually the first item on the checklist when organisers decide on a venue. Indoor lights include signage lights (exit, toilets etc.), as well as those illuminating specific areas such as catering and ticket collection. Outside the venue, lighting is required for venue identification, safety, security and signs.

Once the general venue or site lighting is confirmed, lighting design needs to be considered. The questions to ask when considering lighting are both practical and aesthetic:
- Does the lighting fit in with and enhance the overall event theme?
- Can it be used for ambient lighting as well as performance lighting?
- Is there a back-up?
- What are the power requirements? (Lights can draw far more power than the sound system.)
- Will it interfere with the electrics of other systems? A dimmer board, for example, can create an audible buzz in the sound system.
- Does it come with a light operator — that is, the person responsible for the planning of the lighting with the lighting board?
- What light effects are needed (strobe, cross-fading)? Can the available lights do this?
- What equipment is needed (for example, trees and cans)? Is there a place on the site or in the venue to erect it?
- How can the lighting assist in the safety and security of the event?

The lighting plot or lighting plan is a map of the venue that shows the type and position of the lighting. As Reid (1995) points out, the decisions that the event manager has to make when creating a lighting plan are:
- placement of the lights
- the type of lights, including floods and follow spots
- where the light should be pointed
- what colours to use.

SOUND

The principal reason for having sound equipment at an event is so all the audience can clearly hear the music, speeches and audio effects. The sound system is also used to:

- communicate between the sound engineer and the stage manager (talk-back or intercom)
- monitor the sound
- create a sound recording of the event
- broadcast the sound to other venues or through other media, including television, radio and the Internet.

This means the type of equipment used needs to be designed according to:

- the type of sound to be amplified. This includes spoken word and music.
- the size and make-up of the audience. An older audience, for example, may like the music at a different volume from that preferred by a younger audience.
- acoustic properties of the room. Some venues have a bad echo problem, for example.
- the theme of the event. A sound system painted bright silver may look out of place at a black tie dinner.

The choice of size, type and location of the sound speakers at an event can make a difference to the guests' experience of the sound. Figure 13.6 shows two simplified plans for speaker positions at a venue. The speakers may all be next to the stage, which is common at music concerts, or distributed around the site. They may also be flown from supports above the audience. At a large site, with speakers widely distributed, the sound engineers need to account for the natural delay of sound travelling from the various speakers to the members of the audience.

■ **Figure 13.6**
Two examples of audio speaker layout

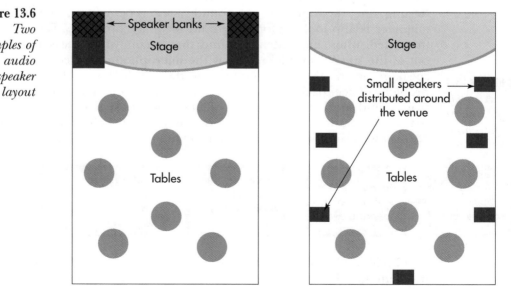

For small events, a simple public address (PA) system may be used. This consists of a microphone, a microphone stand and one or two speakers. It is basically the same as a home stereo system with a microphone added, and generally has only enough power to reach a small audience. The quality of sound produced makes such systems suitable for speeches only.

For larger events that have more complex sound requirements, a larger sound system is needed. This system would incorporate:

- microphones, which may include lapel mikes and radio mikes
- microphone stands
- cabling, including from the microphones to the mixing desk
- a mixing desk, which adjusts the quality and level of the sound coming from the microphones before it goes out the speakers
- an amplifier
- speakers, which can vary in size from bass speakers to treble speakers, and which enhance the quality of the sound within a certain sound spectrum
- a sound engineer or sound technician, who looks after all aspects of the sound, particularly the sound quality that is heard by the audience
- back-up equipment, including spare leads and microphones.

The next step up from this type of system includes all of the above as well as:

- foldback speakers (also called monitors) that channel the sound back to the speakers or performers so they can hear themselves over the background sound
- a foldback mixing desk
- a foldback engineer who is responsible for the quality of sound going through the monitors.

If an event needs a sound system managed by a sound engineer, time must be allocated to tune the sound system. This means the acoustic qualities of the venue are taken into account by trying out the effect of various sound frequencies within the venue. This is the reason for the often-heard 'testing, one, two, one, two' as a sound system is being prepared. The sound engineer is also looking for any sound feedback problems. Feedback is an unwanted, often high-pitched sound that occurs when the sound coming out of the speakers is picked up by the microphones and comes out of the speakers again, thereby building on the original sound. To avoid the problem of feedback, microphones must be positioned so they face away from sound speakers. The tuning of a large sound system is one of the main reasons for having a sound check or run-through before an event. Figure 13.7 shows a simplified sound run-through.

■ **Figure 13.7**
A simple flow chart for sound systems

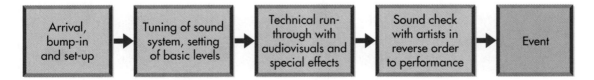

Volume and sound leakage during an event can become a major problem. Local councils can close an event if there are too many complaints from residents. At some venues, for example, there are volume switches that automatically turn off the power if the sound level is too high. At multi-venue events, sound leakage between stages can be minimised by:

- thoughtful placement of the stages
- careful positioning of all sound speakers (including the monitors)
- constant monitoring of the volume level
- careful programming of the events on each stage in a way that avoids interference.

AUDIOVISUAL AND SPECIAL EFFECTS

Many event managers hire lighting and sound from separate companies and integrate these external services into the overall design of the event. However, some suppliers provide both lighting and sound equipment, and act as consultants before the event. These audiovisual companies can supply a fully integrated system of film, video, slides and, often, special effects. However, most audiovisual companies are specialists in flat-screen presentations, and the special effects area is often best left to specialists in each field. Pyrotechnics obviously require different skills and licences from those of ice sculptors, for example. Complex events that use a variety of special effects and audiovisuals require a coordinator who is familiar with the event theme and knows how to link all the specialist areas. This coordinator is called the event producer. Although the terms 'event manager', 'stage manager' and 'event producer' are confusing, they are terms used in the industry. The position of event producer is created when many different specialists are involved in the event. Organisers of corporate events, including product launches and conferences, often sub-contract the audiovisual elements, because the specialist knowledge required means an expert is needed to operate these systems effectively. The decision to use an audiovisual company for an event depends on:

- how the audiovisual presentation fits in with the overall event design
- the budget allocated to the event
- the skills of the audiovisual company, including its technical hardware, software and the abilities of the audiovisual producer and writer.

For large-budget events, the audiovisual company will act as a consultant, with the producer and writer researching and creating a detailed audiovisual script.

Roger Foley of Fogg Production is an expert in the area of 'illuminating art as entertainment and performance'. He regards the essence of an event as the special effects. His aim is to make the event itself a special effect: 'A special effect is anything that is not anticipated or expected. It must heighten the awareness of the viewers and increase their anticipation, sensitivity and receptiveness. The result is to make it easy to get across the message of the event.' Foley emphasises the need to take complete command of all the elements of the special effect. The event producer must know exactly what they are getting when hiring specialists. Fireworks, for example, must be individually listed, fully integrated into the event and not just left to the specialist. The timing of setting off the various devices must be exact, without any gaps.

According to Goldblatt (1997), special effects at an event are used to attract attention, generate excitement and sustain interest. In larger festivals, such as the opening of the Melbourne Festival on the Yarra River, the pyrotechnics become part of the overall logistics planning. Event managers and planners must fully realise the importance of event decoration, scenery and appropriate props as an enhancing tool for the staging of any event.

Because much of the audiovisual and special effects technology is highly complex, it is often 'pre-programmed'. This means that all lighting, audiovisual and sound 'pre-sets' (technical elements positioned before the event) — including the changing light and sound levels, and the cueing of video and slide presentations — can be programmed into the controlling computer. The computer control of much of the audiovisuals means the whole presentation can be fully integrated and set up well in advance. Because these aspects are pre-arranged, including all the cue times, few technicians are needed to control these operations during the event. The disadvantages, however, are that spontaneity can be taken from the event and that, the more complex the technology, the more things can go wrong. Moreover, the technology becomes the master of the cue times, and it is nearly impossible to take advantage of any unforeseen opportunities.

PROPS AND DECORATION

Some events are similar to operatic productions in their use of scenery, stage properties (props) and decoration. Skilled use of these elements can make the attendees feel as though they are in an imaginary world. The audience can often enhance this by dressing the part and becoming part of the entertainment. Themed parties, festivals and dinners are a significant part of the event industry. The way in which these staging elements are combined and their relative emphasis at the event often reflects the personal style of the event company. Malouf (1999) devotes over two-thirds of her book to theming in events, particularly the use of flowers, lights and colour to create a sense of wonder.

CATERING

Catering can be the major element in staging, depending on the theme and nature of an event. Most purpose-built venues already have catering arrangements in place. Parliament House in Canberra, for example, contracts with catering companies. The conference dinners that take place in the Great Hall can use only the in-house caterers. Figure 13.8 illustrates some of the many factors to be considered in catering.

The event producer Reno Dal makes the following points about aspects of catering:

■ My rule for the staff-to-client ratio at a corporate function is:
silver service, 1 to 10 ratio
five-star service 1 to 25 ratio
general catering 1 to 50 ratio.
I emphasise that there should be 'waves of service'. This means that the main course and beverage arrive at the right time and then waiters leave the guests until the appropriate moment for the next course. I like to see each table as a stage, with the placements presented in the same manner as a theatrical stage. The waiters become the performers dressed to the theme. The waiters love it — after all, it's a difficult job at the best of times. ■

■ **Figure 13.8**
Issues to be considered when arranging catering for an event

In-house or contracted?
The advantage of in-house catering is the knowledge of the venue. The advantages of contract catering are: (1) the event manager may have a special arrangement with the caterer that has been built up over time; (2) the event manager can choose all aspects of the catering; and (3) the catering can be tendered out and a competitive bid sought.

Quality control factors to consider
■ Appropriateness and enhancement of the event theme
■ Menu selection and design, including special diets and food displays
■ Quality of staff and supervision
■ Equipment, including style and quantity, and selection of in-house or hired
■ Cleanliness
■ Cultural appropriateness — a major consideration in a culturally diverse society
■ Staff-to-guest ratio

Costs
■ Are there any guarantees, including those against loss and breakages?
■ What are the payment terms?
■ Who is responsible for licences and permits: the caterer, the venue or event management?
■ What deposits and upfront fees are there?
■ What is the per capita expenditure? Is each guest getting value commensurate with the client's expenditure?

Waste management
■ Must occur before, during and after the event
■ Must conform to health regulations and environmental concerns
■ Must be appropriate to the event theme

As Graham, Goldblatt and Delpy (1995) stress, the consumption of alcoholic beverages at an event gives rise to many concerns for the event manager. These include the special training of staff, which party holds the licence (venue, event manager or client), and the legal age for consumption. The possible problems that arise from the sale of alcohol — for example, increased audience noise at the end of the event and general behavioural problems — can affect almost all aspects of the event. Due to the high risk in this area, one event company sends all of its staff to responsible service of alcohol (RSA) training. The decision on whether to allow the sale or consumption of alcohol can be crucial to the success of an event and needs careful thought.

The serving of alcohol can be negotiated with a caterer in a variety of ways. The drinks service can be from the bar or served at the table by the glass, bottle or jug. A caterer may offer a 'drinks package', which means the drinks are free for, say, the first hour of the catered event. A subtle result of this type of deal is that the guests may find it hard to find a drinks waiter in the first hour.

PERFORMERS

The 'talent' (as performers are often called) at an event can range from music groups to motivational speakers to specially commissioned shows. A performing group can form a major part of an event's design. The major factors to consider when employing artists are listed below:

- *Contact* — the event's entertainment coordinator needs to establish contact only with the person responsible for the employment of the artist or artists. This could be the artist, an agent representing the artist, or the manager of a group. It is important to establish this line of authority at the beginning when working with the artists.
- *Staging requirements* — a rock band, for example, will have more complex sound requirements than those of a folk singer. These requirements are usually listed on a document called the spec (specification) sheet. Many groups will also have their own stage plan illustrating the area needed and their preferred configuration of the performance area.
- *Availability for rehearsal, media attention and performance* — the available times given by the artists' management should include the time needed for the artists to set up on stage as well as the time needed to vacate the stage or performance area. These are referred to as 'set-up' and 'pull-down' times. These times need to be considered when, for example, scheduling a series of rehearsals with a number of performing groups.
- *Accompanying personnel* — many artists travel with an entourage that can include technicians, cooks, stylists and bodyguards. It is important to establish their numbers and their roles and needs.
- *Contracts and legal requirements* — the agreement between the event manager and the performers is described in chapter 11. Particularly

important to the staging are union minimum rates and conditions, the legal structure of the artists, and issues such as workers compensation, tax structure and public liability. Copyright is also important because its ownership can affect the use of the performance for broadcast and future promotions.

- *Payment* — most performing groups work on the understanding that they will be paid immediately for their services. Except for 'headline' acts that have a company structure, the 30-, 60- or 90-day invoicing cycle is not appropriate for most performers, who rarely have the financial resources that would allow them to wait for payment.

Performers come from a variety of performance cultural backgrounds. This means different performers have different expectations about the facilities available for them and how they are to be treated. Theatre performers and concert musicians, for example, expect direct performance guidelines — conducting, scripting or a musical score. Street and outdoor festival performers, on the other hand, are used to less formal conditions and to improvising.

Supervision of performers in a small theatre is generally left to the assistant stage manager, whereas a festival stage may not have this luxury and the stage manager may be responsible. Regardless of who undertakes the supervision, it cannot be overlooked. The person responsible needs to make contact with the artists on arrival, give them the appropriate run sheets, introduce them to the relevant crew members and show them the location of the green room (the room in which performers and invited guests are entertained). At the end of the performance, the artists' supervisor needs to assist them in leaving the area.

*T*HE CREW

The chapter on leadership (chapter 6) discussed the role of staff and volunteers at an event. While a large festival or sporting event will usually rely on the work of volunteers, staging tends to be handled by professionals. Dealing with cueing, working with complex and potentially dangerous equipment and handling professional performers leaves little room for indecision and inexperience. Professionalism is essential when staging an event. The staging of a concert performance, for example, will need skilled sound engineers, roadies, security staff, stage crew, ticket sellers and even ushers. (The roadies are the skilled labourers who assist with the set-up and breakdown of the sound and lights.) The crew is selected by matching the tasks involved to the skills of each crew member and ensuring everyone can work together.

The briefing is the meeting, before the event, at which the crew members are given the briefs, or roles, that match their skills. The names and jobs of the crew members are kept on a contact and responsibility sheet.

Neil Cameron, the organiser of many events and lantern parades around Australia and overseas, stresses the importance of being 'brief' at the briefing. His events involve large numbers of performers moving near fire sculptures. These sculptures can be over three storeys high and take weeks to build. He first briefs the support organisations, such as St John Ambulance and the fire brigade, and emphasises the importance of communication and chain of command. At the crew briefing, Neil is conscious of not overloading the leaders with too much information.

The event producer should also not forget that the crew comes with an enormous amount of experience in staging events. The crew can provide valuable input into the creation and design of the event. Interestingly, the changes in the event industry, particularly in the audiovisual area, are reflected in the make-up and number of crew members.

HOSPITALITY

A major part of the package offered to sponsors is hospitality. What will the sponsors expect event management to provide for them and their guests? They may require tickets, food and beverages, souvenirs and gifts. The event may benefit in the long term by also offering hospitality to stakeholders, VIPs and others, including politicians, media units, media personalities, clients of the sponsor, potential sponsors, partners and local opinion leaders. Anyone offered hospitality is referred to as a guest of the event.

The invitation may be the guest's first impression of the event, so it needs to convey the theme of the event. It should create a desire to attend, as well as impart information. Figure 13.9 is a checklist for covering the various elements of hospitality.

In their informative work on sports events, Graham, Goldblatt and Delpy (1995, p. 84) describe the four stages for achieving success in the provision of hospitality to guests. Stage 1 is to know the guests' expectations. Stage 2 is to exceed the guests' expectations, particularly by providing extra amenities. Stage 3 is to be responsive to changes in the guests' needs during the event. Stage 4 is to evaluate the hospitality at the event so it can be improved next time.

Corporate sponsors may have a variety of reasons for attending the event, and these reasons have to be considered in hospitality planning. Graham, Goldblatt and Delpy (1995) suggest reasons including networking opportunities for business, an incentive for a high sales performance, an opportunity for entertaining possible clients, or just the creation of customer goodwill.

The hospitality experience is particularly important at corporate events. In one sense, such an event is centred around hospitality (figure 13.4, p. 426). Being a private function, there is no public and the members of the audience are the guests. Most of the items on the hospitality checklist, from the invitations to the personal service, are applicable to staging these events. For the guests, the hospitality experience is fundamental to the event experience.

■ Figure 13.9
*Looking
after
corporate
sponsors —
a hospitality
checklist*

HOSPITALITY CHECKLIST

Invitations

❑ Is the design of a high quality and is it innovative?

❑ Does the method of delivery allow time to reply? Would hand delivery or email be appropriate?

❑ Does the content of the invitation include time, date, name of event, how to RSVP, directions and parking?

❑ Should promotional material be included with the invitation?

Arrival

❑ Has timing been planned so guests arrive at the best moment?

❑ What are the parking arrangements?

❑ Who will do the meeting and greeting? Will there be someone to welcome them to the event?

❑ Have waiting times been reduced? Will guests receive a welcome cocktail while waiting to be booked into the accommodation, for example?

Amenities

❑ Is there to be a separate area for guests? This can be a marquee, corporate box (at a sporting event) or a club room.

❑ What food and beverages will be provided? Is there a need for a special menu and personal service?

❑ Is there a separate, high-quality viewing area of the performance with good views and facilities?

❑ Has special communication, such as signage or an information desk, been provided?

Gifts

❑ Have tickets to the event, especially for clients, been organised?

❑ What souvenirs (programs, pins, T-shirts, compact discs) will there be?

❑ Will there be a chance for guests to meet the 'stars'?

Departure

❑ Has guest departure been timed so guests do not leave at the same time as the rest of the audience?

THE PRODUCTION SCHEDULE

The terms used in the staging of events come from both the theatre and film production. A rehearsal is a run-through of the event, reproducing the actual event as closely as possible. For the sake of 'getting it right on the night', there may also need to be a technical rehearsal and a dress rehearsal. A production meeting, on the other hand, is a get-together of those responsible for producing an event. It involves the stage manager and the event producer, representatives of the lighting and sound crew or audio-visual specialists, representatives of the performers and the master of ceremonies. It is held at the performance site or stage as near to the time of the event as possible. At this crucial meeting:

- final production schedule notes are compared
- possible last-minute production problems are brought up
- the flow of the event is summarised
- emergency procedures are reviewed
- the compere is introduced and familiarised with the production staff
- the communication system is tested (Neighbourhood Arts Unit 1991, p. 50).

The production schedule is the main document for staging. It is the master document from which other schedules, including the cue or prompt sheet and the run sheets, are created. Goldblatt (1997, p. 143) defines it as the detailed listing of tasks, with specific start and stop times occurring from the set-up of the event's equipment (also known as 'bump-in') to the eventual removal of all the equipment ('bump-out' or 'load-out'). It is often a written form of the Gantt chart (chapter 9) with four columns: time, activity, location and responsibility. Production schedules can also contain a description of the relevant elements of the event.

Two particularly limited times on the schedule are the bump-in and bump-out times. The bump-in is the time when the necessary infrastructure can be brought in, unloaded and set up; the bump-out is the time when the equipment can be dismantled and removed. Although the venue or site may be available to receive the equipment at any time, many other factors set the bump-in time. The hiring cost and availability of equipment are two important limiting factors. In most cases, the larger items must arrive first. These may include fencing, tents, stage, food vans and extra toilets. Next could come the audiovisual equipment and, finally, the various decorations. Supervision of the arrival and set-up of the equipment can be crucial to minimising problems during the event. The contractor who delivers and assembles the equipment is often not the operator of the equipment. This can mean that once equipment is set up, it is impossible to change it without recalling the contractor.

Bump-out can be the most difficult time of an event, because the excitement is over, the staff are often tired and everyone is in a hurry to leave. Nevertheless, security and safety are important at this stage. The correct order of bump-out needs to be on a detailed schedule, which is often the reverse of the bump-in schedule. The last item on the checklist for the bump-out is the 'idiot check'. This refers to the check that is done after everything is cleared from the performance area, when some staff search for anything that may be left.

The run sheets are lists of the order of specific jobs at an event. The entertainers, for example, have one run sheet while the caterers have another. Often, the production schedule is a loose-leaf folder that includes all the run sheets. The cue sheets are a list of times that initiate a change of any kind during the event and describe what happens on that change. The stage manager and audiovisual controller use them.

RECORDING THE EVENT

By their nature, special events are ephemeral. A good quality recording of the event is essential for most event companies, because it demonstrates the ability of the organisation and can be used to promote the event company. It can also help in evaluating the event and, if necessary, in settling later disputes, whether of a legal or other nature. The event can be recorded on video, as a sound recording or as photographs. Making a sound recording can be a matter of simply putting a cassette in the sound system and pressing the record button. However, any visual recording of the event requires planning. In particular, the correct lighting is needed for depth of field. The following factors need to be considered for video recording:

- What is it for — promotion, legal purposes or sale to the participants?
- What are the costs in terms of time and money?
- How will it affect the event? Will the video cameras be a nuisance? Will they need white lighting?
- What are the best vantage points?

Recording the event is not a decision that should be left until the last minute; it needs to be factored into the planning of the event. Once an event is played out, there is no going back.

CONTINGENCIES

As with large festivals and hallmark events, the staging of any event has to make allowances for what might go wrong. 'What if' sessions need to be implemented with the staff. A stage at a festival may face an electricity blackout; performers may not arrive; trouble may arrive instead. Micro-contingency plans thus need to be in place. All these must fit in with the overall festival risk-management and emergency plans. Further, at corporate events in well-known venues, the venue will have its own emergency plan that needs to be given to all involved.

SUMMARY

The staging of an event can range from presenting a show of multicultural dancers and musicians at a stage in a local park, to the launch of the latest software product at the most expensive hotel in town. All events share common staging elements, including sound, lights, food and beverages, performers and special effects. All these elements need to create and enhance the event theme. The importance of each element depends on the type of event. To stage an event successfully, a number of tools are used: the production schedule, the stage plan and the contact and responsibility list, all of which are shown in figure 13.10 (page 440).

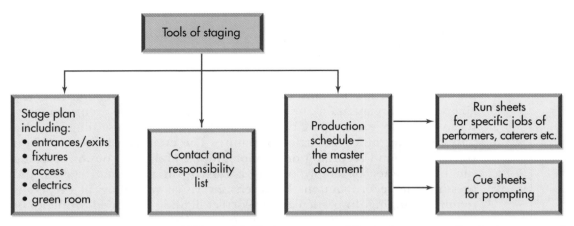

■ **Figure 13.10** *A summary of the tools necessary for staging an event*

Questions

1 Break an event into its staging elements and discuss the relationships between each element.

2 Choose a theme for a company's staff party. How would you relate all the elements of staging to the theme?

3 Compile a stage plan, contact responsibility list and production schedule with the relevant run sheets for:

(a) a corporate party for the clients, staff and customers of a company

(b) a fun run with entertainment

(c) a large wedding

(d) one of the stages for a city arts festival.

4 Discuss the constraints on programming the following events:

(a) a large musical concert in a disused open-cut mine

(b) an association award dinner

(c) a multi-stage arts festival

(d) a rough-water swim

(e) a mining exhibition conference

(f) an air show

(g) a tax seminar for accountants.

5 What is the case for contracting one supplier for all the staging elements? What are the disadvantages?

QFest — a cultural festival
in a remote location

Cue is a small town in the Murchison region of central Western Australia, about 750 kilometres from Perth, on the Great Northern Highway. It was once a major centre in a prosperous gold mining area, but the shift in mining operations to site-based settlements meant it has shrunk significantly. Today, 300 people live in the Cue township and a further 300 people live on pastoral properties in the shire. It is a town of great architectural interest, with its main street lined with attractive, historic buildings.

It is also an important area for Aboriginal people and has a substantial Aboriginal community. There are several important sites in the area, particularly Walga Rock, which has an impressive 'gallery' of rock art, and Wilgie Mia, the oldest mine in the world.

The shire has been trying to raise awareness of Cue as a tourist destination or stopover. Cue is also trying to help to develop businesses in the shire, including eco-tourism initiatives by the Aboriginal community.

In 2001, the then shire president and chief executive officer, inspired by a visiting visual artist, proposed an annual cultural festival as a catalyst for economic development. This was agreed, and the shire proceeded to advertise for a festival coordinator. A team of three people from APP was appointed in late 2001. Reuben Kooperman was the project manager and carried out most administrative functions, as well as coordinating the community consultation. Barry Strickland researched local history and culture, conceived the overall program and provided advice on marketing. (A specialist marketing person was appointed during the process.) Peter Grant was the 'hands-on' festival coordinator, taking care of artist negotiation and booking, contracts, logistics, accommodation, transport, community liaison, keeping people happy and keeping things going.

Festival philosophy

It was clear at the outset that to attract people to a cultural festival in a remote Goldfields location with little or no 'catchment' would be a significant challenge that would require both a unique program and effective, innovative marketing. It was also felt that the program should have an immediate relevance to the local community. These were considered the critical success factors. How the program would work over a four-day period was also important.

Programming approach — theming and event design

The program evolved following research into local history, a consideration of relevant Aboriginal stories and places, and consultation with the community. The

(continued)

first step was the production of a draft program outline that set out the 'artistic product' that was both available and of relevance. This was put forward for discussion and consultation. The consultation process also allowed for the input and development of local ideas. The objective was a varied program of sufficient appeal and uniqueness to attract people from Perth and beyond. The final ingredients included:

- a circus
- Aboriginal theatre
- Aboriginal music
- world music
- contemporary music
- spoken word
- cabaret
- visual arts exhibitions and installations
- community singing
- percussion for children.

Participation by community members in pre-festival activities that led to festival performances with visiting performers was an important mechanism in bringing the community into the 'heart' of the festival.

The choice of a 'cabaret'-style event was the festival's *çoup de grâce*. This arose out of the local community's desire for a fashion parade, Cue's tourism motto ('Queen of the Murchison') and the creative input of the festival coordinators. It took little brainstorming to conceive the 'Queens of the Murchison' — a cabaret show featuring four of Western Australia's most talented drag queens and its leading costumier, tracing the history of women's fashions from colonisation to the present day. The idea was embraced by the community, provided the perfect vehicle for promotion of the festival, and was a spectacular success.

The overall mix was also successful, and the strong Aboriginal content ensured almost unilateral support from the local community.

Venues

The primary venue was a spectacular circus tent set up on a vacant block in the main street. This was used for the circus shows, the Aboriginal theatre performances, the cabaret shows and feature concert performances. It also provided a hub for food and beverage outlets.

Other venues included the Old Gaol, used (as is) for spoken word performances, a pastoral property for a twilight concert (with a flat-bed truck as the stage), vacant shops and a local café for visual arts exhibitions, the 'ghost town' of Big Bell for a ritual burning event, a shearing shed for a bush breakfast, and some heritage buildings for other arts projects. The Shire Hall was used as a back-up venue for a theatre show during an unexpected wind storm. The main street of the town, lined with heritage buildings, hosted a weekend craft market and the children's percussion street parade. The selection of the venues reinforced the festival theme and served to heighten awareness and knowledge of the region.

Programming philosophy

With the likelihood that audiences would be small in the first year(s), it was decided that the program should be 'linear' in nature. This meant that major events or attractions would occur sequentially, so as not to split audiences; the aim was to achieve 'critical mass' for each show.

The linear approach to programming also served to build interest in the festival as the days went by. The first performance was by an Aboriginal theatre group, held in the circus tent. This venue became 'festival central' — the primary venue for most major performances. Performances by the different artistic genres followed, and the momentum of the festival grew.

In parallel with the performances, there were four distinct visual arts exhibitions or installations, each with a particular relevance to the region, the people and the history. One could be witnessed only after dark. All were successful.

Another dimension of the linear-style program was that the festival was designed as a 'journey of discovery' through the region. This 'journey' was achieved by having three major performances outside the town and by including guided tours to the major Aboriginal cultural site in the area.

The concluding event at the festival combined a visual arts project with Aboriginal and world music. During the course of the festival, a group of 40 students from two art schools in Perth had constructed a family of sculptures using found objects among the ruins of a once great mining settlement. These were ceremoniously burnt to the eerie and atmospheric world music sounds of Sirocco, followed by inspirational songs from Aboriginal performer Kerrianne Cox.

Staging of the event — key aspects

Overall, the event was a combination of a variety of performance types held at multiple venues. Each performance required its own technical and staging requirements, ranging from minimal — bare stage, no lights, no public address (PA) system — to complex — a concert PA, a lighting rig, stage props and dressing. The festival coordinator, the technical assistant and the sound engineer managed these requirements.

The elements of the event were selected to showcase the most notable aspects of the region: Aboriginal history and heritage, the natural beauty of the landscape, the history of the area following settlement, and the contemporary face of the town. The combination of these elements provided a strong festival theme.

Safety considerations were important for all component events, particularly the event at Big Bell. The culmination of this event was the ritual burning of 15 sculpture installations across a site of approximately 10 000 square metres, in front of a moving audience of several hundred people. In addition to standby fire trucks, the event was set up to ensure adequate separation of sculptures. Just before the fires were lit, the audience was briefed on what would happen and how, and what was expected of them to maintain the safety of both artists and audience. These procedures were determined well before the event.

Key success factors

Many factors contributed to the successful staging of QFest, including those on the following page.

(continued)

- The *reliability* of the technical crew and equipment was critical. Choices were made to ensure experienced operators with first-class gear filled these positions.
- *Risk minimisation* was considered in relation to all aspects of staging. Known risks were addressed and managed well before the event.
- *Transport* was an issue. Both the location and several venues were remote, so transport arrangements had to allow for this.
- Ensuring the availability and suitable standard of *accommodation* for artists and audience was important to provide a satisfying visitor experience and maximise the chance of return visits.
- *Publicity* was paramount for a new event in a remote location. A widely experienced and innovative marketing specialist managed this activity. The development of a user-friendly website was also important and very successful.

QFest was successful for many reasons. Ultimately, it was the presentation of a unique and multi-faceted program in an exotic location that captured the imagination of those who chose to attend. The logistics and complexities of staging the event were managed using a rigorous project management approach. QFest (www.qfest.com) is an excellent example of the successful marriage of creativity and management.

Reuben Kooperman, APP

Questions

1   How did the logistics influence the staging of the event?

2   Draw and discuss the elements of the staging and how they related to the theme of the festival.

Port Arthur — catharsis
in the community

People in all times and in all cultures have held communal festivals and events. One could say that gatherings of this kind are part of the human story and are built into the human condition. The way in which the community is initially consulted and involved can be vital when it comes to organising and 'staging' a meaningful event. The community's feelings, participation, help and permission can be essential to the success of the event; if the interface between organisers and community is not a good one, the whole project can be jeopardised. In practice, many projects are set up with community involvement as the major aim. Events and festivals can be a wonderful means of bringing people together to express their identity and culture, and perhaps this is most needed when a community has suffered a crisis.

When a gunman shot 35 men, women and children in Port Arthur, Tasmania, on Sunday 28 April 1996, the whole community was shattered. The massacre took place in the historic setting of one of Australia's most brutal penal settlements. It shocked the world. Was it possible for a public event to address the effects of this terrible tragedy?

To stage an event in circumstances such as these can be very difficult. Consultation with the community must be conducted with sensitivity and thoroughness, not only in traumatised communities but in all communities. When staging community events, I do not hold a public meeting and canvass through the press to attract interest. Rather, I find the community leaders one by one, and talk through their feelings and needs. In Port Arthur, the local people wanted to do something to facilitate the healing process but did not know exactly what. When I had had a chance to talk to all concerned, I went away and worked on an idea based on mythology.

Myths and stories can give us insights into the human spirit and a strong thematic base from which to proceed. One great recurring theme that seemed appropriate to the situation was journey into unknown danger, the descent into darkness, and the emergence 'to rebehold the stars' (from Dante's *Inferno*). I suggested taking well-known myths and stories that told of human journeys through difficulty towards eventual triumphant emergence from suffering — Dante, Ulysses and Innana, as well as folk stories from indigenous America and tales from Africa and Australia. This approach would hopefully distance the community from the actual event while demonstrating the capacity of the human spirit to survive pain. With this plan approved by the community, the planning phase began.

(continued)

The community decided to stage the 'Festival of Journeys' on the site where the massacre had taken place. The Port Arthur Authority could not have been more helpful, providing premises and assistance at every level. Credit, too, to the Tasmanian Government, who gave us wholehearted support without knowing whether the event would be successful.

Events and festivals can succeed only when they are very carefully planned and organised. We ordered the tents, food, sound systems and lights, staging and all the other infrastructure needed to hold a one-day festival. We also started to involve the local people, without whose help this could not possibly succeed.

The community members whom we had first approached were now invaluable in establishing further contacts and resources. They gave our presence their blessing, and this made it all much easier. The church, the schools, local artists and musicians, organisations and many individuals helped and guided us through the process of preparation. We worked with many school groups on small theatre shows depicting the stories chosen. We formed a local choir, organised a children's lantern parade, built a large lantern boat, practised shadow puppet performances, rehearsed story telling and conducted all sorts of other activities. We lived in caravans and spent a month in full rehearsal mode. Many problems emerged that were tackled not so much by us as by the community leaders, who tried to alleviate people's fears and worries. It takes courage to walk back into the mouth of the dragon, and I was constantly aware of the particular bravery displayed by the community.

There was one particular problem. After the massacre, the national and international media attention had been horrific for some local people. Their grief and suffering had been exploited in a multitude of ways. As a result, they wanted no publicity for the event and did not want any media to attend. Without publicity, how would people know to come? We needn't have worried. Everyone who lived locally knew about the event and, as a result of the initial consultation process, felt the event would be worth attending. The involvement of young people through the schools was also a guarantee that the parents would support the project.

At last, the day arrived for the festival and, thank goodness, it was a beautiful day. Many people from the community turned up to help us 'rig' the festival, and many brought flowers to decorate the space. As darkness descended, 200 children dressed in white came onto the site carrying candle-lit paper lanterns that they had made. A large lantern ship with poetry of renewal written on the side was carried by 12 local adults and led the parade. The poetry comprised painted messages of hope. The boat was placed on a bonfire and ceremoniously burnt while the choir sang. The various theatre shows and other performances were presented at various locations at the site. Food and drink were enjoyed around the bonfire. The feeling among the people was emotional, but not negative.

The climax of the evening was a bush dance. I had concerns about this: would the community want to dance on the very spot where this terrible tragedy happened? Again, the local people had been our guide and approved the idea. It proved to be one of the most moving moments of my life. People danced and sang, cried and hugged one another, and they expressed their grief and community spirit. A feeling of catharsis swept through us all. It ended with large groups of local people standing together with their arms around one another.

Events and festivals are vital to the life of our community and allow us to express what is important to us. In staging our events, we must have confidence and trust in the communities with whom we work. With the right design and good organisation, we can facilitate wonderful and meaningful experiences for the people of Australia.

Neil Cameron

Questions

1 Neil used mythology as a source for inspiration and a theme. What other areas could an event manager investigate to discover themes?

2 How did the theme of this event influence the way in which it was organised?

3 How was the dignity of the event maintained?

4 What other types of event have this type of theme and why?

REFERENCES

Cameron, N 1993, *Fire on the water*, Currency Press, Sydney.

Goldblatt, J 1997, *Special events: best practices in modern event management*, 2nd edn, Van Nostrand Reinhold, New York.

Graham, S, Goldblatt, J & Delpy, L 1995, *The ultimate guide to sports event management and marketing*, Richard Irwin, Chicago.

Malouf, L 1999, *Behind the scenes at special events*, John Wiley & Sons, New York.

Neighbourhood Arts Unit 1991, *Community festival handbook*, City of Melbourne, Melbourne.

Reid, F 1995, *Staging handbook*, 2nd edn, A&C Black, London.

CIM Rostrum n.d., 'The comprehensive convention planner's manual', vol. 32, Rank Publishing Company, Sydney.

CHAPTER 14

Evaluation
and research

LEARNING OBJECTIVES

After studying this chapter, you should be able to:

■ describe the role of evaluation in the event management process

■ discuss when to evaluate an event

■ understand and discuss the evaluation needs of event stakeholders

■ identify and use secondary research sources

■ create an evaluation plan for an event

■ apply a range of techniques, including the conducting of questionnaires and surveys, in evaluating events

■ describe and record the intangible impacts of events

■ measure the expenditure of visitors to an event

■ prepare a final evaluation report

■ use event profiles to promote the outcomes of events and seek sponsorship

■ apply the knowledge gained by evaluation to the planning of a future event.

INTRODUCTION

Event evaluation is critical to the event management process. Event management is still a young industry, and is struggling in some areas to establish legitimacy and acceptance as a profession. One of the best means for the industry to gain credibility is for events to be evaluated honestly and critically, so their outcomes are known, their benefits acknowledged and their limitations accepted. However, event evaluation serves a much deeper purpose than just 'blowing the trumpet' for events. It is at the very heart of the process where insights are gained, lessons are learnt and events are perfected. Event managers need to be aware of and utilise both primary and secondary research sources in the planning and evaluation of events. Event evaluation, if properly utilised and applied, is the key to the continuous improvement of events and to the standing and reputation of the event industry. As such, it should be a high priority for all event managers to properly evaluate their events and to disseminate this evaluation to their stakeholders and interested groups. If done well, this will not only enhance the reputation of their events, but also their own reputation as true professionals.

WHAT IS EVENT EVALUATION?

Event evaluation is the process of critically observing, measuring and monitoring the implementation of an event, in order to assess its outcomes accurately. It enables the creation of an event profile that outlines the basic features and important statistics of an event. It also enables feedback to be provided to event stakeholders, and plays an important role in the event management process by providing a tool for analysis and improvement.

The event management process is a cycle (figure 14.1, page 450) in which inputting and analysing data from an event allows more informed decisions to be made, more efficient planning to occur and event outcomes to be improved. This applies to individual repeat events, where the lessons learnt from one event can be incorporated in the planning of the next. It also applies to the general body of events knowledge, where the lessons learnt from individual events contribute to the overall knowledge and effectiveness of the event industry.

The Hokitika Wildfoods Festival in New Zealand used the strategic review process in 2003 to identify and address the issues that caused a 50 per cent increase in the number of festival visitors in the previous five years (see case study at the end of this chapter). Marti's Balloon Fiesta at Canowindra in New South Wales used a similar process in 2002 to address the falling numbers and income of the festival, resulting in greater community involvement, a more family-friendly program and reduced entry fees, which contributed to a better overall outcome of the festival in 2003.

Innovations in marketing, programming and staging, as well as improvements in operational issues such as crowd control, risk management and security, quickly ripple through the industry and become universally used and accepted. Sometimes this transfer of knowledge occurs through the movement of event personnel. Di Henry, who successfully organised the torch relay for the Sydney Olympic Games in 2000, went on to organise the torch relay for the Commonwealth Games in Manchester in 2002. Andrew Walsh, who directed the opening ceremony for the Rugby World Cup in Sydney in 2003, went on to become executive producer for the opening and closing ceremonies of the Olympic Games in Athens, Greece, in 2004.

The transfer of Olympic knowledge was formalised by the payment of $3 million dollars by the International Olympic Committee to the Sydney Organising Committee for the Olympic Games (SOCOG) for the intellectual property of the Games, and the establishment of the Olympic Games Knowledge Service based in Lausanne, Switzerland. A further example of this knowledge transfer at a training level was a project funded by the Greek Government in 2000, where 70 Greek students undertook work placement at SOCOG during the preparation and conduct of the Sydney Olympic Games. This was supported by a sports management course at the University of Technology, Sydney. The knowledge and training gained was then applied to the conduct of the 2004 Olympic Games in Athens.

Innovations in event communications, products and technologies are constantly spread and refined throughout the process of event evaluation, which leads to better event planning, implementation and further evaluation. This in turn leads to the improvement of individual events and to an ever-growing and more knowledgeable event industry.

■ **Figure 14.1**
Evaluation and the event management process

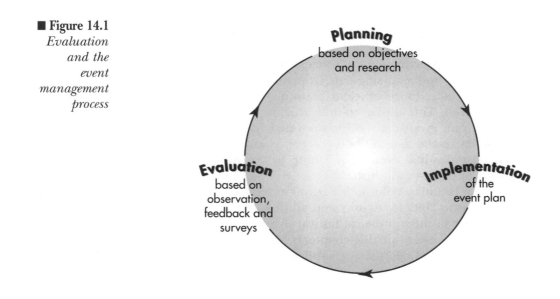

Planning
based on objectives and research

Implementation
of the event plan

Evaluation
based on observation, feedback and surveys

Evaluation is a process that occurs throughout the event management cycle. However, Getz (1997) and others have identified three key periods when it is useful to undertake evaluation.

■ Pre-event *assessment*

Some assessment of the factors governing an event usually takes place in the research and planning stage. This is sometimes called a feasibility study and is used to determine what level of resources an event is likely to require, and whether or not to proceed with the event. A study may involve market research of the probable audience reaction to the event and some research into and prediction of attendance figures, costs and benefits. It will often compare the event with profiles and outcomes of similar previous events. The study may result in establishing targets, or benchmarks, against which the success of the project will be measured.

■ Monitoring *the event*

Event monitoring is the process of tracking the progress of an event through the various stages of implementation, enabling factors governing the event to be adjusted. Ticket sales may be perceived as slow in the lead-up to an event, for example, and this may result in increased advertising or a greater publicity effort. Monitoring the budget may result in the trimming of expenses or the freeing up of money for other areas of expenditure. Observation during the event may lead to changes that improve the delivery of the event, such as adjusting sound volume or altering the dispersal of security and cleaning staff to match changing crowd patterns. This process of monitoring is vital to quality control and it will also provide valuable information for the final evaluation and for future planning purposes.

■ Post-event *evaluation*

The most common form of evaluation is post-event evaluation. This involves the gathering of statistics and data on an event and analysing them in relation to the event's mission and objectives. Key Performance Indicators (KPIs) are sometimes used to translate the event objectives into measures that can be applied to gauge the success of the event. An important aspect is usually a debrief meeting of key participants and stakeholders, at which the strengths and weaknesses of the event are discussed and observations are recorded. Post-event evaluation may also involve some form of questionnaire or survey of the event participants or audience. Such surveys seek to explore participants' opinions of the experience and to measure their levels of satisfaction with the event. They often involve the collection of data on the financial expenditure of the participants, so that the cost can be compared with the revenue generated by the event. The nature of the evaluation will be determined largely by the purpose of the event and the audience for which the evaluation is intended.

REPORTING TO STAKEHOLDERS

One of the prime reasons that event managers evaluate events is to report information back to stakeholders.

- The host organisation will want to know what the event achieved. Did the event come in on budget and on time? Did it achieve its objectives? How many people attended and were their expectations met? For future planning purposes, it might be useful to know where they came from, how they heard about it and whether they intend to return next year.
- The event sponsor may have other measures. Was the level of awareness of the product or service increased? What penetration did the advertising achieve? What media coverage was generated? What was the profile of the people who attended?
- Funding bodies will have grant acquittal procedures to observe and will usually require audited financial statements of income and expenditure, along with a report on the social, cultural or sporting outcomes of the event.
- Councils and government departments may want to know what the impact was on their local or state economies.
- Tourism bodies may want to know the number of visitors attracted to the area and what they spent, not only on the event, but also on travel, shopping and accommodation.

Quantifying and disseminating the outcomes of an event can be very helpful to the event manager in promoting support for and the acceptance of the event. Mercedes Australian Fashion Week has used statistics on media coverage and fashion orders generated by the event very effectively to promote support for the event from sponsors and government. The International Gay Games in Sydney in 2002 used statistics from previous Games in New York and Amsterdam to shore up support for the event.

TYPES OF RESEARCH

Primary research is original research undertaken directly in relation to a project or event. It involves many of the evaluation techniques, such as observation, questionnaires and surveys, which are discussed later in this chapter. Secondary research, undertaken by external organisations or agencies, is not conducted specifically for the purpose of the event, but may be of considerable value and assistance to the event manager. It includes research reports from previous events, information and statistics available from research bureaus, research journals and the Internet.

■ Secondary *research*

Secondary research can be useful throughout the life cycle of the event. However, it is particularly useful before the event in preparing feasibility studies, when existing information may assist the event manager in building up a picture of the event and predicting event outcomes. Some important sources of secondary research will now be discussed.

Research reports from previous events

If the event has been conducted before, then previous event reports and/or discussions with their organisers or staff may be of great assistance to the event manager. Each Australian Masters Games event, for example, is required to provide a detailed report, including the number of event participants and their partners, the number and type of competitions/functions that were conducted, the marketing strategies employed and detailed statements of income and expenditure of the event. By studying these previous event reports carefully, the event manager can form a fairly accurate profile of the event, including likely predictions of attendance figures and budgets. The specifics of the host city's planned event will need to be taken into account, including characteristics and aspects of the location that are likely to influence the event outcomes. If the event has not been conducted before, then studies of similar events or discussions with their event managers may prove rewarding. A new food and wine festival, for example, may be expected to have a similar profile to other existing food and wine festivals, allowing for differences of location, market etc. A conference for one industry group or association may be expected to behave in similar ways to previous conferences for similar groups or associations. By studying carefully what has gone before, an astute event manager may be able to develop a template that may need fine tuning and adjustment, but will provide valuable insights into the likely profile of a new event.

Research bureaus

There are many public and privately funded research organisations that will provide access to valuable data either free of charge or for a modest fee. The Australian Bureau of Statistics, for example, produces detailed information on a wide variety of topics, including Australian social trends, census statistics and how Australians spend their leisure time. Their Directory of Culture and Leisure Statistics provides useful information on topics such as attendance at cultural venues and events, attendance at arts festivals and children's participation in cultural and leisure activities. The Bureau of Tourism Research produces annual national and international visitor surveys, which provide accurate data on visitor patterns and expenditure on a wide range of activities, including travel, accommodation and attendance at festivals and events. The Centre for Regional Tourism Research, part of the Cooperative Research Centre for Sustainable Tourism, has research and information on community events.

Web searches

A web search of similar events will produce a surprising amount of data, including how other event managers have approached the issues of programming, promotion and logistics. Some will even include research reports providing detailed information on event outcomes such as attendance and economic impacts.

Journal databases

Also found on the web are journal databases that will enable event managers to track down research articles in tourism marketing and event-specific journals, which can be of great assistance in researching and planning an event. Some of these articles may be accessed directly from the web or through public and university libraries. Articles can be found on a wide range of event issues, including marketing, sponsorship, audience motivation and satisfaction, event impacts, risk management, harm minimisation and event operations.

By undertaking a thorough scan of relevant secondary research, the event manager can proceed from an informed and knowledgeable position and can often save time and money in devising a primary research and evaluation plan for an event.

■ Primary *research*

An exact event profile and invaluable information for its future planning and improvement can only be obtained by close observation and evaluation of the event. The evaluation of an event will usually be more effective if it is planned from the outset and built into the event management process. Planning should include consideration of:

- what data is needed
- how, when and by whom it is to be gathered
- how it is to be analysed
- what format to use in the final reporting.

Data collection

The process of implementing the event may provide opportunities for useful data to be collected. Participants may be required, for example, to fill in an event registration form, which can be designed to capture useful information on numbers, age, gender, point of origin, spending patterns and so on. Ticketed events allow for a ready means of counting spectators and the ticketing agency may be able to provide further useful information, such as the postcodes of ticket purchasers. For non-ticketed events, public transport and car park figures and police crowd estimates can be used in calculating attendance figures. Event managers should look out for and make use of all opportunities for the collection of relevant data.

Staff observation

An obvious but critical source of data collection is the direct observation of the event. Staff observation and reports may provide information on a number of aspects of the event, including performance quality, audience reaction, crowd flow and adequacy of catering and toilet facilities. However, staff will provide more accurate and useful data if they are trained to observe these issues and are given a proper reporting format, rather than being left to make casual and anecdotal observations. From the outset, staff should be made aware that observation and reporting on the event form part of their role, and they should be given appropriate guidance and benchmarks. They may be given checklists to evaluate items such as performance quality and audience reaction by using a scale of one to five or by ticking indicators such as below average, average, good, very good or excellent.

At Sydney's Darling Harbour, stage managers are required to complete a written report on each event, giving their estimates of attendance figures, weather conditions, performance standards and crowd reaction, and commenting on any unusual occurrences or features. Likewise, security staff are required to report on crowd behaviour, incidents, disturbances and injuries and to estimate the size of crowds with the help of photographs taken at regular intervals by security cameras at strategic locations. By compiling these reports, using statistics from attraction operators, and assessing factors such as competition from other major events in the city, management are able to form profiles of individual events and to track trends over time.

Stakeholder observation

Other key players in an event, such as venue owners, councils, sponsors, vendors, police and first-aid officers, can often provide valuable feedback from their various perspectives.

- Venue owners may be able to compare the performance of the event with their normal venue patterns and comment usefully on matters such as attendance figures, parking, access, catering and facilities.
- Police may have observed aspects such as crowd behaviour, traffic flow and parking and may have constructive suggestions for future planning.
- Councils may be aware of disturbances to the local community or difficulties with street closures or compliance with health regulations.
- Sponsors may have observations based on their own attendance at the event, or may have done their own surveys on audience reaction, awareness levels and media coverage.
- Vendors may have information on the volume of sales or the waiting time in queues that will be valuable in planning future catering arrangements.
- First-aid providers may have statistics on the number and seriousness of injuries such as cuts, abrasions or heat exhaustion that will assist in future planning of safety and risk management.

All of these key stakeholders may have observations on general planning issues such as signage, access, crowd management, communication and the provision of facilities that will have implications for improvement of the event. It is important that their observations are recorded and incorporated into the evaluation and planning stages of the event management process.

De-briefing meetings

All stakeholders should be made aware at the outset that they will be given an opportunity to provide feedback, and that this is a vital part of the event planning process. They should be encouraged to contribute their professional observations and assessments. This may be done at a single 'de-briefing' meeting or at a series of meetings, depending on the complexity of the event. It is often useful for the date and agenda of this meeting to be made known to all parties early in the process, so that if it is not possible for them to communicate their observations during the staging of the event, then they are aware that a suitable forum will be provided during the finalisation of the event. This meeting should ensure neither congratulations nor recriminations overshadow the important lessons that are to be learnt from the event and the consequent changes to be incorporated in future planning. It is important that all parties are heard and their comments are taken into account in the future planning of the event.

The topics to be addressed at the meeting will be determined by the nature and size of the event. However, the checklist in figure 14.2 is a useful starting point.

■ Figure 14.2
Event evaluation checklist

CHECKLIST FOR EVENT EVALUATION			
Aspect	**Satisfactory**	**Requires attention**	**Comments**
• Timing of the event • Venue • Ticketing and entry • Staging • Performance standard • Staffing levels and performance of duties • Crowd control • Security • Communications • Information and signage • Transport • Parking • Catering facilities • Toilets • First aid • Lost children • Sponsor acknowledgement • Hosting arrangements • Advertising • Publicity • Media liaison			

Questionnaires and surveys

Questionnaires can range from simple feedback forms targeting event partners and stakeholders to detailed audience or visitor surveys undertaken by trained personnel. The scale of the questionnaire will depend on the needs and resources of the event. Simple feedback forms can usually be designed and distributed using the event's own internal resources. They may seek to record and quantify basic data, such as the expenditure of event partners, the observations of stakeholders and their assessment of event management and outcomes.

Surveys are used to ascertain reliable statistical information on audience profiles and reaction and visitor patterns and expenditure. They may be implemented by direct interviews with participants or may rely on participants filling in written forms. They may be undertaken face-to-face, by telephone or by mail. Face-to-face interviews will usually generate a higher response rate, but techniques such as a competition with prizes as incentives for participation may improve the response rate of postal surveys. Undertaking effective surveys requires expertise and considerable organisational resources. For event organisers with limited in-house experience and expertise, professional assistance can be called on for tasks, ranging from the design of survey forms to the full implementation of the survey process.

In the case of repeat events, a single well-designed survey may satisfy the basic research needs of the event. Some event organisers may wish to repeat the survey each year in order to compare successive events and to establish trends, or they may want to embark on more ambitious research programs in order to investigate other aspects of the event. Whatever the scale and approach that is decided on, experts such as Getz (1997) and Veal (1997), and the publication by the National Centre for Culture and Recreation Statistics (1997) agree on certain basic factors that should be kept in mind. These are listed below:

- *Purpose* — clearly identify the purpose and objective of the survey. A clearly stated and defined purpose is most likely to lead to a well-targeted survey with effective results.
- *Survey design* — keep it simple. If too much is attempted in the survey, there is a danger that focus will be lost and effectiveness reduced. Questions should be clear and unambiguous and should be tested by a 'trial run' before the actual survey.
- *Size of sample* — the number of participants must be large enough to provide a representative sample of the audience. The sample size will depend on the level of detail in the survey, the level of precision required and the available budget. If in doubt, seek professional advice on the size of the sample.
- *Randomness* — the methodology employed in the selection of participants must avoid biases of age, sex and ethnicity. A procedure such as selecting every tenth person who passes through a turnstile may assist in providing a random selection.
- *Support data* — the calculation of some outcomes will depend on the collection of support data. The calculation of total visitor expenditure, for example, will require accurate support data on the average expenditure of visitors as well as the number of visitors to the event. Then the spending pattern revealed by the survey can be multiplied by the number of visitors to provide an estimate of the total visitor expenditure for the event.

WHAT TO EVALUATE

Events have both tangible and intangible impacts. Surveys most commonly measure tangible impacts such as economic costs and benefits, because these can most easily be measured. However, it is also important to evaluate the intangible impacts of events, even if evaluation needs to be of a narrative or descriptive nature. Some intangibles that are hard to measure include the effect on the social life and wellbeing of a community, the sense of pride engendered by an event, and the long-term impact on the image of a place or a tourist destination.

In a study by Jago et al. (2002) they explain:

> ■ Queensland's Woodford Folk Festival was noted as an example of an event that has successfully enhanced a destination's brand, and that has done so in an appropriate way. Prior to the event's initiation, the destination was synonymous with the Woodford Prison. However, the festival is now so popular with the community and visitors that it has caused the destination's image to change from a negative to a positive one. ■

Goldblatt and Perry (2002) summarise the benefits of an event in Providence, Rhode Island:

> ■ WaterFire has brought a new sense of pride to the citizens of Rhode Island. It has transformed downtown Providence into a safer and busier city with a greater number of elements to experience. Local residents who previously traveled to other states for various forms of entertainment now look to Providence, Rhode Island for entertainment and out-of-state visitors have now made Providence a destination. Providence is no longer viewed as a 'detour' on the way to the Cape Cod or Boston, Massachusetts. WaterFire has allowed Rhode Islanders, for the first time in decades, to feel proud of the city in which they live. ■

While events such as this have undoubted social worth, it would be difficult, perhaps even counterproductive, to quantify them in anything other than descriptive terms. Nevertheless, their cultural meaning and social impacts would need to be taken into account in any serious evaluation of their community impacts.

Measuring visitor expenditure

All event managers should be familiar with constructing a simple financial balance statement of the income and expenditure of events. Until recent times, this form of reporting was considered sufficient, because most events were evaluated on the basis of their cost to the event organisers or their value to the local community. However, the growing involvement of governments, tourism bodies, corporations and sponsors has brought with it an increasing need to consider the wider impacts of events.

The impacts of events on the economy are based primarily on the expenditure of visitors to the event from outside the host community. The National Centre for Culture and Recreation Statistics (1997) has published simple guidelines for measuring the expenditure of festival visitors, which can be applied to most other public events. Their publication outlines a basic methodology and includes sample questionnaires for visitor and resident surveys.

The visitors' survey form aims to identify expenditure on items such as accommodation, food, festival tickets, other entertainment, transport, personal services, films, books and souvenirs. This survey establishes an average expenditure which can then be multiplied by the number of visitors to obtain the total visitor expenditure. The methodology takes into account the complexity of estimating the number of visitors from outside the region. It seeks to distinguish those visitors attracted by the event or who have extended their visit because of the event, from those who would have visited the region anyway.

In the case of a festival that extends for more than one day or that has multiple events, the survey also takes into account the need to identify the number of days or events attended and to weigh this in calculating the results of the survey.

A residents' survey form is also provided to identify residents who 'holidayed at home' because of the event and 'switched' their expenditure, which can then be legitimately attributed to the event. Since it is difficult to determine what they would have spent if they had gone elsewhere, their expenditure is treated the same as that of visitors to the event.

Calculating the economic impact of events from the point of view of cities or governments is complex, as discussed in chapter 2. However, by applying the guidelines and the survey shown in figure 14.3, a simple snapshot of the economic impact of an event can be readily obtained.

■ **Figure 14.3**
Sample event participation survey

1. Gender: Male   Female
2. Age Group: Under 15   15–24   25–44   45–64   65+
3. Highest level of education:
   High School   Private College/TAFE   University
4. Employment status: Full time/Part time/Casual/Student/Unemployed/Senior
5. Household income (AUD):
   0–20 000   21 000–30 000   31 000–40 000   41 000–50 000   50 000+
6. Who are you travelling with today?
   Travelling alone   Adult couple   Family (parents and children)
   Friends or relatives   Club, Society   Business associates
   Other _____ specify
7. What means of transport did you use to come to the event from your home or place of accommodation?
   Car   Bus/coach   Taxi   Walked   Other _____ specify
8. What was the primary means by which you found out about the event?
   Brochures/posters   Newspaper   Radio   TV   Internet
   Tourist Information Centre   Word of mouth   Other _____ specify
9. Have you attended this event in previous years?
   Yes   No   If yes, then which year did you last attend? _____
10. Do you intend to attend the event next year?   Yes   No
    If you answered no, is it because:
    Will not be in the area   Expenses/cost associated with event
    Like to do new things   Program too similar to previous years
    Event not particularly entertaining/enjoyable   Other _____

(*continued*)

11. How would you rate the following aspects of the event?
    very poor   satisfactory   good   excellent
    (a) Venue   (h) Seating
    (b) Parking   (i) Toilets
    (c) Value for money   (j) Shade
    (d) Quality of food   (k) Overall presentation of event
    (e) Variety of food   (l) Crowd management
    (f) Entertainment for adults   (m) Signage/information
    (g) Entertainment for children   (n) Overall site presentation/layout

12. Were there any aspects of the event that you particularly enjoyed?
    _____

13. Were there any aspects with which you were particularly displeased?
    _____

14. Are there any additional comments that you wish to make about the event?
    _____

15. What is your usual place of residence?
    Local
    Elsewhere in Australia — list postcode _____
    Overseas — list country _____

16. Was your visit here today motivated by the event?
    Yes   No
    If not, what was the purpose of your visit?
    Holiday   Visit friends/relatives   Business   Other _____ specify

17. How long are you staying in the region?
    Less than 1 day   1–3 days   3–7 days   7–14 days   More than 14 days

18. If staying more than one day, what type of accommodation are you using?
    Hotel/motel/resort   Guest house/bed and breakfast
    Self-catering cottage/apartment   Caravan park/camping ground
    Backpacker/hostel   Own or family property
    Other _____ specify

19. Please estimate how much you have spent or intend to spend on behalf of
    yourself or others during your visit including transport, food,
    accommodation, souvenirs and entertainment (AUD)
    0–50   51–100   101–150   151–250   251–300   301–500   500+

20. Other than the event, what activities/attractions did you or do you intend to
    engage in during your visit?
    _____

A festivals do-it-yourself economic impact kit can also be downloaded free of charge from the Arts Victoria website although its use in other states is limited due to the use of Victorian economic multipliers in calculating the economic impacts of events.

MEDIA MONITORING AND EVALUATION

Media coverage is an important aspect of an event. This coverage can be either positive or negative depending on the event outcomes, the impact on the community and the kind of relationship built up with the media. It is important to monitor and record this coverage as part of the event documentation. If the event is local, it may be possible to do this by keeping a file of newspaper articles and by listening and looking for radio and television interviews and news coverage. For larger events, it may be necessary to employ a professional media-monitoring organisation that can track media coverage from a variety of sources. They will usually provide copies of print media stories and transcripts of radio interviews and news coverage. Audiotapes and videotapes of electronic coverage can be obtained for an additional charge. This coverage provides an excellent record of the event and can be used effectively in profiling the event for potential sponsors and partners.

A further issue is content analysis of the media coverage, as this is not always positive. Negative media coverage can impact on the reputation of the event and by implication on stakeholders, such as host organisations and sponsors.

Some media monitors attempt to place a monetary value on media coverage, usually valuing it at around three times the cost of equivalent advertising space, on the grounds that editorial is likely to be better trusted by consumers and is therefore worth more. Such valuations should be regarded as approximate only, but may provide a useful comparative assessment of media coverage. The promotional value of the 2003 Lexmark Indy 300 resulting from international print and broadcast media was valued at $15.5 million (see the event profile in chapter 2, page 43).

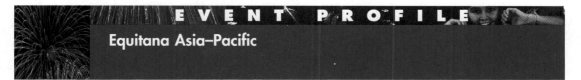

EVENT PROFILE

Equitana Asia–Pacific

This profile examines Equitana Asia–Pacific, held at the Melbourne Exhibition and Convention Centre, 19–23 November 2003.

Background
Equitana was held for the first time in 1972 in Germany. The vision was to bring people together in an exchange of information, ideas and expertise covering all facets of the equine industry. Equitana was first staged in Australia in 1999 and is a biennial event. Before Equitana, the Asia–Pacific region of the industry had no central point of convergence, or any single forum in which to showcase their products, skills, breeds or competitions. This 'equaliser' event has achieved its major goal: to bring the Australian equine industries together in the same successful way as Germany had done.

(*continued*)

Equitana encompasses a number of industry- and public-related events. The unique event formula that combines competition, education, exhibition and entertainment into a four-day equestrian fair has been a great hit with the equine industry and the general public.

Equitana Asia–Pacific's mission and vision statement is:

■ To continue to present this unique event formula by providing a forum for the equine industry. Combining competition, education, exhibition and spectacular entertainment to capture the imagination of all industry stakeholders and general public. ■

Event highlights

The event features four days of action, using the entire Melbourne Exhibition Centre. Competitions include:

- the indoor Polo Skins Tournament run in conjunction with the Victorian Polo Association
- the indoor cross-country championship featuring the world's leading event riders in a 20-obstacle spectacular that is conducted in three connected indoor arenas. Riders included Sydney Olympic individual gold medallist and silver medallist Karen O'Connor from the USA
- World Cup dressage grand prix and freestyle to music
- CSI-W World Cup show jumping
- Cutting Masters — series grand final
- reining championship
- indoor combined driving
- saddlehorse finals
- barrel racing.

Equitana features more than 200 educational presentations, including three major international clinics, plus demonstrations, presentations and lectures from some of the world's best equine specialists. Presenters include:

- Martina Hannöver, German dressage gold medallist and 2003 number one world dressage rider
- Pat Parelli, world famous natural horsemanship trainer
- David and Karen O'Connor, America's most successful husband and wife eventing team
- George Morris, legendary American showjumping trainer
- Andrew Hoy, triple Olympic gold medallist

Equitana is the largest gathering of equine exhibitors in the Asia-Pacific region. It features 16 500 square metres of exhibition space, including four equine education arenas, offering all requirements for the horse, home or stable. A thrilling evening of family entertainment is provided in a 90-minute equine spectacular — the 'Mane Event Variety Special'.

Audience and statistics

The economic impact of Equitana 2003 to the State of Victoria is $10.2 million. The audience was 66 per cent female and 34 per cent male, with total audience numbers up 8 per cent on 2001's official numbers (73 000). Some 56 per cent of audience members were aged 30–49 years old, 42 per cent were from interstate and overseas and 77 per cent were from outside the Melbourne metropolitan area. Eighty per cent of attendees said they would return to Equitana 2005.

In 2003, 95 per cent of competitors returned from 2001. There were 208 individual exhibitors and 8 per cent of exhibitors were international, representing New Zealand, England, Germany, Finland, Scotland, Switzerland, India, South Africa, Canada and the USA. Some 96 per cent of exhibitors met or exceeded their business goals.

Industry, economic and tourism impacts

Equitana Asia–Pacific is the only event of it kind in the Asia–Pacific region that provides a middle ground for the industry to come together.

■ *Economic impact on Victoria — direct and indirect impact ($)*

DIRECT	INDIRECT	TOTAL
$4 452 000	$5 707 000	$10 159 000

The Victorian Government elevated Equitana Asia–Pacific to Hallmark Event status after its inaugural staging in 1999. In addition, the event has won two major tourism awards.

Awards

Equitana has a proven track record, delivering far more than organisers, stakeholders and supporters thought possible:
• Awarded Hallmark Event status by Tourism Victoria in 1999
• Victorian Tourism Finalist Award for Major Event of the Year 2001
• Victorian Tourism Merit Award for Major Event of the Year 1999
• MIAA Winner — Victorian Event of the Year 1999, Major Event category.

Jamie Page, Definitive Events

$\mathcal{E}$VENT EVALUATION
REPORTS AND PROFILES

Once information has been collated from data collection, observation, feedback meetings and surveys, a final event evaluation report should be completed and distributed to all stakeholders. The information should provide a profile of the event, which can be included in the executive summary of the report. This profile can form the basis of a media release promoting the outcomes of the event, and can be used to begin planning for the next event and approaching sponsors. Figure 14.4 provides an example of such a profile.

■ **Figure 14.4**
Profile of the 2003 Rugby World Cup

LOOKING AT THE NUMBERS GAME

Forty-eight games in 44 days. A telling statistic on the scale of the Rugby World Cup (RWC) but one that is only the tip of the iceberg now the dust is settling on the tournament which has been dubbed 'best ever'.

The 600 players involved in the tournament used 64 hotels in which to amass 36 000 hotel room nights. The same players made 980 coach trips and used 900 rugby balls. Once the 700 tonnes of freight had arrived for the teams, they then made use of 150 different training venues.

The training grounds alone provided enough statistics to drive an accountant to drink. The venue used 2040 marker cones and 28 scrum machines. Defence was obviously a factor as teams hit 200 tackle bags, 570 tackle suits and 300 bump shields.

All that training is thirsty work. In order to quench such thirst, the players drank 100 000 litres of water and 100 tonnes of ice. If that didn't cool them off, they could have used one of the 40 ice baths in operation.

It is also sweaty work — but being creatures of hygiene, the players made 900 team laundry washes and 8000 personal washes.

All that hard work put on a great show, with two million spectators attending the RWC. This included 400 jumbos of international tourists and 500 000 Australian beds giving plenty of rest to the 40 000 overseas visitors.

For those at home the action was relayed by one of 1 818 accredited journalists. These guys weren't the only ones working at the venues either. After 10 500 expressions of interest to be a volunteer, 1 000 were appointed as match day assistants, media and accreditation assistants and rugby service managers. The opening ceremony alone was made possible through the efforts of 220 volunteers.

For those not at the game, there were plenty of people tuning in on TV. The RWC final gripped an audience of 4.34 million, making it the most watched television program of the year. Throughout the tournament, 31 525 000 viewers tuned into the Seven Network's coverage.

Our own rugbyworldcup.com. had 495 million hits throughout the tournament, including 44.5 million hits on the day of the final. One tournament can produce a lot of numbers.

(**Source:** *Kaless 2003.*)

FINALISATION

Once the event is over, and before administration is disbanded and preparation for the next event is begun, it is important to tidy up loose ends and to bring the event management process to a satisfactory conclusion. The following information is a useful checklist of tasks to be completed in finalising the event:

• hold a debriefing meeting and allow for feedback by all stakeholders
• settle accounts and prepare an audited financial statement

- fulfil all contractual and statutory obligations
- prepare a full report on event outcomes and distribute it to all key stakeholders
- make recommendations for future refinements and improvements to the event
- thank all staff, participants and stakeholders for their support of the event.

SUMMARY

Event evaluation is a process of measuring and assessing an event throughout the event management cycle. It provides feedback that contributes to the planning and improvement of individual events and to the event industry's pool of knowledge.

Feasibility studies identify the likely costs and benefits of an event and help to decide whether to proceed with it. Monitoring the event establishes whether it is on track and enables the event manager to respond to changes and adjust plans. Post-event evaluation measures the outcomes of the event in relation to its objectives. The exact nature of this evaluation will depend on the perspectives and needs of the stakeholders. The event manager needs to be aware of both primary and secondary research sources and techniques.

A range of techniques is used in event evaluation, including data collection, observation, feedback meetings, questionnaires and surveys. Good evaluation is planned and implemented from the outset of the event management process, with all participants being made aware of its objectives and methodology. As well as tangible impacts, events have intangible benefits that cannot always be quantified and may need to be recorded on a narrative or descriptive basis. These include social and cultural impacts on a community and the long-term profile and positioning of a tourism destination. A key factor in calculating the economic impact of an event is the measurement of visitor expenditure through the use of visitor surveys. The media coverage of an event should be monitored in-house or by using professional media monitors. Once information is gathered from all sources, an event evaluation report should be compiled and distributed to all stakeholders. This report can provide the basis of media releases that promote the outcomes of the event, and can be used in planning for the future and seeking sponsorship. In finalising the event, it is important to tidy up loose ends and apply lessons learnt from the event to the future planning and management of the event.

Questions

1 Imagine a fictional event that you would like to organise. Make a list of the secondary research sources that you would use in researching the event and make a detailed summary of one of these sources.

2 Identify an event that you are familiar with. Design an evaluation plan that will provide a profile of the event and form the basis of a report to key stakeholders.

3 Imagine that you are employing staff to work on a particular event. Design a report sheet for them to record their observations of the event. Decide what aspects you want them to observe and what benchmarks you want them to use.

4 Select an event that you are familiar with, and identify the stakeholders that you would invite to a final evaluation meeting. Write an agenda for the meeting that will encourage well-organised feedback on the event.

5 Imagine that you are a tourist officer for your region. Design a questionnaire for a major local event in order to evaluate the impact of the event on local tourism.

6 Obtain copies of three evaluation reports from libraries or from event organisations. Compare and contrast the methodology, style and format of these reports.

7 Identify a high-profile event in your region, and monitor as closely as you can the media coverage of the event, including print, radio and television coverage.

8 Choose an event that you have been associated with, and assemble as much data as you can on the event. Using these data, create a written profile of the event. Using this written profile as a basis, draft a media release that outlines the outcomes of the event and the benefits to the local community.

Two international conferences:
a delegate perspective

The business events industry is a significant contributor to the Australian economy, and conferences form a large component of this industry. The most recent estimate of the business events industry's economic value to the Australian economy was over $7 billion (Johnson, Foo and O'Halloran 1999). There are a number of key stakeholders in the conference sector. These include the professional conference organisers, associations, conference bureaus, conference centres, local tourism authorities and, finally and perhaps most importantly, the delegate attending the conference.

This case study provides an overview of two large international conferences held at the Melbourne Exhibition and Conference Centre in Melbourne, Victoria in November 2000: the GeoEng2000 conference and the 4th World Stroke Congress. It is based on an industry-commissioned study that produced a report to industry entitled the *Melbourne Convention Delegate Study 2000: decision making in the convention industry*. The industry-commissioning bodies for the study were Arts Victoria, the Melbourne Exhibition and Convention Centre (MECC), Qantas and Melbourne Convention and Visitors Bureau (MCVB). The Co-operative Research Centre for Sustainable Tourism also supported the study.

One of the key aims in undertaking the study was to obtain an in-depth understanding of the motivations and planning processes for international delegate attendance at conferences. The industry partners were also keen to understand the role that Melbourne, as a destination, played in the decision-making process. An evaluation provides powerful information for organisations like MCVB and the MECC, and also provides a means to undertake 'delegate boosting'. Increasing delegate numbers is an important part of the role that these organisations play.

The case study looks at the conference industry from the international delegates' point of view, and covers the decision-making processes of the delegates, their expectations, the role of the destination and the communication cycle. It examines the various components of conventions and the ways conventions can be made more successful. These aims were provided as the brief by the industry partners in the study.

A delegate's perspective

In-depth interviews were the method used in this case study and the aim was to build on quantitative information obtained in *The Melbourne Conference Delegate Study 1999*. Each interview was one hour in duration and, in all, 19 international delegates were interviewed. The findings from these interviews are presented over and provide delegate information on the elements they considered part of a successful conference.

(continued)

The 'average' conference delegate attends between two and four conferences per year, of which at least one will be international. The delegates interviewed for this study were, on average, aged between 30 and 49 years. There were more males than females, but the proportion of female delegates is increasing. This appears to be a typical delegate profile of conferences and is comparable to the results from *The Melbourne Conference Delegate Study 1999*. The occupations of the delegates attending the two conferences of the study were quite different. At the GeoEng2000 Conference, bringing three different societies together for the first time, there was a high number of academics or researchers, whereas the Stroke Congress attracted a greater number of people involved in the medical profession.

The study found that conference delegates are very 'time poor'. It is common for the conference delegate to arrive one or two days before the conference and leave either the day the conference finishes or the day after. This leaves little time for pre- or post-touring. However, there are exceptions, with some delegates arriving in Australia a week beforehand or staying on in Australia for up to a month afterwards. Although some delegates arrived before or departed immediately after the conference, they may have arrived via another destination or stopped somewhere on the way, thus increasing their length of stay away from home. Marketers of conferences could perhaps build on this trend to provide information that will ultimately capitalise on the conference destination.

Conference delegates have certain expectations of what makes a successful conference and these views were expressed in the interviews undertaken. Most delegates expect a conference to be well organised, to cover the appropriate educational material and to provide opportunities for networking. They expect the venue to be large enough to fit the number of delegates in comfortably and for the venue to be easy to move around in. They also expect to be able to find accommodation choices available close to the conference venue, and well-connected transport links to the destination are also highly regarded. The conference delegate also expects to be able to communicate with the conference organisers easily. As a consequence, the role of the Internet has become increasingly important.

The delegates interviewed for the study did not hesitate in recommending the conference they had attended. They were very satisfied with the way the conference had been organised. They attributed this to the content of the conference and the networking opportunities available. Another significant factor was the outstanding organisation of the conference:

■ Organisation and facilities have been tremendous. The organisation is outstanding. There is enough space. Other conferences have been terrible. Everything is sorted. (Deery, Jago & Sokolich 2000) ■

The delegates thought the venue (Melbourne Exhibition and Convention Centre) was a great venue for a conference. They liked the layout of the conference with the exhibition in the middle and the coffee breaks taken in the exhibition area. The GeoEng2000 conference was particularly commended because of the three societies coming together as one and the ability of the venue to cater for such a large group.

The destination of the conference can play an important role in a delegate's decision to attend a conference. For many of the delegates, the destination was very important in deciding to attend the conference — in this case, it was an influencing factor.

For others, it is an opportunity to visit an exotic destination they had not visited frequently and something they may not get to experience again:

■ [It is a] very expensive and long trip, so I can see Australia. [There is] maybe no other opportunity.

Well the opportunity for getting back to this part of the world which I hadn't really seen before, I like to travel and I think that the combination of content plus location was extremely important to me. (Deery, Jago & Sokolich 2000) ■

One of the key elements that, even before the terrorist attacks on the World Trade Center and the Pentagon in the USA, was perceived to be important was that of destination safety. Many of the delegates interviewed for the study stressed the need for a safe conference environment. This included the venue as well as the destination. However, for some delegates, the destination had no effect or was irrelevant and they would attend a conference wherever it was held.

Responding to delegate feedback

The information from this study was provided to the key stakeholders in the study — the convention centre and the convention bureau. For both parties, there was information that provided a useful framework to improve delegate numbers and also increase the level of satisfaction for delegates. The interviews provided an opportunity to understand some of the key drivers for international delegate attendance at conferences. In summary, these included a number of conference attributes such as the greater provision of a dedicated space for delegate Internet facilities, the need for more female-friendly conference facilities such as affordable on-site accommodation and perhaps on-site creche facilities (given the increasing representation of female delegates), the allowance for time-poor delegates to maximise the socialising and networking opportunities, the need for a safe host-country environment and the need to include activities that are culturally host-country-centric. Each of these components provides an opportunity for the conference industry to maximise its potential capacity.

In particular, providing Internet facilities was one tangible change for conference organisers to make. Many of the delegates stated they were required to keep abreast of their work while attending the conference. Communication via email was the key method suggested to allow this to occur.

Another important finding from the interviews was the promotion of Melbourne as a safe destination. Not only was it perceived as being safe, but also extremely interesting, sophisticated and quite different from expectations. From a marketing point of view, this finding provides a distinctive and important advantage of Melbourne over other destinations.

In conclusion, the two conferences discussed, the GeoEng2000 Conference and the Stroke Conference, were highly successful. This was due to the choice of venue, the provision of Internet facilities, the perceived safety of the destination

(continued)

and the fact that delegates perceived the conferences as being well organised. All of these elements assist in conference success, and organisers need to be aware that as these expectations become the norm they will need to be constantly reviewed in order to meet the delegates increasingly higher expectations. Regular evaluations of delegate expectations and levels of satisfaction need to occur to provide a competitive business events sector.

Dr M Deery, Centre for Hospitality and Tourism Research, Victoria University

Questions

1 Who are the key players in the business events industry? You will need to undertake some research to answer this question and to find out the roles of each 'player'.

2 Given the importance of the perceived safety of a conference destination, how should convention bureau and destination management companies market the safety of a destination?

3 Outline the process for organising a successful conference. Include at least three of the issues addressed in the case study.

Hokitika Wildfoods
Festival

Background

Hokitika is a town of 3500 people on the west coast of the South Island of New Zealand. It is home to one of the country's icon events. Each March the town hosts the Hokitika Wildfoods Festival — a celebration of the pioneer wildness of the west coast of New Zealand. The festival is built around wild and challenging food, complemented by entertainment and activities that reflect this history. It is a day of 'testing the boundaries' with sheep's eyes, bull's penises, huhu grubs, and alcohol complete with pickled insects, to name just a few of the offerings.

The festival began in 1990 as a community event to celebrate the 1990 Sesquicentennial and completion of Gibson Quay heritage area. The first festival took place at Gibson Quay and attracted 1800 people and 28 stallholders. Most of those who attended were local residents of Hokitika, with the organisation of the event also conducted by a local.

The event has now grown into an annual celebration, drawing in large numbers of visitors from around New Zealand. It moved to its current site in Cass Square, a larger venue in the centre of town, when the Westland District Council took over the management of the festival in 1992.

The festival has grown from a single-day event based on the food experience to include a number of other events over a four-day period that promote and celebrate this history of toughness, wildness and individuality, still valued by current and former coasters and many others from around the country. The festival program now includes sport, arts and food events offering something for a wide range of target markets and utilising several different locations in town.

A valuable fundraising opportunity for local schools, sports and community groups is provided through the festival and for many, this is the only fundraising required. It is also the highlight for many younger townspeople, providing one of the few large event experiences in the community. For this reason, the event continues to have strong community support despite a negative impact on sales for many local businesses over the festival weekend. Most locals are involved in some way in the lead up or during the event, providing either services, goods or labour.

Festival management

From a New Zealand event perspective, the festival is a major success not only in terms of visitor numbers, but also in event longevity. The 13th staging of the event in 2003 attracted a record 22 000 visitors to town.

(*continued*)

Hokitika Wildfoods Festival organisers have dealt with the growth issues by holding annual evaluation sessions with stallholders, volunteers and key stakeholders, applying the lessons learnt each year to the planning for the following year. In 1997 a comprehensive visitor survey was conducted, with the aim of gaining participant feedback on the event experience.

As a result of the feedback received, small adjustments were made to what was considered a successful formula. However, there were some issues emerging from the survey related to size, perception and infrastructure support which have been monitored as numbers continue to grow.

Issues of growth

The participation numbers at the 2002 and 2003 festivals highlighted a need for a more comprehensive evaluation of both logistics and event risk management. In the last five years the Wildfoods Festival has grown by over 50 per cent. This is a cause for celebration with increased publicity, tourism and income spin-offs for the town. However, this growth has stretched local resources and provided additional challenges for management and the council, who have had to address the negative impacts of a resident population expanding from 3500 to 22 000 over the festival weekend.

Problems that have arisen include:

- changing perceptions of a weekend of drinking, rather than experiencing the food sensation. There has been increased coverage by the media of the wilder side of the festival created by large numbers of young drinkers at the venue and in town.
- lack of accommodation facilities and the resulting problem of 'freedom' camping around town. Some of these camping spots are by the river or sea, creating safety issues if inclement weather arises, along with sanitation, rubbish disposal and vandalism problems due to a lack of any controls.
- an increase in younger visitors. (The total number of people within the 16–24 age group had almost doubled over the five years from 1998 to 2003.) Associated with this problem is dangerous driving, drunkenness, drinking in town rather than attending the event and bringing in alcohol and therefore not contributing money to the local economy. The festival was pitched at the family and mature market and the growing numbers of young visitors are driving the key target market away.
- damage to property and broken glass on beaches and streets due to the open nature of the event. There are many places where people congregate, including the beach, making it difficult to service all areas with rubbish containers, toilets and security services. This is compounded by the freedom camping in these areas.
- increased health and safety risks coupled with tougher legislation and penalties. Legislation changes in New Zealand have put the responsibility back on the organisers of the events to provide a 'reasonable' level of care, with the definition of 'reasonable' not being stated. As a result an organiser can be prosecuted against standards that do not exist or are not comparable with international standards.

- the impact on the town infrastructure and services. With the huge influx of people there is a severe drain on basic services and infrastructure such as water, rubbish and sanitation, as well as the equipment held in a town of this size.

These growing problems meant that an evaluation/review of the strategic direction of the event was needed.

The evaluation

The Westland District Council, the owner and manager of the event, commissioned consultants to undertake a strategic review of the festival and to develop business and marketing plans which would address the issues and take the event forward in a planned way.

The review involved research among a number of groups, including visitors, stallholders, local businesses and community, suppliers, sponsors and stakeholders.

A random sample of visitors was surveyed as they entered the venue and around town, requesting in the first section demographic, event expenditure and services used information, while the second section focused on questions related to the event itself.

Stallholder feedback was secured though a post-event questionnaire which was posted out with specific questions related to expectations, pricing and staffing. The local community, randomly selected from the telephone book, provided feedback through structured phone interviews during which they were asked about their support, attendance, impressions, town impacts and other aspects. The business community was also approached using qualitative research methods with some set, but mainly open-ended questions related to possible changes, future directions, impacts etc.

The final group of suppliers and stakeholders included council units (for example, sewerage, rubbish removal and water), police, contractors, St John Ambulance staff, local hoteliers, security companies and sponsors. Due to the range of event contexts for each group or individual, the research was qualitative, with informal discussions around several key areas.

As a result of the evaluation research, the plans for the 2004 festival have incorporated a number of recommendations which include a site layout review, expansion and focusing of key events over the weekend, adoption of bylaws by council, development of several festival sites and a review of the marketing tools and target markets.

Summary

The Hokitika Wildfoods Festival demonstrates the use of evaluation techniques in the planning and review processes both to (a) substantiate observations or statements and (b) as supporting documentation for recommendations put forward as the basis of the business and marketing plans.

It will be necessary to undertake additional evaluations in the future to measure the success of the strategic review; however, the festival management is confident that the repositioning will be successful in ensuring the ongoing success of the event.

Anne Hindson

Questions

1 What do you see as the successful components of this festival which have seen it grow so quickly?

2 What questions would you include in a visitor survey which would provide the answers sought for this project?

3 For a sample size of 22 000, what numbers of visitors would need to be surveyed to ensure a representative sample?

4 Why would a marketing plan be requested as part of the strategic review and how would it support the business plan?

REFERENCES

Arts Victoria 2004, Home page, www.arts.vic.gov.au (accessed 27 February 2004).

Australian Bureau of Statistics 1997, *Measuring the impact of festivals: guidelines for conducting an economic impact study,* National Centre for Culture and Recreation Statistics, Cultural Ministers Council, Statistics Working Group, Canberra.

Australian Bureau of Statistics 2003, Home page, www.abs.gov.au (accessed 23 October 2003).

Bureau of Tourism Research 2003, Home page, www.btr.gov.au (accessed 23 October 2003).

Centre for Regional Tourism Research 2004, Home page, www.regional tourism.com.au (accessed 3 March 2004).

Davidson, R & Shaw, R 2000, *The Melbourne convention delegate study 1999,* CRC for Sustainable Tourism Pty Ltd, Melbourne.

Deery, M, Jago, L & Sokolich, R 2002, *The Melbourne convention delegate study 2000: decision making in the convention industry,* unpublished industry report.

Getz, D 1997, *Event management and event tourism,* Cognizant Communication Corporation, New York.

Goldberg, JJ 1997, *Special events — best practices in modern event management,* Van Nostrand Reinhold, New York.

Goldblatt, J & Perry, J 2002, 'Re-building the community with fire, water and music. The WaterFire phenomenon', in *Events and place making: proceedings of international research conference held in Sydney 2002,* eds L Jago, M Deery, R Harris, A Hede & J Allen, Australian Centre for Event Management, Sydney.

Hindson, A 2003, *Hokitika Wildfoods Festival,* Christchurch Polytechnic, Christchurch.

Jago, L, Chalip, L, Brown, G, Mules, T & Ali, S 2002, 'The role of events in helping to brand a destination', in *Events and place making: proceedings of international research conference held in Sydney 2002*, eds L Jago, M Deery, R Harris, A Hede & J Allen, Australian Centre for Event Management, Sydney.

Johnson, L, Foo, L & O'Halloran, M 1999, 'Meetings make their mark: characteristics and economic contribution of Australia's meetings and exhibition sector', BTR Occasional Paper no. 26, Bureau of Tourism Research, Canberra.

Kaless, S 2004, 'Looking at the numbers game', http://www.rugby worldcup.com/RugbyWorldCup/EN/Tournament/News/sk+24+11+stats.htm (accessed 3 March 2004).

Veal, AJ 1997, *Research methods for leisure and tourism: a practical guide*, Pitman Publishing, London.

This final part looks at current and emerging topics in festival and special event management. It examines societal trends and their impacts on events, the growth of the event industry, the professionalisation of event management, event franchising, the use of events in skills development and training, information technology, transfer-of-knowledge programs, increased government involvement in events, and the adoption of environmental management practices by events.

15
Issues
and trends

LEARNING OBJECTIVES

After studying this chapter, you should be able to:

- list and discuss the major trends and issues in the event industry

- discuss the changes in society that are affecting the nature of events

- identify and discuss the major factors affecting the growth of the event industry

- list and discuss the factors in event management becoming recognised as a profession

- discuss the impact of information technology on the nature of contemporary events

- describe the impact of risk management on the event industry

- discuss the expansion of event education

- understand and describe the increased government involvement in events

- describe and discuss the factors influencing the adoption of environmental management practices by events.

$\mathcal{I}$NTRODUCTION

This chapter examines current trends and issues in the event industry. A trend is defined as a general direction in which a company or industry is moving. Issues are problems that are common across the industry. The solution to a number of related issues may result in a trend in the industry. The issues outlined in this chapter have a common thread: they are the growing pains of a young industry. As the industry grows, it absorbs older industries and redefines current ones.

$\mathcal{S}$OCIETAL TRENDS AND THEIR IMPACT ON EVENTS

Throughout the developed world, demographic changes are profoundly affecting societies and, consequently, the types of event and festival that will grow in popularity in the future. According to the World Bank (2004), these trends include the ageing of the population, a dramatic decrease in the birth rate, and a significant increase in migration from less developed countries to developed countries.

The ageing of the population is caused by people living longer as a result of improvements in health care (that is, a decrease in the death rate) and a decrease in the number of children born per woman (that is, a decrease in the birth rate). Australia's birth rate fell from 3.2 per woman in 1950 to only 1.8 in 2000, and life expectancy rose by nine years for males and 10 years for females in the same period. This means family size has reduced and probably will continue to reduce, which increases the disposable income per household. Many other developed countries have experienced even more dramatic increases in the average age. In Japan, only 11.6 per cent of the population was 65 years or older in 1989, but over 25 per cent of the population is projected to be in that age category by 2030 (allrefer.com 2004). The 'age pyramid' in developed countries is no longer a pyramid with the largest number of citizens being the youngest; rather, it is bulging around the middle years, as if to represent a stereotypical middle-age spread.

In many developed countries, as in Australia, increased immigration is used to ensure growth in the number of working-age residents. According to the Australian Department of Immigration (2004), immigration was responsible for between one third and nearly half of the population increase for the years 1993–2002.

These demographic changes will have several impacts on events produced in the future. As ethnic groups living outside their country of origin increase in number in host countries such as Australia, the number and scale of events that celebrate these cultures will increase. At the same time, events that celebrate (perhaps in reaction) the dominant or mainstream Anglo-Celtic culture will also increase in importance. The Anzac Day celebrations, for example, continue to grow in size even though it is about 60 years since the end of World War II, and increasing numbers of young Australians visit Gallipoli in Turkey for the Anzac Day ceremony. Other celebrations of the dominant culture that are expected to increase in significance are traditional sporting events (for example, test cricket), commemorations of historic events, and long-standing events such as the Sydney Royal Easter Show.

The demographic bulge (known sometimes as the baby-boom generation) will also affect future festivals and events. This generation's tastes and attitudes were formed in the 1960s and the music, lifestyle and values from that era, along with the events that celebrate them, will gain even more significance in years to come. An excellent example is the Woodford Folk Festival, which gets larger each year.

People in developed nations are also becoming much better educated. Almost one quarter of Australians who leave school now attend university, and this number is expected to grow. According to the government of New South Wales (2004), Australia has more graduates per million of population than the United Kingdom, Singapore, Germany and Hong Kong. This should ensure the market for more cerebral events grows as the proportion of university graduates in the population grows.

THE GROWTH OF THE EVENT INDUSTRY

A major trend worldwide over the past decade was the growth and expansion of the event industry. Having emerged as an industry in its own right through the 1990s, the event sector continues to grow, fuelled by economic growth and the increase in leisure spending in most western countries. In many of Australia's cities and towns, an almost bewildering array of public entertainment events is on offer each weekend, catering to almost every conceivable taste and interest group. Events have become an essential element of contemporary life, linked inseparably with tourism promotion, government strategies and corporate marketing. Major sporting events, along with the marketing campaigns and controversies that accompany them, feature almost daily in our newspapers and electronic media. Corporate use of event sponsorships and event marketing keep events at the forefront of our awareness. The term 'events', along with the associated management process and industry structure, has considerable currency and profile. Many other areas that were previously seen as distinct — such as meetings, conferences, exhibitions, festivals, major sporting fixtures and corporate functions — are now perceived as part of a wider event industry.

Events have become so all encompassing and far reaching that it is almost impossible to accurately gauge the full size of the industry. If a major car company uses an event to launch a new model, it has no responsibility or even desire to notify anyone of this event other than the participants and guests. The event thus remains difficult to identify by anyone attempting to track and quantify the event industry. Nevertheless, evidence of the growth of the industry is overwhelming. The number of events listed by tourism organisations and 'what's on' entertainment directories, compared with the number of 10 years ago, indicates the extent of this increase.

Among the reasons for the virtual explosion of the event industry over the past decade are:

- rising levels of disposable income, combined with increasing time pressure, resulting in the demand for structured, high-quality leisure experiences
- increased government awareness of the tourism and economic benefits of events, leading to further development of government event strategies and funding
- growing corporate affluence and awareness of the marketing power of events, leading to increased use of events both for internal staff training and morale building, and as marketing and communications tools.
- increased awareness of event management as a cohesive discipline with the ability to focus resources and deliver specific objectives.

■ Increased *demand and supply*

This exponential increase in the number of events has created a demand for qualified event managers and for industry suppliers to fill the increasing need for event-related goods and services. The number of venues has increased, both at the level of publicly funded recreation spaces, malls, convention and exhibition centres, and at the level of privately funded meeting facilities in hotels. The need for unique and interesting event spaces has resulted in museums, historic houses, councils, universities and other property holders developing managed special event facilities as an additional revenue stream. A plethora of specialised hire companies, caterers, entertainment agencies, designers, publicists, technical producers, lighting and sound personnel, set builders and pyrotechnicians has also risen to meet the needs of this burgeoning new industry. A glance at the Yellow Pages telephone directory under categories such as event management companies and event suppliers will reveal the size and scope of this recent phenomenon. Event industry associations and directories have struggled to keep pace with this rate of expansion, and event websites such as specialevents.com and worldofevents.net have taken an increasing role in tracking and communicating the growth and changes in the industry.

In a competitive marketplace, the supply of goods and services tends to rise to meet perceived demand; so far, the trend in the demand for event services continues to be upward. Whether this trend continues and how the industry might weather any future downturn in the economy remain the subject of speculation.

■ The growth *of corporate events*

One area strongly fuelling the expansion is the corporate sector. In the halcyon days of the 1980s boom, many companies became involved in event sponsorship, often tailored to the tastes and interests of senior management. With the recession of the late 1980s and early 1990s, there was a general cutback in spending on event sponsorships. As the financial climate improved through the late 1990s, many large companies re-entered the sponsorship market, but with a greater focus and rigour (Geldard & Sinclair 2000). At a time when traditional advertising was perceived to be losing impact as a result of buyer cynicism and market clutter, events were perceived as a means of cutting through the clutter to reach consumers in terms of their own interests and the areas that were important to them. One sponsor might reach motor sport enthusiasts by sponsoring a car race, for example, or another sponsor might increase the profile of a youth-oriented product by sponsoring a rock concert.

Against the background of increasing corporate affluence, companies also expanded their internal use of events to train and reward staff, improve company morale, educate dealer networks and maintain customer relations. In many instances, the corporate sector wholeheartedly embraced events, but with a new rigour. Events were no longer the prerogative of senior management, but were selected and run by marketing departments, and subject to the same return-on-investment analysis used for other marketing areas such as advertising and direct marketing. Figure 15.1 (page 484) is an example of an approval chain for a corporate event. (Chapter 10 also discusses control.)

■ The growth *of international event companies*

As events became established as a significant component of the marketing mix, they became increasingly subject to rigorous evaluation of their outcomes, leading to the need for standardised event management processes. Companies began to create event management teams, often within their marketing divisions. Global companies began to streamline their event production to ensure the delivery of a standard event product over different markets and locations. The launch of a new Mercedes Benz model, for example, would employ the same format and style whether conducted in Berlin, Tokyo, London or Sydney. To be able to deliver a standardised global event product to their clients, some of the larger event companies, particularly in the USA, bought out local event companies in different markets — for example, the large US company Jack Morton purchased Caribiner Wavelength in Sydney, retaining the original company director to manage the new Sydney operation. As this trend towards globalised event management continues, the question of local cultures and differences arises. The same event may not be able to be adapted from, say, Los Angeles to Hong Kong without taking careful account of the individual cultural nuances of each location. Arguably, local companies may sometimes be in a better situation to appreciate and respond to these cultural differences, although the process of standardisation seems likely to continue in an increasingly globalised world.

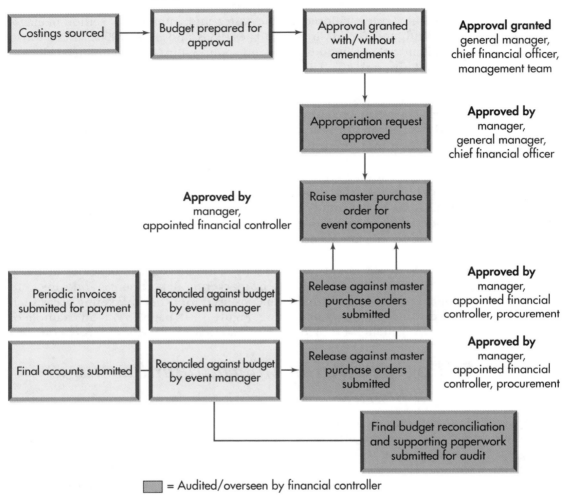

■ **Figure 15.1** *Corporate event financial management*

RECOGNITION OF EVENT MANAGEMENT AS A PROFESSION

When considering the event industry, it is easy to be misdirected and believe it is only about events. Events can be compared to any project-based industry. Civil engineering, for example, is not just about the product; it is a description of the process needed to create that product. Event management, therefore, is about the processes that are used to create and sustain the event. Recognition of this process is the basis for recognising event management as a profession.

A profession is characterised by:

- *a body of knowledge* — this is the library of the profession. It is made up of information from other professions such as logistics, contract management and marketing. Journals and textbooks describe the body of knowledge and continually refine it.
- *a methodology* — this is made up of a series of processes or tasks, which can be described and taught. The risk management process is an example.
- *heuristics* — these are 'rules of thumb', stories and descriptions of experience that can be learned only 'on the job'.

Event management is gradually collating and describing these three areas. In the past, the 'rule of thumb' was the main way of organising events. The recognition and description of the processes used to create the event — that is, the methodology — is the moment when event management progresses from a skill to a profession.

■ The event *management body of knowledge*

The event management body of knowledge (EMBOK) is being defined. Silvers (2003) and O'Toole (2002) have developed categories for the EMBOK, as described in chapter 9. Some of these EMBOK categories overlap and some are common to all. Risk management and logistics, for example, are found in all these areas. Only one area of knowledge (design) deals with what is on at the event.

■ Competency *standards*

Combined with the advance of the EMBOK is the development of competency standards for event management. In Australia, the competency standards were developed in 2000 and are constantly under review. A countrywide competency standard for event management gives the industry a benchmark to measure excellence in management. Previously, this benchmark was the success of the event; however, stakeholders cannot wait until the event to find out whether the event management is competent — by then, it is too late. Linked to the development of standards is the interest in ethical standards for events.

The search for standards has led to the adoption of the Australian and New Zealand Standard (AS/NZS 4360) on risk management in the event context. With a constantly changing business environment, risk management is perceived as the way to handle the uncertainty. The requirement for accountability is a reason for the adoption of International Standards Organisation (ISO) standards. Government departments and large companies are investigating their events to make sure they comply with their organisation's ISO certification.

■ Management *systems*

When this need for standards and competency levels is integrated with the use of software, a management system emerges. PRINCE 2, for example, is a management system that some clients have requested their event management company or event office use. MS Project software is another. Both systems can create status reports. These work-in-progress reports are an example of the need for accountability of event management. They are a response to clients' and other stakeholders' demands to know how the organising of an event is progressing.

A part of the trend of accountability is the need to measure success. The success of an event can be measured by the attitudes of the attendees surveyed after the event. However, attitudes are too intangible to be used in a business case for an event. Many event sponsors thus now regard the economic impact of an event as a key success factor. In the past, there was no accurate way to measure the economic impact, which was often exaggerated and more of a 'wish list'. More accurate methods of measuring this impact are being developed. The V8 Car Race in Canberra was cancelled when the race was evaluated from a cost–benefit viewpoint.

The introduction of methods to measure intangible benefits is another trend in the event industry. Consumer surplus is one such method, whereby the attendees are asked to assess the monetary value of the event to them. If this value exceeds the ticket price, the event is said to have a consumer surplus. The exhibition industry has a number of metrics to value an event. Other metrics include the generation of leads and sales directly attributed to the event. The measurement of intangibles is important in the feasibility study of an event and in the presentation of the business case.

EVENT FRANCHISING

With the development and recognition of a management system comes the ability to transfer this system to other events — that is, the ability to franchise. The successful event or festival becomes a model that can be developed into another event anywhere in the world. The value is not only in the single event, it is in the method used to organise the event. Event franchising is common in the sport industry and exhibitions. The Olympic Games is perhaps the largest example. Numerous sports races, such as the Formula 1 Grand Prix, 'fun runs' and rough water swims, are also franchised events. Further, some corporate events (such as seminars and conferences) are variations on an original model. An example of successful event franchising is the Night of the Ad Eaters. This started as a small event in France and now takes place in 160 cities across 47 countries, including Mongolia, Mexico and Japan.

Again, the value of a management system is illustrated. Without a system, there is nothing to pass on except personal experience.

THE USE OF EVENTS IN SKILLS DEVELOPMENT AND TRAINING

An unexpected opportunity has emerged from the trend towards standards and competency levels. In South Africa, the National Qualification Framework includes the experience and knowledge gained from working on events as credit points towards certification. This opens up a new use for events as vehicles for training.

With major events such as the Cricket World Cup, the South African Government had a platform to train volunteers: 'The National Skills Development Strategy *Skills for productive citizenship for all* has a mission to equip South Africans with the skills to succeed in the global market place' (ICC Cricket World Cup 2003 Organising Committee 2003).

The Training of Volunteers 2003 program was aligned to this skills development strategy. Once volunteers were registered, they were assessed for their current abilities by a process called 'recognition of prior learning'. As they worked on the event, they were trained in the national unit standards:
- caring for customers
- organising oneself in the workplace
- maintaining occupational health and safety
- functioning as a team.

This innovative scheme now allows the South African Government to achieve maximum value from events: major events are used as a way to restructure the new South Africa. The result is that most of the volunteers are young. The skills they learn are not wasted, but rather used towards their careers. At the time of writing, Events Tasmania was investigating a similar scheme.

INFORMATION TECHNOLOGY

Any advance in information technology has an effect on events. Information technology permeates almost all areas of event management, from the sound system used at the event to the ticketing and attendee registration. The software used to manage events has become more sophisticated as the power of the microchip has increased. USI, one of the largest event software companies in the world, claims that the trend is towards 'thin client computing'. This means the software is not on the event management company's computer, but held on the software company's computer and accessed over the Internet by the event company when needed.

A further trend in computing is the growth of the Internet, which is used for research, marketing, communication and reporting. Any one of the knowledge areas of management outlined in chapter 9 can benefit from the Internet. Being so pervasive, the Internet is no longer only a trend.

The use of personal digital assistants (PDA), or hand-held computers, is also increasing at events. These pocket-sized devices can contain all the information about the event. The complete event manual can be placed into a PDA. Information can quickly be retrieved and new data can be entered.

Some events rely on the anonymity of the new media to exist. Rave parties are an example. By using SMS messages, these parties are kept exclusive.

RISK MANAGEMENT

As mentioned earlier, the adoption of risk management is a strong trend in the event industry around the world. Reasons for this trend include the following:

- Event managers are increasingly obligated to produce a risk management plan to gain insurance cover, or to control premium levels.
- Various court cases and coronial inquiries have demanded to sight the risk management plans of the event companies involved.
- Government departments at various levels have adopted a risk management process and require their contractors do the same.
- Occupational health and safety codes recommend the use of risk management.
- State and federal legislation and codes, such as the Commonwealth Criminal Code, call for the use of formal risk management.
- The event manuals published by local councils and state governments, such as the City of Ballarat's *Event planning guide*, ask event managers to produce a risk management plan.
- Government funding bodies and authorities such as the Roads and Traffic Authority request that a risk management plan be produced before giving a grant or approval.

The findings of the coronial inquiry into the death at a Big Day Out concert in New South Wales listed a number of recommendations, including that public events use the Australian Standard AS/NZS 4360 on risk management. The criminal nuisance findings against an event manager in New Zealand are further proof that an event company needs a formal risk management system that can be demonstrated in court.

The above list constitutes the external pressure on event managers to use a risk management plan. However, there are internal reasons as well. A number of event companies have found that the risk standard improves their ability to manage an event. It is a formal way of looking for problems and solving them; it captures the whole process, so that process can be improved for each event. The case study in chapter 11 demonstrates the effective use of risk management as part of general logistics management.

■ The increased *threat to security*

The changing world has introduced a new risk to public and private events — the threat of terrorism. Wars, the 11 September 2001 terrorist attacks in New York and Washington, the Bali bombings and the terrorist attack in

Madrid have all affected events in Australia. Major public events in Australia are now subject to intense security, unheard of a few years ago. Simple matters, such as a car parked outside an event, can now take on an ominous meaning.

THE EXPANSION OF EVENT EDUCATION

The Event Educators Forum (2004) in Australia identified 212 registered training organisations and 23 universities with courses that include significant event management components. Bowdin (2003) estimates that about 140 event-related undergraduate courses are offered by about 29 colleges and universities in the United Kingdom.

Important issues have been (1) where event courses sit in the overall pattern of tertiary education, and (2) what the content of such courses should be. Traditionally, the first generation of event courses comprised individual subjects within wider tourism and hospitality programs. They often emphasised the MICE aspect of events — meetings, incentives, conventions and exhibitions — and focused on the management of meetings and conferences in a tourism industry context. As the definition of events has broadened to include public and government events, new courses have been developed with a wider focus encompassing the full spectrum of event types. These courses sometimes sit within the broader framework of arts, sports and business management programs. More recent courses have been developed as stand-alone programs, encompassing the full range of contemporary events.

TRANSFER-OF-KNOWLEDGE PROGRAMS

Allied to the increase in event management programs has been the identification of knowledge involved in the management of major events, and the formal and informal transfer of this knowledge to other events. The International Olympic Committee (IOC) paid $5 million to the Sydney Organising Committee for the Olympic Games (SOCOG) for the intellectual property arising from the 2000 Olympics. This material was then made available to organisers of both the Salt Lake City Winter Olympics in 2002 and the Athens Summer Olympics in 2004. Known as the Transfer of Know-how (TOK) Program, the knowledge gained from the Sydney Olympic Games was transmitted via 90-plus individual guides and a debrief session by senior managers in Athens in November 2000. This knowledge will form the basis of a generic Olympics management guide, to which successive Olympic Games organisers will add. Olympic Games Knowledge Services, jointly owned by the IOC and Monash Ed (owned by Monash University, Cambridge Consulting Services and Equiset), has been formed to assist in tailoring the TOK Program to the needs of individual Olympic Games and future bidding cities. It will also identify and credit Olympic Games experts and engage them to pass on their experience (Universitat Autonoma de Barcelona Sistems Centrals 2003). The case study on page 500 provides a detailed account of the development of transfer-of-knowledge programs in relation to the Olympic movement.

THE GROWTH OF EVENT RESEARCH

Paralleling the growth in event education and transfer of knowledge has been the growth of academic research on events, leading to a greater understanding of events' contexts, impacts and outcomes. Prior to 2000, event research was generally incorporated in wider fields such as tourism and hospitality, business and economics. In 2000, the Australian Centre for Event Management conducted the first dedicated international event management research conference, 'Events beyond 2000 — setting the agenda'. This conference has continued as a biennial conference, and event management has become increasingly recognised as a distinct field of study. The journal *Festival Management and Event Tourism* has been refocused as *Event Management*, and specialised event research websites such as the worldofevents.net and the European Case Clearing House (www.ecch. cranfield.ac.uk) have been developed. Further, event industry associations such as the International Festivals and Events Association and the International Special Events Society have developed academic research strands in their annual conference programs, with the increasing participation of the academic community.

Much event research is still dispersed over a wide range of journals from allied fields, and some key topics remain underresearched. However, event research is continuing to expand and to provide valuable insights into the behaviour of events, and a better understanding of event management processes and outcomes.

INCREASING GOVERNMENT INVOLVEMENT IN EVENTS

As the benefits and impacts of events have been increasingly recognised, governments at all levels have assumed a growing role in event creation, funding, management and regulation. Most major events — including the

Olympic and Commonwealth Games, the Grand Prix and Expo circuits, and international single-sport championships such as those in soccer, rugby union, athletics, tennis and swimming — are subject to bids by national associations. Given their costs and infrastructure needs, these bids are increasingly supported and/or underwritten by city, state or national governments. The IOC has gone so far as to state that bids to host the Olympic Games will be considered only if they have the full and explicit backing of the host city government. Likewise, many homegrown festivals, community and cultural events seek the financial and organisational support of government. Major conferences and exhibitions also require government assistance through the provision of infrastructure such as convention and exhibition centres, and the support of convention bureaus able to mount bids and orchestrate resources.

■ The creation *of event strategies*

Recognising the social, cultural and economic benefits of these events, but aware of limited funds and conflicting needs, governments at all levels are increasingly devising event strategies to assist policy development and establish funding priorities. The number and extent of these strategies have grown in recent years, with each Australian state having a formal strategy and government event organisation, and with regional cities also starting to develop their own independent event strategies. This situation is mirrored globally, with Scotland and Denmark among several countries to develop event strategies in the recent past. These strategies set out to identify the role of events in their country/state/city, and to provide policy guidelines and action plans for the funding, management, coordination, regulation and promotion of events. These strategies acknowledge the multiple roles of government as event host organisations, funding and regulatory bodies.

■ Event *portfolio management*

Most event strategies acknowledge the advantages of a state or city having a balanced portfolio of events spread across the annual calendar and including different types of event. Event strategies such as that of the New South Wales Government thus attempt to identify and support an annual calendar of events — such as the Sydney Festival, the Sydney Royal Easter Show, the Sydney Gay and Lesbian Mardi Gras, the Sydney Writers' Festival, and Carnivale — as well as one-off special events such as the 2000 Sydney Olympic Games and the 2003 Rugby World Cup. Edinburgh has built on the success and reputation of the established International and Fringe Festivals and the Edinburgh Tattoo to build a year-round calendar, which also includes Hogmanay and the International Jazz and Blues, Science and Book festivals. Well-balanced and well-managed event portfolios have become an indispensable element of city marketing and tourism development, and are increasingly found in most urban and many rural centres.

The coordination *of event infrastructure services*

Staging major events successfully involves coordinating a wide range of infrastructure and support services, including venues, transport and communications, and public authorities such as police, fire, ambulance and emergency services. Many of these services are provided by government, so many event strategies include a 'one-stop shop' approach to their coordination and management. The staging of major events has increasingly underlined the importance of such coordination. The Central Sydney Operations Group (CSOG), which arose from the staging of the Sydney Olympic Games in 2000, is a best-practice example of such a coordination group. CSOG consists of almost 40 government and nongovernment agencies, including landholders, emergency services, traffic and transport agencies, volunteer services and other agencies such as the State Chamber of Commerce and relevant state government departments. According to its terms of reference:

> ■ CSOG provides a forum for a cooperative, coordinated approach between agencies. It is a conduit for organisers of approved events to communicate with government agencies about the possible impacts of the event on government infrastructure and operations. The agencies identify unresolved issues that are addressed in smaller, working groups. CSOG conducts debriefs following major events in order to continually improve their effectiveness, efficiency and safety (Premier's Department 2003). ■

The growth *of government funding for events*

As government involvement in events increased throughout the 1990s, the need for government financial support and funding became increasingly obvious. As a result, many governments at all levels now run funding programs for events. In Australia, these programs range from federal programs (such as Festivals Australia) to state funding through state events corporations and tourism ministries, to local government funding through council event programs. Issues raised by such funding programs include the differing agendas of events, and the differing criteria for selection and evaluation.

At state government level, funding programs acknowledge the role of major events (which are usually funded by events corporations or major event boards) and the more general needs of special interest groups, such as the arts, sport and ethnic communities (which are usually funded by individual ministry programs). At the local government level, the need to create a portfolio of tourism events is often distinguished from the need for events that primarily serve community needs and objectives. In some areas, these two types of event are treated as separate funding programs, each with its own set of objectives and selection criteria. Growing pressures on event funding and competition from other government programs have resulted in an increasing emphasis on rigorous assessment and evaluation procedures. As requirements for funding increase and added pressure is placed on available resources, the need to predict event outcomes accurately and measure results is likely to continue to increase.

THE ADOPTION OF ENVIRONMENTAL MANAGEMENT PRACTICES BY EVENTS

Many event organisers are now consciously seeking to manage the physical environmental impacts of their events, the Olympic Games being perhaps the most notable in this regard. The following discussion identifies a range of factors that have pushed event organisers in this direction.

■ Government *adoption of the principles of ecologically sustainable development*

The principles of ecologically sustainable development were adopted by 182 governments on the signing of the Agenda 21 document at the conclusion of the Earth Summit in Rio de Janeiro in 1992. While not legally binding, the adopted principles carry 'a strong moral obligation to ensure their full implementation' (United Nations 1992, p. 3). Areas covered by this document included solid waste management, the protection of the atmosphere, the protection of the quality and supply of freshwater resources, and environmentally sound management of toxic chemicals. Perhaps not surprisingly, given the impact, size and international nature of Olympic Games, the IOC has been the most proactive of event-based organisations in embracing the principles of ecologically sustainable development. Cities seeking to conduct a winter or summer Olympic Games must now formally address environmental issues in their bid documents (IOC 1999). The Olympic Movement has also developed its own version of Agenda 21 (based on the principles embodied in the more generic Earth Summit document) and has acted to make environmentalism the 'third pillar' of Olympism, the others being sport and culture (Tarradellas & Behnam 2000).

Given the limited published material on the extent to which events (other than the Olympics) have engaged with the principals of ecologically sustainable development, it is difficult to be sure about the impact of these principles in the events area in general. Nonetheless, those organisations involved in the creation and conduct of events in signatory countries would be affected by the efforts of their government (at all levels) to pursue their responsibilities under this agreement. To some extent, the issue of waste management (discussed next) could be perceived as an example.

■ Government *waste reduction efforts*

Rapid economic and population growth in the post-World War period resulted in solid waste becoming a major environmental problem, with government increasing its focus over the last decade on ways in which to reduce waste. Events is an area that has been the subject of such attention because events often involve large numbers of people, and can result in the generation of significant volumes of solid waste. In New South Wales, for example, the Environmental Protection Authority (2004) has provided resources through its Community Waste Reduction Grant Scheme for a number of event-related initiatives, including the Reusabowl project — a mobile automated dishwashing facility that event organisers can hire. Additionally, Resource NSW (the state's waste management agency) operates a waste-wise management program for events, with dedicated staff and supporting publications (Department of Environment and Conservation 2004).

In the United States, there is also evidence that events are being actively targeted for waste reduction purposes. In the state of Wisconsin, for example, the recycling laws require event managers to make provisions for the recycling of:

- glass bottles and jars
- aluminium and steel/tin cans
- plastic containers
- newspapers
- corrugated cardboard
- office paper
- other items, depending on the community (Wisconson Department of Natural Resources 2000).

The following event profile on Taste of Tasmania (a food and wine festival conducted by Hobart City Council) demonstrates how one local authority has sought to engage in the waste reduction process for an event that it owns and operates.

EVENT PROFILE

Taste of Tasmania

In 2000–01, the Taste of Tasmania food and wine festival implemented a significant public waste management program that achieved 75 per cent recovery of waste. Over the past four years, the event generated 275 tonnes of waste, of which 207 tonnes was collected for waste reuse, waste recycling and energy recovery activities.

After 15 years of successful operation, the Taste of Tasmania has gained the status of Tasmania's premier food and wine event. The continual expansion of the event meant that it has been generating greater amounts of waste. It thus needed to meet current practices for waste management, including those for solid waste disposal, recycling and reuse, stormwater and liquid trade waste.

The Hobart City Council's Events and Marketing Unit and Waste Engineering Unit collaborated to introduce a comprehensive waste management and recycling program for the 2000–01 Taste of Tasmania. An assessment of the 1999–2000 event identified five key areas in which it was necessary to demonstrate higher standards of waste management while meeting legislative and regulatory requirements:

1. protecting the stormwater system and the River Derwent from pollution generated from the event
2. ensuring liquid trade waste standards for waste discharged to sewerage systems are met
3. implementing an appropriate resource recovery program, with the majority of waste generated from the event being reused, recycled or used for energy recovery to complement the event's existing use of 100 per cent compostable cutlery and plates
4. developing event-specific stallholder and patron education strategies aimed at avoiding waste, preventing the generation of waste or reducing the volume generated, and ensuring appropriate disposal practices are achieved.

The program implemented for the 2000–01 event resulted in significantly improved waste management at the event. In particular, 45.41 tonnes (or 69.6 per cent) of waste generated by the event was redirected from waste disposal to waste reuse, waste recycling and energy recovery from waste. A large volume of waste was thus recovered to produce value-added products, which would otherwise have gone to landfill, taking up valuable space and adding to greenhouse gas emissions.

Since the 2000–01 event, additional waste management strategies have been put in place to further reduce waste disposal through the identification of other waste streams and the improvement of existing waste management facilities. This work includes implementing an on-site cardboard collection and recycling service, installing stormwater litter traps on six drainage entrances at Princes Wharf Shed 1, and increasing the grease arrestor's treatment capacity by 25 per cent by installing a filter on the outlet of one of the units.

Over the past four years, approximately 275 tonnes of waste have been generated by the Taste of Tasmania. Of this amount, 207 tonnes (or 75 per cent) of waste have been collected for waste reuse, waste recycling and energy recovery activities. The table on page 496 documents the resource recovery and waste disposal of the different waste streams from 2001–02 to 2003–04.

(continued)

■ *Waste recovery at Taste of Tasmania*

WASTE CATEGORY	2001–02 (TONNES)	2002–03 (TONNES)	2003–04 (TONNES)
Refuse (non-recoverable waste)	17.92	14.8	15.77
Glass	44.88	38	35
Compostables	8.7	5.88	7.54
Cardboard	6	4	5.96
Used cooking oil	1.18	1.4	2.2
Total waste	78.68	64.8	66.47
Total amount recovered	60.76	50	50.7

(**Source:** *John Chrispijn, Hobart City Council 2004.*)

■ Cost *savings*

Increasingly, event organisers and event facilities are realising the economic benefits that can result from the adoption of environmental management strategies. Publications such as Chernushenko's (1994) *Greening our games: running sports events and facilities that won't cost the earth* have been making the point for some time that financial savings or avoided costs can flow from the pursuit of environmental programs and principles. An area of note in this regard is the reduction of disposal fees. Calculations by the Californian Showgrounds in 2000, for example, showed that the venue had realised savings of over US$5.5 million over the previous five years due to effective environmental management of its waste stream (Strauss 2000). The decision to purchase reusable items can also serve to reduce or eliminate disposal charges. The 1999 Pan American Games, for example, eliminated disposable plates and cups from its waste stream by purchasing crockery items. At the completion of the event, these items were sold, resulting in a total saving of an estimated $US30 000 over the alternative of disposal (Crawford 2000).

■ Protection *by sponsoring companies of their corporate image*

The extent to which sponsors influence the environmental practices/policies of events is an area that has received little attention, yet sponsor expectations can be an important factor in the uptake by events of environmental programs (Crawford 2000). Goldblatt (1999), for example, posits that major corporations, being sensitive to criticism from consumers, will increasingly require that the events they sponsor meet or exceed certain environmental standards. He also suggests that companies involved in particular environmental strategies — recycling, for example — are likely to want recycling programs to be in place at the event they sponsor. An example of the significance of 'green' policies in attracting sponsorship is the 2000 Sydney Olympic Games: Bonlac Foods, a large multinational corporation, stated that its decision to become an Olympic sponsor was directly influenced by SOCOG's environmental agenda (Green Games Watch 2000, 2004).

■ Increasing *consumer awareness of environmental issues*

The trend towards increasing consumer awareness of environmental issues is well established and, in some contexts, supported by buyer behaviour findings (Minton & Rose 1997; Schlegelmilch, Bohlen & Diamantopoulos 1996). In the context of leisure-based products and services, however, there is little substantive research to indicate whether consumers are influenced by environmental concerns in their decisions to buy/participate in/attend leisure products or services such as events (Hjalager 1996). Nonetheless, Crawford (2000) and others believe that this influence exists, and that event organisers need to ensure they reflect their market's concerns in this area if they are not to experience a consumer 'blacklash'.

■ The influence *of environmental interest groups*

Some events, particularly mega-events, have attracted the attention of environmental interest groups because they exhibit potential to have a negative impact on a community's physical environment, and because they can make significant demands on an area's resources. The first documented protest over the staging of a public event appears to have taken place in Denver, Colorado, when concerned local citizens successfully protested against the staging of the 1976 Winter Games (Chernushenko 1994). Such concern over the impacts of large-scale events has persisted, as reflected in the establishment of Green Games Watch 2000 — a coalition of major state and national environment groups — to monitor the Sydney Olympics (Green Games Watch 2000 2004). The stated aims of this group were to ensure:

- ecologically sustainable development and coordinated planning in the provision and management of Olympic facilities
- government and industry accountability and adherence to environmental guidelines through Green Games Watch's annual audits of performance
- the use of international best practice to showcase Australia's environment industries
- the application of principles of ecologically sustainable development (stimulated by the Olympics) to the metropolitan region to ensure long-term benefits to New South Wales

- the representation of community concerns to ensure long-term benefits for local communities and New South Wales (Green Games Watch 2000, 2004).

The interest, or potential interest, of environmental groups in events focuses the attention of event organisers on environmental issues and pushes them to adopt a proactive stance on environmental matters. Industry associations, such as the International Festival and Events Association are also now acknowledging in their annual industry awards the events that seek to embrace their environmental responsibilities.

SUMMARY

The common solutions to issues and challenges become the trends that help to define an industry. Some of the observable recent trends in the event industry include its rapid growth (particularly corporate events) and the increasing recognition of event management as a profession, as defined by a body of knowledge and the establishment of competency standards and management systems. Other observable trends are (1) event franchising, whereby the model established for an event is on-sold in other markets, and (2) the use of events as vehicles for skills training.

Major influences on the industry include rapid advances in information technology, the changing climate of risk management and the increased international threat to security. In answer to the increasing demands of the industry, event education and research have expanded, and transfer-of-knowledge programs have been developed to help build on the expertise gained from previous events. As awareness of the value of events has increased, governments around the world have become increasing involved in creating event strategies, establishing event portfolios, coordinating event infrastructure services and funding events. Events are increasingly adopting environmental management practices in response to growing awareness in the community and to pressures from governments and sponsors.

Questions

1 Do you think the number of events in your city or region is increasing? If so, what evidence can you offer of this increase?

2 Select an established profession and compare it with event management, using the characteristics of a profession outlined in this chapter. From this comparison, evaluate what you consider to be the progress of event management towards the status of a profession.

3 Identify an event that has been franchised and examine the method of the event. What aspects of the event can be franchised and transferred to a new location?

4   Choose a fairly large recent local event and interview the event manager to establish what risk management was undertaken. Evaluate the risk management of the event using the risk management procedures outlined in this book as a benchmark.

5   Choose a recent major event and investigate the security measures that the event had in place. How do you think increased threats to security might have influenced these measures?

6   Identify a situation in which a senior event manager has taken a position with a new event. What knowledge and skills was this manager able to transfer to the new event?

7   Identify a local or state government body in your region that has developed an event strategy. What are the major elements of this strategy? How is the strategy manifested in a portfolio of events?

8   Identify a body in your region that has been established to coordinate event infrastructure services. Who are the members of this body? With what issues does the body deal?

9   Identify an event in your region that has adopted environmental management practices, and outline the practices that they have adopted.

CASE STUDY ··

Managing the knowledge of
the 2000 Sydney Olympic Games

Event organisations need to effectively capture, share, manage, transfer, use and exploit their corporate information. By doing so, they can operate efficiently, reduce risk, coordinate their strategies, expedite policy implementation and not duplicate effort. Regrettably, managers have not understood the importance of knowledge management until recently; consequently, this facet of event management is often overlooked and underused. However, poor information and knowledge management at any stage can be a major source of risk for an event. Knowledge management is a multidisciplinary approach to achieving organisational objectives by making best use of knowledge. It involves the design, review and implementation of social and technological processes to improve the application of knowledge in the collective interests of the stakeholders (Standards Australia 2003, p. 3).

The Olympic movement, in the lead-up to the 2000 Sydney Olympic Games, recognised the potential gap between professional event management and information/knowledge management. During the Sydney Games and since then, the International Olympic Committee (IOC) has understood that knowledge is too valuable a resource to be left to chance and has improved the management of its knowledge assets. The Olympic movement thus provides a rich case study of event knowledge management.

Every time the games are staged, both winter and summer, there is a new organising committee, the host city and its culture are different, and technology and many other games-related procedures (such as security) have become more complex. Yet, until the 2000 Sydney Olympic Games, few standard operating methods, precedents or documentation — except the *official reports* produced after every games — were passed directly from the IOC or one organising committee to the next. This lack of know-how about the organisational, operational and cultural aspects of past games can be problematic for each new organising committee, which has the challenge of staging the world's most prestigious multisport event.

Added to this pressure is the fact that the event management team grows from a very small number of specialist staff to several thousand, and then rapidly closes down, all in about a seven-year time span (Halbwirth & Toohey 2001). Toffler (1990) calls organisations that grow then shrink (such as the Olympic organising committees) 'pulsating organisations'. Hanlon and Jago (2000) describe their main organisational characteristics as flexible, flat, highly formalised, decentralised (particularly during the peak stage of the event), having teams of people in functional units, innovative and regularly transforming their internal structure. An essential resource in such organisations is information. Its role is multidimensional in connecting and maintaining operational effectiveness and enhancing decision making.

The Sydney Organising Committee for the Olympic Games (SOCOG) exhibited all of the characteristics of a pulsating organisation. Additionally, its corporate governance was complex, embracing government and private sector agency interests. Its stakeholders included governments, sporting organisations, a range of corporate sponsors and broadcast rights holders, the public and the athletes who competed.

While commercial knowledge and sport management expertise were vital to SOCOG successfully staging the games, this achievement was underpinned by effective and innovative information and knowledge management strategies and leadership, including:

- a team of information professionals
- a corporate portal that ensured SOCOG staff had access to consistent, current and approved corporate, operational and public information
- research and retrieval services
- document and records management
- collaborative workspace for the authoring of key documents
- terminology and taxonomy management
- systems and processes to manage the flow of information to and from key stakeholders, such as sponsors and the public information call centre
- a knowledge-sharing culture, built in part via staff social events, cross-functional teams, a corporate newsletter and so on
- induction and orientation sessions for new staff
- a test event for all sports and for a number of key functional areas ('learning from doing')
- debriefing sessions and actioned organisational learning from test events and the games.

In 1998, during a Coordination Commission visit, the IOC praised SOCOG for its progress in its games organisation across its full range of functional milestones and activities. This marked the official beginning of the recognition that the Sydney Games might be a benchmark ('the best ever games') and might be able to provide many lessons for future event organisers. SOCOG agreed to develop a program for collecting and transferring information and know-how to the IOC. In exchange, the IOC contributed $5 million to SOCOG's tight budget. This established, for the first time in Olympic history, a formal transfer of know-how (TOK) agreement. The transfer included the collection of data, information and story via the corporate portal, which was collated into 90 functional area manuals, video footage, face-to-face debriefings with the IOC, Salt Lake City 2004 and Athens 2004 staff, work experience exchanges, and synthesis and analysis of documentation. The result of this process was the transfer to the IOC of hundreds of boxes of documents, electronic files and video footage, images and transcripts.

Each host city contract (which is signed by the IOC, the relevant national Olympic committee and the host city immediately after the games are awarded) contains an obligation to make available to the IOC, within two years after the games, a full and complete official report. Until the 2000 Sydney Olympic Games,

(*continued*)

this report was the only opportunity for the organising committee and its management to document the success (or otherwise) of its achievements in various areas of games organisation. The report also acted as a written legacy of the games which was available internationally. Sydney thus had a requirement to publish its report by October 2002. The result, the *Official report of the Games of the XXVII Olympiad*, contains three volumes: volume one explains the history and organisation of the 2000 Olympic Games; volume two is an account of the 16 days of the sport competition of the games, life in the Olympic Village and Cultural Olympic activities; and volume 3 contains the official results of the sport competition. This results volume is in the format of a compact disc (CD) rather than the traditional book mode of reports of previous games (Toohey 2001). The report is also more widely accessible than other previous reports, because it is available to the general public electronically at www.gamesinfo.com.au. This website also includes an electronic archive of public information related to the Sydney games.

The 2000 Sydney Olympic Games provided a number of information legacies — for example, transfer of know-how, the official report, www.gamesinfo.com.au and a comprehensive archive now managed by the State Records Authority of New South Wales. Post-Sydney 2000, the IOC had the issue of improving its own information and knowledge management as it took ownership of the TOK agreement resources. In 2001, it established the Olympic Games Knowledge Services, which is a joint venture to capitalise on Olympic know-how, create customised information packages for event organisers and continue a program of know-how capture. The IOC also took on a new strategic intent, creating a new division in 2003 that coordinates its information and knowledge assets under the leadership of a director of information management. Further, the IOC recognised the need to include in future host city contracts the obligation for organising committees to manage their information proactively and professionally through archives. All these initiatives have allowed the intellectual know-how and the historical legacy of Olympic material to be available for future use. The IOC is now active in managing its knowledge property.

While these activities have potential for positive outcomes for the IOC and other event organisers, there are ongoing issues and challenges in managing knowledge. Just as staging an Olympic Games requires complex organisation and coordination, so too do the processes of collecting, documenting, disseminating and using relevant information. Before an Olympic Games, for example, staff in various functional areas are understandably more concerned about their own tasks and may not be willing to share their intellectual property or provide input into knowledge-sharing practices. The sheer enormity and complexity of the tasks of Olympic Games organisation means processes are needed for harvesting key information from the vast knowledge bank. Organisers have to be able to sift through material to capture all vital information.

In a world where events are characterised by growing complexity in both their internal and external environments, information and knowledge management provide event managers with a multidisciplinary approach to ensure operational effectiveness, continuous improvement, the mitigation of risk and the streamlining of processes.

Kristine Toohey and Sue Halbwirth, University of Technology, Sydney

Questions

1 Choose a specific event. List the key information resources, channels and processes that would be needed before, during and in the wind-down phases of the event.

2 What are the best ways in which to capture know-how in an event organisation?

3 Why is it important to capture organisational information iteratively, rather than just at the end of the event?

4 How can event staff be encouraged to willingly contribute to knowledge sharing?

REFERENCES

ACT Auditor-General's Office 2003, *Performance audit report — V8 car races in Canberra: Cost and Benefit*, Canberra.

allrefer.com 2004, *Japan: age structure*, http://reference.allrefer.com/country-guide-study/japan/japan67.html (accessed April 2004).

Australian Department of Immigration 2004, *Key fact in immigration*, www.immi.gov.au/facts/02key.htm (accessed April 2004).

Australian Department of Environment and Heritage 2004, *Hobart City Council: taking a holistic approach towards decreasing greenhouse emissions and recycling waste*, www.deh.gov.au/industryeecp/corporate/case-studies/hobart-city.html (accessed 3rd April 2004).

Chernushenko, D 1994, *Greening our games: running sports events and facilities that won't cost the earth*, Centurion, Ottawa, Canada.

City of Ballarat 2003, *Event planning guide*, City of Ballarat Council, Victoria.

Crawford, D 2000, 'Environmental accounting for sport and public events: a tool for better decision making', *Sustainable Sport Sourceline*, May, www.greengold.on.ca/newsletter/index.html (accessed 3 April 2004).

Department of Environment and Conservation 2004, 'Waste Wise Events Program', Government of New South Wales, www.wastewiseevents.resource.nsw.gov.au (accessed 3 April 2004).

Environmental Protection Authority 2004, 'Grants: community waste reduction grants', www.epa.nsw.gov.au/waste/wg-34.htm (accessed 3 April 2004).

Event Educators Forum 2004, www.event.educators.net (accessed 19 July 2004).

Geldard, E & Sinclair, L 2003, *The sponsorship manual*, The Sponsorship Unit, Melbourne.

Goldblatt, JJ 1999, *Special events: best practices in modern event management*, Van Nostrand Reinhold, New York.

Government of New South Wales 2004, *State with the most highly educated population,* www.business.nsw.gov.au/business.asp?cid=163 (accessed April 2004).

Green Games Watch 2000 2004, 'About us', www.nccnsw.org.au/member/ggw (accessed 4 April 2004).

Halbwirth, S & Toohey, K 2001, 'The Olympic Games and knowledge management; a case study of the Sydney Organising Committee of the Olympic Games', *European Sport Management Quarterly,* vol. 1, no. 2, pp. 91–111.

Hanlon, C & Jago, L 2000, 'Pulsating sporting events: an organisational structure to optimise performance', *Events beyond 2000: setting the agenda: proceedings of the conference on event evaluation, research and education,* eds J Allen, R Harris, L Jago & AJ Veal, Australian Centre for Event Management, University of Technology, Sydney, pp. 93–104.

Hjalager, AM 1996, 'Tourism and the environment: the innovation connection', *Journal of Sustainable Tourism,* vol. 4, no. 4, pp. 201–7.

ICC Cricket World Cup 2003 Organising Committee 2003, *Volunteers 2003 training manual,* Johannesburg, South Africa.

International Olympic Committee 1999, *Building a positive environmental legacy through the Olympic Games,* Commission on Sport and the Environment, Lausanne, Switzerland.

Minton, A & Rose R 1997, 'The effects of environmental concern on environmentally friendly consumer behavior: an exploratory study', *Journal of Business Research,* vol. 40, pp. 37–48.

Premier's Department, Government of New South Wales 2003, www.premiers.nsw.gov.au (accessed April 2004).

Night of the Ad Eaters, www.adeaters.com (accessed April 2004).

O'Toole W & Mikolaitis P 2002, *Corporate event project management,* John Wiley & Sons, New York.

Schlegelmilch, B, Bohlen, G & Diamantopoulos A 1996, 'The link between green purchasing decisions and measures of environmental consciousness', *European Journal of Marketing,* vol. 30, no. 5, pp. 35–55.

Silvers, J 2003, *Professional event coordination,* John Wiley & Sons, New York.

Standards Australia 2003, *Knowledge Management Standard* (Interim), AS 5037(int)-2003, Sydney.

Strauss, N 2000, 'The last 10 per cent is the toughest', *BioCycle,* January, p. 35.

Tarradellas, J & Behnam S 2000, *Olympic movement's Agenda 21: sport for sustainable development,* International Olympic Committee, Sport and Environment Commission, Lausanne, Switzerland.

Toffler, A 1999, *Future shock,* Bantam Books, New York.

Toohey, K 2001, *Official report of the Games of the XXVII Olympiad,* Sydney Organising Committee for the Olympic Games, Sydney.

United Nations 1992, *Agenda 21: programme of action for sustainable development*, United Nations Department of Public Information, New York.

Universitat Autonoma de Barcelona 2003, www.blues.uab.es (accessed 20 September 2003).

Wisconsin Department of Natural Resources 2000, 'Special events: recycling and waste management', www.uwm.edu/Dept/besmart//festival/dnrspecial.html (accessed 4 April 2004).

World Bank 2004, *Beyond economic growth*, www.worldbank.org/depweb/english/beyond/global/chapter3_2.html#fig3_4 (accessed April 2004).

INDEX